DENNIS BRUCE

THE WORD OF LIFE

BOOKS BY THOMAS C. ODEN

Systematic Theology
Volume One: The Living God
Volume Two: The Word of Life

After Therapy What?
Agenda for Theology
Becoming a Minister
Beyond Revolution
Care of Souls in the Classic Tradition
The Community of Celebration
Conscience and Dividends
Contemporary Theology and Psychotherapy
Crisis Ministries
Doctrinal Standards in the Wesleyan Tradition
Game Free
Guilt Free
The Intensive Group Experience
Kerygma and Counseling
Ministry through Word and Sacrament
The New Birth (editor)
The Parables of Kierkegaard (editor)
Pastoral Theology
Phoebe Palmer: Selected Writings (editor)
The Promise of Barth
Radical Obedience: The Ethics of Rudolf Bultmann
Should Treatment Be Terminated?
The Structure of Awareness
TAG: The Transactional Awareness Game
Timothy and Titus

The Word of Life

SYSTEMATIC THEOLOGY: VOLUME TWO

Thomas C. Oden

1817

HARPER & ROW, PUBLISHERS, SAN FRANCISCO
New York, Grand Rapids, Philadelphia, St. Louis
London, Singapore, Sydney, Tokyo, Toronto

FIRST EDITION

Library of Congress Cataloging-in-Publication Data

Oden, Thomas C.
   The Word of life.

   (Systematic theology ; v. 2)
   1. Jesus Christ—Person and offices.
I. Title. II. Series: Oden, Thomas C.
Systematic theology ; v. 2.
BT202.0318 1989   232'.8   88-46011
ISBN 0-06-066348-0

89 90 91 92 93 RRD 10 9 8 7 6 5 4 3 2 1

For Edrita

Contents

Working Assumptions

The decisive question of Christian testimony is not whether it is palatable but whether it is true. The vocation of theologian places the writer under obligation to deliver an accurate reading of Christian teaching, even when it points to a narrow way.

There is a crisis in the study of Christ today. It has to do with whether Christ can be known historically, and whether he addresses us as one who is dead or as a living person.

My purpose is to set forth the classical teaching of the person and work of Jesus Christ on which there has generally been substantial agreement between traditions of East and West, Catholic, Protestant, and Orthodox. I will be listening intently for the ecumenical consensus that has been gratefully celebrated as reliable Christian teaching by believers of widely varied social locations and cultural settings and periods — African and Russian, pre-European and European, ancient Near Eastern and modern Asian, as expressed by both women and men, whether of the first, tenth, or twentieth century.

This book is more like a travel guide than a reference work. A travel guide is often taken along to the place visited even if it is dog-eared and coffee-stained. The reference work remains neatly back home on the shelf. I hope this will be a useful traveling advisor and practical resource for anyone seeking to understand or attest Jesus Christ.

Those already motivated to learn of Christ do not mind if others find the details of such an inquiry a bit tedious or demanding. Those already deeply touched by Christ are eager to learn all they can of him. This book is also for those who have tried to pray to Christ but could not, have sought solace in Christ but not experienced it, have puzzled over the death of Christ and felt absurdity.

The Living God (the first volume of this three-volume series) dealt with the doctrines of God, creation, and providence. This volume, *The Word of Life,* plunges into perplexing issues of whether the Word became flesh, whether God has entered history in Christ, and whether that has saving significance for us. (This will be followed by another volume on the Holy Spirit, church, sacraments, and the Christian life—*Life in the Spirit*.) Though integrated into a larger system of theology, this volume can be read as a self-standing argument. It commends but does not require the reading of its companion volumes.

Classic, Consensual, Ecumenical Teaching

My mission is to deliver as clearly as I can that core of consensual belief concerning Jesus Christ that has been shared for two hundred decades—who he was, what he did, and what that means for us today. I seek language that makes plausible today the intent of classical Christianity, while avoiding misconceptions that have become attached to its popular exposition.

I will deal with those teachings on which the central stream of classical exegesis has generally agreed as expressing the mind of the believing church. Readers have a right to expect that I will restrain my own idiosyncratic way of looking at things. My aim is not polemics but peacemaking, not dissent but consensus, not with knocking down other positions, but building up the plausible layers of argument employed in defining the Christian teaching of salvation.

I intend to set forth in connected order those points most commonly held on Christ and salvation. Systematic ecumenical theology looks for a cohesive grasp of the whole of classic Christian teaching, so that each part is seen in relation to the whole. At ambiguous points where that central core is not fully evident, I will either leave the subject for further inquiry or rehearse principal viewpoints that remain in tension.

The most intriguing questions of Christian teaching still echoing through the centuries may be stated in plain, uncomplicated words: Why did God become human? Is Jesus truly God? If so how truly human? If both divine and human, how so? Did God die? What does resurrection mean? Did he pay the penalty for our sins? Is Jesus' mission now complete? Do we pray to Jesus? Can he change our lives? These are among the questions that stimulate this inquiry, intended as much for critical examination by laypersons as clergy, for laity as well are called to attest Christ and teach salvation.

Overcoming the Defensive Posture

This study was written out of a practical, specific motivation to solve a pastoral and teaching problem. Search as I might, I have not been able to find a concise, systematic statement of the meaning of Jesus' authority, life and work that sufficiently attends to classic Christian exegesis (especially of the first five centuries) without getting embroiled in ever-extending modern historical interpretations and debates. This is a modest attempt to supply one.

Why this subject? Recent academic studies of Jesus tend to approach him with a kind of braced defensiveness. They seek to win points with modern consciousness without sufficient disavowal of skewed modern assumptions. They yearn to gain acceptable credentials in the secularizing university, leaving the community of prayer to fend for itself. Amid such defensiveness, only the faint aroma of classical Christianity remains. The pungent smell is of the waste products of modernity.

This defensiveness is illustrated by Paul Tillich's guarded statement that "Faith cannot even guarantee the name 'Jesus' in respect to him who was the Christ" (*Syst. Theol.* II, p. 107). Meanwhile Tillich imagined that Christianity could still speak somehow of "a personal life in which the New Being has conquered the old being. But it does not guarantee his name to be Jesus of Nazareth" (*Syst. Theol.* II, p. 114). The same defensive mentality is even more influentially expressed in Rudolf Bultmann's view that little can be known of Jesus and that Christian teaching can therefore only be derived from the early church's *kerygma*, not from Jesus himself; because we cannot say much about what (*was*) happened to Jesus, we can only assert that (*dass*) something happened that constituted for others a saving event and upon that uncertainty preaching must hinge (*TNT* I, pp. 3–63; *KM*, pp. 34–43). Countless influential studies have followed those of these mentors. The closer they approach Jesus, the more their language becomes strained, forced, guarded, despairing, and strapped by a thousand deadly qualifiers (Marxsen, *BCSP*, pp. 67–76; Käsemann, *ENTT*; Fuller, *FNTC*; Perrin, *MPNTC*; cf. Wink, *BHT*, pp. 2–14).

The opposite attitude is adopted here. I view my task as an extraordinary privilege—that of unapologetically setting forth in an undisguised way the apostolic testimony to Christ in its classic consensual form. I want to show that most of what is enduringly valuable in contemporary biblical exegesis was discovered by the fifth century. Numerous key insights that pretend to be modern discoveries about Jesus were reasonably well understood in the first five centuries of preaching and pastoral care.

There is a shared assumption throughout the classic tradition of the rich validity and authority of canonical scripture. If readers have not gotten far enough in the spiritual journey to see that Scripture is the crucial wellspring of Christian existence and reflection, then this study may not be the place to begin. But any reader who shares that assumption is welcomed to the feast.

This book rejects the assumption that the main task of Christology is to make Jesus easily acceptable to the prejudices of modernity. I will not enter into a game whose rules already make one a loser. I will not seek some new ground for making classical Christianity acceptable to its naturalistic critics, whose appetites can never be satisfied. I will not enter square one.

I pledge not to offer a tedious résumé of all the dismal failures of Christological thinking in the last century. Although I will use contemporary sources where pertinent, I will not be preoccupied with speculative modern critical debates but rather will focus upon the historic Christian consensus concerning how Christ affects humanity. As one who has taught and studied and written on modern existentialism, psychotherapies, and social theories, I have paid full dues to modernity and now turn to the classic wisdoms concerning the way to Christ.

To Whom Am I Reaching Out in Dialogue?

I do not assume that readers already affirm traditional Christian teaching. I wish only to give a fair hearing to the way in which classical Christian teaching has critically reasoned about its own grounding and empowerment. I respect those who apply a strict "hermeneutic of suspicion" to these issues and require evidence to be accurately presented, but only if they apply that same hermeneutic to their own assumptions.

I will do my best to let classic Christianity speak in its own language. For people preparing seriously for baptism or confirmation, this study intends to set forth the essential teachings concerning Jesus Christ. The only partner in dialogue I seek is the honest inquirer, young or old.

Working pastors and those preparing for ministry, whose calling and commitment are to attest Christ's living presence, have remained constantly on my mind throughout these pages. Those preparing for ordination will easily see that this study reviews key issues concerning the person and work of Christ and the doctrine of salvation, sufficiently I hope to assist one amid the hazards of rigorous ordinal examination. These issues are not an ancillary part of ordinal qualification, but at its heart.

The most basic questions about Christ have been asked repeatedly in previous centuries of Christian experience. Surprisingly, the best classic mentors have already anticipated our worst contemporary dilemmas. We view these problems as unprecedented only because we have neglected to consult ancient Christian teachers.

No higher purpose of theology can be conceived than that it might assist persons in teaching and interpreting God's saving action. Works of systematic theology have not characteristically been written in our time as intentional companions to evangelical witness. This one is.

I will not seek to circumvent the traditional language of the church. I do not substitute renewal for resurrection, existential alienation for sin, liberation for redemption, or moral influence for ransom. The witness to God's saving action is best served by letting the tested language of the Christian tradition, which has been refined through many historical and political mutations, speak for itself out of its own power to modern minds struggling with the limits of modernity. If we give it this chance, it will make its own sense to us.

I will not try to constantly offer classic Christianity unneeded crutches to assist it in catching up with the frenzied pace of modernity. My premise is that modernity has much more catching up to do with classic Christianity.

From whatever strand of the Christian spectrum (liberal/conservative, Catholic/Protestant, pious/rational, East/West) readers may come, the hope is that by drinking deeply of classic exegesis they may recognize the best of their own recent traditions as already at home within classical Christianity—a trustable faith with practical social implications that can be embodied in the contemporary world and even be aesthetically enjoyed.

But we cannot take the first step on the journey unless we allow ourselves to be directly addressed by the ancient ecumenical writers. Only by steeping ourselves in their wisdom and joy will this journey become lively and meaningful. These writings are like packages sitting under a tree begging to be opened. To Protestants they offer prodigious gifts awaiting rediscovery. To Orthodox and Catholics they await reappropriation. As a son of the liberal tradition, I reach out constantly on every page for both evangelical and Catholic partners in dialogue.

Is He the Expected One?

That Christianity lives out of Jesus Christ no one denies. That he became identified by his disciples as the Messiah of ancient Jewish hopes is equally plain. But *whether he is or is not the Christ* is not a matter for historical inquiry alone to settle, although historical inquiry must fund its settlement. That question one must finally decide for oneself in honesty based upon fair examination of the facts.

It is not my purpose to try to establish by argument that God is revealed in Jesus—for the obvious reason that no logical argument of itself could convince and no historical evidence in itself can elicit belief. Traditional Christian teaching has clearly understood that one cannot rightly lay hold of faith without the inward empowering of God's own Spirit.

I do not wish to argue this crucial point but simply to make clear the fact that this is what is believed in the Christian community and has been believed in countless cultural and historical settings. That Christ is received as Lord, Son of God, and Messiah in this community is not a compelling argument, but more simply a fact.

My purpose is not to try to substitute rational argument for what Christianity says the Spirit is seeking to do for us. Yet that need not imply that faith might neglect rational argument or empathic discourse, which itself is used by the Spirit to bring us closer to the truth.

The Pyramid of Sources

Embedded in almost every paragraph of these pages are references to classical Christian sources. They point modern readers to a history of dialogue that rightly informs contemporary discussion. The most important service I can render readers is manifested in these quotations and embedded annotations.

To some it may seem amusing—to me it remains a sober, ironic fact—that *this text is an introduction to its annotations*. Only if it succeeds in pointing readers back to Irenaeus, Cyprian, Chrysostom, Macrina, and their companions has it fulfilled my expectation. All it hopes to do is point beyond itself to the texts out of which its argument lives.

The weighting of references may be compared to a solidly grounded pyramid of sources with Scripture and early Christian writers at the base and the most recent interpreters at the narrower apex—a priority that modern theologians have managed to turn upside down when they quote mostly modern and few classical sources. The history of Christian theology is a history of exegesis. What early Christian theology consists of is nothing more than early Christian exegesis. Medieval and Reformation exegesis stands upon the shoulders of these earliest exegetes. The accompanying diagram represents this ordering of sources.

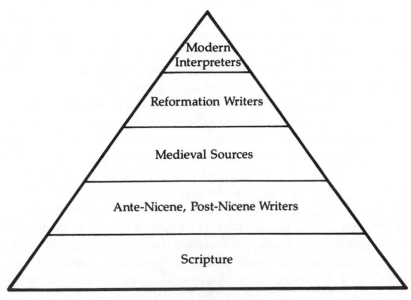

PYRAMID OF SOURCES

Hence primary biblical and classical Christian sources are consistently cited in preference to recent and secondary sources of all kinds. Among classic exegetes, those who have gained the widest consensus are quoted more often than those that have tended to elicit division, speculation, and controversy. Earlier rather than the later sources are quoted wherever possible. Accordingly, only a few modern sources will be noted, not because they are inferior but because they have had less time to affect the consensus. The pyramid implies more attention to Scripture than early church writers, more to ante-Nicene and post-Nicene writers than medieval and Reformation writers, and fewer modern writers. If these ancient references seem at times a bit intrusive, please understand that they are deliberate reminders that continue to knock on the door of the reader's working library.

These classic Christian writers should not be pitted too starkly against Scripture. Their main purpose was to illuminate, order, and explicate the truth of Scripture. In Luther's view, that was precisely what made them "fathers." "All the fathers concede their own obscurity and illuminate Scripture by Scripture alone. And, indeed, that is the right method. Scripture should be placed alongside Scripture in a right and proper way. He who can do this best is the best of the fathers" (Luther, *Reply to Emser*, *WML* III, pp. 277ff.; *WLS* I, p. 88; *WA* 7, 639).

Biblical references are from the New International Version unless otherwise noted. Scripture texts are cited not as wooden, lifeless proof-texts, but as vital *locus classicus* texts upon which numerous previous ancient Christian teachers have repeatedly built, reasoned, and commented. Since the history of Christian teaching is largely a history of exegesis, readers cannot be denied the right to examine the biblical texts upon which Christian teaching is largely a comment. It would hardly be reasonable to provide references to exegetes of the first five centuries, yet inadvertently fail to mention the texts upon which they were commenting. In some cases, a reference will not constitute a support of the point made but will show some variety of opinion (especially where "cf." is noted). Complaints against proof-texting had best not finally result in a disavowal of reference to the very texts out of which theology lives.

A theology intent upon avoiding its textuary is self-limiting and finally cuts itself off from its sources. A theology that limits its referrals only to those texts that are elaborately placed in historical context will finally mutate into a historical, not a systematic, work. Certain nineteenth-century practices of proof-texting (stacking references by the dozen) are rightly rejected. Yet the ancient ecumenical tradition requires theology to show how it bases its conclusions upon canonical texts. We seek accountability to this ancient requirement.

The Promise of Unoriginality

The only promise I try to make to my readers, however inadequately carried out, is that of *unoriginality*. I hope to present nothing whatever original in these pages.

This is not an effort at comedy. Nothing of my own, that would have my initials stamped upon it, is important in this discussion, as I see it. Admittedly the classic language must be reappropriated and articulated in sentences written and organized by some particular person. Yet I hope my own voice does not intrude inordinately upon the likes of Polycarp, Anthony, or Athanasius.

I wish to provide neither a new interpretation of old ideas, nor a new language that is more acceptable for modern sensibilities. Accountability to the ancient exegetes themselves is a large enough task, without adding to it these other heavy burdens. If that seems excessive, it is to some extent a response to a prevailing excess, one that inordinately emphasizes self-expressive innovative exegesis, often exaggerated in self-importance. I do not pretend to have found a comfortable way of making Christianity acceptable to a deteriorating modernity.

Hence I will attempt to constrain the impulse to analyze detailed controversies on specific exegetical points in modern sources. That is not my purpose. Each doctrine has a history of controversy. That history is the subject of historical theology, but that differs from the method of systematic theology (already discussed in *LG*, pp. 317–404), which assumes that it is legitimate to define the purpose of a book of Christian theology as that of simply setting forth classic Christian thinking without becoming intensively preoccupied with each successive stage of development through which each teaching has passed in various traditions, symbol systems, and periods. The author must be informed about these developments but need not burden readers with them.

Readers may be helped by assuming that before each and every paragraph is the hidden phrase: "The principal classical exegetes say . . . " Since it would be tedious to repeat such a reference constantly, I ask your indulgence to say it only once. I fantasize putting a terse disclaimer on the cover advising readers to not buy this book first, but at once go and buy ancient Christian writings and then this one as an ancillary helper.

These principal classical exegetes referred to are those usually designated as the four great ecumenical "Doctors of the Church" of the Eastern tradition (Athanasius, Basil, Gregory Nazianzen, and John Chrysostom), the four "Doctors of the Church" of the West (Ambrose, Augustine, Jerome, and Gregory the Great), and a few others. Among others who have been widely and perennially valued for accurately stating points of ecumenical consensus are Gregory of Nyssa, Hilary, Leo, John of Damascus, Thomas Aquinas, Luther, and Calvin. "Classic" in our definition includes classic Reformation sources.

Consensual documents widely received by the consenting church over a long period of time are valued above statements of individuals. Most important of consensual documents are the decisions of ecumenical councils and the most widely received synods and councils. The method of consensus hinges on the fact of consent (*consentio*, "to be of one mind, to agree," from *com-*, "with," and *sentire*, "feel"). Who gives consent in this consensus? The whole church. How is this consent defined? In correspondence with ancient conciliar consent (*LG*, pp. 321–51).

The term traditionally applied to the classic Christian teachers of the first five centuries is "patristic," in reference to the fathers (from *pater*) of the church. Yet since there were also influential mothers and not fathers alone, we will also speak of the matristic (from *mater*) exegetes and saints such as Macrina, Perpetua, Caecilia of Rome, Agatha of Sicily, Margaret of Antioch, Paula, Eustochium, and Amma Theodora. When the term "patristic" is used it refers to the fathers; when "matristic" is used it refers to key women of the early Christian tradition; the hyphenated "patristic-matristic" refers to both.

Traditional Teaching Addresses Current Issues

Although this inquiry does not focus upon the contributions and critical issues of liberation theology, it makes constant reference to Jesus' profound and unremitting identification with the poor and dispossessed. Those interested in feminist theology and the liberation of women will find in Jesus one who compassionately cared for women and who broke through the prevailing class, race, and gender limits of his day. Those interested in black theology will find in Jesus a fellow sufferer who understood rejection and social alienation. Those interested in process theology can find in the incarnation God's own empathic engagement in the limits of humanity.

In pursuing classical exegesis, it is surprising to find that so many current issues of human controversy are touched and treated. I mention several leading examples to indicate that traditional study is not a flight from relevance. These texts relentlessly address modern and postmodern problems. Note that I have not set out deliberately to focus upon such problems in the interest of relevance—they have necessarily emerged in the interest of accurately setting forth classical exegesis. Among these are questions of sexual equality, poverty and liberation theology, as well as psychological and historical analysis.

Women

Readers particularly interested in how classic consensual writers understood the role of women in salvation history may be alerted to coming sections on whether the incarnation was sexist, whether the virginal conception has meaning for today, and whether women are rightly honored in the salvation event. There are specific sections on classical understandings of the New Eve; sexuality and nativity; a savior born of woman; *theotokos*; and the vulnerability of life at life's beginning and life's end.

Equality

Christology itself raises probing issues about the nature of equality, if the servant mission of the Son is to be taken as a pattern of human relationships. One cannot mine classic Christologies without thinking deeply about the equality and subjection of the Son and what that means for human societies. There are in what follows classic interpretations of the reversal of egalitarian assertiveness, the nature of subjection and subordination, and the humbling of God to servanthood.

Poverty and Liberation

Those interested in liberation theology will find detailed classic discussions of Jesus' identification with the poor; being numbered among the transgressors; voluntary suffering; crucifixion between two thieves; and the social location of biblical critics. Those interested in questions of poverty will find classic exegesis of texts on voluntary poverty, voluntary obedience, voluntary servanthood, the missional implications of lowliness, the obscuration of the divine majesty, and Christ's care of the poor.

Sexuality

There are numerous segments of the ensuing study that inquire into the body language of God; the meaning of the assumption of flesh; sexual metaphors of God's bodily coming; mediation and birth; the consecration of sexuality; the circumcision of the Savior; the psychosexual development of Jesus; the calling to the single state; and the metaphor of seduction.

Psychological Analysis

Those interested in psychological themes will find sections on the temptation of Jesus; the emotive range of the soul of Jesus; the psychosomatic interface and the theandric person; whether the Mediator experienced fear; nonverbal communication; and the recapitulation of humanity.

Historical Criticism

Those interested in historical criticism will find sections on the value of historical method; whether historical verification is possible; the search for the history of Jesus; the unity of the New Testament; the critique of criticism; the lordship of Christ and the history of religions; *monogenēs*; and title Christology.

These topics are mentioned to concede in advance that we are not seeking to demean relevance, even though we do not focus upon it. I made no effort to draw or tilt the discussion toward these issues. They have emerged naturally in the course of following the Vincentian Method (defining theology as a search for ancient ecumenical consensus, first clearly formulated as a method by Vincent of Lerins).

Holding to the Center

A work of this sort is best assessed on the basis of its own stated purpose, not an intention imposed upon it externally by a critic. I would hope that this study could receive the benefit of active criticism on the basis of whether it in fact does what it sets out to do, not what it does not try to do.

The questions of conscience that have accompanied my pursuit of this task include: Have I adequately represented the consensual core of Christian belief that spans the centuries? Have I rightly balanced East and West? Have I inserted nonecumenical voices and pretended that they were consensual? Have I neglected important voices that in fact did represent consensual views? This is what I would most like my critics to help me understand.

My intention has been to sparely quote relatively nonconsensual authors like Origen, Novatian, and Menno Simons, but only on those points at which they generally represent consensual views (see *LG*, p. xii). Novatian was clearly a heretic on church authority, but not on the Trinity, as is generally acknowledged.

The prime criterion is consensuality. If I have failed there, I need the help of others to see how it could be better grasped or achieved. If such a task is not worth doing, I would like to hear the reasons why. I would prefer that the debate focus upon the decisive question of whether such consensus is possible rather than a particular scriptural passage has been rightly understood from some modern critical perspective. I would rather see the study attacked at its center—on the possibility of ecumenical consensus—than on details that miss that central focus. Beyond this I have no right or desire to advise my critics on where my greatest vulnerabilities lie. They will see them quickly enough, and I am aware of many of them. But at least I would like my intention to be clearly understood: the method is Vincentian (Vincent of Lerins, *Comm.*, LCC VII, pp. 37–39, 65–74, as set forth in *LG*, pp. 322–25, 341–51), not Bultmannian, Barthian, Pannenbergian, Marxsenian, Marxist, Lonerganian, or Segundian.

Among those to whom I am most deeply indebted in developing this argument are Father Louis Bouyer, Monsignor Michael Wrenn, Theresa Cuomo Smith, Kenneth Brewer, Kent A. Branstetter, John Franke, Paul Stallsworth, and James Hampson. To Joseph Cardinal Ratzinger I am deeply grateful for his interest in this study. No words can adequately express my reliance upon the person to whom this study is affectionately dedicated, my companion of thirty-seven years, Edrita.

Classic Christianity remains, like Keats's urn, a "still unravish'd bride of quietness," a "foster-child of silence and slow time" ("Odes on a Grecian Urn"). I feel the eccentric longing of Henry Vaughan's "Retreat":

> O how I long to travel back,
> and tread again that ancient track! . . .
> Some men a forward motion love,
> But I by backward steps would move.

CHAPTER 1

Why Christ?

AN UNFORGETTABLE LIFE

Christianity arose out of a particular human life ending in a disturbing, terrible death—then, resurrection. The meaning of Christianity is undecipherable without grasping the meaning of Christ's life and death and living presence.

"Christ is the central spot of the circle; and when viewed aright, all stories in Holy Scripture refer to Christ" (Luther, *Serm. on John 3:14, WLS* I, p. 148; *WA* 47, 66). Luther compared the Scriptures to "A lute player who always plays only one little song"—Christ, promised and sent (*Pentecost Serm., John 3:16* [1532], *WLS* I, p. 147; *WA* 36, 181). It is from Christ that Christianity derives its name, its mission, its identity, its purpose, its very life (Acts 11:26; John 15:1–5; Augustine, *Hom. on the Epist. of John* I, *NPNF* 1 VII, pp. 460–68).

Christian Teaching Is Personally Grounded

Christianity *is* a relation to a person. It is not essentially an idea or institution. It has defined itself in canon and tradition as a relation to Christ. He is the one to whom faith relates and in whom faith trusts. Gustavo Gutiérrez writes: "Being a Christian does not mean, first and foremost, believing in a message. It means believing in a person" (*PPH*, p. 130).

Christian teaching is therefore personally grounded. It lives in response to a personal life yet alive. Christian teaching only serves to show the way that leads to faith in this person. That the Christian community emerges and lives out of personal trust in this person is simply a fact (John Chrysostom, *Hom. on John* LVII, *NPNF* 1 XIV, pp. 204–206).

A consequent discipline—Christology, the study of Christ—has emerged in the attempt to understand this fact. Such an attempt to understand the identity and activity of Christ cannot be incidental to Christian teaching. It is central and specifically required if one is to reflect upon Christian worship, Christian community, or the Christian life. If one remains mute or inattentive at this point, it means that one has elected not to inquire into Christianity. We must try to understand why this person is so important in this religion and why he is finally attested as nothing less than God (Athanasius, *Incarn. of the Word* 15–21, LCC III, pp. 70–75). That is what Christology is all about. Christian teaching and the study of Jesus are inseparably bound.

Christians know God as the One revealed in Jesus. Other ideas of God are measured in relation to that idea of God known in Jesus. The approach to that idea of God knowable only through the history of Jesus must begin with the study of Jesus himself. This is distinguished from the view that assumes that Jesus is not knowable and that therefore one can only begin with the study of others' proclamation about Jesus.

His Uncoercive Influence

It would be difficult to think of a single person who has affected human history more profoundly than Jesus of Nazareth. This alone would make the study of him significant. Yet this is not the primary reason he is studied. He is not studied as Alexander and Napoleon would be studied, for their enormous power or political sway over millions. His influence is not outwardly measured in terms of worldly power (John 18:36) but remains uncoercive, person-to-person, spiritual, subtly transforming, inconspicuous (*Martyrdom of Polycarp*, LCC I, pp. 152–57; Athanasius, *Incarn. of the Word* 46–57, NPNF 2 IV, pp. 61–67; Clare of Assisi, *Testament of St. Clare, Francis and Clare*, CWS, pp. 226–32).

The modern spirit of historical inquiry could not ignore the history of Jesus. His footprints are all over the Western literary, moral, and social landscape, and on every continent. Who has affected history more than he? No other individual has become such a permanent fixture of the human memory. He has been worshiped as Lord through a hundred generations.

Through the centuries Jesus has been memorialized in architecture, painted on frescoes, embedded in stone by mosaic designers, prayed to by opposing armies, praised in conflicting ways by poets, and interpreted diversely by philosophers. Western history would not be Western history without him. It would be strangely unhistorical if the historians accidentally ignored him or decided to study all figures except the one who has affected Western history most. Indeed it is puzzling when his name is carefully avoided in high-school history texts.

The intellectual and moral struggle that has ensued from his life has penetrated every corner of Western intellectual history, psychology, politics, and literature. One cannot understand human history without asking who Christ is and what he did and continues to do. No one is well educated who has systematically dodged the straightforward question of Christology—a question that committed Jews or Muslims may ask and study as seriously as Christians or agnostics or hedonists—Is Jesus the Christ?

Historical inquiry into Jesus cannot avoid at some point overhearing the question Jesus asked to Peter: "Who do you say that I am?" Peter's confession, "You are the Christ, the Son of the living God," remains the concise pattern for subsequent Christian liturgy and confession (Moltmann, *ICT*, pp. 175–78). In saying this, Peter stood in a personal relationship with another person, Jesus Christ—not with an idea, abstract system, or institution, but an actual *you* in a real relationship. The confession was not about Christ, but to him. Peter did not say: "I am willing tentatively to trust the hypothesis that you are the Christ" or "The historical evidence seems to lead to this probable conclusion." One says "You are the Christ" only to one who is alive. If Christ is not alive, forget about Christian confession—there is no one to whom to confess.

The meaning of Jesus' life and death has never been a permanently dead issue to any generation since his appearance. It remains even today a matter of intense debate as to who Jesus was and what his life and death mean. Deeper even than the mystery of his astonishing historical influence is the simpler, starker question that rings through Christian reflection: *Cur Deus homo*? Why did God become human?

The Question Required by the Facts

The Facts Briefly Stated

Date of birth: between 5 B.C. and A.D. 4. Place: Palestine. Ethnic origin: Jewish. Vocation: probably first a carpenter, then a traveling preacher of the coming rule of God. Length of ministry: three Passovers (John 2:13; 6:4; 12:1). Date of death: Friday, 14 Nisan (the first month of the Jewish year), probably, by our calendar, April 7 A.D. 30 (or by some calculations 3 April, A.D. 33). Place of death: Jerusalem. Manner of death: crucifixion. Roman procurator: Pontius Pilate (A.D. 27–33). Roman emperor: Tiberius.

The Decisive Question

Christology focuses not simply upon bare facts, but upon what this life meant and how these events have been interpreted—especially as they come down finally to a single, pivotal question: whether Jesus is rightly understood as the expected Messiah of Israel, Son of God, Lord— or not. There is no way to dodge artfully this question so as to conclude that Jesus might be *partially* Lord or *to a certain degree* the Christ or *maybe* in some ways eternal Son or *perhaps* truly God (Perpetua, *Passion of the Holy Martyrs, Perpetua and Felicitas, ANF* III, pp. 704–706; Justin Martyr, *First Apology* 35, FC 6, p. 72). Finally, he must either be or not be the Messiah. He must either be or not be Lord.

There is no middle way or golden mean. This is the startling question that his life constantly asks. The nearer one comes to him, the more clearly he requires that decision. It is the unavoidable issue that the observer of Jesus' life must finally come up against, for Jesus himself presses and requires that decision. To avoid that issue is to avoid him. To avoid him is to avoid Christianity altogether (Kierkegaard, *TC*, pp. 66–71).

The Incongruity of an Apparent Failure

The portrait of his life among us, as offered by presumably honest eyewitness rememberers, is poignant, simple, and stirring. The closer we come to examine it the more we are likely to be profoundly moved by it.

He was born of a poor family, of a destiny-laden but powerless nation that had long been humiliated and stripped of national pride. The earliest traditions report that he was born in a squalid stable among animals in an out-of-the-way village, a refugee baby of a fleeing family seeking to escape political tyranny and violent religious persecution. He grew up in another obscure Galilean town having the unenviable reputation that "nothing good could ever come from there." He learned to speak a language that has long been virtually forgotten and that never produced a widely read literature. He is never said to have written anything except with his finger in the sand. He was obedient to his parents. He followed the law. He worked with his hands as a common laborer.

He became an itinerant preacher, and was called "rabbi." He had few possessions. He lived constantly among the poor and identified with their lowliness, recognizing them to be uniquely blessed with promise. To them he preached the good news of the coming governance of God. His disciples were not brilliant leaders or worldly-wise strategists. They were simple folk, mostly involved in the fishing trade, a variety of ordinary people, including some reprobates, whose lives were stunned and reshaped by their unforgettable meeting with him.

Even in the face of angry criticism, he did not cease to dine and converse with sinners, to mix with the lowly and disinherited. His closest associates followed him everywhere but often resisted whom they followed. He intentionally took the form of a servant. He washed the feet of his followers. He reached out for other cultures despised by his own people and valued their gifts.

In his company were women who had suffered wrenching social rejection. He considered it an incomparably memorable event that he was anointed with oil by one who was viewed as a woman of ill repute. Of all the people who might have been able to grasp the fact that he was to be anointed to an incomparable mission, it turned out to be a harassed "woman who was a sinner"!

Remarkable things were reported of him. He touched lepers. He healed the blind. He raised persons from the dead. These events pointed unmistakably to the unparalleled divine breakthrough that was occurring in history—the decisive turnaround in the divine-human story of conflicted love. He taught by parables—often simply, sometimes enigmatically. He heralded a new age. He called all his hearers to decide for or against God's coming reign. He called for a high ethic of accountability. His behavior was radically consistent with his teaching.

Unscientific and lacking the advantages of advanced education, he became a controversial teacher. His coming was not publicly celebrated except in one brief ironic moment (his entry into Jerusalem). His ministry was constantly misunderstood by those closest to him and especially by those who had vested interests in the managing of power. He was born to a racial group widely despised and rejected; but he himself became even more despised and rejected by many of his own people.

His enemies plotted to trap him and finally came to take his life. His closest friends deserted him when his hour had come to die. He knew all along that he would be killed. He agonized in a garden. Sweat poured from his face as he approached death. He was betrayed by one of his closest associates. He submitted to a scurrilous trial with false charges.

His end was terrible. His back felt the whip. He was spat upon. His head was crowned with thorns. His wrists were in chains. On his shoulders he bore a cross. Spikes were driven through his hands and feet into wood. His whole body was stretched on a cross as he hung between two thieves. He felt completely forsaken. All the while he prayed for his tormentors, that they might be forgiven, for they knew not what they were doing.

This is a sketch of the Gospels' portrait of Jesus. It is this one whom the disciples experienced as alive the third day after his death. This is the incomparable person we are trying to study, whose extraordinary life we try to understand. The closer we make him the object of our study, the more we become aware that he is examining us.

Is There a Plausible Explanation?

How is it plausible that two thousand years ago there lived a man born in poverty in a remote corner of the world, whose life was abruptly cut short in his early thirties, who traveled only in a small area, who held no public office, yet whose influence appears greater than all others? How is it that one who died the death of a criminal could be worshiped today by hundreds of millions? This is the surprising disjunctiveness of his life, but not its deepest mystery. Why are people willing to renounce all to follow him and even die in his service? How is it plausible that two thousand years later his life would be avidly studied and worshipers would address their prayers to him? What accounts for this extraordinary influence?

Classic Christian teaching answers without apology: what was said about him is true—*he was the Son of God, the promised Messiah, the one Mediator between God and humanity, who as truly God was truly human, who liberated humanity from the power of sin by his death on the cross*. That hypothesis better explains what his life is and means than any alternative. It is theoretically possible for the study of Jesus to function without that hypothesis, but in practice it is exceptionally difficult, for one is forced to stretch and coerce the narratives to make any sense of them at all without that decisive premise. The documents give dogged resistance to the discarding of that hypothesis, because they think they know about his true identity. There is no other or better way to explain his extraordinary life. According to Christian confession, Jesus is either Messiah or nothing at all.

The Subject

Christology is that study that inquires critically and systematically into this person, Jesus the Christ. In him the fitting and true relation between God and humanity is alleged to be knowable. What that means is the subject of Christology.

The Unimportance and Importance of Christology

The systematic study of Jesus' life is less important than trusting in the efficacy of his death. One may be saved by faith without passing an examination on Christology.

Yet his life and death remain the central interest of Christian piety and education. The events surrounding this individual are alleged to stand as the supreme truth of the history of revelation. The study of Christ implies the study of the divine plan for which humanity was created and the purpose anticipatively revealed toward which history is moving. In Christ God actively embraces fallen humanity and enables humanity to respond to God's active embrace.

This is not a study that can be rightly undertaken by those who remain dogmatically committed to the assumption that nothing new can happen in history or that no events are knowable except those that can be validated under laboratory conditions.

The Study Occurs in Relation to a Worshiping Community

Christology is studied within the context of a worshiping community, just as Islamic theology occurs within the community of Islam. One cannot rightly study basketball and never see a basketball game. The "game" in this case is a living person, Jesus Christ. Where that person is regarded as dead, the game is not being played.

The New Testament itself frequently disavows that it contains an entirely new idea or understanding of God, for the one known in Jesus was already revealed in history before Jesus and in the Law and Prophets (Heb. 1:1-5). Yet in Jesus the reality of God is brought home and relationally received in an unparalleled way. The same God of Israel is experienced in an incomparably personal way through Jesus' life, death, and resurrection.

Our purpose is to understand and teach Jesus the Christ as he has been understood and taught by those whose lives have been most profoundly transformed by him. If we were studying Hasidism or Sufism, we would hope the same of a Hasidic or Sufist interpreter. We would want to learn about the *hasidim* from those whose lives most profoundly embody their teaching. Christians also do well to study honestly the Vedics, Tao, Mishnah, Gemara, Tosefta, and Quran, while others are asked to take seriously the New Testament, and let the evidence be fairly presented.

There can be no denying that out of a two-millennia history in which Jesus' life has been at times partially, wrongly, or self-interestedly remembered, vexations for humanity have also flowed—wars, divisions, inequities, and systemic injustices. A poorly developed, ill-formed understanding of Jesus Christ can limit our experience of Christ and collude with social sin. Hence it is imperative to think clearly about him if such distortions are to be avoided.

Ethical Consequences of Christology

Ethical Demands upon Christology

The incarnation is above all God's own act of identification with the broken, the poor, with sinful humanity. God did not enter human life as a wealthy or powerful "mover and shaker" but came in a manger, amid the life of the poor, sharing in their life and identifying himself with the dispossessed. Liberation theology is poised to be profoundly strengthened by dialogue with classic exegesis.

There is embedded deeply in the best of early ecumenical teaching a pungent critique of sexual inequalities and of the propensity of male users of power to abuse that power. Gregory the Theologian argued in the fourth century that "the majority of men are ill-disposed" to equal treatment of women, hence *"their laws are unequal* and irregular. For what was the reason why they restrained the woman, but indulged the man, and that a woman who practises evil against her husband's bed is an adulteress, and the penalties of the law for this are very severe; but if the husband commits fornication against his wife, he has no account to give? I do not accept this legislation; *I do not approve this custom. They who made the Law were men and therefore their legislation is hard on women"* (Gregory Nazianzen, *Orat.* XXXVII.6, *NPNF* 2 VII, pp. 339–40, italics added). When modern secularists assume that only they are capable of providing a critique of the dynamics of social oppression, it is well to be reminded of this powerful history of Christian social criticism.

Christ and Social Reality

Post-Marxist critics were not the first to ask about social location of interpreters or for an ethical clarification of the meaning of Christianity. There have been numerous times when the ethical consequences of the gospel have taken first place in the minds of those inquiring into Jesus Christ (notably Clement of Alexandria, John Chrysostom, Ambrose, Francis of Assisi, Menno Simons, Grotius, Zinzendorf, and the Blumhardts).

In certain periods of Christian reflection, it has become clear that it is not enough to speak of God's own redemptive coming as if it lacked social consequence, but to spell out what that means for the increase of love and justice in society (as did Augustine, Thomas Aquinas, Calvin, Hooker, and Wesley). This was especially an excellence of nineteenth-century Christianity (notably in such figures as W. Wilberforce, Phoebe Palmer, F. D. Maurice, W. Rauschenbusch, and W. Gladden).

P. T. Forsyth has argued that the moralizing of theology is an essential feature of all modern Christian thought (*PPJC*, chaps. 7, 9). This plea for ethical accountability in speech about God is justified. It is a test that much classical Christianity passes better than modern Christianity (Athanasius, *Incarn. of the Word* 46–57, NPNF 2 IV, pp. 61–67). But it also runs the risk of reducing the Word of Life to moralism (cf. Allison, *The Rise of Moralism*).

The Tradition of Voluntary Poverty

Some imagine that a high Christology necessarily tends to be neglectful of moral responsibility. Those who buy into the Marxist view of history tend repeatedly to sound this alarm. Insofar as such a distortion occurs, it is inconsistent with classical Christian teaching, where the assumption prevails that the confession of Jesus Christ as Lord has insistent moral meaning and social implications. Christians who call for an identification with the poor do so out of a long tradition of voluntary poverty, which follows from Christ's willingness to become poor for our sakes.

On Not Confusing the Kingdom of Christ with State Power

Pope John Paul II, having been himself a pastor who struggled under fire against totalitarian regimes, has written of those who "claim to show Jesus as politically committed, as one who fought against Roman oppression and the authorities, and also as one involved in the class struggle. This idea of Christ as a political figure, a revolutionary, as the subversive man from Nazareth does not tally with the Church's catechesis. By confusing the insidious pretexts of Jesus' accusers with the—very different—attitude of Jesus Himself, some people adduce as the cause of His death the outcome of a political conflict, and nothing is said of the Lord's will to deliver and of His consciousness of His redemptive mission. The Gospels clearly show that for Jesus anything that would alter His mission as the servant of Yahweh was a temptation (Matt. 4:8; Luke 4:5). He does not accept the position of those who mixed the things of God with merely political attitudes (Matt. 22:21; Mark 12:17; John 18:36). He unequivocally rejects recourse to violence. He opens His message of conversion to everybody, without excluding the very publicans" (Puebla Address [1979], *CF*, p. 196).

Out of the cauldron of the Nazi struggle, the Barmen Declaration similarly pleaded for a distinction between the gospel and the political order and rightly rejected a political fixation that would assume "that the Church might be permitted to abandon the form of its message and order to its own pleasure or to changes in prevailing ideological and political convictions" (II.4, *BOC* 8.18). Barmen's warning still needs to be heard: "We reject the false doctrine, as though the Church, over and beyond its special commission, should and could appropriate the characteristics, the tasks, and the dignity of the State, thus itself becoming an organ of the State" (II. 4, *BOC* 8.24; cf. R. Shinn, D. Soelle, P. Berger, "A Politicized Christ," *Christianity and Crisis*, 39 [1979]: 50–57).

A Word To Doubters

A central strength of the fiber of liberal faith has been that it has become difficult for liberals to raise the question of God apart from Christ and impossible to raise the question of Christ without probing its moral implications. Some who clearly recognize that Jesus is an excellent teacher and moral example have been unable to grasp, even when they tried, the reasons why Christianity still continues to speak of him as God, Messiah, Son of God, Lord, and Redeemer. Many morally concerned liberal Christians can honestly understand the church's speech about the Father and the Spirit more readily than about the incarnate Son.

This study respects those whose integrity requires that they raise these ethical questions earnestly. To those who look for a time-tested clarification, this study reaches out. Two principles quietly prevail. First, some who wonder despairingly about the mystery of Christ have nonetheless already been deeply affected by him and may by study come to that recognition. Even those who may hate him (however difficult that is to imagine) can by stages move toward recognizing his hidden presence in their lives. Often those who most doubt his claims have been already addressed by those claims or they would not be so earnestly inquiring and doubting. Hence it is rightly said that doubters may be nearer to salvation than those still morally asleep.

Second, some who have been most actively engaged in social justice and political change who deny Christ's deity nonetheless may remain profoundly affected by his continuing presence. Many are struggling for justice because they have first undergone the pedagogy of his meekness, peacemaking, and hope.

This principle, aptly stated by John Knox, remains applicable to a secularizing culture that is once again turning to the study of Christ: "Whether we affirm or deny, the meaning of 'God' is the meaning which Christ has given to the name" (*MC*, p. 7). H. R. Mackintosh remarks in the same vein: "The name of God has the final meaning that Jesus gave it. . . . He is an integral constituent of what, for us, God means" (*PJC*, pp. 290, 292).

Few understood better than Wordsworth how deeply the spiritual affections outdo the reasoning of secularizing humankind:

> Pious beyond the intention of your thought;
> Devout above the meaning of your will . . .
> The estate of man would be indeed forlorn
> If false conclusions of the reasoning power
> Made the eye blind and closed the passages
> Through which the ear converses with the heart.
> ("The Excursion," Book 4)

THE GOSPEL

Jesus Himself Is the Good News

Jesus did not come to deliver a gospel, but to be himself that gospel. The gospel is the good news of God's own coming. The cumulative event of the sending, coming, living, dying, and continuing life of this incomparable One is the gospel.

The gospel does not introduce an idea but a person—"we proclaim *him!*" (Col. 1:28, italics added) The "him" proclaimed is one whose life ended in such a way that all before and after has become decisively illumined.

What was written about him was not written simply as biography, for biographies are written of persons who are dead and quite deactivated. A biography is a written history of a person's whole *bios* ("life"). A biography of a person still alive is by definition incomplete. Rather the gospel is the account of a person who remains quite active, palpably present, whose heart still beats with our hearts, one who died who is now alive (Augustine, *CG* XIII.18–24, *NPNF* 1 II, pp. 254–61; Bonhoeffer, *Christology*).

The Gospel Defined

The Gospel a Summary of the Person and Work of Christ

Reflections on Jesus are often divided into discussions of his person and work, that is, who he was and what he did. The gospel unites these two: the *person* of the Son engaged in the *work* of the servant-messiah. These are one in the good news of human salvation. "Gospel" is the unique term that concisely summarizes and unites the person and work of Christ. Only this person does this work, which constitutes God's good tidings to human history.

"Gospel" (*euaggelion*) is a distinctive New Testament theme, occurring over one hundred times. The term was embedded in Jesus' preaching from the outset. His coming was announced as "good news of great joy that will be for all the people" (Luke 2:10; Cyprian, *Treatises* XII.2.7, *ANF* V, p. 51). "I must preach the good news of the kingdom of God to the other towns also, because that is why I was sent" (Luke 4:43; Tertullian, *Ag. Marcion* IV.8, *ANF* III, p. 355). The medieval Anglo-Saxon root (*god-spell*) meant "good news" or "glad tidings" (Anglicizing the Latin *bonus nuntius*). The gospel, Luther thought, is to be sung and danced (*Intro. to NT, WLS* II, p. 561, commenting upon David bringing the ark to the City of David, 2 Sam. 6:14).

The Second Helvetic Confession sparely defined the gospel as "glad and joyous news, in which, first by John the Baptist, then by Christ the Lord himself, and afterwards by the apostles and their successors, is preached to us in the world that *God has now performed what he promised* from the beginning of the world" (XIII, *BOC* 5.089, italics added; cf. Ursinus, *CHC*, p. 101). God is now fulfilling what had been promised all along (Origen, *OFP* IV.1, pp. 259–64).

The Gospel Expected by the Prophets

The good news of Jesus' coming was understood as fulfillment of prophetic expectation, as in Isaiah: "How beautiful on the mountains are the feet of those who bring good news, who proclaim peace, who bring good tidings, who proclaim salvation" (Isa. 52:7; Irenaeus, *Ag. Her.* III.13, *ANF* I, pp. 436–37). In Isaiah's setting the good news referred to the return of Israel from exile, yet it prefigured Jesus' proclamation of deliverance of all humanity from sin (Augustine, *CG* XVIII.29, *NPNF* 1 II, p. 376; cf. Calvin, *Comm.* III, pp. 99–101).

The Gospel of God

Paul defined the subject of his letter to Rome as the "gospel of God" (Rom. 1:1). Mark probably entitled his narrative "the gospel of Christ" (Mark 1:1). Both thereby stressed the transcendent origin of the events surrounding Jesus of Nazareth.

Various modifiers of the term "gospel" suggest different angles of vision upon the same series of events, viewed as the gospel of the coming of God's righteousness (Rom. 1:17), or the gospel of grace (Acts 20:24), or of power (Rom. 1:16; 1 Thess. 1:5), or of truth (Gal. 2:14; Col. 1:5), or of hope (Col. 1:23). Yet in all these angles of vision it remains the singular gospel of Christ, the good news of God's own coming (John Chrysostom, *Hom. on First Cor.* XV.1–2, *NPNF* 1 XII, pp. 226–28; Melanchthon, *Loci Communes, LPT*, pp. 141–49; Barth, *CD* IV/2, pp. 180ff.).

The Earliest Christian Preaching

The Kerygma of Acts

The earliest interpretations of the meaning of Jesus' life are found in the oral traditions that fed the preaching reported in Acts (M. Hengel, *Acts and the History of Earliest Christianity*). That preaching has been sparely summarized (Dodd, *APD*, pp. 21–24) in these six points:

(1) "God fulfilled what he had foretold through all the prophets, saying that his Christ would suffer" (Acts 3:18; 2:16; 3:24).

(2) This has occurred through the ministry, death, and resurrection of Jesus, of Davidic descent (Acts 2:30–31), "a man accredited by God to you by miracles, wonders and signs" (Acts 2:22).

(3) "God raised him from the dead" (Acts 2:24; see 3:15; 4:10), making him Lord and Christ (Acts 2:33–36), and "exalted him to his own right hand as Prince and Savior that he might give repentance and forgiveness of sins to Israel" (Acts 5:31).

(4) God has given the Holy Spirit to those who obey him (Acts 5:32). "Exalted to the right hand of God, he has received from the Father the promised Holy Spirit and has poured out what you now see and hear" (Acts 2:33).

(5) Christ "must remain in heaven until the time comes for God to restore everything" (Acts 3:21; 10:42). Having suffered as Messiah and having been exalted as Messiah, he would return as Messiah to bring history to a fitting consummation. So:

(6) "Repent and be baptized, every one of you, in the name of Jesus Christ for the forgiveness of your sins. And you will receive the gift of the Holy Spirit" (Acts 2:38).

These points summarize the earliest Christian preaching. Subsequent creedal confession would generally adhere to this sequence and build upon it (J. N. D. Kelly, *Early Christian Creeds; SCD; CC; COC* I).

The Pauline Kerygma

Paul's conversion is usually dated around A.D. 33–35, probably within forty-eight months of Jesus' death. He understood himself to be passing on to others the tradition he had from the earliest time received (1 Cor. 15:1–7; 16:22). Hence the earliest layer of Paul's proclamation could hardly be assumed to have undergone extensive changes, philosophical mutations, or mythic developments that would have required considerable time to emerge and integrate into a community.

The alternative hypothesis is implausible—that Paul might have been surreptitiously passing on to Corinth views that had only later gradually developed between A.D. 33 and 50, for he himself specifically notes that this is the tradition he received, transmitting to Corinth what had been transmitted to him "from the beginning straightway" (*o kai parelabon*, "from the outset," 1 Cor. 15:3; John Chrysostom, *Hom. on First Cor.* XXXVIII, *NPNF* 1 XII, p. 227). Paul specified his primary sources for the oral tradition he passed on, for he personally knew and had received "the right hand of fellowship" from "James, Peter and John, those reputed to be pillars" of the earliest Christian community (Gal. 2:18–19). "What great friends he was with Peter," remarked John Chrysostom (*Hom. on Gal.* I, *NPNF* 1 XIII, pp. 12–13).

The gospel Paul had earlier received and subsequently passed on was carefully preserved in a Letter whose authenticity is undisputed: "Now, brothers, I want to remind you of the gospel I preached to you, which you received and on which you have taken your stand. By this gospel you are saved, if you hold firmly to the word I preached to you. Otherwise, you have believed in vain. For what I received I passed on to you as of first importance: that Christ died for our sins according to the Scriptures, that he was buried, that he was raised on the third day" (1 Cor. 15:1–4).

The Pauline kerygma was collated and summarized by C. H. Dodd:

The prophecies are fulfilled, and the new age is inaugurated by the coming of
    Christ.
He was born of the seed of David.
He died according to the Scriptures, to deliver us out of the present evil age.
He was buried.
He rose on the third day according to the Scriptures.
He is exalted at the right hand of God, as Son of God and Lord of quick and
    dead.
He will come again as Judge and Saviour of men" (*APD*, p. 17).

The Ascription of Lordship

That Jesus was confessed as "Lord" dates to the earliest known record of Christian kerygma. There is one telling Pauline passage that undercuts the common form-critical theory that the ascription of deity only slowly evolved and that lordship was *much later* to be attributed to Jesus (Bultmann, *TNT* I, pp. 121–33). It is a prayer of Paul's of unquestionable authenticity: "If any man love not the Lord Jesus Christ, let him be *Anathema Marana tha*" (1 Cor. 16:22a, KJV), which means: "a curse be on him. Come, O Lord!" (v. 22b). "That Paul should use an Aramaic expression in a letter to a Greek-speaking church that knew no Aramaic proves that the use of *mar (Kurios)* for Jesus goes back to the primitive Aramaic church and was not a product of the Hellenistic community" (Ladd, *TNT*, p. 431). Just as Jesus had been *Mar* (Lord) to the earliest Aramaic-speaking Jerusalem Christians, so did he quickly become confessed as *Kurios* among the earliest Greek-speaking Christians (1 Cor. 1:2; 1 Thess. 1:1; Mark 2:28; cf. *Didache* 10:6; Rev. 22:20; Rawlinson, *NTDC*, pp. 231–37). This Corinthian passage contains strong internal evidence that the earliest Christian proclamation attested Jesus as *Kurios*, confirming Luke's report of Peter's first sermon in Acts 2:36. This earliest Christian confession derives not from others but from Jesus himself, for in debating the scribes, Jesus made it clear that the Messiah was not merely David's son, but David's Lord, implying that he himself was this divine Lord (Mark 12:37; Taylor, *NJ*, pp. 50–51; Ladd, *TNT*, pp. 341, 167–68).

The earliest Christians were rigorously monotheistic, worshiping and proclaiming the one God. As such they worshiped and proclaimed Jesus Christ as Lord (Ursinus, *CHC*, pp. 202–204). The kernel of triune teaching was already firmly implanted in this earliest core of Christian confession (Pearson, *EC* I, pp. 260–75; *LG*, pp. 181–223).

Early Creedal Summaries

Creedal summaries developed from these primitive scriptural confessions. Ignatius (ca. A.D. 35–107) provided this early summary of core events that were to form the second article of the Apostles' Creed on Christ: "Be deaf, therefore, whenever anyone speaks to you apart from Jesus Christ, who is of the stock of David, who is of Mary, who was truly born, ate and drank, was truly persecuted under Pontius Pilate, was truly crucified and died in the sight of beings of heaven, of earth and the underworld, who was also truly raised from the dead" (Ignatius of Antioch, *Trallians* 9:1–2, *CC*, p. 16; *ANF* I, p. 71; J. B. Lightfoot, *The Apostolic Fathers*, 1891, p. 74).

Irenaeus (ca. A.D. 130–200) was firmly convinced that the following confession had been reliably received directly from the apostles themselves and had not passed through a series of dilutions resulting from its development: "The Church, though scattered through the whole world to the ends of the earth, has received from the Apostles and their disciples the faith . . . in one Christ Jesus, the Son of God, who became flesh for our salvation" (Irenaeus, *Ag. Her.* I.x.1, *COC* II, p. 13).

Short creedal summaries were designed to be memorized verbatim at baptism, in order that believers may have "salvation written in their hearts by the Spirit without paper and ink" (Irenaeus, *Ag. Her.* II.4.1, *COC* II, p. 15; O. Cullmann, *Earliest Christian Confessions*). The rule of faith as recalled and passed on by Tertullian was understood by him to be "irreformable" (*irreformabilis; On the Veiling of Virgins* I, *ANF* IV, p. 27).

Far from being appended to Scripture, the creed was understood as a summary of Scripture, containing nothing other than that teaching found in Scripture (Pearson, *EC* I, p. 383). The *Heidelberg Catechism* asks: "What, then, must a Christian believe? All that is promised us in the gospel, a summary of which is taught us in the articles of the Apostles' Creed, our universally acknowledged confession of faith" (II, Q22, *BOConf.* 4.022).

Protestant confessions characteristically accepted the classical Christian teaching of ancient ecumenical formulae "summed up in the Creeds and decrees of the first four most excellent synods convened at Nicaea, Constantinople, Ephesus and Chalcedon—together with the Creed of blessed Athanasius, and all similar symbols," and "in this way we retain the Christian, orthodox and catholic faith whole and unimpaired" (Second Helvetic Confession XI, *BOConf.* 5.078). Orthodox, Catholic, and Protestant doctrinal definitions share this common consensus. It is to these ancient ecumenical formulations and their leading expositors that consensual theology primarily appeals, provided that "nothing is contained in the aforesaid symbols which is not agreeable to the Word of God" (Second Helvetic Confession XI, *BOC* 5.079).

Gospel and Church

It is this gospel that created the church. The gospel does not belong to the church, for the gospel brought the church into being (Eph. 5:23; Col. 1:18–24; Ursinus, *CHC*, pp. 102–104). The church does not possess or own or contain the gospel. The very purpose of the church is to proclaim and make known the gospel (Luther, *Serm. at Leisnig* [1523], *WLS* I, p. 263, *WA* 11, 408; Melanchthon, *Loci Communes, LCC* XIX, pp. 70ff., 84ff.).

The deepest need of humanity is for salvation from sin. This is the quandary to which the gospel speaks. The church that forgets the gospel of salvation is finally not the church but its shadow. The church that becomes focused upon maintaining itself instead of the gospel becomes a dead branch of a living vine. The church is imperiled when it becomes intoxicated with the spirit of its particular age, committed more to serve the gods of that age than the God of all ages (Augustine, *CG* IV, *NPNF* 1 II, pp. 64–83; Kierkegaard, *Judge for Yourselves!; Two Ages*).

KEY TERMS: PERSON, WORK, STATES, AND OFFICES

Shorthand terms have long been used in the ecumenical tradition to encompass large masses of dialogue and consensual thinking in condensed formulae. This section introduces readers to the most important of these terms pertaining to Christ, namely, those distinguishing between Christ's person, his work, his states of descent and ascent, and his offices (prophet, priest, and king). Time is saved by learning these distinctions from the outset.

The Person and Work of Christ

The overall design of classical Christology is essentially simple and need not be confusing even to the novice. It hinges on a simple distinction between who one *is* and what one *does*. A person is not the same as that person's work. *The work (opus) is done by the person (persona*, Gk. *hupostasis) through an office (officium)*. Nothing proceeds rightly in setting forth the work of Christ unless the unique person doing the work is properly identified.

Person and Work Conceptually Distinguishable

The work accomplished by Jesus Christ (including all that has been done for humanity) could not have been done by any other person than one distinctly capable of mediating the alienated relationship between deity and humanity. To mediate that relationship, one must have personal credentials in both humanity and divinity. One must have a particular identity, a unique personhood to do that work (Leo, *Serm.* 27, *NPNF* 2 XII, pp. 139–41; *Serm.* 63, pp. 175-77; Warfield, *The Person and Work of Christ*).

Classic exegetes characteristically began their reflection with a discussion of the distinctive *identity* of Christ, or the *person* of Christ as truly human and truly God—who he is (Augustine, *Trin.* IV, FC 45, 129-79; cf. Novatian, Hilary, and Gregory Nazianzen on second article of the Trinity). If this cannot be systematically established, it is doubtful that there is any viable alternative way to speak of divine-human mediation or of the mediator's activity.

This sequence runs counter to the prevailing modern procedure insisted upon by Harnack, Bultmann, Bousset, Tillich, Pannenberg, Marxsen, and many others, which is characterized by the notion that it is necessary to speak first of the historical activity of Jesus before speaking of his being recollected as the Christ.

Theandric Union

Quietly operating in the overall design of classic teaching is the *principle of economy (oikonomia*—the arrangement, plan, order, design of the foreseeing God, see *LG*, pp. 270–315): the central ordering economic principle of all talk of the *person* of Christ is the union of his humanity and divinity, one person having two natures. This is called the *theandric* (divine-human) *premise*, or the premise of theandric union. Theandric is a contraction of *theanthropos* (God-man; Augustine, *Trin.* I.13, *NPNF* 1 III, pp. 33–36).

The Deity of Christ Is the Premise of His Saving Activity

The mission of divine grace is the central ordering principle of all talk of the *work* of Christ, encompassing his life, death, exaltation, and continuing presence. "The doctrine of the mediator consists of two parts: the one has respect to the person of the mediator; the other to his office" (Ursinus, *CHC*, p. 164). An intrinsic order is here implied. One must first establish the personal identity of the Son, and only on that basis can one consider the work of the Son or the saving action of God in Jesus Christ.

Person and work, though conceptually distinguishable, are intrinsically related, hence inseparable, always appearing together (just as you are premised in what you do, your work cannot be considered apart from you). There is no mediation without this mediator. There can be no doctrine of the person without speaking of his activity, and no doctrine of the work without speaking of the person.

Christ Known Through His Benefits

The saving significance of his work for us is the reason why we study his person, his unique divine-human identity. Melanchthon wrote: "Who Jesus Christ is becomes known in his saving action" (*Loci*, pref., *CR* 21, p. 85). Yet this is not to imply that his saving work predominates, subsumes, or countervenes his deity or divine-human unity, for no one could save except *theanthropos* (God-man).

Terms of the Inquiry Defined

Key Issues of the Person

There is an aesthetically beautiful simplicity in the ordering of classical Christology that examines in sequence three questions: the deity of the person; the humanity of the person; and the unique personal union of God and humanity in one person (Athanasius, *Four Discourses Ag. Arians* III.26–28, *NPNF* 2 IV, pp. 407–22; cf. Novatian, *Trin.* 9–28, *FC* 67, pp. 42–99). There indeed are other ancillary questions associated with the identity of Christ, but no one attentive to Scripture could long avoid these: Is the Son truly God? Is the Son truly human? If both are answered yes, how can these two affirmations be made in the same breath? This is the trajectory that we will track in Part I.

Key Issues of the Work

Only when the classic exegetes had identified the Worker did they speak of the work of the Savior. The *work* of Christ is a phrase that sums up all the saving activity of God the Son on behalf of humanity. Whatever he has done that has saving significance is viewed synoptically as his saving work. Under the rubric of the work of Christ we will focus primarily upon his mission, death, and resurrection, but we will also speak more broadly of his life, teaching, and the events preceding and surrounding his death and exaltation.

Soteriology (the study of salvation, *peri tes sōtērias logos*, concerning the Word of salvation) studies the reconciling *work* this unique Person came to accomplish, the *redemption* of humanity. The Mediator came to mediate between God and humanity in a redemptive work that could only be accomplished by this unique person.

The study of God's saving action includes the work of redemption (the atoning death and victorious resurrection) and the receptive application of that work in the community of faith and the world. The way of entry into the study of salvation is the discussion of the estates and offices of the Redeemer.

This Work Engaged and Completed in Descending and Ascending Phases

For this person to do this work, it was necessary that he come to humanity in a manner fitting to his theandric identity. Humbled from an exalted state, he came to share in our human sphere in life and death. Having accomplished this mission, he returned as resurrected Lord in exaltation.

The redemption envisioned by God in eternity was accomplished in time by his Son Jesus Christ. Hence the whole complex story of his coming and going may be summarized in two basic states or phases:

He must come	He must go
He is sent from the Father	He returns to the Father
The Son who descends	Must ascend

Physics teaches that which goes up must come down. Christology teaches that the Son who descends must ascend. The usual way of expressing these phases doctrinally is:

Humiliation	Exaltation
From incarnation to death	From resurrection to judgment
katabasis (descent)	*anabasis* (ascent)

Thus it is summarily said that the Son appeared in two *states* ("estates" or conditions), first as lowered, then as raised.

Humiliation does not mean that God has been finally degraded, demeaned, or diminished, but rather that God the Son enters our human condition by self-humbling and becoming obedient unto death and burial (Phil. 2:6-9), after which there can be no further humbling. Then he is exalted to return to the bosom of the Father (Hilary, *Trin.* II, XI, *FC* 25, pp. 35-63, 459-500; Longenecker, *CEJC*, pp. 58-63).

The Three Offices

An office is a position of trust, an assigned service or function, with specified duties and authority. The ancient Hebraic offices to which the expected One would be anointed were prophet, priest, and king. These provided a sufficient frame of reference for organizing and summarizing the whole redemptive work of Christ. To these three tasks he was anointed: as prophet he taught and proclaimed God's coming kingdom; as priest he suffered and died for humanity; as king he is exalted to receive legitimate governance of the coming reign of God.

Sequential Correlation of Estates and Offices

Note that there is a sequential correlation between the two estates and three offices: he is *humbled* to undertake his earthly *prophetic* ministry, which ends in his *priestly* ministry; he is *exalted* to complete his *ministry of governance* in guarding and guiding the faithful community toward the fulfillment of the promises of God. One who grasps this sentence thoroughly has already touched the vital center of the inner structure of classic reasoning about the Word of Life. We will make clear each of its elements.

Surveying the Christological Landscape

Summarizing

Looking ahead in overview: Even the novice can distinguish between (1) *the person and work of Christ*, (2) *the two natures of the one person in theandric union*, (3) *death and resurrection as key to the work of Christ*, (4) *the two estates, and* (5) *the three offices by which he accomplished his work*.

These simple terms grasp the essential structure of classical Christology. Everything else falls into place in relation to this fairly uncomplicated structure. This book promises to make these distinctions clear and functional for preaching and pastoral care.

Sources of This Order

The specific order we will follow is a composite of patterns formulated by the most deliberate and intuitive systematic minds of the early periods of Christian teaching: Irenaeus, Tertullian, Gregory Nazianzen, Cyril of Jerusalem, Hilary of Potiers, Augustine, and John of Damascus. Parts of our sequence are found in all of these figures, but in no one in full detail. This sequence owes very little to any writer after the eighth century.

In Thomas Aquinas and John Calvin are found some further refinements of this same primitive sequence. The structure of Thomas Aquinas's treatise on the Savior, for example, falls into two major divisions:

THE MYSTERY OF THE INCARNATION	THE MYSTERY OF REDEMPTION
The person of Christ	The actions and sufferings of Christ
Divine-human union (Christology, *ST* III, Q48–51)	Birth, life, death, exaltation (Soteriology, *ST* III, Q52–55)

Calvin's similar order has profoundly shaped Protestant Christology:

How the two natures of Mediator make one person (Inst. 2.14)	Offices: prophet, priest, king (Inst. 2.15)	How Christ has fulfilled the function of Redeemer to acquire salvation for us by his death, resurrection, and ascension (Inst. 2.16–17)

The Name Jesus Christ Encompasses His Person and Work

Christ (Messiah) is a title, Jesus a personal name. The unified name Jesus Christ welds together the person and office of the Savior. The inclusive name itself reveals the heart of the interfacing of the Jesus of history and the Christ celebrated by faith. Hence to resist calling him simply Jesus Christ, as did Tillich (*Syst. Theol.* II, pp. 136–38, 151–58), is to mistake his proper name.

This office (Christ) cannot be viewed or understood apart from this person (Jesus). The person is never seen or attested "off duty" or as separable from the office, for Jesus is always the sent Son, the anointed One, whose work is the giving of himself, whose person is the Word made flesh, whose enacted word is his life. He cannot be reduced either to Jesus or the Christ. The narratives of Jesus do not mention anything he *did* that could be understood as disconnected from *who he was* as Sent and Anointed One.

Likewise one cannot separate the teachings of Jesus from his person-hood or his personal mediatorial office, as one might view the teachings of Spinoza as to some degree separable from the person or office held by Spinoza. The teachings of Jesus are important to faith not simply because they are great ideas, but because they are the teachings of this incompara-ble Mediator, Jesus Christ. There is no mention of teachings whatever in the Apostles' Creed and no attempt in any of the classic confessions to set forth the teachings of Jesus as conceptually separable from his person and work.

Faith in Jesus Christ is not the acceptance of a system of teaching or doctrine, but personal trust in him based upon an encounter with this liv-ing person whose life is his word and whose word is embodied. His mes-sage is proclaimed only through his action, especially in the events surrounding his death. Jesus not only has a word to speak for humanity but himself *is* that Word. He not only does good works but also is the inestimable good work of God on our behalf.

This is why the most basic form of Christian confession is that *Jesus Christ is Lord* (based on the pivotal recognition that *Jesus is the Christ*). Nothing is more central to New Testament documents than that confes-sion based on that recognition. That Jesus is God and Savior is the essen-tial confession of the World Council of Churches (Amsterdam, 1948). This is a quintessential integrating statement of the person and work of Christ.

Yet modern criticism has sought for a century to pry Jesus loose from his identity as the Christ on the one hand (Harnack and the German liberal tradition focusing upon Jesus' teachings) or from any significant correlation with the historical person of Jesus (Bultmann and Tillich, who had grave doubts that anything at all could be known about Jesus, even though the community's memory of the kerygma could be proximately known).

The "Nicene" (Nicaea-Constantinopolitan) Creed as Organizing Principle of the Classic-Ecumenic Study of Christ

The prevailing organizing structure for the classic sequence of Chris-tian teaching of Christ is found in the second article of the Creed of the

150 Fathers of the Council of Constantinople (traditionally called the "Nicene Creed," but more accurately called the Nicaea-Constantinopolitan Creed of 381, referenced here as the Creed of the 150 Fathers).

This creed may be found in virtually any prayerbook or hymnbook of the Christian tradition—Catholic, Orthodox, liberal or evangelical Protestant. It contains everything essential to this study and to Christology. We will examine each phrase in due course.

The creed has a deliberate overarching structure of three articles of faith in one God: God the Father, God the Son, and God the Spirit. Having already discussed the first article on God the Father in the first volume of this series (*The Living God*), this volume will treat point by point the series of topics of the *second article on God the Son*, leaving it to the third volume to discuss the third article on God the Spirit. In this way it becomes clear how the whole of theology is a preparation for or confirmation of baptism.

Luther thought that "all errors, heresies, idolatries, offenses, abuses and ungodliness in the Church have arisen primarily because this [second] article, or part, of the Christian faith concerning Jesus Christ, has been either disregarded or abandoned" (Luther, J. N. Lenker ed., [1908] XXIV, p. 224, in *CLT*, p. 50). "You must stay with the Person of Christ. When you have Him, you have all; but you have also lost all when you have lost Him" (Luther, *Serm. on John 6:37, WLS* I, p. 149; *WA* 33, 80).

Note that the creed's second article is ordered according to the pivotal twofold division that summarizes classic Christology: the *person* and the *work* of Christ (*who* the Redeemer *is* and *what* the Redeemer has *done* to redeem humanity), distinguishable yet integrally united in a single gospel. In this way the creed provides the core outline of this inquiry (with key Greek and Latin terms), as follows:

OUTLINE OF THE CHRISTOLOGICAL ARTICLE OF THE "NICENE" CREED

PART I. Who Christ Is—Word Made Flesh

    Faith in the One Lord: Truly God, Truly Human

        Personal trust: I believe (*credo*; Gk. *pisteuomen*).
        Belief in one Lord (*in unum Dominum*; Gk. *eis ena Kurion*).

    Confession of the Name Jesus Christ

        I believe in Jesus (*Credo in . . . Jesus*).
        Jesus is the Christ (*Christum*), anointed as proclaiming prophet, self-offering priest, and messianic king.

    One Person: Deity and Humanity in Theandric Union
    Only Son of God (*Filium Dei*; Gk. *ton huion tou theou ton monogenē*).

The Son is eternally Begotten (*unigenitum*; Gk. *monogenē*, "only-begotten").
Of the Father (*ex Patre natum*; Gk. *ton ek tou patros gennēthenta*).
Begotten before all worlds (*ante omnia saecula*; Gk. *pro pantōn tōn aiōnōn*).

True God

The Son is God of God (*Deum de Deo*).
The Son is Light of Light (*Lumen de Lumine*; Gk. *phōs ek phōtos*).

The Nature of Divine Sonship

The Son is true God of true God (*Deum verum de Deo vero*; Gk. *Theon alēthinon ek Theou alēthinou*).
The Son is begotten, not made (*genitum, non factum*; Gk. *gennēthenta, ou poiēthenta*).
The Son is consubstantial with the Father (*consubstantialem Patri*; Gk. *homoousion tō Patri*, of the same essence as the Father).

Creator and Savior as Preexistent Word: The Preincarnational Life of the Son

By the Son were all things made (*per quem omnia facta sunt*; Gk. *di ou ta panta egeneto*).
The Son's mission was for us humans (*qui propter nos homines*; Gk. *ton di hēmas tous anthrōpous*).
He came for our salvation (*et propter nostram salutem*; Gk. *kai dia tēn hēmeteran soterian*).

The Humbling of God to Servanthood

God the Son descended to human history (*descendit*). The descent from heaven (*de coelis*) to earth.

The Incarnation: Truly Human

For us the Son became incarnate (*incarnatus*; Gk. *sarkōthenta*).
Was conceived by the Holy Spirit (*de Spiritu Sancto*).
Born of the Virgin Mary (*ex Maria virgine*).
Was made man (*homo factus est*; Gk. *enanthrōpēsanta*).

PARTS II AND III. Our Lord's Earthly Life—He Died for Our Sins

Our Lord's Earthly Life (Prophetic Office)
His Suffering and Death (Priestly Office)

Jesus was crucified (*crucifixus*).
For us (*pro nobis*; Gk. *huper hēmen*).
Tried under Pontius Pilate (*sub Pontio Pilato*).

Suffered (*passus;* Gk. *pathonta*).
Died and was buried (*sepultus est*).

PART IV. Exalted Lord

[He descended into the abode of the dead (*descendit in inferna* (not
in the Creed of the 150 Fathers, but appearing in the creed of
Rufinus, A.D. 390, and following)].
He was raised again from the dead (*resurrexit;* Gk. *anastanta*).

According to the Scriptures (*secundum Scripturus*).
On the third day (*tertia dei*).
He ascended into heaven (*ascendit in coelum*).

His Coming Kingdom (Regal Office)

He now sits at the right hand of the Father (*sedet ad dexteram
Patris*).
And he shall come again (*et iterum venturus est*) to judge the
quick and the dead (COC II, pp. 57, 58).

Why This Organizing Principle?

"Before you go forth," wrote Augustine, "fortify yourselves with your
Creed," composed of words "scattered throughout the divine Scriptures,"
but which "have been assembled and unified to facilitate the memory"
(Augustine, *The Creed* 1, FC 27, p. 289). The creed is compact, memoriza-
ble, serving the teaching function of bringing together the heart of the
matter of Scripture.

Note that this organizing principle expresses both a logical and a
chronological order. It is *logical* in that it proceeds from Christ's identity
to his activity, from his person to his work, from his being to his doing,
from *who* the Mediator is to *what* the Mediator does to benefit humanity.
This person is required for this saving act, for who else could do this
work of mediation?

There can be no soteriology without Christology, for there is no salvation without a Savior. If Jesus were not truly divine Son, then his atoning
action on the cross would have been insufficient — merely an example of
human heroism or altruistic generosity.

The order of the creed is *chronological* because the story of salvation is
a history — a basic premise of Hebraic religion. History (hence God's salvation) unfolds chronologically as a linear, sequential development. Consequently the study of Christ proceeds according to the order of time
(*chronos*), within which a pivotal moment occurs that divides time —
appearing at the fullness of time (*kairos*).

This historical sequence could be schematized as follows:

DESCENT

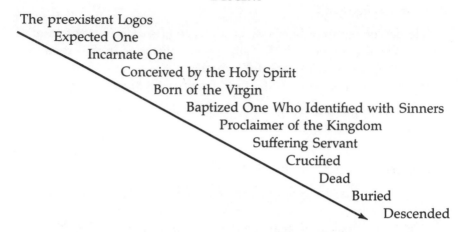

The preexistent Logos
   Expected One
      Incarnate One
         Conceived by the Holy Spirit
            Born of the Virgin
               Baptized One Who Identified with Sinners
                  Proclaimer of the Kingdom
                     Suffering Servant
                        Crucified
                           Dead
                              Buried
                                 Descended

This entire descending sequence is called the humbling (lowering, lowliness, humiliation, or sometimes exiniation) of God, because it takes the story of the Mediator chronologically from preexistence to death, in a descending order from the highest of the high to the lowest of the low. It reveals the lowliness of God to the greatest conceivable extent. In the first three Parts of this study we will take that descent step by step.

Part IV must be portrayed in the reverse ascending order, since it begins in the depths and moves upward toward exaltation into the reception of the Son into the heavenly kingdom; hence it is called the exaltation of the messianic king (read from down to up):

ASCENT

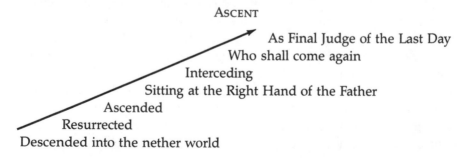

                            As Final Judge of the Last Day
                      Who shall come again
                Interceding
            Sitting at the Right Hand of the Father
        Ascended
      Resurrected
Descended into the nether world

In this way the twofold movement of descent and ascent, the humbling and exaltation of God the Son, provides a way of organizing exceptionally diverse materials of Scripture into a single memorable confession of faith encompassed in the Nicene Creed.

The four Parts of this study may be stated concisely:

He came.
He lived.
He died.
He rose.

The first question to be faced is: Who came?

Part I

WORD MADE FLESH

Four classic questions encompass the teaching about Christ's person: *Quis* (who)? *Quid* (what)? *Quomodo* (how)? *Ad quid* (why)?.

Who assumed humanity in the incarnation?
What nature did the eternal Son assume?
How are deity and humanity united in one person?
Why did the Son become flesh?

Modern journalism quotes this sequence as the essence of good reporting, unaware that it derives from classic Christian theology, which itself sought to report the best of good news.

The four answers may be summarized: (1) the divine Logos assumed (2) human nature, (3) so as personally to unite deity and humanity in Christ, (4) for the redemption of humanity (Athanasius, *Incarn. of the Word*, NPNF 1 IV, pp. 39–53; Pohle-Preuss, *DT* IV, p. 5; cf. Bellarmine, *De Christo* I.1; Franzelin, *De Verbo Incarnato*). This is a high altitude map of the spectacular territory we are now to traverse on foot, traditionally called "the Person of Christ."

CHAPTER 2

The Body Language of God

The premier question of Christology focuses upon the identity of Jesus. Who is this itinerant teacher, Mary's son, the carpenter's son? There is little doubt that such a question was beginning to be asked already during Jesus' own lifetime. It emerged early in Jesus' ministry, continued steadily, and remains vexing to us today. "Who do you think you are?" (John 8:53), they asked of him.

Such questioning was a response to the words and deeds of Jesus and not merely projected upon him decades later by romanticizing rememberers. This question always arises necessarily out of concrete meeting and dialogue with Jesus of Nazareth.

THE DEITY OF CHRIST

Who Can Forgive Sins but God Alone?

Four forms of the same identity question appear in Gospel reports of Jesus. The same question was posed from extremely varied inquirers: by the religious establishment, by civil authorities, by the general populace, and among the inner circle of his disciples. The first task is to show textually the force of the identity question among varied audiences.

Asked by the Religious Establishment

When he healed a paralytic, Jesus said: "Your sins are forgiven." Some asked: "Who is this man who speaks against God in this way. No man can forgive sins; God alone can!" (Luke 5:21, TEV; Calvin, *Comm.* XVI, p. 395; cf. Novatian, *Trin.*, FC 67, p. 54). Later when he pronounced as forgiven "a woman who had lived a sinful life" (Luke 7:37), "the other guests began to say among themselves, *'Who is this who even forgives sins?'"* (Luke 7:49, italics added; Tertullian, *Ag. Marcion* IV.18, ANF III, p. 376; Henry,

CWB V, pp. 656–58). Such questions were dutifully raised by pious defenders of the religious establishment.

Asked by the Civil Authorities

A related question was raised by civil authorities anxious about political succession, legitimated power, order, and authority. Herod jailed and finally beheaded John the Baptist, a relative of Jesus. The theory was being circulated that Jesus perhaps might be John returning from the dead. Herod complained: "I beheaded John. *Who, then, is this* I hear such things about?" (Luke 9:9, italics added). The question of his identity became an urgent matter for civil authorities and ultimately the cause of his death.

Asked by the Populace

The question of Jesus' identity was not merely a matter of private conversation but perplexed the general populace. This became clear at one decisive point—"When Jesus entered Jerusalem, the whole city was stirred and asked, *'Who is this?'*" (Matt. 21:11, italics added; cf. Stott, *BC*, pp. 19ff.).

Asked Within the Inner Circle

A decisive moment in Jesus' ministry came when he put the question squarely to the disciples: *"Who do you say I am?"* (Mark 8:29; italics added). When he told them that he would soon be betrayed, would die, and be raised again, Mark reported candidly that "they did not understand what he meant" (Mark 9:32; Luke 9:45). It was not until the resurrection that his identity was clearly revealed.

This question accompanied the footsteps of Jesus all along the way. And it has hardly lost its force for us today.

The Irreducible Issue

The same vexing question surfaces today for anyone who reads the New Testament texts—"Who is this?" (Mark 4:41; cf. Victorinus, *On the Creation of the World*, ANF VII, pp. 314–43). One cannot easily read the New Testament without taking up this question of Jesus' identity. Moreover it cannot be taken up casually as a purely historical exercise, for to ask "Who is he?" is to ask "Who is God?" and "Who am I myself?"

The Quick Way to End Christology

This question is decisive for classical Christianity. If it should turn out to be the case that Jesus was quite different from who he said he was, then we might as well end this book here and not bother with its remaining pages. If there is a radical gap between who he claimed to be and who he really was, then little remains of the New Testament witness except burdensome bones of moral perfectionism and stuffy bags of sentimental religious trivia. If, on the other hand, it might be possible to demonstrate to fair-minded inquirers that the report concerning Jesus is essentially a truthful recollection, then the consequences of that must reverberate to every dimension of personal and social life.

Does the Question Yield to Evidentiary Analysis?

A fair hearing may be given to this question without necessarily asking about the inspiration of the documents attesting the evidence. The question can be explored as other historical questions are rightly explored—rigorously and fair-mindedly on the basis of the best accumulation of facts we can muster, with a candid, honest assessment of evidence (Origen, *OFP* IV.2-3, pp. 269-312; Eusebius, *CH* I, *NPNF* 2 I, pp. 81-103; Jerome, *Hom. on Mark*, 75-84, *FC* 57, pp. 121-92).

Is it possible to set forth credible evidence that Jesus is the one he is attested to be—the One and Only God become fully human, a historical individual personally uniting two distinct natures, human and divine—so that only this one could be the expected One worthy of worship? That is the only ultimately important subject of the study of the person of Christ. Other questions are made tiny by comparison. If this proves right, then all else follows; if this proves wrong, then nothing else could possibly avail to make Christianity worth pursuing. If true but undemonstrable, then a heavy cloud hangs over Christian testimony. This is in fact the central and decisive question that the New Testament as a whole seeks to answer.

The examination of this sort of evidence will occupy us throughout this volume, but it will focus initially upon three key issues: did Christ's claims about himself correspond with the remembering church's attestation about him? Did Christ's living and dying reveal a character and behavior that corresponds with these claims? In what sense did the resurrection constitute a unique validation of these claims? The historical evidence cannot be fairly assessed without probing these questions (Irenaeus, *Ag. Her.* IV.5-10, *ANF* I, pp. 466-74; Mark 8:29; Matt. 10:32-33; Stott, *BC*, p. 21).

Petition for Illumination

It is fitting that we preface the presentation of this evidence not with prolix methodological considerations, but more directly with simple honest prayer: "God—if you are there!—illuminate this path that we may rightly understand what has happened in the events surrounding Jesus of Nazareth. We seek plain truth. We intend to follow the facts as best we can discern them. Enable us fairly to examine whether the extraordinary claims made about Jesus are true. If you should bring us to the point where it is clear that these claims are true, we will not live as though they were not true but will reorder our lives accordingly" (for classic prayers for illumination of the mystery of Christ, see Augustine, *Confessions*, *LCC* VII, pp. 31, 34, 330–33; *BCP*, "Collects to be Used Throughout the Year"; cf. Stott, *BC*, p. 18).

CLAIMS MADE BY AND ABOUT CHRIST

Was He Inordinately Self-centered?

Prophetic Expectation Fulfilled

Early in his ministry, when Jesus attended the synagogue of his home village of Nazareth, he reportedly read this passage from Isaiah 41:1–2, as recorded by Luke: "'The Spirit of the Lord is on me, because he has anointed me to preach good news to the poor. He has sent me to proclaim freedom for the prisoners and recovery of sight for the blind, to release the oppressed, to proclaim the year of the Lord's favor.' Then he rolled up the scroll, gave it back to the attendant and sat down. The eyes of every-one in the synagogue were fastened on him, and he began by saying to them, 'Today this scripture is fulfilled in your hearing'" (Luke 4:18–21; Tertullian, *Ag. Marcion* IV.8, *ANF* III, pp. 354–55; *Ag. Praxeas* 11, *ANF* III, pp. 605–606; Calvin, *Comm.* XVI, p. 230). The point is unmistakable: Jesus, in Luke's view, thought that Isaiah was referring to him! The climax of the episode is not Isaiah's prophecy but Jesus' response to it.

When he preached the coming governance of God, he assumed that his own ministry inaugurated that governance. Entrance into the reign of God was thought to depend entirely upon how one answers the question—"Who is this one?"—and whether one would be willing to share unreservedly in the coming of God that Jesus' ministry signaled.

His entire public ministry was charged with the energy of fulfillment of prophetic promises. "Blessed are the eyes that see what you see. For I tell you that many prophets and kings wanted to see what you see but did not see it, and to hear what you hear but did not hear it" (Luke 10:23). All four Gospels hold that he assented to the recognition that he was the expected deliverer of Israel (Matt. 16:15–20; Mark 8:29–32, 14:62–63; Luke 9:20–22, 24:46; John 11:25–28).

Faith Attaches Personally to Jesus

Note that Jesus did not ask his hearers to believe merely his teaching, but to believe *in him*. He was less concerned that his miracles be publicly celebrated than that they be inwardly recognized as embodying and attesting his divine mission and sonship. His ministry confronted every hearer with the same simple decision: are you ready to live in the presence of the coming governance of God?

He did not merely call for faith in God generally, as if apart from himself, but rather understood himself to be nothing less than the authentic basis and object of genuine faith in God (John 12:44–50, 15:1–8). Hence one who meets Jesus cannot avoid asking: who is this one? The consequences were assumed to be radical: believing in him would deliver the sinner from sin; failing to believe in him would leave the sinner so mired in sin as to miss eternal life (John 3:15–16, 36).

The Scandal of Self-Reference

It is characteristic of great religious teachers that they are self-effacing. Jesus seems quite different. He was constantly remembered as saying outrageous things about himself, like: "I am the way and the truth and the life. No one comes to the Father except through me" (John 16:6). "Anyone who loves his father or mother more than me is not worthy of me" (Matt. 10:27). These ring with absurdity unless there is a plausible premise behind them that can help them make sense (Stott, *BC*, pp. 18–23).

One of the most immodest and shocking aspects of the New Testament is the frequency with which Jesus makes reference to himself, his mission, his sonship, his coming kingdom. No wonder interpretations of his supposed delusions have been offered by modern psychiatrists whose naturalistic assumptions already rule out taking seriously his own explanation of himself.

The Teacher of Humility

Compounding the irony, all of this was said by one who most earnestly *taught humility* and urged others to "become as little children." Preaching meekness, he warned his hearers against self-centeredness, and when they quarreled over who would be the greatest, he corrected them (Mark 10:35–45).

Either he did not follow his own teaching at all, or there must have been something utterly unique about him that enabled him to teach from a very different premise of authority than anyone else. The most shocking hypothesis is simply to suppose that he was telling the truth about himself and that reports of him were substantially accurate (the faith of classic Christianity).

Did He Himself Make Direct Claims?

The most crucial question is whether Jesus understood himself to be the messiah of historic Jewish expectations. Did he transform the very notion of messiah in accepting that designation? Much of the most penetrating evidence comes from the earliest written Gospel. According to Mark, Jesus understood his ministry as a sign of the end time. His first statement of public ministry, according to the earliest Gospel, was: "The time has come." "The Kingdom of God is near. Repent and believe the good news!" (Mark 1:15).

There can be little doubt that he assumed the title "Son of Man" as particularly definitive of his mission. It was a recognized messianic title from Daniel 7:13, Ezekiel (2:1, 3; 3:1–10; 8:1–12), 2 Esdras 13, and the *Similitudes of Enoch* (Justin Martyr, *Dialogue with Trypho* 31–33, FC 6, pp. 192–97; Gregory of Nyssa, *Ag. Eunomius* III.4, NPNF 2 VI, p. 145; Augustine, *Trin.* II.18, NPNF 1 III, pp. 53, 54; cf. Cullmann, *CNT,* pp. 137–92; H. E. Toedt, *The Son of Man in the Synoptic Tradition;* Taylor, *NJ*). It implied descent from above.

When asked by the high priest before the Sanhedrin: "Are you the Christ, the Son of the Blessed One?" Jesus broke his previous reserve and replied, "I am." "The high priest tore his clothes. 'Why do we need any more witnesses?' he asked. 'You have heard the blasphemy'" (Mark 14:61–62; Clement of Alexandria, *From Cassiodorus, Fragments* 2, ANF II, p. 574).

The most remarkable part of Peter's confession, "You are the Christ" (Mark 8:29), is not so much that Peter said it but that Jesus accepted the ascription, and "warned them not to tell anyone about him" (v. 30; Origen, *Comm. on Matt.* XII.10, AEG III, pp. 151–55). The Jesus of Mark's Gospel was not just another prophet, such as Elijah or John, but the one to whom the prophets attested, less a sign pointing to the door of life than the door itself (Mark 13:4–37; cf. John 10:7–9; Rev. 3:8; Athanasius, *Four Discourses Ag. Arians* I.1–11, NPNF 2 IV, pp. 306–28). We have no earlier or more reliable evidence of Jesus' proclamation than these Markan sayings.

His Unique Sonship

Jesus understood himself to have a unique relation of sonship to God the Father. Much of John's Gospel focuses upon the intimacy and eternality of that relationship. John reported Jesus as saying: "I and the Father are one" (10:30). The text implies mutual, coeternal accountability, with Father and Son assumed to be distinguishable, one sending and one being sent.

Jesus explained to Philip: "How can you say, 'Show us the Father'? Don't you believe that I am in the Father, and that the Father is in me? The words I say to you are not just my own. Rather, it is the Father, living in me, who is doing his work" (John 14:9–10).

He regarded himself as alone able intimately to understand the Father's will and to reveal God: "All things have been committed to me by my Father" (Matt. 11:27). When the seventy-two returned from their mission, Jesus, "full of joy through the Holy Spirit," delighting in his sonship soon to be revealed, said: "No one knows who the Son is except the Father, and no one knows who the Father is except the Son and those to whom the Son chooses to reveal him" (Luke 10:21–22). The Son met and called persons to whom this relationship to the Father would be revealed, who would be able to attest that they had lived in the presence of the Son of God (Matt. 28:16–20; John 17:6–26; Irenaeus, *Ag. Her.* IV.6, *ANF* I, pp. 467–69).

After the Pharisees investigated the healing of the man born blind, Jesus asked him: "'Do you believe in the Son of Man?' 'Who is he, sir?' the man asked. 'Tell me so that I may believe in him.' Jesus said, 'You have now seen him; in fact, he is the one speaking with you'" (John 9:35–37). Either Jesus viewed himself as the Son of Man descended of the Father, or John's account is irreparably flawed and untrustworthy.

Inadequate Hypotheses Concerning His Identity

From the earliest time, there have been alternative hypotheses about Jesus that have been tested and consensually rejected by the believing community. Three such hypotheses recur: that he was not God but was more like God than most of us; that the disciples projected upon him a messianic identity; and that he was demon-possessed. The ancient exponents of these hypotheses were Arius, Ebion, and Jesus' Pharisaic opponents.

Unity of Moral Intent

Jesus did not understand himself to be a mere representative, ambassador, or agent of God, but one in whom the fullness of God is personally present (Col. 1:15–20; Tertullian, *Ag. Marcion* IV.25, *ANF* III, pp. 389–90). It is he who *sent* the Holy Spirit (John 16:7). The diluted view that Jesus merely shared an ethical purpose with God, an agreement with God in moral intent, not personal union with God (Ritschl, *CDJR*, pp. 385–90,

442–80), ignores the force of passages attesting his sonship and coeternality and equality with the Father.

Projection

It is not likely that the unique Father-Son relationship is something that the remembering church later fantasized or manufactured and then projected back upon Jesus after the resurrection. For evidences of the intimate Father-Son relationship appear in the earliest identifiable oral sources that antedate the written sources (Jeremias, *The Parables of Jesus*, pp. 70ff.; F. Hahn, *TJC*, pp. 295–310; V. Taylor, *Mark*, p. 597).

Jesus was distinctly remembered much later by eyewitnesses as having aroused indignation among his adversaries precisely "because he claimed to be the Son of God" (John 19:7; Augustine, *Comm. on John* 116, *NPNF* 1 VII, pp. 425–27). Such an impression cannot easily have been made up, since the motivation to make it up seems wholly lacking and implausible. Jesus as portrayed by John assumed that the encounter with him was indeed an encounter with God, that to know him would be to know God, that loving or hating Jesus amounted to loving or hating God, that trusting Jesus was trusting God (John 8:19; 12:44–45, 14:1–9; 15:23; John Chrysostom, *Hom. on John* LXXIV, *NPNF* 1 XIV, pp. 271–75).

We are pressing steadily toward the question of the deity of Christ. At this point we have not established (or even sought to argue) that Jesus is God, but it is at least clear that Jesus as remembered in earliest texts understood himself as Son of Man, possessing a unique relation of sonship to God the Father, such that our daughterhood or sonship comes to hinge radically upon our response to him. His sonship confronts one with a decision about the meaning and destiny of one's own life, as if that had to be answered in relation to him.

Demonic Possession

The direct question to Jesus, "Who do you think you are?" was frankly asked by his pious opponents in a conversation that centered on the question of whether Jesus might possibly be crazy (or demon-possessed). When he answered, "I am not possessed by a demon," he then added a phrase that convinced opponents that he was indeed crazy: "If anyone keeps my word, he will never see death." At this his learned opponents exclaimed, "Now we know that you are demon-possessed!" They were furious: "Are you greater than our father Abraham! He died, and so did the prophets. Who do you think you are?'" (John 8:49–53). The identity question emerged not from the disciples' claims, but out of a direct encounter between Jesus and interrogators. Jesus' answer astonished them: "My Father, whom you claim as your God, is the one who glorifies me." "Before Abraham was, I am!" (John 8:54, 58; John Chrysostom, *Hom. on John* LV, *FC* 41, pp. 80–85). This caused his shocked hearers to pick up "stones to stone him," for this is what they perceived their duty to be in relation to blasphemy.

It is implausible to argue that the disciples fabricated such a story out of their fertile imaginations, for in a fabrication one must have a motive, and what motive could they have had in inventing such an unlikely story? Either Jesus was indeed blaspheming against the holy divine name, "I am" (= Yahweh, Exod. 3:14), by identifying himself as one existing before Abraham and eternally with deity, or he was revealing something about his identity that stands as the central feature of the gospel.

The "I Am" Statements

John's Gospel is organized around a series of key "signs," each culminating in an "I am" (*ego eimi*) statement reminiscent of the declarations of Yahweh. When he raised a dead man he said, "I am the resurrection and the life" (John 11:25). When he gave sight to the man born blind he announced, "I am the light of the world" (John 8:12). When he fed the five thousand, he declared, "I am the bread of life" (John 6:35). He later said, "I am the door of the sheep" (10:7) and "I am the good shepherd" (10:10).

These are extremely immodest statements if applied to an ordinary human subject. Jesus did not teach as the prophets taught when they pointed beyond themselves to the source of the divine revelation. Rather he taught and spoke in the first person, as Yahweh had spoken in the form of "I am" in the Exodus account of deliverance.

Luther commented on Jesus' statement, "I am the light of the world": "If He had at least expressed it more moderately and modestly and had cast it in a more reasonable form, such as: I am the light of this country, this kingdom, house, people, or of this temple, we would let it pass. But it is pitching the sermon very high to burst into boasting in this way, to take the entire world at a bite. . . . It is the language of presumption thus to stop all mouths" (Luther, *Serm. on John 8:12* [1531], *WLS* I, p. 185; *WA* 33, 511f.).

His Perceived Authority

The Question of Authority

The way he taught people is a clue to the remarkable presence he commanded. "He taught as one who had authority, not as their teachers of the law" (Matt. 7:29; John Chrysostom, *Hom. on Matt.* XXV, *NPNF* 1 X, pp. 171–76). The Temple guards remarked, "No one ever spoke the way this man does" (John 7:46). When he taught in the Temple courts, the religious leaders were amazed and puzzled: "How did this man get such learning without having studied," to which Jesus answered; "My teaching is not my own. It comes from him who sent me" (John 7:14–16). Even those of remote Nazareth "were amazed at the gracious words that came from his lips. 'Isn't this Joseph's son?' they asked" (Luke 4:22).

What was the fulcrum of his weighty authority? It appeared to be greater than the prophets', whose authority was derived from God, for Jesus' authority was derived from his own person. He often said: "Truly, truly I say to you," noticeably not following the prophetic formula of speech that used the phrase: "Thus says the Lord." The "I" is either an extremely egocentric "I" or one that directly illumines his identity (John Chrysostom, *Hom. on John* XLIX, *NPNF* 1 XIV, pp. 176–79).

Resurrection as Ultimate Validation

His identity was not fully grasped by the disciples until the resurrection. Thomas's recognition was particularly dramatic. Having been told by the others: "We have seen the Lord!" (John 20:25), Thomas testily replied: "'Unless I see the nail marks in his hands and put my finger where the nails were, and put my hand into his side, I will not believe it.' A week later his disciples were in the house again, and Thomas was with them. Though the doors were locked, Jesus came and stood among them and said, 'Peace be with you!' Then he said to Thomas, 'Put your finger here; see my hands. Reach out your hand and put it into my side. Stop doubting and believe.' Thomas said to him, 'My Lord and my God!'" (John 20:25–28).

Jesus could have rejected this ascription. Rather he received it, chiding Thomas not for his adoration, but for the tardiness of his belief, delayed by the requirement of having to "see." "Blessed are those who have not seen and yet have believed" (v. 29). One who could welcome such an ascription must either be God or deceiver (John Chrysostom, *Hom. on John* LXXXVII, *NPNF* 2 XIV, pp. 327–29; Kierkegaard, *TC*, pp. 40–71).

Eschatological Judge

The resurrected Lord taught that he would return to judge the world at the end time—a prerogative belonging only to God. Matthew's report of his language is audacious: "Whoever acknowledges me before men, I will also acknowledge him before my Father in heaven. But whoever disowns me before men, I will disown him before my Father in heaven"

(Matt 10:32–33). The Father "has entrusted all judgment to the Son" (John 5:22). "A time is coming when all who are in their graves will hear his voice and come out" (John 5:28–29).

Why Delusion Is an Implausible Charge

All this is very unusual language, especially in the monotheistic Hebraic tradition. It is unconvincing to argue that Jesus did not say these things. They are so extraordinary that it seems implausible that they would have been invented by the disciples and put in Jesus' mouth decades later. The problem with that hypothesis is that it would have tended to discredit the attestors had they not been quite sure that they had heard it the way it was reported. The traditions reported by synoptic writers could have been challenged and corrected by many living eye-witnesses during the period of oral transmission. This is why so much attention is given in the New Testament to accuracy and credibility of testimony (Luke 1:1–4; Mark 1:1; John 15:27, Acts 1:21–22; 1 John 1:1).

These Claims Appear Throughout the Testimony About Him

Such claims are not to be found merely in obscure nooks and crannies of the New Testament or in minor writers. They are found widely throughout all strata of the oral tradition preceding the writing of the Gospels and in all Gospels, and they recur in Paul and John, in Hebrews and Peter, and in both the early and late epistles. The picture of Jesus that confronts us in the New Testament is too consistent to be fantasized or projected, too shocking and unrelenting to be fabricated.

These are the claims that we constantly meet on whatever page we read of the New Testament. Turn to most any paragraph of the New Testament and see if you can read it without the premise that God has come in Jesus and the claim that in Jesus we are being met by nothing less than God.

Only a Bad Teacher Would Lie About His Identity

These claims in themselves cannot be considered reasonable arguments for the deity of Christ, but they do require some reasonable explanation. They defy the premise that Jesus was a great teacher *even if he was not* the messianic Son he claimed to be, for if he were not the messianic Son, then he surely must have been a deluded and deceptive teacher (Justin Martyr, *Dialogue with Trypho* 32–38, FC 6, pp. 194–204; Augustine, *Trin.* III, FC 45, pp. 95–127).

It is a bad teacher who fails to tell the truth about himself. If the centerpiece of his teaching is himself, his own identity, sonship, and messianic mission, and if he is in error about that central premise, then how could he be trusted as a teacher about anything else? Some imagine that the best way to communicate with the modern mind is to speak only of Jesus' teaching and say nothing of his embarrassing alleged identity as eternal Son. But ironically that position is made disreputable by Jesus' own teaching about himself if he is not the One he appears to be.

If he were a man claiming to be God, he would be far more than egocentric—either he must be deluded, or it must be true (Kierkegaard, *TC*, pp. 26–39). In fact, it is a testimony of such incredible, outrageous import that it must be either radically true or radically false. One cannot just take a little snip of this truth and leave the scandalous center of it behind. Only if he was indeed the Christ, the God-man, can he be considered sane.

No Other Evidence of Delusion

Suppose he suffered hallucinatory delusions. Wouldn't you expect other parts of his life to manifest some delusory behaviors? We do not get the impression from any source that he was delusive in any other way. There is no supporting evidence that Jesus was in any way psychologically imbalanced, as one would expect to find in one purported to be seriously deluded (Tertullian, *Ag. Praxeas* 22–24, *ANF* III, pp. 617–21; Stott, *BC*, pp. 28–33).

Everything else we know about Jesus leads us to believe that he was honest, unhypocritical, guileless, and undeceptive. It seems implausible that he who resisted deception so strongly in others would himself become so deceptive. Upon examining the record, some may conclude delusion, but it is also possible that one may conclude with the remembering ecumenical consensus that the delusion of the skeptics is greater than that of Jesus.

ARGUMENTS CONCERNING CHRIST'S DEITY

The primitive Christian community had deep roots in Jewish monotheism. With such a heritage, it must have required an extraordinary motivation to confess Jesus Christ as Lord or speak of him publicly as the one God. The motive would have had to have been powerful enough to overcome rigorous piety and religious training to the contrary.

These witnesses, however, had met him as risen Lord. Only on this eventful and experiential basis were they able to draw the conclusion that he was the heavenly Son of Man, messianic King, Son of God, and indeed truly God (Gregory Nazianzen, *Third Orat. on the Son, Orat.* XXIX; *NPNF* 2 VII, pp. 301–305; *BOC*, pp. 500, 592).

How May It Be Arguably Established That Christ is God?

The Central Feature of Christian Confession

There is little doubt that central to Christian teaching is the confession that Jesus Christ is truly God (Athanasius, *On the Incarn.*, *NPNF* 2 IV, pp. 31–68; Augustine, *CG*, *FC* 24, p. 392). No ancient Christian creed fails to confess the deity of Christ, for that would be to omit the central feature of Christian confession.

Christ is called "God" in precisely the same sense and with the same meaning that the Old Testament applies that address to Yahweh, the one God to whom worship is owed, to whom the divine attributes rightly apply. Accordingly, Jude confessed Christ as "our only Sovereign and Lord," the same One who "delivered his people out of Egypt" (Jude 4–5; Irenaeus, *Ag. Her.* III.6.2, III.19, *ANF* I, pp. 419, 448).

Traditional Reasoning Regarding Christ's Deity

Justin Martyr early grasped the philosophical importance of the liturgical fact that Christians were being baptized not only in the name of the first person of the Trinity, but also the second, not only of the "Parent of all things," but also of "our Saviour Jesus Christ, and of the Holy Ghost" (Justin Martyr, *Apology* 61; Pohle-Preuss, *DT* IV, p. 24, note the genderless *"in nomine Parentis universorum"*; cf. *ANF* I, p. 183). "Notice how David calls Him Lord; he does not call Him son" (*Epist. of Barnabas* 12, *ECW*, p. 211). "Brothers, we ought to think of Jesus Christ as we do of God — as the 'judge of the living and the dead'" (*An Anonymous Sermon, Commonly Called Clement's Second Letter to the Corinthians*, *LCC* I, p. 193).

The Necessity and Limits of Argument

By what argument might it possibly be established that Jesus is God? Classic exegetes thought that no argument of itself could finally instruct the heart adequately. Rather than by argument, such a conclusion can only be a decision of the whole heart and mind, based upon whatever evidences one may be able to bring together to achieve a reliable sense of comprehensive coherence.

Whatever hypothesis best explains the widest range of evidence is the one upon which one may best ground one's active, risk-laden trust. The classic tradition is not without a series of arguments to attempt to grasp and understand what faith knows — that Christ is God (Tertullian, *Apology* 21, *ANF* III, pp. 34–36).

Arguments for Christ's Deity Assuming the Veracity of Scripture

The arguments that most often prevail in classical exegesis usually begin with the premise of the veracity of Scripture. They center in the pivotal point that *the claims so obviously made by and about Jesus cannot be justified unless he is God*. Either this central claim is dead wrong or it must be profoundly right. There is no way for it to be partially (by a few percentage points) right or wrong.

The alternatives are either that Jesus deceived others and himself and permitted his closest companions to entertain an entirely false view of him—*or* he spoke the truth concerning his unique divine sonship in a way that was accurately reflected by honest witnesses (Augustine, *Comm. on John* CXII, NPNF 1 VII, pp. 416–18; M. Lepin, *Christ and the Gospel*, pp. 128ff).

Traditional arguments for the divinity of Christ focus upon five key inferences: *one who is addressed by ascriptions that could only be appropriate for God, who possesses attributes that only God could possess, who does the works only God could have done, who was worshiped as God without disclaiming it, and one who was viewed by the apostles as equal to God must be God*. These five arguments recur in classical exegesis of hundreds of New Testament texts.

The Argument from Ascription

If Jesus Christ is repeatedly *called God* in Holy Writ, then Christ must either be God or the writ is unholy. The pivotal inference is that Christ is reliably knowable as God because Scripture is reliable (Ursinus, *CHC*, pp. 185–92). His deity is taught because it is expressed in Scripture in "lofty utterances" such as "Only-begotten"; "the Way, the Truth, the Life, the Light"; "the Effulgence, the Impress, the Image, the Seal"; "Lord, King, He That is, The Almighty" (Gregory Nazianzen, *Orat.* XXIX.17, NPNF 2 VII, p. 307).

If this inference is to be shown reliable to those who affirm Scripture's veracity, it is necessary to show that Jesus is in fact addressed in Scripture as God (Ignatius of Antioch, *To the Ephesians* 7–15, FC 1, pp. 90–93). The evidence accumulates from a wide variety of sources. Paul speaks of Jesus as the "one Lord, Jesus Christ, through whom all things came, and through whom we live" (1 Cor. 6). Matthew identifies him as the same Immanuel expected by Isaiah (7:14), "God with us" (Matt. 1:23). John calls him the only Son of God, "God the One and Only," the only one to have seen God (John 1:18). There is no accompanying recollection that Jesus protested when these terms were ascribed to him (John Chrysostom, *Hom. on John* LXXXVII, *FC* 41, pp. 458–61; Augustine, *Comm. on John,* John 20:10–29, Tractate CXXI, *NPNF* 1 VII, pp. 438–39).

James refers to him as "Lord of glory" (2:1, KJV). The author of Revelation calls him "King of kings and Lord of lords" (19:16). The Epistle to Hebrews views him as God's "Son, whom he appointed heir of all things, and through whom he made the universe. The Son is the radiance of God's glory, the exact representation of his being, sustaining all things by his powerful word" (Heb. 1:2–3).

The Argument from Divine Attributes

If to him were ascribed *attributes* that could only rightly be ascribed to God, and if canonical Scripture bears truthful witness, then he must be God (Hilary, *Trin.* XI, *NPNF* 2 VII, pp. 64–71; Pearson, *EC* I, pp. 219–30). Among divine attributes repeatedly ascribed to Christ were:

holiness ("the Holy and Righteous One" (Acts 3:14)
underived being (Col. 1:15ff.)
uncreated eternality (John 8:58; 17:5; "the same yesterday and today
     and forever," Heb. 13:8; cf. Heb. 9:14; Hilary, *Trin.* IX.53, *NPNF* 2 IX,
     p. 153)
unsurpassable power (Matt. 28:20; Mark 5:11–15; John 11:38–44;
     Augustine, *CG, FC* 24, pp. 332, 333)
exceptional knowledge (knowing the hearts of all, Acts 1:24; Matt.
     16:21; Luke 68; 11:17; John 4:29, Hilary, *Trin.* IX.62, *NPNF* 2 IX,
     p. 177)
absolute veracity ("the truth," John 14:6)
eternal love ("that surpasses knowledge," Eph. 3:19)

Such testimony could be greatly extended. Conclusion: either Scripture misleads or Christ is God (Ursinus, *CHC*, pp. 186–88).

The Argument from Divine Operations

If it should be the case that Christ in fact *performed actions and operations that only God could do and acted in a way that only God could act,* by forgiving sin (Mark 2:1–12); giving life to the dead; by engendering new life in the Spirit (John 5:21); by being himself raised from the dead (Matt. 28:1–15; Luke 16:1–14; Hilary, *Trin.* III, *NPNF* 2 IX, pp. 62–70; Chemnitz, *TNC*, pp. 37–46), *then he must be nothing less than true God* (Ursinus, *CHC*, pp. 188–89). He who searches the hearts and reveals the thoughts of men, who makes known distant events, who stills the storm, who lays down his life and takes it up again could only be God.

The Argument from Adoration

If Christ was worshiped as God and *unresistingly received worship due only to God* (1 Cor. 11:24, 25; John 5:23; 14:14; Acts 7:59), *then he must either be a blasphemer or God*.

There was little reserve in the adoration given him. That "Jesus is Lord" (Rom. 10:9) is the heart of the Christian confession. John's Gospel states that "He who does not honor the Son does not honor the Father, who sent him" (John 5:23; John Chrysostom, *Hom. on John* XXXIX, *NPNF* 1 XIV, pp. 137-43). This is an especially powerful statement in the light of the perennial hebraic religious antipathy against the worship of a man (recall Paul's refusal of idolatrous worship at Lystra, Acts 14:8-20).

The Argument from Equality

If God the Son is viewed on *equal* footing with God the Father, then he must be a person of the Godhead in an equality that appears to be clearly established in the baptismal formula ("baptizing them in the name of the Father and of the Son and of the Holy Spirit," Matt. 28:19).

It can hardly be ascribed to postresurrection inventions that Jesus clashed with authorities about keeping the Sabbath (R. Brown, *Gospel According to John*, pp. 215-21). These conflicts centered precisely on the question of whether he was implying his own equality with God, a charge that he heard and significantly did not deny (John 5:18). His accusers were determined to kill Jesus, according to John's report, precisely because "he was even calling God his own Father, *making himself equal with God*" (John 5:18, italics added; Augustine, *Trin.* IV.20, *NPNF* 1 III, pp. 83-85; *LG*, pp. 196-99).

Although the Son does not need to grasp at equality with God since he is the eternal Son, that equality is nonetheless assumed even in passages that speak of the incarnation and humble entry of God into human servanthood (Phil. 2:6, 7; Ursinus, *CHC*, pp. 185-87). Spiritual gifts such as faith, hope, and love are given equally by the Father and the Lord Jesus Christ (2 Thess. 2:16).

Christ is equally invoked in Paul's benediction that prays for "the grace of the Lord Jesus Christ," cast in parallel form with "the love of God" and "the fellowship of the Holy Spirit" (2 Cor. 13:14). Christ is addressed as one who is "God over all, forever praised! Amen" (Rom. 9:5).

Those prone to doubt the veracity of Scripture may remain unmoved by such arguments. Yet even doubters are provided by classical Christianity with apologetic arguments from history, philosophy, psychology, politics, and the phenomenology of religion that supplement arguments from Scripture. Two of these types follow, one from experience, one from history.

An Experiential Argument: Redeemed Lives Require a Redeemer

In addition to the above scriptural and traditional arguments, we may rehearse a simple but disarming argument from experience—namely, the experience of the faithful community. This argument is found occasionally in classical exegesis but awaited the tradition following Schleiermacher to come into wide acceptance.

It begins with the fact that the disciples experienced a profound consciousness of redemption. It asks: how did that experience occur? From this it is argued that one's inference may move back from the influence of Jesus upon redeemed persons to the character of his person as influencing cause. He cannot be less than God himself if he influences persons as Redeemer. *If such faith is allowed to search in its own way for who Christ is, the name upon which it insists is God.* No name but God is sufficient. No lesser identity will satisfy (Gregory Nazianzen, *Orat.* XXIX, *On the Son,* *NPNF* 2 VII, p. 307; cf. Liddon, *DL*, pp. 152–208).

This sort of Christology is derived from the fact that people experienced Christ as having the value of God (Ritschl, *CDJR*, pp. 412ff., 448ff.). One cannot predicate of a mere human being the saving efficacy that is known by the redeemed. If Christ is the incomparable enabler of the divine energy that works in believers to change their lives, how can one avoid the conclusion that he himself was divine? One who is obeyed as Lord of one's life, who is trusted for pardon for sins, to whom worship is rightly offered must be God, by whatever name he is called.

The argument was well stated by Wilhelm Herrmann: "This thought, that when the historical Christ takes such hold of us, we have to do with God Himself—this thought is certainly the most important element in the confession of the Deity of Christ. . . . In what Jesus does to us, we grasp the expression God gives us of His feeling towards us, or God Himself as a Personal Spirit working upon us. This is the form in which every man who has been reconciled to God through Christ necessarily confesses His Deity, even although he may decline to adopt the formula" (*Communion with God*, p. 143). Schleiermacher cautiously concluded: "The Redeemer, then is like all men in virtue of the identity of human nature, but distinguished from them all by the constant potency of His God-consciousness, which was a veritable existence of God in Him" (*ChrF*, p. 385).

Those who may doubt that the liberal tradition has a doctrine of the divinity of Christ do well to examine these sources, for they affirm the deity of Christ on the basis of the experience of his influence in the community of faith.

All this means, even in the liberal tradition, that one does not reach deeply enough into the saving significance of Jesus' life by assuming that he was a superbly good man who offered a moral lesson in self-sacrifice or became the best of all teachers who taught the highest ethics or spiritual principles. There is no saving faith without the confession: Jesus Christ is Lord. His work reveals who he is as eternal Son, and on this premise alone do "his benefits interpret His nature" (P. T. Forsyth, *PPJC*, p. 6). Christ's deity is not taught to encourage us to rise to do our best, but to redeem us from our worst (H. D. McDonald, *ADC*, pp. 17–19).

History Itself Vindicates Christ's Deity

Gregory of Nyssa proposed a threefold demonstration from history, empirically discernible, that God became incarnate in Jesus:

Animal Sacrifice Demonstrably Ended

Before Christ came idolatry "held sway over man's life." "But, as the apostle says, from the moment that God's saving grace appeared among men and dwelt in human nature, all this vanished into nothing, like smoke." Writing in the fourth century, Gregory noted that the times could not even be remembered when there was widespread practice of "sacrificing living victims and making foul offerings"–all this had been demonstrably ended by the once-for-all priesthood of Christ.

The Period of Martyrdom Survived

In the period of persecution, the church could not have survived had the incarnation been based upon myth. It is a mockery of the martyrs and failure to listen to the testimony of their lives to assume that their faith was only in a man, not God-man. No hypothesis explains the church's survival of the genocidal history of martyrdom more adequately than that God was in Christ.

The Destruction of Jerusalem

The destruction of Jerusalem was viewed as an unmistakable historical sign that the people of the old covenant had "refused to accept the grace made manifest" (Gregory of Nyssa, *ARI* 18, *LCC* III, pp. 295–96; for similar arguments see Eusebius, *CH* VIII–X, *NPNF* 2 I, pp. 323–87; Augustine, *CG* XVIII, *NPNF* 1 II, pp. 361–96), and that a new covenant had been offered to humanity.

Thus it has been often argued subsequently that by history the deity of Christ is demonstrated—otherwise, reasoned Gregory, how could the force of long-dominant pagan idolatries have been so decisively broken? How could such a fragile persecuted community have survived? And by what alternative hypothesis might the actual historical event of the Diaspora be more plausibly interpreted?

Christ's Deity the Differential Feature of Christianity

The constant testimony of the New Testament to Christ's deity can only be circumvented by directly challenging Jesus' veracity or the apostles' accuracy of reporting, or by some speculative device such as viewing the deity of Christ as a projection of the exuberant hopes of the disciples after the crucifixion. Such a device has been implausibly overused in form criticism and redaction criticism.

The New Testament can hardly be contorted to make sense without the hypothesis that Jesus is God-incarnate (Calvin, *Inst.* 2.12; Wesley, *WJW* II, pp. 352-53). These claims by Jesus and the apostles, taken together, have led Christians to conclude that the valid beginning point for understanding this particular man is plainly and simply that he is truly God while not ceasing to be truly human (Creed of Epiphanius, SCD 13, p. 9; Council of Ephesus, *SCD* 113, p. 50; Council of Chalcedon, *SCD* 148, p. 60).

The deity of Christ is the differential feature of Christianity (Augustine, *Trin.*, FC 45, pp. 52-58; 205, 206). Even Hegel could discern that "the Christian religion has this characteristic: that the Person of Christ in his character of the Son of God himself partakes of the nature of God" (Hegel, "On Philosophy," *On Art, Religion and Philosophy*, 1970, p. 277). "The unity of essence between father and son in the Godhead was discovered even by the Jews in the relation to God which Jesus ascribed to himself (John 5:18)" (Hegel, *The Spirit of Christianity*, OCETW, p. 261).

A suffering messiah who is less than God may elicit our pity or admiration, but not our worship. A messiah to whom one cannot pray is not the Christ of the New Testament (cf. "Whether the Son Is God," *LG*, pp. 196-99). If the Messiah is God's own coming, then Christ is God, according to apostolic reasoning. One who confesses Jesus as Christ confesses Christ as God.

Why the Arian Challenge Was So Decisive

Christ is God—this was the hypothesis that became a battleground in the fourth century and was settled ecumenically thereafter. The Arian controversy is not likely to be precisely rehearsed in postmodern ecumenical

Christianity, since it took shape with the Greek language and its nuances. Nonetheless it has a more general history of recurring sporadically in mutated forms. It was fought through thoroughly in the fourth- century ecumenical consensus by which all subsequent ecumenical consensus has defined itself (First Ecumenical Council, *NPNF* 2 XIV, pp. 3, 163–65; Newman, *Ath.* II, pp. 287–92). Those who flirt with Arianism flaunt the ancient and continuing ecumenical consensus.

Every Christian should know what Arianism is, just as every American learns about the Boston Tea Party, every Pole knows all too well of the Hitler-Stalin Pact, and every Briton understands why the defeat of the Spanish Armada was so decisive. Arianism represented one of the most massive challenges in the early history of the church. But why?

Believers understood themselves to be saved from sin by Jesus' sacrificial death, whose meaning was validated and confirmed in his resurrection. Their faith was based upon Jesus' own interpretation of the relation between his person and work, who he was and what he did. This understanding of salvation by faith in the crucified Lord was repeatedly attested in the apostolic witness and consensually believed in Christian communities, and subsequent worshipers found their own experience corresponding to this testimony. They worshiped him as "Lord and Christ" (Acts 2:36).

Just at this point arrived Arius, offering to these redeemed worshipers "–what? *A creature*–a being who actually had *commenced to live*, a being *made*" (Curtis, *ChrF*, p. 225). Arianism had to be rejected, but doing so was not easy, for the Arian teaching was ingeniously based upon disconnected and distorted scriptural testimony that made it appear to some as apostolic faith (Athanasius, *Four Discourses Ag. Arians*, *NPNF* 2 IV, pp. 303–21; Newman, *Ath.* II, pp. 299–302).

The story is dramatic: a letter was read from Arian bishop Eusebius of Nicomedia, in which he declared that to assert the Son to be uncreated would be to say that he was 'of one substance' (Gk. *homoousion*) with the Father. The letter elicited intense conflict in the council. The very test for which they had been searching was found in the Arian resistance to calling the Son the uncreated God, of one substance, *homoousion*, with the Father. "The letter was torn in pieces to mark their indignation, and the phrase which he had pledged himself to reject became the phrase which they [the First Ecumenical Council] pledged themselves to adopt" (Stanley, *The Eastern Church*, p. 228; for an account of the controversy see Theodoret, *History* I.1–12, *NPNF* 2 III, pp. 33–51; cf. Newman, *Ari.*, p. 252).

In the language of Arius, the Son "is not eternal or co-eternal or co-unoriginate with the Father," for the Son was "created" and "*was not* before His generation" (Arius, *To Alexander, Bishop of Alexandria, TGS,* p. 54, italics added).

Athanasius, to his great credit, found a way of stating the received faith in such a way that it could not be easily distorted, and in precise words: "very God of very God, (*Theon alēthinon ek Theou alēthinou;* Lat. *Deum verum de Deo vero*), begotten, not made, (*gennēthenta, ou poiēthenta;* Lat. *natum, non factum*), being of one substance with the Father (*homoousion tō Patri;* Lat, *unius substantiae cum Patre*)."

The crucial term, "begotten, not made," comes directly from the testimony of John that Jesus was the "only begotten" Son, or the One and Only Son (John 1:14, 18; 3:16; 1 John 4:9). "Not made" means that the Son is not a creature. The Father eternally wills the Son. The Son is without beginning in time. The Father eternally lives by giving; the Son eternally lives by receiving. This generation and begottenness is uncreated. Their relationship is without temporal beginning. This is not a nonsensical or obscure notion but has proven itself extremely fruitful in subsequent Christian teaching for resisting abuses (*Coelestine to the Synod of Ephesus,* NPNF 2 XIV, pp. 220–22; Barth, *CD* I/1, pp. 423–38).

This formula is not only crucial for defense of the church's faith, but also even more enduring practical value in New Testament interpretation, for it illuminates all those sayings of Jesus in which he insists both upon the equality of the Son with the father and the obedience of the Son to the Father (Athanasius, *Defence of the Nicene Definition* III.6–13, NPNF 2 IV, pp. 153–59; cf. Curtis, *ChrF,* p. 229).

When asked why the Council of Nicaea resorted to terms not used in Scripture, Athanasius answered that these definitions were forced upon the council by the evasions of the Arians, who had an Arian double meaning for every other formula proposed. Even these extrascriptural terms express no sense not to be found in Scripture (Athanasius, *Defence of the Nicene Definition* V.18–24, NPNF 2 IV, pp. 161–66).

Arian voices continue to echo among Christological reductionists at the edges of consensual Christianity. The echoes are heard among exegetes who resist the deity of Christ, historical critics who see Jesus only as human creature, social idealists who see Jesus mainly as a means of social improvement, and pantheists who are unable to see the difference between God and the world. If Christ is imagined finally as creature, there is no way to speak of the liberation of humanity from sin.

Christians have long agreed ecumenically to reject Arianism. It has been widely recognized that Arius would have led Christianity into polytheism. It was not an ancillary squabble or casual theory at stake in the Arian controversy, but the vitality of the Christian life. Christ is not a mere man adopted by God as Messiah or a supreme angelic visitor lacking full deity, but God in the flesh, incarnate Lord. Strip the New Testament of this assumption, and you have little left but trivial historical quibbles and moral instructions. Even the moral instruction requires the central premise of the incarnation to be taught intelligibly (Barth, *CD* I/2, pp. 33ff.).

ONE LORD

It is an article of apostolic faith to confess "one Lord" (*Credo in unum Dominum*, Gk. *eis hena Kurion*, Creed of 150 Fathers, *COC* II, p. 58; Apostles' Creed, *SCD* 1, p. 3). How the Father can be Lord and the Son can be Lord was discussed in connection with the triunity of God (see *LG*, pp. 181–225). What did the lordship of Christ mean?

Christ's Lordship

The Aramaic word for Lord (*Mar*) was primitively applied to Christ in Paul's poignant, closing salutation to the Corinthians: "Come, O Lord!" (*Marana tha*, 1 Cor. 16:22). Hence Jesus was called Lord from the earliest known layers of Christian proclamation. It is likely that this phrase was a well-known and available enough tradition that Paul could assume that his Corinthian hearers would understand it (Rawlinson, *NTDC*, p. 235).

Kurios

The most frequent designation for Jesus in early Gentile Christianity was *Kurios* (Lord): "Jesus is Lord" (*Kurios Iesous*) was the received confession of the Pauline tradition. Paul made over two hundred and fifty references to Jesus as Lord in his Letters. "If you confess with your mouth, 'Jesus is Lord,' and believe in your heart that God raised him from the dead, you will be saved" (Rom. 10:9; cf. 2 Tim. 2:22). "No one can say, 'Jesus is Lord,' except by the Holy Spirit" (1 Cor. 12:3; John Chrysostom, *Hom. on First Cor.* XXIX, *NPNF* 1 XII, pp. 170–71). To understand Christ as Lord is to confess that "he was appointed by the Father to have us under his power, to administer the Kingdom of God in heaven and earth" (Calvin, *Catech. of the Church of Geneva*, LCC XXII, p. 96; cf. Baxter, *PW* XVII, pp. 381–412).

Confession of Divinity

To confess Jesus as Lord after his resurrection was to confess his divinity. Prior to the resurrection *Kurios* could have meant "teacher" or "master," but after the resurrection it indicated his present reign in the coming kingdom: "God has made this Jesus, whom you crucified, both Lord and Christ" (Acts 2:36; cf. Phil. 2:9–11; Augustine, CG, FC 24, pp. 331–32). "He really is Lord, not as having step by step attained to lordship, but as having by nature the dignity of being Lord" (Cyril of Jerusalem, Catech. Lect. X.5, LCC IV, p. 134). Kurios quickly came to be used interchangeably with Theos.

Yahweh as Kurios

In over six thousand instances in the Septuagint, Kurios translates the ancient Hebraic tetragrammaton YHWH, the name for Yahweh (Lord) in the Old Testament. Kurios was not a polite vocative reference to human leadership in the New Testament kerygma. It assumed power, sovereignty, the ability to rule. That Jesus is Lord means that he is the One speaking who said: "I am who am," and "I am has sent me" (Exod. 3:14). That Jesus is Lord means that all alternative pretensions to power are finally reduced to nothingness. Augustine argued that this incomparable One (Yahweh, Kurios, Deus) "has nothing for an opposite." "If anyone were to ask us what the opposite of 'white' is we would answer 'black'; if asked the opposite of 'hot' we would answer 'cold'; if asked the opposite of 'fast' we would answer 'slow'; and so on in similar case. But, when asked the opposite of that which 'is', we answer rightly that it is 'nothing'" (Augustine, Faith and the Creed 4.7, FC 27, p. 324).

Lordship Before Time

Christ as Kurios is viewed as pretemporal agent of creation ("through whom all things came," 1 Cor. 8:6; cf. Heb. 1:2–3) and posttemporal agent of consummation (1 Cor. 15:25–28). "Then the end will come, when he hands over the kingdom to God the Father after he has destroyed all dominion, authority and power" (1 Cor. 15:24). It was this Lord who met Paul personally on the road to Damascus and to whom Paul ascribed worship that belongs only to God.

Lordship at the End of Time

The exaltation of the Lord began from the nether world with resurrection, but the full acknowledgment of his lordship will only finally occur in the end of history. Judgment is a function of his lordship in the final day (Rom. 14:10; 2 Cor. 5:10). Peter preached: "Exalted to the right hand of God, he has received from the Father the promised Holy Spirit" (Acts 2:33). Paul wrote: "Therefore, God exalted him to the highest place and gave him the name that is above every name, that at the name of Jesus every knee should bow, in heaven and on earth and under the earth, and every tongue confess that Jesus Christ is Lord, to the glory of God the Father" (Phil. 2:9–11).

Triune Lord

The triune premise holds throughout the confession of Christ's lordship. Jesus has been made Lord (Acts 2:36) while God does not cease to be Lord (Acts 2:39). *Kurios* is ascribed simultaneously to God and to the exalted Christ. Jesus Christ the Lord has himself become the object of worship (Acts 2:21; 3:16), the holy, forgiving, author of life (Acts 3:14–15; 5:31). The believer is one who has received Jesus Christ as Lord (Col. 2:6).

The Lordship of Christ and the History of Religions

Can His Lordship Be Reduced to Historical Determinants?

Modern historical criticism has tended to proceed by assuming that the worship of Jesus Christ as Lord is adequately accounted for by applying to Christianity principles of the transmission and development of religious ideas found operative in human systems of religions generally (Troeltsch, *Christian Thought*, pp. 3–35; Tillich, *Biblical Religion and the Search for Ultimate Reality*; Holdsworth, CG, pp. 7–8). It is thereby argued that Christianity can be explained in a way analogous to the apotheosis of Krishna or the enlightenment of Buddha.

Notably the history of religions school has focused upon the correspondence between Christianity and its history of religions backgrounds. These points of correspondence do not constitute the slightest embarrassment or scandal to classic Christianity, whose testimony has always referred unapologetically to contingent history as the arena of divine redemption. Like Judaism, Christianity has always understood itself as a history of divine-human covenant worked out through a history of salvation.

The Light Enlightens All

No creditable ecumenical teacher ever assumed that Christianity was separable from a history of salvation, or from a universal history in which God is never left without witness in the world (Acts 14:17), who is the light that enlightens all who come into the world (John 1), who is known in various and sundry ways in general human history, yet who has come to be finally known in his Son (Heb. 1). The final revelation of life and light enjoys and asserts an intrinsic correspondence with all forms, intimations, and intuitions of life and light (even the broken refractions) that have previously appeared in the world.

Dialogue with World Religions

On this premise, the dialogue with world religions is not best understood under the metaphor of a diplomatic negotiation of competing interests of varied cultures. Rather it must inquire into the truth of all attested revelations, including Christianity. If the revelation of which Christianity speaks is only for Christians, then there is no compelling need for dialogue. But that does not square with Scripture. The Great Commission is to go to all nations and proclaim the gospel.

Continuing dialogue with Islam, Buddhism, and Hinduism presents a vexing set of challenges to the Christian community to account for its statements about Jesus. Yet in the dialogue with world religions, Christians are tempted to dilute the testimony to the universal relevance of Jesus' coming and diminish crucial New Testament affirmations of Jesus as light and life of the world, eternal Son, and Messiah, so as to focus more amiably upon the moral teaching of Jesus or his extraordinary life.

It remains a pivotal Christian assertion that Christ is the truth even for those who do not recognize him as their truth (Barth, *How to Serve God in a Marxist Land*, pp. 57–58; *CD* I/2, pp. 344ff.; III/1, pp. 83ff.; J. Ngally, "Jesus Christ and Liberation in Africa," *Ecumenical Review* 27, [1975]: 212–19). He is Savior of all humanity even when humanity does not acknowledge his salvation. He remains the Life of the world even if the world remains in darkness (Gutiérrez, *PPH*, pp. 12, 16). The dialogue with world religions cannot begin by softening the good news to be addressed to all.

Light of Light, God of God

Light of Light

What is the import of the ancient affirmation that the Son is Light of Light—*Lumen de Lumine* (Creed of 150 Fathers, *COC* II, p. 58)? "When we look at the sun, we see light: from this light is generated the light visible every where beneath; but both the one and the other is one light, indivisible, and of one nature" (*Russian Catech.*, *COC* II, p. 467). "As the light which comes from another light does not differ from the light from which it came, but is as full a light as that one, so the Son is true God, coming from a true God" (*Gk. Orthodox Catech.* sec. 28, edited by C. N. Callinicos [1953], p. 25).

The metaphor of a perfect mirror provided the context for the confession that the Son is the "image of the Father's goodness" (Hilary, *Trin.* VIII.48, *NPNF* 2 IX, p. 151). Origen described the Son as "the primal goodness," who "being in all respects the image of the Father, may certainly also be called with propriety the image of His goodness. For there is no other second goodness existing in the Son, save that which is in the Father. And therefore it is not to be imagined that there is a kind of blasphemy, as it were, in the words, 'There is none good save one only, God the Father'" (Origen, *Principles* I.2, *TGS*, p. 43; on the image of Father, see Newman, *Ath.* II, pp. 178–83; cf. Augustine, *Trin.*, FC 45, pp. 213–14).

Cyril of Jerusalem astutely noted that "He did not say: 'I and the Father *am* one,' but 'I and the Father *are* one'; that we might neither separate them nor confuse the identities of Son and Father. They are one in the dignity of the Godhead, since God begot God" (*Catech. Lect.* XI, FC 61, p. 226, italics added).

Very God of Very God

That the Son is called "Very God of very God" means "that the Son of God is called God in the same proper sense as God the Father" (*Russian Catech*, COC II, p. 467; see Council of Nicaea, *SCD* 54, p. 26; also *SCD* 13, 86). As Son eternally begotten of the Father he is truly God begotten of the true God (hence *Deum verum de Deo vero;* Gk. *Theon alēthinon ek Theou alēthinou,* Creed of 150 Fathers, COC II, p. 58; see *SCD* 13, 54, 86), consubstantial with the Father (*consubstantialem Patri;* Gk. *homoousion tō Patri,* COC II, p. 58; *SCD* 13, 54, 86; Pearson, *EC* I, p. 239). If Christ is Son of God, he can be no other than God.

CHAPTER 3

Divine Sonship

THE NATURE OF DIVINE SONSHIP

The confession that Jesus Christ is Son of God stands as a key confession of the primitive oral tradition, amplifying other compacted confessions ("Jesus is the Christ," "Jesus Christ is Lord"). John's first Letter states: "If anyone acknowledges that Jesus is the Son of God, God lives in him and he in God" (1 John 4:15; Augustine, *Comm. on First Epist. of John*, Hom. VIII.14, *NPNF* 1 VII, pp. 512–13). The 150 Fathers at Constantinople confessed the Son born of the Father (*ex Patre natum*; Gk. *ton ek tou patros gennēthenta*) by whom were all things made (*per quem omnia facta sunt*; Gk. *di ou ta panta egeneto*; *COC* II, p. 58; 1 Cor. 8:6; *SCD* 13, 54, 86).

The Ascription "Son of God"

"Son of God" is concisely defined by the *Russian Catechism* as "the name of the second Person of the Holy Trinity in respect of his Godhead: This same Son of God was called *Jesus*, when he was conceived and born on earth as man; *Christ* is the name given him by the Prophets, while they were as yet expecting his advent upon earth" (*COC* II, p. 466).

The Title "Only Son"

The Pauline term "his own Son" (*ton heautou huion*, Rom. 8:3; *tou idiou huiou*, v. 31), and the Johannine term "his only Son" (John 1:18) point to the unique pretemporal relation of Son to Father. The Son is unique, one and only (*unigenitum*; Gk. *monogenēs*, "only-begotten") eternal Son, uncreated Son of God (*Filium Dei*; Gk. *ton huion tou theou ton monogenē*, Creed of 150 Fathers, *COC* II, p. 58; cf. Jer. 6:26; Zech. 12:10; *BOC*, p. 414).

Son indicates an eternal relationship, not a temporal beginning point. "Father is not a name either of an essence or of an action, most clever sirs. But it is the name of the relation in which the Father stands to the Son, and the Son to the Father" (Gregory Nazianzen, *Theol. Orat.* XXIX.16, *LCC* III, p. 171; cf. pp. 190–91; Athanasius, *Four Discourses Ag. Arians* I.11–21, *NPNF* 2 IV, pp. 312–19).

There Can Only Be One Monogenēs

"One and only Son" (*monogenēs*—John 3:16, 18) indicates that Jesus is the only one of his class. The daughterhood and sonship in which believers participate is not natural, independent, or autonomous, but entirely dependent upon their relation to this one and only Son of the Father.

The One Son by Nature Distinguished from the Many Sons and Daughters by Grace

Monogenēs (one and only Son) came to have a pivotal function in all subsequent Christian teaching, for it distinguished all "holy men who are called sons of God *by grace*" from the one and only Son, consubstantial with the Father, in whose Sonship our sonship is hidden (*Russian Catech.*, COC II, p. 467; see Augustine, *Trin.*, FC 45, pp. 171–83; Chemnitz, *TNC*, pp. 43, 74, 105).

His eternal sonship is by nature, while the believer's daughterhood or sonship in him is by grace. Calvin refined this distinction: "That we are sons of God is something we have not by nature but only by adoption and grace, because God gives us this status. But the Lord Jesus, who is begotten of one substance with the Father, is of one essence with the Father, and with the best of rights is called the only Son of God (Eph. 1:5; John 1:14; Heb. 1:2), since he alone is by nature his son" (Calvin, *Catech. of the Church of Geneva*, LCC XXII, p. 96; BOC, pp. 18–20).

His Sonship Makes Possible the Sonship and Daughterhood of Believers

God sent his Son "that we might receive the full rights of sons" (Gal. 4:5). The mission of the Son is to bring humanity into a reconciled relation to the Father (John Chrysostom, *Hom. on Gal.* IV, *NPNF* 1 XIII, p. 30). The faithful are called "into fellowship with his Son Jesus Christ our Lord" (1 Cor. 1:9). Through faith and love believers share in the life of fellowship with "the Father and with his Son, Jesus Christ" (1 John 1:3; Augustine, *Comm. on First Epist. of John*, *NPNF* 1 VII, pp. 460–61). "Because you are sons, God sent the Spirit of his Son into our hearts, the Spirit who calls out, 'Abba, Father'" (Gal. 4:6).

The Resurrection Declared What Was Prefigured in the Annunciation and Baptism

He who in due time was declared Son of God by his resurrection had been announced as Son of God at his annunciation and anointed as Son of God at his baptism.

Declared the Son of God by His Resurrection

Paul drew from a pre-Pauline oral tradition in announcing the startling subject matter of the gospel—Christ Jesus, God's Son—"who as to his human nature was a descendent of David, and who through the Spirit of holiness was *declared with power to be the Son of God [huiou theou] by his resurrection* from the dead: Jesus Christ our Lord" (Rom. 1:1-4, italics added). In Jesus we meet a human being descended of David "as to his human nature," whose hidden identity as Son of God was finally revealed in the resurrection.

The resurrection was placed first in Paul's sequence of topics, because only through that lens did the rememberers grasp the events that had preceded it (William of St. Thierry, *Expos. Rom.*, CFS 27, pp. 21-23; Luther, *Comm. on Epist. to Rom.* [1954], p. 20).

Announced as Son of God at His Coming

The annunciation narrative had already presignaled the identity of the coming One, according to the Lucan tradition. Though his divine sonship would not be widely recognized until his resurrection, from the first announcement of the coming of Jesus, the angelic visitor indicated to Mary that "the holy one to be born will be called the Son of God" (Luke 1:35), the "Son of the Most High" (Luke 1:32; Irenaeus, *Ag. Her.* III.9.1; III.10.1 ANF I, pp. 422-23). Human nature was being assumed by and brought into the singular personhood of the Son of God.

Anointed as Son of God at His Baptism

In the narrative of Jesus' baptism, the voice from on high declared: "You are my Son, whom I love; with whom I am well pleased" (Mark 1:11; Matt. 3:13-17; Luke 3:21-22; Lactantius, *Div. Inst.* IV.15; ANF IV, pp. 115f.). The Baptist also "gave this testimony" to the expected one who would "'baptize with the Holy Spirit.' I have seen and I testify that this is the Son of God" (John 1:32, 34).

This did not imply an adoptionist teaching, by which it might be assumed that prior to his baptism Jesus was not the Son of God, but was at that point adopted. Rather he was named what he always was (Hilary, *Trin.* VI.23–36, *NPNF* 2 IX, pp. 106–111; Newman, *Ari.*, pp. 157–58).

Sonship and Time

In the relation of Father and Son, no notion of time appears (Augustine, *Hom. on John*, *NPNF* 1 VII, p. 402). Jesus did not become Son at a particular stage but is eternally and antecedently the Son, whose sonship was affirmed and celebrated at his baptism. "To the extent that He is the Only-begotten Son of God, the expressions 'has been' and 'will be' cannot be employed, but only the term 'is', because what 'has been' no longer exists and what 'will be' does not yet exist" (Augustine, *Faith and the Creed* 4.6, FC 27, p. 323).

The Son enjoyed a pretemporal relation with the Father prior to the incarnation (Rom. 8:3; John 1:1–10; 1 John 4:9–14), coequal and consubstantial with the Father (Augustine, *Hom. on John*, *NPNF* 1 VII, pp. 184, 296, 338), a relation that timebound mortals will never adequately fathom, but to which human speech can joyfully point. The notion of "pre"-temporal is paradoxical, because it must use a temporal prefix ("pre") to point to that which transcends the temporal. Nothing exists "before" time except the triune God.

The Mission of the Son

The Son is God and is with God (John 1:1–5; cf. Augustine, *Trin.*, FC 45, pp. 52–58). Having assumed human flesh, his deity is hidden in obedience to his mission (Calvin, *Inst.* 1.13.7–13; 2.14.5–7).

The Son Was Sent

The mission of the Son is to save humanity. "The Father has sent his Son to be the Savior of the world" (1 John 4:14). "When the time had come, God sent his Son" to "redeem those under law" (Gal. 4:4, 6). This only Son of the Father became flesh, entered history, and shared our humanity (John 1:14–18). God "did not spare his own Son, but gave him up for us all" (Rom. 8:32). The Son is mirror of the Father's heart (*BOC*, p. 419).

The Narrow Way

It was this One who suffered and died: "Although he was a son, he learned obedience from what he suffered and, once made perfect, he became the source of eternal salvation for all who obey him" (Heb. 5:8–9). His way of being a son was not a pampered, favored way, but a hard, narrow way. By this same narrow way do the faithful still enter into daughterhood and sonship, learning responsibility through life experiences suffered. The Son was delivered to death, bore our sins, reconciled us to the Father, and brought us life (Rom. 5:9-11, 8:32), which is lived "by faith in the Son of God" (Gal. 2:20; John Chrysostom, *Hom. on Gal.* II, *NPNF* 1 XIII, p. 22). This One is preached as giver of salvation (Rom. 1:9; 2 Cor. 1:19; Gal. 1:16). Salvation hinges upon the fitting answer to the simple, straightforward question: "Whose son is he" (Matt. 22:41) whose narrow path led to the cross?

Sonship A Self-Designation?

Did Jesus think of himself as Son of God? When tried before the Sanhedrin, charges were made to which Jesus did not reply. Put under oath (Matt. 26:63) he was asked directly the crucial question of his identity as Son: "Are you the Christ, the Son of the Blessed One?" (Mark 14:61). To make sense of this question, a premise is required: someone — either he or another — had claimed that he was the Son of God during his lifetime (Tertullian, *Ag. Praxeas* 16-18, *ANF* III, pp. 611-14).

Jesus' response, according to Mark, finally ended the suspense of the messianic secret: "'I am,' said Jesus. 'And you will see the Son of Man sitting at the right hand of the Mighty One and coming on the clouds of heaven'" (Mark 14:62). Note the shocking parallelism: now I am being judged by you, but at some point you will be judged by the Son of Man who is now being judged. Only God exercises final judgment — hence the charge of blasphemy (Calvin, *Comm.*, XVII, pp. 255-58).

This passage shows the interweaving, interactive quality of the two titles "Son of Man" and "Son of God," their affinity in the minds of the proclaiming church, and their complementarity. The Son of God "has been given authority to judge because he is the Son of Man" (John 5:27; 18:31; Tertullian, *Ag. Praxeas* 23, *ANF* III, p. 610).

Harnack complained that "The sentence, 'I am the Son of God' was not inserted in the Gospel by Jesus himself," but constitutes "an addition to the Gospel." Hence in his view, "The Gospel, as Jesus proclaimed it, has to do with the Father only and not with the Son" (*What Is Christianity?* pp. 92, 154). From Harnack's complaint has emerged a whole scholarly industry — biblical historical criticism's attempt to detach Jesus from divine sonship, a massive hundred-year enterprise that is now facing bankruptcy (Stuhlmacher, *HCTIS*, pp. 61-76; Maier, *EHCM*, pp. 12-26; Wink, *BHT*, pp. 1-15).

It is likely that the acceptance of the title "Son of God" by Jesus has its origin and explanation not in the later memory of the disciples but in Jesus himself (Matt. 11:25f.; Luke 10:21f.; Guthrie, *NTT*, pp. 301-20; T. W.

Manson, *Teaching of Jesus*, pp. 89–115). It is a title that is complementary to and commensurable with "Son of Man" (Eusebius, *MPG* I, p. 185).

The divine sonship theme appeared prominently at the most crucial moments of Jesus' ministry: his baptism, temptation, transfiguration, crucifixion, and resurrection (Mark 1:11; 9:2–8; Matt. 3:13–17, 17:1–8; 27:40). In the temptation narrative Jesus was challenged as Son of God to perform miracles for his own benefit (Luke 4:1–13). He refused. A similar taunt was flung at his crucifixion: "Let God rescue him now if he wants him, for he said, 'I am the Son of God'" (Matt. 27:44). Whether Jesus referred to himself as Son of God remains under debate, but these passages make it clear that Jesus was perceived by rememberers (including detractors) as having received and not disavowed the title Son of God.

The Reliability of Johannine Testimony

As a critical aside, if we were required for critical considerations to rule out John's Gospel in building a Christology, then our resources would be unduly constricted. Some critics have preferred to take John out of their private canon because of its presumed lateness. Hence it cannot be left to uncertainty as to why we regard John's Gospel as a reliable narrative.

Technical studies have shown that John's inclusion of specific topographical and factual details lends overall credibility to his report (Cana, John 2:1–12; the discussions with Nicodemus, 3:1–21, and the Samaritan woman, 4; Bethesda, 5:2; Siloam, 9:7). John reveals meticulous knowledge of Palestinian place names, customs, geographical sites, specific people and private relationships, and the precise movement of people from place to place that could hardly have been invented subsequently (or if invented, what could possibly be the purpose of such invention? Cf. R. D. Potter, *Texte und Untersuchungen* 73 [1959], pp. 320–37). Johannine language is closer to the Dead Sea Scrolls than the Synoptics, thus pointing to its Palestinian origin (though the author was more likely in Ephesus when writing). The Fourth Gospel contains "evidences of a familiarity with Palestinian conditions during our Lord's life which could not have been possessed by one who had not come in personal and contemporaneous contact with them" (Hall, *DT* VI, p. 307; W. F. Albright, "Recent Discoveries in Palestine and the Gospel of John," in W. Davies and D. Daube, *Background of the NT and Its Eschatology*, pp. 170–71). Although debates may continue as to the precise identity of its author, there can be no doubt, based on internal evidence, that it was written by one who had direct eyewitness contact with the events reported.

If John was exceedingly careful in remembering details, but entirely inaccurate in reporting his major subject, Jesus as Son of God, that would suggest a highly unlikely sort of inconsistency. J. B. Lightfoot, C. H. Dodd, C. K. Barrett, G. E. Ladd, R. E. Brown, David Wells, and other scholars have shown that John represents a reliable tradition of memory of Jesus. It cannot count against the Fourth Gospel that some events reported there are not in the Synoptics, for the reverse is also true (many events reported in the Synoptics are not in John — much of Jesus' teaching and public ministry). Some scholars hold that John the disciple wrote the Gospel (Guthrie, *NTI*, chap. 8; L. Morris, *The Gospel According to John*), while others hold that the core of the Gospel is the work of the disciple but it was subsequently rewritten by another hand (R. Brown, *The Gospel According to John* I; cf. J. A. T. Robinson, *Twelve NT Studies*, pp. 94–106; R. Schnackenburg, *The Gospel According to St. John* I, pp. 11–209; A. M. Hunter, *According to John*); others hold a much later authorship.

The likely assumption is that the author lived a long period of time in Ephesus and wrote the Gospel for that audience, with special concern to be faithful in detail to the original events in Palestine with the intent of confirming them in the belief that Jesus is the Messiah, the Son of God. The Gospel shows how missionary teaching was occurring in settings far away from Palestine yet was grounded in the history of Jesus in Palestine (C. H. Dodd, *Historical Tradition in the Fourth Gospel*; L. Morris, *Studies in the Fourth Gospel*; cf. A. J. B. Higgins, *The Historicity of the Fourth Gospel*; J. L. Martyn, *History and Theology in the Fourth Gospel*).

The tendency of some modern critics to discredit the Johannine testimony is unjustified. Although probably written late in the century and with a strong desire to teach the eternal sonship of Christ, its essential understanding of the Christ is fundamentally congruent with that of the other Gospel writers. Its high level of spiritual insight makes it wholly improbable that it might have been a manipulative attempt on the part of a later writer to put words in the mouth of Jesus inaccurately or to serve partisan interests. Where the Fourth Gospel restates points made in the other Gospels, there is reason to believe that it does so more accurately, more precisely, or in more specific detail than the others (C. K. Barrett, *The Gospel According to St. John*, pp. 3–119; W. Sanday, *Criticism of the Fourth Gospel*; cf. G. Ladd, *The NT and Criticism*, chap. 5).

Some modern critics are made uneasy by John's Gospel because it confronts them unmistakably with an exalted Christology and adheres so consistently to the premise that the Word was made flesh and dwelt among us. Some attempts to discredit John's Gospel may be based on resistance to the high Christology more than any internal or external evidence. Classical Christianity has chosen to rely on the historical trustworthiness of John as equal to that of the other synoptic writers. The reliability of John's Gospel is better appreciated when compared with apocryphal writings that are fixated on the miraculous.

Sonship in John's Gospel

John's Gospel requires special treatment on the theme of sonship, since it was for this very purpose that John wrote his Gospel—to make more explicit what had been implicit in the other Gospels—"that you may believe that Jesus is the Christ, the Son of God" (John 20:31; Tertullian, *Ag. Praxeas* 25, *ANF* III, p. 621).

The sonship of Jesus to the Father is the heart of the Johannine tradition. Jesus speaks of God as Father over a hundred times in John's Gospel. John refers to Jesus as "God the One and Only" (John 1:18, or "the only Son" or "the only begotten Son"). The Son's words, accordingly, are God's own words (John 8:26–28). Jesus' critics were offended by the fact that he was "calling God his Father, making himself equal with God" (5:18). "The Father loves the Son" in a special way and "shows him all he does" (John 5:20). Even as he walked toward death, he understood himself to be specially and uniquely loved by the Father (John 10:17; Pearson, *EC* I, pp. 49–69).

His union with God was more than a diffuse sharing in God's purpose. It was such that he was uniquely God, and with God, the Son being in the Father, and the Father in the Son (10:38; 14:10–11). What the Son was about, the Father knew, and what the Father intended, the Son knew (John 10:15; cf. Matt. 11:27), because the Son and the Father are one (John 10:30; Augustine, *Comm. on John*, Tractate 47–48, *NPNF* 1 VII, pp. 259–69).

Yet Son and Father are distinguishable. The Son depends upon the Father for every action. The Father sends, the Son is sent; one commands, the other obeys (John 15:10–20; Tho. Aq., *ST* III Q20, II, pp. 2136–38). "The Son is not the Father, but the Son is of God by nature" (Creed of Council of Toledo [A.D. 400], *SCD* 19, p. 13).

The Peculiar Equality of the Servant Son: Does the Sonship Tradition Reinforce Social Inequalities?

Rich familial images pervaded early Christianity. God as Father paternally sends his Son for redemption; the church as mother maternally nurtures this growth. One cannot understand this paternity without this maternity: "You are beginning to hold Him as a Father when you will be born of Mother Church" (Augustine, *The Creed* 1, *FC* 27, p. 290).

Modern egalitarianism (romanticist, quasi-Marxist, proletarian, and some secular feminist) complaints against Scripture are prone to turn angry and testy. It is said that there is an overemphasis upon super- and subordination and little notion of equality in Christian Scripture and tradition. That is partly due to the modern critical lack of imagination and unwillingness to enter into dialogue with New Testament and patristic-matristic writings on their own terms. The seldom mentioned, but distinctive and beautiful, contribution of Christianity to the teaching of equality is found in its teaching on the servant of God. Equality implies servanthood. But how?

Classical Christian Reasoning About Equality

We find in classic exegesis a powerful statement on equality and subordination in a most unlikely place—triune Christology—for it distinctly belongs to God to be *both equal and less than himself!* "It pertains to the Godhead alone not to have an unequal Son" (Council of Toledo, *CF,* p. 103). In the Godhead all historical inequalities are finally transcended. God the Son is both equal to the Father and less than the Father. The triune logic surprisingly implies and requires that God the Son is by nature equal to the Father, while voluntarily in mission obedient to the Father. In this way the Son can be both congruent within and self-giving to the world. He is one without ceasing to be the other. He calls us friends. By this paradox, the dilemma of equality is turned upside down. Intrinsic equality becomes voluntary poverty and subordination. The formula is so simple in its profundity that it first appears innocuous or unreasonable.

Equality and Servanthood

The *Symbol of Faith* of the Eleventh Council of Toledo will serve as an ecumenical point of reference for rigorous reflection about equality and servanthood:

> Similarly, by the fact that He is God,
>   He is *equal* to the Father;
> by the fact that He is man,
>   He is *less* than the Father.
> Likewise, we must believe that He is both greater
>   and less than Himself:
> for in the *form of God*
>   the Son Himself is greater than Himself
>   because of the humanity which He has assumed
>   and to which the divinity is superior;
> but in the *form of the servant*
>   He is less than Himself, that is, in His humanity
>   which is recognised as inferior to the divinity.

> For, while by the flesh which He has assumed
> He is recognized not only as
>   less than the Father
>   but also as less than Himself,
> according to the divinity He is co-equal with the Father;
> both He and the Father are greater than man whose nature (*quem*)
> the person of the Son alone assumed.
> Likewise, to the question whether the Son might be equal to,
> and less than the Holy Spirit, as we believe Him to be
>   now equal to,
>   now less than the Father, we answer
> according to the form of God He is equal to the Father
>   and to the Holy Spirit;
> according to the form of the servant,
>   He is less than both the Father
>   and the Holy Spirit
>
> (Eleventh Council of Toledo, *CF*, pp. 170-71;
> indentation and italics added).

Equality and servanthood thus belong together and cohere congruently.

THE PREINCARNATIONAL LIFE OF THE SON

Without the premise of preexistence, there can be no talk of the incarnation or Christmas. The temporal birth assumed and required a pretemporal hypothesis: existence of the Logos before the incarnation. If the Savior is God, then that One must be eternal God, hence must have existed prior to incarnation in time, just as he continues in exaltation after his incarnate life (Phil. 2:6-11; John Chrysostom, *Hom. on Phil.* VII, *NPNF* 1 XIII, pp. 212-18).

How Can the Son Be Begotten Before Time?

There Is No Before with Him

The Logos that is eternal by definition must exist before time. This is hardly an optional point of Christian theology. Far from being a tardy accretion of hellenization, the seeds of this premise were firmly embedded in the earliest Christian preaching, for how could the Son be born in time or sent from the Father on a mission to the world if the Son had no life with the Father before the nativity? "Begotten before. Before what, since there is no before with Him? . . . Do not imagine any interval or period of eternity when the Father was and the Son was not," for the Son is "always without beginning" (Augustine, *The Creed* 3.8, FC 27,

p. 295). "The Sources of Time are not subject to time" (Gregory Nazianzen, *Orat.* XXIX.3, *NPNF* 2 VII, p. 302).

The Price of Neglect of This Premise

It might seem that one could politely circumvent this tedious point or dismiss it by alleging that it is a later or inconsequential addition to the earliest tradition. That might be plausible if this theme were not so persistent in the earliest strains of oral tradition, in the New Testament texts themselves, and in all its major writers. As attested by Paul, John, Luke-Acts, Hebrews, and other New Testament writings, the life of the Son of God is antecedent to the incarnation.

The neglect of the premise has more drastic consequences than one might expect, for it amounts to conceding that Christ is not true God. His humbling into incarnate life and death is meaningful only in relation to the Whence from which he came. Lacking the premise of preexistence, the nativity narratives are rendered meaningless. If the Son came into being only at his birth, then there can be no triune God, for the second Person would not be eternal, hence not God (Augustine, *Comm. on John 6:60–72, Tractate* XXVII, *NPNF* 1 VII, p. 175; Chemnitz, *TNC*, pp. 38–39).

If preexistence is denied, then Christ could not have been speaking through the prophets, as New Testament and classic interpreters consistently assumed. If the eternal Son did not exist before his earthly ministry, then the teachings of Paul and John are drastically discredited. This is why the premise of preexistence is so insistent and pervasive in New Testament and ecumenical teaching (Pearson, *EC* I, p. 195; Forsyth, *PPJC*, pp. 261–90). If the Son is divine, he must have been divine from the beginning and from before all worlds (Ursinus, *CHC*, pp. 186–88).

Word as Son

"In the past God spoke to our forefathers through the prophets," but "in these last days he has spoken to us by his Son" (Heb. 1:1–2). The Word of God is spoken through the life of the Son. These two recurrrent terms—Word and Son—are principal titles ascribed to the pretemporal existence of the One who assumed flesh in Jesus. "He is called Son, because he is identical with the Father in essence," and "Word, because he is related to the Father as word to mind" (Gregory Nazianzen, *Theol. Orat.* XXX.20, *LCC* III, p. 191).

Contra Ebionism

The preexistent Logos theme has exercised constraint over the Ebionitic distortion that Jesus was first and foremost a good teacher whose teaching and death later caused his disciples to ascribe to him attributes of divinity (the modern expression of this is the tradition from David F. Strauss to Herbert Braun that seeks to reduce to anthropological determinants all talk of divinity). If Jesus had been remembered as man only, not God-man, there would have been no motivation whatever to speak of his pretemporal existence. His life would have then begun with his birth. But his life could not be eternal *and* begin with his birth. The logic of the earliest kerygma was that God has chosen to come to humanity—not humanity to God. God's sovereign initiative is not finally reducible to social influences of the history of religions.

Preexistence in the Pauline Tradition

That preexistence is not exclusively a Johannine idea is evident from its recurrent treatment in Pauline Letters (1 Cor. 8:6; 2 Cor. 8:9; Eph. 1:3–14). Paul taught preexistence in conspicuous passages.

Equality with God

The Son was "in very nature God," yet "did not consider equality with God something to be grasped" because he already shared fully in the divine life and was willing to become obedient unto death in order that the divine life be manifested to humanity in servant form (Phil. 2:5–11).

Coeternal Creator

Through the Son were created all things visible and invisible. Not only is he "before all things," but also "in him all things hold together" (Col. 1:16; John Chrysostom, *Hom. on Col.* III, *NPNF* 1 XIII, pp. 270-75). The Son who is before all things is coeternal with the Father, hence nothing less than God (Hilary, *Trin.* XII.35–43, *NPNF* 2 IX, pp. 226–29; *BOC*, p. 577; Wesley, *WJW* VI, pp. 426–27). It was through the resurrection that the primitive Christian community came to grasp and confess that the living Lord is eternal Son. The Colossian Letter set forth the crucial analogy between Jesus Christ as first in *creation* and first in *resurrection*, "first-born over all creation" and "the beginning and the first-born from among the dead" (Col. 1:15, 18; Athanasius, *Four Discourses Ag. Arians* II.1–82, *NPNF* 2 IV, pp. 348–93).

Only One Already Existing Could be Sent

"When the time had fully come, *God sent his son*"—only one who already exists could be sent—to be "born of a woman, born under law, that we might receive the full rights of sons. Because you are sons, God sent the Spirit of his Son into our hearts, the Spirit who calls out, 'Abba,

Father'" (Gal. 4:4–5, italics added). There is a triune premise here: the Spirit helps us understand the speech of the Father through the Son, whom he sent, born of woman under law.

The Pre-Pauline Oral Tradition

Allusions to the preexistence of Christ appear embedded in the earliest oral traditions antedating Paul's Letters (Phil. 2:6–11; 1 Cor. 15:47; Col. 1:17; 1 Tim. 3:16; F. Craddock, *The Pre-Existence of Christ*; cf. R. Hammerton-Kelly, *Pre-Existence, Wisdom and the Son of Man*). They are not presented with baroque flourish or as if they were an elaborated extension added later as a result of subsequent reflection. The attestation is attended with no speculative details or mythic ornamentations but rather presented as an element of faith presumably shared by all who proclaim the gospel of God.

The fact that the preexistence theme had widespread currency among the earliest Christian sources and in the most important Christological texts of the New Testament—Paul, John, Hebrews, and the Synoptics—makes it hard to counter it as a later ancillary mythic appendage. Here form criticism is put to a service very different from that assumed by many form critics, namely, that of establishing the early date of the preexistence theme (Taylor, *PC*, pp. 62–78; A. M. Hunter, *Paul and His Predecessors*, pp. 40ff.; C. F. D. Moule, *Colossians and Philemon*, *CGTC*, pp. 58ff.).

Logos Christology

Hebraic Source of Logos Christology

The main stem of New Testament usage of Logos is not Greek but the ancient Hebraic *dabar Yahweh* ("Word of God") by which the world was made and the prophets inspired (Manson, *Studies in the Gospels and Epistles*, p. 118). Although Bultmann had argued for the Hellenistic origin of the Logos language of the New Testament, the more probable origin is Semitic (Cullmann, *CNT*, pp. 249ff.), since John 1:1–3 is best seen in recollection of Genesis 1:1 (Augustine, *Trin.*, FC 45, pp. 281–84, 476–93).

Personification of Logos

In Old Testament usage, the Word of God is not merely an utterance, but can become personified. God's Word can go forth and accomplish its purpose and can be expressed through prophetic witness (Isa. 55:10–11; Jer. 1:4, 2:1). God's Word as Wisdom speaks as a person: "The Lord possessed me at the beginning of his work, before his deeds of old; I was appointed from eternity, from the beginning, before the world began.

When there were no oceans, I was given birth," when "he marked out the foundation of the earth. Then I was the craftsman at his side. I was filled with delight day after day, rejoicing always in his presence, rejoicing in his whole world and delighting in mankind" (Prov. 8:22–30). Wisdom literature may stand as background for John's language (John Chrysostom, *Hom. on John* XV.1, *NPNF* 1 XIV, p. 51).

Logos as Agent of Creation

John's Gospel speaks of the Logos as active agent through whom God created the world ("through whom all things were made," John 1:3). This is consistent with Paul's language, that all things come *from* (*ek*) God the Father *through* (*dia*) Christ the Son: "For us there is one God, the Father, *from* whom all things came and for whom we live; and there is but one Lord, Jesus Christ, *through* whom all things came and through whom we live" (1 Cor. 8:6, italics added; John Chrysostom, *Hom. on First Cor.* XX.6, *NPNF* 1 XII, p. 114).

It is this eternal Word (*logos*) that becomes flesh (*sarx*), contrary to all Hellenistic assumptions and expectations. Were one seeking to accommodate to a Hellenistic audience, one would certainly not say: Logos becomes flesh. It is this enfleshed Logos, the Son, through whom God the Father is revealed (John 1:17–18; Newman, *Ari.*, p. 169). "He is the Son-Word, maker of rational creatures, the Word that hears the Father and himself declares it" (Cyril of Jerusalem, *Catech. Lect.* IV.8, *LCC* IV, p. 103).

Preexistence in Johannine Teaching

Pauline and Johannine views are far less in tension on preexistence than some have imagined. If preexistence receives occasional but crucial reference in Paul, it receives recurrent and decisive reference in John.

The eternal Logos, whose glory the disciples beheld in Jesus Christ, not only appeared in time but also, according to John's Gospel, was "in the beginning." The Logos was God and was with God in the beginning (John 1:1–2), through whom "all things were made; without him nothing was made that has been made" (v. 3). If the Son can be said both to *be God*, and to *be with God* that implies both *unity* with God and *distinguishability* within the Godhead—elementary features of triune teaching.

The relation of Father and Son before the incarnation is expressed in metaphors of love and glory. The Son was preexistently "at the Father's side" (John 1:18, or "in the bosom of the Father," KJV), sharing in the glory (*doxa*) of God the Father (John 11:4, 40; 12:41; 17:5, 22, 24).

The preexistence theme is found in Jesus' own teaching of himself as heavenly Son of Man come down from above (Mark 5:7; 9:7-31; 13:26; 14:61-62). This is consistent with the Johannine recollection of his saying: "Before Abraham was born, I am" (John 8:58; Barth, *CD* I/2, p. 75). The "I am" (*ego eimi*) sayings imply eternality as a distinctive attribute of the speaker (Irenaeus, *Ag. Her.* IV.13.4, *ANF* I, p. 478).

When his "time had come," Jesus is remembered as having prayed to stand once again in the glory of God's presence with the same "glory I had with you before the world began" (John 17:5). The love that the Son experienced from the Father, remembered by Jesus even as he was facing arrest and crucifixion, was from the beginning, "because you loved me before the creation of the world" (John 17:24; Augustine, *Comm. on John*, *Tractate* 109, *NPNF* 1 VII, p. 412-15).

Classical Ecumenic Formulations of the Son's Pretemporal Existence

Only He Existed Before He Was Born

The preexistent Logos was understood by the Nicene Council as the only Son of the Father, begotten not in time, but eternally Son. Hence preexistence is closely connected with the "eternal generation of the Son," resisting the Arian notion that the preexistent Son was created or made and hence not truly God (Athanasius, *Defence of the Nicene Council*, *NPNF* 2 IV, pp. 149-73). Ancient ecumenical teaching holds that the Son is the second of three coequal, distinguishable, but inseparable persons of the triune Godhead, coeternal with the Father and the Spirit. "We say, then, that the divine Person of God the Word exists before all things time-lessly and eternally, simple and uncompounded, uncreated, incorporeal, invisible, intangible, and uncircumscribed" (John of Damascus, *OF* III.7, *FC* 37, p. 281).

Such language does not put the Logos out of reach, for as "He was God before all ages; he is man in this age of ours" (Augustine, *Enchiridion* X.35, *LCC* VII, p. 361). "For He was not first God without a Son [and] afterwards in time became a Father; but He has the Son eternally, having begot Him not as men beget men, but as He Himself alone knows" (Cyril of Jerusalem, *Catech.* XI, *FC* 61, p. 215). Hence the views of Paul of Samosata, Photinus, and Priscillian were rejected insofar as they taught that the Son "did not exist before He was born" (John III, Council of Braga, *SCD* 233, p. 93).

The early Latin hymn writer Prudentius wrote:

> Of the Father's love begotten,
> Ere the worlds began to be,

He is the Alpha and Omega,
  He the source, the ending he,
Of the things that are, that have been,
  And that future years shall see
(trans. John Mason Neale, *HPEC*, p. 63).

The developing recognition of the preexistent divine Logos (*logos asarkos*, "fleshless Word") had to be inferred from the actual existence of the incarnate Logos (*logos ensarkos*, "enfleshed Word"). While incarnation is prior to preexistence in the order of its having become known, preexistence is prior to incarnation in logical and timely order.

Is There Process in God?

If the redeeming purpose is fully intentional in God before creation, the notion of a "growing God" or gradual historically developing maturity in God is made problematic. Jews and Christians do not view God as increasing in justice, struggling to develop mercy, or growing in knowledge. Justice, mercy, and knowing are already incomparably great in God from the beginning and on this basis ever being expressed actively and responsively in each succeeding temporal situation (Irenaeus, *Ag. Her.* IV.2, *ANF* I, p. 465). For "nothing can be added to that which is full" (Gregory Nazianzen, *Orat.* XXVIII.31, *NPNF* 2 VII, p. 300).

The language of Gregory Thaumaturgus of Neo-Caesarea (ca. A.D. 270) is typical. He seems to rule out any notion of process or development in the Godhead: "Neither, indeed, is there any thing created or subservient in the Trinity, nor introduced, as though not there before but coming in afterwards; nor, indeed, has the Son ever been without the Father" (*A Declaration of Faith*, *COC* II, p. 25; cf. *ANF* VI, p. 7). This does not imply a lack of responsiveness in God, whose unchanging covenant love is constant responsiveness. The Aristotelian view that God is incapable of responsiveness would have been thought strange to Jeremiah or Paul or Augustine.

Was the World Begotten with or After the Son?

Among alleged views of Meister Eckart rejected by medieval Christianity (and withdrawn by Eckart when challenged) were views that sound today much like some forms of process theology: the view that "as soon as God was, He immediately created the world," "that the world existed from eternity," and that the instant God begot the Son "He also created the world" (John II, *In Agro Dominico* [1329], *SCD* 501, p. 195). Problems perceived in Eckart's writings were incipient pantheism, failing to distinguish between God and the world, and the misplacement of the eternity of the Son (cf. Calvin, *Ag. the Fantastic and Furious Sect of Libertines Who Are Called 'Spirituals', TAAAL*, pp. 161ff.).

Preincarnation Activity of Christ in Creation, Providence, and Salvation History

The preexistent Son is not portrayed in Scripture as passively immobile, awaiting the incarnate moment to become alive and active, but rather as active in the history of salvation before the incarnation.

As Creator

The Logos is active as *Creator*. It is by God's Word that God creates (John 1:3; Heb. 1:2). Creation has as its purpose the demonstration of God's saving activity, all things having been created "for him" (Col. 1:16). Creation is not autonomously an end in itself but serves the redeeming purpose. Wherever the divine Word is spoken or divine wisdom manifested before the incarnation, there is the Son: "The Father created all things by his Son, as by his eternal Wisdom and his eternal Word" (*Longer Catech. of the Eastern Church, COC* II, p. 468).

As Providential Guide

The Word of Life is continuously present in the sustenance of creation, the whole story of *providence* unfolding in world history, including history prior to and following incarnation and resurrection (Col. 1:17; *LG*, pp. 306–15). The Letter to the Hebrews argues that the Son is "The radiance of God's glory and the exact representation of his being, *sustaining all things* by his powerful word" (Heb. 1:3, italics added; John Chrysostom, *Hom. on Heb.* IV, *NPNF* 1 XIV, pp. 382–88). The central feature of providence was pointedly stated by Pascal: "Without Jesus Christ the world could not continue; for it must needs be destroyed or become a very hell" (Pensées 12, *TGS*, p. 215).

As Revealer

This same eternal Word of God is present and active throughout the *history of salvation*. Classic exegetes viewed the eternal Logos who assumed human nature in Christ as the active, speaking agent of prophecy and as the Angel of Yahweh who appeared repeatedly in the Old Testament narratives, who spoke as God, displayed attributes of God, and identified himself with God (Gen. 21:17–18; Exod. 3:2; Judg. 2:1–4; 6:11–22; 13:3–22; Zech. 1:12–13; 3:1; 12:8). "It was not the Father, then, who was a guest with Abraham, but Christ" (Novatian, *Trin.* XVIII, *ANF* V, p. 629).

In this preincarnate role the preexistent Son acted as messenger of
God (Gen. 16:7–14; 22:11–18; 31:11–13), judge (1 Chron. 21:1–27), en-
courager (1 Kings 19:5–7), and guide of the people of God (Exod. 14:19;
23:20; 2 Kings 190:35; Gregory of Nyssa, *FGG*, pp. 150–53; Ambrose,
Patriarchs, 4.16–7.34, FC 65, pp. 250–61). The Word of God yet to be made
flesh was present in the prophetic, priestly, and governance traditions of
Israel.

Breaking the Double Bind of Contrary Objections to Pretemporality

There are two characteristic ways of attempting to discredit the idea of
Christ's preexistence: by showing that it was a much later addition to the
earliest kerygma or that it was already discoverable in a much earlier form
in the Jewish tradition. Taken together they constitute a double bind, a
"Catch-22." As to the former criticism, the stronger evidence is that preexistence was embedded in the earliest Christian sources and widely held.
Against Bultmann's view that the preexistence theme was a later accretion of the hellenizing church, Martin Hengel has argued that this is a
much earlier idea with Jewish roots and is found in the deepest layers of
oral tradition of Christian preaching anteceding the writing of the New
Testament (*Son of God*, pp. 66ff.).

As to the second part of the double bind, H. R. Mackintosh made
good reply: "That its similarity to a prior idea must discredit the Christian belief could only be conceded on the obviously untenable assumption that no true idea is ever providentially prepared for. It may well be
that certain current Jewish theologoumena [names for God] operated by
suggestion" (*PJC*, p. 450). It seems an unusual and impossible criterion of
authenticity to assume that any idea that has previously appeared invali-
dates its use by a subsequent writer, for that would discredit Gray's
"Elegy" on the comic grounds that every word of it is found in previous
lexicons.

THE HUMBLING OF GOD TO SERVANTHOOD

The Lowering and Raising of the Son

Humiliation and Exaltation

By way of review, the complex issues associated with the study of
Christ are often sorted out into two overarching groups, chronologically
arranged into *two periods* in which the work of *three offices* is accomplished. These two fundamental stages or periods are frequently distinguished in Christ's ministry: the humbling of the Son to servanthood

(including everything leading to his death and burial); and the raising of the Son to governance (everything following after his resurrection; Hilary, *Trin.* IX–XI, *NPNF* 2 IX, pp. 155–217; Newman, *Ath.* 2 I, pp. 218–25). Within this broad frame, Christ's mediatorial work is seen in three offices that correlate generally with this chronological progression: prophetic teaching, priestly sacrifice, and regal governance, schematized as follows:

TWO PERIODS:

Humiliation	Pivot	Exaltation
Birth to	Death	Resurrection

THREE OFFICES:

Prophetic	Priestly	End-time
Teaching	Sacrifice	Governance

The prophetic office is undertaken primarily during the period of humiliation. Reception of the regal office is primarily associated with exaltation. The priestly sacrifice focuses upon the pivotal event—the death of Christ—marking the end of God's humbling and the reversal leading to exaltation.

The Cross Marks the Boundary Between the Two Periods

The salvation event had been prophetically promised to occur through suffering and death (Isa. 53:4–9). Each step of Jesus' life descended toward his death, followed by his descent into the grave. The death of the Savior marked the clear boundary line between the two overarching phases of the Son's ministry, in which divine powers were first withheld, then exercised. The *humiliation* of the eternal Son was marked by a *cessation* of the independent exercise of divine powers in the voluntary acceptance of humanity, birth, finitude, suffering, and finally death and burial (Phil. 2:6–8). His *exaltation* was marked by a *resumption* of the independent exercise of divine powers (Phil. 2:9–11). The Son's exaltation confirmed the hidden meaning of his humiliation (Gregory Nazianzen, *Orat.* XXXVII, *NPNF* 2 VII, p. 339).

The Humbling of the Eternal Son Under Limits of Time

Voluntary, Temporal Humbling

The humbling of God was not an enforced humbling, but an elected, voluntary humbling. The humiliation (*tapeinōsis*) was temporary, lasting from birth to death, or more precisely from the Son's first moment of

conception to his last moment in the grave. The phase of exaltation begins
with his resurrection and continues to the last day.

Humbling to Birth, Then to Death

The eternal Son humbled himself first to birth, then to death, and
only then was exalted to return to glory with the Father. The contrast
between the two overarching phases of mediatorial ministry is based
upon contrasting phrases of Philippians 2: he "made himself nothing" (v.
7), and "Therefore God exalted him" (v. 9). The sequence of conditions
was glory followed by servanthood followed once again by glory.

Descendit de Coelis

The humbling motif is found in the Nicene Creed in the phrase: "He
came down from heaven" (*descendit de coelis*; Creed of 150 Fathers, *COC* II,
p. 58). The descent theme is presupposed in the titles Son of God, Son
of Man, Logos, and Lord, for how could the eternal Son become incarnate as a child without "coming down"—a spatial metaphor of descent, of
self-chosen lowering of power, and of taking upon himself all human
limitations including death? (*Doc. Vat. II*, pp. 563–67).

Kenosis

What is meant by the phrase, he "made himself nothing" (Phil. 2:7;
Gk. *heauton ekenosen*; Lat. *semet ipsum exinanivit*)? Sometimes this is
referred to as the exiniation or self-renunciation of the Son, whose
earthly ministry was characterized by self-emptying (*kenosis*) or voluntary
abnegation of the divine glory (Hilary, *Trin.* IX.48, *NPNF* 2 IX, p. 172).

The Disavowal of Uninterrupted Exercise of Divine Powers

This voluntary renunciation consisted essentially in the *disavowal or
abdication of full and uninterrupted exercise of divine powers*, while the Son
accepted the incarnate life and assumed the form of a servant (John
Chrysostom, *Hom. on Phil.* VI, *NPNF* 2 XIII, pp. 206–12; Newman, *Ari.*,
pp. 163–66; Hollaz, *ETA*, p. 765). It is this self-giving, serving love that
Paul was commending as a primary pattern of human behavior to the
Philippians.

The Hiddenness of Deity in Humanity

This involved the temporary obscuring of the divine sonship, hidden
in the flesh of humanity (Cyril of Alexandria, *Third Letter to Nestorius*, *LCC*
III, pp. 349–54). "He has hidden His majesty in humanity, does not
appear with lightning, thunder, or angels, but as one born of a poor

virgin and speaking with men of the forgiveness of sins" (Luther, *Serm. on John 4* [1540], *WLS* I, p. 154; *WA* 47, 209f.).

Emptying as Filling

The metaphor of voluntary emptying should not be confused with emptiness. Embedded in the metaphor is a paradox, for when one cup is emptied into another, the other becomes full. The self-emptying of the Logos is the filling of the incarnate Son, for in emptying himself, God reveals himself as enfleshed, filling a human body with his fullness.

The Spirit Sustained the Incarnate Son

During his saving mission, the Son "through the eternal Spirit offered himself unblemished to God" (Heb. 9:14). While engaged in his earthly ministry, "God gives the Spirit without limit" to the One sent by the Father (John 3:34; Augustine, *Hom. on John* XIV, *NPNF* 1 VII, pp. 93–99). The humbling of the Son ceased when, upon accomplishing this mission, the Holy Spirit was given to the church as the Son ascended to the Father.

Triune Premise Required

It is well to recall how essential the triune premise is to the incarnation.

The Godhead Not Humbled

It was not the Godhead that became incarnate, but one of the persons of the Godhead. The Godhead as such was not humbled or lowered, but the one person of the Son embracing two natures, wherein the human nature was humbled. Hence it is said that the subject of the humiliation is the human nature, unconfusedly united with the divine nature, which "neither died nor was crucified" (Hollaz, *ETA*, p. 767; Schmid, *DT*, p. 381).

The triune premise impinges everywhere upon Christology: *if God were only one person*, it could not be proclaimed that God both sends and is sent; that God could be both lawgiver and obedient to law; that God could both make atonement and receive it; that God could both reject sin and offer sacrifice for sin; that God could at the same time govern all things, yet become freely self-emptied in serving love (Hilary, *Trin.* IX.38–42, *NPNF* 2 IX, pp. 167–70).

The Word Not Dissipated in Flesh

An exaggerated theory of *kenosis* "which imagines that in Christ the divinity of the Word is lost" must be rejected as a "rash interpretation" of the text. For "Like the doctrine of Docetism directly opposed to it, it makes the whole mystery of the incarnation and the redemption a lifeless and meaningless illusion" (Pius XII, *Encyclical Letter Simpiternus* [1951], *CF,* p. 187; for Chemnitz's rejection of an exaggerated kenoticism, see *TNC,* pp. 280–82).

FORM OF GOD, FORM OF A SERVANT

The locus classicus of this teaching is Philippians 2:5–11:

Have this mind among yourselves, which you have in Christ Jesus, who, though he was in the form of God, did not count equality with God a thing to be grasped, but emptied himself, taking the form of a servant, being born in the likeness of men. And being found in human form he humbled himself and became obedient unto death, even death on a cross. Therefore God has highly exalted him and bestowed on him the name which is above every name, that at the name of Jesus every knee should bow, in heaven and on earth and under the earth, and every tongue confess that Jesus Christ is Lord, to the glory of God the Father (RSV).

The context in which this pivotal passage occurs is an appeal to *follow Christ's way of lowliness.* Paul had just instructed the Philippians to "do nothing out of selfish ambition or vain conceit, but in humility consider others better than yourselves. Each of you should look not only to your own interests, but also to the interests of others" (Phil. 2:3–4).

This way of lowliness was effectively pioneered by Christ himself: "Let this mind be in you, which was also in Christ Jesus" (v. 5, KJV; on meditation on the humiliation of Christ, see Mark the Ascetic, *Letter to Nicolas, Philokal.* I, pp. 155–56; Boff, *LibT.,* p. 26). What follows is quite likely an early Christian hymn or hymnic fragment, used or adapted by Paul, that offers a remarkable glimpse into the view of Christ embedded in the earliest worship of primitive Christian communities.

In the Form of God: Exposition of Locus Classicus—Philippians 2:5–11

Morphē Theou

The One who became Servant was One "Who, being in the very nature God [*morphē Theou*]" (Phil. 2:6)—the preexistent Logos subsisted in the form (*morphē*) of God before the incarnation, in an existence equal to that of God (Council of Ephesus, *SCD* 118, p. 50). "The divine nature was his from the beginning" (Phil. 2:6, *TCNT*).

The same theme recurs in Paul: "There is but one Lord, Jesus Christ, through whom all things came, and through whom we live" (1 Cor. 8:6);

"by him all things were created" (Col. 1:15). Christ pretemporally existed in the form and glory of God.

Equality Assumed but Not Asserted

Christ "did not consider equality with God something to be grasped" (*harpagmon*, "forcibly retained," Phil. 2:6). Recall that the essence of Adam's disobedience had been a presumptuous grasping for equality with God. Oppositely, Christ did not grasp self-assertively at the divine majesty, for he already possessed it (Hilary, *Trin.* XII.6, *NPNF* 2 IX, p. 219).

He Made Himself Nothing

He voluntarily became lowly (*heauton ekenosen*, "He emptied himself," Phil. 2:7, KJV). He did not assert self-interestedly the power he rightly had. He made no display of it. The Son *gave up the independent exercise of divine attributes and powers that constituted his equality with God*. In becoming human, the Logos did not divest the substance of Godhead, which from the moment of conception dwelt in Christ bodily, for we know from other texts that Paul viewed the incarnate Lord as the veritable embodiment of deity (Col. 1:19). The text does not focus specifically upon what was emptied, but rather upon what the self-emptying called forth—the servant life. *Kenosis* did not extinguish the Logos, but the Logos became supremely self-expressed and incarnately embodied in the *kenosis*.

Taking the Form of a Servant

In taking "the form of a servant [*morphen doulou*]" (Phil. 2:7), the contrast is sharpened between one in the form of God who voluntarily takes a constricted, limited form as if slave. He came "not to be ministered unto, but to minister" (Matt. 20:28, KJV). He came among us "as one who serves" (Luke 22:27). Jesus washing the feet of his disciples symbolized his taking the form of a servant (John 13:1–20; Hilary, *Trin.* XI.13–15, *NPNF* 2 IX, p. 207).

The Form of God Not Lost

Augustine warned against exaggerations: "The form of a servant was so taken that the form of God was not lost, since both in the form of a servant and in the form of God He himself is the same only-begotten Son of God the Father, in the form of God equal to the Father, in the form of a servant the Mediator between God and men, the man Christ Jesus" (Augustine, *Trin.* I.7, *NPNF* 1 III, p. 24; cf. *Enchiridion* VIII.35, *LCC* VII, p. 361).

He Who Empties, Receives

The most brilliant analysis of Philippians 2:7 is found in Hilary:

Hence, the emptying of the form is not the destruction of the nature, because He who empties Himself is not wanting in His own nature and He who receives remains. And since it is He Himself who empties and receives, we find indeed a mystery in Him, because He empties Himself and receives Himself, but no destruction takes place so that He ceases to exist when He empties Himself or does not exist when He receives. Hence, the emptying brings it about that the form of a slave appears, but not that the Christ who was in the form of God does not continue to be Christ, since it is only Christ who has received the form of a slave (*On the Trinity* IX.44, FC 25, pp. 334–35).

The New Man Must Participate in the Nature of Humanity

The humiliation was necessary to the mediatorial role: "And in what way could He properly fulfill His mediation, unless He who in the form of God was equal to the Father, were a sharer of our nature also in the form of a slave; so that the one new Man might effect a renewal of the old; and the bond of death fastened on us by one man's wrong-doing might be loosened by the death of the one Man who alone owed nothing to death" (Leo, *Letters,* 124.3, NPNF 2 XII, p. 91).

Made in Human Likeness

Sharing Human Limits

"Being made in human likeness" (*homoioma*, Phil. 2:7), being born, being under the law, undergoing development, he lived in poverty. The Son of God became that particular kind of slave that human finitude requires—under servility to time and space, suffering, and death. It is not merely that the Son became a man—emphasis is rather placed upon the servile limitations that are associated with human life generally, and especially the life of the poor, the neglected, hidden sufferers. "Down, down, says Christ; you shall find Me in the poor; you are rising too high if you do not look for Me there" (Luther, *Serm. on Matt. 22:34–46*, WLS I, p. 206; WA 20, 517f.). "In him God becomes oppressed man" (Cone, *BTL,* p. 215; cf. Boff, *LibT.*, pp. 60–61).

The conditions common to humanity included physical development (being born and passing through stages of growth), intellectual development (learning as humans learn), and even moral development (submitting to parents and to the law), within a distinct historical context, under a particular political regime, of a particular ethnicity, and in a particular family.

As a Man

"And being found in appearance as a man" (Phil. 2:8), that is, "recognized as truly human" (Weymouth transl.). This phrase does not imply that he was not really a man, but underscores the contrast—being God he was found in human form, appeared as such, and was recognizable as such. "His experience was that of every other man, eating, drinking, sleeping, waking, walking, standing, hungering, thirsting, shivering, sweating, fatigued, working, clothing Himself, sheltered in a house, praying—all things just as others" (Luther, *SCF*, p. 144).

He Humbled Himself and Became Obedient unto Death

He Humbled Himself

Though more than human, he was willing to become the least among humanity, despised and rejected (Julian of Norwich, "The Homeliness of God," *IAIA*, p. 89). This humiliation extended over the whole of his earthly life. The cross cast its shadow upon every step of his way from his baptism to his death (Barth, *CD* I/2, pp. 35ff.; IV/4, pp. 52–67).

Obedient to Death

He "became obedient to death—" (Phil. 2:8). "Although he was a son, he learned obedience from what he suffered" (Heb. 5:8). In his active obedience he fulfilled the obligation of the law; in his passive obedience he endured the penalty of human sin. Hence "through the obedience of the one man the many will be made righteous" (Rom. 5:19).

Even Death on a Cross (Phil. 2:8)

The humbling of the Son ends in death by crucifixion, "rectifying that disobedience which had occurred by reason of a tree, through that obedience which was [wrought out] upon the tree [of the cross]" (Irenaeus, *Ag. Her.* V.16.3, *ANF* I, p. 544). He thereby became "a curse for us" (Gal. 3:13).

The Reversal of Egalitarian Assertiveness

Voluntary Obedience of the Son to the Father in Mission

Such was, in brief, the humiliating *schema* (Phil. 2:7, "way or fashion of life") accepted by the Son.

The notion of subordination appears in the sayings of Jesus that he is able to do nothing by himself and that the Father is greater than he (John 5:30; 10:15, 30; 14:28; cf. Matt. 11:27; Titus 2:13; 1 John 5:7). To be subordinated means to be placed in a lower class or order or rank. The subordination of which Paul spoke in Philippians 2:5-8 was a temporary one that ended when Jesus was exalted to the glory of his previous existence.

Eternal Subordinationism Rejected

Subordinationism is that false teaching that argues that the Son is eternally and by nature unequal to the Father (rejected by the Councils of Nicaea and Constantinople, and the Second Helvetic Confession; the tendency is found in Sabellianism, Arianism, and Monarchianism). Any subordinationism that fails to recognize Christ's return to equality with the Father has not been ecumenically received. Instead, the temporal subordination freely chosen by the Son demonstrated missional account-ability by one divine person to another, not of one divine nature to another, for there is only one divine nature.

The Son, Not the Godhead, Humbled

The triune premise must be held firmly in place for such language to make sense. It speaks not of the temporary subordination of one divine nature to another, but of the voluntary, temporary subordination of one divine person to another on behalf of mission, the Son to the Father. Whatever humbling events occurred, the Son in his Godhead retained all that belongs to the nature of God. "Only the Son took the form of a servant in the singleness of person, not in the unity of the divine nature; He took it into what is proper to the Son, not into what is common to the Trinity" (Eleventh Council of Toledo, *CF*, p. 170; see also *SCD* 284, p. 110).

Equalitarian and Missional Implications of Christ's Lowliness

A curious anomaly resulted: "for in the form of God even the Son Himself is greater than Himself on account of the humanity He assumed, than which the divinity is greater; in the form, however, of a servant He is less than Himself, that is, in His humanity" (Eleventh Council of Toledo, *SCD* 285, p. 111; cf. *BOC*, pp. 602–604).

Hence amid the humbling of God, "so far as He is God, He and the Father are one; so far as He is man, the Father is greater than He," and in this paradoxical way, "He was both made less and remained equal" (Augustine, *Enchiridion* 35, *NPNF* 1 III, p. 249). "He is the Mediator, then, in that He is man—inferior to the Father, by so much as He is nearer to ourselves, and superior to us, by so much as He is nearer to the Father" (Augustine, *On the Grace of Christ and on Original Sin* II.33, *NPNF* 1 V, p. 249). In making for himself no reputation and taking the form of a servant, he did not lose or diminish the form of God (*BOC*, pp. 602–605).

The Consequent Moral Imperative

Ethic of Voluntary Servanthood

With this in mind we can now return to the ethical appeal made at the outset of this passage: Paul was calling upon the Philippians to follow Christ's example of lowliness of mind. His object is to elicit among the Philippians a similar attitude of self-submission, hoping that they would walk in humility, considering others better than themselves (Phil. 2:3)—that is what apparently elicited Paul's recollection and insertion of the Christic hymn.

A radical ethical consequence ensues that transmutes a simpler humanistic equalitarianism: as Christ is equal to God, so you are equal to your neighbor, yet Christ did not grasp at that equality but chose the form of a servant; similarly you are not to grasp at equality with your neighbor but to choose the form of a servant in all dealings (cf. Francis of Assisi, *The Admonitions*, *CWS*, pp. 25–29; cf. Augustine, *Since God Has Made Everything, Why Did He Not Make Everything Equal? EDQ* 41, FC 70, p. 74).

The Gradual Unfolding of a Way of Life

The humbling of God is not simply a single event of nativity alone. Rather, having been born into the world, the Son grew to maturity and had to choose again and again the way of the humble One, until such choosing ended in death (John of Damascus, *OF* III.21–29, *NPNF* 2 IX, pp. 69–73; Wesley, *WJW* VI, p. 507). There is a developing ethical dimension in the humbling of God that awaits event after event to unfold in its own characteristic way of life: washing feet, reaching out for the sick and neglected, identifying with sinners, living without material comforts, dying on a cross.

Voluntary Poverty

His poverty consisted in the self-renunciation by which he assumed servant form—he was born in a stable, remained poor throughout his life, worked with his hands in common labor, was without a home of his own, and finally in his crucifixion was stripped of his robe and laid in the grave of another—all signs of poverty, of complete and willing lack of worldly resources. This poverty has made us rich by enabling us to share in his glory by faith (Francis of Assisi, *Admonitions*, *CWS*, p. 32). By his death he purchased life. By his divestiture we gain our inheritance. By his payment, we receive our passage (*viaticum*) to the eternal city (Gregory Thaumaturgus, *Four Hom.* I, *ANF* VI, p. 60; John Chrysostom, *Hom. on 2 Cor.* XIX, *NPNF* 1 XII, pp. 367–69; Gerhard, *LT* III, p. 575; Schmid, *DT*, p. 385).

Paul summarized the teaching of the Son's humbling with this comprehensive metaphor: "Though he was rich, yet for your sakes, he became poor, so that you through his poverty might become rich" (2 Cor. 8:9). The poverty consists not in the involuntary loss of the divine nature, but in the voluntary humbling of the eternal Son.

Sequential Descent of the Son's Humbling

The humbling of the eternal Son proceeded in a sequence of ever-lowering stages culminating in death and burial. Some writers have organized the descent into two phases:

(A) The *self-emptying* (*kenosis, exinanitio*) by which he
    (1) does not grasp for the equality with God due him, but
    (2) makes himself nothing, gives up independent exercise of the divine attributes, by
    (3) taking the form of a servant, living in absolute dependence upon the power of the Spirit, not independently but as a servant,
    (4) being made in the likeness of human flesh, subject to human growth and development; and
(B) The *humiliation itself*, (*tapeinōsis, humiliatio*), by which he
    (5) became obedient, even so far as to
    (6) obey unto death, even the
    (7) death of the cross, so as to become a sacrifice for our sins.

This self-emptying and the humiliation proper are differentiated systematically as between the humiliation of the incarnate person and the humiliation of the redeeming work (Pope, *Compend.* II, pp. 152–56).

Taken together, key events of the humiliation of the Son reported in Scripture are:

conception (Luke 1:31)
a lowly nativity, born in a manger
was made man, born of woman, the seed of Eve (the mother of all living)

became a child (Luke 2:7) "he had to be made like his brothers in every way" to perform his mission "that he might make atonement" (Heb. 2:17–18)

born a Jew, son of the law

voluntary subjection to instruction by parents (Luke 2:51)

economic subjection to poverty

political subjection to unjust political authority

educational subjection to teachers of the law

circumcision, signifying his subjection to law though he was the giver of the law (Matt. 12:8; Mark 2:28)

common labor in a manual occupation

facing ordinary discomforts of human finitude

enduring reproaches and ill-treatment by others, facing social rejection

suffering of body, affect, and spirit–"Because he himself suffered when he was tempted, he is able to help those who are being tempted" (Heb. 2:18)

crucifixion

abandonment in which he, bearing the part of sinners, felt the wrath of God and was not comforted (Matt. 27:46)

finally death, the dissolution of the natural union of body and soul

burial

Why this trajectory and not another? He humbled himself and became obedient to reveal true humanity amid the conditions of history and to become the representative of humanity in the Father's presence, presenting to God the perfect obedience due from humanity (Rom. 6:14; 13:10). What the law was powerless to do "God did by sending his own Son in the likeness of sinful man to be a sin offering" (Rom. 8:3). "God made him who had no sin to be sin for us, so that in him we might become the righteousness of God" (2 Cor. 5:21; cf. Gal. 3:13; 4:4–5).

"God's transcendent power is not so much displayed in the vastness of the heavens, or the luster of the stars, or the orderly arrangement of the universe or his perpetual oversight of it, as in his condescension to our weak nature," wrote Gregory of Nyssa. "We marvel at the way the God-head was entwined in human nature and, while becoming man, did not cease to be God" (ARI 24, LCC III, p. 301).

THE HIDDEN MAJESTY

The divine humiliation was not an impoverishment of God but an incomparable expression of the empathic descent of divine love (Calvin,

Inst., 2.13.3–4). God never did anything in history more revealing of the divine character than to become incarnate and die. By his coming the poor were blessed, the hungry satisfied, weepers brought to laughter, the excluded embraced, and the reviled welcomed (Luke 6:20–23).

The Lowliness of God the Son

Subjection to Infirmities

In his humbling, the eternal Son was not shielded from the infirmities, finitude, temptations, and limitations common to humanity. Jesus fulfilled what had been promised by the prophet: "He took up our infirmities " (Matt. 8:17, quoting Isa. 53:4). Only thereby could he be the One expected by Isaiah, who would be "despised and rejected by men, a man of sorrows, and familiar with suffering" (Isa. 53:3).

The Obscuration of the Divine

At first the mission of the Son was not immediately or flatly to reveal the divinity of the Son, but rather to *obscure it so that the mission might be fully accomplished through suffering and death* (Hilary, *Trin.* IX.6, NPNF 2 IX, p. 157). The divinity of the Son was eclipsed for a season to more fully manifest its glory in due time through the resurrection of the flesh. God the Son assumed human nature for the very purpose that he might experience this humiliation of his human nature on behalf of the redemption of humanity (Council of Ephesus, *NPNF* 1 XIV, pp. 211–13). In this humbling, the divine nature of his person was concealed, not in the sense of being deceptively disguised, but under the assumed servant form (*morphē doulou*) it was simply unrecognizable to self-assertive sinners.

Divinity Expressed Precisely Through Humbling Servanthood

The nature of God did not change in the incarnation. Rather it was precisely the Servant-caregiver who was revealed and became knowable in history. He who is the "same yesterday and today and forever" (Heb. 13:8) became formed in our likeness without ceasing to be unchanging God.

His divinity was not reduced, retracted, relinquished, or suppressed, but enhanced, set forth, offered, and expressed in this particular manner: enfleshed. "He withdrew His power from its normal activity, so that having been humiliated He might also appear to be made infirm by the nonuse of His power. . . . Though He retained His power, He was seen as a man, so that the power would not be manifest in Him" (Ambrose, *Comm. on Phil.* 2, quoted in Chemnitz, *TNC*, p. 493).

The Son permitted his natural human capacities and infirmities to prevail, as if alone in his human nature, for a time withdrawing and withholding from activity the divine virtue dwelling bodily in the human nature (Ambrose, in Schmid, *DT*, p. 383; see Chemnitz, *TNC*, pp. 317, 327, 484, 487–95). Not until the resurrection did he resume the full exercise of divine dominion.

These are the elements that make the central mystery of the incarnation unfathomable to human egocentricity bent on self-assertion. This humbling remains the central datum of Christian proclamation and experience. While lying in the cradle and dying on the cross, he did not cease to be the One in whom the fullness of the Godhead was dwelling bodily (Col. 2:9), in whom "all things hold together" (Col. 1:19). "What is lofty you are to apply to the Godhead and to that nature in him which is superior to sufferings and incorporeal; but all that is lowly to the composite condition of him who for your sakes made himself of no reputation and was incarnate" (Gregory Nazianzen, *Orat.* XXIX.18, *LCC* III, p. 173).

The Voluntary Restraint of Independent Exercise of Divine Powers

Abstinence from Power

In the phase of humiliation the Son "abstains from the full use of the divine attributes communicated in the personal union" (Jacobs, *SCF*, p. 145). By proximate analogy, the heir of nobility may have a great inheritance left to him, yet in his minority he may have only that use of it that is permitted by his guardian.

Glory of the Son Constrained, Then Recovered

In his preexistent form, "being in the very nature God" (Phil. 2:5), the Son was glorified in the presence of the Father with a glory that was voluntarily given up in his earthly life. In humbling himself, the preexistent Logos gave up his divine glory with the Father to take on the form of a servant. He is remembered as having prayed: "And now, Father, glorify me in your presence with the glory I had with you before the world began" (John 17:5).

Theories of Self-Renunciation

There are several theories of this self-renunciation: Anselm argued that Christ appeared or acted as if he did not possess divine attributes. Scholastic Lutheran divines argued that Christ gave up full use of the attributes. Some Protestant writers have argued that the Logos gave up some attributes and retained others (Thomasius, *Dogmatik*, sec. 38–45;

Baillie, *GWC*, pp. 94ff.), while others argued that he gave up all, wherein the Son ceased to be the upholding principle of the world (Gess, *Lehre von der Person Christi*; for Barth's objections to kenotic Christology, see *CD* VI/1, pp. 181ff.).

The centrist tradition carefully defined that he resigned "not the possession, nor yet entirely the use, but rather the independent exercise, of the divine attributes" (Strong, *Syst. Theol.*, p. 703). The Son submitted to the limitations of the messianic mission, reliant upon the power of the Spirit. On certain occasions, on behalf of his mission, he does not abstain from full use but rather exercises divine attributes (as in miracles). He continuously surrendered the exercise of those divine powers and voluntarily accepted birth, limitation, obedience to law, temptation, suffering, and death. The door was narrow (Luke 13:24).

There are indications in Jesus' remembered sayings just before his crucifixion that suggest that he could have exercised this power that was temporarily and voluntarily surrendered: "Do you think I cannot call on my Father, and he will at once put at my disposal more than twelve legions of angels? But how then would the Scriptures be fulfilled that say it must happen in this way?" (Matt. 26:53–54; John Chrysostom, *Hom. on Matt.* LXXXIV, *NPNF* 1 X, pp. 501–506).

The Hidden Majesty

Note the ironies of the hidden majesty that wills to become visible, comprehensible, and existent in time, yet in a lowly way: "Invisible in His nature, He became visible in ours; surpassing comprehension, He has wished to be comprehended; remaining prior to time, He began to exist in time. The Lord of all things hid his immeasurable majesty to take on the form of a servant" (Leo I, *Letter to Flavian* [13 June 449], *CF*, p. 151; see *SCD* 144, p. 58). Kierkegaard chose a parabolic form by which to speak of this obscuration in his unforgettable parable of the king and the maiden (*Phil. Frag.* II, pp. 32–43).

Divine Attributes Hidden

Among attributes possessed by the Son but not fully exercised in his phase of humiliation were omnipotence, omniscience, and omnipresence.

Omnipotence

If fully exercised, the divine omnipotence would have exempted Jesus from suffering for our sins, but this would have run counter to the purpose of his mission. Rather, he was willing to lay down his life, reminding his hearers that "No one takes it from me, but I lay it down of my own accord. I have authority to lay it down and authority to take it up again" (John 10:18). He had no where to lay his head (Matt. 8:26). His lack of power is most poignantly expressed in his cry from the cross: "My God, my God, why have you forsaken me?" (Matt. 27:46)—his dying humanity still refusing to exercise the omnipotence due him and available to him, yet voluntarily surrendered on behalf of his mission of redemption (Chemnitz, *TNC*, pp. 283–85).

Omniscience

"He did assume an ignorant and servile nature, and this is because man's nature . . . does not have knowledge of future events" (John of Damascus, *OF, FC* 37, pp. 324–25). Thus it is said that ignorance was assumed economically by the Lord (Athanasius, *Four Discourses Ag. Arians* I.11, III.28, *NPNF* 2 IV, pp. 333–36, 416–22; Newman, *Ath.* II, pp. 161–72).

In his human nature he chose to remain ignorant of the day on which the final judgment would occur (Matt. 24:36). "No one knows about that day or hour, not even the angels in heaven, nor the Son, but only the Father" (Mark 13:32). Hence it is wise to resist the pious notion that "the soul of Christ was ignorant of nothing but from the beginning knew in the Word everything, past, present, and future, that is to say everything which God knows with the 'knowledge of vision'" (Benedict XV, *Decree of the Holy Office, CF*, p. 182).

Some have on the other side of excess argued that Jesus knew no more than the average Jew of his time (C. Gore, *Lux Mundi*; cf. Hodgson, *Doctrine of the Atonement*, p. 26). However, the New Testament picture of Jesus is more complex: in some passages he knows what is going on in the minds of others and knows future events; in other passages he expresses surprise at learning something by observation or he professes ignorance and asks questions that assume he did not know the answer (Athanasius, *Four Discourses Ag. Arians* I.11, *NPNF* 2 IV, pp. 333–36; J. S. Lawton, *Conflict in Christology*; Taylor, *PC*, pp. 286–306).

This troublesome point is greatly illumined by the triune premise (and confusing without it): the divine Logos eternally experiences full awareness of the cosmos, yet as incarnate Logos united to Christ's humanity he has become voluntarily subjected to human limitations, ignorance, weakness, temptation, suffering, and death. As eternal Son he is equal with God in knowing and foreknowing, but in the mystery of his humiliation he is servant, obedient, willing to be vulnerable to time and finitude. As conceived in the womb, as born of Mary, as child of Joseph, the eternal Logos gave up or constrained or temporarily abnegated the full and independent exercise of eternal foreknowing, so as to become a little child

(Gregory Nazianzen, *Fourth Theol. Orat.*, *NPNF* 2 VII, pp. 315–17). Hence the paradox (ethically the same as in Phil. 2:1–11): unless we become as little children (as did the eternal Son) we will not behold the meaning of God's coming governance.

John Chrysostom offered a pastoral reason why the saying that the Son "knows not the day or hour" was providentially given for the good of the disciples: to diminish anxiety, for if everyone "knew when they were to die, they would surely strive earnestly at that hour" (John Chrysostom, *Hom. on St. Matt.* LXXVII.1, *NPNF* 1 X, p. 463).

In assuming flesh the Son assumed that ignorance proper to humanity, demonstrating his love of humanity by participating in human limitations of knowing, "for since He was made man, He is not ashamed, because of the flesh which is ignorant, to say 'I know not,' that He may show that knowing as God, He is but ignorant according to the flesh" (Athanasius, *Four Discourses Ag. Arians* III.43, *NPNF* 2 IV, p. 417; see also III.42–53). "He knows as God, and knows not as Man" (Gregory Nazianzen, *On the Holy Spirit* 30.15, *NPNF* 2 X, p. 463; cf. Brunner, *Med.*, pp. 363–65). The Son does not know future events according to his human nature but by the divine nature that he shares with the Father (Basil, *Epist.* 236, *NPNF* 2 VIII, pp. 276–78).

A major exegetical breakthrough on this point occurred with Gregory the Great. In commenting on Mark 13:32 and in seeking to counter the error of the Agnoetes (that there is no sense in which the Son knew the day of judgment), Gregory insightfully wrote: "This can also, therefore, be understood in a more subtle way by saying that the only begotten Son incarnate, made perfect man for us, knew the day and hour of judgment *in* His human nature but did not know it *from* His human nature. What He knew therefore *in* His humanity He did not know *from* it, because it is by the power of His divinity that God-made-man knew the day and the hour of judgment. . . . Thus it is that He denied having the knowledge which He did not have from the human nature by which He was a creature" (*Letters*, *To Eulogius* [A.D. 600], *CF*, p. 164). "For, just as we say a day is happy not because the day itself is happy, but because it makes us happy, so the omnipotent Son says He does not know the day which He causes not to be known, not because He himself is ignorant of it, but because He does not permit it to be known at all" (*Letters*, *To Eulogius*, *CF*; *SCD* 248, p. 97).

The Damascene's distinction was similar: "While His human nature did not of its essence have knowledge of future events, the Lord's soul, by reason of its union with God" did have such knowledge (John of Damascus, *OF*, *FC* 37, p. 325).

Omnipresence

He was not everywhere, but in a specific time and place, in the scandal of particularity that accompanies incarnational revelation (John 11:21). During the time of the earthly ministry of the incarnate Lord, the Logos did not cease to be. While the Logos continues to live eternally, the incarnate Logos suffers on earth (Origen, *OFP*, pp. 12–154, 316–17).

Note that the divine attributes of holiness, love, and justice are exercised during his earthly ministry, but those divine attributes enabling the full exercise of unlimited power, knowledge, and presence are restrained. In the incarnation the Son of God took upon himself the weakness of humanity; he did not relinquish the strength of God (Stone, *OCD*, p. 66; cf. D. G. Dawe, *The Form of a Servant: A Historical Analysis of the Kenotic Motif*).

> Mild He lays His glory by,
> Born that man no more may die,
> Born to raise the sons of earth,
> Born to give them second birth
> (C. Wesley, "Hark the Herald Angels Sing").

The State of Exaltation

Having laid aside the infirmities of the flesh, the Son received and resumed the full exercise of the divine glory, which had been voluntarily given up in the humiliation. In his state of glorification, he laid aside suffering and humiliation and human infirmities, and in his state of majesty he was received again in glory. The exaltation, to be further discussed in connection with the resurrection and ascension, consists of three phases:

1. The divine reversal: "Therefore God exalted him to the highest place" (Phil. 2:9).
2. The bestowal of Lordship: "And gave him the name that is above every name" (Phil. 2:9). The name is Lord (*Kurios*), which is the Greek translation of Yahweh. What the Son did not self-assertively gain by "grasping" or "snatching" (equality with God), he received upon completion of his mission by the gift of the Father (Augustine, *EDQ* 50, *FC* 70, p. 84).
3. The homage of universal acknowledgment: "That at the name of Jesus every knee should bow, in heaven and on earth and under the earth, and every tongue confess that Jesus Christ is Lord, to the glory of God the Father" (Phil. 2:9–10). The homage is offered

both now and in the future, currently by the church and ultimately by the cosmos.

The events of this exaltation (*hupsosis*) unfold in dramatic scope: the
Son descended into the nether world whereby he conquered death; rose
again from the dead, whereby his messianic vocation was confirmed;
ascended into heaven, whereby he returned to glory; and sits at the right
hand of the Father, whereby he receives power and governance, glory
and dominion from the Father in the kingdom of grace, power, and glory.
These four topics will be dealt with in Part IV (Cyril of Jerusalem, *Catech.
Lect.* XIV, *FC* 64, pp. 52ff.; Tho. Aq., *ST* III, Q56–59, II, pp. 2326–38; Hollaz, *ETA*, pp. 777–89; Schmid, *DT*, pp. 379–81).

CHAPTER 4

The Incarnation

The word "incarnation" (Gk. *sarkosis*, Lat. *incarnatus*) means enfleshing, or becoming flesh, the union of human nature with the divine in one person. The term "flesh" points to our entire created (not fallen) human nature. It signals that in the assumption of humanity "nothing was lacking that belongs to human nature" (Augustine, *Enchiridion* X.34, *LCC* VII, p. 360).

Key teaching: in the fullness of time, the eternal Son assumed human nature without ceasing to be God (John 1:17; Augustine, *Comm. on John*, *NPNF* 1 VII, p. 237; *BOC*, p. 20).

Incarnation is the necessary premise of any further episode of the unfolding Christ event (Archelaus, *Disputation*, *ANF* VI, pp. 220-22; Lactantius, *Div. Inst.*, *ANF* VII, p. 125; Liddon, *DL*, pp. 100ff.). Since the incarnation is the antecedent basis of all other speech about specific acts pertaining to God's coming, it must be studied, guarded, and transmitted carefully (Hilary, *Trin.* IX.55, *NPNF* 2 IX, pp. 174-75; Chemnitz, *TNC*, pp. 147-48, 210-11). It finally renders hazardous, though not impossible, any exclusive "Christology from below" in the sense of a Christology that would begin with the human Jesus (Pannenberg, *JGM*, pp. 33-37).

WAS MADE MAN

According to creedal summaries: God the Son was made human (*homo factus est*; Gk. *enanthrōpēsanta*), or became incarnate (*incarnatus*; Gk. *sarkōthenta*) by the Holy Spirit (*de Spiritu Sancto*), and was born of the Virgin Mary (*ex Maria virgine*). The saving event was for us humans (*qui propter nos homines*; Gk. *ton di hēmas tous anthrōpous*). He became incarnate for our salvation (*propter nostram salutem*; Gk. *dia ton hēmeteran sōterian*, Creed of 150 Fathers, *COC* II, p. 58; cf. pp. 11-61).

The Scriptural Teaching of Incarnation

Pauline Teaching

Paul wrote and probably even sang of One "Who, being in very nature God," became "made in human likeness" (Phil. 2:6-7). The incarnation is metaphorically expressed in Paul's phrase: "Though he was rich, yet for your sakes he became poor, so that you through his poverty might become rich" (1 Cor. 8:9). Paul did not invent this tradition but received it from the early Christian preaching prior to his conversion.

The Pauline tradition interpreted the incarnation in comprehensive cosmic terms: God has seen fit in the fullness of time "to bring all things in heaven and on earth together under one head, even Christ" (Eph. 1:10), in whom "all things hold together" (Col. 1:17). "For in Christ all the fullness of the Deity lives in bodily form" (Col. 2:9).

The Johannine Teaching on Incarnation

The testimony of John on incarnation generally concurs with that of Paul, yet it is expressed differently. John's Gospel was primarily interested in the way in which the divine *doxa* (glory) shines through the veil of *sarx* (the flesh) and dwells in it. "The Word became flesh and made his dwelling among us" (John 1:14; John Chrysostom, *Hom. on John* XII, *NPNF* 1 XIV, pp. 40–43; Gutiérrez, *PPH*, p. 13).

John's primary purpose was not to write a scientific or heroic biography of an eminent moral leader, but to reveal this pivotal truth of Jesus' distinctive personal identity: He is "from above" (John 6:33), preexistent Logos (John 8:42), sent by the Father to the self-alienated world of *sarx* (John 1:14; 5:23-38), who left the Father's presence and glory (John 6:62; 8:38) and descended from heaven into the human-historical sphere (John 3:13; 6:33).

An ancient objection (not lately invented by Tillich, Bultmann, or J. A. T. Robinson) asks: If he is everywhere, how could he be said to have "come *down*"? The *Russian Catechism* answers: "It is true that he is everywhere; and so he is always in heaven and always on earth; but on earth he was before [the incarnation] invisible; afterwards he appeared in the flesh" (*COC* II, p. 468).

That the Son was *sent* by the Father is a notion that occurs forty-two times in John's Gospel (e.g., 3:17; 9:39; 10:36). The Father's sending *is* the incarnation (Augustine, *Hom. on John* XXXI, *NPNF* 1 VII, pp. 211, 227). The Sent One is the one and only Son of God (*monogenēs*, "unique Son," "only begotten Son," "the Only Son of the Father," John 1;14, 18; 3:16, 18;

1 John 4:9). It is this one who becomes *sarx* (John 1:14; cf. 19:17, 34, 37), fully *anthropōs*, human in every way.

Assumptio Carnis

Incarnation focuses upon the joyful mystery of the announcement that God takes on our humanity (John Chrysostom, *Hom. on John*, NPNF 1 XIV, p. 107; Baxter, *PW* XXI, pp. 314–18). More broadly, the discussion of incarnation may include the redemptive necessity, compassionate motivation, missional purpose, and significance of that event, and its chosen means of virginal conception.

Incarnation Defined

The *Russian Catechism* defines incarnation: "The Son of God took to himself human flesh without sin, and was made man, without ceasing to be God" (*COC* II, p. 471). For classic discussions of the incarnation, see Athanasius (*Incarn. of the Word*, NPNF 1 IV, pp. 36–67), Ambrose (*The Sacrament of the Incarn. of our Lord*, FC 44), and Anselm (*On the Incarn. of the Word*, TIR, pp. 5–36, CDH; for medieval discussions see Richard of St. Victor, *Trin.* LCC X, pp. 324–32; Peter Lombard, *De Incarnatione Verbi*, MPL CXCII, p. 757; LCC X, pp. 334–52; Tho. Aq., *ST* III, Q1–26).

At once, God is man, man is God (Augustine, *Hom. on John*, NPNF 1 VII, p. 413). "Nor did he lose what he was, but he began to be what he was not" (Faith of Damascus, *SCD* 15, p. 11). Similarly Origen, in transmitting the tradition he received, stated that God "was made man, was made flesh [Lat. *homo factus incarnatus est*], although he was God; and being made man, he still remained what he was, namely, God" (*FP* I, pref., 3, p. 3; cf. *COC* II, p. 23).

Body as Communicator

God used risk-laden body language to communicate to humanity. "Since human nature is essentially composite, and can neither express itself nor receive anything—cannot even think or aspire,—except by use of the physical organism and of its material environment, God adapts His method to the nature which He has created, and uses what we have to use—the human body—as the instrument of His self-manifestation, of redemption, and of sanctifying grace" (Hall, *DT* VI, p. 78; cf. Fulgentius, *Incarn.* MPL LXV, pp. 103–20; Thornton, *The Incarnate Lord*).

The Assumption of Humanity

The incarnation occurred not by conversion of divinity into flesh but by the assumption of humanity into God (Athanasius, *On the Incarn. of the Word* 14–15, *NPNF* 2 IV, pp. 43–44; Heppe, *RD*, p. 414). God became flesh not by changing into another reality, but by assumption (*assumptio carnis*), by entering the human mode of being without ceasing to be God. Remaining what he was, he became what he was not (Hilary, *Trin.* III.16, *NPNF* 2 IX, p. 66; Athanasius, *Four Discourses Ag. Arians* I.35, *NPNF* 2 IV, pp. 326–27). "What He was He continued to be; what He was not He took to Himself" (Gregory Nazianzen, *Orat.* XXIX.19, *NPNF* 2 VII, p. 308).

The Creed of Epiphanius confessed that God "was made man, that is, assumed perfect human nature, soul and body and mind, and all whatever is man except sin, not from the seed of man nor by means of man, but having fashioned unto himself a body into one holy unity; not as he lived in the prophets and talked and worked in them, but became man completely ('for the word was made flesh,' he did not submit to any alteration, nor did he change his own divine nature into human nature); he combined both the divine nature and the human into the only holy perfection of himself; (for there is one Lord Jesus Christ, and not two)" (*SCD* 13, p. 10).

Avoiding Distortions

The Fourth Ecumenical Council of Chalcedon, A.D. 451, found it necessary to define incarnational teaching so as to protect it against gross distortions. Jesus Christ is "consubstantial with the Father [*homoousion tō patri*] according to divinity, and consubstantial with [*houoousion hemin*] us according to human nature" (Chalcedon, *SCD* 148, p. 60). Outler's translation continues: "thus like us in all respects, sin only excepted. Before time began [*pro aiōnōn*] he was begotten of the Father, in respect of his deity, and now in these 'last days,' for us and on behalf of our salvation, this self same one was born of Mary the virgin, who is God-bearer [*theotokos*] in respect to his human-ness [*anthrōpotēta*]" (Chalcedon, *CC*, p. 36).

Classic Protestant definitions of incarnation do not differ significantly from these ancient ecumenical definitions: "The incarnation is a divine act, by which the Son of God, in the womb of His mother, the Virgin Mary, took into the unity of His person a human nature, consubstantial with us, but without sin, and destitute of a subsistence of its own, and communicated to the same both His divine person and nature, so that Christ now subsists forever, as the God-man, in two natures, divine and human, most intimately united" (Hollaz, *ETA*, p. 665; Schmid, *DT*, p. 303; cf. Ursinus, *CHC*, pp. 196–202; Barth, *CD* III/4, pp. 337ff.; IV/2, pp. 36ff.; H. Relton, *A Study of Christology*).

Is a Reasonable Approach Possible?

Anselm set out to articulate a rational method of establishing "by necessary reasons (Christ being put out of sight, as if nothing had ever been known of him) that it is impossible for any man to be saved without him." He attempted rigorously to think and write *"as if nothing were known of Christ,"* so as to come to the necessary conclusion "by clear reasoning and truth" that "a Man-God" was required for salvation (*Cur Deus Homo*, LCC X, p. 100, italics added).

Yet the nearer he approached, upon being asked to provide reasons for faith in the incarnation, he stated modestly: "I am afraid to handle 'the things that are too high for me.' If someone thinks, or even sees, that I have not given him adequate proof, he may decide that there is no truth in what I have been saying, and not realize that in fact my understanding has been incapable of grasping it" (*Cur Deus Homo*, LCC X, p. 102). He knew how much he regretted seeing a bad artist paint an ugly form. He was afraid that he would be such an artist in theology in using frail words to portray this incomparable Subject.

The question around which Anselm's great book revolves is: "For what reason or necessity did God become man," when God could have restored life to the world "by a sheer act of will"? (*Cur Deus Homo*, LCC X, p. 101). He sought to show that "it was quite impossible for him to save man in some other way" (*Cur Deus Homo*, LCC X, p. 107).

The Mystery of the Incarnation

A Mystery When Best Explained

Incarnation remains a mystery even when best explained (Gregory Thaumaturgus, *Four Hom.* III, *ANF* VI, p. 67; Lactantius, *Div. Inst.* IV.8, *ANF* VII, p. 106). Reverence forbids the pretension that human knowledge is competent to make a minute or exhaustive scrutiny of the empirical or physical dimensions of this mystery (Maximos, *Various Texts, Philokal.* II, pp. 167–68). "How silently, how silently, the wondrous gift is given!" (Phillips Brooks, *HPEC*, p. 68).

The incarnation remains incomprehensible to sensory-based reason (Hilary, *Trin.* I.12; II.33, *NPNF* 2 IX, pp. 43, 61). Human language is pressed and stretched to "feel what I can ne'er express, yet cannot all conceal" (Byron, "Childe Harold's Pilgrimage," canto 4).

The Mystery of Godliness Is Great

Even the New Testament writers recognized that the mystery would not be resolved by ever-extending logical or historical analysis. "Beyond all question, the mystery of godliness is great: He appeared in a body, was vindicated by the Spirit" (1 Tim. 3:16). "Let us grant that God can do something which we confess we cannot fathom. In such matters the whole explanation of the deed is in the power of the Doer" (Augustine, *Letters* 137.2, *FC* 3, p. 24; Barth, *CD* I/2, pp. 124ff., 172ff.). The unfathomable mystery of the incarnation is a perennial theme of classical Christianity (Tertullian, *Apology* XXI, *ANF* III, pp. 33–36; Hilary, *Trin.* I.12, *NPNF* 2 IX, p. 43; Augustine, *Hom. on John*, *NPNF* 1 VII, pp. 111, 197).

The Rhetoric of Paradox

It was inevitable that such a premise would generate a paradoxical tradition of rhetoric: "Teacher of children became Himself a child among children, that He might instruct the unwise. The Bread of heaven came down to earth to feed the hungry" (Cyril of Jerusalem, *Catech. Lect.* XII.2, *FC* 61, p. 228). "The Word, though remaining what It was, became what It was not" (Theophilus of Bulgaria, *Enarratio in Evangelium Ioannis* I 14, *MPG* Vol. 123, p. 1156). "He, while being perfect God, became perfect man" (John of Damascus, *OF* III.1, *FC* 37, p. 269; Baillie, *GWC*, pp. 106–21).

"Reason stumbles at this article." The question of *how* the incarnation occurred, "you are to believe, not to know and to understand, until the solution appears on the blessed Day of our redemption" (Luther, *Christmas Serm. on John 1:1–14* [1541], *WLS* I, p. 150; Kierkegaard, *TC*, pp. 40–56). "According to our nature, then, He offered Himself that He might do a work beyond our nature" (Ambrose, *The Incarn. of our Lord* 6.54, *FC* 44, p. 240).

The mystery of the incarnation is not adequately grasped under the general philosophical idea of "the New Being, who conquers existential estrangement," especially if such a New Being is in no way necessarily correlated with Jesus of Nazareth (Tillich, *Syst. Theol.* II, p. 114). Tillich has ruled himself out of consensual Christianity by arguing that "the assertion that 'God has become man' is not a paradoxical but a nonsensical statement. It is a combination of words which makes sense only if it is not meant to mean what the words say" (Tillich, *Syst. Theol.* II, p. 94). If the incarnation remains an obstacle to some sincere modern intellects, it deserves both a serious clarification and a fair hearing. This is what we seek.

Is It Fitting That God Became Human?

Why Not Salvation by Fiat?

If God had the power to save humanity by fiat, by a simple sovereign act, then "why did God take a tedious, circuitous route, submit to a bodily nature, enter life through birth, pass through the various stages of development, and finally taste death?" (Gregory of Nyssa, *ARI* 15, *LCC* III, p. 291). Gregory argued that God's saving action had to be consistent with God's character as "not only powerful, but also just and good and wise," and these in their most congruent relationship (*ARI* 20, *LCC* III, p. 296).

But how could it be consistent with God's wisdom and power that God should become human? From one viewpoint it might seem unfitting, recalling that God from all eternity had been without flesh. Since God and flesh are infinitely different, it might seem the height of absurdity that "He should be hid under the frail body of a babe" (Volusianus, *Epist.* CXXXV, *To Augustine*; cf. Berkouwer, *Person of Christ*, pp. 352–55), for it seems "not becoming that He who surpassed the greatest things should be contained in the least" (Tho. Aq., *ST* III Q1.1, II, p. 2025).

Goodness Communicates Itself

Yet it was "most fitting that by visible things the invisible things of God should be made known" (Tho. Aq., *ST* III Q1.1, II, p. 2025; Rom. 1:20). If the very nature of God is goodness, what belongs to goodness befits God.

Hence it was fitting for God to become human because "it belongs to the essence of goodness to communicate itself to others," and particularly to those creatures most capable of responding. The mystery of incarnation does not imply that God became "changed in any way from the state in which He had been from eternity," but rather the incarnation occurred through God's "having united Himself to the creature in a new way," a way fitting to God for the salvation of humanity (Tho. Aq., *ST* III Q1.1, II, p. 2026; cf. Augustine, *Trin.* XIII, *FC* 45, pp. 369ff; Dionysius, *Divine Names* IV [SPCK, 1975], pp. 86–130; N. Pittenger, *The Word Incarnate*).

It was appropriate to the mystery of divine love that the Son would make our nature his own (Tho. Aq., *ST* III Q1, II, pp. 2025–32, 2305). By this condescension God brought human history to a decisive climax and reversal (Arnobius, *Ag. Heathen* 55–65, *ANF* VI, pp. 429–33; Augustine, *Trin.*, *FC* 45, pp. 396–403). The incarnation was a stooping down of compassion, not a defect of power (Leo, *Tome*, *NPNF* 2 XIV, p. 255; see Maximos, *Philokal.* I, pp. 245–52).

Why Delayed?

Augustine sought to answer the question: "Why did the Lord Jesus Christ come so long after man sinned, and not in the beginning?" Humanity had to pass, as does youth, through its own sequence of developing stages and ages. The teacher had to come in the time of humanity's youth and readiness to learn. So history was kept under the law as if under a tutor until the One would come whom the tutor served (*EDQ* 44, *FC* 70, pp. 75–76).

The Empathic Mediator

The Human Face of God

Job had long ago complained that God "is not a man like me that I might answer him, that we might confront each other in court. If only there were someone to arbitrate between us, to lay his hand upon us both" (Job 9:32–33). Now just such a One has appeared in Jesus, through whom the goodness of God is communicated to humanity, and the flesh of humanity is assumed by God the Son (Tho. Aq., *ST* III Q4–6, II, pp. 2056–60; cf. Calvin, *TAAAL*, pp. 106–19).

No more complete revelation of God's empathic love is possible than this: that God shares our human frame, participates in our human limitations, enters into our human sphere (Tertullian, *Apology* II, *ANF* III, p. 18; Chemnitz, *TNC*, pp. 39–46; cf. Oden, *KC*, chaps. 2–3; Cone, *BTL*, pp. 215–17; Anne Carr, "The God Who Is Involved," *Theology Today* 38 [1981]: 314–28).

The Suffering Physician

Augustine was amused at those patients whose physician makes them "rather grudge that we be healed than help our cure" (Augustine, *CG* IX.17, *NPNF* 1 II, p. 176). Humanity receives extraordinary treatment from the empathic divine Physician who is willing to come into the sphere of the epidemic to share personally the diseased human condition. He "measures all by comparison with his own suffering, so that he may know our condition by his own, and how much is demanded of us, and how much we yield" (Gregory Nazianzen, *Theol. Orat.*, XXX.6, *LCC* III, p. 181). They are narrow-minded who "define God's majesty from its inability to share the properties of our nature" (Gregory of Nyssa, *ARI* 27, *LCC* III, p. 305).

God's Empathy a Wholly Voluntary Act

A key component of the idea of incarnate divine empathy is that the enfleshing was completely voluntary and in no way coerced (Hilary, *Trin.* XI.8-9, *NPNF* 2 IX, p. 205; L. Hodgson, *And Was Made Man*). The Son did not have to come to us; he chose to. This act of divine mercy humanity did not deserve (Hilary, *Trin.* II.25, *NPNF* 2 IX, p. 59). The salvation event begins in an initiative taken not by "human decision or a husband's will, but born of God" (John 1:13).

None of us had the choice of whether or not to be born—with one exception: "He [Jesus] was not born without His will. None of us is born because he will, and none of us dies when he will: He, when He would, was born; when He would, He died: how He would, He was born of a Virgin; how He would, He died on the cross" (Augustine, *On the Creed* 8, *NPNF* 1 III, p. 371). Only the Son elected human life from eternity.

God's New Beginning

The end of salvation is already grasped primordially and attested anticipatively in the enfleshing of the Word. The consummation of history is anticipated in the coming of the eternal Son.

The advent of Christ had long been pledged by the prophets and angelic hosts as promised salvation. The hope of God's own incarnate coming had been deeply but inconspicuously embedded in various prophetic witnesses (Tertullian, *Ag. Marcion* III, *ANF* III, pp. 321-44; Lactantius, *Div. Inst.* IV.5-19, *ANF* VII, pp. 105-21; Hilary, *Trin.* V, *FC* 25, pp. 133-62; Ambrose, *Cain and Abel*, *FC* 42, pp. 359-437). Isaiah especially had foretold that a human child would be born who would be called Mighty God (*el gibbor*, Isa. 9:6). The name "Immanuel" (Isa. 7:14) prefigured that it was nothing less than God who promised to come to deliver humanity. It was a human child that was called "God with us."

Without this mediation, salvation is impossible. "For if Christ is God, as He truly is, but did not assume manhood, then we are strangers to salvation" (Cyril of Jerusalem, *Catech. Lect.*, XII.1, *FC* 61, p. 227). To those who wonder whether incarnation is possible, classical Christian teachers reply that without it redemption is impossible (Augustine, *Hom. on John*, *NPNF* 1 VII, pp. 347-48).

THE MEDIATOR

A mediator (*mesites*) is one who interposes between two parties at variance to reconcile them. To mediate is to act as the intermediary in effecting peace or reconciliation (Augustine, *CG, FC* 14, pp. 99–101, 303–308, 335ff.; Tho. Aq., *ST* III, Q26.1, II, p. 2158). In the political sphere, a mediator intervenes between quarreling, alienated powers so that by means of the reconciling offices of mediation, the quarrel may end.

The quarrel in this case is that between God and humanity occasioned by the history of sin. Christ is sole mediator between God and humanity (Augustine, *Enchiridion* X.33, *LCC* VII, pp. 359–61; *Canons and Decrees of the Council of Trent*, transl. H. J. Schroeder, 1941, Session 5, pp. 22–23). "He is the mediator between God and man, because He is God with the Father, and a man with men. A mere man could not be a mediator between God and man; nor could a mere God. Behold the mediator: Divinity without humanity cannot act as mediator; nor can humanity without Divinity; but the human Divinity and the Divine humanity of Christ is the sole mediator between Divinity and humanity" (Augustine, *Serm. on NT Lessons* XLVII, *NPNF* 1 VI, p. 412; Pohle-Preuss, *DT* V, p. 11). The incarnation itself is the beginning of this mediation, uniting humanity and deity in one person, bringing God to humanity, and humanity to God (Baxter *PW* IX, pp. 33–34; *Doc. Vat. II*, pp. 112, 586).

The mediation occurred as an event in time. There was "one mediator between God and men, the man Christ Jesus, who gave himself as a ransom for all men—the testimony given in its proper time" (1 Tim. 2:5–6). No one could overcome the divine-human estrangement unless able to so take "what was ours as to impart what was his to us, and to make what was his by nature ours by grace" (Calvin, *Inst.* 2.12.2; Barth, *CD* IV/3, pp. 278ff.).

Cur Deus Homo?

Why did God assume our common humanity? "The sole purpose of Christ's incarnation was our redemption" (Calvin, *Inst.* 2.12.4). He came first to live and and then to die for others (Hilary, *Trin.* II.24, *NPNF* 2 IX, p. 58; Augustine, *Trin., FC* 45, pp. 387–403). The means by which God chooses to effect the redemption of humanity is congruent with the essential nature and attributes (love, holiness, and power) of God (Augustine, *Trin., FC* 45, pp. 145–47).

"God the Word was made man for this reason," wrote John of Damascus, "that that very nature which had sinned, fallen, and become corrupt should conquer the tyrant who had deceived it" (*OF* III.12, *FC* 37, p. 293). Augustine summarized: "That men might be born of God, God was first born of them" (*Hom. on John* II.15, *NPNF* 1 VII, p. 18).

Born of Woman That Humanity Might Be Born of God

He came "that there might be a way for man to man's God through a God-man" (Augustine, *CG* 11.2, *NPNF* 1 II). "The Word had to become flesh that He might unite in Himself the alliance between earthly and heavenly things by incorporating the pledges of both parties in Himself, thus uniting God with man and man with God" (Novatian, *Trin.* 23, *FC* 67, p. 85).

No one burdened with human imperfections can represent imperfect humanity in the presence of God. But God's own humanity has come openly to view in Jesus of Nazareth (Lactantius, *Div. Inst.* IV.9, *ANF* VI, pp. 109–10, 126; Ambrose, *The Prayer of Job and David*, *FC* 65, pp. 401–20).

God's Fullness Dwells in Him

Aristotle had assumed that in the vast gulf that separates God and humanity nothing like friendship or reconciliation could be possible. Yet in Christian teaching, "Both the one who makes men holy and those who are made holy are of the same family. So Jesus is not ashamed to call them brothers" (Heb. 2:11).

Christ is Mediator, not fleshless Logos, but God-incarnate (Augustine, *CG* IX.15, *NPNF* 1 II, pp. 173–74; Tho. Aq., *ST* III, Q26.2, II, pp. 2159f.). "For God was pleased to have all his fullness dwell in him, and through him to reconcile to himself all things, whether things on earth or things in heaven, by making peace through his blood, shed on the cross" (Col. 1:19–20). One who meditates on the incarnate mystery becomes increasingly aware of ever more astonishing facets of it (Tho. Aq., *Disputations*, *TATT*, pp. 282–94; *SCG* IV.54).

The Necessity of Incarnation as Premise of Redemption

He Came to Die

Scripture states the point starkly: he came to die (Athanasius, *Four Discourses Ag. Arians*, III.58, *NPNF* 2 IV, p. 425). The relation between his birth and death can be stated schematically:

MYSTERY OF INCARNATION	THE MYSTERY OF PASSION
He came	to give his life as ransom (Mark 10:45)
To this end I was born	Crucify! Crucify! (John 18:36; 19:6)
God sent his Son	to redeem (Gal. 4:5)
God so loved	that he gave his only Son (John 3:16)

He humbled himself   becoming obedient unto death (Phil.
                             3:8)
The reason he appeared: to destroy the devil's work (1 John 3)

The sacrificial-mediatorial reason for the incarnation is stated directly in the Letter to the Hebrews: "Since the children have flesh and blood, he too shared in their humanity so that by his death he might destroy him who holds the power of death" (Heb. 2:14). "For this reason he had to be made like his brothers in every way, in order that he might become a merciful and faithful high priest in service to God, and that he might make atonement for the sins of the people. Because he himself suffered when he was tempted, he is able to help those who are being tempted" (Heb. 2:17–18).

The Intrinsic Connection of Incarnation and Atonement

The purpose for which the Son came was clearly set forth by the Gospel writers: "the Son of Man did not come to be served, but to serve, and to give his life as a ransom for many" (Matt 20:28). "For God did not send his Son into the world to condemn the world, but to save the world through him" (John 3:17). The redemption for which the incarnation occurred has universal significance for the whole of human history (Hilary, *Trin.* II.24–28, *NPNF* 2 IX, pp. 58–60; cf. G. Hendry, *Gospel of the Incarnation*).

Anticipating the cross, Jesus said: "The hour has come for the son of Man to be glorified" (John 12:23). "It was for this very reason I came to this hour" (John 12:27). Only the incarnate mediator could also be the mediator of the sacrifice so essential to the atonement (Tho. Aq., *ST* III Q1, II, p. 2026; Leo, *SCD* 143, p. 58; see also *SCD* 251, 253, 333).

No Mediator Without Birth and Death

Redemption could only occur through sacrifice. There could be no dying Mediator without the Mediator's birth. Hence the Son's death and birth are intrinsically connected (Chemnitz, *TNC*, pp. 220–22; cf. R. Brown, *The Virginal Conception and Bodily Resurrection of Jesus*).

Necessity of Incarnation

Augustine's gift for epochal summary will help us grasp the intrinsic connection of the incarnate person and mediatorial office: "Now when Adam was created, he, being a righteous man, had no need of a mediator. But when sin had placed a wide gulf between God and the human race, it was expedient that a Mediator, who alone of the human race was born, lived, and died without sin, should reconcile us to God" (*Enchiridion* 108, *NPNF* 1 III, p. 272; cf. Diadokos, *On Spiritual Knowledge, Philokal.* III, p. 280).

Calvin stated the point with extraordinary precision: "In short, since neither as God alone could he feel death, nor as man alone could he overcome it, he coupled human nature with divine that to atone for sin he might submit the weakness of the one to death; and that, wrestling with death by the power of the other nature, he might win victory for us." Thus he "took the person and the name of Adam in order to take Adam's place" (*Inst.* 2.12.3; cf. Peter of Damaskos, *Treasury, Philokal.* III, pp. 125–28).

Purposes of the Mediation

Scriptural Teaching on Why God Became Human

Why then did God become human (*cur Deus homo*)? Varied perceptions of the purposes of the incarnation have been summarized by complementary scriptural texts:

To reveal God to humanity (John 1:18; 14:7–11).

To provide a high priest interceding for us able to sympathize with human weaknesses (Heb. 4:14–16).

To offer humanity a pattern or example of the fullness of human life (1 Pet. 2:21; 1 John 2:6).

To provide a substitutionary sacrifice adequate for the sins of all humanity (Heb. 10:1–10).

To bind up the demonic powers (1 John 3:8).

To provide for humanity a final judge at the end time (John 5:22–27).

The Damascene's Summary

John of Damascus could be counted upon to bring these together in an economic pattern: "The Son of God became man in order that He might again grace man as He had when He made him. For He had made him to His own image, understanding and free, and to His own likeness, that is to say, as perfect in virtues as it was possible for human nature to be, for these virtues are, as it were characteristics of the divine nature—freedom from care and annoyance, integrity, goodness, wisdom, justice, freedom from all vice. Thus, He put man in communion with Himself. . . . But, since by transgressing the commandment we obscured and canceled out the characteristics of the divine image, we were given over to evil and stripped of the divine communion. . . . But, since He had shared with us what was better and we had not kept it, He now takes His share of what is worse, of our nature I mean to say, that through Himself and in Himself He may restore what was to His image and what was to His likeness" (*OF* IV.4, *FC* 37, pp. 337–38).

Prefigurative Types

"The inexpressible beauty of our redemption" was expressed by Anselm in these typic parallels:

> Death entered through one man's obedience
> Life is restored through one man's obedience
>
> Sin came through the temptation of a woman
> Salvation came through one born of woman
>
> The enemy conquered humanity by tasting of a tree
> Christ conquered the enemy by bearing suffering on a tree
> (*Cur Deus Homo, LCC* X, pp. 104–105).

Why This and Not Another Mediator?

No mere mortal could save humanity while humanity itself was mired in the history of sin: "The wounds of mankind are beyond our healing," remarked Cyril of Jerusalem. "The evil cannot be repaired by us" (*Catech. Lect.* XII, *FC* 61, p. 231; Brunner, *Med.*). "Who could accomplish this, unless the Son of God should become also the Son of man, and thus receive to himself what belongs to us, and transfer to us that which is his" (Calvin, *Inst.*, Bever. 2.12.2; Augustine, *CG, FC* 14, pp. 99–101, 303–308, 335ff).

The Incarnation Reveals True Humanity

In becoming human, God teaches by embodiment the doctrine of true humanity. The incarnation has vast importance beyond Christology, strictly speaking, for it also teaches us about our very selves (Gregory Nazianzen, *Fourth Theol. Orat., On the Son, NPNF* 2 VII, pp. 309–18; Barth, *The Humanity of God*). Hence incarnation belongs to anthropology, not theology alone.

Before his conversion Augustine had been afraid "to believe Him to be born in the flesh, lest I should be compelled to believe Him contaminated by the flesh" (*Confessions* V.10, *NPNF* 1 I, p. 86). After his conversion, he learned that if the incarnation showed us nothing else it sufficiently revealed these "two wholesome facts"—"that true divinity cannot be polluted by flesh, and that demons are not to be considered better than ourselves because they have not flesh" (*Augustine, CG* IX.17, *NPNF* 1 II, p. 176; cf. *CG, FC* 14, pp. 170–72; *CG, FC* 24, pp. 137–41).

The incarnation could not have assumed the nature of a buffalo or rock or tree or even an angel, but only of a human being. Luther must have smiled when he preached: "It is not for the angels to be proud of Christ's incarnation, for Christ did not assume an angelic but a human nature. Therefore it would not be a surprise if the angels looked at us with envy in their eyes because we human beings, creatures far inferior to them and sinners besides, are placed above them into an honor so high and great. They worship Christ, who has become our Brother, our flesh and blood" (Luther, *Serm. on Col. 1:18–20*, WLS I, p. 153; WA 45, 306).

CONSEQUENT ISSUES OF THE INCARNATION

Several vexing issues emerged and had to be answered in the course of explicating the scriptural teaching of incarnation. Did Jesus gradually or instantly become God-man? Was the incarnation unique and unrepeatable? If the nativity attests a temporal birth, how can one say that the Son was pretemporally begotten of the Father? Did the whole of the Godhead assume flesh? Would there have been an incarnation if there had been no fall? (For classic responses to standard objections against the incarnation see, Lactantius, *Div. Inst.*, ANF VII, p. 124; Augustine, *Trin.* XIII.9–20, NPNF 1 III, pp. 173–82; Baxter, PW XXI, pp. 314–18.)

Did Jesus Gradually Become God?

Christianity speaks of God becoming man, not a man becoming God. The idea is not that a particular man comes nearer and nearer to God until, being filled with increasing divine abilities or powers, gradually becomes so conjoined with God as to become God. Such reasoning appeared in fifth-century adoptionism and recurred in popular nineteenth-century liberalism. Yet it runs against the grain of the language of the New Testament, where there is hardly more than a hint of adoptionism.

It was considered a standard counter-ecumenical teaching that "Christ is not God made man, but a man made God; for they [false teachers] have dared to say that it was not the pre-existing Word that became man, but that a certain man was crowned by advancement" (Cyril of Jerusalem, *Catech. Lect.* XII.3, FC 61, pp. 228–29, an issue to be further developed in connection with Jesus' baptism).

Does God Do This Often?—or Was the Incarnation Utterly Unique?

Did God become human only once? Or can we expect repeated incarnations? Nothing is more characteristic in the history of religions than the thought of the union of God and humanity. In some traditions this occurs

by the *apotheosis* (deification) of the human who ascends to become a god
and in others by the alleged descent of one or more of the gods to live
with humans (but not *as human!*). Evidence for the recurrence of these
notions may be found the world over in almost every known period of
human history.

The Bible recognizes that such expectations had been generally present in human history. When Paul preached at Lystra, the crowd had
"shouted in the Lycaonian language, 'The gods have come down to us in
human form!'" (Acts 14:11), and they called Paul Hermes and Barnabas
Zeus, an impression that the apostles sought immediately to correct.
Hence it is evident that, even in the earliest Christian preaching, such
general expectations or presentiments of apotheosis or polytheistic
descent were available and latent in human society. Often they became
blended with complex thoughts of transmigration of souls and with
nativistic animisms.

Hindu religion has a great variety of avatars, one of which (Krishna) is
represented as biting the heel of a serpent. Such intuitions were viewed
by early exegetes as evidence for the conviction that the first promise of
the overcoming of the tempter made to Eve (Gen. 3:15) had become
known and diffused throughout all cultures of human history (Irenaeus,
Ag. Her. V.21, ANF I, pp. 548–50; Tertullian, *On the Apparel of Women* I,
ANF IV, pp. 14–18; John Chrysostom, *Hom. on Gen.* XVII, FC 74, pp.
236–46). The prophet Habakkuk indeed spoke of the expected One as
"the Desire of all nations" (Hab. 2:7, KJV).

Reports of alleged apotheosis and polytheistic descent are many, but
these all differ markedly from the incarnation. The incarnation speaks of
the one true God who becomes flesh and suffers and dies in history
without ceasing to be God. Thus polytheistic myths of divine-human
intermixing, apotheosis, and simple deification of a human are all distin-
guised from and finally rejected by the teaching of incarnation.

The once-for-all condescension of the one and only Son (*monogenēs*) to
assume human nature was thus understood to be a unique, singular,
unduplicatable historical occurrence. He is the only Mediator, not one
among many (Tho. Aq., *ST* III Q26, II, pp. 2158–63; Calvin, *Inst.* 3.20.19).
In our later discussion of the resurrection we will show how the revelation of God in Jesus is understood to be unique, unprecedented, and
insurmountable in relation to the history of religions.

How Is Generation Both Eternal and Temporal?

If the nativity attests a temporal birth, how can one say that the Son
was pretemporally begotten of the Father?

The Two Nativities

A twofold generation is posited of the Son: an eternal generation through which Christ is Son of the Father; and a generation in time through which Christ is son of Mary, a man born of woman (Augustine, *Hom. on John, NPNF* 1 VII, pp. 69–71, 267, 298). Hence it should not be surprising that ancient ecumenism confessed that Christ had *two nativities, eternal as God and temporal as man* (John of Damascus, *OF* III.7, *FC* 37, p. 283; Lateran Council [649], *SCD* 257, p. 102).

Ecumenical Settlement

The Second Council of Constantinople (A.D. 553) had firmly settled this point ecumenically by confessing "that God the Word was twice begotten, the first before all time from the Father, non-temporal and bodiless, the other in the last days when he came down from the heavens and was incarnate by the holy, glorious, *theotokos*, ever-virgin Mary, and born of her" (*CC*, p. 46; see *SCD* 214, p. 86). "For, He who before all ages was called the only begotten, in time became the first born; the only begotten on account of the substance of the Godhead, the first born on account of the nature of the body which He assumed" (Eleventh Council of Toledo, *SCD* 285, p. 111).

This teaching cannot be stated more beautifully than by the ancient formularies. Language that to the doubtful may seem disingenuous to the ecumenical teachers has seemed wonderfully symmetrical, aesthetically balanced, and typologically ingenious in speaking of "two births of the one our Lord Jesus Christ Himself, one incorporeal and eternal from God the Father before all ages, the other, corporeal and in the last age, from holy Mary, ever virgin, Mother of God; and one and the same Jesus Christ our Lord and God, one in being with the Father as to His divinity, one in being with men and with His mother as to His humanity, subject to suffering in His flesh while He is impassible in His divinity, limited in His flesh while He is illimited in His spirit, at once created and uncreated, earthly and heavenly, perceptible by sense and by intellect, bound by space and beyond space" (Lateran Council [649], *CF*, p. 166; Hilary, *Trin.* IX.51–54, *NPNF* 2 IX, pp. 173–74).

Council of Toledo

"By the fact that He has come forth from the Father without a beginning, He is said only to be born, not to be made or predestined; but by the fact that He was born from the Virgin Mary, we must believe that He was born and made and predestined. Yet, in Him both births are wonderful, because He was begotten from the Father without a mother before all ages, and in the end of the ages He was generated from a mother without a father. He who inasmuch as He is God created Mary, inasmuch as He is man was created from Mary. He is at once the Father and the Son of His Mother Mary" (Eleventh Council of Toledo [675], *CF*, p. 170; also Gregory Nazianzen, *Orat.* XXIX.19, *NPNF* 2 VII, p. 308)!

Study the playful ironies of the following schematic of the two births drawn from Toledo:

THE INCARNATE SON WAS PARADOXICALLY:

Father of the Mother	Son of the Mother
Without a Mother	Without a Father
Begotten from the Father	Generated from a Mother
As to divinity	As to humanity
One in being with the Father	One in being with humanity
Incorporeal birth	Corporeal birth
Born not made	Born and made
Before all ages	In the last age
Illimited in his Spirit	Limited in his flesh
Uncreated	Created
Impassible	Subject to suffering
Beyond space	Bound by space

The analogical imagination soared symmetrically in a way that entranced and energized the ancient orthodox mind: "For, as Eve was formed from Adam without carnal conjunction, so did this one bring forth the new Adam in accordance with the law of gestation but surpassing the nature of generation. Thus, He who is without a mother begotten of a father was without a father born of a woman. And because it was of a woman it was in accordance with the law of gestation; while, because it was without father, it surpassed the nature of generation" (John of Damascus, *OF* IV.14, *FC* 37, p. 364; see Cyril of Jerusalem, *Catech. Lect.* XI, *FC* 61, p. 215).

Eternally Begotten?

The doubtful protested that if the Son is said to be born, did he not have a beginning and thus is a creature? The ecumenical teachers never tired of clarifying that they spoke of an *eternal begetting that never had a beginning in time*. If this distinction is not grasped, the student of classic Christianity will be forever puzzled by confusions between eternal and temporal begetting.

Again, Toledo stated the point in its consensually mature form: "The Son was born, but not made, from the substance of the Father, without beginning, before all ages, for at no time did the Father exist without the Son, nor the Son without the Father. Yet the Father is not from the Son, as the Son is from the Father, because the Father was not generated by the Son but the Son by the Father. The Son, therefore, is God from the Father, and the Father is God, but not from the Son" (Eleventh Council of Toledo, CF, p. 103).

Eternal begetting is not subject to time. Temporal begetting occurs in time. Cyril warned: "Now when you hear of God begetting, do not fall athinking in corporeal terms, or risk blaspheming by imagining corruptible generation. 'God is a Spirit.' Divine generation is spiritual. Bodies are begotten from bodies, and there has to be an interval of time for it to be completed. But time does not come into the begetting of the Son from the Father. . . . For what he is now, that has he been timelessly begotten from the beginning. . . . For God was not at first childless, and then after [a] lapse of time became Father, but he had his Son from all eternity, not begetting him as men beget men, but as he alone knows who begat him true God before all ages. . . . Do not compare it with teachers 'begetting' disciples. . . . So the way in which the Father begat the Son is not attainable by human analogy. . . . It is enough for us that we should know that God has begotten one only Son" (Cyril of Jerusalem, Catech. Lect. XI.7-12, LCC IV, pp. 141-45).

"He has never begun nor ceased to be born" (Eleventh Council of Toledo, CF, p. 103). He was not first born as an ordinary man of the holy Virgin and then the Word descended upon Him, but having been united with the flesh in the very womb itself, he is said to have submitted to a birth according to the flesh, as appropriating and making his own the birth in the flesh (Cyril of Alexandria, Five Tomes Against Nestorius, LCC II, p. 350-51; cf. Pearson, EC I, pp. 244-48).

The Father did not exist an instant before the Son, for both are eternal, being God. "Do not imagine any space of eternity in which the Father was and the Son was not. Since when the Father was, since then the Son. And what is that 'since,' where is no beginning? Therefore ever Father without beginning, ever Son without beginning. And how, thou wilt say, was He begotten, if he have no beginning? Of eternal, co-eternal" (Augustine, On the Creed 8, NPNF 1 III, p. 371).

As early as the late second century, counter-ecumenical speculations about how the Son was begotten had to be resisted: "If anyone, therefore, says to us, 'How then was the Son produced by the Father?' we reply to him, that no man understands that production, or generation, or calling, or revelation, or by whatever name one may describe His generation, which is in fact altogether indescribable. Neither Valentinus, nor Marcion, nor Saturninus, nor Basilides, nor angels, nor archangels, nor principalities, nor powers (possess this knowledge), but the Father only who begat, and the Son who was begotten" (Irenaeus, *Ag. Her.* II.28, *ANF* I, p. 401).

The generations of the Son were distinguished by Hilary as pretemporal (eternal generation of the Son), temporal (incarnate Son), and posttemporal (exalted Lord): "It is one thing, that He was God before He was man, another, that He was man and God, and another, that after being man and God, He was perfect man and perfect God" (Hilary, *Trin.* IX.6, *NPNF* 2 IX, p. 157).

The Fourth Lateran Council (1215, against the Albigenses) concisely defined three persons in one essence: "the Father from no one, the Son from the Father alone, and the Holy Spirit equally from both: and without beginning, always, and without end; the Father generating, the Son being born, the Holy Spirit proceeding" (Fourth Lateran Council 1, *TGS*, p. 122).

That such masterworks of typic definition may seem boring to modern impatience is admitted. But they continue to claim the meditative attention of anyone seeking to understand classic Christianity.

Is the Incarnation a Work of the Triune God?

The incarnation is a work of the triune God, the Son being sent by the Father by the power of the Spirit (Augustine, *Trin.*, *FC* 5, p. 479). Not the whole Godhead but the Son only assumed human flesh, which the Father formed in the Son through the conceiving work of the Spirit in the Virgin. The Father willed the Son's coming, and the Spirit enabled the conception. The Father prepared the body for the Son, the Son assumed it, and the Spirit conceived and enabled it (*Leiden Synopsis* XXV, 6–8, in Heppe, *RD*, pp. 413–15; Cocceius, *Summa Theologiae* [1665], LVIII, p. 12).

Lacking the premise of triunity, God could not at the same time be sovereign and empty himself in servanthood; nor both send and be sent; nor be both lawgiver and obedient to law; nor both offer himself as a sacrifice and receive that sacrifice (Augustine, *Trin.*, *FC* 45, pp. 62–63, 396–401, 484–86; Boyce, *AST*, p. 272).

The assumption of flesh is peculiar to the Son. The will to redeem proceeds from the entire Trinity (Peter Lombard, *Sent.* III.5 in Chemnitz, *TNC*, p. 40; Gerhardt, *LT* III, 413, in Schmid, *DT*, p. 303). The cause of conception was the Holy Spirit, while the material matrix was the womb of a lowly maiden.

"To us there is one God the Father, from whom are all things, and one Lord Jesus Christ, through whom are all things, and one Holy Ghost, in whom are all things" (Gregory Nazianzen, *Serm. 39.12, in OF,* FC 37, p. 288). John of Damascus added: "And the 'from whom,' 'through whom,' and 'in whom' do not divide the natures" (*OF* III, FC 37, p. 288).

Did the Whole Godhead Assume Human Flesh?

The error of Patripassianism insisted that it was the Father himself, not the Son incarnate, who suffered upon the cross. "If anyone says that in the passion of the cross it is God Himself who felt the pain and not the flesh and the soul which Christ, the Son of God had taken to Himself — the form of servant which He had accepted as Scripture says (cf. Phil. 2.7) — he is mistaken" (Council of Rome, *Tome of Damascus* 382, CF, p. 147; cf. Jung Young Lee, *God Suffers for Us,* pp. 23–79).

It is not Deity as such but the Logos that became flesh, so as to be God manifested in the flesh (1 Tim. 3:16). It is the *logos* who was from the beginning, was with God and was God (John 1:1), was before Abraham (John 8:58), who existed in the form of God (Phil. 2:6), being of one substance (*homoousios*) with the Father, who became flesh in time (John 1:14; see Calvin, *Inst.* 2.13–14; *Leiden Synopsis* XXV, 10, in Heppe, *RD,* p. 415; Pearson, *ECI,* pp. 215–19). John's Gospel does not say that the divine nature as such became flesh or that the whole Godhead became flesh, but the Word became flesh (John 1:14). The divine nature subsisted of itself before the assumption and during the union (Chemnitz, *TNC* 23, pp. 287–313; J. H. Heidegger, *Corpus Theologiae* [1700], XVII, p. 36, Heppe, *RD,* p. 415).

Augustine brilliantly employed the analogy of speech to set forth the unchanging integrity of God throughout the incarnation: "For just as our word in some way becomes a bodily sound by assuming that in which it may be manifested to the senses of men, so the Word of God was made flesh by assuming that in which He might also be manifested to the senses of men. And just as our word becomes a sound and is not changed into a sound, so the Word of God indeed becomes flesh, but far be it from us that it should be changed into flesh. For by assuming it, not by being consumed in it, this word of ours becomes a sound, and that Word became flesh" (Augustine, *Trin.,* FC 45, p. 477).

"Without suffering change the very Person of the Word became Person of the body," argued the Damascene. "The Word, while being God, was made man without suffering change," but this does not imply that "the Godhead was made man"; rather it means that "the Godhead was united to humanity in one of Its Persons" (John of Damascus, *OF* III.11, FC 37, p. 291; Tho. Aq., *ST* III, Q1, II, p. 2025).

Those views were rejected that said "that the Word of God dwelling in human flesh took the place of the rational and spiritual soul, since the Son and the Word of God did not replace the rational and spiritual soul in His body but rather assumed our soul (i.e., a rational and spiritual one) without sin and saved it" (Council of Rome, *Tome of Damascus, CF,* p. 147). "We do not proclaim Him God alone stripped of our humanity, nor do we despoil Him of His divinity and proclaim Him man alone" (John of Damascus, *OF* III.7, *FC* 37, pp. 283–84).

While incarnate, the Son was truly God. Scripture does not teach that his divinity ceased, was cast aside, absorbed, or left behind. As incarnate Lord he acted in a way that only God can act: forgiving sin, giving life to the dead, revealing the secret thoughts of persons, dividing loaves and fishes, and laying down his life and taking it up again.

Assuming Unfallen Freedom, Would the Incarnation Have Been Necessary?

Would the Son have become incarnate even if humanity had not sinned? It is possible that without sin, there might have been no incarnation? Thomas Aquinas answered no, "that the Incarnation was ordained by God as a remedy for sin, and that if no sin had come in, the Incarnation would not have taken place" (*ST* III, Q1.3, II, p. 2028). Duns Scotus answered yes. Hilary had also argued that the incarnation was independent of the fall and did not have sin for its cause (*Trin.* XI.49, *NPNF* 2 IX, p. 217; see Intro. lxviii).

This question, being so speculative, cannot attain certainty, and no article of faith may hinge upon any proposed conclusion. Human reason is not sufficiently equipped to probe the mind of God so as to pretend to know what God might have done if all human history had been fundamentally different than it is.

Yet the question recurs in history out of both speculative and practical concerns. The Thomist/Scotist controversy reappeared in disguised form in the seventeenth-century battle between scholastic Lutherans and Calvinists, Arminius and Dort, and in the eighteenth between Wesley and the Calvinists.

The order of the divine decrees according to the Scotists (Duns Scotus, *Commentaria in Quatuor Libros Sententiarum* III.7.3; cf. Suarez, *De Incarnatio* 5) was first the incarnation, then the permission of the sin of humanity, then the mission of Christ. Creation was for Christ's sake. The incarnation was preordained independent of the fall. The motive for the incarnation was the manifestation of the divine glory.

The order of decrees for Thomists was: creation, permission of sin, and only then the incarnation. The fall is a condition of the incarnation. The motive for the incarnation was compassion for the misery of humanity. The creed appears to prefer this order, speaking of One "who for us men and for our salvation descended from heaven" (Creed of 150 Fathers, *COC* II, p. 57; cf. Ambrose, *On the Sacrament of the Incarn.* VI.56, FC 44, p. 240).

An ancient Latin Easter hymn had the wit to celebrate the irony of a happy failure (Adam's) from which redemption could arise: *"O felix culpa quae tantum ac talem meruit habere redemptorem"*—"O happy fault, which deserved to have so great and glorious a Redeemer" (Daniel, *Thesaurus Hymnologica* [5 vols., Halle: Anton, 1844–56] I, c., p. 303; this theme, found in Augustine, Rupert of Deutz [*De Trinitate*, III.20], Julian of Norwich [*IAIA*, p. 116], and Hugh of St. Victor, was treated by John Donne, *Selected Works* [1839], *Serm.* I, pp. 303–306; cf. Milton, *Paradise Lost* XII.469–72). Wesley concluded: "For if Adam had not fallen Christ had not died" ("God's Love for Fallen Man," *Serm.* II, *WJWB*, p. 425).

Are There Sexual Implications in God's Bodily Coming?

The incarnation was not sexless. God did not hesitate to identify himself with the very flesh that is so profoundly associated with sexuality and so easily corrupted by sexual self-assertion.

Novatian responded to those who hate the body and consequently the fact that God came to humanity in bodily, human form in this imaginary dialogue with the "counterfeit Christ, devised somehow from old wives tales": "And if you hate the body, what are you doing with the semblance of a body? . . . For you ought to have hated even the imitation of a body, if you hated its reality. . . . Surely, if birth was odious to you because you hated the Creator's ordinance of marriage, you should have refused to assume even the very resemblance of a man born according to the Creator's ordinance of marriage" (*Trin.* 10, FC 67, p. 45).

Gregory of Nyssa undefensively held that the incarnation implied sexual differentiation. "The only thing alien to the Divine is evil. Nature is not evil. . . . There is only one way for a man to enter life. . . . [Our opponents] are *offended at the means of the visitation. What other method, then, of entering life do they prescribe for God?* They fail to realize that the whole anatomy of the body is uniformly to be valued . . . the generative organs have the future in view, and it is by them that the succession of the race is maintained" (Gregory of Nyssa, *ARI* 28, *LCC* III, p. 306, italics added).

THE HUMANITY OF CHRIST

Jesus was not partially or occasionally human. The human nature

assumed by the Logos included all that properly belongs to humanity—
everything we share when we speak of ourselves as human beings—yet
without defect or sin (Augustine, *Enchridion* X.34, *LCC* VII, p. 360; Benedict XIV, *Profession of Faith*, *SCD* 1463, p. 358).

Was He Fully Human?

The creed of Epiphanius (second form, A.D. 374) stated that the Logos
"assumed a perfect man, soul and body and mind (spirit), and all that
belongs to man, without sin" (*COC* II, p. 36; cf. *BOC*, p. 586). The
"human nature which he assumed" he "did not destroy" (Augustine,
Letters 137.3, *NPNF* 1 I, p. 476).

That the affirmation of Jesus as truly human was a part of the core of
Christian confession from the earliest memory of him is seen in John's
First Epistle, which commends this test of faith that had been passed
down from earlier oral tradition: "This is how you can recognize the
Spirit of God: Every spirit that acknowledges that Jesus Christ has come
in the flesh is from God" (1 John 4:2). This was an anti-Docetic test
(Augustine, *Hom. on the Epist. of John*, *NPNF* 1 VII, p. 499; Calvin, *Comm.*
XXII, pp. 230–38).

Palpable, fleshly humanity is what is meant by the word *sarx*,
"flesh"—the human condition—when it is said that the Word was made
flesh and dwelt among us (John 1:14; John Chrysostom, *Hom. on John* XII,
NPNF 1 XIV, pp. 40–43). The implication is not that a Divine person coin-
habited a human body with another human person so as to be two distinct persons with one name, but rather the one name, Jesus Christ,
made reference to a single person, God made flesh (Tho. Aq., *SCG* IV,
pp. 64–74).

Jesus was called and called himself a human being, man (*anthropon*,
John 8:40). Pilate, who sought to discern his true identity and colluded in
allowing his death, said of him, "Behold the [*anthropos*] man!" (John 19:5
KJV; Vulg: *Ecce homo!*)—a fully human being, an extraordinary statement
of humanity ("true man," Quicunque Creed, *SCD* 40, p. 16; see also *SCD*
13, 18, 25, 33, 111, 114; consubstantial with the nature of man, Chemnitz,
TNC, pp. 56–57). This affirmation of genuine humanity is implied in the
creed's simple confession: *Credo in . . . Jesus* (Creed of 150 Fathers, *COC* II,
p. 58).

Thomas Aquinas defined the essential point: "God has now shown us
the high place human nature holds in creation, for he entered into it by
genuinely becoming man" (Tho. Aq., *ST* 3a.i.2, *TATT*, p. 279, referring to
Augustine, *OTR* XVI, pp. 26–28). There is a broader, more general sense
in which God dwells in all humanity or lives in the hearts of all

believers—that of course is true, but this general meaning is not what is referred to in the incarnation of the Son in Jesus Christ, the unique, once-for-all coming of God to human history (*Doc. Vat. II*, pp. 220–21).

Was the Incarnation Sexist?

Did God show sexist bias or partiality against females or males in the birth of the incarnate Lord? The classical exegetes reasoned that both maleness and femaleness were honored equally in the incarnation: God's "temporal plan ennobled each sex, both male and female. By possessing a male nature and being born of a woman He further showed by this plan that God has concern not only for the sex He represented but also for the one through which He took upon Himself our nature" (Augustine, *On Faith and the Creed* 4.9, FC 27, p. 326; cf. *NPNF*: "that dispensation has honored both sexes, at once the male and the female, and has made it plain that not only *that sex which He assumed* pertains to God's care, but also *that sex by which He did assume* this other, in that He bore [the nature of] the man [*virum gerendo*], [and] in that He was born of the woman," 1 III, p. 325, italics added). This is part of the reason why a renewed emphasis on the virgin mother is due in a contemporary theology of the incarnation that is attentive to sexist bias (cf. Augustine, *Since God Has Made Everything, Why Did He Not Make Everything Equal?*, EDQ 41, FC 70, p. 74; Tho. Aq., *ST* III Q1.5–6 II, pp. 2030f.).

Mary is female, Jesus is male. God's way of coming involves both genders in a particular way fitting to those genders: female, for the birthing of the God-man without human father, and male, for the mission of the anointed messianic servant, according to the Jewish expectation of a male of Davidic descent. "He did not despise the male, for he assumed the nature of a man, nor the female, for he was born of a woman" (Augustine, *Letters* 3; cf. Suarez, *De Incarnatio* III.3; C. Pesch, *Institutions Propaedeuticae* [Friburg: Herder, 1894] IV, pp. 209ff.; Pohle-Preuss *DT* V, p. 18).

The core of this classic feminine/masculine incarnational equilibrium is found in Paul's Letter to the Galatians: "But when the time had fully come, God sent his Son, born of a woman, born under law, to redeem those under law" (Gal. 4:4). Paul says: born of a woman, a particular woman, without male assistance, not born of woman and man.

If one takes the premise that the incarnation required birth and that giving birth cannot be done by males—there is no way physiologically—it forms a plausible hypothesis for explaining why the Savior was male: *if the mother of the Savior must necessarily be female, the Savior must be male, if both sexes are to be rightly and equitably involved in the salvation event*, according to classical interpretation. This hypothesis reverses the sexism argument by making the female birth-enabler the primary basis upon which the incarnate Lord was more plausibly to be male (this in addition to the Hebraic assumption that the Messiah would be of the male line of David).

That God was not ashamed of female and male bodies, or of human embodiment, or of sexuality was one of the main purposes of the incarnation. Augustine must have been in a playful mood when he wrote: "Now the reason why the Holy Spirit was not born of a dove, whereas Christ was born of a woman, is this: The Holy Spirit did not come to liberate doves [!], but to declare unto man innocence and spiritual love, which were outwardly symbolized in the form of a dove. The Lord Jesus Christ, having come to liberate human beings, including both men and women destined for salvation, was *not ashamed of the male nature, for He took it upon Himself; or of the female, for He was born of a woman*" (Augustine, *The Christian Combat* 22, FC 21, p. 338, italics added; see also OTR XIV, p. 27).

Augustine delighted in imagining that the ancient tempter was exasperated by the thought that both the female and male sex were being decisively used by God for human salvation, for "there is a profound mystery that, as death had befallen us through a woman, Life should be born to us through a woman. By this defeat, the Devil would be tormented over the thought of *both sexes, male and female*, because he had taken delight in the defection of them both. The freeing of both sexes would not have been so severe a penalty for the Devil, unless we were also *liberated by the agency of both sexes*" (Augustine, *The Christian Combat*, 22, FC 21, pp. 338–39, italics added). Both sexes can relish the fact that this fifth-century saint savored this particular reflection upon divine equity.

Gregory Nazianzen resisted the idea of making woman responsible alone for the temptation of Adam: "The Woman sinned, and so did Adam. The serpent deceived them both; and one was not found to be the stronger and the other the weaker. . . . Christ saves both by His Passion . . . let the one flesh have equal honour" (*Orat.* XXXVII.7, NPNF 2 VII, p. 340; Tho. Aq., SCG IV, pp. 206–208, 257–62).

The deeper conflict being dealt with in the incarnation is not the difference between the sexes, however, but the divine-human controversy resulting from sin. The mediation of this post-Adam, post-Eve controversy required a mediator who was fully human. Julian of Norwich envisioned in Christ a humanity that both encompasses and transcends sexual differentation: "I am, as I hope, a member of this 'man,' by the mercy of God, for the blessed comfort I saw is large enough for all of us" (*RDL* 79, p. 226).

Was Humanity an Absolute Mediatorial Requirement?

The mediator between God and humanity would have to be nothing less than God and nothing less than fully human, otherwise this mediatorship would have been impossible, for how can one mediate in a conflict in which one has no capacity to empathize with one or the other side?

The key text is from the Pauline tradition: "For there is one God and one mediator between God and men, the man Christ Jesus" (1 Tim. 2:5). No mediation between God and humanity is possible if the mediator lacks full participation in one side.

The mediatorial requirement was brilliantly formulated in Hebrews: "Since the children have flesh and blood, he too *shared in their humanity* so that by his death he might destroy him who holds the power of death" (Heb. 2:14, italics added). How could one destroy the power of death without being truly God? And how could the mediator have gained the trust of perplexed humanity unless our humanity had been genuinely shared?

Hence Christ's full humanity became axiomatic for classic Christology: "For if Christ is God, as He truly is, but did not assume manhood, then we are strangers to salvation" (Cyril of Jerusalem, *Catech. Lect.* XII, FC 61, p. 227). Mediation must come through a human being (Tho. Aq., ST III Q2.5–6, II, p. 2158; cf. J. Cobb, *Structure of Christian Experience*; D. Griffin, *A Process Christology*).

Paul had early recognized that it is (ironically) possible to summarize salvation history in this way: by *one representative human person* (Adam) sin appeared in history. This is matched by the deepening irony that by *one representative human person* (Christ) grace appeared in history (Rom. 5:15). It could not have happened either through the agency of some suprapersonal angel or impersonal "Force," for since sin had been personally conceived and willed, salvation must be personally embodied and enacted. "For since death came through a man, the resurrection of the dead comes also through a man" (1 Cor. 15:21).

The law could not do it. "What the law was powerless to do in that it was weakened by the sinful nature, God did by sending his own Son in the likeness of sinful man to be a sin offering" (Rom. 8:3). Thereafter Christianity has relied upon this searching typological parallelism between the old humanity, which all humans share, and the new humanity of the man born of woman to redeem those under law.

"If He lacked anything as man, then He did not redeem all, and if He did not redeem all, He deceived us, since He said that He had come to save all men. But, since it is impossible for God to deceive, He did not deceive us" (Ambrose, *Letters* 48, FC 26, pp. 126–27).

Was His Humanity Ordinary or Extraordinary?

Ordinary Humanity

First it must be noted that Jesus' humanity was entirely ordinary. Jesus is pictured as a normal person in unmistakably human terms—going to weddings, visiting friends, eating and drinking, getting tired and napping. All the familiar elements of human nature are found in Jesus: body, soul, will, and spirit (Matt. 16:12, 26; 26:38; Luke 23:46). Scriptures speak of a real person having all things requisite for human existence, not an ephemeral but a real body, not an angelic but a rational human soul (*psuchē*; Council of Toledo, *SCD* 25, p. 14; see also *SCD* 111, 148, 216, 255, 283). Everything that we as human beings experienced in the normal course of being human, Jesus also experienced, sin excepted (Calvin, *Catech. of the Church of Geneva*, LCC XXII, p. 97; *Two Discourses on the Articles*, LCC XXII, pp. 40–42).

Extraordinariness

Yet at the same time this human life was utterly extraordinary, since unfallen. The narratives were aware that Jesus, recollected as being wholly without sin, exhibited and lived out precisely that kind of humanity that had been primordially given to human history before our fall, to our first parents prior to their disobedience, unsullied by sin. Yet this did not diminish but intensified his humanity (J. Knox, *The Humanity and Divinity of Christ*; H. Johnson, *The Humanity of the Saviour*).

Unfallen Integrity

Paradoxically, the uncorruptible divine Logos assumed not only our fragile, vulnerable, created human nature, but also that which stands against our created human nature—sin and the consequences of sin—while yet not contributing further sin to the history of sin. God participated in our ambiguous, sin-drenched, human condition, yet without sin. God the Son embraced all that was common to humanity (infirmity, hunger, pain, and suffering from the consequences of other's sins, ending in death—all that every ordinary human being experiences) after the fall, excepting sin (Ignatius, *Trallians* 9, *ANF* I, p. 70; Irenaeus, *Ag. Her.* V.xiv.3, *ANF* I, pp. 541–42). Precisely amid this assumption of the flesh, the state of integrity of original human nature was maintained (Chemnitz, *TNC*, pp. 53–54).

Like Us, Jesus Did Not Experience Everything: The Scandal of Particularity

No Individual Experiences Everything All Individuals Experience

To say that Jesus shared our humanity does not imply that he experienced every possible human experience—for we know that he was not an architect or thief; he was not married; he possessed no wealth. These are all human experiences that Jesus apparently did not have. But *neither does any other human being experience all that is possible for all human beings, so in that sense he was more like us*—by sharing in human limitation—than if he had specifically (unimaginably!) shared in every possible human experience of every time and place. His earthly life did not occur in both the first and fifteenth centuries in both Iceland and China—but neither did anyone else's.

The Contrary Hypothesis

If one hypothesizes that to be representative he must have done everything possible that any human being could have done, then one would have already thrust him into some sort of nonhistorical status. Try the hypothesis that to be representative human he must have undergone my particular personal history and your personal history and that of your brothers and sisters and your father and mother, that he must be Hispanic and Korean and black and Polish—such a thought is absurd, and would be nothing like our own temporally placed humanity. One cannot be human without being a particular human being. He shared sufficiently in human experience to teach us that he is one of us, even unto death.

The Mediator's Particularity

He is more like us by living in a particular time and place. He would have been less like us if he had spent his earthly ministry in all times and places. This is in part what is meant by the phrase the "scandal of particularity"—that God comes to us in a special time (when the hour had come) and a special place (the Holy Land) to a specific woman birthing a particular child, yet in a way that bestows significance upon all other times and places (Luther, *Comm. on Gal.*, P. Watson, ed., pp. 353–59).

What makes God's coming scandalous is that it is particular to a time and place. What makes it revelation is that it bestows significance upon all other times and places.

Jesus came, like all of us, through a particular historical lineage. One way the Gospels sought to demonstrate to hearers the humanity of Jesus was by setting down his genealogy. Luke's account demonstrates that he stood in a natural succession from David (3:23–38), and Matthew shows his lineage from Abraham (1:1–17). This (in addition to establishing Davidic descent) was the Evangelists' way of saying: we are dealing here with a human being.

Two parallel points follow: Jesus had a living human body and embodied human emotions or "soul." He was rooted in nature and capable of self-transcendence (Niebuhr, *NDM* I), having finite freedom (Kierkegaard, *SD*). "The body's bulk, to be sure, is circumscribed by its particular parts, but the soul is free to embrace the whole creation by the movement of thought. It ascends to the heavens, sets foot in the depths, traverses the dimensions of the world" (Gregory of Nyssa, *ARI* 9, *LCC* III, p. 287). Jesus lacked neither.

THE EMBODIED WORD

The Embodied Word:
The Mediator Assumed an Ordinary Human Body

The Range of Bodily Experiences Reported

There can be no doubt that the Jesus of the Gospels had a real, not an imagined or fantasized, human body. Jesus' body was truly human flesh (Council of Constantinople II, *SCD* 216, p. 86; see *SCD* 20, 255ff., 393, 422; Gregory Nazianzen, *Orat.* XXIX, XXXVIII, *NPNF* 2 VII, pp. 301–309; 345–50). He was reported as experiencing hunger, love, fear, and sorrow (Innocent III, *SCD* 422, p. 167) and as having made reference to his own ordinary body and its members: head, hands, feet, blood, and bones (Matt. 26:12; Mark 14:8, 24; Luke 24:39). "And perhaps he goes to sleep in order that He may bless sleep also; perhaps He is tired that He may hallow weariness also; perhaps He weeps that He may make tears blessed" (Gregory Nazianzen, *Orat.* XXXVII.2, *NPNF* 2 VII, p. 338).

Contra Docetism

Embedded in the Gospel narratives is a determined struggle against a Doceticism (*dokesis*, "appearance, semblance, illusion") that would suppose that since matter is intrinsically evil, Jesus Christ could not have had a human, material body, a fleshly existence; rather his body was a mere phantasy (*dokema, phantasma*; probably referred to in 1 John 4:3, 2 John 7; cf. Calvin, *TAAAL*, pp. 111–18).

Oppositely, the Gospels constantly portray him as living a thoroughly human, bodily existence: he was conceived in a womb and born when a census was being taken; his penis was circumcised when he was an infant. He grew in stature—he did not come full grown. He got hungry, thirsty, and weary (Creed of the Council of Toledo [A.D. 400], *SCD* 20, p. 13). His body was nourished by ordinary food and rested by ordinary sleep; his spiritual relation with the Father was refreshed by prayer, like us. In saying "I thirst" (John 19:28), he revealed his affinity to everyone whose throat has become parched, who has desired a drink of water on a hot day. The human body of the Savior was neither imaginary nor celestial (Leo, *Symbol of Faith*, *SCD* 344, p. 141; see also *SCD* 20, 462, 710; Council of Florence, *SCD* 710, pp. 227–28).

The Son's Passability and Death

A more difficult point viewed in the light of the glory of his sonship was: he experienced bodily pain. He felt exhaustion, for example, when his bodily powers failed and he was unable to carry the cross. He was wounded and hurt when nailed to the cross.

The most decisive proof of his humanity is simply that he died. There is no doubt either to the eyes of faith or to historical investigation that Jesus died. The death of Jesus unmistakably marks him as one of us (Tho. Aq., *ST* III Q50, II, pp. 2293–98). The well-established facts that he suffered and died were what made his messianic identity most vexing to explain to those who had been nurtured by contrary expectations.

The scandal that had to be clarified was that the eternal Son suffered. "Although he was a son, he learned obedience from what he suffered" (Heb. 5:8). It was fitting that God should have made "the author of their salvation perfect through suffering" (Heb. 2:10). Why? Because only on this basis would he be *"able to help* those who are being tempted" (Heb. 2:18, italics added; Pearson, *EC* I, pp. 326–34)). Under Roman guard headed toward his execution, the fettered bishop of Antioch observed: "If the things He did were done by our Lord merely in appearance, then I am in chains merely in appearance" (Ignatius, *To the Smyrnaeans* 4, *FC* 1, p. 119).

Christology is finally theodicy. The teaching of the humanity of Christ penetrates a point that runs deeply through Christian care of souls: since he suffered through temptation, he is able to help all who suffer through temptation. Not a minor point. He suffered the risks and vulnerabilities of human existence, and because of this we can identify with the God who identifies with us (Tho. Aq., *ST* III Q14, II, pp. 2101–104).

This teaching of the suffering of the incarnate Lord is utterly distinc-

tive of Christianity. It is not to be found (except prefiguratively) in Judaism and absolutely not in Islam. Hinduism and Buddhism are inclined to
find the notion of the suffering, dying incarnate God rather impossible
and disgusting.

The Risen Body Not an Apparition

Even in the case of the resurrected body, the New Testament texts
went out of their way to make clear that the risen body of Jesus was not
an apparition or incorporeal spirit. On the road to Emmaus "while they
were still talking about this [the crucifixion], Jesus himself stood among
them and said to them, 'Peace be with you.' They were startled and fright-
enend, thinking they saw a ghost." To this Jesus replied: "'Touch me and
see; a ghost does not have flesh and bones, as you see I have'." He asked
them for something to eat, and "they gave him a piece of broiled fish, and
he took it and ate it in their presence" (Luke 24:36–43).

When the disciples saw Christ walking on the lake toward them after
his death, "They were terrified. 'It's a ghost' they said." "It is I," Jesus
replied (Matt. 14:26–27). The "I" had a recognizable voice, that of an
embodied person.

The Enlivened Word:
The Mediator Assumed a Human Soul, Spirit, and Will

Soul is that without which the body is a corpse. Soul is the animating,
enlivening dimension of human existence. Jesus Christ possessed not
only a human body but (like all of us) a human soul—that liveliness without which the body is unresponsive (hence dead; Tho. Aq., ST III Q15, II,
pp. 2104–12; Chemnitz, TNC, pp. 58–59).

Emotive Range

That implies that Jesus, like the rest of us, experienced the whole
range of human emotions—whatever living persons experience. A good
sampling of this emotive repertoire is reported in the Gospels: Mark
reports that he experienced pity (1:41), anger (3:5), deep sighing (7:34),
compassion (8:2), surprise (6:6), and disappointment (8:17; 9:19). Jesus is
portrayed in Luke as experiencing joy (10:21), distress (22:15), and love
(7:36–50). "These emotions are certainly not falsely ascribed to Him"
(Augustine, CG 14.9, NPNF 1 II, p. 269; cf. FC 14, pp. 369–70). "He
assumed all the natural and blameless passions of man. This is because
He assumed the whole man and everything that is his," except sin,
"including hunger, thirst, fatigue, pain, the tears, the destruction, the
shrinking from death, the fear, the agony, from which came the sweat-

ing" (John of Damascus, *OF, FC* 37, pp. 323–24; Council of Toledo, *SCD* 20, p. 13).

Jesus Wept

Even more poignantly he wept, "deeply moved in spirit and troubled" at the death of his dear friend Lazarus, the brother of Martha and Mary (John 11:33–35). And finally he showed deep filial concern for his mother while hanging on the cross (John 19:25–26).

Contra Apollinarius

Hence the view of Apollinarius had to be rejected that Christ had no human *psuchē* (soul), the divine nature having completely taken the place of the human soul. That was unacceptable to the remembering church who had heard the Gospels read and knew that Jesus had a human *psychē*, the full range of affective experience, and fully human emotions (Newman, *Mix.*, pp. 324–26).

Hence Apollinarianism was rejected by the Fourth Ecumenical Council of Chalcedon, which affirmed that Jesus was true God, truly human, with soul and body, of one essence with the Father as touching his Godhead, and of one essence with us as touching our humanity, like us in all things except sin. These scriptural terms came to be remembered, something like ecumenical multiplication tables. The ecumenical councils sought to formulate in a clear and precise way (so as to be not easily misinterpreted) the crux of the testimony of Scripture as shared by the believing church.

Tempted

Discussion of the temptation narratives will come later, but it is fitting here to note that Jesus was not remembered as being immune to experiencing the full power of temptation. He possessed all those capacities that temptation would seek to make instruments of sin. He possessed those same capacities by which, through grace, we are enabled to overcome temptation.

The pictures we are given in the temptation narratives and Gethsemane are of genuine, not superficial or charadelike, temptations. The Christ of Scripture was liable to all of these subtle influences and temptations of the psychosomatic interface that so uniquely accompany ordinary human existence (but not animal or angelic existence, because beasts and angels do not experience the clash of the psychosomatic interface so drastically as this unique human *compositum*).

His Mind

Jesus' soul was a human soul, Jesus' emotional life a human emotional life (Tho. Aq., *ST* III Q15, II, pp. 2104–12). Jesus experienced ordinary human mental processes and intellectual life (Council of Constantinople II, *SCD* 216, p. 86; see also *SCD* 13, 255, 422, 429) and not merely a sensitive or animal soul (*SCD* 710). Jesus' human soul, like all human souls, did not previously exist, as did the the eternal Son before the incarnation (Vigilius, *Canons Ag. Origen, SCD* 204, p. 84). There was in him, concluded Augustine, "a whole soul, not merely the irrational part of the soul, but also the rational, which is called mind" (*On the Gospel of St. John*, Tractate XXIII.6, *NPNF* 1 VII, p. 153).

Do His Prayers Reveal His Humanity?

He prayed

Without *psuchē* (soul, the animating, moving, responsive, emotive dimension of human existence), what could the Gospel writers have meant when they reported that Jesus prayed? Surely his prayers were not a pretense. His prayers reveal a soul heavy with human burdens, capable of joy in God, happy to withdraw from the world for a time to converse with the Father.

He prayed not only for others, but for himself, when he said: "My soul is overwhelmed with sorrow to the point of death" (Mark 14:34). "He fell to the ground and prayed that if possible the hour might pass from him" (Mark 14:35). How can one read the account without feeling with him the full burden of his human situation at that time? What other purpose might these details have been recorded than to show the Savior as one of us, fully human, sharing our human condition, our agony, this same one being none other than God?

John Chrysostom marveled at the canonical providence that Matthew would demonstrate Christ's sharing in our humanity in a quite different way than John: Matthew by anxiety over future torment, John by grief over history's distortions; Matthew "by the agony, the trouble, the trembling, and the sweat; but John by His sorrow. For had He not been of our nature, He would not once and again have been mastered by grief" (*Hom. on John* LXIII.2, *NPNF* 1 XIV, p. 233).

The Human Will in Prayer

In praying he "became a model for us, He taught us to ask of God. . . . He actually had two wills that are natural and correspond to His nature and are not mutually opposed. 'Father,' he says as being consubstantial, 'if it be possible,' not because He did not know—and what is impossible for God?—but to instruct us to put the divine will before our own" (John of Damascus, *OF* III.24, *FC* 37, p. 329). It was his fully human *psuchē* that longed, prayed, pleaded, agonized, and was tempted to despair, yet that finally was willing to affirm, "Yet not what I will, but what you will" (Mark 14:36).

Such Prayer Could Only Emerge out of the Actual, Human Psychosomatic Interface

Only a human person could suffer in this way, not animals or angels. Animals, lacking language for awareness of the future, cannot agonize in spirit. And supratemporal intelligences or incorporeal creatures such as angels, lacking bodies, could not suffer what a body suffers. Jesus' agony in the Garden reveals the difficulties intrinsic to the composite (psychosomatic) character of human existence. If Christ were God without being at the same time human, he would not be thus limited, dependent, faced with a horrible prospect of death, subject to the control of others. But Christ is God while being at the same time human, limited, dependent, facing suffering and death. This point alone singles Christianity out as something quite distinct from other major world religions.

Did the Mediator Experience Fear?

There are two kinds of fear. Jesus experienced one kind but did not experience the other, according to classical exegesis.

Not Neurotic Anxiety

Jesus did not experience unnatural fear—neurotic anxiety—or unreasonable or disproportional anxiety about contingencies he had to face. Even though he at times hid himself (as a reasonable response to real threat or because he was aware that "his hour had not yet come"), there is no evidence that he was inordinately afraid or overly anxious in an exaggerated sense (Athanasius, *Four Discourses Ag. Arians* III.29, *NPNF* 2 IV, pp. 423, 425; Augustine, *EDQ* 33, *FC* 70, pp. 62–63). This conclusion could be derived inductively from the texts or deductively from the theandric premise.

Natural Fear

Yet Jesus did experience reasonable fear, proportional to actual threat, as seems indicated by John's Gospel: "Now my heart is troubled, and what shall I say? 'Father, save me from this hour'? No, it was for this very reason I came to this hour" (John 12:27; Athanasius, *Contra Apollinaris* I.16; II:3, 10, 13; cf. Matt. 26:39; Mark 15:34; John 11:35).

He is like us in that he experienced that "natural fear when the soul is unwilling to be separated from the body because of the natural feeling of affinity and kinship implanted in it by the Creator" which "shrinks from death. . . . On the one hand, by desiring both food and drink and sleep and by being naturally acquainted with these He showed His inclination for the things which sustained His nature; on the other, He showed His disinclination for things destructive of His nature" (John of Damascus, *OF* III.23, *FC* 37, p. 327; cf. Spinoza, *Ethics*, Hofner Library of Classics II, pp. 163-77).

How Was Humanity Recapitulated in Him?

Recapitulation

Justin Martyr, Irenaeus, Tertullian and, Athanasius all commented upon the Pauline texts implying that Jesus Christ recapitulated humanity. The kernel of this idea is that God "made known to us the mystery of his will according to his good pleasure, which he purposed in Christ, to be put into effect when the times will have reached their fulfillment—to *bring all things in heaven and on earth together under one head*, even Christ" (Eph. 1:10, italics added).

Accordingly Christ gathered up (re-headed) all things in himself. "God recapitulated in Himself the ancient formation of man, that he might kill sin, deprive death of its power and vivify man" (Irenaeus, *Ag. Her.* III.xviii.7, *ANF* I, p. 448). The Son recapitulated "the long line of human beings and furnished us *in compendio* with salvation; so that what we had lost in Adam—namely, to be according to the image and likeness of God—that we might recover in Christ Jesus" (*Ag. Her.* III.xviii.1, *ANF* I, p. 446).

Recapitulation of Stages of Human Development

Christ was thought by Irenaeus and Gregory Nazianzen to have passed through every stage of life from birth to death in order that he might sanctify each stage. "For that which He has not assumed He has not healed; but that which is united to His Godhead is also saved. If only half Adam fell, then that which Christ assumes and saves may be half also; but if the whole of his nature fell, it must be united to the whole nature of Him that was begotten, and so be saved as a whole" (Gregory Nazianzen, Epist. 101, *NPNF* 2 VIII, p. 440). "That which has not been assumed has not been healed. And so, He assumed the whole man," the

Damascene argued, "in order that He might grace the whole with salvation" (John of Damascus, *OF* III.12, *FC* 37, p. 318). The Son honored all human conditions by in principle assuming them all (Gregory Nazianzen, *Orat.* XL, *NPNF* 2 VII, p. 360).

The Holy Reversal of Each Stage

As a person he went through "the various stages of his life." Each step, however, constituted a unique reversal of ordinary expectations and a consequent liberation: "He determined to be poor. . . . All the things which men unrighteously desired to possess, he did without and so made them of no account. All the things which men sought to avoid and so deviated from the search for truth, he endured and so robbed them of their power over us." Accordingly he "refused to be a king," did not marry, "bore with insults", and while "They thought a cross the most shameful form of death: He was crucified" (Augustine, *OTR* XVI, pp. 26–28). The modern study of moral development and Christian psychogenetic development has yet to enter into dialogue with this powerful ancient ecumenical interpretation.

How Was Humanity Honored in His Coming?

Humanity is incomparably honored in the incarnation, for God made flesh divine, without providing occasion for the worship of the creature.

The Glorification of Human Nature

This had profound personal, experiential relevance for Augustine: "Why should there be such great glory to a human nature—and this undoubtedly an act of grace, no merit preceding it—unless it be that those who consider such a question faithfully and soberly might have here a clear manifestation of God's great and sole grace, and this in order that they might understand how they themselves are justified from their sins by the selfsame grace which made it so that the man Christ had not power to sin?" (Augustine, *Enchiridion* XI.36, *LCC* VI, p. 362).

The whole nature of humanity was taken up by God the Son. Augustine summarized: "By the Holy Spirit there was granted to us so great humility on the part of so great a God, that He deemed it worthy of Him to assume the entire nature of man" (*totum hominem*; Augustine, *On Faith and the Creed* IV.8, *NPNF* 1, III, p. 325). Leo thought the incarnation made us partners in the divine nature: "Know your worth, O Christian; you are made a partner of the divine nature" (*Serm.* 21.3; quoted in Tho. Aq., *ST* 3a.i.2, *TATT*, p. 279; cf. *NPNF* 2 XII, p. 129).

God Came Closer Than the Enemy

"The devil came close to us; but he did not come so close as to assume our nature. For although he fell through pride and thereupon persuaded man also to fall away from God, he nevertheless did not become man and did not come so close to us as did God's Son, who became our flesh and blood" (Luther, *Serm. on the Annunciation, Luke 1:26–38* [1534], *WLS* I, p. 153; *WA* 37, 336).

Deification of Incarnate Humanity

Irenaeus stated the principle of deification (*theosis*) of the incarnate humanity in a way that became prototypical for others: he became "what we are, that He might bring us to be even what He is Himself" (Irenaeus, *Ag. Her.* V.pref., *ANF* I, p. 526; cf. Tertullian, *Ag. Marcion* V.17). In this way Christ recapitulated humanity (Irenaeus, *Ag. Her.* III.19.1, *ANF* I, p. 449; V.pref. p. 526; V.16.2, p. 544; V.21.1, p. 549).

Athanasius developed this theme: "He was made man that we might be made God; and He manifested Himself by a body that we might receive the idea of the unseen Father; and He endured the insolence of men that we might inherit incorruptibility" (Athanasius, *Incarn. of the Word* 54, *NPNF* 2 IV, p. 65). "He deified that which He put on" (Athanasius, *Four Discourses Ag. Arians* I.42, *NPNF* 2 IV, p. 330; Maximos, *Various Texts, Philokal.* II, pp. 177–78).

In this he enhanced the glory of being human (Hilary, *Trin.* IX.40, *NPNF* 2 IX, p. 168) and thereby brought human nature into the divine nature (Hilary, *Trin.* IX.4, 51–54, *NPNF* 2 IX, p. 156).

Is the Humanity of Christ to Be Worshiped?

Christianity struggled to clarify the special nature of the glory of human nature in Christ (Chemnitz, *TNC*, pp. 325–26, 399–400) and the adoration of the humanity assumed by the Son (Hugh of St. Victor, *OSCF*, pp. 280–84; Chemnitz, *TNC*, pp. 338–39). This humanity was not like a piece of clothing to be subsequently thrown away. The Logos determined to be one with humanity continuing after the resurrection. The resurrection is *of the body* and occurred "through a man" to whom ultimately all things are to be made subject (1 Cor. 15:21–28). Hence the humanity of Christ as directly united with divinity is rightly adored as the subject of true worship, with one adoration, not two (Council of Ephesus, *SCD* 120, pp. 50–51; see also *SCD* 221, 224).

Does Christianity therefore worship a man? "We do not worship a creature. Far be the thought! For such an error belongs to heathens and

Arians. But we worship the Lord of Creation, Incarnate, the Word of God" (Athanasius, *Letter to Adelphius*, chap. 3, *NPNF* 1 IV, p. 575).

James Montgomery celebrated Christ's humanity magnificently:

> What is the thing of greatest price,
>   The whole creation round?
> That which was lost in Paradise,
>   That which in Christ is found:
> The soul of man—Jehovah's breath—
>   That keeps two worlds at strife:
> Hell moves beneath to work its death,
>   Heaven stoops to give it life.
> God, to reclaim it, did not spare
>   His well-beloved Son;
> Jesus, to save it, deigned to bear
>   The sins of all in one.
> The Holy Spirit sealed the plan,
>   And pledged the blood divine,
> To ransom every soul of man—
>   That price was paid for mine
>   (*PS*, p. 41).

The Detached Humanity in Modern "Christ"ologies

The Modern Separation of Jesus' Humanity from His God-Manhood

A major deficit of modern views of Jesus Christ is that his humanity is affirmed in such a way as to detach it from the theandric person.

Modern writers are prone to assume that if you have the human Jesus, that is all you need and perhaps all you can ever have (if you have that!). The classic teaching of the union of the one and only divine-human Person is dissected and detached, and only on this misunderstood basis does it appear to be boring to those who finally come to view Jesus only as a moral hero or religious genius. Such interpreters are prone to place their faith not in him (the unique divine-human Person), but in his ideas or ideals and imagine that they share with him the faith he had.

The Resulting Diminution of Christianity

Such a detachment systematically ignores the central theme of the New Testament. It has to work hard to read the New Testament from these alien presuppositions. From its origins, Christianity has worshiped Jesus as the Christ, the Son of the living God, the fullness of God made manifest in history. To change this is to change Christianity so much that it becomes virtually unrecognizable. Those who set aside Christology by focusing on the human side alone, abstracted from the God-man unity, have altered Christianity beyond recognition.

Neither Hero or Genius

Those who treat Jesus essentially as a moral or political guide, as a heroic fashioner of history, or as a spiritual genius cannot avoid that fact that he intends to meet them as infinitely more—as the only Son of God. Faith receives his own invitation to "come unto me" (Matt. 11:28), not fit him into our categories. "We must not force Him, so to say, to be the mere hero or genius He has no interest in being. To-day as of old He hides Himself from those who would take Him by violence to make Him king" (Mackintosh, *PJC*, p. 292; cf. Kierkegaard, *On Authority and Revelation*).

Heroes come to accomplish their own will—Jesus came not to do his own will, but that of the heavenly Father. Geniuses are prone to be contemptuous of those in darkness. Jesus came to meet and care for those in darkness, to wash their feet, to share their lives with them, to live among the poor.

CHAPTER 5

The Manner of God's Coming

The means by which God chose to come into the world would be, according to prophetic expectation, a virginal conception and birth. Mary is celebrated as remnant of Israel. The New Israel dawns with her radical attentiveness, receptivity, and trust in God (Gregory Thaumaturgus, *Four Hom.* I, *ANF* VI, pp. 58–60; Barth, *CD* I/2, pp. 138ff.). She is the daughter of Zion with whom God makes a new beginning with humanity (Isa. 1:8; Zech. 9:9).

THE VIRGINAL CONCEPTION

A Natural Birth of Preternatural Conception

The conception was preternatural—exceeding natural explanation. The birth was natural.

The Triune Initiative

The birth of Jesus is viewed by the ancient ecumenical consensus as the creative act of the triune God through the initiating agency of God the Spirit (Tho. Aq., *ST* III Q31–33, II, pp. 2183–2200). In this lowly birth the Holy Spirit enabled the eternal Son to take on human nature without ceasing to be God (Tho. Aq., *ST* III Q20–25, 32–33, II, pp. 2136–56, 2192–2200).

Absence of the Earthly Father

God's own initiative is intensified by the absence of the earthly father. The conception was without coitus of any kind (Chemnitz, *TNC*, pp. 38–39, 208–10). "Without any intercourse with a man, her virgin womb was suddenly impregnated" (Lactantius, *Div. Inst.* 4.12, *ANF* VII, p. 110).

Jesus' birth was a birth in ordinary human flesh of a normal human mother who was a virgin.

Fitness of Bodily Means

This was not a diminution of sexuality, but an exaltation and celebration of the human body as the means God chooses to become knowable and palpably present in history, through a man born of woman. The virginal conception was not a repudiation of maleness, but a sign of the grace of God toward all humanity, male and female. It does not commend sexual asceticism generally or condemn sexual passion but rather is a testimony to God's compassion for the fallen world and determination to save it from folly and sin. The fitness of these bodily means (God's embodiment through a human body normally born) has been repeatedly affirmed by the apostolic witness and early Christian tradition.

Prominently Attested, Liturgically Crucial Testimony

Testimony to the virginal conception is considered important enough to be numbered among the spare articles of faith of the creed and has remained an anchor of the Christian year for over seventeen ecumenical centuries.

Prominently Selected As a Creedal Article of Faith

The testimony is crucially located among irreducible articles of faith. These articles have been considered essential to baptism at least since the fourth century and probably much earlier.

Even though the Apostles' Creed itself is very short, with no room for talk about such weighty matters as atonement or justification, it does make room for the crucial affirmation that Jesus was *conceptus de Spiritu Sancto, natus ex Maria virgine* ("conceived by the Holy Spirit, born of the Virgin Mary," *Symbolum Apostolicum*, COC II, p. 45). The most widely received ancient creeds confess the virgin birth as an article of faith (see the second-century rule of faith as reported by Irenaeus and Tertullian; cf. Rufinus, *Rule of Faith*, COC II, p. 53).

So crucial is this testimony that it is often thought that those who reject the special conception are likely to fail to grasp the broader significance of the incarnation and thus of the resurrection. The Reformed theologian E. W. Sartorius wrote: "Those who deny the birth of the God-man of the Virgin Mary, will always question also the pre-existence and deity of Christ in general" (*The Doctrine of Divine Love* [1884], p. 138; Jacobs, *SCF*, p. 146).

Continuous Proclamation

The testimony to the conception has been a continuous feature of Christian proclamation since the oral traditions antedating Luke's and Matthew's Gospels. Admittedly it is likely that some believed in the resurrected Lord without hearing or knowing of the unique conception, for it was not the special conception but the resurrection that persuaded them that Jesus is the Christ, the Son of God. Yet testimony from the first century onward has been constantly accompanied by attestation of the virginal conception as a fit means of God's own coming. Whatever moderns may think, there is no doubt that the core proclamation of the church from very early times has included a witness to one "born of the virgin Mary."

Widely Attested in Varied Sources

The received tradition is a sufficient testimony not limited to a single author, but so dispersed that it cannot be regarded as idiosyncratic. Surprisingly there is more information in the New Testament about the virgin birth than about the Lord's Supper (D. A. Edwards, *The Virgin Birth in History and Faith*, chap. 3; Ramm, *EC*, p. 71). The virgin birth is sometimes rejected by critics as an unreliable account on the grounds that so little mention is made of it in the New Testament, but few would think the accounts of the Lord's Supper are made dubious by their paucity of reference. Pivotal doctrines do not require many, but pivotal, reference.

A Key Liturgical Event

The birth narrative has come to form an integral part of classic Christology. Liturgically the Feast of the Nativity (Christ-mass) is a focal point of the seasonal cycle of celebrations of the Christian year. If ignored or dismissed, a crucial link between Christology and liturgy is omitted (Tho. Aq., *ST* III Q29–30, II, pp. 2175–83; J. G. Machen, *The Virgin Birth of Christ*; H. von Campenhausen, *The Virgin Birth in the Theology of the Ancient Church*).

Distinguishable from Miraculous Births in the History of Religions?

Commonness of Miraculous Birth Narratives

Myths of miraculous birth are said to be common in the history of religions. They express the desire of fallen human history for a new beginning, for moral purity. There is probably a distinct hope for human renewal that accompanies every human birth. It is not surprising that in the history of religions generally that hope would be asserted on an idealized or cosmic scale — especially amid certain periods of historical despair and awakening hope.

Israel too had hopes of this sort (Isa. 7:14; 54:1; Jer. 31:1–21), but Israel transmuted these metaphors and gave them a totally different (historical-eschatological) meaning and import. Israel expected a palpable, actual, coming event in history, God's own new beginning, not a demigod or mythic idea.

Nativity Not Analogous to a Sexually Active Deity Fertilizing to Produce a Demigod Son

The extrabiblical antecedents often symbolize the pantheon as horny, quasi-sexual agents who are attracted to human sexual partners and whose fertilizing power bears quasi-divinized births. This premise remains quite alien to the New Testament birth narratives. In Luke and Matthew, God is not the biological father of Jesus so as to make Jesus half God, half human. Rather Jesus is fully human, fully God. The narrative does not imply that a new Son of God is begotten who never before existed — rather it speaks of the eternal Son of God who without benefit of genital sexuality assumes human flesh in the conception and birth of this person.

There is no clear or adequate parallel in the history of religions' myths of virgin births, for what is celebrated here is that "God was manifest in the flesh" (1 Tim. 3:16, KJV) to suffer for the salvation of humanity. The Son, "who, being in very nature God" took "the very nature of a servant" (Phil. 2:6–7). Pagan pieties knew nothing of incarnation in this lowly sense.

Old Testament Expectations

First Announced to the Mother of All Living

The first announcement of God's saving intention came to the first woman, not the first man. The earliest gospel or embryonic anticipation of the gospel (the Protoevangelium of Genesis 3:15) was directly addressed not to Adam but Eve, in a promise to the mother of all living that from her seed would come the promised One who would overcome the tempter of humanity (John Chrysostom, *Hom. on Gen.* XVII, FC 74, pp. 236–45; J. Marckius, *Compendium Theologiae* XVIII, 19; Heppe, *RD*, p. 411). The *Russian Catechism* asks: "Why was Jesus Christ called *the seed of the woman*? Because he was born on earth *without man*" (*COC* II, p. 470). Cyril of Jerusalem thought it significant that in paradise Eve was "still a virgin; for it was *after* his expulsion from Paradise that 'Adam knew Eve his wife'" (*Catech. Lect.* XII, FC 61, p. 230; cf. Menno Simons, *Brief and Clear Confession*, CWMS, pp. 432–33).

Virginal Conception Unlike Old Testament Barrenness Narratives

The Old Testament reports a number of miraculous births, each one signaling a turning point in salvation history: Sarah belatedly bore Isaac (Gen. 18), Hannah belatedly gave birth to Samuel (1 Sam. 1–3), and an anonymous mother had Samson (Judg. 13). These were not virginal conceptions, however. In each case the mother had been barren and had abandoned all hope of having a child. God made the impossible birth possible, elevating the lowly to put down the rich and mighty (1 Sam. 2:7; Luke 1:52). In each case the child played a major role in the fulfillment of divine promise.

The virgin birth of Jesus differs from all these partriarchal miraculous birth narratives, which focus upon barrenness overcome through divinely enabled human sexuality and human fathering without specifically disclaiming male sexual initiative. Impotence is overcome through potency—quite different from virginal conception.

The Coming of Immanuel

The Language of Virginity—Almah, Parthenos

"Virgin" (*almah*, root word: "concealment," Song of Sg. 1:3; *bethulah*, root word: "separated," Judg. 21:12) in the Old Testament generally meant a woman who has not had sexual intercourse with a man. It may also refer to a young maiden or woman of marriageable age (*almah*, "virgin, maiden," never signifies a married woman, but always a maiden for whom virginity was presumed, Gen. 24:43). The pivotal passage in Isaiah 7:14 uses *almah* (LXX, *parthenos*).

Virginity also symbolized the people of Israel as betrothed to God (Isa. 62:4–5; Jer. 18:15). Later *parthenos* would be applied metaphorically to the church (2 Cor. 11:2–3) and to the faithful (Rev. 14:4). The Greek word *parthenos* ("virgin," Matt. 1:23) refers to a chaste unmarried maiden in its New Testament references. Long before modern conflicts over this word, Cyril of Jerusalem had remarked of the supposed improvers of Christianity that "it has long been their custom to resist the truth perversely; they say the text is not 'the virgin,' but 'the damsel'" (*Catech. Lect.* XII, FC 61, p. 240; and so the controversy still simmers today over the translation of Isa. 7:14).

Immanuel

To clarify Jesus' messianic identity, Matthew specifically quoted Isaiah's prophecy (7:14) that "'The virgin will be with child and will give birth to a son, and they will call him Immanuel,' which means 'God with us'" (Matt. 1:23; Origen, *FP* IV.1, p. 263). It is only if God *is* with us that he can rightly be *called* "God with us" (Novatian, *Trin.* 12, *FC* 67, p. 50). This birth was thought by Isaiah to be a "sign" (*oth*), addressed to "the house of David" (v. 13), not merely for Ahaz in the singular but to "you" in the plural. Classical exegetes followed Matthew in regarding Isaiah's prophecy as a type pointing beyond the circumstances of Ahaz to the Expected One (Irenaeus, *Ag. Her.* III.21, *ANF* I, p. 451; Eusebius, *MPG* II, p. 54).

Luke's Nativity

The Birth of John the Baptist

Key features of Luke's narrative preceding Jesus' nativity are that the birth of John the Baptist was foretold; Elizabeth was barren; she was a descendant of Aaron; the angel Gabriel appeared to the priest Zechariah announcing God's good news that Elizabeth would bear a son who will be great in the sight of the Lord, who would make ready a people prepared for the Lord; and that Zechariah could not speak until the birth of John.

The Annunciation

Gabriel appeared to Mary, a virgin (*parthenos*) pledged to marry Joseph, a descendant of David. It was announced that "you will be with child and give birth to a son, and you are to give him the name Jesus. He will be great and will be called the Son of the most High. The Lord God will give him the throne of his father David, and he will reign over the house of Jacob forever; his kingdom will never end" (Luke 1:31–33). "Hail Mary, full of grace, the Lord is with thee," is thus the opening moment of the salvation event as trustfully received by an attentive, grace-filled human agent (Tho. Aq., *ST* III Q30, II, pp. 2178–83).

"'How will this be,' Mary asked the angel, 'since I am a virgin?'" (Luke 1:34; note that *parthenos* here cannot possibly be translated "young woman," for that cannot fit the context). "The angel answered, 'The Holy Spirit will come upon you, and the power of the Most High will overshadow you. So the holy One to be born will be called the Son of God.'" "For nothing is impossible with God" (Luke 1:35, 37). The narrative says nothing descriptively about how specifically this overshadowing would occur. It simply focuses upon what has been made possible by God. Little more is known of the conception than that it occurs by the power of God the Spirit who would immediately "come upon" (*epeleusetai*) the virgin.

Woman Honored in Conception

Tertullian ingeniously noticed that it was *not virginity* as such *but woman* that was being honored in the annunciation: "I recognize, too, the angel Gabriel as having been sent to 'a virgin.' But when he is blessing her, it is 'among women,' not among virgins, that he ranks her: 'Blessed art thou among women'"; for "if Mary is here put on a level with a 'betrothed,' so that she is called a *woman* not on the ground of being a *female*, but on the ground of being assigned to a husband, it immediately follows that Christ was not born of a *virgin*" (Tertullian, *On the Veiling of Virgins* 6, ANF IV, p. 31; Luke 1:28). It was not Mary's relation to her husband that was honored or her virginity, but her being a woman, capable of trust in God.

Mary steps forward as "a woman who was poor, who toiled with her hands, who was harassed and persecuted, who was exiled," "the *woman of the Magnificat*—the prophetic woman of liberation" (Boff, *LibT.*, p. 27; cf. R. Ruether, "She's a Sign of God's Liberating Power," *Other Side* 104, [1980]: 17–21; J. Alfaro, "The Mariology of the Fourth Gospel," *Biblical Theology Bulletin* 10 [1980]: 3–16).

Luke's Intention to Produce an Eyewitness History

Luke's narrative is told from Mary's point of view. Mary herself may have been one of the eyewitnesses Luke referred to as those from whom he gathered his information. Luke's prologue clearly indicated his intention to write only about that which he had "carefully investigated" concerning "everything from the beginning" of these events "just as they were handed down to us by those who from the first were eyewitnesses" (Luke 1:2).

Luke regarded the nativity as a straightforward historical account. If there had been an extended oral tradition intervening between eyewitnesses and Luke's account, it seems unlikely that Luke would have specifically said that he got the account from direct eyewitnesses. It is also likely that some speculation would have attached to the story if it had taken a longer time to develop, but the story is plainly told without speculation or artifice.

As a reporter-historian (and probably as physician [Col. 4:14]) with access to eyewitnesses (Luke 1:1–4), Luke was highly trusted. He seems least likely to be among those that might be prone toward gullibility or distortion of received reports. Distinct Hebraisms in the text (such as the Davidic inheritance, Luke 1:46–55) resist the interpretation that this was a story invented by the later hellenizing church to explicate its Christological dogmas.

Matthew's Nativity

Born of Mary

Matthew's narrative is apparently independent of Luke's, hence corroboratory, again affirming the special conception. His genealogy ends with an atypical, curious reference to "*Joseph, the husband of Mary, of whom was born Jesus, who is called Christ*" (1:16, italics added). It is rare in ancient literature to find a man publicly identified primarily by means of his relation to his wife. Matthew then relates how the birth came about: "Mary was pledged to be married to Joseph, but before they came together, she was found to be with child through the Holy Spirit" (1:18).

The fact that Matthew's account seems to be written distinctly from Joseph's point of view has led some to surmise that the source of this narrative could have been Joseph himself. If it is assumed that Matthew the tax-collector wrote it, his working with documents in a profession in which accuracy of record was crucial may stand as a plausible reason why he was selected or chose to write the Gospel narrative. It is not unreasonable to assume that as an early disciple he could have personally known members of this extended family, many of whom survived Jesus, and thus could have received this tradition directly from them.

The Dream of Joseph and the Naming of Jesus

The angel appeared to Joseph in a dream and explained that he had no reason to "be afraid to take Mary home as your wife, because what is conceived in her is from the Holy Spirit. She will give birth to a son, and you are to give him the name Jesus" (1:20–21), a name that held the clue from the outset to his identity—he will save (John of Damascus, *OF* II.2, FC 37, p. 269; Tho. Aq., *ST* III Q37, II, pp. 2219–23).

Hence even from the outset it is fitting that he be addressed as Savior (Martin I, Lateran Council [A.D. 649], *SCD* 269–271, pp. 101–106; see also *SCD* 1, 251, 253, 337). Cyril of Jerusalem pointed out that "it was not by men that he was named Jesus" but by the unexpected divine visitor, who then gives the reason for this name: "for he shall save his people from their sins" (*Catech. Lect.* X.12, *LCC* IV, pp. 136–37; see *Heidelberg Catech.* II,

Q29, *BOConf* 4.029). His name signals that he was "born to save" (*Russian Catech.*, *COC* II, p. 466).

The Legal Father

In taking special note that Joseph, following the commandment of the angel, "called his name Jesus" (Matt. 1:25), the implication was that Joseph would accept legal responsibility for Jesus. It was then immediately specified that Joseph "had no union with her until she gave birth to a son," precluding any notion that Jesus had an earthly father. Wherever Jesus is described as the "son of Joseph" (Luke 2:27, 33, 41, 43, 48; Matt. 13:55), the reference is to Joseph as legal not biological father, for otherwise Luke and Matthew would clearly be inconsistent with their own account (the same reasoning also applies to John 1:45; 6:42).

Prophetic Reference

The messianic promises were widely known in popular late Judaic piety: Micah foretold that the Savior would be born in Bethlehem (Matt. 2:4-6). Malachi had prophesied that a forerunner like Elijah would prepare the way for deliverance (Mal. 3:1; 4:5; Matt. 3:10-12; *Russian Catech.*, *COC* II, p. 472). Isaiah had written: "For to us a child is born, to us a son is given, and the government will be on his shoulders. And he will be called Wonderful Conselor, Mighty God, Everlasting Father, Prince of Peace. Of the increase of his government and peace there will be no end" (Isa. 9:6-7). It is presumptuous to decide in advance that Isaiah determined Matthew's perception of the birth of Christ, rather than that the event itself called forth a reasonable recollection of that prophecy—for about such matters honest historians can only vaguely speculate.

Is Mark Silent?

When it is suggested that Mark does not report the birth narrative, it should also be noted that Mark does not report anything at all from the first thirty years of Jesus' life (circumcision, obedience to parents, or his growth as a lad). On closer inspection Mark may not be so silent as supposed, for he pointedly refers to Jesus in an unusual reference as "son of Mary," contrary to usual Jewish custom that identified the son by relation to the father, oddly leaving Joseph's name out of the account (Mark 6:3). Hence it is possible that Mark, too, had access to the nativity narrative in some form, even if it did not fit in with the purpose of his particular task of writing.

Matthew and Luke, who probably had Mark's Gospel in hand as they wrote, both thought it useful and necessary to add on the nativity narra-

tive. Does this mean that the narrative is late and hence of less importance? Or does it mean that they thought the nativity narrative was in fact
necessary, and that in Mark's account something important had been
missing on that point that was widely shared in the prevailing oral tradition? The latter seems more probable, for if they had thought otherwise,
why would it even appear in their texts? For whatever reason, Luke and
Matthew did not want to leave out the nativity accounts that were lacking
in Mark's version.

Further, it is often supposed that neither John nor Paul make any
reference to the birth of Jesus. Yet a careful examination of John 1:13, 6:42,
Romans 1:2–4, and Galatians 4:4 makes it imperative that one not judge
too quickly.

Johannine References

The birth narrative was almost surely known in some form to John,
whose prologue on the incarnation assumes a parallel between the
believer's regeneration and the coming of God into the world.

The Prologue's Peculiar Phrase: "Not of Natural Descent"

The prologue replaces the nativity narrative, focusing not upon the
mode of God's becoming flesh but upon the *incarnation itself*, which
requires some appropriate mode of entry into the world that is consistent
with the preexistent Son becoming human. It stretches credulity to imagine that John would celebrate the unparalleled event of the preexistent
Son of God becoming human by means of ordinary coitus.

In the prologue, the believer's new birth in faith is seen under the
analogy of the coming of God into the world. In developing the theme of
"Word made flesh," John writes: "Yet to all who receive him, to those who
believed in his name, he gave the right to become children of God—
children *born not of natural descent, nor of human decision or a husband's will,*
but born of God" (John 1:12–13, italics added; see W. Elert, *Der Christliche
Glaube*, 1960, p. 310; cf. Metzger, *TCGNT*, pp. 196ff.). Why is the "husband's [sexual] will" prominently inserted into the prologue? The analogy seems to be between the eternal Son who came into the world
unrecognized and the children quietly born of God who come into being
through faith. If so, there is another level of this analogy between the Son
of God born without a husband's sexual initiative and children of God
born of spirit. This suggests that John also may have had access to the
nativity narratives and understood himself to be here complementing
them, certainly not contradicting them.

Resistance to the Divine Mission by Jesus' Opponents

The question of Jesus' birth may have already been a subject of debate during Jesus' lifetime, as was suggested by the opponents of Jesus who said: "Is this not Jesus, the son of Joseph, whose father and mother we know? How can he now say, 'I came down from heaven'?" (John 6:42). This was said by his detractors who "were not as yet able to hear of that marvelous birth. And if they could not bear to hear in plain terms of His birth according to the flesh, much less could they hear of that ineffable Birth which is from above" (John Chrysostom, *Hom. on John* XLVI, *NPNF* 1 XIV, p. 164).

Pauline References

The Salutation of Romans

Paul speaks with great precision of the descent of Jesus in Romans: the gospel has to do with God's own Son, "who as to his human nature was a descendant of David, and who through the Spirit of holiness was declared with power to be the Son of God by his resurrection from the dead: Jesus Christ our Lord" (Rom. 1:2–4). Why would Paul assume a distinction such as *"as to his human nature* a descendant of David" unless he had access to some sort of genealogical or birth reports? Paul's access to the tradition of Davidic descent suggests that genealogies like those of Matthew and Luke or some similar tradition may have been available to Paul.

Galatians 4

The passages in Galatians 4 are more intriguing and more crucial. Paul specifically quotes the virginal passage from Isaiah 54 to his congregation in Galatia. Isaiah had prophesied that a barren woman who had never born a child would burst into song and would "have no labor pains" in giving birth, for "more are the children of the desolate woman than of her who has a husband" (Gal. 4:27, quoting Isa. 54:1). In commenting on this passage, Paul went out of his way to make note of the difference between a "son born in the ordinary way" and "the son born by the power of the Spirit" (Gal. 4:29). He was trying to teach the Galatian church that they were the children of this free woman, "the Jerusalem that is above" who is "free" and who is "our mother," whom God had given extraordinary birth by the Spirit.

Elsewhere, Paul made reference to Sarah's giving birth in Romans 4, where Abraham was regarded as father of all the faithful, since when "his body was as good as dead—since he was about a hundred years old—and that Sarah's womb was also dead," yet "he did not waver through unbelief regarding the promise of God" (Rom. 4:19–20).

These references strengthen the hypothesis that Paul may have had access to some form of the nativity narratives and was assuming that his audience was already familiar with Sarah's childbearing of Isaac, which was viewed as a prefiguring of Christ. In both cases the new beginning that God makes is not a part of the stream of historical causes but comes wholly and unexpectedly from God. The direction of these birth narratives goes contrary to the history of religions hypothesis that these metaphors were borrowed from available cultural sources (usually argued as Hellenistic) and exhaustively explained by them.

God Sent His Son Born of Woman

The crucial Pauline reference is from the same passage in Galatians: "When the time had fully come, God sent his Son, born of a woman" (4:4). Why not "man and woman"? The omission of the father in this reference makes it particularly unusual and noteworthy. The Father sends the Son by the power of the Spirit, and without mention of male sexuality woman gives birth.

The verb "born" (*genomenon*) in this passage is the same one used in Philippians 2:7: "born to be like other men." It is fitting that one equal with God should be born and become flesh in a distinctive way—the holy God through lowly birth. This is consistent with the theme of reversal common in the nativity images: no room at the inn, born of poor parents in a remote village, and the flight to Egypt.

THE SAVIOR'S BIRTH AS EVENT

The Extended Family—Source of Birth Narratives?

The Holy Family

Much of the extended family of Jesus appears to have been involved in the messianic event—John the Baptist, Mary, Joseph, Elizabeth, Zechariah, Simeon, Anna, the apostle John, his brothers James, Joses, Judas, and Simon—all were part of a single family. Jesus' sisters are also occasionally referred to (Mark 6:3; Matt. 13:56). Mary's sister (Jesus' aunt), John reports, was with her at the crucifixion (19:25). Although many of the family were earlier unbelievers (Mark 3:21, 31; John 7:5), they later shared significantly in the mission of the church (Acts 1:14; 1 Cor. 9:5).

Mary or other family members could have been the direct source of the birth narratives. The presence of Jesus' mother and brothers, especially James (Acts 1:14; 15:13–21; Gal. 1:19; 2:9), in the early circle of leading rememberers makes it unlikely that legendary materials about Jesus' origin would have been invented and left unchallenged by these prominent living persons during the decades following Jesus' death (Africanus, *Epis. to Aristides*, AEG I, p. 206; cf. Raymond Brown, *The Birth of the Messiah*).

Only gradually, at some point subsequent to the resurrection, did the birth narratives become a consistent and standard part of the core of Christian proclamation. How could it have been otherwise? Only Mary and Joseph and perhaps a few others would have been privy to these events prior to the time when their significance would become plausible.

The reason that much of the New Testament does not appear to be preoccupied with the virgin birth may have been that open proclamation sought to maintain a quiet reserve about public discussion of such private matters out of respect for Mary and other members of the family, perhaps in connection with the supposed "illegitimacy" question that opponents might have sought to exploit. Already in John 8:41 the opponents of Jesus were hinting at his "illegitimacy," and that charge continued to be made by opponents of Christianity well into the second century. Such a charge would hardly have been invented by Christians, and it is unlikely that it would have been invented by opponents of Christianity unless there had been something about Jesus' origin that was known to have been unusual (Brown, *Birth of the Messiah*; cf. Augustine, *Comm. on John* XLII, NPNF 1 VII, pp. 235–40; Pius II, *Epist. Cum Sient*, SCD 717f., p. 232).

Mary's Recollections

Luke in fact specifically mentions that "Mary treasured up all these things and pondered them in her heart" (Luke 2:19; cf. 2:51). This appears to present Mary as the almost exclusive custodian of the mystery of Jesus' birth until the time came for a clearer proclamation. This may explain why the publicly shared tradition of the nativity was relatively slower in forming than that of the resurrection. Lateness does not imply inauthenticity but reserve.

The Contrary Hypothesis

If one takes the hypothesis that Jesus was not born of a virgin, a greater difficulty arises, namely, that an unmarried couple would be chosen to give life to the Son of God who is without sin, the One who would forgive the sins of others, who without the premise of the virgin mother would have been legally treated as an illegitimate son born out of wedlock—hardly a probable hypothesis and one not made more plausible by the failure of the modern "sexual revolution." Due to the alleged teachings (subsequently renounced) of Zaninus of Pergamum (Zanini de Solcia) it became necessary in 1459 formally to declare the premise of the illegitimacy of Jesus an outrageous view (Pius II, *Epis. Cum Sicut, SCD* 717, p. 233).

The Limits of Alternatives

The Logical Alternatives

It is theoretically possible to hypothesize that God could have entered human history in some other way than by virginal conception, but objections mount as one considers the alternatives. The formally conceivable ways of being born are reduced to only two: normally, of one male and one female parent; or virginally, of a female parent alone. There is no third for the simple reason that *male sexuality cannot give birth alone.*

Hence if both sexes are to be honored in the incarnation, and *if the one giving birth must be female*, then the one sex remaining—the one to be born—would have to be male. If one hypothesizes that both the mother of God-incarnate and God-incarnate might have been female, this would have been less representative of humanity than a man born of woman (Gal. 4:4). Long before modern feminism, Augustine had thought seriously about this: "Mankind's deliverance had to be evidenced among both sexes," hence if the incarnate one is male, "it reasonably followed that the deliverance of the female sex be seen by that man's birth from a woman" (Augustine, *EDQ* 11, *FC* 70, p. 42).

Why Without Human Father?

Several reasons are offered by classic exegetes as to why Christ was born without human father:

(1) The principle of parsimony is at work here: God only uses what God needs for human salvation. God does indeed need female sexuality for the birthing, for birth is impossible without a mother. But male sexuality did not qualify as absolutely required in the same way that a mother is *sine qua non* to a birth. The question of classic exegetes concerning the manner of God's coming is: what is the most fitting way for the incarnation to occur? An eternal Son who descends from heaven to become incarnate does not need and can do without the complications of male sexuality.

(2) More significantly, the fatherless Messiah points beyond human fathering to the heavenly Father, who sends the eternal Son whose mission is enabled by the Spirit. In all of this there is a marked absence of erotic assertiveness so characteristically correlated with male sexuality or claims of merit to which male spirituality is prone.

(3) To be qualified as mediator he must be without sin. The human nature of Christ must be set apart and preserved from defilement by sin. A divine-human mediator engendered by male genital sexuality with its prevailing tendency to focused assertiveness and propensity toward pride, lust, and idolatry would have seemed implausible to ancient minds. This does not imply that human generation as such is defiled or in itself vicious, but that sexuality, both male and female, has become willfully distorted by the disobedience that followed the fall. A new beginning was needed.

(4) If he is to follow as the type of Melchizedek, who was without father, the Savior must be without father (Heb. 7:3).

(5) Christ was one person, not two. Logically, had he been born both of the Holy Spirit and of a human father, it might be argued that he was two persons, not one. Such incipient Nestorian reasoning was circumvented altogether in the special conception (Pearson, *EC* I, pp. 301–10; II, pp. 203, 230). So this was uniquely "a fatherless birth to Him Who was born of the Father before the ages" (*Gk. Orthodox Catech.* 32, p. 26).

The Ebionite Challenge

The challenge to the virginal conception is ancient. Already in the second century Ebionites were arguing that Jesus "was begotten by Joseph," thus "setting aside the testimony of the prophets," denying the eternal Logos in Jesus (Irenaeus, *Ag. Her.* III.21, *ANF* I, p. 451; cf. Council of Rome, *Tome of Damascus, SCD* 63, p. 31). Had this route been taken it would have been far more difficult to view Jesus as the new head of humanity supplanting Adam.

A Counter-Docetic Statement: Truly Born

An Actual Human Birth Points to Jesus' Humanity and Historicity

It is ironic now to realize that the birth narratives probably were not first proclaimed and transmitted to underscore Jesus' divinity, but his humanity. The primitive church was doing battle with Docetic views that doubted that the Savior could have been born at all. It is less pivotal in the narrative that Jesus was conceived *without* a father than that Jesus indeed *had* a mother and was conceived at all and born.

The counter-Docetic motif shines through the primitive rule of faith recalled and passed on by Ignatius of Antioch to the Trallians, where it is affirmed that Jesus Christ "is of the stock of David, who is of Mary, who was truly born, ate and drank" (Ignatius, *Trallians* 8:1–2, *CC*, p. 17; see also *COC* II, pp. 11–12; cf. Ignatius, *Smyrna* I.1, *ANF* I, p. 86; H. von Campenhausen, *The Virgin Birth in the Theology of the Ancient Church*).

The birth narratives rejected the view that Jesus was so divine that he could not have been born at all. He was "born from her truly and properly," "lest one should believe that from the Virgin He took on a mere appearance of flesh or in some other way a flesh which was not real, as Eutyches irreverently declared" (John II, *Letter to the Senate of Constantinople* [534], *CF*, p. 156). "He truly fed upon her milk" (Cyril of Jerusalem, *Catech. Lect.* IV.10, *LCC* IV, p. 104). "He did not pass through her as the sun shines through a glass, but brought her virgin flesh and blood with Him" (Luther, *Epiphany Serm. on Matt. 2:1–12* [1538], *WLS* I, p. 152, *WA* 46, 136; cf. Calvin, *Inst.* 2.13.4). Christianity is not embarrassed by the womb of Mary or chagrined that the Savior was normally born.

Doctrinal Cohesion

It is difficult to imagine how any alternative view could provide sufficient doctrinal cohesion. The virgin birth helps makes sense out of a whole series of doctrines. The correspondence of this teaching with other key points of doctrine may be summed up as follows: it is consistent with the witness to the preexistent Logos. It is consistent with the witness to the humanity of Christ. It is consistent with the witness to the deity of Christ. It is consistent with the teaching of the one and only divine-human Person. It is consient with the teaching of the sinlessness of Christ. It is consistent with the teaching of the new birth. Hence it is thought to be an apt way of understanding the beginning of God's saving act (Calvin, *Inst.* 2.13.3; 3.20.22).

The New Eve

Eve and Mary

Eve is not to be viewed alone, in isolation from Mary. Mary fulfills promises given to Eve.

The human condition has become neurotically tangled and knotted by the history of sin. "The knot of Eve's disobedience was loosed by the obedience of Mary. For what the virgin Eve had bound fast through unbelief, this did the virgin Mary set free through faith" (Irenaeus, *Ag. Her.* III.22, *ANF* I, p. 455; *Doc. Vat. II*, pp. 87–90; cf. R. D. Laing, *Knots*).

Note the parallelisms: the fall occurred by false belief; the incarnation began with true belief. Tertullian wrote: "What had been reduced to ruin by this sex, might by the selfsame sex be recovered to salvation. As Eve had believed the serpent, so Mary believed the angel. The delinquency which the one occasioned by believing, the other by believing effaced" (*On the Flesh of Christ* 17, *ANF* III, p. 325). As destruction of the old humanity occurred through the disobedience of a virgin, so the redemption of the world occurred through the obedience of a virgin (*Doc. Vat. II*, pp. 87–90; Cocceius, *Summa Theologiae* IV, p. 79, in Heppe, *RD*, p. 422).

The Back Reference from Mary to Eve

Hence Irenaeus spoke of "the back-reference from Mary to Eve" (Irenaeus, *Ag. Her.* III.22, *ANF* I, p. 455). This means that one best understands Eve from Mary, not alone Mary from Eve. Those who criticize Christianity for having a sexist view of Eve's fall may have forgotten the special role of Mary in the recovery of humanity from Eve's fall. Eve alone is an incomplete story. Mary is "the new Eve believing God's messenger with unhesitating faith" (*Doc. Vat. II, Dogmatic Constitution Lumen Gentium* 63, *CF* 718, p. 210). The narrative of Eve cannot rightly be read without thinking of Mary, as Adam's story is similarly incomplete apart from Christ.

Conception by Attentive Hearing

The bodily locus of the virginal conception was not portrayed in early Christian art as the vagina, but the ear: *"The conception was by hearing,"* as distinguished from the birth, which "was by the usual orifice through which children are born, even though there are some who concoct an idle tale of His being born from the side of the Mother of God" (John of Damascus, *OF* IV.14, *FC* 37, p. 365; italics added). In early iconography the Holy Spirit is not portrayed as coming into Mary's body physiologically by sexual transmission, but spiritually by attentive hearing. The birth was by "the usual orifice," the uterine birth canal; but the conception was by right hearing of the Word of God. Accordingly, Mary remains in Christian memory the primary prototype of human readiness to receive God's coming (Julian of Norwich, *IAIA*, pp. 161–62; cf. L. Boff, *The Maternal Face of God*). The gift of God's coming can only be received, it cannot be acquired.

Points to Justification and the Exclusion of Merit

There is nothing that Mary does beforehand that qualifies her as worthy for this decisive role, except to trust in God's promise, as did Abraham. Protestants have laid stress upon the meaning of the virgin birth as the exclusion of all human effort, parallel to the teaching of justification by faith alone without works of merit. This theme was anticipated by patristic writers, as when Hilary spoke of the incarnation as the sublime moment "when human nature without any precedent merits of good works, was joined to God the Word in the womb of the Virgin" (*Trin.* 15.26, *NPNF* 2 III, p. 224).

The Conception Uncoerced

The virginal conception occurred by consent, not coercion. The virgin Mother was receptive to the divine address, willing to trust God's purposes. As the incarnation was voluntary, so was the virginal conception. Mary was willing to be the human bodily means by which the Word became flesh, even as the Son became flesh voluntarily. Mary consented to divine persuasion rather than yielded to divine coercion. The overshadowing was not analogous to rape but involved consent.

The will of the virgin was not sanctified as a result of a decreed special privilege apart from her own willing or as an exemption from the destiny common to all humanity, but because she was responsive to God as an expression of her liberty; she consented, without impairment of the liberty that made her human. "It was only after having instructed her and persuaded her that God took her for His Mother and borrowed from her the flesh that She so greatly wished to lend Him" (Cabasilas, in M. Jugie, "Homilies mariales byzantines," *Patrologia orientalis* XIX, 3 [1925], p. 463, in Lossky, *MTEC*, p. 141).

Is Faith Mothered by Jesus' Care?

Sexual differentiation is both honored and transcended in gospel of Christ. Julian of Norwich astutely recognized that the mothering metaphor belongs also to "Jesus our true mother in nature from our first making. He is our true first mother in grace by the taking of our created nature." "A mother's service is nearest, readiest and surest. It is nearest because it is more natural. It is readiest because it is most loving. And it is surest because it is most true. This office no one but him alone might or could have performed to the full. We realize that all our mothers bear us for pain and what is that? But our true mother, Jesus—All love—alone bears us for joy and for endless living, blessed may he be! Thus he sus-

tains us within himself in love and hard labor, until the fulness of time,"
nurturing with sacramental food (Julian of Norwich, *RDL*, pp. 190–92).

Is Sexuality Diminished in the Nativity?

The virginal conception is not an embarrassed attempt to avoid sexuality. To the contrary, according to Gregory of Nyssa: "By the generative organs the immortality of the human race is preserved, and death's perpetual moves against us are, in a way rendered futile and ineffectual. By her successive generations nature is always filling up the deficiency. What unfitting notion, then, does our religion contain, if God was united with human life by the very means by which our nature wars on death" (*ARI* 28, *LCC* III, p. 307). Sexuality is not diminished but affirmed in the incarnation.

Adam's Creation Prefigured Christ's Birth

The Birth of Adam and Christ Compared

It seems odd that some are quick to affirm that God could breathe life and created goodness generally into all humanity, yet find it difficult to affirm that God could act specially or directly to breathe life into the Savior in a way distinctly befitting his mediatorial role. How it is that some readily affirm that God created Adam, but find it wrenching to hear that God might have taken some special initiative to create the New Adam? Why is the special conception of the Savior intrinsically a less plausible miracle of creation than the creation of humanity?

Compare the Genesis narrative of the surprising creation of Adam and Eve with the Lucan-Matthean nativity narratives telling the surprising story of God's own direct and special initiative in the birth of the Savior. In both cases natural material was utilized to fulfill a preternatural purpose—the body of Adam made from mud; the body of Jesus born through an ordinary period of gestation and delivery.

The Miracle of Human Creation Itself Prefigurative of the Miracle of the Birth of Jesus

Ancient exegetes marveled that the miracle of human creation was itself prefigurative of the miracle of the birth of Jesus, just as the fall of Adam became prefigurative of restoration in Christ, and the Protoevangelium to Eve was prefigurative of the annunciation and of Mary's responsiveness to God's will to renew humanity (Rom. 5:14; 1 Cor. 15:22, 45; 1 Tim. 2:11–15; Irenaeus, *Ag. Her.* III.19–23, *ANF* I, pp. 448–57; John

Chrysostom, *Hom. on First Cor.* XXXIX, *NPNF* 1 XXI, pp. 233–43; *Hom. on Tim.* IX, *NPNF* 1 XIII, pp. 435–37).

The Event and Its Meaning

Established by Canon

Jerome's language displayed the high regard for canonical Scripture that prevailed in ancient ecumenism: "We believe that God was born of the Virgin, because we read it" (*The Perpetual Virginity of Blessed Mary* 21, *NPNF* 2 VI, p. 344). Classical exegetes assumed that the historicity of the virgin birth was firmly established quite simply by canonical authority (Ursinus, *CHC*, pp. 205–207).

Yet the simple fact that the narrative is found in Scripture does not make it immune to historical investigation. Faith seeks to make such a historical investigation on the basis of the fullest possible assessment of evidence. Yet this must not be a limited inquiry that would rule out the possibility of the alleged event before one makes the investigation.

The Reductionist Bias:
Shall the Special Conception Be Ruled Out A Priori?

The birth narratives have indeed found their way into the canon. They cannot belatedly be arbitrarily weeded out of the canon on the grounds that they do not fit neatly into an empiricist worldview. The historicity of these reports is subject to continuing investigation and debate and not easily resolved exclusively on historical or evidentiary grounds (V. Taylor, *Historical Evidence for the Virgin Birth*; D. Edwards, *Virgin Birth in Faith and History*; cf. J. Orr, *Virgin Birth of Christ*; J. G. Machen, *Virgin Birth of Christ*). Yet if one begins by assuming dogmatically that there can be no miracle and most definitely no virgin birth, then has not a philosophical predisposition prevailed over inquiry into history? Is one then making a fair and open historical inquiry?

Christianity does not take special pleasure in seeing natural or biological law circumvented. Yet nature is not best defended by trying to prove philosophically that God cannot act either within or beyond it. Augustine argued that no miracle could be known without the reliability of natural law (*Trin.* III.5–9, *NPNF* 1 III, pp. 59–63; *CG* X.13–32, *NPNF* 1 II, pp. 189–204).

It is indeed probable that some Christians in the first century accepted Jesus as Lord who had not heard of the virginal conception. Hence, it is arguable that the belief in its historicity is not indispensable to faith and is not an absolute article of faith necessary for salvation.

THE MANNER OF GOD'S COMING

Yet if the event is interpreted away as merely projection or myth or incidentally functional for a particular audience (Tillich, *Syst. Theol.* II, p. 160; Bultmann, *TNT* I, pp. 50, 131), the nativity narrative is in effect disowned. Those who carve away from the narrative all historical reference by regarding it merely as a symbol of hope or myth of fulfillment tend to leave the narrative bereft of meaning, even if they try to salvage it in some other way.

That it has been considered an article of faith by the mainstream of ecumenical Christianity is nonetheless evident from its persistence in the creedal traditions. The virgin birth remains an intensely symbolic article, yet it did not function merely as an abstract symbol in classic Christianity but purported to attest an event.

Why the Genealogies?

Accompanying the nativity narratives are genealogies that raise intriguing questions.

Why Are Such Notorious Sinners Included in the Genealogies?

One remarkable fact of the genealogies is that they are not embarrassed by the notorious sinners in the messianic line. Luther commented: "The first thing to be noted in the lineage of Christ is the fact that the Evangelist lists in it four women who are very notorious in Scripture: Thamar, Rahab, Ruth, and Bathsheba. But nothing is said about the women of good repute: Sarah, Rebecca, Leah, and Rachel. Now Jerome and others have been concerned about the reason why this was done. I hold that the first group was mentioned because these women were sinners and that Christ also wanted to be born in that large family [*Geschlecht*] in which prostitutes and fornicators are found in order to indicate what a love He bore sinners" (Luther, *Serm. on Matt.* [8 September, 1522], *WLS* I, p. 151; *WA* 10 III, 327).

Why Two Different Routes of Davidic Descent?

The main purpose of both genealogies was to establish Davidic descent, to show that Jesus fulfilled the messianic expectations of Israel (Irenaeus, *Ag. Her.* III, 16–17, *ANF* I, pp. 441–45; Pearson, *EC* I, p. 313). Matthew's registry of Davidic descent moves from past to present through Joseph, son of David. Luke's registry of Davidic descent is from present to past through Heli, the father of Mary. Matthew's descent begins with Abraham and proceeds to Christ. Luke's begins with Christ and recedes all the way back to Adam (Tertullian, *On the Flesh of Christ* 22, *AEG* I, pp. 203–204; Origen, *John* I.4, *AEG* I, p. 202; *Hom. 28 on Luke, AEG* I, pp. 206–209).

Is Joseph Only Legally in the Descent?

Does Matthew's genealogy, which traces Jesus' ancestry not through Mary but through Joseph, inconsistently imply that Joseph was Jesus' physiological father ("inconsistently" because Matthew makes it abundantly clear that Joseph "had no union with her," Matt. 1:25)? The explanation is rather that it was the prevailing custom to trace lineage not through the mother but through the father's side, and without such patrilineal tracing first-century readers might have found the genealogy puzzling and implausible.

The Damascene commented: "One should know, however, that it was not customary for the Hebrews, nor for sacred Scripture either, to give the pedigrees of women. . . . Consequently, it was sufficient to show the descent of Joseph" (John of Damascus, OF IV.14, FC 37, p. 362; cf. Eusebius, CH I.7; Tho. Aq., ST III Q31, II, pp. 2185–87). The "descent is reckoned by the male line," but this is only "as far as the political order is concerned," for this legal status "does not gainsay the fact that the woman's seed must share in the act of generation" (Calvin, Inst. 2.13.4). So Matthew recorded the Abrahamic and Davidic descent of the Messiah, and then described his birth and infancy as a fulfillment of Old Testament prophecies (Origen, Comm. on Matt. 1:1 18, AEG I, pp. 201–202; Ambrose, Comm. on Matt. 1, MPL XV, pp. 1593–1610).

Luke's genealogy arguably traces Jesus' line through Mary (due to the ambiguous phrase "son of Heli," [Luke 3:23], for Joseph was arguably Jacob's son by birth [Matt. 1:16], and Heli's son by marriage; yet others argue that Luke also traces through Joseph by assuming that the Jacob of Matthew 1:16 and the Heli of Luke 3:23 were brothers, one being Joseph's father and the other his uncle). Luke clarified that Jesus was not literally or biologically the son of Joseph but "was thought" to be the son of Joseph (Luke 3:23; Eusebius, Quaestiones ad Stephanum 2–3, MPG 22, pp. 892ff., 958ff.). The syntax before "Joseph" in the phrase "He was the son, so it was thought, of Joseph" (3:23) links Jesus directly with Heli, according to some, and would thus take Joseph altogether out of Luke's genealogical line (Africanus, Epist. to Aristides, AEG I, pp. 204–206; see also Eusebius, CH I.7). Hence it is argued that Matthew's genealogy follows the line of Joseph (Jesus' legal but not biological father), while Luke follows the line of Mary.

Such judgments, however, remain clouded with uncertainty. According to one ancient tradition, "Herod indeed destroyed the genealogies, hoping that he would then appear as well born as anyone else. But a few careful people preserved private genealogies, either from recollections of the names or from copies; among them are those which are called *desposunoi* because they belong to the Saviour's family" (Africanus, *Epist. to Aristides, AEG* I, p. 206). In the absence of fuller information, it is extremely difficult to find a theory that adequately harmonizes the genealogies, yet classic exegetes argued that they are not intrinsically contradictory (Eusebius, *Questiones ad Stephanum, AEG* I, pp. 207–209).

Better to approach the identity of the Child poetically than as a matter of historical evidence:

> What Child is this, who, laid to rest,
> On Mary's lap is sleeping?
> Whom angels greet with anthems sweet,
> While shepherds watch are keeping?
>
> This, this is Christ the King,
> Whom shepherds guard and angels sing:
> Haste, haste to bring Him laud,
> The Babe, the Son of Mary.
>
> Why lies He in such mean estate
> Where ox and ass are feeding?
> Good Christian, fear: for sinners here
> The silent Word is pleading
>   (William C. Dix, *MH*, p. 109).

THE MOTHER OF THE SAVIOR

The discussion of Mary the mother of the Savior is complementary to the discussion of Jesus Christ the Son. The problem many Protestants have had with the Roman Marian tradition is that it has seemed at times to have become inordinately detached from its Christological center or disconnected unproportionally as a separate subject of inquiry.

Two movements have occurred simultaneously in recent years to correct this disproportion: Protestants have sought to reaquaint themselves with classical Christian reasoning about Mary; and Catholics under the guidance of the Second Vatican Council have reintegrated Marian teaching into Christology, rather than appearing to view it as relatively unconnected (*Lutherans and Catholics in Dialogue* I–III; Outler, *A Methodist Observer at Vatican II; Doc. of Vat. II*, pp. 85–96).

The consensual teaching concerning Mary upon which Christians generally agree is the chief interest of this discussion. Is there an ecumenical teaching on Mary generally received by Catholics, Orthodox, and

Protestants? The place to begin is with the *theotokos* doctrine largely shared by East and West.

In What Sense Did the Virgin Give Birth to God?

Theotokos *as a Self-limited Formulation with Disclaimers*

In ascribing to Mary the term *theotokos*, "bearer of God," there has never been intended the slightest implication that Mary gave birth to the Godhead, but only to the incarnate Son (Council of Ephesus, *NPNF* 2 XIV, pp. 206–215; Athanasius, *Four Discourses Ag. Arians* II.14f. *NPNF* 2, IV, pp. 348–57; Luther, *WLS* III, p. 1255; *WA* 45, 558; cf. *Expos. Isaiah 53* [1550], 23, 476).

"We do not, however, say that the Virgin Mary gave birth to the unity of this Trinity, but only to the Son who alone assumed our nature" (Eleventh Council of Toledo, *CF*, p. 170; *SCD* 284, p. 110). The intention is accurately stated by John II (A.D. 533–535), that Mary is "truly the one who bore God, and the *Mother of God's Word*, become incarnate from her" (*Epist.* 3, *SCD* 202, p. 83, italics added; see also *SCD* 20, 91, 111, 113, 144). "We do not say that God was born of her in the sense that the divinity of the Word has its beginning of being from her, but in the sense that God the Word Himself . . . did in the last days come for our salvation to dwell in her womb" (John of Damascus, *OF* III.12, *FC* 37, p. 292; Cyril of Alexandria, *Third Letter to Nestorius*, *LCC* III, pp. 349–54; Chemnitz, *TNC*, p. 101).

Triunity and Nativity: The Birth of the Son Enabled by the Spirit

The Spirit "gave her [Mary] the power both to receive the divinity of the Word and to beget" (John of Damascus, *OF* III.2, *FC* 37, p. 270). The Holy Spirit is the Sanctifier in the Christian economy, who enables creatures to receive the holy One. The Holy Spirit hallowed the flesh, the womb into which our Lord entered and set apart the mother for her incomparable function (Tho. Aq., *ST* III Q35, II, pp. 2203–10). "For the holy Virgin did not give birth to a mere man but to true God, and not to God simply, but to God made flesh" (John of Damascus, *OF* III.12, *FC* 37, p. 292).

"These are interior subtleties of the Redemptional economy of the Triune God which none who would understand the Scriptures may despise, though none can find them out unto perfection" (Pope, *Compend.* II, p. 151). We are dealing with a mystery without analogy, "neither grasped by reason nor illustrated by example. Were it grasped by reason, it would not be wonderful; were it illustrated by example, it would not be unique" (Eleventh Council of Toledo, *CF*, p. 169; see *SCD* 282, p. 110).

Protestant Reception of Theotokos

Among Protestants, Zwingli early argued that "the Virgin should be called the Mother of God, *Theotokos*" (*An Expos. of the Faith*, LCC XXIV, p. 256), a view affirmed by Luther and uncontested by Calvin (*Inst.* 2.14.4; *BOC*, p. 595). Barth regarded it as "a test of the proper understanding of the incarnation" that "we do not reject the description of Mary as the 'mother of God'" (Barth *CD* I/2, p. 138).

Why "*Theotokos*"?—Nestorius and Cyril

The Nestorian Formula Threatened the Personal Unity of Christ

Recall that it had been asserted by the Nestorians that there were two persons, a divine person distinguished from a human person, that this human person was conceived by the Virgin Mary and born, and that the divine person was later added or appended in some way to this human person. The crisis emerged when Anastasius publicly denied to Mary the title, "Mother of God" (or "bearer of God," *Theotokos*)—the implication being that she was not mother of God but only of Christ (*Christotokos*) to whom the person of the Word of God had united himself. This amounted to saying that Christ is two persons, one divine and one human.

The Council of Ephesus

It was principally to guard the teaching of the distinctive unity of the Person of Jesus Christ against Nestorianism that "Mother of God" was applied to Mary. "For, as He who was born of her is true God, so is she truly Mother of God" (John of Damascus, *OF* III.12, *FC* 37, p. 292). Cyril of Alexandria and the Council of Ephesus (A.D. 431) cut through to the essential point, that the one born of the Virgin was Son of God at the time of his conception and birth.

The formula of the Council of Ephesus established that Mary was the Mother of God "according to his human nature," but not so "according to his divine nature": "She brought forth, according to the flesh, the Word of God made flesh" (Cyril of Alexandria, *Third Letter to Nestorius*, LCC III, pp. 349–54; Council of Ephesus, *SCD* 113, 114, p. 50; Jacobs, *SCF*, p. 135). Hence *theotokos* "does not mean that the nature of the Word or His divinity received the beginning of its existence from the holy Virgin, but that, since the holy body, animated by a rational soul, which the Word united to Himself according to the hypostasis (*kath'hupostasin*), was born from her, the Word was born according to the flesh" (Cyril of Alexandria, *Second Letter to Nestorius*, *CF*, p. 149).

The Typological Imagination

The virginal conception became the basis for the vast exercise of poetic and typological imagination in early Christianity: "In this the Mother of God, in a manner surpassing the course of nature, made it possible for the Fashioner to be fashioned" (John of Damascus, *OF* III.12, *FC* 37, p. 295). "Without leaving the bosom of the Father, the Word came to dwell uncircumscribed in the womb" (John of Damascus, *OF* III.7, *FC* 37, p. 282; X.34, *LCC* VII, p. 360). While "as God, He had no mother," yet "as a man on the cross" Jesus "acknowledged His human mother and commended her in a most human fashion to the Apostle He loved most" (Augustine, *Faith and the Creed* 4.9, *FC* 27, p. 326).

St. Methodius of Olympus, a martyr of the Diocletian persecution (d. ca. 311), gave this poetic eulogy to the Blessed Virgin:

> Thou art the circumscription, so to speak,
> of Him who cannot be circumscribed;
> the root of the most beautiful flower;
> the mother of the Creator;
> the nurse of the Nourisher;
> the circumference of Him who embraces all things;
> the upholder of Him who upholds all things by His word;
> the gate through which God appears in the flesh;
> the tongs of that cleansing coal;
> the bosom in small of that bosom which is all-containing . . .
> Thou hast lent to God, who stands in need of nothing,
> that flesh which He had not,
> in order that the Omnipotent might become
> that which it was his good pleasure to be. . . .
>
> Thou hast clad the Mighty One with that beauteous panoply
> of the body by which it has become possible
> for Him to be seen by mine eyes. . . .
>
> Hail! hail! mother and handmaid of God.
> Hail! hail! thou to whom the great Creditor of all
> is a debtor
>   (*Orat. Concerning Simeon and Anna* 10, *ANF* VI, p. 390).

Divergent Views of the Mother of the Savior

The points at which differences remain between Protestants, Catholics, and Orthodox largely have to do with the degree to which it is possible or necessary to extend the teaching of *theotokos* to include other affirmations such as Mary's sinlessness, immaculate conception, perpetual virginity, and bodily assumption into heaven.

The Eastern Marian Tradition

John of Damascus stated the classic consensus that Christ "was conceived in the immaculate womb of the Virgin, not by the will of man, nor by concupiscence, nor by the intervention of a husband, nor by pleasurable generation, but of the Holy Ghost" (John of Damascus, *OF* III.2, *FC* 37, p. 269; cf. Origen, *Ag. Celsus* VI.34–36, *ANF* IV, pp. 588–89). The medieval scholastics of the West generally argued that Mary herself was free from all sin, original as well as actual (Tho. Aq., *ST* III Q27, II, pp. 2163–70; cf. Anselm, *VCOS*, pp. 50–63).

Eastern Orthodoxy has generally taught that "She remained and remains a virgin before the birth, during the birth, and after the birth of the Saviour; and therefore is called *ever-virgin*" (*Russian Catech.*, *COC* II, pp. 471–72). The impeccability of the virgin was not widely discussed in the East, where dogmatic definitions did not specifically exempt Mary from the general truth that "death came to all men, because all sinned" (Rom. 5:12).

A twelfth-century panegyric to Mary (attributed to Peter of Damaskos) reflects the essential basis of a profound Eastern Marian piety ordered in relation to Christ's lordship: "Blessed Queen of the universe, you know that we sinners have no intimacy with the God whom you have borne. But, putting our trust in you, through your mediation we your servants prostrate ourselves before the Lord: for you can freely approach Him since He is your son and our God" (*Treasury of Divine Knowledge, Philokal.* III, pp. 129–30).

The Protestant Marian Tradition

Protestants have debated whether Mary remained perpetually a virgin (Zwingli asserted that she did, *Opera* III [Tiguri, 1581], p. 188; Peter Martyr thought not, cf. Heppe, *RD*, p. 422). Some Reformed scholastics have argued that the doctrine of perpetual virginity is not necessary, but probable, for which affirmation or denial is not a matter of an article of faith, yet it has remained as a pious belief of many that Mary "after untainted parturition retained the bloom of virginity" (Heidegger, *Corpus Theologiae* [1700] XVII, p. 18; Heppe, *RD*, p. 423).

Protestants have shifted the question of Mary toward a relatively greater soteriological emphasis upon the *benefits* received from "the holy conception," wherein the Mediator "covers over with his innocence and perfect holiness the sinfulness in which I have been conceived" (*Heidel-*

berg Catech. Q36, *BOC* 4.036; cf. H. Küng and J. Moltmann, *Mary in the Church*).

The Roman Marian Tradition

Key affirmations of the Marian tradition in Roman Catholic teaching are:

(1) The perpetual virginity of Mary, "her virginity remaining equally inviolate after the birth" (Lateran Council [A.D. 649], *CF* 703, p. 201; see also *SCD* 256, p. 102), and equally inviolate before birth, in birth (Siricius, *Epist. 9 to Anysius, SCD* 91, p. 39; *SCD* 282; Augustine, *Concerning Faith of Things Not Seen* 5, *NPNF* 1 III, p. 339; Tho. Aq., *ST* III Q28.4, II, p. 2170), and "after childbirth" (Sixtus IV, *Cum Praeexcelsa* [1476], *SCD* 734, p. 236). The view "that Mary seems to have brought forth many children" is rejected on the grounds that the term "brothers" (*adelphoi*) can also mean more generally "relatives" or "cousins" (Siricius, *SCD* 91, p. 39; cf. Matt. 12:46–49; 13:55; Mark 3:31–34; 6:3; John 7:3; Luke 8:19–21; Acts 1:14; M.-J. Lagrange, *Comm. on St. Mark*, pp. 79–93).

(2) Mary's freedom from original sin was "preserved immune from all stain of original sin" (Pius IX, *Bull Ineffabilis Deus* [1854], *CF* 709, p. 204; *DS* 2803), hence conceived immaculate (Sixtus IV, *SCD* 734, 735, pp. 236–37; see also *SCD* 792, 1073; Tho. Aq., *ST* III Q31, II, p. 2186). The Roman teaching of the virgin's bodily assumption into heaven is that Mary, "when the course of her earthly life was finished, was taken up body and soul into the glory of heaven" (Pius XII, *Apostolic Constitution Munificentissimus Deus* 1950, *CF* 715, p. 207; see *SCD* 2291, 3031, 3903).

(3) Mary's active intercession continues for all humanity, so as to play a leading role in Christ's redemptive work (Council of Nicaea II, *NPNF* 2 XIV, pp. 533–34; Sixtus IV, *Cum Praeexcelsa, SCD* 734, p. 236). Irenaeus had early approached this delicate point indirectly, that "Through her obedience she became cause of salvation both for herself and for the whole human race" (*Ag. Her.* III, 22.4, *ANF* I, p. 455). She was later viewed as the "primary minister in the distribution of the divine graces" (Pius X, *Encyclical Letter Ad Diem Illum* [1904], *CF* 712, p. 206; *DS* 3370), the mediatrix of all graces (*SCD* 1940, 1978) and in that special sense a coredemptrix with Christ (*SCD* 1978), yet such language is used so as to "in no way diminish or add to the dignity and efficacy of Christ the one Mediator" (*Dogmatic Constitution Lumen Gentium* 62, *Doc. Vat.* II, *CF* 717, p. 209).

"The Credo of the People of God" summarizes current Roman teaching: "Because of her close and indissoluble connection with the mystery of the Incarnation and Redemption the most Blessed Virgin Mary, the

Immaculate, at the end of her earthly life was assumed body and soul into heaven, and so became like her Son, who himself rose from the dead, anticipating thereby the destiny of the just. We believe that the most holy Mother of God, the new Eve, the Mother of the Church, continues in heaven her maternal role towards the members of Christ, in that she cooperates with the birth and growth of divine life in the souls of the redeemed" (Paul VI, *Doc. Vat.* II, p. 391).

Marian Teaching More Generally Agreed Upon

Among Marian teachings of ancient and modern Roman Catholicism with which Protestants have less difficulty in agreeing are the following:

(1) Mary is a type of womanhood that transcends the setting of a particular culture. "First, the Virgin Mary has always been proposed to the faithful by the Church as an example to be imitated, not precisely in the type of life she led, and much less for the socio-cultural background in which she lived and which today scarcely exists anywhere. She is held as an example to the faithful rather for the way in which in her own particular life, she fully and responsibly accepted the will of God (cf. Luke 1:38); because she received the word of God and acted on it; because charity and a spirit of service were the driving force of her actions; because she was the first and the most perfect of Christ's disciples. All of this has a permanent and universal exemplary value" (Paul VI, *Apostolic Exhortation Marialis Cultus* [1974], *AAS* 77, sec. 35–36, pp. 113ff.; *CF* 719, pp. 210–11).

Christians in many different cultures, historical periods, and social settings have seen "in Jesus' mother the outstanding type of womanhood and the prominent example of a life lived according to the Gospel," yet in celebrating her faith the church "does not bind herself to any particular expression of an individual cultural epoch or to the particular anthropological ideas underlying such expressions" (Paul VI, *Apostolic Exhortation Marialis Cultus* [1974], *AAS* sec. 35–36, pp. 113ff., *CF* 719, p. 211).

(2) Mary is a "type of the Church, or exemplar, in the order of faith, charity and perfect union with Christ" (*Dogmatic Constitution Lumen Gentium* 63, *Doc. Vat.* II, *CF* 718, p. 209; cf. Ambrose, *Concerning Virgins* II.2, *NPNF* 2 X, pp. 374–76). Insofar as the mystery of the church may be understood through metaphors of motherhood and virginity, Mary stands out as "an eminent and unequalled exemplar of both motherhood and virginity" (*Dogmatic Constitution Lumen Gentium* 63, *Doc. Vat.* II, *CF* 718, p. 210). Mary is understood "not merely as a passive instrument in the hands of God, but as freely co-operating in the salvation of mankind by her faith and obedience" (*Dogmatic Constitution Lumen Gentium* 56, *Doc. Vat.* II, *CF* 716, p. 209).

(3) Mary remains for many a sign of hope amid the crisis of modern man, "torn as he often is between anguish and hope, defeated by the sense of his own limitations and assailed by limitless aspirations, troubled in his mind and divided in his heart, uncertain before the riddle of death, oppressed by loneliness while yearning for fellowship, a prey to boredom and disgust. She shows forth the victory of hope over anguish, of fellowship over solitude, of peace over anxiety, of joy and beauty over boredom and disgust" (Paul IV, *Apostolic Exhortation Marialis Cultus* [1974], *CF* 720, p. 211).

Theology of Christmas

One can ask about the *meaning* of the virginal conception even if the *fact* or historicity of that event has not been universally established. The question of why the church remembered Jesus as born of a virgin and what that *meant* remains intriguing, whatever the status of historical evidence. The persistence and ecumenical reception of the doctrine in the absence of certain forms of demonstrable historical evidence make for an important historical fact in itself.

The Liturgical Persistence of the Nativity

The extraordinary liturgical importance of the virgin birth for the celebration of the incarnation at Christmastide makes the teaching hard to dismiss. Or if one attempts to dismiss it, one does so at the risk of resisting a broad church consensus that is written into the most widely shared baptismal and catechetical confessions of historic Christianity.

Anchor of the Christian Year

There are many in the modern world who know very little about Jesus other than the birth narratives, yet they know these by heart. Jesus' life begins with incarnation and ends with resurrection. These two events form the two key moments of the Christian year—Christmas and Easter. The virgin birth and the bodily resurrection are anchor points of the salvation event (cf. R. E. Brown, *The Virginal Conception and the Bodily Resurrection of Jesus*). It is fitting that the salvation event begin and end appropriately. It seems implausible to retain the resurrection as a key point of confession yet rule out the nativity narratives as having no theological value.

Metaphors of Nativity

That the birth was attested in Bethlehem (literally "the house of bread," from whom comes the Bread from heaven, John 6:32–33) and of

Davidic descent was from the outset viewed as fulfillment of messianic prophecy (Mic. 5:2; Matt. 2:2, 6; 1 Sam. 16:18; Luke 2:4). The angelic hosts celebrated his coming (Luke 2:10–14; Tho. Aq., *ST* III, Q36.5 II pp. 2214–15). The stories of Simeon and Anna in the Temple (Luke 2:22–39) and the wise men (Matt. 2:1–11; Isa. 9; Tho. Aq., *ST* III, Q36 II, pp. 2210–18), indicate that he came as a light both to Jews and Gentiles—the whole world (Hag. 2:6–9; Tho. Aq., *ST* III, Q37.3–4 II, pp. 2221–23). The gifts of gold, frankincense, and myrrh were gifts befitting his hidden royal identity yet to be revealed.

Why did this teaching appear so early, and why has it been sustained so tenaciously? The incarnation was such a unique event that it was unthinkable that it could have been treated merely as an ordinary birth. Characteristically the church has not argued for the moral uniqueness of Jesus on the basis of a biological theory of the uniqueness of his birth. Rather it has simply pointed to the mystery of God's coming in our midst, in God's own way and time (Baxter, *PW* XIX, pp. 70-73).

Christ's Birth and the Christian's Rebirth

Finally, Christ's birth anticipates and makes way for the rebirth of the believer: "O holy Child of Bethlehem! Descend to us, we pray; Cast out our sin and enter in; Be born in us to-day" (Phillips Brooks, *HPEC*, p. 68). This is the church that, imitating his mother, daily gives birth to his members yet remains virgin (Augustine, *Enchiridion* 37–57, *NPNF* 1 III, pp. 250–56; cf. *BCP*, "Collect for Christmas Day").

> Gentle Mary laid her Child
> Lowly in a manger
> There He lay, the undefiled,
> To the world a Stranger.
> Such a Babe in such a place,
> Can He be the Saviour?
> Ask the saved of all the race
> Who have found His favor
> (Joseph S. Cook, *MH* 107).

Leo wrote (beautifully): "In adoring the birth of Our Savior, we find ourselves celebrating our own nativity; for the birth of Christ is the birth of the Christian people, and the Christmas of the Head is the Christmas of the Body" (Anger, *MB*, p. 43n).

CHAPTER 6

One Person—
Truly God, Truly Human

Four elementary scriptural teachings are essential for understanding the distinctive personhood of Christ:

1. Christ is truly God.
2. He is truly human.
3. He is one person.
4. There are in him two distinct natures, divine and human (*SCD* 18, 20, 33, 42, 111, 143, 148), clearly distinguishable and substantially different (Lateran Council [A.D. 649], *SCD* 260, p. 102), yet undivided, inseparable, and unconfused (*SCD* 148, 288, 290; *BOC*, p. 592).

Having discussed the first two points, we now turn to the last two.

The subjects now to be addressed are among the most difficult in biblical teaching, for an attempt is being made to show how Jesus is truly God yet truly human as one person. It might seem merciful to say: "Skip these pages and go on to the temptation narrative." But one who wishes to understand classic thinking about Christ cannot skip over that part where the unity of his divinity and humanity is congruently interpreted and duly qualified. As multiplication tables must be memorized to be functionally applied, so in the study of ecumenical theology, one saves time by doing something like memorizing formula-like codes showing basic consensual definitions in summary form (Seven Ecumenical Councils, *NPNF* 2 XIV).

No code phrase has been more widely useful to classic Christology than *two natures, one person* (Council of Chalcedon, *SCD* 148, p. 61; *Russian Catech.*, *COC* II, p. 471). To make this puzzling formula presently useful is the purpose of this chapter.

SCRIPTURAL GROUNDING OF THE PERSONAL UNION

Christ is as simply God as if he were not man, and as simply man as if he were not God (Newman, *Ath*. II, p. 326). First it must be established that the theandric premise is required by Scripture itself, not merely an appendage of tradition added to Scripture.

The Union of Two Natures in One Person in Scripture

The Scriptures represent Jesus Christ as having a divine nature and a human nature in a single undivided personality (John 1:1-18; 9:48-59; Hilary, *Trin*. VIII.13, *NPNF* 2 IX, p. 141). The notion that two natures are united in one person is constantly assumed though not formally defined in the New Testament.

The Hypostatic (Personal) Union

This scriptural teaching has become known in the tradition as the *personal union of the divine and human natures*, or the *hypostatic* (= *personal*) *union*, from *hypostasis*, or personal subsistences in the Godhead, as distinguished from their common essence or substance (*ousia*) as God (Chalcedon, *CC*, pp. 35-36; II Constantinople, *CC*, p. 46). Christ's personhood is as singularly unified as any one person can be, yet in a profound, mysterious union of humanness and deity (Tho. Aq., *SCD* IV, pp. 152-55, 175-82; *BOC*, p. 472, 515).

Is He One or Two?

The personal union is not a conflation or mixture of two composite things so the person could be said to be part human, part divine (Chalcedon, *CC*, p. 36; Hooker, *Laws of Ecclesiastical Polity*, bk. V, chaps. 51-56; Owen, *Person of Christ, Works* I, pp. 223ff.). "What He was He laid aside; what He was not He assumed; not that He became two, but He deigned to be One made out of the two" (Gregory Nazianzen, *Orat*. XXXVII.2, *NPNF* 2 VII, p. 338).

Predicates Applied to One Person as Human, as Divine

In the New Testament, predicates are constantly applied to the one person that are taken from either or both the human nature and/or the divine nature. In some passages these two natures are held in tension in a single compact phrase, such as: they have "crucified the Lord of glory" (1 Cor. 2:8). It is not uncommon to hear Jesus Christ attested as truly God in one passage, truly human in another, and both in the next (John 11:1–43). The one subject, Jesus Christ, is described as divine and human.

Theanthropos

Hence the redeemer is called *theanthropos*, God-man, the single person being undivided. The unitive term "God-man" (or God-as-a-man) is preferred to the more general "God-in-humanity" or "godly person" because these phrases might be used equally to speak of the union of Christ with every believer, while no believer is rightly spoken of as "God-man."

Union, Not an Oscillation

Nor did the incarnate One oscillate between being partly or occasionally God and partly or occasionally human (Newman, *Ath.* II., pp. 240–42). To allege this obscures the central paradoxical point of Christ's existence: he was always God and nothing less, expressed within the frame of time and structures of human consciousness.

The New Testament actively proclaimed the full deity and full humanity of the Lord and left for later reflection the formal definition of their precise correlation (Hilary, *Trin.* IX, *NPNF* 2 IX, p. 155–81; Wells, *PC*, pp. 65–66). Scripture repeatedly portrays Jesus Christ as one person, a single subject self, an undivided personality in whom these two natures are inseparably united (Ursinus, *CHC*, pp. 208–12; G. Berkouwer, *The Person of Christ*).

Technical language eventually became necessary to defend against ingenious distortions of central scriptural teaching. It is useful today to see how this technical language stood as a reasonable defense of scriptural teaching.

Texts Expressing Union

Scripture teaches the union but does not use specific defensively oriented language to describe the mode or manner in which that union is actualized. The purpose of Christology is rightly to reflect upon that union so as to guard against distortions and enable its truthful proclamation (Tho. Aq., *SCG* IV, pp. 57–74, 174ff.; Newman, *Ath.* II, pp. 191–93; 223–25).

Prophetic Expectation of Immanuel

There is already embedded in the messianic prophecy of Isaiah the rudiments of the two-natures teaching: the one promised will be *vere homo*, a truly human child born, and *vere Deus*, truly divine, to be called

Mighty God (Isa. 9:6). The name "Immanuel" anticipates the union: "The virgin will be with child and will give birth to a son, and will call him Immanuel" (Isa. 7:14; Irenaeus, *Ag. Her.* III.21, *ANF* I, pp. 451-54). The mystery of the God-man was thus prophetically announced. The prophetic testimony, seen in the light of its fulfillment in the New Testament, seems clear in retrospect, but the distinctive way of God's coming would remain an enigma until the coming of Jesus (Gregory Thaumaturgus, *Four Hom.*, *ANF* VI, pp. 58-71).

The scriptural testimony to the union of divine and human natures in the person of Christ was clearly formulated in the Epistles and narratively corroborated in the Gospels:

The Personal Union in Pauline Teaching

1. The divine Son is of Davidic descent. In Romans, Paul spoke of Christ as a descendant of David according to his human nature (1:3) and Son of God according to the Spirit of holiness (1:4)—dual sonship that required dual natures in a single person. Paul did not hesitate to speak in the same breath of the "human ancestry of Christ, who is God over all" (Rom. 9:5).

2. He is crucified Lord. He is "Lord of glory" whose human body the rulers of this age have crucified (1 Cor. 2:8; John Chrysostom, *Hom. on First Cor.* VII, *NPNF* 1 XII, pp. 35-36).

3. He is sent Son. What the law could not do, "God did by sending his own Son in the likeness of sinful flesh" (Rom. 8:3). Hence the Savior who appears within the distortions of human history is at the same time nothing less than God's own Son.

4. He is reconciler on the cross. The dual nature of the person of Christ is expressed throughout the New Testament Epistles, but nowhere more explicitly than in Colossians as "the image of the invisible God, the firstborn over all creation," in whom "God was pleased to have all his fullness dwell, and through him to reconcile to himself all things" (Col. 1:15-20), but this could only occur "through his blood, shed on the cross" (v. 20).

5. As form of God, he took the form of a Servant. The same personal union is reflected in Philippians' description of Christ as being in very nature God (*morphē theou*), yet with respect to his humanity "made himself nothing, taking the very nature of a servant [*morphēn doulou*], being made in human likeness" (Phil. 2:6-8).

6. He is one Mediator. The Pastorals also reflect the view that Christ is one person uniting two natures, for in Christ we behold "one God and one mediator between God and men, the man Christ Jesus, who gave

himself as a ransom for all men" (1 Tim. 2:5), who "appeared in a body, was vindicated by the Spirit" (3:16). All these phrases of the Pauline tradition require the theandric premise.

The Union in Hebrews

A more systematic development of Christ's two natures in one person is found in the Epistle to the Hebrews. The first chapter asserts and celebrates Christ's divinity ("his Son, whom he appointed heir of all things," Heb. 1:2), the second chapter develops Christ's humanity ("he too shared in their humanity," 2:14), and the remaining passages set forth the mystery of the interfacing of the two natures—"the Son of God" who is able "to sympathize with our weaknesses" (Heb. 4:14–16; 3:1; Luther, *Lectures on Hebrews* 3, *LW* 29, pp. 143–44; *BOC*, p. 489). This one person, sent from God to humanity, is the representative of humanity and as such the high priest petitioning from man to God, who "through the eternal Spirit" offered his humanity "unblemished to God" (Heb. 9:14).

The Hypostatic Union in John

The prologue of the Gospel of John attests that the Logos, the one and only God, became flesh. The union of the human and divine natures is viewed as the dwelling of God among us (John 1:1–18). The divine Logos was not diminished by the union with the flesh. To behold the Son is to behold the Father (John 14:9). The Son is given authority to bestow life (John 5:24, 40; 6:27; 10:10), to judge (5:22), to answer supplications (14:14; 15:7). Faith in the Son is the same as faith in God (John 12:44; 14:1; Augustine, *Comm. on John* LIV, *NPNF* 1 VII, pp. 296–99).

Two Language Strata United

The Theandric Premise Necessary for Reading the New Testament

Scriptural attestations to Jesus Christ are characterized by the constant use of both language strata—human and divine. Hardly a page of the New Testament lacks implicit reference to the Christ who is true God without ceasing to be truly human and unreservedly human without ceasing to be eternal Son.

Names and titles are ascribed to this one person that reveal or imply the union of the two natures—Jesus Christ, Son of God, Son of Man, Word become flesh, the Lamb slain for the redemption of the world. Yet in all these ascriptions, it is always assumed that we are speaking of a single person, one Mediator, one self, the one and only Son (Second Council of Constantinople, *CF*, p. 161; Grensted, *The Person of Christ*).

The Singular 'I'

If one should hypothesize that Jesus Christ is two persons, one would expect him to say of himselves, "we," but this never occurs. The Son is "I," the Godhead is "we." In the Son's dialogue with the Father, there is a clear sense of "I" (Gregory Nazianzen, *Orat*. XXXVII.2, *NPNF* 2 VII, p. 338).

The union is so permeant that readers of Scripture cannot always easily separate out what Christ says of himself *as God* and what he says of himself *as human*. When the Scripture student keeps clearly in mind that though divine this one is human and though human this one is divine, then the Scriptures make immediate sense and each narrative unfolds plausibly (Athanasius, *Four Discourses Ag. Arians* I, *NPNF* 2 IV, pp. 306–43).

Lacking the Premise, Textual Confusion Prevails

Distinctive qualities of both humanity and deity are ascribed to the unifying person in a way that makes little sense unless one assumes that these two natures were united in a single person.

He is paradoxically "before Abraham" yet "born in a manger," "suffered under Pontius Pilate" yet "the same yesterday, today, and forever." The rhetoric of the New Testament constantly juxtaposes the two natures in a way readers find inescapable. Only the theandric premise can allow these highly varied ascriptions in a given text to make sense.

The one who upholds all things by the word of his power is the same one who grows in the womb of Mary. He who knows all from the foundation of the world declares as man that he does not know the day or hour of judgment. He who created all has no where to lay his head. He from whose hand comes all things is the same one who agonized in the Garden. The eternal One who cannot change or suffer prays that the cup might pass from him. The eternal One who is unlimited in power suffers and dies. The one who is crucified and buried is the same one in whom the eternal life of God remains and works.

These statements are neither contradictions nor absurdities, seen in the light of the permeant logic of the divine-human personal union. Only with the two-nature/one-person hypothesis do these Scriptures make sense. Lacking the premise of permeant union, the scriptural testimony to him will be found constantly confusing, a maze of internal contradictions (cf. Harvey, *HB*, pp. 13–35). With this premise, the scriptural testimony has economy, beauty, and cohesion (Gregory Nazianzen, *Fourth Theol. Orat. on the Son*, *Orat*. XXX, *NPNF* 2 VII, pp. 310–12; cf. Boyce, *AST*, p. 288).

Summarizing, in the person of Christ there are two natures—the human nature and the divine nature—taken up into the unity of the person. Christ communicated his glory to our human nature by assuming our humanity; he possessed divinity by nature and humanity by grace.

THE ONE PERSON

Simplistic phrases such as "the dying God" should be avoided because they collapse triunity into sonship and the deity of Christ into his humanity. Rather than the "death of God," classic exegetes spoke more precisely of the God-man "according to his humanity" who suffered and died. Yet the scriptural texts do not intend that the interpreter artificially bifurcate Christ's divine acts from his human acts, for this tends to rend the union of his person.

Much current biblical criticism assumes that the humanity of Christ can be detached as an object of historical study like any other historical object to be assessed, criticized, manipulated, and judged. This rends the personal union assumed in the texts. Having reviewed the basic scriptural testimony to the union, it now is fitting to set forth some major ecumenical definitions that sought to clarify that union. All ecumenical formulations sought accountability to Scripture as expressive of the one mind of the believing church. They are best understood as attempts at consensual exegesis.

The Nature of Theandric Union

Theandric union is a simple idea, though its simplicity encases a mystery. It is nothing more than the idea that one person is both human and divine, uniting God and humanity in one individual.

One Person of Two Natures

As one person Christ is "the whole God man and the whole man God" (Gelasius, *SCD* 168, p. 71), consubstantial with God and with man (Council of Chalcedon, SCD 148, p. 61; see also *SCD* 220, 257). In Christ we have to do with only one person (Council of Toledo, *SCD* 20, p. 14; see also *SCD* 42, 143, 215ff.), yet in him divinity and humanity are personally united (Council of Ephesus, *SCD* 11, p. 49; see also *SCD* 13, 215ff., 257, 259, 288ff.).

Not Godly, but True God

It is inexact to think of the Christ of Scriptures merely as godly (*theophoros*; Council of Ephesus, SCD 117, p. 50), for the two natures are united according to subsistence (*hupostasis*); hence the union is termed a hypostatic (personal) union (Council of Constantinople III, *SCD* 289–93, pp. 113–15; see also *SCD* 13, 111, 115f., 148, 216ff., 226, 288), which began with the incarnation (Vigilius, *SCD* 204f., p. 84, see also *SCD* 111, 234, 250).

No serenity or beauty of poetic expression exceeds Gregory the Theologian on this point: "That which anoints is called Man, and makes that which is anointed God. He is the Way, because He leads us through Himself" (Gregory Nazianzen, *Orat.* XXX.21, *NPNF* 2 VI, p. 317).

Not Two Sons

As God, the Son knew that he was human; as human, he knew that he was God, hence one encompassing two. He was not two Sons, but one uniting two. "For both are God, that which assumed, and that which was assumed; two Natures meeting in One, not two Sons (let us not give a false account of the blending)" (Gregory Nazianzen, *Orat.* XXXVII.2, *NPNF* 2 VII, p. 338).

The Logos is united not with an individual person that existed prior to the God-man, but with a human nature that had no separate identity before union with the divine, for Jesus' human body had not existed eternally, but was born in time. Hence there are not two conscious persons, but a single conscious person uniting the divine and human natures. It is not one or the other nature that speaks when Jesus Christ speaks, but one person bearing the congruent imprint of two natures. He is a particular human being and Son of God, but not two persons, since it is the integrity of the one person in both his humanity and deity that makes him a single "I" (Second Council of Constantinople, *CC*, pp. 46–49).

He speaks as "I" whether in his human or divine voice, there being only one "I," not two; for if there were two "I"s, there would have been at Nazareth two persons. He unites in one person the utterly diverse characteristics needed for his mediatorial work (Tho. Aq., *ST* III Q17–19, II, pp. 2122–33).

Problems of Disavowal of Either Union or Difference

Classical exegetes carefully steered a middle course between two hazards: the *denial of the union* of God and humanity in Christ and the *denial of the distinguishability* of deity and humanity in Christ. It was to provide guidance for this trajectory that the ecumenical definitions developed the "one person in two natures" formula, so that the biblical testimony would not be skewed in either oversimplified direction.

Distinctions Enabled by the Formula

By the two-nature hypothesis, Christ is *distinguished both from other human persons and from the other persons of the Trinity*: "On the one hand, He is joined to the Father and the Spirit by His divinity, while on the other He is joined by His humanity to His Mother and to all men. However, because of the fact that His natures are united, we say that He differs both from the Father and the Spirit and from His Mother and other men" (John of Damascus, *OF* III.3, FC 37, p. 275; see also III.7, p. 282).

The Psychosomatic Analogy to the Divine-Human Permeation

All Analogies Are Inadequate

The unity of the human and divine natures of Christ is a mystery without adequate empirical analogy. The Colossian Letter attests "the mystery of God, namely, Christ, in whom are hidden all the treasures of wisdom and knowledge" (2:2).

The Psychosomatic Analogy Preferred

Yet the one analogy that ancient exegetes thought came closest to expressing the union of Christ's person is that of the psychosomatic (soul-body, freedom-nature) interface that every human being already knows (and is!).

Gregory of Nyssa opened up the issue in this way: "If you inquire how the Deity is united with human nature, it is appropriate for you first to ask in what way the soul is united to the body" (Gregory of Nyssa, *ARI* 11, LCC III, p. 288). The "Athanasian Creed" (Quicunque) summarized this analogy: "For as the reasonable soul and flesh is one man, so God and Man is one Christ" (*COC* II, p. 69).

Augustine gave definitive expression to the psychosomatic analogy of divine and human natures in Christ: "But there are some who request an explanation of how God is joined to man so as to become the single person of Christ, as if they themselves could explain something that happens every day, namely, how the soul is joined to the body so as to form the single person of a man. For, *as the soul makes use of the body in a single person to form a man, so God makes use of man in a single Person to form Christ. In the former person there is a mingling of soul and body; in the latter Person there is a mingling of God and man.* . . . The one process happens daily in order to beget men; the other happened once to set men free" (*Letters* 137, FC 20, p. 26, italics added; see also Chemnitz, *TNC*, pp. 95–100, 296–97).

As Psuche to Soma, So Divinity to Humanity

No human being can lack a body. No human being can lack a soul, for that is what makes the body live. The *psuchē* (*anima*, soul) sees only with bodily eyes and hears only with bodily ears. Similarly Jesus Christ saw, heard, and even suffered and died as a human being. The Word dwelt in flesh, just as our souls dwell in our bodies. As the soul-body interface pervades every moment of human selfhood, so the divinity-humanity of Christ pervades every moment of his unique personhood (Hugh of St. Victor, *OSCF*, pp. 236–39). As *psuchē* transcends *soma*, as imagination soars above finitude, so does the divine nature of Christ transcend the limits of human finitude in the man Jesus.

The Familiar Interface

Accordingly there is a profound similarity (acknowledging differences) between this everyday human body/soul permeation and the unique mystery wherein God becomes human. The human *psuchē* acts and suffers through the body in ways that require a body, yet always such action and suffering has an interfacing spiritual dimension that transcends the body. The human spirit (*pneuma*) is precisely characterized by that interface (Kierkegaard, *SD*, pp. 146, 147).

Every human being already knows something of the complexity and mystery of the psychosomatic interface in him- or herself. We know how subtly our bodies are affected (moment by moment) by our spirited or dispirited condition. We know how deeply psychosomatic factors affect the health and malaise of the body, its immune systems, often causing allergies, ulcers, headaches, and nausea.

One's own bodily nature grounds one's capacity for self-transcendence. Yet imagination and freedom transcend finitude and body. These two always exist in intense and delicate interfacing (cf. Nemesius, *On the Nature of Man*; Niebuhr, *NDM*). The complexity and subtlety of this interface is something like that between the divine and human natures of the one person, Jesus Christ. Grace-enabled freedom receives and owns the body willingly, as did the Son receive life willingly from the Blessed Mother. This is what human freedom is constantly choosing: *either* to receive joyfully *or* waste in despair over one's own living body (Kierkegaard, *Either/Or* I; *SD*; *The Concept of Anxiety*).

The "entire and singular unity of Person" was explicated by Vincent of Lerins in this ingenious way: "For the conjunction has not converted and changed the one nature into the other (which is the characteristic error of the Arians), but rather has in such wise compacted both into one, that while there always remains in Christ the singularity of one and the self-same Person, there abides eternally the characteristic property of each nature; whence it follows, that neither does God (the divine nature) ever begin to be body, nor does the body ever cease to be body. This may be illustrated in human nature: for not only in the present life, but in the future also, each individual man will consist of soul and body; nor will his body ever be converted into soul, or his soul into body" (*Comm.* 13, *NPNF* 2 XI, p. 141).

The Limits of the Analogy

Like all analogies, this one needs to be used with constraint. The body-soul analogy is not to be equated with the divine-human union because (1) soul is not uncreated—for God alone is uncreated; (2) our bodies are unlike Christ's body in that in them the Logos has not become incarnate; and (3) our bodies and souls interface in such a way that the right balance is constantly prone to being upset by the history of sin and personal sin, unlike Christ's humanity and divinity, which appear to be steadily cooperative (Tertullian, *On the Soul*, *ANF* III, pp. 181–241; Augustine, *On Two Souls*, *NPNF* 1 IV, pp. 95–107; Heppe, *RD*, p. 430; Bucanus, *ITLC* II, p. 15). Hence the correspondence is best viewed circumspectly as an analogy and not an equation, for God is not soul and humanity is not body. Analogy differs from equation precisely in its dissimilarities.

Other Analogies

The Eucharistic Analogy

Another analogy appeared repeatedly in classic attempts to clarify the union of two natures in Christ: the divine-human unity of Christ's person is like the divine-human action in the Eucharist.

It will suffice to quote John of Damascus, who drew the analogy in this way: "Now, bread and wine are used because God knows human weakness. . . . He does through the ordinary things of nature those which surpass the natural order. . . . However, should you inquire as to the manner in which this is done, let it suffice for you to hear that it is done through the Holy Ghost, just as it was through the Holy Ghost that the Lord made flesh subsist for Himself and in Himself from the blessed Mother of God. And more than this we do not know, except that the word of God is true and effective and omnipotent, but the manner in which it is so is impossible to find out. What is more, it is not amiss to say this, that *just as bread by being eaten and wine and water by being drunk are naturally changed into the body of the person eating and drinking and yet do not become another body* than that which the person had before, so in the same way are the bread of the offertory and the wine and water supernaturally changed into the body and blood of Christ by the invocation and coming down of the Holy Ghost, yet they are not two bodies, but one and the same" (*OF* IV.13, *FC* 37, pp. 357–58; italics added).

Inadequate Analogies to the Union

The union is not like a physical union, as when form and matter are united. Nor is it like a union of friends. It is a more profound union than the *henosis* of two persons in marriage (Origen, *De Principiis* II.6, *ANF* IV, p. 282), for the unity of marriage leaves husband and wife "even after their union, two persons" (Nestorianism asserts two persons), nor is it "one nature being mingled or absorbed by the other" (Monophysitism asserts one nature; *Gk. Orthodox Catech.* 33, p. 27). Christ is more profoundly and intrinsically one person than two marriage partners are one person.

Rather Christ's personal union is a union that can only exist in one distinctive person in whom there is an intimate and perpetual conjunction of divine and human natures in one individual, wherein the human nature was assumed by the *logos* so as to be the *Word in person* (*enhupostatos logo*; Augustine, *Hom. on John*, *NPNF* 1 VII, p. 413; see Heppe, *RD*, pp. 431–32).

The three major problems of formulae for the union are that they run the risk of inordinately divinizing the human, humanizing the divine, or dualizing the one person. It is to these problems that we now turn.

Recurrent Misunderstandings of this Union

The two-nature/one-person formula has remained the stabilizing center of ecumenical Christology for almost two millennia. It has repeatedly been tested by challenge. This section seeks to show the perennial nature of these challenges and how they remain pertinent today.

Did the Divine Attributes Disappear in the Union?

Some challengers to ecumenical Christology have persisted in holding that the Logos has become reduced to the limits of human nature, disavowing eternality, destitute of divine attributes. They say that the divine nature became dormant, paralyzed, or even nonexistent during Christ's earthly ministry.

There is no exegetical warrant for this conclusion, for in Scripture it is precisely the Word that has become flesh to dwell among us, not the

Word that ceased to be in becoming flesh. The New Testament does not imply that the Logos in becoming flesh temporarily quit being Logos and began being merely a man. Rather "the Word became flesh and dwelt among us" (John 1:14, RSV). The central point is that God became flesh without contradiction or negation of either deity or humanity (1 Tim. 3:16; 1 John 4:2; John 1:14).

Was the Incarnation Incomplete?

Some hold that the union between humanity and deity in Christ was not completed in the incarnation, but was only gradually seeking to be realized (Schleiermacher, *ChrF*, pp. 377–90). Some have argued that it was only belatedly in the resurrection, not the incarnation, that the union could become realized (Pannenberg, *JGM*; cf. I. A. Dorner, *History of the Development of the Doctrine of the Person of Christ* I, p. 123). Yet Paul commends the mind of Christ, who "in very nature God" was found in human form as servant (Phil. 2:7). The classic consensus held that the incarnation was not incomplete, but fully manifest in the nativity.

Was the Trinity Altered in the Incarnation?

Some versions of kenotic (divine self-emptying) theory suppose that the Trinity must have been altered in number during Jesus' earthly ministry. This was firmly countered by the Second Council of Constantinople: "For the Holy Trinity, when God the Word was incarnate, was not increased by the addition of a person" (CC, p. 48). God remained triune and the trinity became most profoundly expressed through the incarnation.

Do Ancient Council Definitions Remain Viable?

Criticism of the personal union of Christ is often based upon some repeatedly disavowed misunderstanding of it. Some criticize Chalcedon's teaching as dualistic, as a dissection of the whole, a fissure of the person (each of which the formula itself specifically rejected!). Some think it amounts to duplicity. Some view it as two abstractions instead of one reality, or two halves instead of one personal whole, wherein God now acts, and now man acts. Each of these criticisms was specifically anticipated in the precise formulation of Chalcedon, in its attempt to move cautiously between duplex personality and impersonal manhood (Leo, *Tome*, LCC III, pp. 359–71; cf. Mackintosh, *PJC*, p. 296; Aldwinckle, *MTM*, pp. 35–43).

That the classic Christological formulae have undergone various reinterpretations in their long history remains a testimony to their vitality, not deadness. "The fact that each reasoned view of Christ should call for criticism and modification at the hands of later ages, so far from being an embarrassment, is a profound testimony to the magnitude of the theme" (Mackintosh, *PJC*, p. 300). It exudes inordinate optimism, however, to conclude that "each new conception of Christ we form, only to dismantle and reshape it later on the score of inadequacy, gives place to one always more broad and deep and high" (Mackintosh, *PJC*, p. 302). Such optimism is belied by the weakness of Christology in our time. Personal salvation, however, is not dependent upon the precise acceptance of a particular Christological formula or definition of the Person, but rather upon active faith in the Person himself.

Limits of Reflection upon the Union

The Personal Union Not Subject Finally to Empirical-Rational Dissection

Only dead things can be dissected. The worshiping and reflecting community is invited to celebrate and study and revel in this living mystery, not as something fully comprehensible to objective analysis, but as a divine gift for joyful contemplation (*BOC*, pp. 489, 597, 609). Modesty of expression remains a radical intellectual requirement in the presence of this incomparable Person. This mystery was already being acknowledged in New Testament times: "Beyond all question, the mystery of godliness is great: He appeared in a body" (1 Tim. 3:16; cf. Newman, *GA*).

Not Ancillary

This union of humanity and divinity in Christ is not an incidental or ancillary aspect of Christian proclamation, not an odd accommodation to myth, but rather the heart of faith, a hinge point for subsequent profound knowledge of God revealed in history, for the Father is recognized through the Son (Matt. 11:27), the Word of Life, "that which was from the beginning, which we have heard, which he have seen with our eyes, which he have looked at and our hands have touched—this we proclaim" (1 John 1:1).

The Struggle the Texts Require

The ordinary reading of the New Testament becomes increasingly problematic and confusing to the extent that any of three concessions are granted: that Jesus lacks humanity, deity, or personal union. The texts will fight any reader all along the way if any of these are conceded. With such a concession, a major retrogression has occurred that finally tends to make Christology formally and logically impossible (Harvey, *HB*, pp. 275–89).

Yet it is not likely that inquirers into Christianity will ever cease raising questions about the unique theandric person. Luther commented wryly: "I know nothing about the Lord Christ that the devil has failed to attack" (*Table-Talk*, *Veit Dietrich* [20 April–16 May 1532]; *WLS* I, p. 147; *WA-Tischreden* 1, #269). "Now he does not want to allow that He is God, then, again, he does not want to allow that He is man" (Luther, *Serm. on Col. 1:9–20*, *WLS* I, p. 146; *WA* 45, 295).

The Classic Hermeneutic

The Honest Money Changer

The skilled biblical hermeneut, like a skilled and honest money changer (according to Athanasius's happy analogy), must attend carefully to the context of each scriptural passage concerning Christ, as to whether it has particular reference to his humanity, deity, or divine-human interface. "Expressions used about His Godhead and His becoming man are to be interpreted with discrimination and suitably to the particular context. . . . He who expounds concerning His Godhead is not ignorant of what belongs to His coming in the flesh; but discerning each as a skilled and 'approved moneychanger,' he will walk in the straight way of piety; when therefore he speaks of His weeping, he knows that the Lord, having become man, while He exhibits His human character in weeping, as God raises up Lazarus" (Athanasius, *On the Opinion of Dionysius*, chap. 9, *NPNF* 2 IV, p. 179). The dishonest money changer constantly shortchanges either the divine or the human aspect. The honest money changer keeps the two currencies (divinity and humanity) in fitting congruence as one reads narrative after narrative.

Texts Variously Refer to Christ's Deity, Humanity, or Union

The Formula of Union between Cyril of Alexandria and the bishops of Antioch, A.D. 433, advised the biblical interpreter to be attentive to whether a narrative had reference primarily to the one person or one of the two natures: "As for the words of the gospels and of the apostles concerning the Lord, we know that theologians have considered some as *common* because they are said of the *one person* (*prosopon*), while they have distinguished others as applying to the *two natures* (*phuseis*), reserving those which befit God to Christ in His *divinity*, while assigning those which are lowly to Christ in His *humanity*" (*CF*, p. 1510, italics added; Gregory Nazianzen, *Orat.* XXIX.17, *NPNF* 2 VII, pp. 307–308).

Classic exegetes recognized that language was early applied to Christ in reference to varied contexts before and after his incarnation and resurrection. The continuing problem for any reader of Paul or Mark or John is that it often happens that "sometimes indeed when teaching about the supreme nature, he is completely silent about the human nature, but sometimes when treating of the human dispensation, he does not touch on the mystery of His divinity" (John IV, *Epist. to Constantius* [A.D. 641], *SCD* 253, p. 101).

Four Generic Ways of Using Language About Christ

Hence it became a subtle task of Christian reflection to sort out the different classes or "generic modes" or ways of speaking of Christ. By the eighth century, these four standard classes had been astutely outlined by John of Damascus, the most systematic of the later Eastern patristic theologians. Accordingly, varied references are made to Christ in relation to four stages.

Things may be said of Christ in reference to:

I. *Before* the incarnate theandric union so as to show
   A. Consubstantiality with the Father
   B. The perfection of the Person
   C. The mutual indwelling of the Persons in one another
   D. The subordination of Son to Father
   E. The will of the Father as fullfilled by the Son, or
   F. The fulfillment of prophecy, or
II. *During* the time of incarnate union so as to indicate
   A. The deification of the flesh, or
     1. By assuming the human
     2. By uplifting the human
   B. The humbling of the Word
     1. By abasement
     2. By assumption of the flesh, or
     3. By kenosis, or
   C. Permeation of both deity and humanity in the union
     1. By uniting
     2. By anointing
     3. By an intimate conjoining
     4. By permeating, or
     5. By mutual indwelling, or
III. *After* the Union, so as to show the
   A. Divine nature, or
   B. Human nature

       1. Spoken of him naturally
         a. of his birth
         b. growth
         c. progress with age
         d. hunger, thirst, weariness, fear, sleep
         e. death
       2. Ascribed to him fictionally "as if" human only (Luke 24:28)
       3. Things spoken in the matter of association and said relatively
       4. Things spoken by reason of distinctions in thought
       5. Things spoken to strengthen faith
       6. Things spoken with reference to his ethnic identity, or
    C. One Person displaying both divinity and humanity, or
  IV. *After the Resurrection*
    A. As pertaining to divinity, or
    B. As pertaining to humanity
       1. As actual but not according to nature (as eating after the resurrection)
       2. As actual and according to nature (as passing through closed doors)
       3. As simulated or intentionally fictional (as when he "acted as if he were going farther," Luke 24:28), or
    C. As pertaining to both natures.

A careful interpreter will attend to which of these positions was implied by a particular saying of a particular writer. The classic hermeneutic is this: varying types of ascriptions concerning Christ may be rightly applied only in relation to the context in which they occur, whether before or after the incarnation or resurrection (John of Damascus, *OF* IV.18, *FC* 37, pp. 376–83; *NPNF* 2 IX, pp. 90–92). This ancient theandric premise needs to be better correlated with current Scripture studies.

THE INTRAPERSONAL PERMEATION

In seeking to set forth a plausible theory of the personal union consistent with Scripture and resistent to distortion, the classic exegetes (of East, West, and of the Protestant era), have applied a carefully devised logic of permeation that still deserves study. Scholastic teachers sought to show how Christ's deity affected his humanity, what his humanity meant in relation to his deity, and how the permeation communicated itself to the actions of the single, unified person.

To permeate is to spread, to become diffused, or to penetrate (*per* + *meare* = "to pass through") something. The interpenetration of divinity and humanity of Christ in one person refers to the diffusion of each nature in the other. The Greek terms expressing this union were *koinonia* ("communication, communion") and *poieo* ("to do") or *koinopoiesis* ("communicative action" or "communication of acts"). They are referred to more commonly in the Latin as *communicatio idiomatum* ("communication of idioms or attributes," or *genus idiomaticum*, Hilary, *Trin.* IX.15–20, *NPNF* 2 IX, pp. 160–61; Tho. Aq., *ST* III Q16, II, pp. 2112–22; Chemnitz, *TNC*, pp. 162–64; Barth, *CD* IV/2, pp. 73ff.).

Properties of Each Nature Predicated of the Other

The mediatorial work required a spontaneous sharing of properties of both natures within the one person. Hence the attributes of both divinity and humanity may be predicated of the same person. This is what is meant by *communicatio idiomatum*—the communication of divine and human properties fully and unitively to the single person. From the unity of the person of the Mediator there follows a communication of idioms, or reciprocal predication of properties and operations (Council of Ephesus, *SCD* 116–24, pp. 50–51; see also *SCD* 16, 201, 222, 224). The properties of each nature are predicated of the other. Calvin held to "such a connection and union of the Divinity with the humanity, that each nature retains its properties entire, and yet both together constitute one Christ" (*Inst.* II.14.1, Bever.; cf. *BOC*, p. 593).

This is a technical point that may cause confusion if not clarified: the one person embraces two natures and their *idiomata*, their distinctive (from *idios*, pertaining to self, one's own, private or distinctive [Luke 9:10; 10:23]) properties. In the one person, Jesus Christ, we see attested constantly a communication of properties (*koinonia idiomaton*) or attributes, so that the one person may be called just as easily "Jesus" as "the Christ." All acts of the Mediator require a conjoint but distinct operation of each of the natures (Pearson, *EC* I, pp. 244–53).

"And thus, Christ—which name covers both together—is called both God and man, created and uncreated, passible and impassible. And whenever he is named Son of God and God from one of the parts, He receives the properties of the co-existent nature, of the flesh, that is to say, and can be called passible God and crucified Lord of Glory—not as being God, but in so far as the same one is also man. When, again, He is named Man and the Son of Man, He is given the properties and splendors of the

divine nature. He is called Child before the Ages and Man without beginning. . . . Such, then, is the manner of this exchange by which each
nature communicates its own properties to the other" (John of Damascus, *OF* III.4, *FC* 37, p. 276; *BOC*, p. 597).

This permeant logic gradually entered into the life of piety, prayer, and
counsel. How do we speak of the One who shapes the life of prayer as
God, man, or God-man? "Let Christ raise you by that which is man, lead
you by that which is God-man, and guide you through to that which is
God" (Augustine, *On the Gospel of St. John*, Tractate 23:6, *NPNF* 1 VII, p.
153). The multilevel relation of believers to Christ is profoundly glimpsed
in Christ's prayer to the Father: "I in them and you in me" (John 17:23).

Perichoresis: Where Divinity and Humanity Interfuse

Paul taught that "in Christ all the fullness of the Deity lives in bodily
form" (Col. 2:9). Church teaching interpreted this to mean that the divine
nature penetrates and perfects every aspect of the human, and the
human is pervaded by the divine (John of Damascus, *OF* III.8 *FC* 37, pp.
284–86). This was powerfully conveyed by the term *perichoresis* (Lat. *cir-
cumincession*, an embracing movement, "a proceeding around," or "walking about all sides"), literally the existence of persons in one another.

The *perichoresis* or active intermingling of the natures was that abundant interpenetration or immission by which the divine nature of the Son
pervaded inwardly the human nature so as fully to impart his divinity to
his humanity and his God-manhood to every aspect of his action (Koenig, *TPA*, p. 126; Schmid, *DT*, p. 306). In this way the deity participated
in the Passion of the humanity and the humanity in the majesty of the
deity without blurring or confusing either. Qualities of either nature may
by this logic (a distinctive Christo-logic) be ascribed to the one person
(Newman, *Ari.*, pp. 171-74).

The Lutheran Formula summarized that "the entire fulness of the
divinity dwells in Christ, not as in other holy men and angels, but bodily
as in its own body, so that, with all its majesty, power, glory, and efficacy,
it shines forth in the assumed human nature of Christ, when and as He
wills, and in, with and through it, exerts its divine power, glory and
efficacy, as the soul does in the body and fire in glowing iron" (*Formula of
Concord*, Jacobs, ed. [1882], p. 636, cf. *BOC*, pp. 604–608; Chemnitz, *TNC*,
p. 396).

Iron being "incessantly heated"–*penetrated by fire while remaining
iron*–was the analogy most often used to make this point (Origen, *De
Principiis* II.6, *ANF* IV, p. 283; Maximus, *Disputatio cum Pyrrho*, *MPG* 91,
p. 337C; *BOC*, pp. 603–604). "While we speak of the cut burn and the

burnt cut of the red-hot knife, we nevertheless hold the cutting to be one operation and the burning another" (John of Damascus, *OF* III.19, *FC* 37, p. 323). In this analogy the red-hot knife is Jesus Christ—the knife his humanity, the heat his divinity—cutting and burning are distinguishable but inseparable. "For the two natures are one Christ and the one Christ is two natures" (John of Damascus, *OF* III.19, *FC* 37, p. 322; cf. Chemnitz, *TNC*, pp. 229–30).

Yet such analogies require discernment: "Now, examples do not have to be absolutely and unfailingly exact, for, just because it is an example, one must find in it that which is like and that which is unlike. For likeness in everything would be identity and not an example, which is especially true with divine things. So, in the matter of theology and the Incarnation, it is impossible to find an absolutely perfect example" (John of Damascus, *OF* III.26, *FC* 37, pp. 331–32).

His Human Nature Endowed with Requisite Gifts for Mission

The theandric union had effect upon Jesus' human nature by enabling gifts requisite for his earthly mission.

Personal Gifts Given

Jesus was adorned with extraordinary gifts for his mission. These gifts were as complete as can or need be given to a human being. They were sufficient to the salvific mission. They were given contextually as needed from the time of birth, yet these gifts had to be allowed to grow in time and emerge as competences ordinarily emerge in the development of a human person. Hence Scripture portrays Jesus paradoxically as full of grace from birth, yet also capable of growing in grace through the years (Luke 2:40, 52; Origen, quoted in Corderius' *Catena*, *AEG* I, p. 273; cf. Origen, *Homélies sur S. Luc* [1962], Hom. XIX–XX, pp. 279–89).

The Spirit Enabling the Son

During his earthly ministry, the communication of divine power to the human Jesus was administered by the Holy Spirit, upon whom he constantly relied. Jesus taught, acted, and suffered what the Spirit enabled, directed, and permitted (Acts 1:2, 10:38). "For the one whom God has sent speaks the words of God, for God gives the Spirit without limit" (John 3:34). While being empowered by God the Spirit, Jesus taught and acted not simply as a prophet (speaking for God), but as God (Luke 5:20–21), from whom power was perceived as streaming forth immediately from his person (Luke 6:19).

Fully Given, Yet Voluntarily Constrained

The Son is attested as having been unreservedly given the power of miracle, the power to know and do as God, yet this power was voluntarily constrained, under the principle of *kenosis*, amid a self-chosen, humble mission of servanthood. Even then, there was sufficient impartation of divine empowerment to Jesus as was needed for each stage of the fulfillment of his office of Mediator.

Types of Knowing Differentiated

Protestant scholastics distinguished three types of knowing in the theandric person—experiential, donative, and infused knowing. By *experiential* knowedge he knew ordinary things knowable in the light of nature through sense experience, reason, and the grasping of the relation of cause and effect. This means that Christ learned by his experience just as we do. By *donative* knowledge, Christ as human knower received the gift (*donum*) of extensive but not inclusive perception. He saw but did not always understand as finite knower what he knew (hence it was remarked by Jesus according to Mark 13:32 that "No one knows about that day or hour, not even the angels in heaven, nor the Son, but only the Father"). He saw history "as a whole, but not wholly" (Wollebius, *CTC*, in *RDB*, pp. 89–95; cf. Heppe, *RD*, p. 436). By *infused* knowledge he, as human, knew whatever pertained to the divine purpose yet could not be seen without the aid of divine grace (Wollebius, *CTC* in *RDB*, p. 67; cf. Chemnitz, *TNC*, pp. 100–102). By these means the grace of union with the divine *logos* was imparted developmentally to Jesus' human nature (sometimes called the communication of grace to Jesus, or *communicatio gratiarum*).

Who Suffers—God, Man, or God-man?

This premise affected thinking about who suffered in the suffering of Christ. Luther drew the distinction carefully: "If I believe that only the human nature has suffered for me, I have a Saviour of little worth. . . . It is the [theandric] person that suffers and dies. Now the person is true God; therefore it is rightly said: 'The Son of God suffers.' For although the divinity does not suffer, yet the person which is God suffers in His humanity. . . . In His own nature, God cannot die; but now God and man are united in one person, so that the expression 'God's death' is correct, when the man dies who is one thing or one person with God" (Luther, quoted in the *Formula of Concord*, *BOC*, pp. 631–32).

As human, Jesus exercised divine attributes (yet was self-constrained in their use on behalf of his mission) through his divine nature. The Savior could suffer, be powerless, and die as a human being, not in his divine nature, but through his possession of humanity. Similarly his soul could feel anguish from bodily pain, which lacking body it would not feel. So although in his divine nature he was insensible to pain, the God-man was capable through the divine-human union to suffer pain (for discussions of passability, see John Chrysostom, *Hom. on John* LX, *NPNF* 1 XIV, pp. 217–27; Strong, *Syst. Theol.*, p. 697; cf. Jung Young Lee, *God Suffers for Us*).

The Damascene's theological scalpel cut precisely: "It was in one nature that He worked miracles and in another that He endured suffering" (John of Damascus, *OF* III.3, *FC* 37, p. 274). Ironies abound in consequence: "Wherefore, the Lord of Glory is even said to have been crucified, although His divine nature did not suffer; and the Son of Man is confessed to have been in heaven before His passion, as the Lord Himself has said" (John of Damascus, *OF* III.3, *FC* 37, p. 274, cf. John 3:13). "The same one person is at once uncreated in its divinity and created in its humanity" (John of Damascus, *OF* IV.5, *FC* 37, p. 339).

Gregory the Theologian played out a series of intriguing juxtapositions solved by the permeation:

He hungered—but He fed thousands. . . .
He was wearied, but He is the Rest of them that are weary. . . .
He was heavy with sleep, but He walked lightly over the sea. . . .
He prays, but He hears prayer.
He weeps, but He causes tears to cease.
He asks where Lazarus was laid, for He was Man; but He raises Lazarus, for
  He was God.
He is sold, and very cheap, for it is only thirty pieces of silver; but He
  redeems the world. . . .
As a sheep He is led to the slaughter, but He is the Shepherd of Israel, and
  now of the whole world also.
As a Lamb He is silent, yet He is the Word. . . .
He is . . . wounded, but He healeth every disease. . . .
He dies, but He gives life. . . .
If the one give you a starting point for your error, let the others put an end to it
                    (Gregory Nazianzen, *Orat.* XXIX.20, *NPNF* 2 VII, p. 309).

Suppose a mathematician has been struggling to understand a vast body of perplexing data. He sits facing the pile of numbers and equations. Someone hands him a formula that could make instant sense of the entire mass, but he refuses to try the formula because it is written on yellowed paper. That is the situation of modern New Testament theology in refusing to use the classic logic of permeation.

Formal Definitions of the Personal Union

Ecumenical council definitions sought to define faith in such a way that it would not be easily distorted. Their definitions were largely elicited and required by persistent distortions that did not reflect the consensual mind of the believing church.

The Definition of Chalcedon

The Fourth Ecumenical Council (A.D. 451, SCD 148, pp. 60–62) defended the scriptural teaching of the personal union of Christ by defining it as:

- unconfused (*asunkutōs*), with no mixing of the two natures, which remain distinct even while they are in communion (against the Eutychians)
- unchanged (*atreptōs*), in the sense that the deity is not transmuted into humanity, nor humanity into deity (against the Eutychians)
- indivisible (*adiairetōs*), unable to be divided—the personal union is never at any point split apart (against the Nestorians)
- inseparable (*achōristōs*), undissolved through eternity, perpetual (against the Nestorians)

Rejected Options

Chalcedon was intensely economical in ruling out rejected options. The Eutychians tended to confuse the natures; the Nestorians tended to divide the person (Ursinus, *CHC*, pp. 196–202). The rejected options may be summarized in this simple schema:

Heresies that reject Christ's humanity:
    Docetists (Christ as not fully in flesh)
    Apollinarians (Logos replaces human spirit)
    Eutychians (Christ as a single mixed nature)
Heresies that reject Christ's divinity:
    Eutychians (Christ not fully divine, but mixed nature)
    Ebionites (Jesus as natural son of Joseph and Mary)
    Arians (Christ as creature, not eternal)
Heresies that reject Christ's personal union:
    Nestorians (Christ as two persons)

Ecumenical orthodoxy maintains Christ as truly human, truly God, one person. Each nature remains whole, unimpaired, and distinct from the other without confusion. The divine nature remains uncreated, infinite, almighty, and all-wise, while the human nature retains its own properties—those characteristic of all human existence—created, finite, and subject to time and death.

To allay distortion, the formula had to be precise: Jesus Christ "must be acknowledged in two natures, without confusion or change, without division or separation. The distinction between the natures was never abolished by their union but rather the character proper to each of the two natures was preserved as they come together in one person (*prosopon*) and one hypostasis" (Council of Chalcedon, *CF*, pp. 154–55; cf. A. Grillmeier, *Christ in Christian Tradition*; Aldwinckle, "How Definitive Was Chalcedon?" *MTM*, pp. 35–43; A. Harnack, *History of Dogma*; R. V. Sellers, *The Council of Chalcedon*).

Gregory the Theologian mused: "By some He is honoured as God but confused with the Father; by others He is dishonoured as Flesh, and is severed from God. . . . Which shall He forgive—those who falsely contract Him, or those who divide Him? For the former ought to have made a distinction, and the latter to have made a Union, the one in number, the other in Godhead" (Gregory Nazianzen, *Orat.* XLV.27, *NPNF* 2 VII, p. 433).

Intimacy of the Union

Whatever unites human beings through their participation in human nature is precisely the human nature experienced by Jesus. Whatever distinguishes one person from another also distinguished Jesus from all other human persons, for there was only one Jesus of Nazareth.

The most essential distinctions were tightly compacted in these phrases of the Quicunque Creed (A.D. 440), which confesses:

Our Lord Jesus Christ the Son of God is
both God and man;
God of the substance of the Father, begotten before time,
and man of the substance of his mother born in time;
perfect God and perfect man,
consisting of a rational soul and human body;
equal to the Father in his divinity,
less than the Father in his humanity;
who, although both God and man, is not two but one Christ;
one, however, not by the conversion of the Godhead into flesh
but by the assumption of manhood into God.
Wholly one, not by fusion of substance but by unity of person. For as the
  rational soul and the body are one man,
so God and man are one Christ

(*TGS*, p. 102; *SCD* 40, p. 16).

(Similar definitions were widely received by Protestant formularies.)

"He is a man who is of man," and "he is God who is of God," Novatian had written. The typic symmetry of Novatian's language is worth enjoying: "In the same manner that He, as Man, is the Son of David, so is He also, as God, called the Lord of David. And in the same manner that He, as Man, is made under the Law, so is He also, as God, declared to be the Lord of the Sabbath. . . . In the same manner that He, as Man, ascended into heaven, as God, He first descended from heaven. In the same manner that he, as Man, goes to the Father, so as a Son obedient to His Father shall he descend from the Father. . . . However, when you read about both these truths, there is danger that you will believe not both of them but only one" (Novatian, *Trin.* 11, FC 67, pp. 46–47).

The Second Council of Constantinople (A.D. 553) defended the union of the two natures from distortion in these terms: "If anyone, while using the phrase 'in two natures,' does not confess that the one Jesus Christ our Lord is acknowledged in divinity and humanity, signifying thereby the distinction of the natures of which the ineffable union was made without any confusion, without either the Word being transformed into the nature of the flesh or the flesh being translated into the nature of the Word—for each of the two remains what it is by nature, even after the union according to the hypostasis has taken place—but if he applies the phrase to the mystery of Christ as meaning a division into parts," such a position must be rejected (Second Council of Constantinople, *Ag. the Three Chapters*, CF, p. 161).

The saving mediatorial work "becomes impossible if one separates the two natures of Christ, as Nestorius did, or if one only ascribes to Him one divine nature, like the Monophysites, or if one curtails one part of human nature, like Apollinarius, or if one only sees in Him a single divine will and operation, like the Monothelites. 'What is not assumed cannot be deified'" (Lossky, *MTEC*, p. 154, quoting Gregory Nazianzen, *Epist.* 101; cf. *Letters on the Apollinarian Controversy*, NPNF 2 VII, pp. 437–45). "For each of the two natures performs the functions proper to it in communion with the other; the Word does what pertains to the Word and the flesh what pertains to the flesh" (Leo I, *Letter to Flavian of Constantinople* [13 June 449], CF, p. 152).

DIVINE AND HUMAN WILL IN THE SON

That Jesus had a human *will* is evident from his Gethesmane prayer, "Not my will but yours be done" (Luke 22:42), yet from that same passage it is also evident that *his human will was unremittingly consecrated to follow the divine will.* "For I have come down from heaven not to do my will but to do the will of him who sent me" (John 6:38; Athanasius, *Four Discourses Ag. Arians*, III.58–67, *NPNF* 2 IV, pp. 425–31).

The obedient, responsive, self-emptying service of the Son, according to Philippians 2, provides the pattern for human willing in faith. This pattern is offered not merely as an idea or formal doctrine, but an embodied ethic of service in which one freely wills to become poor and obedient (John Chrysostom, *Hom. on Phil.* VII, *NPNF* 1 XIII, pp. 212–18; Lossky, *MTEC*, p. 145), as the Word of Life walked and showed the lowly way of serving love.

Human Will in the Son

Jesus' Human Will Obeyed His Divine Will

On this scriptural basis, it became a distinctive point of ecumenical confession that Jesus had two wills—his human will being obedient to the divine will in him—"his human will following, and not resisting or opposing, but rather subject to his divine and all-powerful will" (Third Council of Constantinople, *CC*, p. 51). "The two wills proper to the two natures are different, but He who wills is one" (Lossky, *MTEC*, p. 146; see Gregory Nazianzen, *Fourth Theol. Orat.*, *Orat.* XXX, *NPNF* 2 VII, pp. 313–17; Tho. Aq., *ST* III Q18, II, pp. 2125–31).

Prevenience of the Divine Will

The divine will always "goes before" or "prevenes" (leads the way) for the human will, so that the human will may choose freely in accord with the divine will. The pattern is the Gethsemane prayer, in which death is faced and resisted in a way fitting to human nature and then freely offered up to God. "And when He begged to be spared death, He did so naturally, with His divine will willing and permitting, and He was in agony and afraid. Then, when His divine will willed that His human will choose death, the passion was freely accepted. . . . And so, the Lord's soul was freely moved to will, but it freely willed those things which His divine will willed" (John of Damascus, *OF* III.18, *FC* 37, pp. 319–20).

Freedom Preserved in the God-man

Jesus' will was not simply an automated or programmed response as in animal instinct, but genuine human volition. The distinction between brute appetite and free will was ably summarized by the Damascene: "He willed freely with His divine and His human will, for free will is absolutely inherent in every rational nature. After all, of what good can rationality be to a nature that does not reason freely. Now, the Creator has implanted a natural appetite in *brute beasts* which constrains them to act for the preservation of their own nature. For, since they lack reason, they cannot lead; rather, they are led by their natural appetite. Whence it is that the instinct to act arises simultaneously with the appetite, for they enjoy neither the use of reason nor that of counsel or reflection or judgment. For this reason they are neither praised and deemed good for practicing virtue nor punished for doing evil. The *rational nature*, however, has its natural appetite, which becomes aroused, but is guided and controlled by the reason," and it is on this basis that "the rational nature is both praised and deemed good for practicing virtue and punished for practicing vice" (*OF* III. 18, *FC* 37, pp. 320–21, italics added.).

The Rejection of Single-Will Christology: Monothelitism

On this premise, the Third Council of Constantinople (A.D. 681) rejected a one-will Christology (Monothelitism), which taught that in Christ there was not a divine will and a human will, but only one (*monos*) will (*thelein*). Against this view, the council declared: "Each nature wills and works what is proper to it, in communion with the other. On this principle we glorify two natural wills and operations combining with each other for the salvation of the human race" (*CC*, pp. 52–53; cf. *CF*, p. 172; see also John Chrysostom, *Hom. on John* XXX, XLV, *NPNF* 1 XIV, pp. 104, 161–62, 184; Chemnitz, *TNC*, pp. 223–38, 270–71).

How Could One Having Two Natures Exercise a Personal Free Will?

Willing Belongs to Personhood

It is God's nature to will. It is also human nature to will. Willing, like knowing, belongs to the human condition, human personhood. One who wills is called a person. Yet it is possible for one will to remain free while voluntarily obeying another.

"To will is inherent to all men" (John of Damascus, *OF* III.14, *FC* 37, pp. 297–99). How one wills particularly in a given situation depends upon judgment, not nature, and upon self-determining freedom, not external causal determinations alone. "If man is by nature volitive, the Lord, too, is by nature volitive, not only in so far as He is God but also in so far as He was made man. For just as He assumed our nature, so also has He assumed our natural will" (John of Damascus, *OF* III.14, *FC* 37, p. 299).

Two Wills Unite in One Person

Since Christ is one person, not two, "the divinely willing in Him and the humanly willing are one and the same." Nevertheless, since he has two natures, we speak of Christ (and Christ alone) as uniquely having two wills, human and divine (unique because in no other has God assumed humanity). Hence Christ's willing is said to be of two natures and in two natures (Lateran Council, *SCD* 259, p. 102; see also *SCD* 462, 708). Each nature retains its own properties (Council of Constantinople II, *SCD* 290, p. 114; see also *SCD* 258, 262, 290), including its proper faculties of knowing and willing (Lateran Council, *SCD* 263–66, p. 103; Agatho, *Roman Council* [A.D. 680], *SCD* 288, p. 113; see also *SCD* 344).

That Protestant formularies followed this ancient ecumenical teaching is seen typically in the Westminster Confession: "Christ, in the work of mediation, acteth according to both natures; by each nature doing that which is proper to itself; yet by reason of the unity of the person, that which is proper to one nature is sometimes, in Scripture, attributed to the person denominated by the other nature" (Article VIII, *CC*, p. 205).

The Mediatorial Work Required the Cooperative Permeation of the Two Working Wills

Divine Working and Human Working in Jesus Christ

The alliance of divinity and humanity was cooperatively required for the mediatorial work in a communication of activities (*communicatio operatio,*) a unified action of the two natures resulting from their personal union in Christ, wherein the natures act together in the activity of either (Chemnitz, *TNC*, pp. 203–30, 245–46; Barth, *CD* IV/2, pp. 73ff., 104ff.).

Scriptural Grounding

"My Father is always at his work to this very day, and I, too, am working" (John 5:17). "Whatever the Father does, the Son also does" (John 5:19; cf. Augustine, *The Creed* 2.5, *FC* 27, p. 294). "The Father is in me, and I in the Father" (John 10:38). "For the very work the Father has given me to finish, and which I am doing, testifies that the Father has sent me" (John 5:36; Augustine, *Hom. on John* XXIII, *NPNF* 1 VII, pp. 150–57). "For just as the Father raises the dead and gives them life, even so the Son gives life" (John 5:21).

On the basis of these texts, the classical exegetes affirmed "two operations" (or working wills) in Christ. "While the power of working miracles was an operation of His divinity, the work of His hands, His willing, and His saying: 'I will. Be thou made clean,' were operations belonging to his humanity. . . . For, since in His divinity He is consubstantial with God the Father, He will also be equal to Him in His operation. On the other hand, since in His humanity He is consubstantial with us, He will also be equal to us in His operation" (John of Damascus, *OF* III.15, *FC* 37, pp. 305–306, quoting Matt. 8:3; see Tho. Aq., *ST* III Q19, II, pp. 2131–36).

Community of Action of the Two Natures

Every discrete act or work of the Mediator required this co-willing and co-working of the two natures (Chemnitz, *TNC*, pp. 215–30). "For, since He is consubstantial with God the Father, He freely wills and acts as God. And, since He is also consubstantial with us, the same one freely wills and acts as man. Thus, the miracles are His, and so are the sufferings" (John of Damascus, *OF* III.14, *FC* 37, p. 296).

Summarizing, just as there are two wills in Christ, we are also led by the texts to hypothesize that there are two *actions* without division or confusion, a divine action and a human action, hence two operations (Honorius, *Two Wills and Operations*, *SCD* 251–52, pp. 99–100; see also *SCD* 144, 264ff., 288f., 291f.). The two wills do not act contrary to each other (Agatho, *Roman Council*, *SCD* 288, p. 113; see also *SCD* 251f., 289ff.), the divine action constantly enabling the human action of the one divine-human person.

THE STATUS OF HUMANITY IN THE UNION

God did not choose to become enfleshed in a brute beast, but in human form, for animals are less capable of imaging the divine nature. If God became a frog, it would first be necessary to give the frog speech and moral awareness in order for God to become revealed to or through the frog.

But human nature, as originally given, is already capable of communication with God, of partaking of the divine life (2 Pet. 1:4). God became human, not a rock or hummingbird or spider, because humanity is already made in God's image.

It is on this basis that God assumed human nature without ceasing to be God, not diminishing but enhancing the human condition. Humanity is not less but more human through God's enfleshment.

Yet under the conditions of the fallenness of history, the capacity of humanity to image or reflect God has become grossly distorted. This is why Christ, the perfect image of God according to which humanity was originally made, is said to have restored that lost image by assuming human nature and filling it with the divine life, enabling genuine human faith, hope, and love. Hence the incarnation is said to embody the fulfillment of humanity and to express the truly human.

Why a Union That Included Human Nature Was Necessary for Salvation

Mediation Required Union

There can be no mediation between God and humanity without positing a mediator capable of empathy with ordinary humanity and of equal dignity with God (Phil. 2:6–11; Heb. 2:17–18). As human, he is capable of making intercession and sacrificial offering for humanity; as divine Son his act of sacrificial offering has infinite value to the Father. "For we do not have a high priest who is unable to sympathize with our weaknesses, but we have one who has been tempted in every way, just as we are—yet was without sin" (Heb. 4:15).

If the one who died on the cross were only human and not Son of God, the death could not serve sufficiently as an act of atonement for the whole world. If the one who died were only God and not human, there would have been no basis for celebrating the empathy of God with humanity. Only a mediator fully divine and fully human could undergo the experience necessary to save humanity.

The Person Enables What the Work Requires

Here the unifying principle of Christology again emerges: *What the mediatorial work requires, the mediatorial person supplies*: being very God while being thoroughly human (Rom. 1:3–4), equal with God, empathic with humanity (Phil. 2: 6–7)—distinguishable yet inseparable in one person—Word made flesh (John 1:14; Pope, *Compend.* II, p. 110).

Triune Teaching Presupposed in Theandric Union

Theandric Logic Intertwines with Triune Logic

It is fitting here to review the basic features of triune teaching. God is one, as Father, Son, and Spirit—three persons. One of these persons (not Father or Spirit, but Son) became flesh. Three persons did not become flesh and dwell among us, only one.

In becoming human, the Son did not become less than God. By virtue of his human experience, he thought, willed, and acted just as a human being would, subject to temptation, suffering, and death. By virtue of his divine nature, he thought, willed, and acted just as God would, exercising wherever necessary whatever divine attributes were required for the mediatorial mission.

Here the theandric logic and the triune logic necessarily interface: *Christ is one person, two natures; God is three persons, one in essence.* If God were only one person, God could not send, yet be sent; be both the Giver of law and obedient to it; both offer intercession for humanity and receive the prayers of humanity; both justify and sanctify, making just and making whole.

Distinct Without Separation

Schematically, triune teaching affirms one God in three persons:

God the Father	God the Son	God the Spirit
	Word Made Flesh	
	One Person Uniting Two	
	Natures, Divine and Human	

"The three Persons of the Holy Trinity are united without confusion and are distinct without separation and have number without the number causing division" (John of Damascus, *OF* III.6, *FC* 37, p. 278). "Number belongs to things which differ. . . . It is by that in which they differ that things are numbered. . . . Now, whereas the Lord's natures are hypostatically united without confusion, they are divided without separation by reason and way of their difference. . . . In so far as they are one, they have no number. For we do not say that Christ's natures are two Persons" (John of Damascus, *OF* III.8, *FC* 37, pp. 284–86).

Adoration of Christ's Humanity in the Union

The debate concerning the adoration of the humanity of Christ can be assessed only on the basis of these premises. When Christ is worshiped, he is not worshiped just as the divine nature of eternal Son, but as incarnate (enfleshed!) Lord. Accordingly it was judged to be a false teaching that "to adore directly the humanity of Christ" is "always to render divine honour to a creature" (Pius VI, *Constitution Auctorem Fidei*, *CF*, p. 179). That would amount to denying the unity of the person, and signal a reversion to Nestorianism (as the Synod of Pistoia, 1786, seemed to be leading).

The Damascene summed up centuries of debate: "And we do not say that His body is not to be adored, because it is adored in the one Person of the Word who became Person to it. Yet we do not worship the creature, because we do not adore it as a mere body, but as being one with the divinity" (*OF* III.8, *FC* 37, p. 285).

Part II

OUR LORD'S EARTHLY LIFE

Between Jesus' birth and death are a series of events oddly unmentioned by the creeds: the early events of his life, his baptism, temptation, his manner of life, and his healing, teaching, and proclaiming activity. We have considered the incarnation and its crucial theandric premise. On this basis we are prepared to focus upon issues of his earthly life and ministry.

CHAPTER 7

The Proclaimer Proclaimed

Classic writers regarded as a fundamental challenge to Christianity the view that Jesus was significantly different from the scriptural report of him. Paul wrote that if Jesus was not raised, then faith is in vain and the believer is to be pitied (1 Cor. 15:19).

Classic exegetes did not look for or discover any gross or distortive difference between the Jesus who actually lived and the Jesus portrayed in the Gospels. It is fatuous to criticize the writers of the first five centuries for not using historical methods that were only gradually developed in Western history and only became widely used since the nineteenth century.

The early Christian teachers fused the various canonically received pictures of Jesus in a single Gestalt (Tatian, *Diatessaron*; Augustine, *The Harmony of the Gospels*, NPNF 1 VI, pp. 77–232). Some found interesting the task of trying to sort out significant differences between various strains of the received tradition. There is some evidence that an oral tradition undergirding the written texts was recognized. Origen, Athanasius, Jerome, and Augustine carried on early forms of textual and literary criticism.

THE SEARCH FOR THE HISTORICAL JESUS – OLD, NEW, AND POSTCRITICAL

The recollection of Jesus' earthly life was dominated by the interpretation of the events surrounding his death. His life was viewed by its earliest rememberers as decisively illuminated by his death and resurrection.

Little was recorded about his life that did not serve the interest of the primitive faith of the Christian community in proclaiming the crucified as risen Savior. In Paul's writings there appears to be rather minimal historical interest in the details of his development or activities, excepting those surrounding his death and resurrection.

The Need for a Reliable Narrative of His Life

In the decades following his death, there emerged a felt need for some trustworthy account of the whole course of Jesus' ministry. The Gospel writers preserved many sayings and reliable narratives of his life and work from oral traditions based on eyewitness reports.

The Reliability of the Narratives

The Gospel writers were not trying to write scientific biographies. They were rather serving the interests of the proclaiming community, especially showing how Jesus' life and death fulfilled Hebraic prophecy. This does not imply that their views were distorted by proclamation, but that they had a distinct teaching purpose and evangelical intent.

As the Epistles and Gospels were being written, many remaining eyewitnesses were still alive. At the time of Paul's writing to Corinth, "most" of the "more than five hundred" witnesses to the resurrection were "still living" (1 Cor. 15:6). This must have restrained the authors from private embellishments and speculations, for if their account could have been easily denied by living eyewitnesses, how could they have expected to be taken seriously?

Between Birth and Death

It may seem odd that creeds and catechisms leap directly from incarnation to crucifixion. Calvin's catechism ventured plainly to address this curious question: "Why do you make the transition forthwith from birth to death, omitting all the story of his life?" The unambiguous answer: "Because nothing is dealt with here, except what so pertains to our redemption, as in some degree to contain the substance of it" (Calvin, Catech. of the Church of Geneva, LCC XXII, p. 98).

From Christmas to Easter

This surprising answer was given because incarnation and resurrection already hold all the essential clues to the meaning of his earthly ministry. These two mysteries, celebrated at Christmas and Easter, are the anchor events of Christian year and of the life of Jesus. Their interpretation is essential for Christian belief (BOC, pp. 413–15).

The interpretation of the events of Jesus' earthly ministry is fundamentally illumined by his divine sonship and resurrection. No one's salvation depends upon specific or detailed historical knowledge of the events of his earthly life. This is why the Apostles' Creed "passes at once in the best order from the birth of Christ to his death and resurrection" (Calvin, Inst. 2.16.5).

The Emergence of Modern Portraiture of Jesus

The overall result of modern Jesus criticism has been disappointing. The case does not stand much differently now than it did in 1906 when Albert Schweitzer dourly wrote: "There is nothing more negative than the result of the research into the life of Jesus. The Jesus of Nazareth who appeared upon the scene as the Messiah, proclaimed the morality of the kingdom of God, founded the kingdom of Heaven upon earth and died to consecrate his work never existed. He is a figure sketched by rationalism, brought to life by liberalism and clothed by modern theology with historical scholarship. This image has not been destroyed from the outside; it has collapsed internally, shaken and riven by the actual historical problems" (*The Quest of the Historical Jesus*, p. 388; cf. J. Peter, *Finding the Historical Jesus*). The collapse to which Schweitzer referred (of the liberal picture of Jesus) has once again recurred in new form in the inability of form criticism and redaction criticism to provide a plausible ground for Christian preaching and worship.

It is not our purpose to provide a thorough review of this scene, but it is necessary to set the question of the historical Jesus in the context of recent study of him. There has emerged in modern Christian history an abundant variety of differing pictures of Jesus (H. R. Niebuhr, *Christ and Culture*; Bornkamm, *JN*; H. Anderson, ed., *Jesus*). It is useful briefly to review how the Jesus portraiture of modern historical research emerged.

The Enlightenment Moralization of the History of Jesus

The turn to modernity began with the eighteenth-century Enlightenment, wherein the attempt was increasingly made to approach Jesus not as *theanthropos* or enfleshed Son of God but as moral teacher. Among circles most strongly influenced by Enlightenment thinking, Christ's divinity and theandric union were of decreasing interest. Their focus shifted largely to his earthly life, supposed personality, the sources of his ideas, his political interests, teachings, and moral significance.

H. S. Reimarus (1694–1768) was among the first in the modern period to seek to distinguish sharply the actual historical personage of Jesus from the pictures of Jesus found in the Gospels (*Apology for Rational Worshippers of God*; cf. D. F. Strauss, *H. S. Reimarus und seine Schutzschrift*, 1862; Jeremias, *Das Problem des historischen Jesus*, pp. 6–8). The fantasy that has driven certain speculative historians for two centuries thereafter is the thought that they might discover through historical study some real Jesus that could stand as a distinct improvement over the less palatable Christ attested in Scriptures.

Subjectivizing Shift Following Schleiermacher

Schleiermacher sought to resist the excesses of the rationalistic Enlightenment and balance them with an appeal to an experienced Redeemer, but he did not attempt to recover the full weight of the doctrines of Trinity, preexistence, eternal sonship, and incarnation. The tradition following Schleiermacher tended to narrow statements about Christ to inferences from the consciousness of human experience of the transition from guilt to redemption. Thus our consciousness of salvation becomes the base point, not God's saving action.

From Hegel to Harnack

In the period following Hegel, a supposed "great advance" occurred. Christology became a subject that was preemptively undertaken outside the circle of the worshiping community. With Hegel and those following immediately after him (Strauss, Feuerbach, Bauer, Biedermann, and others), there appeared an armada of modern "Christologies" determined to take charge of university studies in religion.

Since the resultant "Christ" had become completely altered, their whole view of Christianity became altered, for there is no way to change the teaching concerning Jesus Christ without changing every other aspect of Christianity—its teaching of Trinity, creation, providence, human existence, salvation, ethics, the church, ministry, and sacraments. An abandonment of classic teaching concerning Jesus Christ is tantamount to the abandonment of historic Christianity.

Hegel employed classical Christian language but reconceived Christ as a philosophical principle, a symbol of world process through which reason was becoming self-realized through the conflicts of history. David Friedrich Strauss followed by presenting a "Jesus" without any supposed mythical elements, which essentially meant all that Strauss's naturalistic biases found unacceptable. These were followed by a long string of "lives of Jesus" (Renan, Edersheim, Glover, Weiss), mostly amounting to humanistic biographies lacking almost all reference to Christ's eternal sonship, the premise so crucial to New Testament writers. Ritschl followed Kant in attaching to Jesus the idea of the perfect moral personality who founds a universal moral community to work toward the kingdom of God on earth (Ritschl, *CDJR*, pp. 448ff.; Kant, *Religion with the Limits of Reason Alone* [1793; Open Court Press], pp. 52ff.).

The Moralistic Christ

These long-standing modern trends have resulted in an overriding tendency to project upon the history of Jesus a modern moral perspective alien to the texts themselves—a human striving for salvation, the desire for moral self-redemption, and the increasing politicization of theology. Feuerbach and Freud concluded that all references to God are merely projections of human needs. In doing so they unconsciously followed the lead of early Christian "hermeneutics of suspicion" against the pretended efficacy of pagan idolatries of civil religion (Justin Martyr, Athenagoras, Hippolytus, Tertullian, Athanasius).

The moralistic Christ that emerged out of the period of German liberalism has indeed been in disrepute since Schweitzer among scholarly circles but still plays sentimentally in the churches of liberal Christianity. "The Christ that Harnack sees, looking back through nineteen centuries of Catholic darkness, is only the reflection of a Liberal Protestant face seen at the bottom of a deep well" (G. Tyrell, *Christianity at the Cross-Roads*, p. 44; cf. J. L. Segundo, *The Historical Jesus of the Synoptics*).

The Quest "Simplified" by the Peremptory Abandonment of the Theandric Premise

Twentieth-century liberal studies of Jesus have almost entirely unburdened themselves of the very theandric premise that enables the texts to be coherently interpreted, thereby making Christology virtually an anomaly. The New Testament has become plagued with absurdities, lacking the premise that the text considers essential.

The Historical Jesus and the Kerygmatic Christ

Martin Kähler distinguished between scientific history and theologically interpreted history, positing a radical difference between the *historische* Jesus and the *geschichtliche* Christ (*The So-called Historical Jesus and the Historic Biblical Christ*, 1892). At that point, it had not yet become fully evident that the "historical Jesus" was largely a fantasy based upon philosophical biases and not upon fair or adequate historical investigation.

Schweitzer's Reversal of the Quest

The liberal refashioning of Jesus effectively ended (not popularly but in the scholarly world) with Albert Schweitzer's *Quest of the Historical Jesus*, which described Jesus as one who expected the end of the world soon, but was mistaken in that expectation. Schweitzer left behind him a "cemetery of departed hypotheses" (Anderson, *Jesus*, p. 138).

The life of Jesus movement (from Strauss through Renan and Wrede) was in Schweitzer's view an exercise in modern literary imagination that said more about modernity than about Jesus. Renan viewed Jesus as the noblest of all men and the type of the evolution of the human race, but not God-incarnate. Schweitzer focused upon the very feature that liberal pictures of Jesus had most neglected: his imminent eschatology, especially in passages that expected immediately the apocalyptic woes of the last days; when the end did not appear, he surrendered himself to martyrdom, unaware that he would be later called the Christ.

Bultmann's Evisceration

By the time of Bultmann, the proclamation of the early church had replaced Jesus as the object of intense study. Bultmann considered the historical criticism of the Gospels a scientific matter and the kerygma embedded in the Gospels as an existential matter for personal decision. Accordingly, faith in the kerygma is not subject to historical verification. Criticism cannot embarrass faith. There is a salvation event, but it does not include a resurrection, only a cross as an event that took place in history. The resurrection occurred to the disciples, not to Jesus. Little can be known of Jesus except that he elicited the kerygma. Preaching may still point to a bare *that* (*Dass, that* Jesus elicited the kerygma), but not to *what* he did or said. Jesus is posited as that event from which the kerygma derived its interpretation (Bultmann, *TNT* I; *Essays Philosophical and Theological; Jesus Christ and Mythology*). "To believe in such an eviscertated *Dass* is to us certainly a crucifixion of the intellect, for it asks us to believe in an event from which every shred of the personal must be abstracted" (Ramm, *EC*, p. 156).

Tillich's Logos Asarkos

Tillich took these speculative formulations and further exaggerated them with his extreme principle that "the Christ is not the Christ without those who receive him as the Christ"; for without "believing reception," "the Christ would not have been the Christ" (*Syst. Theol.* II, p. 99). A whole generation of Protestants wrongly learned that one can get along quite well in Christology without Jesus.

The New Quest

Käsemann opened up a new form of the quest for the historical Jesus when he sought to develop further knowledge of the historical element in the history of Jesus (*ENTT,* pp. 15–47; cf. Bornkamm, *JN*; Robinson, *NQHJ*; Harvey, *HB*, pp. 174–96). The old liberal search for the historical Jesus was based upon a high valuation of the differences between the teaching of Jesus and supposed deteriorations in teaching by the apostles.

The new quest affirmed greater continuity between the proclaimed one and the proclaimer.

In summary: "Old Liberalism thought it had discovered an ethical prophet. Schweitzer discovered an apocalyptic Jesus, who he himself admits is not a help but an offense to modern man. Bultmann became skeptical of ever reconstructing the historical Jesus. The post-Bultmannians, illustrated by Bornkamm and Robinson, have found an existential Jesus who achieved authentic existence" (Ladd, *TNT,* pp. 178–79). The "historical Jesus" that has emerged has become a "fifth Gospel and the test of the other four" (H. Schlier, *Das Ende der Zeit* III, p. 11; Stuhlmacher, *HCTIS,* p. 71).

What was thought to be a simplification (the mandatory and absolute abandonment of the theandric premise) had the unintended effect of making New Testament interpretation much more strained, defensive, and complicated. The text stubbornly insists upon divine sonship, and to study the text without its essential premise is to search despairingly for an alternative to its premise. Under such circumstances, the text has only one means by which to defend itself against alien interpreters—its own tough, resilient language.

A postcritical inquiry into the life of Jesus is due. It can only be postcritical by proceeding as the texts themselves proceed—with, not without, the theandric premise.

THE PROCLAIMER OF GOD'S COMING
UNDERSTOOD AS GOD'S OWN COMING

The postcritical study of the historical Jesus has not yet begun in our time, because the theandric union has not been taken seriously. Once the documents' own central premise is received as a possible hypothesis, even tentatively, then the historical study of Jesus can resume.

If we take the New Testament rather than modern naturalistic reductionism as our starting point, then everywhere we turn in the texts we are being met by one who is thoroughly human who claimed to be God, was attested as Son of God, and according to Christian confession was God-incarnate. Little attempt is made in the texts to theorize about how that could or could not be. No attempt is made to protect Jesus from the charge of paradox, for he was a *skandalon,* "a stumbling block to Jews and foolishness to Gentiles" (1 Cor. 1:23; Kierkegaard, *TC*).

Two certainties are most deeply shared by all writers of the New Testament: that Jesus was fully human, and that in him God has personally appeared into our midst. Christian teaching seeks to account for that unusual confluence of testimony. The way is narrow that leads to an adequate statement of Jesus Christ, that avoids the polar errors of diminishing either his humanity or deity.

The Approach "From Below"

Does one begin the study of Jesus Christ from the side of his divinity or humanity? Is it necessary to begin with the preexistent Logos, as did John's Gospel, and proceed toward the incarnation, or with the history of Jesus and ask how he came to be worshiped as Lord? This is the problem of a "starting point" (it sounds more weighty in German: *Anfangspunkt*).

Our thesis: *Christology "begins" neither with divinity or humanity abstractly, but by meeting Jesus Christ, the unique theandric person, God-man, one person divine and human.*

The Question of a Starting Point in Christology: Jesus or Eternal Son?

In recent decades the teaching of the incarnation has hardly been universally accepted as a self-evident starting point for Christology. Modernity has instead spawned a series of approaches that begin with the man Jesus and attempt to show how deity came to be ascribed to him. Hence they are called *Christology from below.*

One theologian in our time, Wolfhart Pannenberg, has more astutely than others developed a Christology from below that, on historical-critical grounds, argues from the history of Jesus to the deity of Christ without falling into either Docetism or Ebionism. Pannenberg develops a "Christology 'from below,' rising from the historical man Jesus to the recognition of his divinity," a procedure that is "concerned first of all with Jesus' message and fate and arrives only at the end at the concept of the incarnation" (*JGM*, p. 33).

Pannenberg has resisted a Christology "from above" on three grounds: it begins and proceeds circularly by already presupposing the deity of Jesus; it circumvents the need for understanding the complex relation between Jesus and Judaism; and it tends to imply that one can stand in the position of God.

The Theandric Response

Classic Christology (moving neither unilaterally from below or above but from the theandric person) answers: (1) The apostles and ancient church teachers did not begin by simply presupposing Jesus' deity but rather set forth a chronicle of the events of history—centering in the resurrection—that constituted their reason for receiving Jesus as God's own embodied Word. (2) The ancient exegetes such as Origen, Irenaeus,

Athanasius, Ambrose, Augustine, and Jerome were constantly searching the early Hebraic and later Judaic sources for prefigurations and anticipations of Jesus' ministry. They do not characteristically detach Jesus from his Hebraic or Judaic context. (3) No exegete stands in the position of God, but those who understand that God has spoken through his Word made flesh have a historical datum to deal with: the God-man, a person who was born and died not outside, but in history.

Limitations of Christology "From Below"

The attempt to devise an adequate Christology "from below" runs up against three persistent limitations: (1) Such a procedure has great difficulty from the outset even locating Jesus in history utilizing recent critical methods. (2) Heated speculative-critical questions abound as to how attributions of deity ever came to be applied to Jesus during the period of the oral tradition preceding our written documents. Hence (3) it typically ends with feeble and uncertain affirmations of the divinity of Christ, the keystone of traditional Christology (see Bultmann, *TNT* I, pp. 3–63; W. Marxsen, *BCSP*; H. Conzelmann, *TNT*, pp. 72–86; W. Kümmel, *The Theology of the New Testament* [1974], pp. 105–25; and their critics Guthrie, *NTT*, pp. 401–407; I. H. Marshall, *ONTC*; C. F. D. Moule, *OC*). So what appeared to be a constructive renewal of Christology ended either by denying Christ's deity altogether or losing it in a mass of critical speculation. In the hands of criticism, the classical Christian affirmation of the true humanity of *theanthropos* quickly becomes whittled down to the mere humanity of an itinerant preacher.

Critics who elsewhere reject "above" and "below" as valid spatial metaphors for the God/world relation oddly accept this metaphor here and propose to make it the primary distinction between types of Christology. The "from below"/"from above" distinction follows in form, though not in specific argument, numerous treatises of the turn of the century (Grensted, *Person of Christ*; Glover, *The Jesus of History*; Denny, *Jesus and the Gospel*; Dorner, *A System of Christian Doctrine*).

The Theandric Starting Point

The modern progression from Jesus' certain humanity to his uncertain divinity needs the corrective of classic Christianity. There we meet Jesus Christ always already as divine-human Mediator.

Classic Theandric Teaching Lives Out of a Cohesive Personal Unity That Binds Together the Approaches "From Above" and "From Below"

Theanthropos is always one person, human and divine, hence neither from below reductionistically or from above exclusively, but always an actual, historical, divine-human person. Yet God's saving action is not directly accessible to objective historical investigation, if that investigation proceeds with criteria that, ruling out God, thereby rule out *theanthropos*.

Can a Historically Grounded Procedure Find the Way?

The classic mediatorial view, however, does not impede or deny inquiry into the historical process through which Jesus was received and recognized as divine Son. Critical inquiry can explore within reasonable limits the oral traditions wherein Jesus was received in due time as Son of God, without denial of the personal union of God-man. These are complementary required tasks.

The Historical Question and the Offense

One can sit comfortably in an easy chair and ask historical questions without any commitment or moral response. With the historian's hat on, one can play at the puzzle of trying to understand the sequence of events by which Jesus came to be called Christ, the Son of God. It is possible to raise fine and intriguing historical questions without ever being required to make any personal decision about them.

The irony is that when we meet the Jesus of the text, he is constantly calling us to a decision about him. Historical scholarship wants to suspend judgment while these facts are being examined. Yet the decisive question persists in the New Testament texts: by whomever ascribed, is Jesus the Christ? The Jesus of the texts presses us closely: you must decide, yes or no—one not with me is against me. The historical questions of chronology and sequence are manageable and tame in relation to the unruly, demanding, decisive *skandalon* of the Gospel question: is Jesus the Anointed One?

Is "From Below" Ruled Out?

The deeper sympathies of this study are with the classical procedure that begins, as did John's Gospel, by speaking first to last of the embodied Word made flesh. It is possible, however, without denying that commitment, to include in the study of Christ a careful textually grounded inquiry into the history of Jesus, a history that moves inexorably toward his death. The events surrounding his death came to impinge upon the terms that his rememberers used to describe and report him. Yet such an examination is prone to forget the theandric union that alone makes the text worth reading if the text itself is telling the truth.

Christology cannot rule out "inquiry from below" without ruling out historical inquiry. But classical Christianity sees history and historical inquiry being transmuted by the fact of *theanthropos*, the decisive historical datum to be inquired into, insofar as historical inquiry can approach revelation.

With this preliminary framing of the question, we are ready to ask:

How Did the Proclaimer Become the Proclaimed?

How did it occur that Jesus Christ, who preached the coming kingdom of God, was suddenly after his death declared as Lord of that kingdom? Christology seeks to account for this reversal.

Basic Options

Some say the resurrection did not happen to Jesus, but only to those who remembered him. He was later proclaimed as Messiah and much later as God by those whose faith had emerged after his death (Bultmann's view).

Some say Jesus understood himself as Lord, Messiah, and Son of God. Hence the basic assumptions of Christology concerning Jesus' divine-human identity are found in Jesus' own life and proclamation, not exclusively in postresurrection insight of the disciples (the classical view).

Some say Jesus did not regard himself as Lord, but after his resurrection was so regarded by his disciples. Hence Christological reasoning begins with the event of Jesus' resurrection. Jesus' divine sonship becomes rightly identified only in the light of Jesus' resurrection (Pannenberg).

We will show in due course our reasons for regarding the first view (that of Bultmann, Braun, Buri, Marxsen, and Tillich) as unable to account for the power of the early Christian witness. We will follow the second view (classical Christian writers and, among recent writers, Barth, Manson, Taylor, Ladd, Guthrie, Wells, and Ramm) and include within it certain aspects of the third view (Pannenberg, Moltmann, Braaten).

What Part Did Jesus Himself Have in the Formation of Christology?

The roots of the early development of Christology may be found in the way Jesus himself impacted the historical transition from Jesus the proclaimer of the kingdom to Jesus the One proclaimed as Anointed of God to inaugurate the kingdom as God's own coming to save humanity.

Jesus himself played the decisive role in the transition from preacher to Preached One. The teaching and transfiguration narratives suggest that he was actively preparing his disciples for the events surrounding his death. The recognition of his messianic identity was not determined exclusively by the disciples' postresurrection insight, but by Jesus' own

leading, guiding, and teaching of the disciples before and after the resurrection. The pivotal transition is *from* Jesus' preaching of the kingdom *to*
the church's memory of Jesus viewed primarily but not exclusively
through the lens of his death and resurrection. (On the beginnings of
Christology, see Bultmann, *TNT* I; Cullmann, *CNT;* Longenecker, *CEJC;*
Fuller, *FNTC;* J. A. T. Robinson, *Twelve NT Studies; The Human Face of God;*
Marxsen, *BCSP;* Marshall, *ONTC;* C. F. D. Moule, *OC;* J. Knox, *The Humanity and Divinity of Christ;* H. Conzelmann, *TNT;* V. Taylor, *The Formation of
the Gospel Tradition;* Braaten, *ChrD* I, pp. 483–88; Perrin, *MPNTC.*)

Sequence of the Transition from Proclaimer to Proclaimed

Before the Resurrection

Most agree that the proclamation of the reign of God is the central feature of Jesus' public ministry. He came preaching the kingdom. There is
hardly a firmer point of consensus in modern Scripture studies.

A crucial reversal occurred in Jesus' ministry. The expected and coming kingdom was recognized as God's own coming. That means the kingdom appears when God appears. The kingdom is inaugurated when
God's own power is incomparably and personally manifested. Those
who order their lives in relation to the kingdom live as open to the coming of God.

Jesus' preaching awakened and intensified the expectation of God's
own imminent coming, nothing less. His acts of healing and exorcism
were signs of God's own coming. His parables pointed to the way God
comes to humanity.

Jesus' proclamation of the coming of God required of his hearers a
decision for or against that coming. Every decision must be made now,
for no remaining time is left before God's own coming. Since God's coming was imminent, all were called urgently to repent and trust in God's
emergent rule. To delay is to say no.

After the Resurrection

After the resurrection the rememberers looked back at the times
before the resurrection. Thereafter their lens for viewing the life of Jesus
was the resurrected Lord. What they remembered as occurring before the
resurrection was affected in a decisive way by the present risen Lord and
the abundant recollections of his appearances.

Such a postresurrection frame did not distort but intensified their
acuity of perception of earlier events. Some press this point inordinately
so as to claim that the disciples after the resurrection lost all touch with

the actual historical reality of Jesus, and all they could remember was the Jesus they romanticized through the memory of the resurrection. The resurrection, indeed, transmuted their understanding of Jesus' ministry, for it declared that he was Son of God. Yet that was hardly a diminution of insight (except by a curious definition of insight), but rather an eye-opener, wherein they more fully realized what had been happening to them all along. Years later, having proclaimed this everywhere they could, they wrote the documents we now have as our only access to these events.

Jesus had announced the coming of God, the kingdom of God. The rememberers of Jesus looked back to him as the Anointed One who fulfilled the promises God had made to Israel. Jesus proclaimed the coming God. His rememberers viewed him as the One through whom God had come. Jesus announced the rule of God at hand. The rememberers of Jesus understood that he was God's own coming and that God's salvation of humanity would be finally completed by his coming again on the last day.

The disciples did not invent this insight without Jesus (Taylor, *LMJ*). Rather Jesus nurtured and elicited this recognition in both his earthly and postresurrection ministry (Luke 9:45–47; 24:44–45; Irenaeus, *Ag. Her.* V.1–3, *ANF* I, pp. 526–30; Henry, *CWB* V, p. 843).

The Relation of Jesus to the Coming of God

We approach the decisive question of the role Jesus played in God's coming. Did Jesus merely point to God's coming, or was he in his person God's own coming? That in fact was the decision put to the disciples after the resurrection.

If I Heal, Then the Kingdom Has Come

Remember that John the Baptist also had preached the imminent coming kingdom of God. Jesus was not regarded merely as one who pointed to a coming kingdom, but as one who inaugurated the kingdom and established it, the One through whom God's own coming became decisively manifested. Jesus proclaimed: "But if I drive out demons by the finger of God, then the kingdom of God has come to you" (Luke 11:20) — widely acknowledged even by critics as embedded in the earliest layer of sayings of Jesus in the oral tradition.

This and similar sayings may be the core layer of the earliest ascriptions of deity to Jesus. Here may lie the most primitive Christology embedded quietly in his eschatological proclamation of God's imminent coming. Accordingly, the decision one makes for or against Jesus entirely determines one's relation to God's coming. Even critics who view ascriptions of deity to Jesus as being of a much later period nonetheless view Jesus as the one through whom the kingdom comes (Bultmann, *TNT* I, pp. 33–36; Marxsen, *BCSP*, pp. 31–32).

What specifically happened to enable the rememberers to move from their memory of Jesus the proclaimer to the worship of Jesus as Anointed of God? The short answer: resurrection. The longer and more precise answer will have to await the examination of numerous biblical texts relating to events surrounding Jesus' death.

Jesus as God's Own Coming

The heart of the matter is this: *the proclaimer of the coming of God became understood as God's own coming through his death and resurrection*, which stood as a demonstration—God's own historical way of proving—that he was the expected one of Israel, anointed to inaugurate God's kingdom, to bring salvation, and to offer a special priesthood of sacrifice for the sins of humanity. *The cross was viewed as a sacrifice for humanity's sin and the resurrection as a vindication of Jesus' earthly ministry and deity. The single event of cross/resurrection constituted an unprecedented victory over sin, guilt, and death and a binding up of the power of evil.*

In this way the history of Jesus and God's own coming coalesce. The one person is both proclaimer and proclaimed. The preaching of Jesus was gradually transformed, by his own instruction, into the church's preaching about Jesus. Hence there is no need for classical Christianity to defensively resist the inquiry into the history of Jesus—indeed it has not resisted such inquiry in most of its history. But we do have a right to expect an accurate, unprejudiced evidentiary examination and historical inquiry. His preresurrection history is the ground upon which his postresurrection memory was possible. These matters remain subject to honest and rigorous historical inquiry.

The Confession of Lordship

It did not take the disciples long to learn to say, "Jesus is Lord" (Rom. 10:9; 1 Cor. 12:3; Phil. 2:11). This learning did not emerge gradually over decades through a slow hellenization process or gradual accretions of messianic insight. Rather it came abruptly for many and with great power in the immediate awareness of the risen Lord present amid the remembering community. The confession "Jesus is Lord" could easily have been made on the very day the resurrected Lord was first met, and in some it must have occurred earlier. There is no sufficient reason to imagine that it was a long-delayed insight.

Searching the Scriptures

This explains why the early rememberers were found so diligently "searching the scriptures" (John 5:39, RSV)—namely, Hebrew Scriptures, especially in the tradition of messianic expectation, to gain a deeper grasp of how those expectations were being fulfilled, how the prophets had pointed to the Christ, how the promises of the God of Abraham, Isaac, Jacob, David, and Isaiah were being fulfilled in "these last days" (Heb. 1:2; Origen, *De Principiis* IV.18–23, *ANF* IV, pp. 367–74, 477, 550).

They did not search the Scriptures to concoct supposed events that occurred to Jesus. Rather the events that occurred to Jesus caused them to search the Scriptures to understand better what had actually happened to him. They first beheld his entry into Jerusalem and only then recalled its connection with Zechariah's prophecy (9:9).

Can New Testament Testimony Be Trusted?

The Short Time from Jesus to Paul

Can New Testament reportage be trusted? The longer the time between the events and the documents reporting them, the more problematic are the reports. One case in point deserves special note—the chronological placement of Paul's testimony.

If Mark wrote near the destruction of Jerusalem (A.D. 70) then there would only be about forty years in which mutations of the tradition could have taken place. If Paul began writing about A.D. 50, there remain only twenty years to fill with hypothetical developments. If 1 Corinthians 15:1–7 is correct in identifying the central tradition that Paul received (not one that he subsequently invented), that tradition apparently dates only a few dozen months after Jesus' death (Ramm, *EC*, pp. 121–23).

The Pace of Communication

It is well also to remember the slower pace of transportation and communication, as well as the limits of publishing, and the slow diffusion of ideas in the first century. Hence it is unlikely that vast changes in the memory and interpretation of Jesus could have occurred quickly and become widely diffused over vast areas. It is a mistake to impose upon the first century our twentieth-century assumptions about the immediacy of communication from one country or culture to another.

On these grounds, Herbert Butterfield has argued that the essential interpretation of Jesus was largely settled within the first twenty years after Jesus' death (*Writings on Christianity and History*). If so, there is little to recommend the highly speculative theories of Bultmann and others that enormous mutations of consciousness had time to take place between Jesus and the memory of Jesus (see Hengel, *Between Jesus and Paul*).

The Practice of Detailed Memorization

Note further that the Jewish pedagogy of that period stressed perfect memorization of long passages of sacred writing (B. Gerhardsson, *Memory and Manuscript*). It is hard for us to imagine a culture that puts a high value upon the accurate recollection of oral traditions, for we are constantly dependent upon written and electronic communications of all sorts (M. Wilson, "The Jewish Concept of Learning: A Christian Appreciation," *Christian Scholars' Review* 5:350–63). Our modern memories are not nearly as well developed as the functional memories of those committed to sustaining a tradition of testimony.

The Basis for Trust

Classical Christianity proceeds with a general trust in the reports about Jesus. It is based not only on the trustworthiness of eyewitnesses, but also on a recurrent *a priori* argument concerning providence: if God determines to offer salvation to humanity in Christ, and if that offer must be transmitted through first oral and then written testimony, then it is not plausible that God would allow that testimony to be falsified. God would not come to humanity in a costly way, only to allow humanity to immediately forget, misunderstand, or distort it. God's own Spirit would not allow the church to be led drastically astray in the recollection and canonization process. That argument proceeds from the premise that the Spirit created the church. This stands against the view that "we can no longer assume the general reliability of the Synoptic tradition about Jesus" (Käsemann, *ENTT*, p. 34).

RISEN LORD INTERPRETER OF HIS HISTORY

Was it the case that a series of distinctly different (even competing) Christologies developed in the trajectory of early Christian preaching? Did Christologies emerge in the early Palestinian context that were substantively different from those of the Gentile mission, moving from a focus upon Jesus' death to his exaltation and belatedly to the message of redemption (Fuller, *FNTC*, pp. 243ff.; Marshall, *ONTC*; Hahn, *TJC*; see also Cullmann, *CNT*; J. A. T. Robinson, "The Most Primitive Christology of All," *Journal of Theological Studies* 7 [1956]:177–89; G. B. Caird, "The

Development of the Doctrine of Christ in the NT," in N. Pittenger, ed., *Christ for Us Today*)?

The narratives of apostolic preaching in Acts resist the notion that the basic core of Christological teaching required a long period of development. Obviously there could not have been a complete comprehension in earliest Palestinian Christianity of all the issues that would later develop in the Gentile mission. But the nucleus of the preaching of the Gentile mission was already present in the Palestinian church, and the preaching of Acts provides glimpses of its earliest tendencies. "The lordship of Christ is a case in point. It is tampering with the evidence to suggest that this was not grasped by the Palestinian church" (Guthrie, *NTT*, p. 403; cf. Acts. 2:36).

The Risen Lord as His Own Interpreter

It was the risen Lord who interpreted the history that had gone before him (Luke 24:25-27). The resurrected Lord led the church to an interpretation of Jesus' ministry, not the other way around (that the church was led by emergent challenges in the culture to interpret Jesus as having been resurrected — a fantastic hypothesis for which no adequate evidence exists).

Admittedly there is no revelation without interpretation. It was Jesus, present through the power of the Spirit, who did the interpreting, according to the memory of the apostles. Accordingly, Paul wrote: "We have not received the spirit of the world but the Spirit who is from God, that we may understand what God has freely given us. This is what we speak, not in words taught us by human wisdom but in words taught by the Spirit, expressing spiritual truths in spiritual words. The man without the Spirit does not accept the things that come from the Spirit of God, for they are foolishness to him, and he cannot understand them, because they are spiritually discerned" (1 Cor. 2:12-14).

Jesus both fulfilled and interpreted messianic expectations in his own distinctive, unconventional way, resisting plausible but mistaken interpretations. The Expected One was always presenting himself in unexpected ways (Newman, *GA*, pp. 448-52). When God is the teacher, the learner is not in control of the learning (Kierkegaard, "A Project of Thought," *Phil. Frag.*).

Jesus Himself Provided the Structure of Interpretation for Christian Teaching

That Christ is alive remains the chief premise of Christian teaching. Lacking that premise, Christianity is easily turned into tedious moral obligations, pretentious sounding historical research, unsufferably vague speculative philosophy, or desperate self-help psychology.

Can Jesus Be Explained?

The question "Can this person (Jesus Christ) be explained?" raises the larger question of whether any person can be explained. To explain (*explanare*) literally means to flatten out or make something level or plain so as to bring it down to ordinary understanding. To explain something is to classify it. While any person's actions may be explained to some extent, no person can be explained exhaustively. One explains finally only things, not persons.

Jesus, being unique, fits even less neatly into our preset categories, since there is no class into which he can readily be placed. Theandric personal union happened only once. Christianity asks that Jesus first be met and then interpreted, not first explained and then sought.

A Flat "Explanation"

A standard, late eighteenth-century Enlightenment attempt at a flat explanation of Jesus, however, remains fixed dogma in certain elite circles. The explanation runs this way: the extraordinary admiration of the disciples for their leader gradually turned into reverence, which evolved into superstition, which then projected miracles onto previously innocuous events. Such an explanation says more about the explainers than about the one being explained.

Christ in Search of His Searchers

The more plausible evidence indicates that the theandric person himself provided unity and interpretation to the experiences of the disciples, engendering radical confidence and hope, knitting them into a community of proclamation that "turned the world upside down" (Acts 17:6). It was Jesus himself personally who first called forth and addressed the consciousness of the witnessing, remembering church, not the remembrance that invented the mission.

There are indeed differences in reports about Jesus. Their very diversity lends strength to the authenticity of their testimony. The diversity of documents and witnesses makes their underlying personal unity all the more impressive.

These literary differences come out of varied authors speaking to varied audiences, speaking within different cultural settings and employing different conceptual resources to state effectively in alternative contexts the good news of God's coming. The differences do not arise out of different Christs. One Jesus Christ was being interpreted in many ways, times, places, and languages.

Sources Attesting Jesus' Self-Interpretation

There are four main groups or types of New Testament sources to which Christian teaching returns in seeking an understanding of Christ's self-attestation: (1) the Pauline tradition, including the pastoral Letters; (2) the Johannine writings; (3) the synoptic Gospels and Acts; (4) a miscellany of shorter Letters, including notably the Letter to the Hebrews, James, Jude, and 1 and 2 Peter.

Though distinguishable, they are not completely independent of each other. The references of this study seek to show incrementally that the New Testament sources constitute a single stream whose unity of direction is powerful enough to include, absorb, and provide corrective cohesion for numerous varieties of interpretation.

Each witness met the living Lord in his own way; hence he viewed the salvation event in his own way and described with his own language what he understood to have happened. The attempt to press all these testimonies into a single language mold or mechanical harmony cannot be the legitimate task of exegetically grounded Christian teaching. The remembering church has always found nourishment precisely in the variety of these testimonies—in some periods some witnesses are stressed more than others, but in time the whole canon is needed for an adequate mosaic of Christ.

Christianity need not assume that the New Testament is a neatly designed, logically ordered systematic treatise, either of divine utterances about humanity or human utterances about God, all of which chime in perfect harmony. Systematic theology is an extension of baptismal formula, creed, and catechism, which themselves are "an epitome and brief transcript of the entire Holy Scripture" (Luther, *Large Catech.*, intro., *WLS* I, p. 124; *WA* 30 I, 128). Scripture wishes "to interpret itself by a comparison of passages" (Luther, *Comm. on Deut.*, *WLS* I, p. 96, *WA* 14, 556).

Classical Christian teaching bases its understanding of Christ upon the biblical record. Exegesis proceeds in relation to texts. If classical Christology is to be overturned, it must be overturned on the basis of the texts to which it understands itself to be accountable. If scholars look at these texts and do not like what they see, if the portrait does not appeal to them, they do well to resist the temptation to "retouch it, lest they be found guilty of trying to correct the Wisdom of God by the wisdom of man" (W. M. Horton, in the Foreword to J. W. Bowman, *The Intention of Jesus*).

Unity of Faith Enabled by Christ Himself, Not His Apostles

Diversity Celebrated

The unity that coheres in Jesus himself takes diverse expressions in the New Testament. Unity is not uniformity.

The complex unity of the New Testament is not wooden, lockstep uniformity. Christ is not attested with a single monotonous voice, but with a vast choir of voices in a cast of thousands, all of whose performances are not wonderful. There are villians, bums, heroes, and ordinary folk in the drama Scripture attests—the drama of God's own coming.

The Canon Not a Single Document

The Bible is not a single book, but (as *biblus* itself suggests) a library. The New Testament, from which most of our knowledge of Jesus of Nazareth is derived, is itself a library of documentary resources that attest Jesus.

Listening to Premodern Texts

The New Testament writers were actively engaged at the time of their writing in a continuing dialogue with specific audiences. They sought by means of letters, narratives, and expositions to convince particular hearers in particular cultures of the truth they beheld.

Sometimes the first-century language they used can be easily transferred to twentieth-century settings; at other times that is quite difficult due to changed historical settings, values, symbol systems, language, and assumptions. If we read the New Testament at all, at some point in listening in upon this dialogue, we realize that it profoundly involves us and requires us to join in it in our own way, even if that means fighting it.

The Personal Unity of Canonical Diversity

Jesus himself is the personal center of cohesion of these diverse writings. The cohesion of New Testament documents is seen in the one person to whom they all refer and who elicited and made possible these interpretations. That cohesion is not best grasped by juxtaposing texts merely as scholastic proof-texts, but personally—by penetrating to the singular person, Jesus, to whom the kerygma witnesses (Taylor, *LMJ*).

The preceding issues awaken fundamental questions not only about how far the earthly life of Jesus is historically knowable, but moreso whether any event is historically knowable. If we are to deal fairly and sufficiently with his earthly life, it is necessary to discuss the relation of faith and historical inquiry.

A PERSONAL INTERLUDE: A PATH TOWARD POSTCRITICAL CONSCIOUSNESS

That this writer has once again committed the sin of authorship deserves some explanation. If the company one constantly keeps is John Chrysostom, Augustine, Kierkegaard, and Newman, then perhaps one may be treated gently who writes overmuch. We can all sympathize with Karl Barth's picture of God amused by the theologian bringing his dogmatics by the wheelbarrow to heaven. And Thomas Aquinas ended his enormous *Summa* with the remark that "all I have written now appears to be of little value" in relation to the vision of God.

The reader's burden may be slightly lightened by a brief autobiographical excursus. It seems pertinent at this point, because the steps ahead will challenge some exaggerated forms of biblical criticism. Only some account of the personal side of my long identification with biblical criticism will help the reader see that I do not approach the subject from the outside, but as a long-time participant and erstwhile advocate of radical biblical criticism. As I look back at the trajectory of my adult life, one name weaves in and out almost from the beginning: Rudolf Bultmann.

It surely is obvious that many premodern Christian thinkers have had decisive effect upon this study (Augustine, Gregory Nazianzen, Thomas Aquinas, Calvin, and others). But at this juncture I want to try to be accountable as to how I have been shaped by contemporary theologians, both in constructive and deconstructive ways.

Five theologians have personally shaped my thought and work in unparalleled ways, and they hiddenly appear on almost every page. They are Albert Outler, Rudolf Bultmann, H. Richard Niebuhr, Karl Barth, and Will Herberg. Those who might misperceive this effort under the rubric of neoorthodoxy, I hope, will remember my stubborn criticisms of neoorthodoxy in *Agenda for Theology*.

My first and best teacher of Christian theology was and is Albert C. Outler, who awakened my love of Augustine, of Wesley, of the promise of dialogue between Christianity and contempoary psychotherapy, and who has given me frequent and decisive guidance on matters of faith and ethics. The first irony is that it was that most un-Bultmannian theologian, Albert C. Outler, who first introduced me to Bultmann in 1952.

The one theologian whose work caused the New Testament to come alive for me in the early 1950s was Rudolf Bultmann. From my principal Bultmannian mentors, Joseph W. Mathews and Edward C. Hobbs, I proceeded from Texas to Yale eager to study Christian existentialism—Kierkegaard, Bultmann, and Heidegger especially, under H. Richard Niebuhr. I found Niebuhr to be surprisingly resistant to Bultmann. Niebuhr insisted that I study Barth, which I did chiefly with Hans Frei, and eventually when I decided to write my dissertation as a comparative study of Bultmann and Barth, my heart was Bultmannian. It took months of ambivalent study to enter empathically into the Barthian project. Yet by the time I had completed my dissertation, I had largely shifted from a primary orientation toward Bultmann to a primary orientation toward Barth on grace and Richard Niebuhr on cultural relativism.

After I began teaching I revised the Bultmann portion of my dissertation for publication and sent the draft to Bultmann, who played an important role in my early life by writing a long and thoughtful reply to my study, which was included as a part of my first scholarly book, *Radical Obedience: The Ethics of Rudolf Bultmann*. I now find myself in the odd place of belatedly resisting the very person who first brought my work to the attention of others by very generously taking me seriously as a young scholar. I had already developed by 1959 some criticisms of Bultmann, to which he responded patiently and thoughtfully. As late as the mid-sixties I continued writing and speaking in defense of what I would call a moderate Bultmannian position in theology, seeking to defend Bultmann against Ogden's and Buri's insurgency from the left, and Schniewind's and Thielicke's from the right.

As the sixties progressed (or fell to pieces) the tenor of my work was increasingly more Barthian than Bultmannian, as is evident from *The Crisis of the World and the Word of God* (1962) and my first two books on theology and psychotherapy, *Kerygma and Counseling* (1966) and *Contemporary Theology and Psychotherapy* (1967), which treated of both Barth and Bultmann as well as Tillich, Rogers, Teilhard de Chardin, and others. By the time I wrote *The Structure of Awareness* (1968), the Barthian influence had reached its zenith and was soon to recede. When I was asked by Martin Marty to write *The Promise of Barth: The Ethics of Freedom*, I had already begun to experience serious doubts about Barth's unrelenting campaign against synergism. It took many years before I discovered the rich synergism of the Eastern church fathers as a corrective (especially the Cappadocians and John of Damascus). Fortunately I was able to meet both Barth and Bultmann on my sabbatical year in Germany in 1965 to 1966, as well as to have substantive conversations with Hans Georg Gadamer in Heidelberg and Wolfhart Pannenberg in Mainz.

Coming to Drew University in 1970 brought me into the orbit of a uniquely brilliant individual whose influence on my life and theology was decisive: Will Herberg. Several others influenced me profoundly—especially John Ollom, James O'Kane, Edward Leroy Long, and Bard Thompson, but none more fundamentally than Will Herberg, who did more for me intellectually in the six years of our close friendship (1971–1977) than did any other person during that time, by requiring me to ground my thinking in classical sources. Ironically my chief mentor since Outler in classical Christianity was not a Christian but a conservative Jew.

Herberg made me think through for the first time the strained vulnerabilities of my native, long-seated liberalism. He turned my political thinking more toward neoconservative political sources (Thomas Aquinas, Burke, Madison, Newman, and the mature Reinhold Niebuhr). This trend had already begun in the late sixties but, having been untutored, bore little fruit except what was embryonically visible in *Beyond Revolution*. In 1970 I was far left of center politically, drawn constantly toward socialist politics, and still quasi-Bultmannian in theology. By the time Herberg finished with me, I had become skeptical about the entire Bultmannian enterprise. By the time of *Roe v. Wade*, I had given up situation ethics altogether in a revulsive response to the awareness that I had long uncritically supported liberalized abortion legislation. By the early seventies, I had come to accept Pannenberg's account of the resurrection as a historical event—a most un-Bultmannian idea.

This excursus I hope will give readers at least some confidence that I do not enter into the discussion of the Jesus of history without being instructed in form criticism, for I have spent a large part of my professional life studying its major exponent—Rudolf Bultmann.

Here is how the reversal occurred: I had spent the first fifteen years of my professional life trying to live out the critical method (Oden, *RO*; "The Gnostic Dialogue," *CTP*, pp. 102–11; *SA*, pp. 107–24). I considered it my duty to bring to each text of theology a critical attitude, requiring that text to conform to my assumptions about the world. I was determined not to accept any reports that could not be fitted into my modern worldview (according to Troeltsch's law of analogy). Furthermore, I was mentored (especially by Bultmann, Tillich, Heidegger, and Rogers) to understand that what it meant to be a theologian was to struggle to create something new, to develop a new theology, to see things differently than any others had seen things before and thereby to offer my personal skill and subjective experience as a theologian to the emergent world. The result was that my relation to my sources became less a dialogue than a filtering process by which I permitted these sources to speak to me only insofar as they could meet my conditions, my worldview, my assumptions as a modern man. This is the modernity that for me ended in the late sixties, whose end it took some time for me to realize.

By the middle of the 1970s the idea had gradually begun to dawn upon me with increasing force that it is not my task to create a theology. Newman taught me that the deposit of truth is already sufficiently given, fully and adequately. What I needed to do was to listen. But I could not listen because I found my modern presuppositions constantly tyrannizing my listening.

During the mid-seventies I was keenly aware of the disintegrating moral foundation of the type of theology I had internalized (that of Bultmann, Tillich, and the late Bonhoeffer)—secularization theology—a theology ready to accommodate to rapid secularization. I was becoming aware of the bankruptcy of my political commitments.

Then while reading Nemesius something clicked. I realized that I must listen intently, actively, without reservation. Listen in such a way that my whole life depended upon hearing. Listen in such a way that I could see telescopically beyond my modern myopia, to break through the walls of my modern prison, and actually hear voices from the past with different assumptions entirely about the world and time and human culture. Then I began reading the decisions of the ancient Ecumenical Councils.

Only then in my forties did I begin to become a theologian. Up to that time I had been teaching theology without ever having sufficiently met the patristic mentors who could teach me theology.

This reversal filled my inquiry with new energy. In the fifteen years since this decisive turn I have written *Agenda for Theology* (which narrates this reversal), *Pastoral Theology, Care of Souls in the Classic Tradition*, two works on theology in the Wesleyan tradition (one on Phoebe Palmer, another on doctrinal standards), four volumes on *Classical Pastoral Care*, and the begining of this systematic theology.

My redirection is in part a hermeneutical reversal by which I learned to listen to premodern texts. But that way of stating it is far too weak, unless one understands that embedded in the deepest idea of listening is obedience (*hupokoa*). I find it difficult to convince colleagues that the most important single lesson I have learned hermeneutically is obedience to the text. Carl Rogers taught me to trust my experience. The ancient Christian writers taught me to trust that Scripture and tradition would transmute my experience.

IMPLAUSIBLE PRETENSIONS OF THE CRITICAL STUDY OF JESUS

The Prevailing Idea of Historical Criticism of Documents Attesting Jesus

The Prevailing Myth of the Myth About Jesus

What view of Jesus generally prevails in the historical biblical criticism of the last fifty years, as taught widely in universities and seminaries? It runs something like this:

Jesus was an eschatological prophet who proclaimed God's coming kingdom, called his hearers to decide now for or against that kingdom. After he was condemned to death and died, the belief emerged gradually that he had arisen. Only after some extended period of time did the remembering community develop the idea that Jesus would return as the Messiah, Son of Man. Eventually this community came to project its eschatological expectation back upon the historical Jesus, inserting in his mouth the eschatological hopes that it had subsequently developed but now deftly had to rearrange so as to make it seem as if Jesus himself had understood himself as Messiah. Only much later did the Hellenistic idea of the God-man, the virgin birth, and incarnation emerge in the minds of the remembering church, who again misremembered Jesus according to its revised eschatological expectation.

The disciples are implicitly pictured as either disingenuous or stupid or outright liars, and Jesus as naively being deceptively used by his closest followers.

The Implausibility of the Myth

How such a vacuous, implausible interpretation could have come to be widely accepted is itself perplexing enough. Even harder to understand is the thought that the earliest rememberers would actually suffer martyrdom for such a flimsy cause. One wonders how those deluded believers of early centuries gained the courage to risk passage into an unknown world to proclaim this message that came from an imagined revolution of a fantasized Mediator. The "critical" premise itself requires a high threshold of gullibility.

Yet it is no exaggeration to say that these views prevail in many if not most modern universities where bibical studies are fragmentarily occurring within the prevailing naturalistic assumptions of modernity. Biblical studies in prestigious seminaries doggedly track this pattern.

To anyone accustomed to allowing historical documents to speak for themselves, such an interpretation seems patently absurd. It seems to ordinary Christians more plausible to believe that God became flesh than to credit such a circuitous series of hypotheses and speculations. This in fact is why the believing church has paid so little attention to historical criticism, and why it is so seldom preached and is virtually unpreachable (Maier, *EHCM,* pp. 11–26; cf. Ebeling, *WF,* p. 328; G. Klein, *Bibelkritik als Predigthilfe).*

The Embarrassing Correspondence with the Official Marxist View of Jesus

Some would prefer it not be mentioned in polite company that the continuing official Soviet Communist view of Jesus corresponds almost hand in glove with this curious view: the Jesus portrayed in the New Testament is a second-century mythical projection of writers whose views can best be explained in terms of social location, economic determinism, and class conflict (Marx, "Luther as Arbiter Between Strauss and Feuerbach," *Writings of the Young Marx* [Doubleday, 1967], pp. 94–95; Lenin, "Socialism and Religion," *Soviet Encyclopedia,* s.v. "Jesus").

The University in Which Jesus is Studied: The Myth of Tolerance

The Roots of the Tolerance Ethic

The ethic of tolerance was largely, though of course not wholly, spawned by Christianity. The university as a context for the relatively free market of ideas is largely an invention of medieval Christianity with beginnings in Paris, Oxford, Padua, and Prague. Later the Renaissance universities sought to integrate Christian learning with the wisdom of the ancients (H. Rashdall, *The Universities of Europe in the Middle Ages* I, pp. 38ff.; P. Stuhlmacher, *HCTIC*, pp. 22–36). In religious toleration movements, leading roles were played by Menno Simons (*Appeals for Toleration, Foundation of Christian Doctrine, CWMS*, pp. 190–221), John Milton (*Areopagitica*), Lord Baltimore, Jeremy Taylor (*The Liberty of Prophesying, TPW* I, pp. 499–642), Richard Baxter, Joseph Butler, and Roger Williams — all grounded in classic Christian teachings of salvation.

Modernity has taken this toleration ethic, gradually forgotten its roots, imagining that it did not exist before modern times, and, under the pretense of a secularized toleration, has proceeded to rule out ancient Christian wisdom systematically from its curricula, preventing its being taught even as a hypothesis in tax-supported education. Academic Christianity has hoped that it might gain working credit with modern Enlightenment advocates who think of themselves as tolerationist, but who have difficulty tolerating even the most bland or preliminary inquiry into God.

The Truncated University

Meanwhile the disciplines of the modern university have become increasingly trapped in empiricist methodological reductionisms. Philosophy dutifully ceased speaking of wisdom or the meaning of history and confined its work largely to the analysis of language or logic. Psychology in the empiricist tradition has tried to reduce human behavior to discrete calculable determinants, objectifiable in terms of laboratory experimentation. In due course historical analysis was drastically infected by the empiricist passion to quantify historical data and to rule out evidence deemed unqualified under empirical assumptions.

It is in this sort of truncated university that Christian teaching has recently sought wherever possible to speak the truth about Jesus Christ. To seek a hearing in historical circles, its own methods have inadvertently become correspondingly reductionistic.

An Admonition

Classic Christian teaching of Christ must never again try to gain credentials in an ailing university at the cost of selling its birthright. Christ brings a view of universal history, creation to consummation, that can never be reduced to the methods of naturalistic reductionism.

Can Classic Christology Make Peace with Biblical Criticism?

Several obstacles remain in the debate with historical biblical criticism.

Biblical Criticism's Continued Addiction to Dated Critical Methods Elsewhere Rejected

The study of Jesus has long suffered from an overdependence upon archaic methods of literary criticism once attempted but long rejected by the mainstream of literary criticism. Shakespearean studies went through a period of utilizing these methods of extreme skepticism, only to give them up finally as fruitless and speculative. Yet New Testament literary criticism still remains fixated upon such idiosyncratic methods (R. M. Frye, "Literary Criticism and Gospel Criticism," *Theology Today* 36 [1979]:207–19; John Knox, *Christianity and Criticism*, 1952).

Historical biblical critics have a penchant for holding on to distortions that fit their predispositions long after the facts should have dispelled those distortions. For example, it was once thought that there was a pre-Christian Gnostic redeemer myth, which was later adapted to the memory of Jesus' death (Bultmann, *TNT* I, pp. 129–36, 164–85, 199–204, II, pp. 6, 12, 66; Oden, *CTP*, pp. 102–11). Lately it has become clear that textual fragments that point to a redeemer among Gnostic sources were derived from early Christian preaching, not vice versa. It was once held that the virgin birth narratives had numerous parallels in history of religions. Now it is clear that the New Testament nativity narratives differ markedly from the lusty mythic generativity of the Greek pantheon and that the literary roots of New Testament narratives come from the Old Testament, not Hellenistic influences. It was once widely thought that pre-Pauline Hellenistic Christian congregations infused the memory of Jesus with Hellenisms. Now it is clear that "these Hellenistic congregations were invented by German scholars in the early years of this century" (Neill, *TGI*, p. 61). The most unlikely of all premises is that faith manufactures its own data.

Attachment to Historicism

Historical biblical criticism has adapted hand in glove to the hubris of deteriorating modernity (H. Frey, *KJKEK*, pp. 92–124). In the struggle to gain respectability for religious studies in secular universities with a long record of barring religion in the name of toleration, there has been special pressure on biblical studies departments to dissociate from any sort of theological stigmatization and to assert inordinately the scientific character of the discipline.

Gregory applied a bittersweet analogy to similarly distorted dialogue in his day: "For indeed a little wormwood most quickly imparts its bitterness to honey; while not even double the quantity of honey can impart its sweetness to wormwood" (Gregory Nazianzen, *Flight to Pontus* 12, *NPNF* 2 VII, p. 207).

The Hidden Confessional Addictions of Criticism

The irony deepens when it is recognized that leading historical biblical critics in fact belong inconspicuously to some confessional body and despite disclaimers still tend sentimentally to express the prejudices of those confessions. The most influential are Lutheran and Reformed, and the laggards until recently have been Roman Catholics, Anglicans, Methodists, and Orthodox. Inadvertently, much of the anti-Catholic, anti-Orthodox, antipatristic bias that is so rife in historical criticism comes from hidden Protestant confessional roots, not liberal roots. Protestant evangelical scholars are gradually learning to recognize some of these inveterate biases.

Now at long last the hermeneutic of suspicion needs to be applied to the social location of the advocates of the hermeneutic of suspicion. Such a critique of criticism is needed, as has occurred so many times before in church history (e.g., Tertullian against Marcionism, Athanasius against Arius, Augustine against Manicheanism, Luther against the medieval scholastics, and Wesley against Dort).

Bultmann, Käsemann, and Ebeling have argued that historical criticism stands as a bulwark against works-righteousness that destroys false guarantees for faith (Bultmann, in Bartsch, ed., *KM*, pp. 208–11; Käsemann, *ENTT*; Ebeling, *WE*, p. 56). In practice criticism has become for its professorial practitioners a justifying work.

Tilting the Playing Field

The Modern Portraiture of Jesus

We violate a primary ethical demand upon historical study if we impose upon a set of documents presuppositions congenial to us and then borrow from the canonical prestige of the document by claiming that it corresponds with our favored predispositions. That lacks honesty. The modern attempt to study Christ has done this repeatedly. The text has often become a mirror of ideological interest: Kant's Christ becomes a strained exposition of the categorical imperative; Hegel's Christ looks like a shadow-image of the Hegelian dialectic. Schleiermacher's Christ is a reflection of the awkward mating of pietism and romanticism; Strauss's Christ is neatly weeded of all supernatural referents. Harnack's portrait of Christ looks exactly like that of a late nineteenth-century German liberal idealist; and Tillich's Christ is a dehistorized existential idea of being that participates in estrangement without being estranged.

Amid such reductionisms, the meaning of Christ is never entirely lost (that fortunately is not within the power of the critics), but it is repeatedly skewed, repainted, "improved," modernized, crippled, and distorted.

The historical biblical critic was "not nearly so interested in being changed by his reading of the Bible, as in changing the way that the Bible was read in order to conform it to the modern spirit." Like a business experiencing bankruptcy, historical biblical criticism "still has an inventory of expensive parts, a large capital outlay, a team of trained personnel, a certain reputation," but it lacks one thing, "the ability to fulfill its purpose—effectively to produce and compete on the relevant market" (Wink, *BHT,* pp. 1, 13).

Classic Christianity wishes to allow the New Testament to speak for itself, instead of through these two-hundred-year-old mirrors, filters, and fog machines. Permitting the text to speak on its own terms is the task of exegesis (Irenaeus, *Ag. Her.* II.27, *ANF* I, pp. 398–99; Augustine, *On Christian Doctrine* I, *NPNF* 1 II, pp. 515–22).

On Covert Advocacy Hidden Within Criticism

Historical biblical criticism has been allied with polemical concerns since its eighteenth-century inception as an ideological agent of "Enlightenment." It has expressed a determined interest from the beginning in discrediting not merely the authority of Scripture, but authority in general—all authority as such. Just read the biographies of Reimarus, Rousseau, Lessing, Strauss, Feuerbach, and of course Nietzsche (cf. Jacques Derrida, *The Ear of the Other*). It has operated especially as a partisan "ideology for the demystification of religious tradition." Its "attempted mastery of the object was operationally analogous to the myth of Satan and the legend of Faust." It is astutely described as the strike force of modernity, "the *Wehrmacht* of the liberal church" (Wink, *BHT,* pp. 4, 10–11).

The modern critics of Scripture are another mutation of those described by Gregory Nazianzen. He provided a stunning social location profile of the rebellious "improvers" of religion in his time "who have endured no inconvenience for the sake of virtue, who only begin to study religion when appointed to teach it, and undertake the cleansing of others before being cleansed themselves; yesterday sacrilegious, to-day sacertodal; yesterday excluded from the sanctuary, to-day its officiants; proficient in vice, novices in piety; the product of the favour of man, not of the grace of the Spirit; who, having run through the whole gamut of violence, at last tyrannize over even piety; who, instead of gaining credit for their office by their character, need for their character the credit of their office" (Gregory Nazianzen, *On the Great Athanasius* 9, NPNF 2 VII, p. 271).

Reversal of the Hermeneutic of Suspicion

The hermeneutic of suspicion has been safely applied to the history of Jesus but not to the history of the historians. It is now time for the tables to turn. The hermeneutic of suspicion must be fairly and prudently applied to the critical movement itself. This is the most certain next phase of biblical scholarship—the criticism of criticism. Why has it taken so long?

Social Location of Critics

One obvious neglected arena is the social location of the quasi-Marxist critics of the social location of classic Christianity, who hold comfortable chairs in rutted, tenured tracks. These writers have focused upon the analysis of the social location of the writers and interpreters of Scripture. Yet that principle awaits now to be turned upon the social prejudices of the "knowledge elite"—a guild of scholars asserting their interest in the privileged setting of the modern university. The hermeneutic of suspicion needs to be directed toward the critics that have recently rediscovered this familiar theme (it may be found previously in Hippolytus, Luther, and Kierkegaard), yet who imagine it as a recent invention (Fuchs, *Hermeneutik*, pp. 131–35; cf. Ricoeur, *History and Truth*, pp. 21–82; *Interpretation Theology*; Gadamer, *Truth and Method*; Wells, PC, pp. 65–66). Athanasius, before Marx, argued that the gods had social utility and, before Feuerbach, that the gods were projections of human psychological needs (*Contra Gentes* 15–18, NPNF 2 IV, pp. 12–14).

Peer Group Values in Biblical Criticism

Biblical criticism "sought to free itself from the community in order to pursue its work untrammeled," and hence has become "cut off from any community for whose life its results might be significant. . . . The community of reference and accountability became, not the liberal church, but the guild of biblical scholars" who had a vested professional interest in building influence in the university, in perpetuating their schools and methods, and in enforcing conformity to peer-group values (Wink, *BHT*, pp. 10–11; cf. P. Ricoeur, *The Bible as a Document of the University*).

John Chrysostom grasped the dynamic that the economic status of the interpreter shapes his interpretation. This is why he commended voluntary poverty. The motivation to discover unprecedented critical findings increases as professional advancement is held out as a reward for original research. This perennial habit of the German academic tradition has led biblical criticism to new ecstasies of faddism, where the actual history of Jesus vanishes in a pile of theories and speculations as to the redactive transmission of the tradition of testimony about him. At long last the historian's Pyrrhic victory over the evidence has finally been announced —that there is nothing knowable of Jesus.

It is hardly probable that Holy Writ has been inspired, provided, traditioned at high cost, and defended for twenty centuries for no better purpose than to keep historians busy or advance academic careers.

In honest historical labor the facts are attentively followed. In speculative advocacy criticism, by contrast, the text is preyed upon by ideological interests. Such a "critic" is apt to exude outrage over the redactor's political predispositions, social location, sexism, and cultural borrowings, as if the critic possessed an obviously superior set of moral values by which the sacred text may now at long last be cleverly measured and found wanting.

While criticizing the author's hidden social location or supposed predisposing tendencies, the critic often reveals blatant predisposing interests (Käsemann, *Jesus Means Freedom*; *ENTT*). Gregory Nazianzen understood himself to be living in just such a time, when everyone presumed to be an original teacher instead of being taught of God (*Flight to Pontus* 8, *NPNF* 1 VII, p. 206).

The High Priest of Historicism

The Inner Sanctum

The faith of historical biblical criticism has become fixated upon a curious game, seeking to resurrect not Jesus Christ but its own fantasized "historical Jesus" as an object of its historical curiosity. Amid this attempted burial and resurrection, the historian seeks to remain tightly in control of what is admitted as evidence and of judgments about the evidence.

No one else beside this high priest may now enter this inner sanctum. "Only the historian can answer" (Bultmann, *TNT* I, p. 26). Only New Testament specialists, according to this bias, have any right to enter into the Christological arena (Wink, *BHT*, pp. 8–10; cf. P. Stuhlmacher, *HCTIS*).

Criticism as Proselytism

"Bluntly stated, biblical criticism was a certain type of evangelism seeking a certain type of conversion." It has now, like revivalism, become bankrupt, having been "married to a false objectivism, subjected to uncontrolled technologism, separated from a vital community, and has outlived its usefulness" (Wink, *BHT*, pp. 14–15). Jesus had harsh words for such obstructionists: "Woe to you experts in the law, because you have taken away the key to knowledge. You yourselves have not entered, and you have hindered those who were entering" (Luke 11:52).

The comedy of making secularized proselytism look like scientific inquiry is a little like "those persons who in the theatres perform wrestling matches in public, but not that kind of wrestling in which the victory is won according to the rules of the sport, but a kind to deceive the eyes of those who are ignorant in such matters, and to catch applause" (Gregory Nazianzen, *Ag. Eunomians*, *Orat.* XXVII.2, *NPNF* 2 VII, p. 285).

There still remain in excellent universities courageous scholars who, while earnestly affirming classical Christianity, continue to be deeply engaged in critical studies, though often bearing the marks of pariahs among certain self-contained critical elites (see G. Wainwright, *Doxology*; G. Lindbeck, *The Nature of Doctrine*; D. Wells, *PC*; Clark Pinnock, *The Scripture Principle*; Ramm, *EC*; Guthrie, *NTT*; Ladd, *TNT*; Marshall, *IBHJ*; Henry, *GRA* IV, pp. 7–68). They may feel as did Gregory describing his own historical situation surrounding the Second Council of Constantinople, A.D. 381: "that which the palmerworm left did the locust eat, and that which the locust left did the caterpillar eat; then came the cankerworm, then, what next I know not, one evil springing up after another"—all for our "testing and refining" (Gregory Nazianzen, *Orat.* XLII.3, *NPNF* 2 VII, p. 387).

CHAPTER 8

The Public Ministry of Jesus

Following the childhood narratives, Jesus' public ministry began with his baptism, immediately followed by the powerful narrative of his temptation.

Our thesis: each step of his ministry of proclamation and teaching pointed inexorably toward his final days in Jerusalem.

There is no compelling need for Christology to discuss in detail each event of Jesus' earthly ministry. Rather the focus is primarily upon those aspects that most strongly affect the Christian teaching of salvation.

CHILDHOOD NARRATIVES: CIRCUMCISION, FLIGHT, OBEDIENCE, GROWTH

The childhood of Jesus was understood as the beginning of his Passion, the initial steps of his road to crucifixion. As he was destined to be rejected on the cross, so was he early already being rejected by the political authorities, Herod (Matt. 2:3), and Archelaus (Matt. 2:22; cf. Cone, *BTL* pp. 204–205). His circumcision prefigured his death as a setting aside of the flesh. By his flight to Egypt his life was preserved for the hour that was to come. His active obedience to law in his earthly life readied him for his passive obedience in death (Calvin, *Inst.* 2.16.5-7).

Hence the childhood narratives in the Gospels convey profound meaning for salvation history (Tertullian, *On the Flesh of Christ* 2, *ANF* III, p. 522). They are not merely trivial stories. They recollect Jesus' childhood from the special viewpoint of his death and resurrection.

The Circumcision of Jesus

The initiation into the Hebrew covenant community carried with it the obligation to follow the way of holiness, putting away sin.

Circumcision Under the Old Covenant

Circumcision, the rite of the removal of the foreskin of the male penis, was a sign of God's covenant with Abraham (Gen. 17:11), "an everlasting covenant between me and you and your descendants after you for the generations to come, to be your God and the God of your descendants after you" (Gen. 17:7). By that rite it was being signaled to the circumcised that Yahweh alone would be their God, whom they would serve and trust (Augustine, *CG* XVI.27, *NPNF* 1 II, pp. 326–27). Circumcision is a sanctification metaphor, analogous to the setting aside of something for holy use (oil, bread, wine, water, or temple).

The Consecration of Sexuality

Since sin impinges everywhere in human life, it is likely to impinge most significantly upon that most erotic and generative aspect of human life: sexuality.

Without any harm to sexual function, the circumcision of males aimed symbolically at consecration of that organ by which life itself is reproduced, which because of its extraordinary creative power and goodness is most likely to be corrupted by idolatry and sin. Hence circumcision suggests the putting away of carnal lust (Col. 2:11) and more generally the setting aside or putting off of sinful flesh.

Circumcision of the Heart

To circumcise the heart is to so renew it constantly in obedience that its inveterate obstinacy will gradually atrophy (Deut. 10:16), that all one's redeemed powers may be fully consecrated to God (Exod. 6:12; Lev. 19:23; Deut. 30:6; Wesley, *WJW* V, pp. 203–209). Thus circumcision anticipatively symbolized purity of heart or purification of the whole person in readiness for the divine address (Jer. 9:25), a responsive willingness to hear and obey God (Jer. 6:10). The rite primarily signified the gracious movement of God to humanity and only in a secondary and responsive sense the obedient answerability of humanity to God (Gen. 17:1–14; Jer. 4:4; Rom. 2:25–29; Acts 15:5; Gal. 5:3; *BOC*, pp. 134, 188, 213).

Jesus Was Circumcised

The law required that "every male among you who is eight days old must be circumcised" (Gen. 17:12). Thus not only Jesus (Luke 2:21) but also John the Baptist (Luke 1:9), Paul (Phil. 3:5), and presumably all the apostles were circumcised at eight days (Origen, *On Luke, Hom. XIV, AEG* I, p. 250).

That Jesus was circumcised points to his active obedience to the full requirement of the law (Justin Martyr, *Dialogue with Trypho 67, ANF* I, pp. 231-32; Hugh of St. Victor, *OSCF,* pp. 188-90). This event is prominently celebrated in the Christian year on January 1, New Year's Day, the ancient Feast of the Circumcision, eight days after Christmas.

Circumcision in Christ

Circumcision in the New Covenant

Circumcision under the conditions of the new covenant was to become an inward sign of the righteousness of faith (Rom. 4:10-12), not an outward work of merit or an occasion for boasting. Without the obedience of faith, Paul says, circumcision becomes uncircumcision (Rom. 2:25-29). Insofar as it might suggest that we gain merit by works, it is to be resisted (Gal. 5:2ff.), but its true meaning should be recognized and respected (Col. 2:13; Isa. 52:1).

Analogies of Circumcision, Baptism, and Crucifixion

Only after Christ's death could the special meaning of his circumcision be more fully discerned. It would then be understood that the believer's circumcision is (far from an outward act) not only a spiritual act of putting off the flesh or shedding of blood for the covenant, but moreso it is precisely Christ's circumcision (Cyprian, *Treatises, Testimonies, ANF* V, p. 508).

Christ was "circumcised"–his flesh separated–in the most radical way by his death. His circumcision is reckoned or imputed to all believers. "In him you were also circumcised, in the putting off of the sinful nature, not with a circumcision done by the hands of men but with the circumcision done by Christ, having been buried with him in baptism and raised with him through your faith in the power of God, who raised him from the dead" (Col. 2:11-12; cf. Tertullian, *On the Resurrection of the Flesh* XXIII, *ANF* III, p. 561). That blood was shed in circumcision was to become a significant aspect of its Christian reinterpretation.

The crucial analogies are as follows:

IN CIRCUMCISION UNDER THE LAW

Body trimmed	Heart made full
Blood is shed	Life is promised
The sinful nature cut off	Consecrated to covenant

Libido constrained	Spirit prepared
The will purified	The new will freed
Passion constrained	Passion consecrated to right use

SO CHRIST CRUCIFIED WAS

Buried	Raised

SO IN BAPTISM THE BELIEVER IS

Buried with him	Raised with him
The old life put away	New life received
Sin cut away	The way of holiness established

The Damascene carefully honed the analogy between circumcision and baptism: the circumcision was given to Abraham "as a sign separating him and his offspring" from the Gentiles. "It was, moreover, a figure of baptism. For just as the circumcision does not cut off a useful member of the body, but only a useless superfluity, so by the holy baptism we are circumcised from sin, and sin clearly is, so to speak, the superfluous part of desire and not useful desire. For it is quite impossible that any one should have no desire at all nor ever experience the taste of pleasure. But the useless part of pleasure, that is to say, useless desire and pleasure, it is this that is sin from which holy baptism circumcises us" (John of Damascus, *OF* IV.25, *NPNF* 2 IX, pp. 97-98). In the circumcised heart, passion and desire remain, but they are channeled toward moral and spiritual usefulness (Catherine of Siena, *Pray.*, pp. 214-15).

Presentation at the Temple

Consecration of the Firstborn Male

Jesus was presented in the Temple on his fortieth day as a son of Torah, faithfully honoring the tradition of the older economy of salvation (Irenaeus, *Ag. Her.* III.10, *ANF* I, p. 425; Bernard, *MPL* 183, pp. 133-38). "When the time of their purification according to the law of Moses had been completed, Joseph and Mary took him to Jerusalem to present him to the Lord (as it was written in the Law of the Lord, 'Every firstborn male is to be consecrated to the Lord')" (Luke 2:22-23; Exod. 13:2, 12). All this was done "in keeping with what is said in the Law" (Luke 2:24; Tho. Aq., *ST* III Q37, II, pp. 2219-23).

The poverty into which Christ was born is revealed in that the family could not afford a lamb for offering, but only "a pair of doves" (Lev. 12:8; Origen, *Leviticus, Hom.* VIII.4, *AEG* I, p. 252; Cone, *BTL*, pp. 204-206).

Bonaventure commented: "It was not enough for the teacher of perfect humility, who was equal to the Father in all things, to submit himself to the humble Virgin. He must submit himself also to the Law, that he might redeem those who were under the Law" (*Tree of Life*, *CWS*, p. 131; Gal. 4:5).

Simeon and Anna

In Jerusalem Simeon had long been devoutly awaiting the consolation of God's own coming (Isa. 52:9). "It had been revealed to him by the Holy Spirit that he would not die before he had seen the Lord's Christ. Moved by the Spirit, he went into the temple courts. When the parents brought in the child Jesus to do for him what the custom of the Law required, Simeon took him in his arms and praised God, saying: 'Sovereign Lord, as you have promised, you now dismiss your servant in peace. For my eyes have seen your salvation, which you have prepared in the sight of all people, a light for revelation to the Gentiles and for glory to your people Israel'" (Luke 2:26–32). Simeon recognized that "the thought of many hearts will be revealed" in relation to this child (Luke 2:35; Cyprian, *On the Mortality* 3, *ANF* V, p. 470).

The elderly prophetess Anna, who had been worshiping in expectation "night and day, fasting and praying," met the parents and "spoke about the child to all who were looking forward to the redemption of Jerusalem" (Luke 2:38; Tertullian, *On Fasting* 8, *ANF* IV, p. 107). In these events, Joseph and Mary did "everything required by the Law of the Lord," and returned to Nazareth (Luke 2:39).

The Flight to Egypt

Joseph, Mary, and Jesus are portrayed as a refugee family, escaping to Egypt to evade Herod's bloody search. It seems fitting that one who had no place to lay his head would be from the outset a part of a refugee family fleeing persecution by a self-serving, tyrannical political power (Matt. 2:13–18; Origen *Ag. Celsus* I.66, *AEG* I, pp. 267–68; Proba, *Cento*, 346–75).

This, says Matthew, was to fulfill the expectation of the prophet Hosea: "Out of Egypt I called my son" (Hos. 11:1; Matt. 2:15). This phrase, originally applied to Israel being called out of Egypt under Moses, was viewed by Matthew as applying to Jesus called out of Egypt to undertake his messianic vocation. The displaced immigrant family withdrew to Nazareth after Herod's death (Matt. 2:19–23).

The Passover in Jerusalem and the Questioning of the Rabbis in the Temple

Questioning of the Rabbis

In Luke's account, the boy Jesus at twelve was found "sitting among teachers, listening to them and asking them questions" (Luke 2:46). He instructed the rabbis not by high-handed assertions but by tempered questionings, in a way that "stimulated them to enquire into things which so far they could not know whether they knew or not" (Origen, *Luke, Hom.* XX, *AEG* I, p. 275).

The Learning of Obedience

By his listening to the doctors in the Temple and asking them questions (Luke 2:41–51; Edersheim, *LTJM* II.10), the Gospel underscores that he submitted to the rigorous conditions under which human intellect develops. That he astonished them with his understanding is evidence of his full use of intellectual competencies under the enabling of the Spirit. He was willing to undergo gradual human development so that he could share fully in all the ordinary stages of human growth (Luke 2:40; cf. 1 Sam. 2:26). Thus the eternal Son, in humbling himself to share in the human condition, went through an education; he studied, listened attentively, learned obedience (Heb. 5:8), and was taught by degrees to pray, to read, to meditate on Holy Writ, serving a real apprenticeship as a carpenter (Mark 6:13).

Aware of His Unique Filial Relation

His answer to his mother, "Why were you searching for me? . . . Didn't you know I had to be in my Father's house?" (Luke 2:49), suggests that as a youth he was already aware of his distinctive mission and unique filial relation to God.

He Grew in Wisdom and Stature and in Favor with God and Men

Subjection to Parents

Jesus is remembered as a dutiful son in relation to his parents, a fit expression of the humble human coming of God the Son in time. "Then he went down to Nazareth with them and was obedient to them" (Luke 2:51). It was for our salvation that the Lord became "subject to creatures," for "he had taken upon him human nature on the condition of being subject to parents." Hence so should we voluntarily and cheerfully take on the ordinary duties of life in service with accountability (Calvin, *Comm.* XVI, p. 172).

"Jesus grew" (Luke 2:52; Calvin, *Inst.* 4.16.18). Origen explained that Jesus did not appear as a full grown man, but even while he was "yet a child, since He 'emptied Himself,' kept advancing," for "after emptying Himself He was gradually taking again the things of which He had voluntarily emptied Himself" (*Comm. on Jer.*, *Hom.* I.7, *AEG* I, p. 277). "He increased in stature of soul, and His soul became great by reason of the great and mighty works which He did" (Origen, *Lev.*, *Hom.* XII.2, *AEG* I, p. 277).

The logic of the humbling of God is characterized by surprise and reversal: as God, the Mediator does not advance but descends into ignorance and humiliation. As man, the God-man advances in wisdom and stature to demonstrate his full participation in the human condition (Athanasius, *Four Discourses Ag. Arians* III.42-53, *NPNF* 2 IV, pp. 416-22).

Virtue Chosen

Human beings are not born virtuous. Virtues can only develop through risk-laden decision making. "The being born, ye have; but also the growing, ye ought to have; because no man begins with being perfect" (Augustine, *On the Creed* 8, *NPNF* 1 III, p. 372; cf. Julian of Norwich, "The Discipline of Mutability," *IAIA*, p. 92). Jesus' moral excellence, like all human moral excellence, grew through choices of will.

If Jesus "grew in wisdom and stature" (Luke 2:52), he must have been subject to the normal laws of psychological development, the same processes through which humans generally move to maturity. "He is said to have progressed in wisdom and age and grace, because He did increase in age and by this increase in age brought more into evidence the wisdom inherent in Him, further, because by making what is ours altogether His own, He made His own the progress of men in wisdom and grace" (John of Damascus, *OF*, *FC* 37, p. 326).

JESUS' BAPTISM

Jesus' baptism inaugurated his ministry and began the messianic age (Matt. 3:13-4:11; Mark 1:9-13; John 1:32-34; Barth, *CD* IV/4, pp. 15ff.). Prophetic expectation held that the messianic age would begin with the outpouring of the Spirit (Joel 2). The public designation or sealing of Jesus' messianic office occurred in his baptism with the descent of the Spirit (Tho. Aq., *ST* III Q39, II, pp. 2228-35). His baptism constituted his ordination to his public ministry, prefigured his death and the sacramental coming of the Spirit to the worshiping community succeeding him, anticipating the rites of Christian baptism, confirmation, and holy orders.

Confluence of Symbolic Elements in Jesus' Baptism

Jesus' baptism intensively combined several elements of weighty prophetic-symbolic significance:

The Baptism of John

"His own baptism by John is one of the most certainly verified occurrences of his life" (Bornkamm, *JN*, p. 54). John's ministry bridged the Old and New Testaments in two ways: by epitomizing the prophetic tradition under the old covenant and by preaching repentance looking toward the new (Tho. Aq., *ST* III Q38, II, pp. 2223–35). In receiving John's baptism, the Lord's identity began to be recognized in a preliminary way. He was "marked out to His forerunner, who before knew him not; and that forerunner in his turn marked Him out to the world, which also in another sense as yet knew Him not" (Pope, *Compend.* II, 206; cf. John Chrysostom, *Hom. on John* XVI, *NPNF* 1 XIV, pp. 55–60).

To Fulfill All Righteousness by Identifying with Sinners

When Jesus "came from Galilee to the Jordan to be baptized by John," John "tried to deter him, saying, 'I need to be baptized by you.'" Jesus insisted that "it is proper for us to do this to fulfill all righteousness" (Matt. 3:13–15; Augustine, *EDQ* 58, *FC* 70, pp. 103–108). This interaction between John and Jesus contained a weighty moment: John protested that Jesus was no fit candidate for the baptism of repentance, and Jesus insisted upon identifying with sinners "to fulfill all righteousness" (Hugh of St. Victor, *OSCF*, pp. 291–93). Jesus' baptism was not to signify repentance of his own sins, but his compassionate identification with the consequences of sin in human history.

Jesus was baptized in the very river by which Israel had entered Canaan. Christian baptism enables the crossing of another river (from sin to grace) so as to make the transition into the reign of God's love, prefigured by the Israel's crossing into the promised land (Josh. 3:17; 4:1–24; Ps. 114:3–5; 2 Kings 5:14).

The Descent of the Spirit

The Opening of Heaven

"As he was praying, heaven was opened and the Holy Spirit descended on him in bodily form like a dove" (Luke 3:11; Matt. 3:16). The divine-human intercourse, which through sin had become constricted, was through Christ's baptism opened (Matt. 7:7-8; 27:52; John 9:10-32).

In Jesus' baptism, the Spirit descended. This anticipates what is to occur in Christian baptism, wherein the enabling Spirit is given to the believer. In this way the descent of the Spirit is not for Jesus alone, but for all those whose lives are hid in him by faith.

Descent of the Dove

The Spirit appeared in the figure of a dove to welcome humanity to the peace of God that was already at work in Christ (Origen, *Canticles, Hom.* II.12, *AEG* I, p. 307; Hippolytus, *Theophany* VI, *AEG* I, p. 303; Calvin, *Comm.* XVI, *Harmony*, p. 204). "For the dove's body has no gall in it. So after the deluge by which the iniquity of the old world was purged away, after, so to speak, the baptism of the world, the dove as herald proclaimed to the earth the assuagement of the wrath of heaven—sent forth from the ark and returning with an olive branch, which is a sign of peace even among the nations" (Tertullian, *Baptism* VIII, *AEG* I, p. 304; cf. *ANF* III, p. 673; Augustine, *EDQ* 43, *FC* 70, pp. 74-75; cf. Catherine of Siena, *Pray.*, pp. 152-53).

Spirit-anointed

After Jesus' baptism, his teaching and healing ministry proceeded with the awareness that "The Spirit of the Lord is on me, because he has anointed me to preach good news to the poor" (Luke 4:18, quoting Isa. 61:1). Jesus' baptism was an anointing or ordaining to the role of Messiah–Suffering Servant.

Sonship Attested

"I baptize with water," the forerunner attested, "but among you stands one you do not know. He is the one who comes after me, the thongs of whose sandals I am not worthy to untie." It is he "who will baptize with the Holy Spirit" (John 1:26-27, 33). "I have seen and I testify that this is the Son of God" (John 1:34). Isaiah had looked toward the time when it would be said of the anointed One: "Here is my servant, whom I uphold, my chosen one in whom I delight; I will put my Spirit on him and he will bring justice to the nations" (Isa. 42:1).

The Triune Presence

A voice from heaven confirmed the extraordinary significance of this event: "This is my beloved Son, with whom I am well pleased" (Matt.

3:17, RSV; cf. Mark 1:11). All three persons of the Trinity are present in the Evangelists' testimony attesting and celebrating the sonship: "As soon as Jesus was baptized, he went up out of the water. At that moment heaven was opened, and he saw the Spirit of God descending like a dove and lighting on him. And a voice from heaven said, 'This is my Son, whom I love; with him I am well pleased'" (Matt. 3:16-17). As the triune God affirmed Jesus' baptism, so Christian baptism occurs in the name of God the Father, Son, and Spirit (Hilary, *Trin.* VIII.25, *NPNF* 2 IX, p. 144).

The Spirit Enabled Jesus' Ministry

Gifts Requisite to Messianic Mission

The baptism of Jesus not only marked him as the coming Messiah but also supplied him with gifts of the Spirit requisite to his messianic mission. In Jesus' baptism by the Holy Spirit, his human nature was being equipped with everything needed to fulfill his ministry. "Now that the full time is come, for preparing to discharge the office of Redeemer, he is clothed with a new power of the Spirit, and that not so much for his own sake, as for the sake of others" in order that "believers might learn to receive" (Calvin, *Comm.* XVI, *Harmony,* p. 204). Similarly in Christian baptism, believers are being equipped with gifts requisite to their vocation (Eph. 4:11-13).

Sevenfold Gifts

The sevenfold gifts of the Spirit, according to prophecy and classical exegesis, were bestowed upon Jesus at his baptism. As a shoot "from the stump of Jesse, from his roots a Branch will bear fruit. The Spirit of the Lord will rest on him—the Spirit of wisdom and of understanding, the Spirit of counsel and of power, the Spirit of knowledge and of the fear of the Lord—and he will delight in the fear of the Lord" (Isa. 11:1-2). These gifts (wisdom, understanding, counsel, fortitude, knowledge, piety, and fear of the Lord, as rendered by Bonaventure, *Tree of Life*, CWS, p. 174) were yet to be distributed to the church. In due time the church was to receive "an anointing from the Holy One" (1 John 2:20; Acts 2:1-13) to share in Christ's gifts.

The Sign: Water

Water is the sign of baptism, as wine and bread are the signs of the Eucharist. The baptism of Jesus was necessary not that Christ be purified, but that he once for all consecrate the sign of baptism—water—which was to become the grace-laden instrument of the sanctification of humanity (Hugh of St. Victor, *OSCF,* pp. 301-10). "He was baptized as Man—but He remitted sins as God—not because He needed purificatory rites Himself, but that He might sanctify the element of water" (Gregory Nazianzen, *Orat.* XXIX.20, *NPNF* 2 VII, p. 308).

Cleansed or Cleansing?

In Jesus' baptism alone (as distinguished from ours) the pure water symbolized not the need for his being cleansed from sin (for he was without sin), but rather his own unpolluted purity, which cleanses from sin. Thus Christ was not himself regenerated in the baptism by John, but submitted to identify with sinners and to offer an example of humility, just as he submitted to death not as the punishment for his own sin, but to take away the sin of the world: "For baptism found in Him nothing to wash away, as death found in Him nothing to punish. . . . Both baptism and death were submitted to by Him not through a pitiable necessity, but of His own free pity for us" (Augustine, *Enchiridion* 49, *NPNF* 1 III, p. 253).

Cleansing Water Consecrated

By this act the water of baptism became set aside, consecrated to a special purpose—to bring the cleansing power of the Spirit to humanity (Julian of Norwich, *IAIA,* p. 132). Water, an ordinary and common element yet necessary for human life, was thereby extraordinarily honored and blessed in baptism with symbolic excellence that it had not previously had, as a means of grace by which not only physical but spiritual life would be bestowed upon humanity (Bonaventure, *Tree of Life, CWS,* p. 133).

Water Suggests the Seeking of Lowliness

But the figure of water penetrated more deeply. Jesus in being baptized assumed symbolically the self-effacing position of identifying with the sin of humanity, yet he did so in a way that already pointed toward the reconciliation of that sin, since he was at that moment being designated as messiah to redeem sin. As water runs downward, not upward, so Jesus' incarnation was first to be a humbling, downward movement toward suffering and death, even as Christian baptism is a sharing in his way of lowlines, meekness, and peace.

Numbered Among the Transgressors

Identification with Sinners

His baptism was a body language statement that he was willing to become fully identified with the condition of humanity suffering under the consequences of sin (Tertullian, *On Baptism* X–XIII, *ANF* III, pp. 673–75; Barth, *CD* IV/4, pp. 52ff). He was baptized not to cleanse himself but to identify with our alienated, corrupted human condition. It was for others rather than for himself that Jesus was baptized.

Even at his baptism Jesus was identifying with the suffering servant of Isaiah, in that he was "numbered with the transgressors" from the outset, already on the road toward pouring "out his life unto death" and bearing "the sins of many" (Isa. 53:12; cf. Matt. 3:15). Moreso, baptism itself is a burial symbol; for one is burying the body under (not earth but) water.

The Coronation-Ordination to Suffer Redemptively

The words of the heavenly voice, "This is my beloved Son, with whom I am well pleased" (Matt. 3:17, RSV), are derived from two texts widely appropriated by the messianic tradition: Psalm 2:7, the *coronation* formula of the messianic King of Israel, and Isaiah 42:1, the *ordination* formula of the Servant of the Lord.

The conflation of these two formulae did not occur accidentally or frivolously. It alluded to the fact that the messianic King would be, far from a victorious political deliverer, a suffering servant who would die as a ransom for many. Many attempts would be made to sever these intertwining roles (notably Peter's protest that the Son of Man should not die and the crowd's fascination with Jesus as conquering king but rejection of Jesus as suffering Servant).

The temptation narrative, which directly follows Jesus' baptism, underscores this irony, for the tempter immediately thereafter tempted Jesus to use the power of his messianic authority for some purpose other than his servant mission.

Christian Baptism Prefigured

Jesus' baptism foreshadowed major features of the Christian sacrament of baptism. In being baptized, Christ himself undertook and fulfilled what was later required of all (Augustine, in *MB*, p. 45n; Bonaventure, *Tree of Life*, *CWS*, p. 133). Christ's baptism stands as the inauguration of the sacrament of baptism in which all the faithful participate, and through it are incorporated into Christ. In Christ's baptism, he was metaphorically buried under the waters of the old Adam and rose as new humanity. In his baptism he prefigured his body, the church, which through baptism receives the Holy Spirit (Hugh of St. Victor, *OSCF*, pp. 282–89).

Why Was He Baptized?

"The general reason why Christ received baptism was, that he might render full obedience to the Father; and the special reason was, that he might consecrate baptism in his own body, that we might have it in common with him." He who "had not need of baptism" received what was "suitable to the character of a servant," "for the sake of others" (Calvin, *Comm.*, *Harmony*, XVI, p. 202). "Baptize Me, John," wrote Hippolytus of Jesus, "that none may despise baptism" (*Theophany* IV.5, *AEG* I, p. 300).

Was Jesus Adopted as Messiah at His Baptism?

Rejection of Adoptionism

Notions of baptismal adoption based upon the gradual development of Jesus' consciousness (Cerinthus, in Irenaeus, *Ag. Her.* I.21, I.26, *ANF* I, pp. 345–47, 352; Hippolytus, *Ag. All Her.* VII.21, *ANF* V, p. 114) were carefully considered by ecumenical councils and rejected. "This Son of God is also Son by nature, not by adoption" (Eleventh Council of Toledo, *CF*, p. 102; Hadrian I, *Letter to the Spanish Bishops* [A.D. 793], *CF*, p. 174; see also *SCD* 143, 299, 309ff.). "He is not the putative Son of God, but the true Son, not the adoptive Son but the real Son, for He was never estranged from the Father because of the man [human nature] which He assumed" (Council of Friuli [A.D. 796 or 797], *CF*, p. 1750; Methodius, *Symposium* VIII.9, *AEG* I, p. 308).

Jesus Not a Man Made God

Christianity does not attest a man who became God, as if it happened "that a certain man was crowned by advancement," so that "Christ is not God made man, but a man made God" (Cyril of Jerusalem, *Catech. Lect.* XII, *FC* 61, p. 228; cf. Schultz, *Gottheit Christi*, pp. 725–26). "His sonship is by nature, ours by adoption" (Council of Toledo XI [675], *SCD* 276, p. 107).

He did not acquire divinity (Athanasius, *Four Discourses Ag. Arians* I.37–38, *NPNF* 2 IV, p. 328). "The Jewish mind was by its very constitution incapable of applying to God the category of creation" (Mackintosh, *PJC*, p. 423). "We do not say that man became God, but that God became man.

For, while he was by nature perfect God, the same became by nature perfect man. . . . Thus, He anointed Himself—as God, anointing His body
with His divinity, but as man, being anointed" (John of Damascus, *OF*
III.2, *FC* 37, pp. 270, 272). Only the One divine human Person could be
both as God the anointing agent and as man the one anointed.

Sonship Not "Earned" or "Developed"

Jesus did not "earn" his baptismal messianic identification by rightly
developing his human soul so as to become worthy of divine adoption.
The Second Council of Constantinople specifically rejected the view that
he "freed himself gradually from interior inclinations and, having improved through the progress of his works and having become irreproach-
able in his conduct, was baptised as a mere man in the name of the Father
and of the Son and of the Holy Spirit; who received through baptism the
grace of the Holy Spirit and was deemed worthy of divine adoption;
who, much like an image of the emperor, is worshipped in the person of
God the Word; who after the resurrection became perfectly steadfast in
his thoughts and wholly impeccable" (*Against the Three Chapters, CF*,
p. 162). A parent cannot adopt a boy who is already his son (Tho. Aq., *ST*
III Q23.4, I, p. 2149; Garrigou-Lagrange, *CS*, p. 505).

Modern Adoptionism

The modern form of adoptionism is reflected in the tradition following
Schleiermacher, for whom Jesus' consciousness of God was such that
through it we come to increased God-consciousness. According to this
view, Christology begins not with the preexistent Logos, but with a present experience of the new life as immediately dependent upon Jesus'
consciousness of God. By taking us up into the energies of his God-
consciousness, he reconciles, saves, and brings persons into vital union
with God.

Jesus' Baptism Anticipatory of His Atoning Work

The High-Priestly Role Prefigured

The high priest was always washed before being anointed. Hence the
anointing of Jesus' messianic mission was preceded by this washing—
baptism. Hence the washing by John of Jesus constituted a prefigurative
fulfillment of the high-priestly role he was to take in his death.

The Cross Prefigured

In this paradoxical way, the baptism of Jesus already prefigured and anticipated the cross. Later John would write: "This is the one who came by water and blood—Jesus Christ. He did not come by water only, but by water and blood" (1 John 5:6). The water is the water of his baptism and the blood is the blood of his atonement. Water symbolized the beginning of his messianic ministry in baptism, blood the ending of that ministry in death. Jesus did not merely initiate the messianic office but made it a finished work on the cross.

THE TEMPTATION OF JESUS

In preparation for his public ministry, Jesus underwent a rigorous period of testing or trial—the temptation (*peirasmos*) in the wilderness. These assaults continued for forty days and nights—a period of fasting that came to prefigure the Lenten season of self-examination. "For forty days he was tempted by the devil" (Luke 4:2; cf. Matt. 4:1–11), reminiscent of Moses (Exod. 24:18; 34:28) and Elijah (1 Kings 19:8). In the desert he was "with the wild animals, and the angels attended him" (Mark 1:13), just as the people of God had been attended in the desert (Exod. 23:20, 23; 32:34).

Jesus was "led by the Spirit into the desert to be tempted" (Matt. 4:1). As the Lord led the people of God under Moses into the desert for testing for forty years, so was Jesus led to be tested by Satan for forty days. "Remember how the Lord your God led you all the way in the desert these forty years, to humble you and test you in order to know what was in your heart, whether or not you would keep his commands" (Deut. 8:1–5). This trial was a part of the divine purpose—to demonstrate that the Son was unswervingly responsive to his mission (Eusebius, *PG* II, p. 166).

There is no tendency to romanticize the struggle of temptation. In the Lord's Prayer he taught believers to pray that they not be led into temptation (Matt. 6:13; Baxter, *PW* XIX, pp. 155–56). And at Gethesemane he instructed his disciples to "Pray that you will not fall into temptation" (Luke 22:40).

Tempted as We Are?

The temptation that was unresisted by Adam and so led humanity to destruction (Gen. 3) was resisted by Christ so as to lead humanity to redemption (Augustine, *CG* XIII–XIV, *NPNF* 1 II, pp. 245–83). In this way he became the way of life for believers facing temptation (Gen. 22:1; 1

John 3:8). By destroying Satan's works, his ministry of reconciling God and humanity began.

Extent of His Temptation

As his ministry proceeded relentlessly toward the cross, Jesus was frequently challenged, buffeted, and "tempted" by detractors, the scribes and lawyers (Mark 8:11; Luke 10:25–29) who sought to cause him to make self-incriminating statements (Mark 12:15; Luke 23:2), prematurely declare his messianic identity, or say things that would show that he was not a true teacher of Israel.

Ultimately he would be "tempted in every way just as we are"–not spared the trials of body and spirit that accompany human existence generally–yet he would remain "without sin" (Heb. 4:15). Only this hard route would demonstrate his moral readiness for the ministry of redemption of humanity, which included his empathic capacity to be touched with the feeling of our infirmities.

Necessary to Mediatorship

A necessary part of Jesus' mediatorial role was that, like us, he struggled against sin and temptation. He voluntarily entered into that human (all-too-human) arena of genuine temptation, so as to become victorious over sin (Hegemonius, *Acts of Archelaus* 60, *AEG* I, p. 320; cf. Barth, *CD* IV/1, pp. 257ff.). "Because he himself suffered when he was tempted, he is able to help those who are being tempted" (Heb. 2:18; Gregory Nazianzen, *Orat.* XXX, *Fourth Theol. Orat.*, *NPNF* 2 VII, p. 312; Mark the Ascetic, *On the Spiritual Law, Philokal.* I, pp. 119–20). Faith perceives a gracious correspondence between the reality of his temptation and his real ability to help human freedom prone to fall.

Was His Temptation Genuine?

The temptation narratives assume that Jesus' temptations were real, not imagined. He entered the gravitational field of genuine temptation, but was sufficiently centered in his own filial self-identity and vocation that he never succumbed to any degree. His temptations were real appeals to his real freedom. His resistance was a real act of freedom in saying no on behalf of a larger yes to his vocation (Origen, *OFP*, pp. 215–18; J. Edwards, "Temptation and Deliverance," *Works* II, pp. 227–31; Barth, *CD* VI/1, pp. 258–60).

On the one hand, Jesus may be said to have been more profoundly tempted than fallen humanity, for his greater powers were tempted to greater abuse; his greater insight recognized more clearly than those bound by sin the compulsive, wrenching, trapping power of pride and sensuality. On the other hand, he is said to be less viably tempted than fallen humanity inasmuch as he consistently resisted the gravitational pull of temptation more than we whose imaginations have become perennially distorted in excessive pride and sensuality (Baxter, *PW* XIX, pp. 154–56; Newman, *PPS* V, pp. 120–27).

His sinlessness did not impair the value of his moral example, nor did it diminish his capacity for sympathy with the human condition. His temptation was real and required choice and effort to overcome. A faith that remained forever unchallenged would be a faith untested and inadequately experienced, hence unprepared for mediatorial work (Julian of Norwich, *Aphorisms*, *IAIA*, p. 190).

The Nature of Temptation: Was It Impossible for Him to Sin?

Several perplexing questions arise directly out of the assertion of his unsullied righteousness. First, is temptation even possible where sin is impossible?

Temptation Must Be Posited as Possible for Him

Arguably, there could have been no genuine temptation of Jesus had he not been subject to some possibility of spiritual pride, fatigue of spirit, or inordinate desire. If he were in his human nature absolutely immune to any potential pride or sensuality, then what could the temptation have meant, and how could he then have been truly like us, sharing our infirmities?

The Analogy of Metal Testing

Temptation was compared by ancient Christian writers to the testing of a metal. Gold may go through rigorous types of testing to establish its authenticity, but in a true test, *if* it is indeed gold, there is *no actual possibility* of outcome (though one might hypothesize a theoretical possibility) other than that it be and remain gold. It goes through the examination, a real test, but the inevitability of genuine gold passing that test is already given from the beginning.

By analogy, however severely our Lord may have been tested, if he is the eternal Son, there is no viable possibility (although a theoretical possibility can be conceived) that he would ever fail the test of moral and spiritual accountability (Pss. 12:6; 66:10; Prov. 25:4; Isa. 1:25; Zech. 13:9; 1 Pet. 1:7; 4:12; Augustine, *Comm. on Psalms* 12, *NPNF* 1 VIII, p. 45; Calvin, *Comm.* VII, pp. 79–80; Henry, *CWB* IV, p. 1467; Wesley, *ENOT*, p. 1718). But that could not be determined unhistorically or by simple fiat in advance. Rather, as in the case of the quality test of a metal, the material must go through real testing in order to be fairly evaluated.

Impeccability Necessitated Morally but Not Externally

In the Son's case, it was inevitable that he would pass the test of sinlessness, being who he was, but still it cannot be said that his will was by external necessity driven to impeccability. Impeccability is a condition that can only be chosen, not externally caused. The impossibility of Christ committing sin is best viewed as a moral choice, not an externally necessitated impossibility. It is an impossibility that arises from the radical clarity of his own will, which was so permanently directed toward good by the power of the Spirit that it was morally inconceivable that he should fall into sin.

Further, impeccability was a condition he was required continuously to choose (Tho. Aq., *ST* III Q41, II, pp. 2240–45). "Moralists distinguish two kinds of freedom of the will—the lower kind whereby it is free to choose evil as well as good, and the higher kind whereby, having definitely chosen good, it makes the choice of good a permanent act, and moreover, chooses between different means which are all free from evil. In this higher sense the human will of Christ was free" (Stone, *OCD*, p. 81).

Inevitable but Not Necessary

Hence, even as *our sin* is rightly said to be "inevitable but not necessary" (Niebuhr, *NDM* I, pp. 255–60), *his sinlessness* may oppositely be said to be (due to his unique personal identity) *inevitable but not necessary. His sinlessness is not necessitated because it is an act of freedom, but inevitable because it is the freedom of the eternal Son.* Hence the outcome of his temptation was "certain (not necessary)" (Curtis, *ChrF*, p. 249). Newman drew the distinction precisely: he assumed a nature "of itself peccable," such that, "if it had not been His, might have sinned" (*SN*, p. 148).

The Persistence of the Mistaken Idea That Sin Follows Necessarily from Temptation

Due to the persistent corruption in the actual history of ordinary human freedom, by frequent observation we tend to associate temptation with its apparent inevitable consequence—sin. So wherever there is genuine temptation, we have come to expect that in due time (by the iron rule of Murphy's Law) there is bound to be sin somewhere along the way. The experience is all too familiar: manifold temptations finally lead at some point to a fall. But with Jesus, the case has to be stated differently: there was no external necessity that he would or would not sin, but it was morally inevitable (being who he was) that he would uprightly pass the trial of temptation, whatever it might be (Augustine, *CG*, *FC* 14, pp. 108–109).

Are Saints More Ignorant of Temptation Than Sinners?

It is not the case that only sinners are capable of being tempted. If it is asserted that temptation is real only if one does in fact sin, then that leads to an awkward conclusion—that the most compulsively addicted sinners are the profoundest experts on temptation and its best interpreters. That is hardly born out by experience (Newman, *Mix.*, pp. 97–99; cf. Ramm, *EC*, p. 81). It is not the case that Jezebel, Ahab, and Judas understood temptation better than Noah, David, and Job simply because they yielded to it more profoundly. If the sinner yields to temptation and the saint resists temptation, on what basis may one conclude that the sinner knows the real nature of temptation but the saint does not? Both know the nature of temptation—they differ only in that one yields and the other does not.

The Subtle Metaphor of Seduction

The metaphor of seduction enables a closer view of the dynamics of temptation. It does not have to be sexual seduction—any form of seduction will do. The seductions most prevalent in Scripture have to do with pride, not sexuality. But since sexuality perennially is more intriguing than pride, we will take advantage of its accessibility as an example.

When Evil Appears Good

Seduction draws freedom into a realm in which evil appears good. Seduction's very purpose is to make evil look better than it is, even supremely good. That is precisely how it intends to function.

It is possible for a virtuous person who in theory could be seduced to enter into the arena of seduction and feel the tentative attraction of this apparent good, yet still be able to resist. Whether the attraction becomes stronger or weaker depends upon that person's free response. So in this sense it was possible for Jesus to enter into the realm of real attempts at seduction, to be truly tempted, yet remain without sin.

Seduction Requires Collusion

But nobody simply "gets seduced" as a wholly passive matter. The essence of a successful seduction is a collusion of wills in which one will is drawn to concurrence by another, where one woos the will of another into cooperative consent (Hugh of St. Victor, *OSCF*, pp. 122–24; Goethe,

Faust; Kierkegaard, *Repetition*). Seduction is not a coercion of will, but a drawing or tempting of that will (Newman, *PPS* V, pp. 120–27; cf. Tillich, *Syst. Theol.* II, pp. 33–36).

If it were the case that one always succumbs whenever one is tempted, then there would hardly be any residue of freedom left to be tempted, for freedom would thereby have sold itself out and become already enslaved. That could hardly be called temptation. Always to succumb is not to be tempted but to be a pushover. Genuine temptation presupposes some freedom to resist it (Tho. Aq., *ST* III Q41, II, pp. 2240–45). Augustine accordingly sought to discriminate between three different stages of temptation: suggestion, imagined pleasure, and consent (Augustine, *On Continence*, NPNF 1 III, pp. 380–93; cf. John of Damascus, *On the Virtues*, *Philokal.* II, pp. 337ff.), only the last of which is actual sin.

There Was No Collusion by Jesus with Evil That Seemed Good

In each of the three temptations of Jesus, the tempter sought to present evil in the guise of good. The tempter is metaphorically portrayed as deceiver, who deliberately engages in the trick of seducing (*planaō*, 2 John 7; Titus 1:10; Rev. 12:9; 20:3–10) where the worse choice always looks better than it is. Jesus did not to any degree collude with such deception. He exercised his freedom not to collude, thereby not abusing his freedom through collusion.

God Permits Freedom to Be Tempted, But Does Not Directly Tempt

God is not the tempter, but it is clear that God allows circumstances in which rational creatures can be tempted (Baxter, *PW* XIX, p. 155). Why? To strengthen character and moral fiber. As a trial of virtue, temptation becomes an occasion for spiritual growth, without which the human spirit would be less strong and morally vital (Newman, *US*, p. 142). Temptation is therefore in the long run for our good, though it is not directly initiated by God.

Why the Premise of Temptability Is Preferred to Its Alternative

Imagine a form of so-called human freedom that could not be tempted. That would lack all the qualities necessary for the growth and strengthening of freedom and virtue. One protected from all forms of temptation will not grow. The moral musculature will not be exercised and will atrophy. "He who has not been tempted knows nothing," Luther remarked. "For this reason the Psalter in all its words treats of practically nothing but temptation, tribulation, and affliction and is a book full of concern about them" (*Table Talk*, *WLS* III, p. 1351, *WA-Tischreden* 5, no. 6305).

Jesus was truly tempted and capable of being tempted. This draws us closer to him as one of us.

The Sexuality of Jesus

Hypotheses Concerning Jesus' Psychosexual Development

As shown above, Jesus was not exempt from those interpersonal developments that accompany human existence generally. If so, Jesus' physical, psychological, and sexual development occurred as they do in normal human development. This is a deductive statement derived from classic Christian premises already established but not made explicit in classic sources.

Thus if sexual fantasy is assumed to be a normal part of human experience, it need not be systematically denied of Jesus. But whatever sexuality Jesus is thought to have had speculatively, it must be assumed to be consistent with the assumptions and principles that we have previously set forth as requisite to Christology: that he was fully human, sharing in our human frame, hence including latent sexuality and temptation, yet without sin; that he was truly the Son of God who assumed human flesh; and that the Spirit was providing him with gifts requisite to his ministry, including the gift of continence insofar as sexual self-constraint may have been necessarily required for the fulfillment of his particular messianic mission.

No Human Being Experiences Everything—A Principle Applicable to Sexuality

It is a firm principle of our humanness that we do not live in every age, do not speak every language, do not do every deed or experience every experience.

The fact that Jesus' sexuality did not take all possible forms is more like our sexuality than unlike it, for our sexuality does not and cannot take all possible forms. Just as we cannot be both male and female, both unmarried and married, so neither could he be.

We have established the point that Christ experienced the usual range of physical and emotive responses and vulnerabilities common to humanity—hunger, thirst, sleep, grief, pain. "Surely he took up our infirmities" (Isa. 53:4), but that does not imply that Jesus had every single particular disease or felt every single type of pain there is to feel. It is more rather than less like our humanity that he had specific periods of grief or pain or a parching thirst at a particular time, not some abstract, general, nonhistorical pain or thirst (John 19:28; cf. Augustine, *Hom. on John* CCXIX, *NPNF* 1 VII, pp. 433–34).

This same must be said of his specific mode of sexuality: his, like ours, was not everything but something—not male *and* female, but male, not married *and* unmarried, but unmarried. It does not count against Jesus' humanity that he did not become married or sexually active or that he did not have children, unless one wishes to argue the absurd premise that all singles are less than human or that celibates are second-class humans— an objectionable premise that Christianity rejects.

Jesus' sexuality was lived out in a particular way consistent with his mission and self-understanding. Being in the marital covenant, for whatever reasons, was not the way God chose to become human—Jesus' sexuality was lived out in the unmarried state. This is simply one of two affirmable modes of being sexual. Chaste celibacy is not the preferred mode for everyone for the comic reason that, if absolutely preferred, a completely celibate generation would be the last one.

Modern Distortions of Sexual Consciousness

Modern consciousness, shaped by post-Freudian values and assumptions, has become fixated on active sexual self-expression (whether based upon fidelity or not and often caring less about fidelity than self-expression) as the presumed basis for health. This is the source of incalculable social pain in our time. Modernity is thereby prone to assume that the celibate mode is intrinsically unhealthy and inadequate. According to these premises, Jesus might be viewed as grossly disadvantaged in psychological understanding by never having more fully experienced sexuality. Christianity celebrates sexuality not merely as a form of hedonistic self-expression but within a network of covenant relationships. Christianity values sexuality both in its marital expression of covenant fidelity and in its equally valid form of freedom from marital commitments (provided one is called to singleness).

The Calling to the Married or Unmarried State

Celibacy is a state to which some are called and others are not. For those called to marriage, the celibate state is inferior; for those called to celibacy, the married state is inferior. One is not intrinsically inferior or superior to the other; it depends entirely upon which estate it is to which one is called.

Some apostles were married (Matt. 8:14; 1 Cor. 9:5) and some were not. Paul was unmarried but commended marriage for church leaders (1 Tim. 3:1–3; Titus 1:6). Those who absolutely "forbid people to marry" were considered "deceiving spirits" and "hypocritical liars, whose consciences have been seared as with a hot iron" (1 Tim. 4:1-3).

Freedom—the Special Value of the Unmarried Life

Without devaluing marriage, the special value and calling of the unmarried life was clearly stated by Paul: "I would like you to be free from concern. An unmarried man is concerned about the Lord's affairs—how he can please the Lord" (1 Cor. 7:32), while the married person who is called by God into marriage is rightly and necessarily "concerned about the affairs of the world—how he can please his wife—and his interests are divided" (v. 33). Celibacy is an act of freedom, enabling detachment from worldly entanglements and singleness of mind and heart, but this does not imply that marriage is sinful or less worthy for those called to marriage (1 Cor. 7:9, 28, 36, 38; Hugh of St. Victor, OSCF, pp. 325-43).

Similarly, when asked by his disciples whether "it is better not to marry," Jesus replied cautiously: "Not everyone can accept this word, but only those to whom it has been given" (Matt. 19:11). There are various ways to come to celibate life: some appear born not to marry, others have been deprived of the capacity to marry, others (as Jesus himself) voluntarily choose not to marry on behalf of the freedom that enables special service to the coming reign of God. These have given up one freedom to receive the gift of another freedom: "For some are eunuchs because they were born that way; others were made by that way by men; and others have renounced marriage because of the kingdom of heaven. The one who can accept this should accept it" (Matt. 19:11-12). The celibate life is a gift, a freedom, a commended option for those who are called to celibacy, but is not absolutely preferred for all.

Finally, it is a completely improbable speculative hypothesis determined largely by modern sexual assumptions that Jesus might have been homosexual or might have been married. These are distinctly fantastic projections that have no premodern antecedents and for which there is no plausible evidence.

The preceding observations about Jesus' sexuality are intended to prepare the way for more deliberate consideration of the temptation narratives of Matthew, Mark, and Luke.

Three Forms of Demonic Temptation of the Messianic Servant

No sooner was Jesus baptized to messianic office than he was "immediately beset by temptation" (Tertullian, Baptism 20, AEG I, p. 313). All three synoptic Gospels report that he was tempted immediately after his baptismal commissioning to servant messiahship, signaling that his temptation was connected intrinsically with his vocation.

The three forms of demonic temptation portray Jesus wrestling with his messianic vocation—whether to follow this calling to servant-messiahship or to interpret the messianic role in terms of creature comforts, miraculous power, or conquest according to popular expectations (Matt. 4:1–11; Mark 1:12–13; Luke 4:1–13). These three temptations may be regarded as representative of human temptation generally, yet are presented situationally as messianic temptations to divert his messianic calling to save humanity.

Jesus was tempted to use his extraordinary powers for ends other than those for which they were given: to prove his sonship by a work of power that would guarantee creature comforts (turning stone into bread); to personal abuse of spiritual power (letting the angels catch him from falling from the top of the temple); and to worship rebellious and illegitimate authority for the sake of world dominion (getting power by worshiping Satan).

The disciples also wrestled with analogous questions of vocation, for they persisted in thinking of the coming kingdom in lesser terms and resisted the suggestion that the messiah would suffer and die.

The Temptation to Channel the Messianic Role Toward Creature Comforts

Having fasted during a forty-day period in preparation for his public ministry, Jesus was very hungry, for "it belongs to a man to suffer hunger when fasting." It was under these conditions that the tempter seized the opportunity to attack—"For as at the beginning it was by means of food that [Satan] persuaded [Adam and Eve], although not suffering hunger, to transgress God's commandments, so in the end he did not succeed in persuading Him," the New Man, though he was hungry, to turn stones into bread (Irenaeus, *Ag. Her.* V.21, *ANF* I, p. 549; Newman, *PPS* VI, pp. 6–8).

When tempted to turn stones into bread, Jesus answered, "Man does not live on bread alone" (Luke 4:4; cf. Deut. 8:3). Creature comforts, such as food, are not finally the source of life, and with these alone, one does not fully live.

The Temptation to Exercise His Divine Powers Disobediently

Jesus was tempted to exercise wonder working (thaumaturgy) as a way of validating his messianic mission. The scene is the holy place in the holy city: "Then the devil took him to the holy city and had him stand on the highest point of the temple. 'If you are the Son of God,' he said, 'throw yourself down. For it is written: 'He will command his angels concerning you, and they will lift you up in their hands, so that you will not strike your foot against a stone'" (Matt. 4:5–6; cf. Mark 1:12–13; Luke 4:1–13). The tempter reinforced this temptation by quoting Holy Writ (Ps. 91:11–12), yet not quoting it accurately and leaving out a phrase not suited to his purpose, having "read the Scriptures, not in order to be made better by the reading of holy things, but to destroy them who cling to the letter" (Origen, *Hom. on Luke* XXXI, *AEG* I, pp. 316–17).

Jesus squarely resisted this temptation, answering, "Do not put the Lord your God to the test" (Luke 4:12; Deut. 6:16). This answer countermands the demonic pretense that God can be effectively tempted. Anyway, it is less faith than presumption to put oneself deliberately into a situation of peril – to jump off and speed toward the ground – only for the purpose of offering the angels an occasion for stopping the descent at the last moment.

The Temptation to Idolatry, Worshiping Illegitimate, Demonic Power

The tempter then revealed who he truly was (for "'Satan' signifies an apostate," Irenaeus, *Ag. Her.* V.21, *ANF* I, p. 549), by showing Jesus "in an instant all the kingdoms of the world. And he said to him, 'I will give you all their authority and splendor, for it has been given to me, and I can give it to anyone I want to. So if you worship me, it will all be yours" (Luke 4:5–7). This was the tempter's last ploy, and he was willing to make it risking all. The kingdoms shown Christ were those ruled by the tempter himself, by covetousness, by vainglory, the means through which he reigned in the world (Origen, *Hom. on Luke* XXX, *AEG* I, pp. 315–16).

Jesus answered: "Worship the Lord your God and serve him only" (Luke 4:8; cf. Deut. 6:13; 10:20). "The pride of reason, therefore, which was in the serpent, was put to nought by the humility" found in Christ (Irenaeus, *Ag. Her.* V.21, *ANF* I, p. 549).

All three temptations offered Jesus the glory of ruling without suffering and dying. This is precisely the deception that sought to divert him from the mission on which he had been sent by the Father, the distinctive vocation of servant Messiah. The deceiver's intent was to disqualify the Savior and thereby thwart God's redemptive design (Augustine, *Comm. on Psalms* 8, *NPNF* 1 VIII, p. 32.

Why tempted? He was "tempted that by His overcoming we may overcome" (Origen, *Hom. on Luke* XXIX, *AEG* I, pp. 314–15). Gregory Nazianzen summed it up, that in being tempted he "overcame him who had overcome" (*Flight to Pontus* 24, *NPNF* 2 VII, p. 210). It was fitting, thought Irenaeus, that the tempter should "be bound with the same chains with which he had bound man, in order that man, being set free, might return to his Lord, leaving to him (Satan) those bonds by which he himself had been fettered, that is, sin" (Irenaeus, *Ag. Her.* V.21, *ANF* I, p. 550). Having failed, "the devil left him, and angels came and attended him" (Matt. 4:11).

THE SINLESSNESS OF JESUS

Church teaching affirms that Christ was conceived, lived, and died without sin (Creed of Epiphanius, *SCD* 13, p. 9; see also *SCD* 18, 65, 148, 251), received in full measure the gifts of the Spirit for accomplishing his mission (Council of Rome [382], *SCD* 83, p. 33), and was never unmanageably captive to his passions, although he experienced normal human emotions (Council of Constantinople II, *SCD* 224, p. 89). He did not need purification (Alexander VIII, *SCD* 1314, p. 340) and hence did not offer sacrifice on his own behalf because, being without sin, he had no need for it (Council of Ephesus, *SCD* 122, p. 51; Menno Simons, *Incarn. of Our Lord*, *CWMS*, p. 794).

The sinlessness of Jesus is traditionally argued from two viewpoints: first, deductively from premises previously established and, second, inductively from direct testimony of friends and indirect testimony of opponents.

Classic Deductive Arguments

(1) The most straightforward way to think about the sinlessness of Jesus is deductively on the basis of premises previously established: *if God does not will contrary to God's will, and if sin is to act counter to God's will, then the God-man would not sin.* This is a simple deduction having nothing to do with empirical evidence or testimony—a tight syllogism with a major premise (the divine will does not will against itself), a minor premise (sin is defined as willing against the divine will), and a conclusion (the eternal Son would not sin). The patristic writers did not think one would go far astray by such reasoning.

(2) Another type of deduction brings us closer to salvation history: *only the sinlessness of the eternal Son could be the fitting moral foundation for his atoning work.* Such a deduction was early intuited as the remembering community began to reflect upon Jesus' death: "Such a high priest meets our need—one who is holy, blameless, pure, set apart from sinners,

exalted above the heavens" (Heb. 7:26). The high-priestly atonement under Mosaic law was enacted by one who had been properly cleansed ceremonially. Such is the only kind of priest that could have done what needed to be done for us and our salvation.

(3) The most striking deduction concerning his sinlessness was based upon the extraordinary premise that he understood himself to have legitimate *power to forgive sins*. He was remembered as such both by friends and detractors. This elicited great difficulties.

It is not surprising that the early rememberers would reason deductively: how could anyone presume to forgive sin unless he himself were without sin? If one should view him as sinner, it would make implausible the view that he had power to forgive others' sin.

Conclusions Based on Observation and Testimony: Inductive Arguments and Attestations

Are we justified on the basis of the reported evidence in concluding that statements about Jesus' sinlessness were later accretions projectively attributed to him by a romanticizing church that overlooked or failed accurately to remember his sins? The breadth and nature of evidence for his impeccability is such that it is difficult to argue that it had no basis in Jesus' actual life.

Why It Is Unlikely That the Testimony to Impeccability Was Deluded

Deluded people may claim to be sinless, but they usually do not convince anyone beside themselves. That is why we call them deluded. But in Jesus' case, many appear to have been radically convinced—so much so that they were willing to sell all, deny themselves, bear their cross, and go abroad to proclaim this message at great risk—that Jesus was what he said he was. The rememberers perceived in him no discrepancy between what he claimed and what he did. And the fact that his claims were so extensive makes it even more remarkable that he was perceived as sinless. His character was congruous with his claims (Matt. 27:3, 19; Cyprian, *Treatises* XII.2.15, *ANF* V, pp. 521–22; cf. Stott, *BC*, p. 34).

Were There Unremembered Offenses?

There is no doubt that Jesus was attested as sinless. The question remains as to whether the accounts were accurate recollections. The primary basis upon which one seeks to assess the truth of historical statements of this sort is the evidence that accumulates during one's public life.

It remains an astonishing fact that the most remembered life in history was not remembered to have harmed anyone or shown any elements of moral venality or reprehensibility. Neither friends nor foes remember or report him as sinner. To establish this point, two complementary approaches were pursued in classic exegesis: lack of testimony against and ample testimony in favor of impeccability.

Testimony of Enemies: What Those Who Resisted Him Said of Him

Surveillance Was Intense

Recall that when Jesus was under fire from the scribes and Pharisees and finally on a formal trial for his life, many charges were hurled at him. They were constantly trying to trap him in his own words (Mark 12:13). They watched him, surveilled him constantly, looking for some slight misstep (Mark 3:2).

In a trial one would expect all pertinent charges to be declared. There were plenty of opportunities to dredge up skeletons that might have otherwise been in his closet. If it were the case that his life had been sullied by sin, wouldn't it be likely that in all of those hostile encounters some of those charges would have surfaced? If attempts were made to cover up, wouldn't the authorities have had all the resources to get to the bottom of it?

The Telling Absence of the Charge of Hypocrisy

Suppose he had been guilty of hypocrisy. Suppose he called others to repent yet remained impenitent or called others to love yet remained unloving. Wouldn't one expect some charge of hypocrisy to surface during the heat of embittered debate?

It would have been an extrordinary hypocrisy indeed if this man, who assumed the power to forgive sin, had sinned. He must have included himself in the call to be radically honest and in the call to perfect love. Thus he would have been an easy target for the charge of hypocrisy if there had been any doubt among his contemporaries about the consistency of his behavior with his teaching. Recall that the synoptic Gospels regularly report opinions of detractors, yet there is no hint of any charge of this sort.

Each Presumed Fault a Deeper Good

It is an intriguing fact that, amid all the controversy about him, Jesus was not plausibly charged with moral or character fault, excepting the spurious charges of blasphemy and sedition that finally resulted in his death. He was indeed charged with gluttonous eating and drinking and mixing with sinners, with obscure forms of Sabbath breaking, and chiefly with blasphemy. Yet in each of these cases, the charge itself was a distinct badge of honor in relation to his hidden identity and mission. He was a "friend of sinners," harlots, and publicans because he invited them to enter God's kingdom, not because he was being corrupted by them. He did not truly break the law by healing on the Sabbath but fulfilled it. To forgive sins was God's own prerogative, and he was blaspheming only if he was not indeed God-incarnate (Gregory Nazianzen, *On His Father's Silence*, NPNF 2 VII, p. 252). Each alleged moral deficit was a necessary part of his teaching ministry.

Did Jesus have lapses into undesirable behaviors? Some have argued that Jesus was not unambiguously good according to the reports about him, for he became angry, drove merchants away from the Temple with a whip, spoke harshly to his mother, and broke the Sabbath law. Yet in each of these cases, what seemed to be a questionable behavior was at its depth an excellent act that only appeared deficient when detached from its context (Bonhoeffer, *Christology* [London: Collins, 1966], p. 112; Aldwinckle, *MTM*, pp. 195–99).

The Verdict of Detractors

It is instructive and even moving to listen carefully to the final verdicts of his enemies who colluded in Jesus' death. Judas cried out, "I have betrayed innocent blood" (Matt 27:3). Pilate queried, "What crime has he committed?" and protested, "I am innocent of this man's blood" (27:23–24). He declared: "I have examined him in your presence and have found no basis for your charges against him" (Luke 23:14). Pilate's wife said, "Don't have anything to do with that innocent man" (Matt. 27:19). Herod cleared him of charges, as Pilate remarked, "Neither has Herod [found any basis for the charges], for he sent him back to us; as you can see, he has done nothing to deserve death" (Luke 23:15). The centurion at the cross declared, "Surely this was a righteous man" (Luke 23:47). This is an astonishing confluence of testimony among precisely those who had conspired in bringing his life to a bloody end.

What Those Who Best Knew Him Said of His Character

The Disciples' Testimony Based upon Intimate Knowledge

The disciples of Christ walked daily and lived closely with him, sharing a common purse. They ate together, labored, risked, and traveled together for three years (Acts 1:21–22). Being a disciple was not a casual relation. The disciples must have had the opportunity to see him under all sorts of conditions, in fair and foul weather, struggling and relaxing, at weddings and upon the death of a friend.

Would not it be expected that such familiarity would breed contempt? It did not happen in this case. They were leading witnesses to his perfect love and holiness.

It is worth recalling that the disciples were steeped in the Jewish tradition of the ubiquity of sin, which assumed that "there is no one who does good, not even one" (Ps. 14:3). They had to go against all that they had learned about the universality of sin to assert the impeccability of Jesus, but they did precisely this—the facts of the case warranted it. John wrote: "In him is no sin" (1 John 3:5). Earlier in the same Letter this same author had said of all others, "If we claim to be without sin, we deceive ourselves" (1 John 1:8). Even the thief sized him up instantly, according to Luke: "this man has done nothing wrong" (Luke 13:41; Cyril of Jerusalem, *Catech. Lect.* XIII, FC 64, p. 6).

Early Preaching of Jesus' Unblemished Righteousness

Both Peter and Stephen referred to Jesus as "the Righteous One" (Acts 3:14; 7:52). Calling hearers to follow in the steps of Jesus' example of sacrificial service, the Letter of Peter declared: "He committed no sin, and no deceit was found in his mouth" (1 Pet. 2:21–22, quoting Isa. 53:9). He was compared to "a lamb without blemish or defect" (1 Pet. 1:19). Only one who was "righteous" could die "for the unrighteous" (1 Pet. 3:18; Barth, *CD* III/2, pp. 441ff.; cf. Heb. 4:15).

Paul followed the earliest tradition of Christian recollection of Jesus when he wrote that "God made him who *had no sin to be sin for us*, so that in him we might become the righteousness of God" (1 Cor. 5:21, italics added). Only one who "had no sin" could be in a position to "condemn sin." Yet only one who shares our human condition could save. These were the very conditions requisite for being mediator.

What Christ Is Reported to Have Said of Himself

Did Christ's humility prevent him from telling the truth about his own sinlessness? The question arose obliquely in Jesus' ministry when a woman caught in adultery was brought him. He said, "If any one of you is *without sin*, let him be the first to throw a stone at her," and they "began to go away one at a time, the older ones first, until *only Jesus was left*" (John 8:7, 9, italics added). Jesus bluntly asked his detractors after this incident: "Can any of you prove me guilty of sin?" (John 8:46). Note the counterpoint of these two texts in the same passage: no one in the circle of accusers was without sin. All went away in response to the question except one—Jesus. And those who had gone away were challenged to prove him guilty of sin (Origen, *De Principiis* II.6.4, *ANF* IV, p. 283).

When they "did not understand that he was telling them about his Father," he declared plainly, "I always do what pleases him" (John 8:27, 29). In this way, "He placed Himself in a moral category by Himself," for "although He abhorred self-righteousness in others, He detected none in Himself when He declared Himself to be righteous" (Stott, *BC*, pp. 36–37). For this reason, there is no recollection of his asking forgiveness of his own sins, though he asked for others' sins to be forgiven of God.

Further, there is no evidence of any inward struggle with guilt over moral failure. Those who have walked the furthest on the way of holiness are those likely to be most keenly aware of their own guilt. St. Teresa of Avila, for example, understood most acutely how distant she was from the full possibility of life in Christ, but it was not because she was living distantly from that life but so near it (Teresa, *Life*, *CWST* I, pp. 179–290). This was not morbid preoccupation with guilt but simply the expression of a daily life lived so near to God that she was more painfully aware of each small increment of distance from God than others might have known in a lifetime. Yet Jesus, whose closeness to God the Father could hardly be questioned, showed no evidences of such guilt or remorse or distance but rather sustained the closest filial relation.

The Estimate of Jesus' Character

These exegetical perplexities remain:

(1) Why did Jesus remark, "*Why do you ask me about what is good?*" When Jesus responded to the rich young ruler who had addressed him as "Good Teacher," his response pointedly affirmed that "No one is good—except God alone" (Mark 10:18). Was Jesus saying that he, too, was not good, or not as good as God (as the Arians argued)? Jesus was here challenging the young man about his assumptions about what is good in order better to call him to repentance. The question, "Why do you call me good?" was a query addressed the young man, not a statement about Jesus. It sought a thoughtful, serious answer. Its teaching purpose was to confront the young man with his own predicament, not to talk about Jesus' moral virtue or status (Clement of Alexandria, *Rich Man* 8, *AEG* IV, p. 235; cf. Warfield, *Christology and Criticism*, pp. 97–148). Matthew's narrative of the same incident put precisely this interpretation upon Jesus' question: "Why do you ask me about what is good?" (Matt. 19:16; John Chrysostom, *Hom. on Matt.* LXIII, *NPNF* 1 X, pp. 387–91). That is far different from a disavowal of personal goodness.

(2) *Did Jesus' participation in a sinful society make him unavoidably a sinner?* If simply being born into a society already makes one a sinner, then sin finally has nothing to do with free choice. If every society is thought to be by definition equally sinful—according to some grim logic of equality— and in such a society sin is automatically and necessarily transmitted in an absolutely equal way to every person prior to any act of freedom, then it would have to be asserted that either Jesus was somehow immune to society's evil influences or he was sinner. Neither of these conclusions is consistent with testimony about him. The deeper answer hinges on the Spirit's constant enabling and shepherding of his free soul, providing him with requisite gifts for ministry, enabling him to resist temptation of every kind, including evil that might result from collusion with social injustices.

(3) *Does Jesus become less human by having not sinned?* If we say that Jesus is not fully human because he never sinned, then we have made a grossly un-Hebraic statement about humanity—namely, that because human nature is created sinful, God as Creator created sin (as opposed to the biblical view of God-given freedom as ever prone to the abuse of freedom).

To require of Jesus that he take on our sinful, fallen nature in order to be fully human is not to make Jesus more fully human but less human. That oddly amounts to requiring that humanity *must* miss its mark (*hamartia*) if it is to be human! That is patently self-contradictory, hence in error.

SON OF MAN

The importance of the title "Son of Man" is clear from its frequency of use in the Gospels—over fifty times excluding parallel sayings.

The Most Primitive Layer of Christological Titles

A Title of Descent-Ascent

A crucial feature of the Johannine use of the "Son of Man" title was the assumption that he who had descended from heaven would ascend once again (John 3:13; cf. Daniel 7:13, 14; Augustine, *Comm. on John*, Tractate 12, *NPNF* 1 VII, p. 8). Jesus said to Nathanael: "You shall see heaven open, and the angels of God ascending and descending on the Son of Man" (John 1:51; reminscent of Jacob's ladder), suggesting that the Son of Man is the gate of heaven, the unique personage wherein humanity and deity come into concourse and union.

The preexistence, descent, and ascent of the Son are encompassed in this unusual name: "No one has ever gone into heaven except the one who came from heaven—the Son of Man" (John 3:13). "I came from the Father and entered the world; now I am leaving the world and going back to the Father" (John 16:28). The transcendent identity of the Son of Man is not merely an insight of recent criticism but was clearly grasped by the fourth century: "He is called Son of Man, not as having had His generation from the earth, as each one of us, but as 'coming upon the clouds of heaven' to judge the living and the dead" (Cyril of Jerusalem, *Catech. Lect.* X, *FC* 61, p.197).

Repeatedly Self-referenced by Jesus

The title "Son of Man" is most frequently reported as being used by Jesus himself. It is found in all Gospels repeatedly (from Jesus' lips sixty-five times!). Often viewed as a transition title, "Son of Man" appears to have been utilized almost exclusively by Jesus himself and by the earliest pre-Pauline tradition, but it does not appear in the Letters of Paul and did not find its way into the creeds (I. H. Marshall, ed., *New Testament Interpretation* [1977], pp. 79ff.). Use of the title in the New Testament period appears to have diminished soon after Jesus' death. The strong suggestion is that this was a title that Jesus used, not one that was later ascribed to him, and for reasons that as yet seem unclear, the hellenizing church did not find it useful in its context. The fact that it was not used by others of Jesus lends strength to the authenticity of its earlier usage by him.

It may be that the hellenizing Church found the title "Christ" a better ascription for preaching and apologetics than "Son of Man," and since most of its more crucial nuances are encompassed by the term *Christos,* "Christ" became normative in a way that "Son of Man" may have earlier been. The hypothesis is implausible that the remembering church invented this title and put it in the mouth of Jesus, for if that were so, one would expect to find it commonly in use in the hellenizing church, and this is dramatically not the case.

The Secret Revealed

The most plausible conclusion is that by using the term "Son of Man," Jesus was pointing to his messianic role but transmuting it in an unusual manner. The title carried distinctly supernatural nuances.

Perhaps he did not want to call himself "Messiah" during his public ministry because of potential popular distortions inconsistent with his mission. "He called himself the Son of Man because this title made an exalted claim and yet at the same time permitted Jesus to fill the term with new meaning. This he did by coupling the role of Son of Man with that of the Suffering Servant" (Ladd, *TNT*, p. 158; see also pp. 147–58). The unique sort of messiah Jesus became ran against popular Jewish hopes. He would suffer and die before he would be raised again to inaugurate the reign of God.

The kingdom comes in unexpected form and works secretly, hiddenly, like yeast. As end-time Son of Man, Jesus would return to judge and finally to bestow the kingdom, but before his death and resurrection, he was the Son of Man living as a man among men and women and would suffer and die for others. The messianic secret is that the heavenly Son of Man was already unexpectedly present in human history, moving inexorably toward the hour in which all would be revealed.

There is an anticipatory motif (awaiting confirmation by subsequent events) in many Son of Man sayings that appear to belong to the earliest stratum of recollection. Jesus said, "Whoever acknowledges me before men, I will also acknowledge him before my Father in heaven. But whoever disowns me before men, I will disown him before my Father in heaven" (Matt. 10:32, utilizing "Q"; see Mark 8:28; Luke 9:26). Mark's version states: "If anyone is ashamed of me and my words in this adulterous and sinful generation, the Son of Man will be ashamed of him when he comes in his Father's glory with the holy angels" (Mark 8:28). The saying is valued by form critics as embedded in the deepest layer of tradition coming from Jesus (Bornkamm, *JN*, p. 228; cf. Bultmann, *TNT* I, pp. 28ff.; H. E. Toedt, *The Son of Man in the Synoptic Tradition*, pp. 329–31). "The substitution in Matthew's version of the 'I' of Jesus for the 'Son of Man' shows how the post-Easter community understood and transformed the saying of Jesus" (from Mark 8:38 to Luke 9:26 and Matt. 10:32; Pannenberg, *JGM*, pp. 59–60). On these grounds it seems clear that Jesus identified his mission with that of the Son of Man, but that only became fully clear to the disciples after the resurrection.

The Background of Daniel and Enoch

It is reasonable to assume that Jesus' audience was familiar with the Old Testament title "Son of Man," especially that found in Daniel 7. In Daniel's vision, the Son of Man was seen "coming with the clouds of heaven. He approached the Ancient of Days and was led into his presence. He was given authority, glory and sovereign power; all peoples, nations and men of every language worshiped him. His dominion is an everlasting dominion that will not pass away, and his kingdom is one that will never be destroyed" (Dan. 7:13–14). Many elements of Jesus' identity and ministry are thereby anticipated: Son of the Father, recipient of an eternal kingdom; presented before the Ancient of Days; ruler of a reign of peace that would extend to all nations, never to end. The Son of Man was expected to represent those who have remained faithful to God, who share in the kingdom of which the Son of Man will be ruler, who will stand in God's presence (Dan. 7; Irenaeus, *Ag. Her.* III.19, IV.33, *ANF* I, pp. 449, 506–509; Tertullian, *On the Flesh of Christ* 15, *ANF* III, p. 534).

The Similitudes of Enoch present a Son of Man figure that displays many features similar to that portrayed in the Gospels: in *Enoch*, the Son of Man was a messianic title indicating a pretemporal heavenly figure who would descend to earth, judge the nations, inaugurate the kingdom of glory, and clothe the righteous with robes of glory, who would share in fellowship with the Son of Man eternally (*Enoch* 46:48; 62:6–16; 69:26–29). It is possible that both Jesus and Enoch were relying upon a common, as yet unidentified source. Antecedents of the Son of Man tradition in 4 Ezra (composed before the end of the first century A.D.) could have influenced Jesus. It is doubtful that there was a single common usage of the title "Son of Man" in Jewish apocalyptic circles of the first century, but rather a series of independent exegetical uses of Daniel 7 (N. Perrin, *Rediscovering the Teaching of Jesus*, pp. 164–73).

Son of Man Sayings

Son of Man sayings fall into three phases.

The Earthly Son of Man

Some sayings refer to Jesus' earthly ministry (Mark 2:12; Luke 7:34; 9:58). The Son of Man came to seek and save the lost, was conscious of his mission as messianic redeemer (Luke 19:10); came eating and drinking, calling all to repentance (Matt. 11:19); claimed and evidenced authority to forgive sin (Mark 2:10 and parallels); was Lord of Sabbath; was able to interpret scribal regulations (Mark 2:27 and parallels); yet had nowhere to lay his head (Matt. 8:20). After the transfiguration, there were few Son of Man references to Jesus' earthly ministry; rather they focused upon his coming suffering and death and return in glory.

The Suffering and Dying Son of Man

Some sayings refer to the impending suffering, death, and resurrection of the Son of Man (Mark 9:9; Luke 17:24–25; 24:7). Recollecting Isaiah 53, Jesus combined the Son of Man type with the suffering Servant: "For even the Son of Man did not come to be served, but to serve, and to give his life as a ransom for many" (Mark 10:45; cf. Isa. 53:10–12).

Jesus thereby radically transformed the prevailing messianic expectations of Israel. The Son of Man was a pretemporal heavenly being who comes in poverty, humility, and vulnerability as a man for others. At Caesarea Philippi it may have been first understood that the Son of Man would be like the suffering Servant of Isaiah 53. Thereafter it was said that the Son of Man "must suffer" (Mark 8:31); be delivered into the hands of men and the chief priests (Mark 9:31; 10:33); and be condemned to death, (Matt. 20:18; Luke 18:31); remain three days in the earth (Matt. 12:40; Irenaeus, *Ag. Her.* III.12.5, *ANF* I, p. 442), and rise again (Mark 10:33).

The End-Time Coming of the Son of Man

Some sayings point to the future activity of the Son of Man as Judge and Savior, coming in glory to inaugurate the reign of God (Mark 8:38; 13:26; Luke 12:8; Augustine, *CG, FC* 24, p. 33). The Son of Man will come at an unexpected hour (Luke 12:40; Matt. 24:44); and will come soon (Matt. 10:23; 16:28; Mark 9:1); will come with clouds and great glory (Mark 8:38 and 13:16 with parallels); and will sit at the right hand of power (Mark 14:62 with parallels). Those who acknowledge the Son of Man will be acknowledged by him before the angels of God (Luke 12:18; cf. Ladd, *TNT*, pp. 149–51).

At his trial his identity became clarified: Jesus was asked by the high priest whether he was the Messiah, Son of God. At this crucial point, Jesus stated outright what Messiah means: "'I am,' said Jesus. 'And you will see the Son of Man sitting at the right hand of the Mighty one and coming on the clouds of heaven'" (Mark 14:62). Now they judged him; soon he would judge them.

In Revelation, the redeemer appears in his final manifestation in human form as "someone 'like a son of man'" (Rev. 1:13), the "Alpha and the Omega," "who is, and who was, and who is to come, the Almighty" (v. 8).

It is likely that Jesus applied this term to himself and that his audience had a clear idea of what he meant (Marshall, *ONTC*, p. 79; M. D. Hooker, *The Son of Man in Mark*; F. H. Borsch, *The Son of Man in Myth and History*; G. Vermes, *Jesus the Jew*, p. 186; cf. H. E. Toedt, *Son of Man in the Synoptic Tradition*; Hahn, *TJC*). It suggested his identification with humankind as a whole and anticipated the typology that Paul would later develop between Adam and Christ (Rom. 5:12–21; 1 Cor. 15:45–49).

THE JOURNEY TOWARD JERUSALEM

From Jesus' baptism with water to his baptism with blood on the cross, there was a gradual recognition among the disciples that an unparalleled event was occurring. That evolving recognition is what the Gospel writers sought to narrate and make plausible. The transfiguration was a moment of extraordinary clarity in previsioning this end.

The death of Christ completed his humble engagement in his earthly ministry. Each step of his earthly journey pointed anticipatively toward the atoning work of his death. Each crucial event leading up to this supreme act of self-giving was laden with meaning.

Peter's Confession

The Recognition of the Messianic King

Just before the transfiguration, the Galilean ministry had climaxed at Caesarea Philippi. Jesus and his disciples had been preaching in the vicinity of the northwestern border of Palestine. The preaching ministry that had begun in Galilee was soon to turn toward Jerusalem.

In preparation for that final struggle, Jesus sought to make clear to his closest disciples exactly what was at stake in his mission. At Caesarea Philippi he asked: "Who do you say that I am?" Peter answered boldly with words that were to become the heart of the most basic Christian confession: "You are the Christ" (Mark 8:29). It was because Peter "replied for the rest of the Apostles" and ultimately for the rest of humanity, that "he is called the foundation" (Ambrose, *Incarn. of Our Lord* 4.33, FC 44, p. 231; Baxter, *PW* XVII, pp. 477-79). Jesus received this affirmation with a saying that would greatly affect the history of the church: "Blessed are you, Simon son of Jonah, for this was not revealed to you by man, but by my Father in heaven. And I tell you that you are Peter, and on this rock I will build my church, and the gates of Hades will not overcome it. I will give you the keys of the kingdom of heaven; whatever you bind on earth will be bound in heaven, and whatever you loose on earth will be loosed in heaven" (Matt. 16:17-19).

The Suffering Messiah

Peter's answer was indeed correct, but without sufficient understanding of what it implied in terms of suffering or self-denial. Jesus then "began to teach them that the Son of Man must suffer many things and be rejected by the elders, chief priests and teachers of the law, and that he must be killed and after three days rise again" (Mark 8:31; cf. Matt. 16:13-23; Luke 9:18-22; Tho. Aq., *ST* III Q46, II, pp. 2264-65). Late Judaic expectation had not anticipated a suffering and dying messiah. It had focused upon the Davidic king who was to reign, not die (Ladd, *TNT*, p. 330). Gradually it became clearer to some disciples, although it was still kept from general knowledge, that it is only through suffering and death that the Son of Man would fulfill his mission (Pearson, *EC* I, pp. 157, 317; Marshall, *ONTC*, pp. 63–97).

Willingness to Die as the Distinguishing Mark of Discipleship

Those who would accompany him in this mission must be willing to follow his path of self-giving for others: "If anyone would come after me, he must deny himself and take up his cross and follow me. For whoever wants to save his life will lose it, but whoever loses his life for me and for the gospel will save it" (Mark 8:34–35). Willingness to suffer and if necessary die on behalf of the truth of God's coming thereafter became the distinguishing mark of discipleship.

Martyrdom Neither Sought or Avoided

Yet even this step must be rightly and carefully taken, for "the law of martyrdom alike forbids us voluntarily to go to meet it (in consideration for the persecutors, and for the weak) or to shrink from it if it comes upon us; for the former shows foolhardiness, the latter cowardice" (Gregory Nazianzen, *Orat.* XLIII.6, *NPNF* 2 VII, p. 397). Jesus' willingness to die was neither masochistic nor craven.

Transfiguration Prefigured Exaltation

Jesus' decision to go to Jerusalem was illuminated by a crucial event that prefigured his exaltation: the transfiguration.

Definition

The transfiguration is that event on a mountain in northern Galilee in which Jesus was "transfigured" (*metamorphoō*), or transformed, in conversation with Moses and Elijah, and a voice from heaven affirmed his divine sonship (Matt. 17:1–8; Mark 9:2–8; Luke 9:28–36).

"After six days Jesus took Peter, James and John with him and led them up a high mountain, where they were all alone. There he was transfigured before them. His clothes became dazzling white, whiter than anyone in the world could bleach them. And there appeared before them Elijah and Moses, who were talking with Jesus" (Mark 9:2–1; Tertullian, *Ag. Marcion* IV.22, *ANF* III, pp. 383–84; Baxter, *PW* XVIII, pp. 467–77). According to Luke's report, "They spoke about his departure"—*exodus* (death)—"which he was about to bring to fulfillment at Jerusalem" (Luke 9:31; Bonaventure, *Tree of Life, CWS,* p. 135). He revealed to a select audience his messianic identity, the necessity of his coming death, and his resurrection according to Scripture (John Chrysostom, *Hom. on Matt.* LVI-LVIII, *NPNF* 1 X, pp. 345-63; Barth, *CD* III/2, pp. 478ff.).

Divine Sonship Confirmed from on High

As at his baptism, once again "A voice came from the cloud: 'This is my Son, whom I love. Listen to him!'" (Mark 9:7). "My Son" is a messianic identification. The divine sonship that had been designated in Christ's baptism was being reconfirmed in the transfiguration soon to lead toward the cross (Tho. Aq., *ST* III Q45, II, p. 2260-64). With this confirmation it became clear that the final battle for human redemption was about to be joined and that it would require the death of the Messiah (Chemnitz, *TNC*, pp. 430-31).

Its Historicity Attested

If there existed any debate on the fringes of the postresurrection community as to whether the transfiguration event really occurred, the Second Letter of Peter sought to conclude it. That Letter went out of its way to counter such doubts and attest the truth of the transfiguration: "We did not follow cleverly invented stories when we told you about the power and coming of our Lord Jesus Christ, but we were eyewitnesses of his majesty. For he received honor and glory from God the Father when the voice came to him from the Majestic Glory, saying, 'This is my Son, whom I love; with him I am well pleased.' We ourselves heard this voice that came from heaven when we were with him on the sacred mountain" (2 Pet. 1:16-18).

This writer appears to be deliberately protesting the interpretation that the transfiguration was something that had been fancifully thought up, psychologically projected, or invented for some manipulative purpose. He spoke as an eyewitness who, by beholding this event, had attained increased certainty of Jesus' messianic vocation.

A Foretaste of Glory

Just before the transfiguration, Jesus had said, "I tell you the truth, some who are standing here will not taste death before they see the Son of Man coming in his kingdom" (Matt. 16:28). This was said to prepare them for the ensuing Passion (John Chrysostom, *Hom. on Matt.* LVI, *NPNF* 1 X, pp. 345-51). The transfiguration was a preview of the kingdom, the Lord appearing in a vision of glory (Baxter, *PW* XVIII, pp. 462-67). On the mount of transfiguration those closest disciples who would soon taste the blood and death of persecution were allowed for a moment to taste the glory to come (Bede, *Comm.*, on Mark 8:39; cf. Tho. Aq., *ST* III, Q45, III, p. 2261).

"Therefore it was fitting that He should show His disciples the glory of His clarity (which is to be transfigured), to which He will configure those who are His." The transfiguration "signified the future clarity of the saints" and represented "His body's future clarity" (Tho. Aq., *ST* III, Q45.1, 2, II, pp. 2261–62). Clarity implied the agility, sublety and impassibility of the glorified body (cf. Maximos, *Four Hundred Texts, Philokal.* II, pp. 134–35; Gregory the Great, *Moralia on Job* XXXII, LF 21).

"Thou wast transfigured on the mountain, O Christ our Lord, and the glory has so caught the wonder of Thy disciples, that when they see Thee crucified they will understand that Thy Passion is voluntary, and they will proclaim to the world that Thou art truly the Splendour of the Father" (Hymn for the Feast of the Transfiguration, *Menologia*, in Lossky, *MTEC*, p. 149).

THE ANOINTED ONE

"Messiah" is among the most important of all titles or concepts in Christian teaching. By it the person of Jesus is rightly identified in relation to the history of Jewish expectation (Pearson, *EC* I, p. 142). The New Testament was written in order that hearers might believe that Jesus is the Christ (John 20:31; Irenaeus, *Ag. Her.* III.16.5, *ANF* I, p. 442).

At Caesarea Philippi Jesus straightforwardly raised the central question: "Who do you say I am?" (Mark 8:29). All Christian creeds confess Jesus as *the Christ. Credo . . . in unum Dominum Jesum Christum* (Creed of 150 Fathers, *COC* II, p. 58). What does that mean?

For What Purposes Was the Messiah Anointed?

What Christ Signifies

The name Christ "signifies that he is anointed by his Father to be King, Priest and Prophet. How do you know this? Because Scripture applies anointing to these three uses; and also because it often attributes these three offices to Christ" (Calvin, *Catech. of the Church of Geneva*, LCC XXII, p. 957). "The title 'Christ' pertains to these three offices: for we know that under the law prophets as well as priests and kings were anointed" (Calvin, *Inst.* 2.15.2).

One Title for Three Offices

The systematic connection must be clearly established between the title "Christ" and the three offices. Classic Protestant teaching is best stated by the *Heidelberg Catechism:* "Why is he called Christ, that is, the Anointed One? Because he is ordained by God the Father and anointed with the Holy Spirit to be *our chief Prophet and Teacher,* fully revealing to us the secret purpose and will of God concerning our redemption; to be *our only High Priest,* having redeemed us by the one sacrifice of his body and ever interceding for us with the Father; and to be *our eternal King,* governing us by his Word and Spirit, and defending and sustaining us in the redemption he has won for us" (II, Q31, *BOConf.* 4.031). Though challenged by some interpreters (especially as to the prophetic office), we will seek to show why this structure deserves continued development.

Christos

Messiah (Gk. *Christos,* Heb. *Mashiah,* "anointed") was the Expected One, Son of David anointed to be the deliverer of Israel (Augustine, *CG, FC* 14, pp. 47–56). The resurrection would both confirm and clarify the messianic ascription. Peter proclaimed after the resurrection: "God has made this Jesus, whom you crucified, both Lord and Christ" (Acts 2:36)—"that is, *Anointed*" (Tertullian, *Ag. Praxeas* 38, *ANF* III, p. 625; J. Knox, *Jesus: Lord and Christ).*

Christ a Proper Name

By the time of writing of the early Pauline Letters, *Christos* had become a proper name, intricately welded with the name "Jesus" for all who attested the resurrection. Paul more often spoke of Jesus Christ, Christ Jesus, or Christ than simply Jesus. It is likely that *Christos* became a proper name amid increased engagement with hellenized cultures in which the nuances of "Messiah," so well known among pious Jews, would not have been so clearly understood by Gentiles. The disciples were first called *Christianoi* ("Christians") not in Palestine but in Antioch (Acts 11:26; Theophilus, *To Autolycus* I.1, 12, *ANF* II, p. 89, 92).

Anointed by God

Classical exegetes insisted that his identity as Anointed One comes not from human hands, but from God alone: "He is called Christ, not as having been anointed by human hands, but anointed eternally by the Father to His High-Priesthood over men" (Cyril of Jerusalem, *Catech. Lect.* X., *FC* 61, p. 197; Augustine, *Trin.,* *FC* 45, pp. 515–16).

Athanasius argued that Christ did not become so only when named by others, but was so before being thus humanly confessed (Athanasius, *Ag. Apollinaris* 2:1–2). The same issue that continues in post-Bultmannian circles has been recurrent in historic Christianity: did Jesus disavow the title that was later ascribed to him? Did Jesus become the Christ only when called the Christ? The ecumenical consensus held: "We say that the Son and Word of God became Christ the instant that He came to dwell in the womb. . . . It is when the Word was made flesh that we say that He received the name of Christ Jesus" (John of Damascus, *OF* IV.6, *FC* 37, p. 340; cf. Gregory Nazianzen, *Orat.* XXX.21, *NPNF* 2 VII, p. 317; Cyril of Alexandria, *To Emperor Theodosius* 28; *To the Empresses* 13), not when others perceived him as Christ.

The Expected One in the Prophetic Tradition

There is no doubt that Jesus was *called* the Christ. The harder question of Jesus' messianic identity is: how could Jesus have been called the Christ if he in fact suffered and died contrary to Jewish messianic expectations? The answer requires tracing the course of messianic expectations from the Old Testament, through later Judaic writings, to the prevailing expectation of the New Testament period.

If we had in hand only the Old Testament texts expecting the messiah and knew nothing yet of the New Testament, we would still know a great deal about the Expected One. He would be anointed, set apart as servant of God to bring deliverance to captives (Ps. 89:3–4; Isa. 9–11; Jer. 30:8–9; Ezek. 37:21–23; Pearson, *EC* I, p. 142). Jeremiah expected one whose name would be "The Lord Our Righteousness" (Jer. 23:6). Micah expected that the ruler of Israel would come from Bethlehem (Mic. 5:2). Haggai expected that One "desired of all nations" would come bringing the glory and peace of God (Hag. 2:6–7). Malachi expected a messenger who would prepare the way for the Lord, an angel of the covenant who would appear in the Temple. Isaiah prophesied of "A voice of one calling: 'In the desert prepare the way for the Lord; make straight in the wilderness a highway for our God'" (Isa. 40:3).

It was clear from prophetic utterance that the whole world, Jews and non-Jews, would benefit from God's own coming (Isa. 42:1–17; 49:6–13; Jer. 16:19–21; Mal. 1:11). In all these ways the prophets expressly taught of God's own future coming. These were not a single, cohesive tradition, but a starburst of diverse forms of hope.

That the Expected One would have a distinctive kingly role is repeatedly made clear (Isa. 57:9; Jer. 23:5; Hos. 3:5; Mic. 4:8–9; Zech. 9:9). *Isaiah* expected a king in the line of David who would cleanse from sin, gather Israel, bring peace, and reign forever (Isa. 11). Upon him the "Spirit of the Lord will rest" (11:2; Calvin, *Comm.* VII, pp. 370–96).

Zechariah expected the messianic king to ride into Jerusalem on "a colt, the foal of a donkey" as a sign of victory, bringing salvation, peace, and the rulership of God over the earth (Zech. 9:9–10; Justin Martyr, *First Apology* 35, *ANF* I, p. 175; *Dialogue with Trypho* 53, *ANF* I, pp. 221–22).

Daniel prophesied that the Anointed One would be a ruler who was expected to appear 490 years ("seventy sevens" or seventy weeks, Dan. 9:24–25) after the rebuilding of Jerusalem (Clement of Alexandria, *Stromata* I.21, ANF II, p. 329). Early Christian exegetes thought that Daniel's prophecy must either have been realized during the period in which Jesus lived or remain forever unrealized (Clement of Alexandria, *Stromata* I.21, *ANF* II, p. 329; Origen, *De Principiis* IV.1, *ANF* IV, p. 354).

The messianic hope expected "one who will build a house for my Name, and I will establish the throne of his kingdom forever. I will be his father, and he will be my son" (2 Sam. 7:13–14; cf. Matt. 1:1; Mark 1:11; Heb. 1:5). Pious Jews in Jesus' time were intensely aware of these allusions and expectations.

The messianic king was viewed in *Psalm 2* under two principal metaphors: "Son" of the Father (Ps. 2:8), and "Anointed One" destined to rule nations (Ps. 2:2, 8) as king whose kingdom would be inaugurated in a particular place, Jerusalem (Ps. 2:6; cf. Acts 4:25–28; for expositions of Ps. 2, see Augustine, *Expos. Ps.*, *NPNF* 1 VIII, pp. 3–5; Luther, *Comm. Ps. 2*, *LW* 12, pp. 3–97). That this Expected One would be God is clear from the name "Immanuel" (Isa. 7:11), and from other prophetic titles ascribable only to God: "Mighty God," "Everlasting Father" (Isa. 9:6).

Isaiah more than any other source stressed that the Expected One would suffer for us. The innocent victim would take the place of the guilty. On him their sins would be laid. He would be wounded for our transgressions (Isa. 53).

The Expected One Immediately Prior to Jesus' Coming

The Qumran community looked for an Anointed One, "the Messiah of Righteousness," "the Branch of David" (4Q *Patriarchal Blessings*, Ladd, *TNT*, p. 138n; A. Dupont-Sommer, *The Essene Writings from Qumran*, p. 314–16). The *Apocalypse of Baruch* and 4 Ezra gave form to intense apocalyptic expectations of messianic coming that were current in the period in which Jesus lived, of one who would judge the nations and inaugurate an enduring reign of peace. The *Similitudes of Enoch* spoke of a preexistent heavenly Son of Man whose mission would be to establish the reign of God, a commentary on Daniel's vision of the Son of Man (*Enoch* 48:10; 52:4).

The synoptic Gospels provide evidence that a messiah was expected prior to Jesus' coming (John 1:20, 41; 7:31; Luke 3:15), to be born in Bethlehem (John 7:40–42; Matt. 2:5) of obscure origin (John 7:27). It was assumed that he would come from the line of David (Matt. 21:9; 22:42). Herod and the Pharisees were acutely aware of these prophecies and feared that they would have political consequences (Matt. 2:1–18; John 11:47–48), and at one crucial point in Jesus' ministry it appeared as if they might (after the miracle of the loaves and fishes the people were ready to make Jesus their king by force, an interpretation Jesus resisted and disdained). It gradually became evident that his messianic kingship is "not of this world" and is not to be achieved by coercion (John 18:36). When the people "intended to come and make him king by force," Jesus "withdrew again to a mountain by himself" (John 6:15; John Chrysostom, *Hom. on John* XLII, FC 33, p. 432).

The Identication of Jesus as Messiah

Messianic Expectation During Jesus' Ministry

Intense expectation accompanied Jesus' ministry. The first thing Andrew did after spending a day with Jesus was to "find his brother Simon and tell him, 'We have found the Messiah' (that is, the Christ)" (John 1:40–41). The next day Philip, having been called by Jesus, "found Nathanael and told him, 'We have found the one Moses wrote about in the Law, and about whom the prophets also wrote'," whom Nathanael called "Son of God" and "King of Israel" (John 1:43–50; John Chrysostom, *Hom. 20 on John*, FC 33, pp. 193–201).

Entry into Jerusalem

Jesus' final entry into Jerusalem was interpreted by many as the coming of the messianic king of prophetic expectation (John 12:13–15). In sharp contrast with the power of worldly kings, the messiah was expected to come gently with righteousness, bringing salvation (Zech. 9:9). The messianic expectations of the people overflowed in the shout: "Blessed is he who comes in the name of the Lord! Blessed is the coming kingdom of our father David" (Mark 11:9–10; cf. Ps. 118:25–26). Days later it would be evident how shallow were these expectations, when the crowd shouted once again, but for Jesus' crucifixion (Mark 15:13).

The Identification at the Trial

When accused before Pilate, Jesus was directly asked, "Are you the king of the Jews?" (John 18:33). He indirectly answered, "You are right in saying I am a king, and for this I came into the world, to testify to the truth" (John 18:37). In Mark's account, Jesus answered more directly,

"Yes, it is as you say" (Mark 15:2). In Matthew's account there is a fuller explanation: "'Yes, it is as you say,' Jesus replied. 'But I say to all of you: In the future you will see the Son of Man sitting at the right hand of the Mighty One and coming on the clouds of heaven'" (Matt. 26:64), which caused the high priest to charge blasphemy. Jesus' execution was due to this acknowledgment that he understood his ministry as that of the Messiah, Son of Man. The formal accusation was sedition, in relation to the alleged claim that he was a pretender to kingship and hence a threat to government (Mark 15:26).

Jesus' Use of the Term "Messiah"

Jesus himself used the term "Messiah" with restraint, and for good reason. If the people had been given the signal that he was Messiah, it is quite possible that it would have been instantly misinterpreted as a signal for political rebellion or an intensification of the expectation for a worldly kingdom, which ran contrary to Jesus' mission. Since the popular meaning of the term "messiah" was quite different from the actual mission of the Messiah, Jesus understandably did not make frequent public use of that term, and his messianic identity emerged only slowly and at first only with a few selected disciples.

He was regarded by apostolic testimony as Messiah, yet a Messiah who transformed prevailing messianic expectations by his death and resurrection (Eusebius, PG I, p. 193; Ursinus, CHC, pp. 171-72). It is unconvincing that the Messiah himself would have remained ignorant of his messianic vocation, as claimed by some critics.

The Messianic Secret

When Jesus performed miracles, he often warned his hearers to keep quiet and avoid public notice. The leper was given a "strong warning: 'See that you don't tell this to anyone'" (Mark 1:43-44; Tertullian, Ag. Marcion IV.9, AEG II, p. 154). Jairus was strictly forbidden from telling others about the raising of his daughter (Mark 5:43; Jerome, Hom. 77 on Mark, FC 57, pp. 148-51). After Peter's confession, Jesus warned the disciples "not to tell anyone about him" (Mark 8:30; cf. 9:9).

The modern theory that Jesus altogether rejected the designation of Messiah (Bultmann, TNT I, pp. 26-32; Cullmann, CNT, pp. 122-25; Pannenberg, JGM, p. 31) was anticipated by early critics of Christianity who did not follow the received tradition (see Irenaeus, Ag. Her. III.1-4, ANF I, pp. 414-17; Justin Martyr, Dialogue with Trypho 35-40, FC 6, pp. 200-209). Jesus understood himself as Messiah, but not the political messiah of popular expectation. His messianic mission led not to a political kingdom but to a crucifixion, not to living powerfully but dying powerlessly, not to a crown of majesty but of thorns.

Jesus was conscious of his messianic vocation from the outset of his mission. It is not a consciousness formed only after Jesus' resurrection in the minds of the disciples (as some theories of the "messianic secret" hold, cf. W. Wrede, *The Messianic Secret*, accepted as a central fact of "critical orthodoxy"; cf. Ladd, *TNT*, p. 170). He accepted the messianic title, blessed his disciples when they recognized it, and finally under oath on trial accepted it. But prior to his trial, he was cautious about this disclosure because he knew how distortedly it might be perceived.

NAMES AND TITLES ASCRIBED TO THE ANOINTED ONE

Metaphors abound in describing who Jesus was and is: the rock of our salvation, the foundation on which the church is built, chief cornerstone, the head of the body, the vine that takes leaf, bridegroom of the end-time banquet, brother of his disciples, and friend of sinners (1 Pet. 2:6; Eph. 1:22; Luke 7:34; Matt. 25:6; John 20:17). He is the physician of souls, the fountain of cleansing, the bread and water of sustenance, the door of access to life with God. The variety of his names and titles is as intriguing as a puzzle asking to be put together.

Jesus is servant, suffering Servant, servant of the Lord, minister, counselor, peacemaker (Isa. 42–43; Rom. 15:8; Acts 3:26). His very name, Jesus (from Jehosua or Joshua), means Savior (Matt. 1:21). He is the Help of the Lord, the Prince of Salvation. As Son of the Father, beloved of the Father, uniquely related to the Father, he is the Word of God, preexistent Logos (John 1:1–18), "the radiance of God's glory and the exact representation of his being" (Heb. 1:2).

As Messiah, Jesus is the Lord's anointed agent of salvation, author of salvation (Heb. 3:2), Redeemer, Mediator (Isa. 59:20; 1 Tim. 2:5), Light of the world, the Desire of the nations, the Expected One of Israel (Isa. 17:3; Hag. 2:7). He was called "Jesus Christ the Righteous" (1 John 2:1), the Righteous One (Acts 3:14), Sanctifier, the Holy One (Heb. 2:11; 1 John 2:20), who presides over our justification in the court (as the "guarantee of a better covenant," Heb. 7:22), and our sanctification in the Temple (as "priest forever," Heb. 7:17). Jesus is the "author and perfecter of our faith" (Heb. 12:2), "the mediator of a new covenant" (Heb. 12:24), "the way and the truth and the life" (John 14:6), or, more simply, "the life" (John 11:25).

The Study of Titles and Metaphors Applied to Jesus

The intense study of these ascriptions has been central to classic

Christian teaching of Christ, illuminating to the mind and elevating to the spirit. The study of Christ is diminished when these ascriptions are neglected (Taylor, *NJ*).

The variability of the ascriptions is due to the determination of Christ to meet each person on his or her own ground. Cyril summarized: "The Savior comes in various forms to each man for his profit. For to those who lack joy, He becomes a Vine; to those who wish to enter in, He is a Door; for those who must offer prayer, He is a mediating High-Priest. Again, to those in sin, He becomes a Sheep to be sacrificed on their behalf. He becomes 'all things to all men' remaining in His own nature what He is. For so remaining, and possessing the truly unchangeable dignity of the Sonship, as the best of physicians and a sympathetic teacher, He *adapts Himself to our infirmity*" (Cyril of Jerusalem, *Catech. Lect.* X, *FC* 61, p. 198; italics added).

The titles ascribed to Christ are not used because they adequately designate his reality, but because they point inadequately to him by the only means available—words:

Having no other words to use, we use what we have.
Thou art called the Word, and Thou art above Word;
Thou art above Light, yet art named Light;
Thou art called Fire not as perceptible to sense, but because Thou purgest light
   and worthless matter;
a Sword, because Thou severest the worse from the better;
a Fan because Thou purgest the threshing-floor, and blowest away all that is
   light and windy, and layest up in the garner above all that is weighty and
   full;
an Axe, because Thou cuttest down the worthless fig-tree, after long
   patience. . . . ;
the Door, because thou bringest in;
the Way, because we go straight;
the Sheep, because Thou art the Sacrifice;
the High Priest, because Thou offerest the Body;
the Son, because Thou art of the Father
                     (Gregory Nazianzen, *Orat.* XXXVII.4, *NPNF* 2 VII, p. 339;
                                       italics and paragraphing added).

Cyril warned against diminishing the ascriptions by squeezing out of them their metaphorical functions: "He is called a door. But you must not think of a wooden door. You must think of a spiritual door that reasons, and is alive, and knows all about those that enter" (Cyril of Jerusalem, *Catech. Lect.* X.3, *LCC* IV, pp. 131–32).

The Filial Center of the Titles

The Distinctive Usage of Abba

The Son-Father relationship is expressed in Jesus special use of the Aramaic *Abba*, a highly personal form of address to God, in petition and intercession. That Jesus himself, and not just the rememberers of Jesus, used this term is strongly indicated by internal evidence in the synoptic Gospels. Even the Gentile congregations must have had to overcome cultural resistance in stubbornly retaining its use (Gal. 4:6; Rom. 8:15).

Distinctive of Jesus

There is *"no analogy at all* in the whole of Jewish prayer for God being addressed as Abba" (Jeremias, *The Prayer of Jesus*, p. 57). This lack of analogy is due to very good reason—Jewish aversion to familiarity with Yahweh. Jesus used this most personal and intimate term, almost in defiance of the prevailing Jewish aversion, and did so regularly. This pattern is recalled in all four Gospels (Mark 14:36; Matt. 6:9; 11:25–26; 26:24, 39, 42; Luke 10:21; 11:2; 22:42; 23:34; John 17, passim).

The Privileged Use of Abba

Paul went out of his way to explain to his Roman readers that Christians can use the term *Abba* of God because they now participate in a relationship with God the Father that has been made possible by Jesus, the Son. Human fatherhood is now understood by analogy to the divine Fatherhood made known through the Son (Rom. 8:15; Gal. 4:6; cf. Mark 14:36; Irenaeus, *Ag. Her.* V.8.1, *ANF* I, p. 533; Barth, *CD* I/1, pp. 93–95, 279–80; III/4, pp. 245–46).

Matthew further developed this point in recalling Jesus' startling instruction that the privileged term *Abba* not be used of earthly fathers: "And do not call anyone on earth 'father,' for you have one Father, and he is in heaven" (Matt. 23:9). The analogy of fatherhood was to be read from God's fatherhood to human fatherhood, not the other way around. One can best understand one's own father in relation to God's own parenting, not God in the light of a particular father's parenting.

Titles as a Congruent Mosaic Complex

Issues Embedded in Titles

Central elements of Christian teaching are compacted in the several major titles repeatedly attributed to the messianic Lord. Taken together (and in most cases even taken separately) they embrace key affirmations of the Christian teaching of Christ: his preexistent sonship, his humble coming in the flesh, his suffering, death, and resurrection, his prophetic, priestly, and regal ministries, his unique role as divine-human mediator and reconciler, his union with the faithful, and his future offices of judgment and consummation. Each title forms a colorful fragment in the mosaic of a larger unified vision of the saving event (Lactantius, *Div. Inst.*, FC 49, pp. 271–79). Separately each is intriguing; together they are beautiful.

History of Development Embedded in Titles

Each title has its own history of transmission and development against the backdrop of Jewish hopes and Hellenistic assumptions. Yet in every case the history of that term was transmuted by the ministry of Jesus, so that his stamp was placed ever after upon it—for how can one now think of the term "Christ" without relating that ascription to Jesus?

The Organization of the Titles

One convenient way of roughly organizing the more than one hundred overlapping titles applied to Jesus follows along lines suggested by Cullmann:

1. Titles that apply to the *pretemporal, prehistorical existence* of the Logos (Word, Son of God)
2. Titles pertaining to his *future consummative work* (Messiah, Son of Man, king)
3. Titles pertaining to his *earthly ministry* in history (Suffering Servant, prophet, priest), and
4. Titles pertaining to his *present lordship* (Lord, Savior; Cullmann, *CNT*; cf. Hahn, *TJC*; Wells, *PC*, p. 67).

Their Passage Through Various Cultures and Languages

There were at least three distinguishable cultures through which these titles passed: (a) Palestinian Judaism, which spoke Aramaic and stressed Jesus' earthly ministry and Parousia; (b) Hellenistic Judaism, which spoke Greek, used the Septuagint, and developed a two-stage Christology of the earthly ministry and heavenly reign; and (c) Hellenistic Gentile Christianity, which spoke Greek, had less direct contact with Judaism, and stressed preexistence, incarnate life, and heavenly reign (Marshall, *ONTC*, p. 28, Fuller, *FNTC*). The one Lord was being attested in differing cultural contexts.

Historical inquiry has sought to define in which of these circles various titles emerged and to what extent they emerged directly out of the ministry of Jesus (Hahn, *TJC*). Disputants in title Christology can generally be divided into those who locate the roots of these titles in Jesus himself and those who locate these roots in one or more of these later remembering communities (Fuller, *FNTC*; Ramm, *EC*, p. 108; Marshall, *ONTC*, pp. 11–43).

In this chapter we have covered a broad range of issues concerning our Lord's earthly life. Beginning with the childhood narratives (circumcision, flight, his youthful obedience to law, and his growth), we proceeded to the beginning of his public ministry in his baptism, accompanied by the inward struggle with temptation, and examined the claims of his sinlessness. At long last, the earlier Galilean ministry of proclamation turned toward a decisive journey toward Jerusalem. Gradually being revealed was his identity as the Christ.

The purpose of his coming still awaited completion. All was in readiness for the sacrifice for which he was sent by the Father to humanity. He came not only for the purpose of living amid and for sinners, but also dying for sin.

CHAPTER 9

The Work He Came to Do

Christ and salvation would tend to become split apart were it not for this cohesive principle: only the Mediator can do the work of mediation. Only one who *is* truly human and truly God in personal union is able to *do* what is needed for salvation. Hence the *person* of Christ is the requisite premise for the *work* of Christ. The personal union of deity and humanity is the basis upon which salvation is brought to humanity. The work of Christ is the end for which the Son was sent. This work is now to be considered.

The main concept that seals the unity between person and work is the concept of office (Heb. *kahan*, or ministry; Gk. *diakonia*) to which the Christ was anointed. "He is the Christ, anointed not simply with oil, but with the Holy Ghost, to be the Highest Prophet, Priest and King, and raise us through these three offices from our fall" (*Gk. Orthodox Catech.* 28, p. 24).

OFFICES OF THE ANOINTED ONE

Anointed as Mediator

The Mediatorial Office

Jesus was anointed to mediate between the righteousness of God and the wretched history of sin. The office of Christ is one of mediation between God and humanity—hence called the mediatorial office (Augustine, *Trin.* IV.8, *FC* 45, p. 145; Ursinus, *CHC*, pp. 164–72; Brunner, *Med.*, pp. 399–416). Fulfilling the mediatorial office is the declared purpose of the incarnation. The Son of God assumed human nature "that he might reconcile the Father to us and become a sacrifice" (Leo, *Serm.* 38, *NPNF* 2 XII, pp. 141–45; Augsburg Confession, III, in Schmid, *DT*, p. 338).

Three Ministries of the Mediatorial Office

The Son of God became incarnate to do the threefold work of messianic prophet, priest, and king. His work consisted in the fulfillment and consummation of the prophetic office, the priestly office, and the kingly office, to which servants of God in the Old Testament were anointed.

The overarching theme of Christ's saving work is this: *Jesus first appeared as a teacher in the prophetic office; then as high priest and lamb sacrificed in his suffering and death; and finally by his resurrection received his kingdom and remains active in his office of cosmic governance, as eschatological ruler in this kingdom.* "The office enjoined upon Christ by the Father consists of three parts," wrote Calvin, "prophet, king, and priest" (*Inst.* 2.15.1).

Mediatorial Summary

This shorthand way of summarizing all essential phases of Christ's activity as Mediator brings together diverse themes of Scripture: as prophet he revealed the divine will; as priest he made provision for the redemption of sin; as king he applied and completed that redemption (Newman, *SD*, pp. 52–62; Dorner, *System of Christian Doctrine* IV, pp. 247–340).

This schema will help summarize the threefold office of the Mediator:

PROPHET	PRIEST	KING
To teach	To sacrifice	To empower
Christ preaches	Christ atones	Christ governs
Pedagogy	Expiation	Guidance and protection
Earthly ministry	Dying ministry	Glorified ministry
Messianic beginning	Messianic act par excellence	Messianic consummation
Mosaic type	Aaronic type	Davidic type
The Rabbi	The Lamb	The end-time Governor
God revealed	Humanity redeemed	Redemption applied

Jesus incomparably fulfilled and consummately enacted these three offices as: a prophet like Moses whom God has raised up from among his own people (Acts 3:22); "a priest forever in the order of Melchizedek" (Heb. 7:17); and "King of kings" (Rev. 17:14).

Sequential Reception of the Three Ministries

Sequential Order of the Offices

There is an implicit chronology in this sequence: in his earthly ministry Jesus first appeared primarily as prophet, then in his suffering and death as priest, and only then in his glorification as ruler of the spiritual kingdom (Chemnitz, *TNC*, pp. 334–38; Thielicke, *The Evangelical Faith* II, pp. 342–421). These occur in due order.

The chief reason for his coming was to save sinners. This focused on his priestly office, the center of his mediatorial vocation. Yet this priestly role was held in reserve during most of his earthly ministry, until the events of his trial, suffering, and crucifixion. It was only slowly, by degrees, that the hidden work of salvation became revealed, beginning with prophetic teaching, climaxing in priestly sacrifice, and becoming consummated in eschatological judgment and empowerment.

Anointed at Baptism

The public designation or sealing of his mediatorial office occurred at Jesus' baptism (Matt. 3:17), but his mediatorial mission was not recognized until the transfiguration (Matt. 17:5) and then only partially. A voice from on high in both passages confirmed his identity and mission: "This is my Son, whom I love; with him I am well pleased" (Matt. 17:5; cf. 3:17). His baptism not only signaled the public beginning of his messianic vocation, but also provided him with all spiritual gifts necessary to fulfill his mission.

Sequential Assumption of the Offices

After his baptism he assumed in successive stages the offices of prophet, priest, and king, building gradually to dramatic climax. From his baptism to Holy Week he undertook primarily a prophetic office as teacher and lawgiver. During his last week of earthly ministry, Passion Week, and especially in his prayer of consecration (John 17), he assumed the high priestly office, and in dying offered himself as a sacrifice for the sins of the world. By his resurrection he assumed legitimate governance of the future of history.

All of this is set forth in the Gospels. In the Letters, which look back upon the significance of these events, he was assumed to have already ascended to heaven to continue in the discharge of all these offices: teaching through the Spirit; interceding for the world; and judging in glory.

The Three Ministries as Organizing Principle of Christ's Mediatorial Work

A Continuous Tradition

The three offices of his mediatorial work are fully treated in Scripture and tradition. The division of the messianic task into these three offices is richly anticipated in the Jewish tradition and its rabbinic interpreters and developed by major voices of the Christian tradition from Eusebius and Cyril of Jerusalem through Augustine and Thomas Aquinas (Augustine, *Harmony of the Gospels* 1.3, *NPNF* 1 VI, p. 79; Tho. Aq., *ST* III, Q22.1, II, p. 2142; cf. *Doc. Vat. II*, pp. 29, 141, 237–38). By the time of Luther and Calvin it had become a central organizing structure of Protestant Christological teaching. It reappears in both scholastic orthodox and liberal Protestant writers. Even those who resist the three-office formulation nonetheless make frequent use of its categories, for it is virtually impossible to speak of the Christ of the New Testament without his teaching, sacrificial, and governance functions and metaphors.

Mosaic, Aaronic, and Davidic Types Fulfilled

The classical exegetes sought the truth of Hebraic prophecy, priesthood, and divine governance by looking at these ancient offices in the light of the ministry of Jesus. They viewed Moses as the prophetic type of Christ, who appeared as the new Lawgiver, and the Fulfiller of prophecy. They viewed the Aaronic, Levitical, and Melchizedek priesthoods as the anticipatory type of Christ, who completed and typified the priestly office. And they viewed David as the anticipatory type of Christ as promised messianic king, anointed receiver of the coming messianic kingdom. Accordingly, Christ was understood as already present anticipatively in and through the ministries of Moses, Aaron, and David. The classical exegetes read the law and prophets, the priestly institutions, and messianic hopes as a history in which Christ himself was already active.

A Triple Cure for Sin Required

It is said that a triple cure for the recalcitrance of sin was needed to sweep away the intricately layered misery of the history of sin: as prophet Christ had to penetrate the self-deceptions of sin, effectively calling humanity to repentance; as priestly sacrifice, Christ took our sins upon himself and reconciled us to God; as legitimate recipient of final authority and power, he began to reorder the distorted powers at work in the world, and he continues to do so.

"Our minds were confused; as Teacher and Prophet, He undertook to enlighten us by His wonderful teaching. Our hearts were corrupt; as High Priest and Mediator, He undertook by His precious blood, to purify them. Our wills were held bound by the Devil; as an all-Holy King, He undertook to drive out the Devil, and release us from bondage" (*Gk. Orthodox Catech.* 30, p. 25).

Through his prophetic office he radically interpreted the law, and saved human flesh from egocentric lawlessness. As priest, through atonement and intercession, he saved sinners from crippling guilt. As spiritual king, through just rule, he is saving history from the despair of disorder. In all three offices taken together he saves the world from sin (Ambrose, *Flight from the World*, FC 65, pp. 288–96; Pearson, *EC* I, pp. 366–69).

Key Loci of Apostolic Teaching

The apostles declared Jesus to be prophet, priest, and king, as messianic fulfillment of each. Jesus was incomparably a prophet (Acts 7:37), and in his prophetic and teaching offices he is called rabbi, master, teacher, apostle, and minister. His prophetic work led to the cross, where he became the "high priest whom we confess" (Heb. 3:1), God's own Mercy-seat or "sacrifice of atonement" (Rom. 3:25), a living "sacrifice to God" (Eph. 5:2), the Lamb of God who takes away the sin of the world (John 1:29; Rev. 5:6), our advocate with the Father (1 John 2:2), "the Shepherd and Overseer" of our souls (1 Pet. 2:25). By his resurrection he was declared "King of kings and Lord of lords" (1 Tim. 6:15), the captain of salvation (Heb. 2:10), "Prince and Savior" who brings "forgiveness of sins to Israel" (Acts 5:31), end-time judge to whom "the Father has entrusted all judgment" (John 5:22), who came not to judge but to save the world.

This threefold anointing has served for centuries as a way of summarizing the vast range of biblical teachings of salvation. Christ proclaimed the *truth* for which he finally gave his *life* so as to show the *way* to the kingdom. Hence his ministry became the royal way, the prophetic truth, and sacrificial life (John 14:6).

Hebraic Roots of Anointing to Office

The *Russian Catechism* explains: "*Anointed* was in old time a title of *kings, high-priests, and prophets.* Why then, is Jesus, the Son of God, called The Anointed? Because to his manhood were imparted without measure all the gifts of the Holy Ghost; and so he possessed in the highest degree the *knowledge* of a prophet, the *holiness* of a high-priest, and the *power* of a king" (*COC* II, p. 466).

The Oil of Anointing

Anointing was a symbol of consecration to God, especially to office for divine service. As water was a symbol of cleansing, blood a symbol of expiation, and light a symbol of divine illumination, so was an *anointing oil* the principal symbol of consecration to office (Pearson, *EC* I, pp. 167, 178–80). The Exodus account provided instructions for the making of "a sacred anointing oil, a fragrant blend, the work of a perfumer" (including fine spices, myrrh, cinnamon, cane, and olive oil) to anoint the Tent of Meeting, ark, and altar. "You shall consecrate them so they will be most holy, and whatever touches them will be holy" (Exod. 30:22–29).

This fragrant anointing oil was used for the solemn consecration of prophets, priests, and kings. Elijah anointed Elisha to be prophet and Hazael to be king (1 Kings 19:16). Priests were anointed both with oil (symbol of consecration) and blood (symbol of expiation, Exod. 30:30; Lev. 8:30). When David was anointed by Samuel as king, "from that day on the Spirit of the Lord came upon David in power" (1 Sam. 16:13). Requisite gifts for the fulfillment of the office were expected to accompany the anointing.

Late Judaic Messianic Expectations of an Anointed Deliverer

Passages from the prophets and messianic Psalms nurtured later Judaic expectations for the Anointed One. This Expected One would be anointed: "to preach good news to the poor" (in the prophetic tradition, Isa. 61:1); "to put an end to sin, to atone for wickedness" (in the priestly office, Dan. 9:24); and to receive the kingdom of peace (in the regal office, Pss. 2:2; 45:6–7).

Prevailing Messianic Assumptions Immediately Prior to the New Testament

All three of these offices appear in the expectations of the period immediately preceding the New Testament, where the popular hope of messianic fulfillment was intensified, for they are assumed in New Testament texts.

The messiah was expected as a *prophet* who would come to "explain everything to us" (John 4:25), who would teach, who would "give his people the knowledge of salvation" (Luke 1:77). Some expected that the prophet "Elijah must come first" (Matt. 17:10), before or in connection with the appearance of the messianic king.

The remnant of Israel who most fervently awaited the messiah applied *priestly* metaphors to that expectation of one who would redeem

Israel "through the forgiveness of their sins" (Luke 1:77), as "Lamb of God" who would "take away the sins of the world" (John 11:27).

As *king* he was expected to be "born king of the Jews" (Matt. 2:2), as seed of David, born in Bethlehem (John 7:42; Matt. 12:23).

The Three Offices Transmuted in Christ

In fulfilling the offices Christ changed them decisively. He *teaches* not with mere words but as God's own living Word to human history; he *intercedes* not as the Levitical high priest with animal sacrifice, but by the sacrifice of his own body; and he *governs* not as the rulers of this world but as legitimate heir of divine empowerment (Ursinus, *CHC*, pp. 170-76).

The Unity of the Three Offices

The Offices Uniquely Cohere in Jesus Christ

The three offices of the Expected One uniquely cohere in the ministry of Jesus. As the "one mediator between God and men" (1 Tim. 2:5), he is at the same time the teacher of true religion, expiator of sin, and bearer of legitimate authority to guide and judge future history.

No one before Jesus had adequately united the three offices. Moses, the prototype of the prophet and lawgiver, was neither priest nor king. Aaron, the priest, was neither prophet nor king. David, the prototype of the messianic king, was not a priest. Ezekiel came closer to integral fulfillment of the offices, for as prophet he was also priest, but not king. In one figure alone were all offices adequately united, sufficiently displayed, and fully consummated—Jesus Christ.

All Three Offices Cohere in His Work

In these three complementary ways, he uniquely embodied the "wisdom of God" so as to become simultaneously "our righteousness, holiness, and redemption" (1 Cor. 1:30). Jesus is not just a king without being a priestly king, for his kingship cannot be understood without his suffering, atonement, and intercession. He is not just a priest without prophetic truth, for his priesthood is made understandable by his pungent, parabolic teaching of the kingdom and call to repentance. He is indeed a king, but a caring, interceding, shepherding, priestly king (like Melchizedek) who loves those he admonishes, rules, and guides. In this way all three offices cohere in one mediator, unifying a single act of divine-human mediation. "I tell you that many prophets and kings wanted to see what you see but did not" (Luke 10:23).

The Danger of Loss of Cohesion

Whenever one of these three functions has tended to become excessive, imbalanced, or detached from the others, there has emerged a history of distortion. Misjudgments have occurred because one or another office has been neglected, falsified, or exaggerated.

The history of Christian teaching of the work of Christ has repeatedly had to resist such imbalances. Post-Kantian Protestant liberalism so stressed the prophetic, teaching office as to neglect the priestly office. Some forms of Protestant scholasticism and pietism so stressed the sacrificial substitutionary atonement and eschatological triumphalism as to neglect the prophetic office. The social gospel movement stressed the earthly relevance of the kingship of Christ and Jesus as a teacher of social justice to the neglect of the priestly office. Schweitzer stressed the eschatological kingdom, but concluded that Jesus was a misinformed teacher. Some post-Tridentine teaching neglected the prophetic office by its intense focus upon Jesus' priestly, sacramental ministry. A balanced teaching of salvation depends upon holding these three ministries in proper tension and equilibrium.

CHRIST AS PROPHET: THE TEACHING OFFICE

The prophetic office of Christ refers to the work of Christ in *revealing* fully the divine truth to humanity, *proclaiming* the divine plan of redemption, and *calling* all to accept the salvation offered.

The prophetic office was fulfilled by means of Jesus' *words* (Matt. 7:28–29), *deeds* (John 10:25), and the *example of his life* (1 Pet. 2:21–23). This prophetic work occurs not merely by words but also through active deeds and through the witness of an entire life that walked in the truth and willingly suffered for the truth.

Definition of the Prophetic Office

A prophet is one who speaks for God, an authoritative teacher of God's will, who serves as a channel of communication between the divine and human spheres, so as to bring to light what had remained in darkness (Ursinus, *CHC*, pp. 172–73). By the prophet a divine message (Heb. *dabar*, "word"; Gk. *logos*) from God, an oracle of Yahweh, is communicated through a human messenger (Heb. *nabi*; Gk. *prophētēs*) or seer (Heb. *roeh*), who speaks for divine revelation. In a wider sense, prophet signifies a teacher (Gk. *didaskalos*; Lat. *magister*).

Publication

Intrinsic to the messianic office is the work of publication or proclamation—making public the knowledge of the events of salvation, promulgation of the saving work of God in history. The purpose of prophetic work is to bring humanity to the knowledge of God's saving action (Ambrose, *On Belief in the Resurrection* II.66–75, NPNF 2 X, pp. 184–86).

Dependent upon Revelation

The work of prophecy is possible only where revelation occurs. Prophecy is not a form of knowing that human initiative may actively seek or commence to lay hold of. The prophetic act occurs only through the electing wisdom of God and human receptivity to the divine address. The prototype for all prophetic speech is the receptivity of the eternal Son to the will of the Father (Augustine, *CG* XVIII.27–35, NPNF 1 II, pp. 375–82).

Spirit and Prophecy

Prophetic activity requires the outward promulgation of the truth of the divine address amid the cortingencies of human history. Without the inward work of the Spirit penetrating the heart and mind, such a word could never become outwardly spoken. The prophetic word is lifeless without the Spirit, who awakens the capacity for the hearing of the word (Augustine, *The Spirit and the Letter* 1–6, LCC VIII, pp. 195–99; Barth, *CD* I/2, pp. 83–87; IV/3, pp. 13f.).

Prophetic Witness Continuous

"By providing his people with an unbroken line of prophets," God has "never left them without useful doctrine sufficient for salvation" (Calvin, *Inst*. 2.15.1). Disclosures of the meaning of history have been offered by the prophets through attested dreams, theophanies, visitations, and appearances, such as the burning bush and the pillar of cloud and fire.

The messiah was expected as an incomparable teacher of truth. The Mosaic tradition had long expected the Lord to raise up for Israel a prophet like Moses "from among your own brothers" to whom "you must listen" (Deut. 18:15). This text entered into the messianic tradition and was applied directly to Jesus (Acts 3:22). Isaiah expected a prophetic-messianic deliverer whom God would anoint to "preach good news to the poor," an expectation Jesus regarded as fulfilled in his own ministry (Luke 4:21).

Christ as Prophet

Since he himself is the truth, only he can adequately reveal the truth. Jesus Christ fully possessed the gift of prophecy and vocation of teacher. "For this reason I was born, and for this I came into the world, to testify to the truth" (John 18:37).

Calvin summarized: prophecy is "an office of teaching bestowed upon the Son of God for the benefit of his own [people], and its end is that he illumine them with the true knowledge of the Father, instruct them in truth, and make them household disciples of God" (Calvin, *Catech. of the Church of Geneva*, LCC XXII, p. 96).

Was Jesus a Prophet?

Since it has sometimes been debated as to whether he was indeed rightly viewed as a prophet, it is fitting to set forth this testimony.

Confluence of Testimony

(1) That Jesus was viewed *by the people* as a prophet seems clear from numerous texts. After the feeding of the five thousand, the people "began to say, 'Surely this is the Prophet who is to come into the world'" (John 6:14). Jesus made no protest when the Samaritan woman said to him, "I can see that you are a prophet" (John 4:19). He was popularly regarded by the people as a prophet, even though this perception became distorted by triumphalist hopes: "'Surely this is the Prophet who is to come into the world.' Jesus, knowing that they intended to come and make him king by force, withdrew again to a mountain by himself" (John 6:14–15). Jesus reminded his hearers often of the ancient prophets and was hailed as a prophet (Matt. 16:13–14; Mark 6:15; Luke 7:16; Lactantius, *Div. Inst.*, FC 49, pp. 261–79).

(2) That Jesus was viewed more circumspectly *by the apostles* as a prophet seems evident from Peter's speech to the people of Israel: "For Moses said, 'The Lord your God will raise up for you a prophet like me from among your own people; you must listen to everything he tells you'" (Acts 3:22, quoting Deut. 18:15; cf. Stephen's speech to the Sanhedrin, Acts 7:37). It was with Moses and Elijah (prophetic prototypes) that Jesus had spoken in the transfiguration. The coming messianic deliverer had been expected to appear as a prophet like Moses or Elijah (Acts 3:22). After Philip was called by Jesus, he said to Nathanael: "We have found the one Moses wrote about in the Law, and about whom the prophets also wrote" (John 1:45; cf. Luke 24:27).

(3) The Gospel traditions reported that *Jesus made reference to himself* as

a prophet: "Only in his home town and in his own house is a prophet without honor" (Matt. 13:57; Mark 6:4). "I must keep going today and tomorrow and the next day—for surely no prophet can die outside Jerusalem!" (Luke 13:33; Pearson, *EC* I, pp. 169, 366).

More Than a Prophet

Yet as fulfiller of the prophetic type, Jesus was (like John the Baptist, to whom prophecy had pointed) "more than a prophet" (Matt. 11:9), for "of none of the Prophets was it said: that 'the Word was made flesh'" (Ambrose, *Incarn. of Our Lord* 6.48, *FC* 44, p. 237; John 1:14). The Mediator was not merely God-inspired, but God-incarnate.

The prophets characteristically said "Thus says Yahweh." Jesus by contrast characteristically said: "Truly I say to you" and "I am." No prophet except of a unique sort would say, "Thus I say."

The prophets pointed beyond themselves to One who by his divine sonship would bring salvation to fallen history: "In the past God spoke to our forefathers through the prophets in many times and in various ways, but in these last days he has spoken to us by his Son" (Heb. 1:1–2). The voice from on high commanded hearers to listen to him not as prophet alone but as Son: "This is my Son, whom I love: with him I am well pleased. Listen to him!" (Matt. 17:5; cf. Matt. 3:17).

Himself the Truth

Jesus not only spoke, but was the truth enfleshed, God's own Word of truth. He did not merely teach revelation by words, but was himself that revelation, a living Word, the Word of Life (1 John 1:1; 1 Pet. 1:23). "I am the way and the truth and the life. No one comes to the Father except through me. If you really knew me, you would know my Father as well" (John 14:6–7). One cannot come to faith without trusting personally in Jesus Christ or receive the gospel without receiving him personally.

His Authority as Mediator

All the other prophets were humans speaking for God. The only Mediator was the God-man speaking for God to humanity and to God for humanity (Leo, *Serm.* XXVII, *NPNF* 2 XII, pp. 139–41).

The incomparable credential of Jesus' prophetic teaching was the personal union of deity and humanity in him. He promised that "when he, the Spirit of truth, comes, he will guide you into all truth" (John 16:13). The truth to which the Spirit would guide is the truth made known personally in him. Of no other prophet could that be said. As such Jesus was prophet par excellence, the incomparable interpreter of God. "I do nothing on my own but speak just what the Father has taught me. The one who sent me is with me" (John 8:28–29).

Was Christ's Prophetic Office Embedded in the Rule of Faith?

Even though the prophetic office was not specifically defined in the creeds, it appears embedded in the rule of faith in many of its earliest received forms. The rule of faith as received by Tertullian recalled that the very One who "was always heard in the prophets" had "lived (appeared) as Jesus Christ" and "preached the new law and the new promise of the kingdom of heaven; wrought miracles; was nailed to the cross" (*Prescription Ag. Her.* 13, *COC* II, p. 19). That Jesus continued after the New Testament to be understood and remembered as prophetic herald and teacher is seen in the second article of the creedal formula of Justin Martyr (ca. A.D. 163), which confessed that we worship "the herald of salvation and teacher of good instructions" (*CC*, p. 18).

Prophetic Teaching of Law and Gospel

Jesus was the last prophet and the first preacher of the gospel. His ministry united law and gospel. His ministry made clear both the inner requirement of the law, and what God has done that the law could not do to fulfill the requirement of the law for sinners.

Jesus' Teaching of the Law

Jesus taught Torah in a penetrating new way by republishing it without the elaborate ceremonial or forensic extensions that had been so characteristic of the tradition of the scribes and Pharisees. His teaching went to the heart of the law, its spiritual meaning and center, its radical character as divine demand (Augustine, *Our Lord's Sermon on the Mount* II.21–25, *NPNF* 1 VI, pp. 58–63). This reinterpretation of the law occurred primarily in the Sermon on the Mount, but more generally through his entire earthly ministry of proclamation and teaching (Baxter, *PW* II, pp. 222–38; Wesley, *Serm.* I, *WJWB*, pp. 466–698).

His preaching constantly appealed to the Old Testament Scriptures in such phrases as: "Have you never read in the Scriptures . . ." (Matt. 21:42). His teaching focused upon opening up the meaning of the Scriptures: "Then he opened their minds so they could understand the Scriptures" (Luke 24:45). "It is written" was constantly on his lips (Mark 7:6; 9:12; 11:17; 14:21, 27). Yet he criticized a shallow, merely external application of ceremonial and forensic law, addressing its deeper spiritual and moral meaning.

Not to Abolish but to Fulfill the Law

"Do not think that I have come to abolish the Law or the Prophets; I have not come to abolish them but to fulfill them. I tell you the truth, until heaven and earth disappear, not the smallest letter, not the least stroke of a pen, will by any means disappear from the Law until everything is accomplished" (Matt. 5:17). His behavior conformed to the law "that by obeying the Law He might perfect it and bring it to an end in His own self, so as to show that it was ordained to Him" (Tho. Aq., *ST* III, Q40.4, II, p. 2239). "God sent his Son, born of a woman, born under law, to redeem those under law" (Gal. 4:4-5).

The End of the Law

In teaching the law, he taught with authority because he himself was the end of the law (John Chrysostom, *Hom. on John XII, NPNF* 1 XIV, p. 41). That Christ is the end of the law (*telos gar nomou*, Rom. 10:4) means:

(1) That Christ is the end of our despairing struggle for righteousness based upon our own merit. "For Christ means the end of the struggle for righteousness-by-the-Law for everyone who believes in him" (Rom. 10:4, Phillips).

(2) That he came to fulfill the meaning of the law by putting his own body on the line. Everything previously encompassed by the divine requirement codified into law was summed up in his embodied life and finished, dying work (Matt. 3:15).

(3) That he came to conclude its culture-bound, transient ceremonial functions. As code of a particular theocracy, the old covenant was transcended (Rom. 5:12-20).

(4) That he came to reinterpret the moral vitality of the law in relation to the emerging age of God's righteous love. The ethical depth of the law was sharpened, the simplicity of its demand condensed.

Jesus did not abolish but intensified the moral law written on the heart, now seen more clearly in the context of grace. The believer who looks "intently into the perfect law that gives freedom, and continues to do this" will be "blessed in what he does" (James 1:25). The law remains as a schoolmaster leading to Christ to teach sinners their sin and as a guide in the way of holiness (Leo, *Serm.* LXVI.5, *NPNF* 2 XII, p. 176; cf. Calvin, *Inst.* 2.1-4).

Jesus Proclaimed the Gospel

Hence the distinction: "For the law was given through Moses; grace and truth came through Jesus Christ" (John 1:17). His central prophetic task was to teach the good news of redemption by himself being that good news. The teaching of law is sometimes called the strange work of Christ, subordinate to his proper work, to preach the gospel (*Formula of Concord, BOC*, pp. 107–13, 365–418; Jacobs, *SCF*, p. 164).

The gospel, as good news of redemption through Christ's atoning death, could not be fully preached prior to the cross. Yet in his own synagogue he said of Isaiah 61:1–2: "Today this scripture is fulfilled in your hearing" (Luke 4:21). Then he "went throughout Galilee, teaching in their synagogues, preaching the good news of the kingdom" (Matt. 4:23).

Types of Prophetic Activity Fulfilled

Teaching, Predicting, Healing

The prophets of ancient Israel had characteristically fulfilled their office by *teaching, foretelling, healing,* or some combination of these functions. Similarly Jesus went about doing good in all of these forms (Matt. 5:17; 13:57; 24:8–9)—he taught the multitudes (Matt. 5–7), revealed things hidden (Matt. 24:1–51), and engaged in a ministry of healing that attested his identity as messianic king (Mark 1:30–42; Matt. 9; Luke 8:27–48). Through his *teaching* he instructed the community of faith in all things necessary for salvation. He displayed an unexcelled grasp of the meaning of universal history as the arena of divine self-disclosure, so as to prognosticate and *foretell* future events. Through *healing* he attested the power of the Spirit at work in his ministry (Moltmann, *ICT*, pp. 178–94). In these three ways he followed and transmuted the extraordinary functions of the ancient Hebrew prophets.

The Word Immediately Embodied and Attested Mediately

Jesus fulfilled the prophetic office both directly and indirectly. His prophetic work proceeded by direct embodiment, *immediately* exhibiting God's holy love through interpersonal meeting. He taught the whole counsel of God by embodying it nonverbally. In Jesus the prophetic revealer comes not in speech alone, but in person.

His prophetic office continued indirectly as *mediated* through the apostles and their faithful successors, and hence through the witness of all whose lives are hid in Christ in all periods of church history. This mediation is concisely expressed in John's Gospel: "As the Father has sent me, I am sending you" (John 20:21). "For I gave them the words you gave me" (John 17:8).

Hence the office of ministry today is called to be accountable to this apostolic teaching, which is promised and empowered to continue until the final days. Christian teaching receives analogous gifts of the Spirit, is anointed in an analogous way, and is ordained to participate in his own mission of prophetic witness and proclamation. The prophetic task of the church, however, cannot be autonomously politicized as if separable from the living Christ, lest branch be cut from living Vine.

The Ongoing Character of Christ's Prophetic Work

Jesus' prophetic mission may be traced through a series of stages from his baptism and public teaching, through the prophetic pedagogy of his death, and finally his resurrection, ascension, and session. Jesus' prophetic ministry formally began when he was endued with the power of the Spirit at his baptism. His earthly prophetic ministry ended with the cross, where the Word of God was spoken nonverbally in and through the exceptional events surrounding his death.

His teaching continued during his resurrection appearances (Luke 24:45). The preaching and teaching of the gospel continued in the acts of his apostles, who wrought "even greater things than these" under the power of the Spirit (John 14:12). His prophetic office continues in the Spirit-enabled life of the church. After the resurrection and ascension he continues through the Spirit to teach the church, thus providing the worshiping community with an ongoing prophetic ministry, insofar as the church seeks to teach the world the Lord's teaching. Christ's revelation of the Father to the faithful community will continue to unfold until the end time: "Now we see but a poor reflection, then we shall see face to face" (1 Cor. 13:12). He came to fulfill what was "written in the Prophets: 'They will all be taught by God'" (John 6:45; Isa. 54:13).

HIS MANNER OF LIFE, TEACHING, AND MIRACLES

An extensive treatment could be offered of details of Jesus' earthly ministry, preaching, teaching, way of life, and mighty works. In its detailed form, however, this is beyond the scope of this work.

Since the heart of the saving work of Christ is his atoning death, the events of his life are considered here especially as they relate to his atoning work. Hence these matters will receive only brief, yet it is hoped salient, reference.

His Manner of Life

Characteristic of his manner of life was its congruence with his mission, its rhythm of prayer and activity, its voluntary poverty, and its compassion.

His Life Congruent with His Identity and Mission

The day-by-day life of the Mediator would necessarily manifest the goodness, love, justice, and holiness of God in human terms. He would be expected to embody that mission in a particular time, culture, and setting. He not only taught the way of life but lived the Way and offered himself to humanity as the Way (John 14:6).

Jesus' manner of life and conversation with the world were entirely congruent with the ends for which he became incarnate. These ends were to proclaim the truth by himself being the truth, to seek out the lost, free humanity from sin, enable sinners access to God, and to make God's holy love known by allowing himself to be known amid the conditions of ordinary human life.

The Rhythm of Prayer and Activity, Engagement and Withdrawal

The Son's activity moved in a rhythm of engagement and withdrawal, rest and action, prayer and teaching (Tho. Aq., *ST* III, Q40.1, II, p. 2236). It is not to be neglected that he withdrew from intense activity for communion with the Father in prayer, nor is it an embarrassment that he sat down with sinners (Matt. 9:10), for he had come purposely to meet and save them.

His manner of life in this respect was contrasted with that of John the Baptist, who came fasting. Jesus came eating and drinking (John Chrysostom, *Hom. on Matt.* XXXVII, *NPNF* 1 X, pp. 243–50). "John drank neither wine nor strong drink: because abstinence is meritorious where the nature is weak. But why should our Lord, whose right by nature it is to forgive sins, avoid those whom He could make holier than such as abstain?" (Bede, *Comm.* on Matt. 9:14). As when Christ fasted for his temptation it was not for his own repentance but that others might not disobey, so with similar irony he "ate with sinners, that you might discern His sanctity" (Bede, *Comm.* on Mark 2:18; see also Tho. Aq., *ST* III, Q40.3, II, pp. 2237–38).

His Poverty

It was fitting that Christ should lead a life of poverty in the world, in order to show that abundant life is not dependent upon the accumulation of wealth. He became poor for our sakes that through his poverty we might be rich (2 Cor. 8:9). He had "a poor maid for His Mother, a poorer birthplace," and he voluntarily chose "all that was poor and despicable, all that was of small account and hidden from the majority, that we might recognize His Godhead to have transformed the terrestrial sphere" (Tho.

Aq., *ST* III, Q40.3, II, p. 2239; Cyril of Alexandria, Council of Ephesus, *Serm*. III.10.9, *NPNF* 2 XIV, pp. 201–42).

He avoided both "abundance of riches and beggary," wrote Thomas, "since abundance of riches is an occasion for being proud; and beggary is an occasion of thieving" (Tho. Aq., *ST* III, Q40.3, II, p. 2239). His poverty was voluntary. He was willing to receive "the necessaries of life" from those who had sufficiency (namely, certain women who ministered to him of their substance, Luke 8:2–3; Tho. Aq., *ST* III, Q40.3, II, p. 2239).

His Compassion

His manner of life revealed a person of deep and constant compassion, attentive especially to the lowly, needy, and sick. He forgave those who had lived disreputable lives. He had time to talk with women whose marriages were troubled (John 4:15–30) and to reach out for children (Mark 10:13–16). He provided food where there was hunger (John 6:1–15) and wine at a wedding when the supply had run out (John 2:1–11). He became a symbol of hope to lepers, the blind, epileptics, the poor and dispossessed. Mark reports after the healing of a deaf mute: "People were overwhelmed with amazement. 'He has done everything well,' they said" (Mark 7:37).

His Teaching

His teaching occurred by precept and example. He taught by parables both to penetrate to guileless hearers and to protect the truth from distortion by detractors. His teaching was punctuated by signs and mighty deeds that attested the special empowerment of his mission. He called all hearers to repentance as the primary requirement of participating in the coming governance of God.

The Calling and Training of the Twelve

From his portrayal in the Gospels it appears that Jesus intended from the outset to initiate an ongoing community of faith that would continue to embody his ministry after his death and resurrection (Matt. 28:20; John 20:21). This community was to share in his prophetic teaching, his priestly sacrifice, and his inauguration of the rule of God, under the empowerment of the Spirit that was promised to lead them into all truth (John 16:12–13; 14:26).

As he taught and preached, it became clear that he was in the process of forming a community of faith that could not be fitted neatly into the traditions and institutions of late Judaism but that would address all humanity with the coming of God's love. He engendered a new covenant community that would reshape the Jewish ethos. Personal, trusting response to himself was required to enter this community.

The training of the Twelve occurred didactically and experientially by proximate association with him. They listened to him teach and watched him respond to human needs and deal with adversaries. They beheld his steady compassion. They shared in his life of prayer and service, healing and witness (Luke 6:12; 6:28; 9:28). They received his instruction on missionary preaching and action (Luke 10:1–16; Matt. 4:19).

He Taught with Authority

His manner of teaching was simple, profound, and direct. Even the Temple guards who had been sent to arrest him reported back to their superiors: "No one ever spoke the way this man does" (John 7:46).

"The crowds were amazed at his teaching, because he taught as one who had authority, and not as their teachers of the law" (Matt. 7:28–29; Luke 4:32). "The Jews were amazed and asked, 'How did this man get such learning without having studied?'" (John 7:15). Nicodemus addressed him as "Rabbi" and as "a teacher who has come from God" (John 3:2). He taught in the synagogues, gathered disciples, and debated with scribes concerning Scripture like other rabbis, yet he was different from them in that he taught in the open fields, showed particular concern for women and for the poor, and profoundly identified with sinners, tax collectors, and disreputable folk (Bornkamm, JN, p. 57).

The Manner of His Teaching

His way of teaching was distinctive. As prophesied in one of the messianic psalms, the lips of the Expected One would be "anointed with grace" (Ps. 45:2). He was acquainted with grief and knew the human heart. He deftly dealt with opponents and legalists. He grasped the essence of rabbinic teaching without being deluged by it. He penetrated illusions without becoming trapped in them. He employed symbolic and demonstrative teaching when useful, yet he also taught directly. Even if these dialogues may have been refracted through the memories of the redactors, readers of the Gospels get a sharp picture of Jesus as an apt and ready raconteur not to be outdone.

The Parsimony of His Teaching

In Jesus we have a teacher who "has taught neither too much nor too little. He has taught me to know God the Father, has revealed Himself to me, and has also acquainted me with the Holy Spirit. He has also instructed me how to live and how to die and has told me what to hope for. What more do I want?" (Luther, *LW* 22, pp. 255–56). His sayings are memorable for their compact pungency. This helped to ensure their authenticity in the transmission of the oral tradition.

His Teaching Adapted to Hearers

He adapted his teaching to the capacities of those he taught. He did not teach them all at once but proceeded gradually and in awareness of their prejudices and limitations. "I have much more to say to you, more than you can now bear. But when he, the Spirit of truth, comes, he will guide you into all truth" (John 16:12–13).

The meaning of his ministry was not fully clear until after his death. His own resurrection was his greatest teaching. He promised that his ministry of teaching would be followed by a ministry of reminding: "the Holy Spirit, whom the Father will send in my name, will teach you all things and will remind you of everything I have said to you" (John 14:26).

He Spoke in Parables

The parables illustrated various aspects of the coming reign of God. They used common things to attest God's coming: the surprising growth of mustard seed (Mark 4:30–32); the woman who joyfully recovered a lost coin (Luke 15:8–10); the father who joyfully received back a lost son (Luke 15:11–32); a forgiven debtor who throws in prison one who owes him a pittance (Matt. 18). He spoke of new wine in old wineskins (Luke 5:37–38); moneylenders (Luke 7:41–43); rich fools (Luke 12:16–21); the sower and soils (Mark 4:3–8, 14–20); tenants (Matt. 21:33–44), and banquets (Matt. 22:2–14). The parables pointed to the resurrection: "Though I have been speaking figuratively, a time is coming when I will no longer use this kind of language but will tell you plainly about my Father. In that day you will ask in my name" (John 16:26).

His Teaching Written Not on Paper but in the Experience of the Faithful

St. Thomas argued poignantly that since the most excellent teaching cannot be expressed in writing but only in life, it was fitting that Christ did not directly commit his teaching to writing, so that it could be primarily imprinted on the hearts of hearers (Matt. 7:29; Tho. Aq., *ST* IIIa, Q42.1; Pohle-Preuss, *DT* V, p. 146).

John concluded his Gospel by saying that "the whole world would not have room for the books that would be written" if everything Jesus did or taught "were written down" (John 21:25). Augustine commented that John was speaking not merely of the world not having space for such writings, but moreso "that they could not be comprehended by the capacity of the readers" (*Comm. on John*, Tractate CXXIV.8, *NPNF* 1 VII, p. 452). This is why Christ's teaching had to be written in the experience of believers, so that "You show that you are a letter from Christ, the result of our ministry, written not with ink but with the Spirit of the living God, not on tablets of stone but on tablets of human hearts" (1 Cor. 3:3).

Addressed to the Jews First

It was fitting that Christ was sent first to the lost sheep of the house of Israel (Matt. 15:24). His preaching was directed first to Israel, to demonstrate that the promises of God to Israel were being fulfilled in him. He proceeded in right order by making known God's own coming first to the Jews, then to be "transmitted through them to the Gentiles" (Tho. Aq., *ST* III, Q42.1, II, p. 2246). Isaiah had prophesied that "They will proclaim my glory among the nations" (66:19). It was fitting that the news of God's coming should reach the world by means of the people God chose.

Paul explained: "Christ has become a servant of the Jews on behalf of God's truth, to confirm the promises made to the patriarchs so that the Gentiles may glorify God for his mercy" (Rom. 15:8–9). Jesus' mission at first focused upon Israel, as "servant to the circumcised" (Rom. 15:8, Weymouth). Jesus spent most of his teaching ministry "in the area of Zebulun and Naphtali" (Matt. 4:13) as prophesied by Isaiah (9:1–2), so it was said that from Galilee "the people living in darkness have seen a great light" (Matt. 4:16).

Then to the Gentiles

"He did not wish His doctrine to be preached to the Gentiles before His Passion" (Tho. Aq., *ST* III, Q42.1, II, p. 2246). It was only after his Passion that he said to his disciples: "go and make disciples of all nations" (Matt. 28:19). It was for this reason that shortly before his death, when certain Gentiles wished to see Jesus, he said: "I tell you the truth, unless a kernel of wheat falls to the ground and dies, it remains only a single seed. But if it dies, it produces many seeds" (John 12:24). "He called Himself the grain of wheat that must be mortified by the unbelief of the Jews, multiplied by the faith of the nations" (Augustine, *Comm. on John*, Tractate LI.9, *NPNF* 1 VII, p. 285; quoted in Tho. Aq., *ST* III, Q42.1, II, p. 2246).

His Miracles

Jesus' proclamation was attended by "miraculous powers" (Matt. 13:54, 58) and "miraculous signs and wonders" (John 4:48). Jesus' mighty works were remembered and interpreted in relation to his resurrection as signs of the new age, the coming kingdom. They resist all those powers that resist God's coming: guilt, sickness, death, self-deception, and the demonic grip that sin has on human behavior (Eusebius, *PG* I, p. 124; Bonaventure, *Tree of Life, CWS*, pp. 134–35; Pearson, *EC*, I, pp. 154, 171).

Hence his miracles were regarded as seals of the prophetic office. Nicodemus voiced this connection directly: "Rabbi, we know you are a teacher who has come from God. For no one could perform the miraculous signs you are doing if God were not with him" (John 3:2). The purpose for which the signs and miracles were reported is clearly stated by John: "that by believing you may have life in his name" (John 20:31).

Miracles alone, however, cannot impart faith, but only confirm it. Amid temptation, those who came to faith from miracles alone will not remain steadfast (*BOC*, p. 213).

Healing, Nature, and Resurrection Miracles

Miracles reported of him (many more perhaps being unreported) fall into three types:

MIRACLES OF HEALING

the blind (Matt. 9:27–31; Mark 8:22–26; John 9:1–7)
the lame (Luke 13:11–13)
lepers (Mark 1:40–42; Luke 17:11–19)
paralytics (Luke 5:18–25)
bleeding (Mark 5:25–29)
deafness and muteness (Mark 7:31–37)

MIRACLES SHOWING COMMAND OVER THE FORCES OF NATURE

feeding the five thousand (Mark 6:35–44) and four thousand
   (Mark 8:1–9)
quieting the storm (Mark 4:37–41)
walking on water (Mark 6:48–51)
the catch of fish (John 2:1–11 21:1–11)

MIRACLES OF RAISING THE DEAD

Jairus's daughter (Mark 5:22–24)
the widow's son at Nain (Luke 7:11–15)
Lazarus (John 11:1–44)

Mighty Works Not Ends in Themselves

Jesus appears not to have performed miracles miscellaneously or without purpose. Rather, each one responded to some special need or served some special purpose in pointing to the coming reign of God. He did not draw attention to himself as a worker of miracles. Rather each miracle was a specific response to some personal, social, or contextual need.

He apparently did not think of these works as the most crucial aspect of his ministry, but rather subordinated them to his proclamation and call to decision. Any supposed "faith" that would be founded on them alone would be insufficient. He did not encourage others to interpret his mission essentially as one of signs and wonders, but rather he hoped that the signs would lead to faith (John 4:48). He often commanded that those healed should not speak of it to others, lest false expectations be engendered (Mark 1:44; 3:11; Matt. 12:15–21; 14:13–16).

Early Summaries of Christ's Earthly Ministry

The miracle stories were enmeshed in the earliest layers of Christian preaching. Peter assumed that his audience at Caesarea was already quite familiar with "what happened throughout Judea"—that "God anointed Jesus of Nazareth with the Holy Spirit and power, and how he went around doing good and healing all who were under the power of the devil, because God was with him" (Acts 10:38). "Jesus of Nazareth was a man accredited by God to you by miracles, wonders and signs, which God did among you through him, as you yourselves know" (Acts 2:22).

Jesus' ministry was summarized by Matthew: "Jesus went throughout Galilee, teaching in their synagogues, preaching the good news of the kingdom, and healing every disease and sickness among the people. News about him spread all over Syria, and people brought to him all who were ill with various diseases, those suffering severe pain, the demon-possessed, those having seizures, and the paralyzed, and he healed them" (Matt. 4:23–24). These were victims of the "strong man" (the demonic enemy), whom a stronger One was binding up (Mark 3:27). The miracles confirm the power of God's own coming. The healing acts of Jesus were so integrally related to his proclamation and life, that without these acts it could hardly be viewed as the same ministry.

Signs, Wonders, and Demonstrations of Power and Deity

The miracles were viewed as signs (*sēmeia*) of God's coming and of his saving mission, as wonders (*terata*), and as demonstrations of power (*dunameis*). They were means by which his teaching and identity were presented and interpreted. They point out who Christ is (Brown, *The Gospel According to John*; K. H. Rengstorf, Article on *sēmeion*, *TDNT*, 7:200–68; Aldwinckle, *MTM*, pp. 194–211).

The miracles were taken by beholders as sufficient demonstration that he was of God: "Nobody has ever heard of opening the eyes of a man born blind. If this man were not from God, he could do nothing" (John 9:32–33; Hilary, *Trin.* III, *NPNF* 2 IX, pp. 62–70; Baxter *PW* XX, p. 362; Barth, *CD* III/2, pp. 62–63). The miracles he performed were done "as though of His own power, and not by prayer, as others do" (Tho. Aq., *ST* III, Q43.4, II, p. 2252), not by receiving power from another.

Was It Fitting That Christ Perform Miracles?

At first it might seem that it was not fitting for the Christ to perform miracles, since he himself had said, "A wicked and adulterous generation looks for a miraculous sign" (Matt. 16:4), and admonished those who, unless they would see miraculous signs and wonders, would "never believe" (John 4:48).

Yet it was fitting that Christ did perform miracles, that "we may believe that what he says is from God, just as when a man is the bearer of letters sealed with the king's ring" (Tho. Aq., *ST* III, Q43.1, II, p. 2250). For this reason he said: "But if I do it, even though you do not believe me, believe the miracles, that you may know and understand that the Father is in me, and I in the Father" (John 10:38).

Incarnation and Resurrection as Supreme Among Mighty Works

God's personal coming was itself the miracle of miracles, especially his birth and resurrection—the beginning and ending of his earthly ministry. These are necessary articles of faith for the remembering community and hence are included in the rule of faith. Among all the miracles, the incarnation and resurrection continue to have distinctive status in the liturgical year.

Incarnation and resurrection thus are rightly viewed as the supreme, incomparable miracles of Christian testimony. Incarnation and resurrection were alleged to have happened not merely in the minds or fantasies of the rememberers but in and to the bodies of Mary and Jesus (Augustine, *Concerning Faith of Things Not Seen, NPNF* 1 III, pp. 337–43; *Of Holy Virginity, NPNF* 1 III, pp. 417–19; cf. Barth, *Rudolf Bultmann, Ein Versuch Ihn zu Verstehen*). Yet that which would be implausible if predicated of an ordinary human person was thought to be entirely plausible when predicated of the divine-human person (Augustine, *On the Profit of Believing, NPNF* 1 III, pp. 363–66; Mackintosh, *PJC*, p. 316).

"When we look at the two limits of our human life, we observe the nature of our beginning and our end. Man begins his existence in weakness and similarly ends his life through weakness. But in God's case, the birth did not have its origin in weakness, neither did the death end in weakness. For sensual pleasure did not precede the birth and corruption did not follow the death" (Gregory of Nyssa, *ARI, LCC* III, p. 289).

As to other miracles surrounding the life of Jesus, they must be viewed in relation to their being signs of God's own coming, purposeful in relation to the mission of the Son. They are proper and natural and fitting to the Anointed One.

Can Miracle Be Defined a Priori as Impossible?

If one takes the view of David Hume, that a miracle cannot by its very nature be authentically reported, then miracle must be *prima facie* removed in advance from all inquiry and all potential historical occurrences. Modern physical science is less prone to make such sweeping preemptive judgments.

The nineteenth-century controversy over the possibility of miracles was largely a squabble about a definition. If miracle is defined as suspension of natural law, then it could be asserted that such a suspension is impossible and miracles could be ruled out on the grounds that they have no analogy in normal human experience. Rather, the biblical texts themselves are not concerned with whether natural law can be suspended, but with a simple observed, attested fact: Jesus healed the sick. There is less resistance to talk of miracles now than in the late nineteenth century. Why? In part because physics has probed further into its own vulnerable paradigms and because quantum physics and parapsychological, psychokinetic, and telepathic studies have provided tentative premises that challenge less flexible conceptions of physical causation.

Jesus' Miracles Preternatural, not Contranatural

What is natural to God is unnatural to autonomous human nature. Nothing is more natural to God than to be raised from the dead should God come to earth and die. Nothing is more natural to God than to be born in an extraordinary way, should God become enfleshed.

What seems supernatural to human view is only natural to God. Incarnation and resurrection were not against nature, but merely consistent with God's nature. In both cases the natural forces were not blocked or stultified. The child grew; the body died. But the coming of God to human history stamped these birth and death events with a distinctive imprint. How else could God have come and gone? God came and left in a fitting way that both transcended and used natural human capacities, but that in no way denied or subverted natural human capacities (Lactantius, *Div. Inst.*, FC 49, pp. 280–84, 309–11; Barth, *CD* I/2, pp. 266ff.).

The classical exegetes argued on triune grounds that acts natural to God are equally natural to Christ, for capacities belonging to God belong to Christ. If interpreters later conclude that from their point of view these acts were deemed supernatural (above nature) or preternatural (beyond nature, inexplicable in terms of the common order of nature), they mean that they transcend ordinarily perceived natural human abilities, but not that they were unnatural to Christ or impossible for God.

In an intelligible world, all effects occur as a consequence of causes or actions of an agent. These causes and effects may occur at extremely different levels of causal agency: by physical, chemical agents (studied by physics and chemistry), by living agents (biology), by moral human agents (history), and by God (theology). Everything that happens occurs as a work or operation of an agent by whose power that particular operation is achieved. Nothing occurs either in the natural order or those moral and spiritual orders that transcend natural order that violates the various natures of the agents in those orders (Hall, *DT* VI, p. 321). If one grants that the agency of God functions "naturally" in a different way than chemical agents function naturally in the laboratory or than human agents function in history, then there is no problem with saying that miracle is natural, as long as one recalls that it is natural to God.

If one were to assert that Jesus as a man unassisted by God (not Godman) performed miracles of which simple humanity is intrinsically incapable, that would be self-contradictory and impossible, being *contra naturam*, a reversal of the order of nature, against the capacity of his nature as a man. But such miracles are not ascribed to Jesus in the Gospels.

That Jesus' miracles were preternatural (exceeding natural agency), not contranatural, implies that they attest a power in him exceeding and transcending ordinary natural human powers. Jesus was not proclaimed or self-interpreted as a human magician or spiritual adept who had learned to manipulate psychic forces in unusual ways, but the Son of God enfleshed. The power of his mighty works was not grounded in his human soul but in his deity, which was voluntarily constrained during his earthly ministry (Hilary, *Trin.* VII.26–36, *NPNF* 2 IX, pp. 130–33).

The miracles were as natural for the Son as creating was for the Father. Hence to describe them as supernatural is to select a human vantage point from which to view them.

CHRIST AS TRUE PRIEST

The priestly office of the Son functions in three ways: (1) he makes perfect satisfaction to God the Father through his suffering and death on the cross; (2) he intercedes with the Father for the contrite in heart, in order to (3) bring the blessing of redemption to humanity.

Christ's *priestly* ministry focused primarily upon a single event: his self-giving death as a sacrifice for sin. Why does Christ suffer? Luther answered: "To carry out His office as Priest; and He intends not only to pray for sinners but also to sacrifice His body and life on the altar of the cross" (*Lenten Serm.*, Luke 23:26–31, WLS I, p. 180; WA 52, 799).

By his *prophetic* office, the *priestly*-sacrificial work of Christ had already been announced and predicted, but was not definitively assumed until the last week of his suffering and death. Only after his resurrection would it become clear that his role as messianic *king* was intricately woven with his suffering death. Hence these three offices penetrate each other: the prophetic ministry pointed toward his coming priestly ministry, which in turn made possible his ministry of governance.

Sacrifice, Intercession, Blessing: The Threefold Function of Priestly Ministry

Summary of the Priestly Office

Christ's ministry was anticipated by the Old Testament sacrificial system in which the priest was commissioned to *offer sacrifice, make intercession, and bless the people*. Hence the priestly office may be summarized as that of making atonement, intercession, and benediction (Ursinus, *CHC*, pp. 174–75).

Christ's work reappropriated the threefold function of the high priest in Jewish tradition: to present annually the atoning sacrifice for the whole congregation; to intercede for the faithful; and to bless the people (Lev. 4:16–18; Council of Ephesus, *SCD* 122, p. 50; see also *SCD* 333, 430; Augustine, *CG*, FC 24, pp. 36–39). These three distinctively priestly roles were consummately enacted by Christ (Lactantius, *Div. Inst.*, FC 49, pp. 271–79). This is a stable theological structure that is reflected in various texts of Scripture.

The Work of a Priest

What does a priest do? Priesthood is by Calvin's definition that "office and prerogative of presenting oneself before the face of God to obtain grace, and of offering sacrifice, which may be acceptable to him" (Calvin, *Catech. of the Church of Geneva*, LCC XXII, p. 95; see also *Inst.* 2.12.4; Augustine, *Trin.*, FC 45, pp. 30–31). "Christ's office as a priest is that according to which Christ, the only mediator . . . by His most exact fulfillment of the law and the sacrifice of His body, satisfied, on our behalf, the injured divine justice, and offers to God the most effectual prayers for our salvation" (Hollaz, *ETA*, p. 731; Schmid, *DT*, p. 346). "The priestly office is to provide full satisfaction in our place [*loco nostro*] before God, and to intercede for us" (Wollebius, *CTC* 17, *RDB*, p. 98).

Protestants may be surprised that Luther expressed such a high view of priestly action: "The priest comes forward to take all the shortcoming of the people upon himself as if they were his very own and pleads with God on their behalf. From God he receives the word with which he is to comfort and help everybody. The name 'priest' is therefore, still more lovely and consoling than the names 'father' and 'mother'; nay, this name brings us all the others. For by the fact the Christ is Priest He turns God into our Father" (Luther, *Comm. on Gen. 14:17-24*, *WLS* I, p. 190; *WA* 24, 280f.; *LW* 2, 372f.).

The Whole of Time Embraced by Christ's Priestly Action

As incomparable high priest for the sinful world, Christ sufficiently fulfilled all three of these crucial priestly functions. He voluntarily undertook the mission received from the Father by offering himself as a sacrificial Lamb to atone for the sin of the world, dying for all once for all (as a finished work spoken in *past* tense). He now intercedes in the presence of God for the reconciliation of penitents (in the *present* tense attentive to current need and succor). He blesses human history by redeeming it and promises the final blessing of eternal life and the fulfillment of the reign of God (to be consummated in the *future* tense). His cross is his finished priestly work, his heavenly intercession his present priestly work, and his blessing will ultimately consummate his future priestly work (Wollebius, *CTC* 17, *RDB*, pp. 98–110; Pearson, *EC* I, pp. 172, 367).

The priestly work is therefore already accomplished on the cross, yet still being executed through Christ's intercession with the Father and blessing through the Spirit. While satisfaction is a finished work on the cross, intercession and blessing are continuing activities in the divine presence and amid the blessed community (Gregory Nazianzen, *Fourth Theol. Orat., Orat. XXX, NPNF* 2 VII, pp. 314–15; *BOC*, pp. 118, 148, 158, 259–60, 414–17). Thus the whole of time is embraced by Christ's priestly work.

Set Apart for Priesthood

Priesthood implies a set-apartness or ordination to the service of God, sometimes called unction (an act of anointing). Christ's set-apartness for his priestly service began at the moment of his incarnation, coinciding with the inception of theandric union. He was from birth set apart for priestly service. At his baptism he first exercised the office for which he had been set apart from birth.

"When Christ came into the world, he said: 'Sacrifice and offering you did not desire, but a body you prepared for me'" (Heb. 10:5; cf. Ps. 40:6). Christ's priesthood, therefore, was not to be viewed strictly under the Levitical sacrificial model but was to be offered through his own body (John Chrysostom, *Hom. on Heb.* XVII, *NPNF* 1 XIV, pp. 446–50). The fitting of his body for the cross began at his birth.

The Son did not ordain himself but was sent by the Father. "No one takes this honor [priesthood] upon himself; he must be called by God, just as Aaron was. So Christ also did not take upon himself the glory of becoming a high priest. But God said to him, 'You are my Son,'" and called to be "a priest forever, in the order of Melchizedek" (Heb. 5:4–6; Eusebius, *MPG* I, pp. 25–28; Tertullian, *Answer to the Jews* 2, *ANF* III, pp. 152–53). Whereas Levites were anointed with visible oil, the incarnate Son was anointed with the invisible oil of divinity (Exod. 29:1–10; Lev. 8:1–8; Heb. 5:1–9; Lactantius, *Div. Inst.* IV.14–16, *ANF* IV, pp. 113–118; Clementina, *Recognitions* I.46, *ANF* VIII, p. 89).

Christ's Priestly Work of Sacrifice

"Priest" and "sacrifice" are intrinsically interrelated terms.

Priest and Sacrifice

It is the priest who makes sacrifice on behalf of another. It is Christ who as high priest makes sacrifice on the cross for the sins of humanity (Ambrose, *Flight from the World*, FC 65, pp. 290–96).

In Christ "the same one was to be both priest and sacrifice," wrote Calvin. "Christ plays the priestly role, not only to render the Father favorable and propitious toward us by an eternal law of reconciliation, but also to receive us as his companions" (*Inst.* 2.15.6; see also Tho. Aq., *ST* III, Q22.3, II, pp. 2143–44). "The separating medium is sin, the reconciling Mediator is the Lord," Augustine wrote. "To take then away the separating wall, which is sin, that Mediator has come, and the priest has Himself become the sacrifice" (*Hom. on John* XLI.5, *NPNF* 1 VII, p. 231).

Cross as Altar

Christ was stretched out on the cross as a victim on an altar. "Therefore in the cross on which Christ has suffered we should see nothing but an altar on which Christ sacrifices His life and discharges His priestly office also by praying that we may be rid of sins and freed from eternal death" (Luther, *Serm. on Matt.* 27:33–56, *WLS* I, p. 191; *WA* 52, p. 239).

Sacrifice the Basis of His Intercession and Blessing

Through his satisfaction, Christ made a once-for-all offering of himself. It is on the basis of this self-offering that he intercedes for us and continues to advocate the cause of sinners in the Father's presence. This intercession leads to that ultimate benediction, which is to be consummated finally in the blessing of his return (Newman, *PPS* II, p. 42; VI, pp. 241–42; *SN*, p. 304; Baxter, *PW* VII, pp. 205–208).

By satisfaction he paid the price or ransom for the sins of the world. Through intercession he enables the faithful to obtain the gifts of the Spirit so that God's uprighting action can be rightly applied to them, that his sacrifice may become effective (Eusebius, *PG* I, pp. 184, 197; Pearson, *EC* I, pp. 173–78).

Sacrifice belongs quintessentially to the humble descent of the Redeemer. Intercession belongs more explicitly to his exaltation and ascension.

The Temple Matrix

The Temple in the Old Covenant

Much of the metaphorical matrix for interpreting the Christ event derives from the principal scene of the high-priestly function in Judaism—the Temple—the holy place where God is present and revealed. Since this scene fuels the Christian teaching of salvation in so many ways, it is essential that the student of Scripture understand the altar, the tabernacle, and the high priest in the Levitical tradition and how these were received and reshaped in Christianity.

The Focus of Temple Worship

At the inner core of the Temple stood the altar. Archeological excavations indicate that it was the earliest center of the ever-extending Temple apparatus. The antiquity of this sacrificial function is suggested in the Genesis report that "Noah built an altar to the Lord and, taking some of all the clean animals and clean birds, he sacrificed burnt offerings on it" (Gen. 8:20).

The Design of the Temple

The Temple set aside space for holy functions. Its design set up intentional barriers to secular functions.

(1) The Court. The Temple had a court where the covenant people entered and assembled. A laver (a place of cleansing) stood at the entrance, and there was an altar of burnt offering.

(2) The Sanctuary. Into the sanctuary proper only priests were admitted. On the table of unleavened bread were placed twelve loaves, renewed every Sabbath. The light of the Spirit beamed forth from seven lamps on a golden candlestick. The air was filled with the odor of incense emitting from an altar of incense.

(3) The Most Holy Place. Into the Most Holy Place only the high priest entered once a year, into the place of the ark of covenant. The glory of God rested upon the kapporeth or mercy-seat, which covered the record of transgression from God's eyes. "There, above the cover between the two cherubim that are over the ark of the Testimony, I will meet with you" (Exod. 25:18, 22; Pope, *Compend.* II, p. 245). Such an environment was presupposed in the early church's reference to Christ as a temple.

Christ as Temple

In Christianity, the dying, rising, incarnate Son himself is viewed as temple: "Destroy this temple, and I will raise it again in three days" (John 2:19). His human nature, which is our own nature, became the holy place in which "The Word became flesh and made his dwelling among us. We have seen his glory, the glory of the One and Only, who came from the Father" (John 1:14).

Hence it may now be said that "the tabernacle of God is with men" (Rev. 21:3, KJV). "Jesus Christ has come in the flesh" (1 John 4:2). "A new and living way" has been opened for us "through the curtain, that is, his body, and since we have a great priest over the house of God, let us draw near to God with a sincere heart in full assurance of faith, having our hearts sprinkled to cleanse us from a guilty conscience and having our bodies washed with pure water" (Heb. 10:20–22).

The Body of Christ as Temple

The body of Christ, from another viewpoint, is the church, those whose lives are hid in Christ. He is the church's glory. Hence to the church at Corinth Paul could write: "For we are the temple of the living God" (2 Cor. 6:16); and to the Ephesian church: "In him the whole building is joined together and rises to become a holy temple in the Lord" (Eph. 2:21). Similarly First Peter addressed the church: "You also, like living stones, are being built into a spiritual house to be a holy priesthood, offering spiritual sacrifices acceptable to God through Jesus Christ" (1 Pet. 2:5).

Christ's Priestly Work of Intercession

The essence of the Mediator's intercession is: "I pray for them" (John

17:9). His sacrifice is the objective basis upon which this advocacy occurs. Thus "if anybody does sin, we have one who speaks to the Father in our defense—Jesus Christ, the Righteous One. He is the atoning sacrifice for our sins" (1 John 2:2).

The Ministry of Intercession

Interceding is precisely what priests are called and authorized to do. Christ's continuing intercession is something that only the eternal Son can do. The principal feature of the session of Christ ("sitting at the right hand of God") is that he enters into an intercessory ministry for humanity in the presence of the Father (Calvin, *On Reform*, *SW*, pp. 143–44; Wollebius, *CTC* 18, *RDB*, p. 109). "He prays *for* us, as our *Priest*; He prays *in* us, as our *Head*; He is prayed to *by* us as our *God*" (Augustine, *Comm. on Ps. 85*, quoted in Schmid, *DT*, p. 368).

Advocacy for Sinners

In interceding, Christ presents himself before the Father on our behalf. "He entered the Most Holy Place once for all by his own blood, having obtained eternal redemption" (Heb. 9:12). In him we have an Advocate, an intercessor, a *parakletos*, who speaks to the Father on our behalf (1 John 2:1). He can intercede for us because he is "touched with the feeling of our infirmities" (Heb. 4:15, KVJ). He bears in heaven the marks of the wounds he received from us (Ambrose, *Comm. on Luke 10*, *MPL* 15, pp. 1527ff; Pohle-Preuss, *DT* V, p. 136).

How Long Does He Intercede?

The intercession for the faithful in which Christ was once engaged on earth (John 17) continues until the last day in the heavenly sphere. The Son's intercession does not end with his earthly ministry or at the cross, but continues in the presence of the Father.

After his resurrection and ascension, according to Paul, he "who was raised to life—is at the right hand of God and is also interceding for us" (Rom. 8:34). "In him and through faith in him we may approach God with freedom and confidence" (Eph. 3:12). This intercession continues from the ascension to the final days. Christ is "a priest forever" (Heb. 5:6), having "a permanent priesthood" (Heb. 7:24; Barth, *CD* II/1, pp. 152ff.; IV/1, pp. 314ff.).

Prayer in Christ's Name

He offers the prayers of the faithful to the Father. Hence Christians call upon the Father in the name of Christ. "My Father will give you whatever you ask in my name" (John 16:23; cf. v. 26). Christ mediates and enables the appropriation of his merit to the faithful (Chemnitz, *TNC*, pp. 411–14).

Faith's Ultimate Confidence in His Intercession

The effect of his intercession is to increase faith's joy, trust, and capacity for risk. Key intercessory texts are found in Hebrews: "Let us then approach the throne of grace with confidence, so that we may receive mercy and find grace to help us in our time of need" (Heb. 4:16). "Therefore he is able to save completely those who come to God through him, because he always lives to intercede for them" (Heb. 7:25). For this intercession Christ entered not "a man-made sanctuary," but "he entered heaven itself, now to appear for us in God's presence" (Heb. 9:24).

For Whom?

Christ intercedes for sinners, for the whole world, especially for penitent and contrite supplicants, and for his people as a whole. Christ's intercession shapes and informs the pattern and content of the church's daily intercession.

For Sinners

Christ intercedes not only for those most responsive to grace, but for sinners, following the pattern of the suffering Servant who "made intercession for the transgressors" (Isa. 53:12). Christ's intercession is for all sincere penitents (typified by the unmeritorious thief in Luke 23:34). Christ intercedes for all humanity, yet it is said that those who do not believe do not enjoy the effect of his intercession (Quenstedt, *TDP* III, p. 257; Schmid, *DT*, p. 368).

For the Faithful

Christ intercedes especially for the church, for "those you have given me" (John 17:9, 24). He intercedes not only for the immature in faith that they may be brought fully to repentance and faith (Luke 13:8), but also for believers that they may be kept deeply rooted in faith (John 17:8–11). He intercedes for those in union with the community of faith (John 17:21) and in union with Christ himself (John 17:13–18), that they might be made holy (John 17:19).

He asks of the Father "that the love you have for me may be in them and that I myself may be in them" (John 17:26; Barth, *CD* III/1, p. 221). During his earthly ministry he is reported as praying for particular persons—for Peter (Luke 22:32), for the community of faith who have believed in him (John 17), for those who crucified him (Luke 23:34), and for the world. There is comfort and security in the promise that "Whoever comes to me I will never drive away" (John 6:37).

For All

By analogy the Christian community is called to intercede for all sorts and conditions of humanity: "I urge, then, that requests, prayers, intercession and thanksgiving be made for everyone" (1 Tim. 2:1).

Believers become intercessors by virtue of their participation in Christ. Christ's intercession forms the basis upon which the believing community intercedes. Christ's intercession enables, engenders, and makes acceptable the worship of the people of God who "are being built into a spiritual house to be a holy priesthood, offering spiritual sacrifices acceptable to God through Jesus Christ" (1 Pet. 2:5).

Thus "it is the duty of the entire Christian family" and is not limited to clergy to participate "in the mysterious priesthood" (Pius XI, *Encyclical Letter Miserentissimus Redemptor* [1928], *CF* 657, p. 184). Hence the whole people of God and not clergy alone are called "a chosen people, a royal priesthood, a holy nation, a people belonging to God" (1 Pet. 2:9).

The Empathic Intercession of God

The reconciling sacrifice has a triune premise: it occurs by the sending of the Father, the obedience of the Son, and intercession of the Son by the power of the Spirit.

The Spirit Empowers Intercession

Not only does God the Son make intercession for us but so does the Spirit: "We do not know what we ought to pray for, but the Spirit himself intercedes for us with groans that words cannot express. And he who searches our hearts knows the mind of the Spirit, because the Spirit intercedes for the saints in accordance with God's will" (Rom. 8:26–27).

Father, Son, and Spirit join acts of intercession for us: the Father hears, the Son advocates our cause, and the Spirit prompts our hearts to speak rightly. God's empathic care intercedes when we cannot even understand ourselves adequately: "He my cause will undertake, my interpreter will be" (J. Monsell, *HPEC*, p. 122; Clement of Alexandria, *Stromata* VII.7, *ANF* II, pp. 532–37).

Son in Heaven, Spirit in the Heart

The intercession of Christ and the Spirit are complementary—the Spirit in our hearts and the ascended Son in the presence of the Father. Hence it is said that there are two intercessors, one eternally in the temple of the celestial city and the other temporally in the temple of our hearts, both agreeing, both groaning for our redemption, both enabling communion with the Father. By the work of Son and Spirit we have an introduction, access (*prosagoge*), a right of humble approach to the Father: "For through him we both have access to the Father by one Spirit" (Eph. 2:18; cf. *The Liturgy of James*, ANF VII, pp. 537–50).

The Empathy of God

The real and accurate empathy of the triune God is manifested in the joint intercession of Son and Spirit to the Father. It is as if God feels with us precisely and accurately in our struggle. This is a distinctive aspect of Christian teaching not easily duplicated in the history of religions. God is with us precisely amid our temptations, intimately experiencing with us our special personal difficulties, and imparting strength for good choice. God the Spirit is privy to the secrets of our hearts. God the Son knows what it means to be tempted and to suffer. The point is succinctly stated in Hebrews: "Because he himself suffered when he was tempted, he is able to help those who are being tempted" (Heb. 2:18).

Christ's Priestly Work of Blessing

Blessedness flows from God's own sacrificial intercession. The blessing of God in Christ is the sum of all that has been obtained through his sacrificial act.

Benediction in the Priestly Tradition

Benediction attests divine acceptance of the reconciling act. In the Jewish tradition the signaling of this blessing was a crucial priestly duty (Ambrose, *Jacob*, FC 65, pp. 151–69; *Flight from the World*, FC 65, pp. 316–19). It is to this end that priests of the Torah were called and appointed: "God has chosen them to minister and to pronounce blessings in the name of the Lord" (Deut. 21:5; Henry, *CWB* I, pp. 807–808). Doxology, wherein God is blessed or praised by the people, is distinguished from benediction, wherein it is God who blesses the people.

Aaron's blessing is the Levitical prototype of priestly blessing: "Then Aaron lifted his hands toward the people and blessed them" (Lev. 9:22). When Moses and Aaron came out of the Tent of Meeting, "they blessed the people; and the glory of the Lord appeared to all the people" (Lev. 9:24).

Through Moses the Lord gave Aaron instruction on the threefold form of blessing: "This is how you are to bless the Israelites. Say to them: 'The Lord bless you and keep you; the Lord make his face shine upon you and be gracious to you; the Lord turn his face toward you and give you peace'" (Num. 6:22–26). Classic Christian exegesis interprets the three-fold blessing in relation to the triune premise: the Lord as providential keeper of all by the Father, the Lord as the grace and mercy known to sinners through the Son, and the Lord as the peacemaking gift of the Spirit (Ambrose, *Of the Holy Spirit*, NPNF 2 X, pp. 109–15, 150–51; Henry, *CWB* I, pp. 587–88; cf. Barth, *CD* III/2, pp. 580–82).

The Blessing of Christ

Christ has "blessed us in the heavenly realms with every spiritual blessing" (Eph. 1:3). Apostolic benedictions (such as those found in 1 Cor. 1:3; 2 Cor. 3:14) are offered on the basis of Christ's sacrifice and continuing intercession, not simply as a humanly conceived blessing.

Christ's blessing is imparted through the Holy Spirit, through whom all benefits of the Son's coming are applied. Hence in summary: "The Blessing of the Gospel is obtained by Jesus the Priest, announced by Jesus the Prophet, and imparted by Jesus the King through the Mediatorial Spirit of the new economy of grace" (Pope, *Compend.* II, p. 244). Christ was viewed by analogy to the pattern of Melchizedek who met Abraham and "blessed him" (Gen. 14:17–20; Heb. 7:1).

The aim of the priestly work of Christ is to deliver to humanity his "very great and precious promises, so that through them you may participate in the divine nature" (2 Pet. 1:4); and so "through him to reconcile to himself all things, whether things on earth or things in heaven, by making peace through his blood, shed on the cross" (Col. 1:19; G. Wainwright, *Doxology*).

Christ's Distinctive Priestly Identity: The Order of Melchizedek

By Adam's fall the whole of humanity became alienated from the holy God. But Yahweh chose the people of Israel as a nation of priests, elected for service representatively from the whole of humanity. Yahweh set aside Levi as a priestly tribe and Aaron as a priestly family out of which the high priest (whose type Jesus Christ would fulfill) was chosen.

Christ's priesthood was not exclusively understood in the tradition of Aaron or Levi, however, but even more distinctively "in the order of Melchizedek" (Ps. 110:4; Heb. 7:3). This was shorthand language used by the Letter to Hebrews to show that (1) Jesus' unique ministry is holy and spotless, not one made by a priesthood tainted by self-interest; (2) it is eternal in the heavens and not merely one that occurs in time and on earth; (3) it is a once-for-all offering, not one requiring seasonal repetition; (4) it is a regal priesthood, for Melchizedek ("King of righteousness") was both king and priest, of unknown genealogy, hence anticipatory of the eternal sonship of Christ, who was, like Melchizedek, "the king of peace"; (5) it was Melchizedek who offered bread and wine (Gen. 14:18) prefiguring the Supper of the Lord; and (6) it was Melchizedek who blessed and received tithes from Abraham, who was ancestor to both Aaron and Levi, thus indicating that his priesthood is older and greater than the Levitical one. By this astonishing coalescence of vectors Melchizedek was understood as the "first priest of all priests of the most high God" (Theophilus, *To Autolycus* 31, *ANF* II, p. 107).

This signaled that Christ transcended usual Jewish expectations about a regularized line of succession in priesthood, for his priestly offering, like Melchizedek's, was without immediate predecessors, directly from God (Tho. Aq., *ST* III, Q22.6, II, pp. 2146–47; Heppe, *RD*, p. 458).

Having described generally Christ's priestly office, we turn now to the discussion of those events by which this office was performed in the death of Jesus. After we have done that, we will discuss the exaltation to regal office to consummate his governance.

Part III

HE DIED FOR OUR SINS

The primitive Christian confession received by Paul was "that Christ died for our sins according to the Scriptures, that he was buried, that he was raised on the third day" (1 Cor. 15:3–4).

That Christ died "for our sins" is an article of faith confessed in every creed and taught in every catechism. There can be no adequate recollection of Jesus without confessing the meaning of his suffering and death (Augustine, *CG* XIII, XVII, *NPNF* 1 II, pp. 245–61, 337–60; Pearson, *EC* I, pp. 347–51).

CHAPTER 10

The Death of Jesus

Jesus' death has never been considered an omissible or incidental part of the story, since it was the very purpose for which the Word was made flesh — that he might "suffer death, so that by the grace of God he might taste death for everyone" (Heb. 2:9; Baxter, *PW* XIX, pp. 73–76; Barth, *CD* II/2, pp. 748ff.). It was not an easy death. That he suffered punitively for us in his death is intrinsic to the meaning of his death.

HE SUFFERED

His suffering is incorrectly viewed as primarily bodily pain (although indeed it was that). Rather Jesus absorbed the full force of human anger and aggression and drew it into the sphere of divine love.

The sufferings of his whole life, particularly those of his last days, embraced the full range of human agonies — physical and emotive, retrospective and prospective, personal and interpersonal, inward and outward (John Chrysostom, *Hom. on Matt.* LV, *NPNF* 1 X, pp. 338–44; Catherine of Siena, *Pray.*, pp. 170–80). In Judas's betrayal, Peter's denial, the Sanhedrin's trial, the mockery of soldiers and insults by onlookers, the suffering he endured involved the full range of human rejection, hatred, abuse, deception, and vindictiveness.

The Road to Golgotha

A Passion Story with an Introduction

The Gospel narratives have been described as a Passion story with an extended introduction. The space Mark gives to the Passion is about three-fifths of the total, Matthew two-fifths, and Luke at least a third (John Chrysostom, *Hom. on Matt.* LIV–XC, *NPNF* 1 X, pp. 334–534; Augustine, *Serm. on NT Lessons* XLVI, *NPNF* 1 VI, pp. 408–11; L. Morris,

The Cross in the NT; Ladd, *TNT*, p. 183; Stott, *BC*, p. 87). John's Gospel is divided into two approximately equal halves: the signs of God's coming and the end of his coming (or Book of the Signs and Book of the Passion; John Chrysostom, *Hom. on John* XXII–XXIV, *NPNF* 1 XIV, pp. 79–86).

Why the Gospels Were Written

One of the main reasons why the Gospels were written down at all was to provide some explanation of how it could possibly be that Jesus is both messianic Son *and* that he suffered and died. These colliding assertions created a dilemma of implausibility that required something to be said (Calvin, *Comm.*, *Harmony* XVI, pp. 299–304; Guthrie, *NTT*, pp. 21–37).

In retrospect, every event prior to Jesus' death pointed inexorably toward his death as a date to be kept, a target to be reached, an hour that was coming (John 1:39; 2:4; 11:9; 16:4; John Knox, *The Death of Christ*). In considering whether to go to the Feast of Tabernacles, Jesus explained: "The right time for me has not yet come; for you any time is right. The world cannot hate you, but it hates me because I testify that what it does is evil. You go to the Feast. I am not yet going up to this Feast, because for me the right time has not yet come" (John 7:6–8). His decision to go to Jerusalem was irreversibly laden with the prospect of death.

He Must Suffer

Accordingly, Jesus' suffering was considered a necessary and intrinsic part of his messianic ministry. "The Son of man must [*dei*] suffer" and "be killed" (Mark 8:31). There was no alternative.

It is unlikely that this was a saying attributed to Jesus later by the remembering church for these reasons: the hellenizing church did not characteristically use or easily find useful to their proclamation the "Son of Man" title—other titles were more easily adaptable to their purposes. There was no previous or prevailing analogy in Judaism of the merging of the Son of Man with the suffering Servant theme (Ladd, *TNT*, pp. 155–58). Repeatedly Jesus had tried to draw his disciples closer to the truth of this paradox. The enigma was not that the Messiah was coming, but that he must suffer and die.

Jesus preached that the reign of God was breaking through presently in the unfolding events of his ministry, leading to the crescendo of his death. He viewed his ministry in relation to poignant Old Testament metaphors of vicarious atonement (Mark 10:45; 14:24; Isa. 53; Exod. 32:30–32). He is portrayed as aware that these Scriptures were pointing toward him and being fulfilled in him.

From Caesarea Philippi, he moved inexorably toward his "hour," which had not yet come. Finally with the cross in view he would declare: "Father, the hour has come" (John 17:1, RSV). As he entered Jerusalem for his last tumultuous days, he stated that "it was for this very reason I came to this hour" (John 12:27). When Peter tried to defend him, Jesus said, "Put your sword away! Shall I not drink the cup the Father has given me?" (John 18:11).

Passion: The Humble Descent of the Son

Passion Defined

Jesus' Passion is what he suffered as distinguished from action, or what he did. Passion ("suffering," *pascho*, "to suffer"; Lat. *passus, passionem*), may be viewed in either a narrower or broader way.

In its narrower definition, Jesus' Passion focused intensively upon *a single week* of his life—his last struggle ending on a cross. The week prior to his death was filled with numerous events that clarified his messianic identity and saving work (Lactantius, *Div. Inst.*, FC 49, pp. 284–315). It is in this narrower sense that the term "Passion" is most often used liturgically to point to his priestly-sacrificial ministry.

In its broader definition, however, Jesus' Passion included all the afflictions he suffered during *his whole incarnate life*—including his temptation, his being despised and rejected, reproached and plotted against (Matt. 12:24; John 7:1; 8:6; 9:16), and his suffering of physical pain, hunger, fatigue, and poverty (Augustine, *CG*, FC 14, pp. 487–89; FC 24, pp. 130–37, 160–71). That he must endure hostile opposition was symbolized early in Matthew's narrative of Herod's massacre of innocents at Bethlehem. That he would have nowhere to lay his head was foreshadowed early by the flight of his family to Egypt (Matt. 2:13–18; Origen, *Ag. Celsus* I.66, *ANF* IV, p. 426).

The Sufferer Was God-incarnate

He suffered like others suffer, but his suffering was interpreted as differing from others' in that through it the innocent Son bore "the sin of the world" (John 1:29). Others suffer as humans. He suffered as *theanthropos*. Others suffer through an ambiguous mixture of human guilt and innocence; he suffered innocently, without the slightest admixture of guilt (Pearson, *EC* I, pp. 316–32). That he was eternal Son gave eternal meaning to his temporal suffering (Newman, *Mix.*, p. 321).

Passibility of Christ's Humanity

The unique way he suffered must be understood in relation to his unique personal identity as incarnate Lord, for Christ is said to be passible (able to suffer) according to his human nature, impassible (incapable of suffering) with respect to the divine nature (Hilary, *Trin.* X.23–49, *NPNF* 2 IX, pp. 187–217; Chemnitz, *TNC*, pp. 210–29; Ursinus, *CHC*, pp. 212–14).

His entire earthly ministry was concisely summarized by Paul: he "humbled himself and became obedient unto death" (Phil. 2:8). The full extent of his humiliation was seen in his unjustified execution and innocent death. There human hatred did all the damage it could do to the Only Son of God (Newman, *PPS* VI, pp. 41ff., 73–76).

Stages of Descent and Reversal

Four points in particular are distinguished in speaking of the *descent* or humiliation of the eternal Son:

his birth,
　　the travail of his life,
　　　　his death and burial, and
　　　　　　his descent into the abode of the dead.

For human eyes to see, the descent of the Son reached its completion in the burial, the literal descent of his body into the sepulchre. Yet for the spiritual world, the descent was further extended into the nether world. This phase ended the account of his humiliation, and with this reversal began his exaltation.

The descent into the nether world paradoxically combined his deepest abasement with his victory over sin and death. In a similar way, the incarnation had combined the glory of the divine condescension of the Son with the abasement of his lowly birth—in poverty, under the law, with no room in the inn. Having discussed his birth and life, our present focus is upon the events immediately leading to his death.

Identification with the Lowly

Throughout his suffering he identified with sinners. "God made him who had no sin to be sin for us, so that in him we might become the righteousness of God" (2 Cor. 5:21). This is the vocation that he assumed and accepted at his baptism, the vocation that continued until he uttered, "It is finished" (John 19:30).

The Washing of Feet

The singular event that epitomized dignity expressed through lowliness was of *footwashing*, which he commended as a prime example to his disciples. Metaphors of lowliness are particularly offensive to modern egalitarianism, which so loves equality that it resents servanthood.

Just before the Passover feast, knowing that his time had come and that he was soon to be betrayed, he "wrapped a towel around his waist," "poured water into a basin and began to wash his disciples' feet, drying them with the towel that was wrapped around him" (John 13:4–5). By this means he showed his willingness to stoop and serve. He prototypically taught and enacted the way of lowly service. "Do you understand what I have done for you?" "Now that I, your Lord and Teacher, have washed your feet, you also should wash one another's feet" (John 13:12–14).

The Passion Anticipated by His Baptismal Identification

The same lowliness that was to be finally manifested on the cross had been already anticipated in Jesus' *baptism*, by which he chose to be "numbered with the transgressors" (Isa. 53:11). What happened on the cross was consistent with all that had happened previously in his lowly way of life. Hence the Passion, broadly understood, encompassed his entire incarnate life (Pearson, *EC* I, pp. 316–34).

Jesus' Suffering Prophetically Foretold

Although the suffering and sacrificial death of the messiah had been anticipated in prophecy, it required the actual event before those prophecies could be adequately understood. The retrospective analysis of messianic prophecies that pointed toward the cross became an intensive preoccupation of early Christian preaching.

Triumphal Entry Prophesied

Zechariah had prophesied the coming of Zion's King: "See, your king comes to you, righteous and having salvation, gentle and riding on a donkey, on a colt, the foal of a donkey," who will "proclaim peace to the nations" (Zech. 9:9–10). Jesus' entry into Jerusalem was remembered as fulfilling this prophecy. In Zechariah's oracle concerning the destruction of Jerusalem's enemies, he had prophesied that the people of Israel would mourn for the one they pierced, "as one mourns for an only child, and grieve bitterly for him as one grieves for a firstborn son" (Zech. 12:10).

Temple Cleansing Prophesied

The cleansing of the Temple fulfilled Isaiah 56:7: "my house will be called a house of prayer for all nations." The sanctuary was thereby prepared for the coming kingdom. "With good reason, then, all the Gospels connect the story of the cleansing of the temple with Jesus' dispute with the leaders of the nation about the 'authority' which entitles him to this action" (Bornkamm, *JN*, p. 159; Mark 9:27ff.).

Conspiracy and Trial Prophesied

Jesus' prediction that "one of you will betray me—one who is eating with me" (Mark 14:18) echoes Psalm 41:9. The conspiracy recalled Psalm 31:13–15: "They conspire against me and plot to take my life. But I trust in you, O Lord; I say, 'You are my God. My times are in your hands.'" The "thirty pieces of silver" recalled Zechariah 11:12. Similarly: "They gave me vinegar for my thirst" (Ps. 69:21). "All who see me mock me; they hurl insults, shaking their heads" (Ps. 22:7).

Suffering Servant Prophesied

Isaiah in particular had prophesied concerning one who would be "pierced for our transgressions," "crushed for our iniquities" (Isa. 53:5).

In the narrative of Pilate's discussion with the Jews concerning what to do about Jesus, whether he was rightly charged or a criminal, whether to execute and who had jurisdiction (John 18:28–31), John explained the importance of these events for salvation history: "This happened so that the words Jesus had spoken indicating the kind of death he was going to die would be fulfilled" (John 18:32).

Actual, Voluntary, Innocent, Purposeful Suffering

Four assumptions illuminate Christ's suffering: he suffered truly, voluntarily, innocently, and meaningfully by divine permission. An adequate doctrine of the cross requires that all four points be held closely together.

Truly

His sufferings were real, not imagined. He was indeed "a man of sorrows, and familiar with suffering" (Isa. 53:4). If this suffering and death had been a fantasy, there could be no satisfaction for sin. He actually suffered (*passus, pathonta*—Creed of 150 Fathers, *COC* II, p. 58), not in a pretended but "a real suffering and death" (*Russian Catech.*, *COC* II, p. 475; Council of Constantinople II, *SCD* 222, p. 88; see also *SCD* 20, 86,

480). If he did not truly suffer he has "misled us, by exhorting us to endure what He did not endure Himself" (Irenaeus, *Ag. Her.*, III 18.6, 7, *ANF* I, p. 447; cf. Moltmann, *The Experiment Hope*, pp. 69–84).

Voluntarily

His suffering was not involuntary, but voluntarily accepted on behalf of humanity ("Then he said, 'Here I am, I have come to do your will,'" "And by that will, we have been made holy through the sacrifice of the body of Jesus Christ once for all," Heb. 10:9–10; Cyril of Jerusalem, *Catech. Lect.* 13.6, *NPNF* 2 VII, pp. 83–84; Lateran Council [649], *SCD* 255, p. 102; see also *SCD* 717). Jesus was not merely passive victim, but active Victor (Whale, *PT*, p. 40), willing through love to lay down his life for others, even as others sought to take it away by force. He was not externally compelled to be baptized with the baptism of sinners, to set his face steadfastly toward Jerusalem or go to Gethsemane, or drink the cup of suffering. Rather he received and drank that cup not because he liked to suffer—the very thought caused him to sweat profusely—but rather because it was an intrinsic part of the purpose of his mission to humanity (Catherine of Siena, *Pray.*, pp. 17–18, 174).

Innocently

Without the premise of innocence he could not have served adequately as unblemished Lamb (Heb. 7:26; see the argument on the sinlessness of Jesus, chapter 8).

Meaningfully by the Father's Permission

These sufferings were allowed to happen according to a hidden divine purpose and permission, not by fate, chance, or absurd accident; they have meaning in relation to the history of salvation. "This man was handed over to you by God's set purpose and foreknowledge" (Acts 2:23).

The Supper and Its Meaning

The Last Meal

Jesus celebrated his last meal with his disciples in intense expectation of the coming reign of God, aware that he would soon leave them. "I will not drink again of the fruit of the vine until that day when I drink it anew in the kingdom of God" (Mark 14:25). This meal took place near the time of the Passover festival, in which a Passover lamb was sacrificed in remembrance of the liberation of the people of Israel from Egypt. "Jesus gives himself, in the form of bread and wine, as one given over to death" (Bornkamm, *JN*, p. 161).

Earliest Layer of Interpretation: Words of Institution

The earliest oral tradition anteceding the New Testament written documents reflects intense interest in the interpretation of events surrounding Jesus' death. This tradition funded the recollections of Paul, Mark, Luke, and Matthew of the words of Jesus at the Last Supper. These "words of institution" indicate a tradition that we have every reason to believe goes directly back to the earliest Christian memory of these events.

Mark 14:24 reports that Jesus said to his disciples at their last supper: "This is my blood of the covenant which is poured out for many." Matthew 26:28 adds: "for the forgiveness of sins." Paul's version states: "'This cup is the new covenant in my blood; do this whenever you drink it, in remembrance of me.' For whenever you eat this bread and drink this cup, you proclaim the Lord's death until he comes" (1 Cor. 11:25–26).

Hence there can be little doubt that the cross was being interpreted as a redemptive event even in the earliest identifiable strains of oral tradition anteceding the New Testament documents. Further discussion of the Last Supper will be included in the next volume of this series.

UNDER PONTIUS PILATE

The events surrounding Jesus' death were not done in a corner. They occurred under governmental authority, with the blessing of the highest religious leaders, in a capital city, as the result of a formal trial ending in a torturous public death. These events became common knowledge in the Roman world (cf. Hengel, *Crucifixion*, pp. 2–21; W. Barclay, *Crucified and Crowned*).

The Plot: What Forces Conspired to End Jesus' Life?

Powerful forces colluded in ending Jesus' life: the Sanhedrin, the Pharisees, priests and scribes, and the Roman authorities.

The priestly establishment sought to take Jesus' life because he had challenged their authority, especially in his teaching of the law, triumphal entry into Jerusalem, and cleansing of the Temple. The scribes and Pharisees resisted Jesus because he opposed their finely nuanced interpretation of the law. The political establishment wanted tranquility, which they saw him upsetting. The Sanhedrin sought to end Jesus' life because his popularity had made him dangerous to them and threatened their leadership roles. "The elders of the Jews and the scribes hated him, because he rebuked their false doctrine and evil lives, and envied him, because the people, which heard him teach and saw his miracles, esteemed him more than them; and hence they falsely accused him, and condemned him to death" (*Russian Catech.*, *COC* I, p. 474).

John's Gospel gives us a realistic glimpse into the cynical and hysterical political reasoning of his opponents: "Then the chief priests and the Pharisees called a meeting of the Sanhedrin. 'What are we accomplishing?' they asked. 'Here is this man performing many miraculous signs. If we let him go on like this, everyone will believe in him, and then the Romans will come and take away both our place and our nation.' Then one of them, named Caiaphas, who was high priest that year, spoke up, 'You know nothing at all! You do not realize that it is better for you that one man die for the people than that the whole nation perish.'" "So from that day on they plotted to take his life" (John 11:47–50, 53).

This is why "Jesus no longer moved about publicly among the Jews. Instead he withdrew into a region near the desert, to a village called Ephraim" (John 11:54).

He Faced His Own Death

How did Jesus face the prospect of his own death? Long before his triumphal entry, Jesus had recognized that there was a definite plot against his life. The Gospels offer strong clues that he had grown poignantly aware of the approaching crisis (Matt. 12:50; 26:38; Mark 12:33; Luke 22:44).

That Jesus expected a sudden and violent end that would bring grief to his companions seems clear from his pointed reference to the messianic bridegroom, that "the time will come when the bridegroom will be taken from them, and on that day they will fast" (Mark 2:20). Recalling Zechariah 13:7, he told his disciples at the Last Supper: "'You will all fall away,' Jesus told them, 'for it is written: "I will strike the shepherd, and the sheep will be scattered"'" (Mark 14:27).

There is no maudlin tendency in the Gospels to present Jesus as an idealized martyr or Stoic dying hero. The predominating metaphors are those of Savior, sacrificial Lamb, and Redeemer, whose vocation as a Servant would be fulfilled only through suffering and death. There is no tendency either to present Jesus as an ascetic loner unconsciously seeking pain or a personality tilted toward masochism. Jesus could see his death coming. Jesus did not, like Socrates, calmly face his death but agonized intensely over it and cried out in the face of death, showing the full extent of his sharing our natural human resistance to pain and death (Cullmann,

CNT). "I have a baptism to undergo, and how distressed I am until it is completed!" (Luke 12:50; Tertullian, *On Baptism* 16, *ANF* III, p. 677; *Of Bodily Patience* 13, *ANF* III, pp. 715–16).

The events were concisely recounted. They moved gradually to an irreversible climax—from Gethsemane to trial to cross.

Gethsemane and Arrest

There is profound human tension in the narrative of Gethsemane: "Now my heart is troubled, and what shall I say? Father, save me from this hour? No, it was for this very reason I came to this hour" (John 12:27–28).

The Cup

All synoptic Gospels report Jesus' agony in the Garden of Gethsemane, where he prayed that his Father would "take this cup from me" (Mark 14:36; cf. Luke 22:42; Matt. 26:39). There was deeper meaning in his dying than simply a terrible physical death.

The cup was a metaphor of punishment, of divine retribution for sin (V. Taylor, *Mark*, p. 54). The picture of Jesus in Gethsemane reveals his awareness of the awful reality of impending death, yet he maintained unfailing obedience to his mission (Mark 14:26–42; Calvin, *Inst.* 2.16). Sweat poured from his face like "drops of blood falling to the ground" (Luke 22:44; Bonaventure, *Tree of Life*, CWS, pp. 141–42; Chemnitz, *TNC*, p. 63).

The Abandonment

Matthew reported Jesus' poignant words at Gethsemane, reaching out for human companionship: "My soul is overwhelmed with sorrow to the point of death. Stay here and keep watch with me" (Matt. 26:38; see Newman, *Mix.*, pp. 324–40). Yet he was in effect deserted by his disciples when they were overcome with sleep. How was it known and who could have reported that he prayed, "Let this cup pass," if his disciples were asleep? It could have been made known to a disciple later.

The Arrest by Night

He was betrayed and gave himself up voluntarily (Gregory Nazianzen, *On the Theophany*, NPNF 2 VII, p. 350). He "did not defend himself, but stood to submit to judgment" (Calvin, *Inst.* 2.16.5; Matt. 27:12–14).

He was surrounded by soldiers and bound with chains. When the betrayer came with "men of blood" (Ps. 54:24) "by night with torches, lanterns and weapons to seek his life," he "offered himself to them," healing instantly the ear of the servant cut off by his disciple, "and he restrained the zeal of his defender who wanted to injure the attackers" (Bonaventure, *Tree of Life*, *CWS*, pp. 142–43).

The Trial: Public Condemnation Under Civil Authority

Why do the creeds insist as an article of faith that he was tried *under Pontius Pilate* ("*sub Pontio Pilato*"; Creed of 150 Fathers, *COC* II, p. 58)?

Datability of the Salvation Event

This locates the salvation event as a datable event of history. Christianity, like Judaism, is a historical religion. The redemption of the world is an event located in ordinary human history (*Russian Catech.*, *COC* II, p. 474). It occurred "under Pontius Pilate," pointing to the historical concreteness of this event attested by eyewitnesses (Apostles' Creed, *SCD* 2, p. 4; Council of Constantinople II, *SCD* 222, p. 88; see also *SCD* 20, 86, 255). Christian teaching differs radically from pagan deliverance myths in that its salvation event is the only one with a historical date (cf. Ursinus, *CHC*, pp. 217–19; cf. Dorothy Sayers, *The Man Born to Be King*).

The Time of His Death

Nisan was the first month of the ancient Jewish year. The festival of Passover was celebrated in mid-Nisan. It was on the fourteenth day of Nisan that "Christ our Passover lamb, has been sacrificed" (1 Cor. 5:7; John 18:28), that "Christ died for our sins according to the Scriptures, that he was buried" (1 Cor. 15:3). Jesus died as "lamb of God" (John 1:29, 36) on the day when paschal lambs were sacrificed. As the birth of the Savior was an actual event that occurred on a particular day in history (Clement of Alexandria, *Stromata* I.21, *ANF* II, p. 333) so was his death (Origen, *Ag. Celsus*, *ANF* IV, pp. 411–12, 442–45; Eusebius, *CH*, *NPNF* 2 I, pp. 88–91).

The synoptic Gospels speak of the crucifixion as on the preparation of the Sabbath and not the feast day itself (Matt. 26:5). Hence it appears that the Last Supper was, as John indicated, "just before the Passover feast" (John 13:1). This is why early calculations indicated that the crucifixion took place on fourteenth of Nisan, quite probably Friday, April 7, in the year of Rome 783, A.D. 30. Theologically the more crucial point is not the date, but that God's saving sacrificial action occurred in history on a particular day, not abstractly or symbolically in some mythical or nonhistorical realm. The event is datable with reasonable accuracy (Eusebius, *CH* I.9–II.7, *NPNF* 2 I, pp. 96–110).

Ironies of Official Condemnation

Another reason for confessing that this event occurred "under Pontius Pilate" is stated by Calvin: "That we may know his death to be connected with his condemnation. . . . He died so that the penalty owed by us might be discharged, and he might exempt us from it. But since we all, because we are sinners, were offensive to the judgment of God, in order to stand in our stead, he desired to be arraigned before an earthly judge, and to be condemned by his mouth, so that we might be acquitted before the heavenly tribunal of God." He was "condemned in the presence of an earthly judge, that we should be absolved before the judgment seat of our God" (*Scots Confession* IX, *BOConf.* 3.09; cf. 4.038). It was crucial that his death be public, not natural, but at the hands of others (Athanasius, *Incarn. of the Word* 21–25, *NPNF* 2 IV, pp. 47–49).

Ironies of Official Accountability

It was Pilate who actually held civil responsibility for the execution of Jesus as seditious zealot, yielding to pressure from the Sanhedrin, even though he knew that Jesus was innocent. Ironically, Pilate both bore "testimony to his innocence" and at the same time formally condemned him. Both acts were "by the same judge to make it plain that he suffered as our surety the judgment which we deserved" (Calvin, *Catech. of the Church of Geneva*, LCC XXII, p. 98; *Inst.* 2.16.5). To be "acquitted by the same lips that condemned him" (Calvin, *Inst.* 2.16.5; Matt. 27:23; John 18:38) brought to mind the vicarious metaphor of the Psalms that the servant of God *repaid* what he did *not steal* (Ps. 69:4; Tertullian, *An Answer to the Jews* X, *ANF* III, p. 165; Henry, *CWB* III, p. 493).

Ironies of the Charges

Although the official charge was sedition, the central event of the trial was "Jesus' own confession before the high priest that he is the Messiah, a confession made openly for the first time" (Bornkamm, *JN*, p. 163). Jesus was condemned on the charge of blasphemy by the Sanhedrin for his claim to be the heavenly Son of Man and for his offending statement that those who now were judging him would soon be subject to judgment from the Son of Man (Mark 14:62).

When Pilate quipped, "You are a king," Jesus answered: "You are right in saying I am a king. In fact, for this reason I was born, and for this I came into the world," and for the same reason he was crucified: "to testify to the truth" (John 18:37).

Mocked as Pretended King and Scourged

Jesus was clothed in a robe of purple (John 19:1–4) and mocked as King of the Jews while being struck and spat upon. Victims were routinely tortured by whipping. It is likely that Jesus' blood flowed freely from this scourging, hence he became too weak to carry his cross all the way to Golgotha (cf. Isa. 53:7). "As they led him away, they seized Simon from Cyrene, who was on his way in from the country, and put the cross on him and made him carry it behind Jesus" (Luke 23:26). Simon, from North Africa, a passerby, likely a Passover pilgrim (his sons Alexander and Rufus may have been known to Mark and Paul, Mark 15:21; Rom. 16:13), was "compelled to carry his cross" (Matt. 27:32, RSV), a scene ever thereafter imprinted on the mind of the remembering church.

The messiah was not supposed to be demeaned or die. Jesus' ministry would radically transform Jewish expectations about the messianic king through his death.

CRUCIFIED, DEAD AND BURIED

Jesus did not choose his manner of death. Athanasius employed the simile of the good wrestler to show his readiness to meet the challenge in whatever form. The death that was chosen by others was intended to disgrace him, yet it preserved his body undivided and proved the ultimate trophy in the struggle against the power of death (Athanasius, *Incarn. of the Word* 21–24, NPNF 2 IV, pp. 47–49).

The Crucifixion

His Whole Body and Soul Suffered

From the time of his arrest until his death, he suffered with relentless intensity. Western art has envisioned every misery of body and soul being encompassed: his wrists were bound in chains; his face was spat upon; the flesh of his back was lashed and left bleeding from a Roman whip; his shoulders felt the heavy cross; his eyes could not help beholding corruption, hypocrisy, deception, and the grief of his mother; he heard the hateful rejection of the crowd that earlier had adored him; and on his head was placed a crown of thorns (Catherine of Genoa, *Spiritual Dialogue*, CWS, p. 108; Wollebius, *CTC*, 18, *RDB*, p. 101; Cynthia Maus, *Christ and the Fine Arts*).

His Demeaning Execution

He was executed by a most horrible means (Athanasius, *Incarn. of the Word* 24–25, *NPNF* 2 IV, pp. 49–50). His whole body, "already a mass of wounds," was "stretched and tortured on the cross" (Quenstedt, *TDP*, p. 66; Jacobs, *SCF*, p. 148; Prudentius, *Poems* II, *FC* 2); his limbs almost torn apart by his own weight; his hands and feet nailed to wood. His side was gashed with a spear. Although the Gospel narratives were not seeking intentionally to show that every cell of his body and every recess of his soul was assaulted by human aggression, they in fact did so merely by telling what happened.

His Thirst

One of the most excruciating forms of suffering in crucifixion was extreme thirst. When Jesus, parched with thirst, craved for relief, he was offered only strongly spiced wine mixed with gall, an anesthetic he refused (Matt. 27:34), as he was willing to be fully conscious until his death.

His Torturous Death

The physiological processes accompanying crucifixion are too gruesome to detail. Death by crucifixion usually took two days. Its length and horror were precisely what commended it as a public political punishment. In Jesus' case it was a matter of hours. The cause of death was blood loss, shock, exposure, and dehydration. Legs were sometimes broken with hammers to induce death if the process took too long—Jesus died before this was required.

There is in the Gospel narratives no sentimental idealization of the cross, as later developed. Their focus was upon its saving significance and worth. Despite the fact that the cross was bloody and torturous, it was an event through which God's glory shined (Calvin, *Inst.* 2.16.6; Barth, *CD* IV/1, pp. 178ff., 343ff.).

Paul wrote defiantly: "May I never boast except in the cross of our Lord Jesus Christ, through which the world has been crucified to me, and I to the world" (Gal. 6:14). Luther stressed the personal significance of the cross for believers: "I believe that He bore His cross and passion for my sins and the sin of all believers and thereby has consecrated all sufferings and every cross and made them not only harmless, but salutary and highly meritorious" (*Brief Explanation*, *WML* II, p. 370).

Had he not died, he could not have risen. It was necessary that he die at the hands of others, for he came to receive death as the due of others.

His death had to be a public death, in order to be a condemnation for others.

He Took Our Curse upon Himself

Why the Cross and Not Some Other Form of Death?

"Is there something more in his being crucified than if he had died some other death?" asks the *Heidelberg Catechism*. Answer: "Yes, for by this I am assured that he took on himself the curse which lay upon me, because the death of the cross was cursed of God" (Q. 39, p. 44; Ursinus, *CHC*, pp. 218-19), for "he hung upon the tree to take our curse upon himself; and by this we are absolved from it" (Calvin, *Catech. of the Church of Geneva*, LCC XXII, p. 98; Gal. 3:10). Hanging on a tree was purposefully intended to expose the corpse to ultimate disgrace (Deut. 21:22-23).

"A form of death had to be chosen in which he might free us both by transferring our condemnation to himself and by taking our guilt upon himself. If he had been murdered by thieves or slain in an insurrection by a raging mob, in such a death there would have been no evidence of satisfaction," but by his arraignment as a criminal we know that as one innocent he voluntarily "took the role of a guilty man" (Calvin, *Inst.* 2.16.5). He suffered "the most extreme form of death in order that His martyrs would fear no kind of death" (Augustine, *The Creed* 3.9, FC 27, p. 297; *EDQ* 25, FC 70, p. 51).

Why Between Two Thieves?

That he hung between thieves fulfilled the prophecy that "he was numbered with the transgressors. For he bore the sin of many, and made intercession for the transgressors" (Isa. 53:12; Mark 15:28; Calvin, *Comm.* VIII, p. 130). Even there, on the cross, he continued his ministry of pardon and reconciliation.

Why "King of the Jews"?

The Roman custom was to hang a sign around the neck of a criminal under execution. Jesus' sign read: "Jesus of Nazareth, the King of the Jews" (John 19:19). The religious authorities protested, but Pilate insisted. Pilate's inscription was viewed by the church as an ironic declaration of Jesus' true identity to the whole world.

Why the Prayer for His Persecutors?

The very rabble who were rejecting his testimony were at the same time paradoxically offering up the victim who would redeem. It is amid these ironies that classic exegetes stood amazed: those who most radically symbolized the sin of the world through their very act of absurd rejection played bit parts in the story of the salvation of humanity. He who knew what was in the human heart prayed for his persecutors: "Father, forgive them, for they do not know what they are doing" (Luke 23:34; Pope, *Compend.* II, p. 162).

Cross as Symbol

Christianity once for all transformed the symbolic signficance of crucifixion, which until the time of Jesus had been a demeaning symbol of political repression. Its distinctive shape—"the four arms converge in the middle"—became a universal symbol of "the one who binds all things to himself and makes them one," wrote Gregory of Nyssa. "Through him the things above are united with those below, and the things at one extremity with those at the other. In consequence it was right that we should not be brought to a knowledge of the Godhead by hearing alone; but that sight too should be our teacher" (*ARI* 32, *LCC* III, p. 311).

The cross teaches those "rooted and established in love" "to grasp how wide and long and high and deep is the love of Christ" (Eph. 3:18). "Make this sign as you eat and drink, when you sit down, when you go to bed, when you get up again, while you are talking, while you are walking; in brief, at your every undertaking" (Cyril of Jerusalem, *Catech. Lect.* IV.14, *LCC* IV, p. 106).

Classic exegetes thought it an intimation of "the kind of death he was going to die" when he said, "I, when I am lifted up from the earth, will draw all men to myself" (John 12:32). "For if He came Himself to bear the curse laid upon us, how else could He have 'become a curse,' unless He received the death set for a curse? and that is the Cross," Athanasius reasoned. He came to call all, both Jew and Gentile, to himself. Note that "it is only on the cross that a man dies with his hands spread out" to encompass all (Athanasius, *Incarn. of the Word* 24, *NPNF* 2 IV, p. 49)!

His Cry on the Cross

The pathos of his human suffering was poignantly expressed in his cry: "My God, my God, why have you forsaken me?" (Mark 15:34; Matt. 27:46, quoting Ps. 22:1). That this cry was reported to Gentile audiences in its original Aramaic, "*Eloi, Eloi, lama sabachthani?*" is a clear indication that it belonged to the earliest tradition and had been often repeated in the earliest Christian preaching. "At the height of his agony he did not cease to call God his God" (Wollebius, *CTC* 18, *RDB*, p. 100).

The Remnant

The paradox is that the dying by which he totally identified with sinful humanity left him totally isolated from those with whom he was identified. It was a lonely death, with jeers from the soldiers, rejection from the crowd, the priestly caste pretending righteousness, and the political order washing its hands. Even a thief hanging near him gave him a hard time. This is what it meant in part to be "forsaken"—to be the remnant of Israel. But was he forsaken by the Father, as the verse seems to imply?

His Humanity Revealed

Ambrose viewed the cry as a prototypical moment of God's assumption of the flesh of humanity and identification with the sin of humanity, in this case verbal sin: "According to the flesh, He was forsaken, who according to divinity could have been neither deserted nor forsaken. . . . These words ['Why hast thou forsaken me'] are said according to the flesh, which are very foreign to the fullness of His divinity, for the words of sins are foreign to God, since the sins of words are also foreign to Him; but since I [Christ] have assumed the sins of others, I have assumed also the words of others' sins, so that I say that I, who am always with God, have been forsaken by God the Father" (Ambrose, *Incarn. of Our Lord* 5.38, FC 44, p. 233; cf. Moltmann, *The Experiment Hope*, pp. 69–84).

He Learned Obedience

Some writers argued that his abandonment was a part of his learning obedience. Maximos the Confessor wrote that it is only when God apparently abandons us that he saves us, as in Jesus' death and in the testing of Job and Jacob. Abandonment "made Job a pillar of courage and Joseph a pillar of self-restraint" (*Four Hundred Texts on Love, Philokal.* II, p. 112).

Not a Final Abandonment by the Father

His cry from the cross did not imply a literal abandonment of the Son by the Father. It is not "as if, when Jesus was fixed upon the wood of the cross, the Omnipotence of the Father's Deity had gone away from Him; seeing that God's and Man's Nature were so completely joined in Him that the union could not be destroyed by punishment nor by death" (Leo, *Serm.* 68.1, NPNF 2 XII, p. 180). "It was not he who was forsaken either by the Father or by his own Godhead," wrote Gregory Nazianzen. "But, as I said, he was in his own person representing us. For we were the forsaken and despised before" but now by his representative act saved (*Orat.* XXX.5, LCC III, p. 180).

That the Scriptures Might Be Fulfilled

The psalm quoted (22:1) is a messianic reference. It helped the readers of Matthew and Mark—who were well acquainted with the messianic aspect of the Psalms—make the crucial connection: Jesus is the Expected One of Israel. The same psalm also includes reference to the messianic Son's hands and feet being pierced: "They have pierced my hands and my feet. I can count all my bones; people stare and gloat over me. They divide my garments among them and cast lots for my clothing" (Ps. 22:16-18).

Empathic Comfort for Suffering Believers

Calvin urged against a diluted explanation: "Christ was so cast down as to be compelled to cry out in deep anguish: 'My God, my God, why hast thou forsaken me?' Now some would have it that he was expressing the opinion of others rather than his own feeling. This is not at all probable, for his words clearly were drawn forth from anguish deep within his heart." Yet this was not "a despair contrary to faith," for "all that he voluntarily suffered for us does not in the least detract from his power." Rather "this Mediator has experienced our weaknesses the better to succor us in our miseries" (Calvin, *Inst.* 2.16.11-12).

In the light of this cry, no believer is in a position to say that one's own hour of darkness is darker than that of God the Son. In whatever anguish, the believer can recall that he or she is crying out in companionship with One who also experienced abandonment and who continued nonetheless to pray to the Father.

Temptation Faced and Overcome

The meaning Irenaeus attributed to this cry is cast in the form of a dialogue of the Son with the Father: "Why dost thou present me with such a horrible face and aspect of Thy wrath and indignation, as though that moment Thou were about to desert me or such as is wont to belong to one who would desert? Hence they are words of struggle and temptation, not the words of a desperate spirit; so also the voice of faith rings at the same time in this utterance, while he called God his God and perseveres in prayer" (*Ag. Her.* I.8.1, *ANF* I, p. 327; Heppe, *RD*, p. 465).

Sonship Uninterrupted Through Struggle and Temptation: My God

Although on the cross Jesus was struggling with the temptation to despair, he did not succumb. He overcame the temptation by trust in the enabling power of God the Spirit. The evidence for this is that even at the height of his agonies he did not cease to call the Father "*my* God." His

suffering was mitigated by his uninterupted sonship to the Father, affirming even then "*my* God" (Wollebius, *CTC* 18, *RDB*, p. 100; Calvin, *Inst.*
2.16.12).

No matter how many commentaries we may read, it is impossible for
us to know—sitting in an armchair—how forsaken he was and what that
meant. However deep it was, it was God-incarnate who was experiencing
that forsakenness.

> Upon the cross of Jesus
>   Mine eyes at times can see
> The very dying form of One
>   Who suffered there for me;
> And from my smitten heart with tears
>   These wonders I confess:
> The wonders of redeeming love,
>   And my own worthlessness . . .
> Content to let the world go by,
>   To know no gain nor loss,
> My sinful self my only shame,
>   My glory all the cross
>   (Elizabeth C. Clephane,
> "Beneath the Cross of Jesus," *HPEC*, p. 150).

His Death

A Real Death

Jesus died in six hours. The spear in his side was a test to see if he was
dead. The water mingling with Jesus' blood was a "Sign to all attesting
eyes, of the finished sacrifice" (Venantius Fortunatus, paraphrased by
Richard Mant, *HPEC*, p. 131; on the miracle of blood and water from his
side, see Newman, *Mir.*, pp. 356–58; cf. Innocent III, Letter to the arch-
bishop of Lyons [1202], *SCD* 416f., p. 164; Clement V, Errors of Olivi, *SCD*
480, pp. 189–91).

His death, like the death of any human being, required and involved
the dissolution of the natural union between his soul and body. It did
not, however, imply the dissolution of the union between the divine
nature and the human nature that were united in him (Tho. Aq., *ST* III
Q50–51, II, pp. 2293–99). "Thou, of life the Author, death didst undergo"
(Venantius Fortunatus, *HPEC*, p. 156; *Faith of Damascus*, *SCD* 16, p. 10; see
also *SCD* 3–40, 42, 286, 344, 422).

Without Death Not Fully Human

Early critics of Christianity complained that Christ "ought never to have experienced death." Gregory of Nyssa ingeniously observed a deeper logic of divine empathy, that "the birth makes the death necessary. He who had once decided to share our humanity had to experience all that belongs to our nature, how human life is encompassed within two limits, and if he had passed through one and not touched the other, he would only have half fulfilled his purpose, having failed to reach the other limit proper to our nature" (*ARI* 32, *LCC* III, pp. 309–10).

His Death a Victory

His death is portrayed in the Gospels as a struggle with the demonic powers, not simply with physical suffering or social rejection. Hence his death, as wretched as it was, was at the same time viewed as an incomparable victory, not simply over suffering, but through suffering over evil (*Doc. Vat. II*, pp. 15–17). By means of his death the ruler of this world was being "driven out" (John 12:31) and "now stands condemned" (John 16:11).

Isaac Watts wrote in 1707:

> When I survey the wondrous cross
>   On which the Prince of glory died,
> My richest gain I count but loss,
>   And pour contempt on all my pride.
> Forbid it, Lord, that I should boast,
>   Save in the cross of Christ, my God:
> All the vain things that charm me most,
>   I sacrifice them to his blood.
> See, from his head, his hands, his feet
>   Sorrow and love flow mingled down!
> Did e'er such love and sorrow meet?
>   Or thorns compose so rich a crown?
> Were the whole realm of nature mine,
>   That were an offering far too small;
> Love so amazing, so divine,
>   Demands my soul, my life, my all
>   (*HPEC*, pp. 136–37).

It Is Finished

His life had come to an end, but moreso, the purpose and mission for which he had come had been completed and the prophecy looking toward him had been fulfilled (Ursinus, *CHC*, pp. 220–22). "By the departing word 'It is finished,' Christ indicates that all scripture is fulfilled. He says in effect: World and devil have done as much to Me as they were able to do, and I have suffered as much as was necessary for the salvation of men . . . and no one need argue that something still remains to be fulfilled" (Luther, *Serm. on John 19:30, WLS* I, p. 195; *WA* 28, 406).

His saving work was complete. The ransom for sin had been paid. The penalty for sin had been endured. The full fury of human hostility toward God had been spent. The divine-human enmity was at end. Redemption was sufficiently and perfectly accomplished.

> Mark the miracle of time,
> God's own sacrifice complete;
> "It is finished!" hear him cry;
> Learn of Jesus Christ to die
> (James Montgomery,
> "Go to Dark Gethsemane,"
> *HPEC,* p. 135).

His death was compared in the Letter to Hebrews with a sacrificial offering made by the high priest: "But when this priest had offered for all time one sacrifice for sins, he sat down at the right hand of God. Since that time he waits for his enemies to be made his footstool because by one sacrifice he has made perfect forever those who are being made holy" (Heb. 10:12–13; Council of Trent, *SCD* 938, p. 288; *SCD* 951, p. 292).

Preaching in A.D. 350 near the place where Jesus died in Jerusalem, with all the residual memories of these holy sites Cyril said: "This Golgotha, sacred above all such places, bears witness by its very look. The most holy Sepulchre bears witness, and the stone that lies there to this day. The sun now shining bears witness, that failed, then, during the hour of his saving passion. Darkness bears witness, that lasted then from the sixth to the ninth hour, and the light that shined forth again from the ninth hour till evening" (Cyril of Jerusalem, *Catech. Lect.* X.19, *LCC* IV, p. 139).

Darkness spread over the country at the hour of his death. "When the sun saw its master being dishonoured, it shuddered and ceased to shine" (Cyril of Jerusalem, *Catech. Lect.* IV.10, *LCC* IV, p. 105). The curtain of the Temple that veils the Holy of Holies was torn asunder (Mark 15:38). It was there that the high priest had offered expiatory sacrifice on the Day of Atonement.

No testimony to the finished work excels that of Gregory the Theologian: "Many indeed are the miracles of that time: God crucified; the sun darkened and again rekindled . . . the veil rent; the Blood and Water shed from His Side; the one as from a man, the other as above man; the rocks rent for the Rock's sake; the dead raised for a pledge of the final Resurrection of all men; the Signs at the Sepulchre and after the Sepulchre, which none can worthily celebrate; and yet none of these equal to the Miracle of my salvation. A few drops of Blood recreate the whole world, and become to all men what rennet is to milk, drawing us together and compressing us into unity" (Gregory Nazianzen, *Orat.* XLV.29, *NPNF* 2 VII, p. 433)!

Over a millennium passed before Luther's echo could be heard: "The Person is eternal and infinite, and even one little drop of His blood would have been enough to save the entire world" (Luther, *Comm. on Isa. 53:5*, *WLS* I, p. 196; *WA* 40, III, 717).

> Let me hew thee, Lord, a shrine
> In this rocky heart of mine. . . .
> Myrrh and spices will I bring,
> True affection's offering;
> Close the door from sight and sound
> Of the busy world around;
> And in patient watch remain
> Till my Lord appear again
> (Thomas Whytehead,
> "Resting from His Work Today,"
> *HPEC*, p. 152).

Buried

Why "Buried"?

It is not a minor point that the creed insists that Christ was buried (*sepultus est*; Gk. *taphenta*, Creed of 150 Fathers, *COC* II, p. 58; Ancient Western Form of the Apostolic Creed, *SCD* 2–4, pp. 4–5; see also *SCD* 20, 86, 255, 344; Bonaventure, *Tree of Life*, *CSW*, pp. 157–58).

The *Heidelberg Catechism* asks: "Why was he 'buried'?" and answers plainly: "To confirm the fact that he was really dead" (Q 41, *BOConf.* 4.041; Ursinus, *CHC*, p. 225).

It was fitting that Christ was buried. Christ willed the solitude of the grave, wrote Thomas, in order that he might experience full solidarity with the human condition, that we might know the completeness of his engagement in the human condition, and offer us the hope of one day rising through and with him (Tho. Aq., *ST* III Q51, II, pp. 2298–2301; cf. Pearson, *EC* I, pp. 372–74). "He was buried that he might witness that our sins were buried" (Wollebius, *CTC* 18, *RDB*, p. 103)!

"Behold, He who holds all creation in His hand, is held within the tomb. The Lord who covered the heavens with beauty is covered with a stone" ("Hymn for Good Friday," quoted in Lossky, *MTEC*, p. 150). The repose of God in the tomb reminded the patristic teachers of the resting of God on the first Sabbath. As God the Father rested on the seventh day of creation, Jesus the Son rested from all his works on the Sabbath day, Holy Saturday, the seventh day, the day of God's own rest, the day blessed by God.

Did His Body See Corruption?

The ancient writers held to this precise distinction: the Lord's body experienced genuine death and destruction (*phthora*) in the sense of death as separation of soul from body, but not corruption (*diaphthora*) in the lengthy or extensive sense of the "dissolution of the body and its reduction to the elements of which it was composed" (John of Damascus, *OF*, III.28, *FC* 37, p. 333; Acts 2:27). This was in order to fulfill prophecy (Ps. 15:10) and make way for the ensuing stages of the history of salvation.

Believers' Experiential Participation in His Death

There is a sense in which the faithful now experience themselves as presently entombed with Christ—spiritually dead to sin, buried with him, gone from the world, hidden in him, totally unresponsive to sin (Maximos, *Four Hundred Texts, Philokal.* II, pp. 126–27). "For you died, and your life is now hidden with Christ in God. When Christ, who is your life, appears, then you also will appear with him in glory" (Col. 3:4; Hugh of St. Victor, *OSCF* I.8, pp. 146–47).

Baptized with Him in Death

Baptism means just this: dead to sin, buried with Christ, and raised with him to new life. "We were therefore buried with him through baptism into death in order that, just as Christ was raised from the dead through the glory of the Father, we too may live a new life. If we have been united with him in his death, we will certainly also be united with him in his resurrection. For we know that our old self was crucified with him so that the body of sin might be rendered powerless, that we should no longer be slaves to sin—because anyone who has died has been freed from sin" (Rom. 6:4–7; cf. Koyama, *WT*, pp. 209–24).

> Baptized into thy death we died,
>   And buried were with thee,
> That we might live with thee to God,
>   And ever blest might be
> (Christopher Wordsworth, "The Grave Itself a Garden Is," *HPEC*, p. 152).

Did God Suffer and Die?

The Early Emergence of the Question of the Death of God

Even in early centuries the opponents of Christianity were saying: "If Christ is God, and Christ died, then God died" and "if God cannot die and Christ is said to have died, Christ cannot be God because God cannot be understood to have died." Novatian answered that "what is God in Christ did not die, but what is Man in Him did die" (*Trin.* 25, FC 67, pp. 88–89). It was the incarnate Son and not the Father who suffered death upon the cross and became a true sacrifice (Clement of Rome, SCD 42, p. 20; Council of Ephesus, SCD 122, p. 50). Such a formulation was possible only on the basis of two familiar premises: a theandric Christology and a triune Godhead.

How the Theandric Premise Impinges on the Issue

The Son "died according to the assumption of our nature, and did not die according to the substance of eternal life. . . . He himself, by a kind of new operation, though dead, opened the tombs of the dead, and indeed his body lay in the tomb, yet He himself was free among the dead" (Ambrose, *Incarn. of Our Lord* 5.37, FC 44, pp. 232–35).

It is Christ's human nature that died, for the divine nature cannot die. The classical exegetes carefully ascribed the Passion to the human nature, but the efficacy of the Passion to the divine. It was not the Godhead but the Son who suffered in the humanity that was united with divinity in Jesus Christ (*BOC*, pp. 598–600). "He it was Who suffered and yet suffered not. Suffered, because His own Body suffered, and He was in it, which thus suffered; suffered not, because the Word, being by nature God, is impassible" (Athanasius, *Letter to Epictetus*, chap. 6, NPNF 2 IV, p. 572).

How the Triune Premise Impinges on the Issue

It was only on the triune premise that classic Christian scholars could find an exegetically sound approach: "Christ, while being two natures, suffered in His passible nature and in it was crucified, for it was in the flesh that He hung on the cross, and not in the divinity. Should they say, while inquiring of us: Did two natures die? We shall reply: No, indeed. Therefore, two natures were not crucified either, but the Christ was begotten, that is to say, the Divine Word was incarnate and begotten in the flesh, and He was crucified in the flesh, suffered in the flesh, and died in the flesh, while His divinity remained unaffected" (John of Damascus, OF IV.8, FC 37, p. 342).

Leo explained: "As was fitting to heal our wounds, one and the same 'mediator between God and men, the man Christ Jesus' (1 Tim. 2:5) could die in one nature and not in the other. The true God, therefore, was born with the complete and perfect nature of a true man; he is complete in his nature and complete in ours" (Leo I, *Letter to Flavian*, 13 June A.D. 449, *CF*, p. 152).

The Death of God?

Luther did not back away from the careful use of the phrase "the death of God"–rightly understood: "For God in His own nature cannot die; but now, since God and man are united in one Person, the death of the man with whom God is one Thing or Person is justly called the death of God" (Luther, *On the Councils and Churches*, 1539, WLS I, p. 198; cf. WML V, p. 223). "For though suffering, dying, rising are attributes of the human nature alone, yet since Christ is the Son both of God and of Mary in one indivisible Person with two distinct natures, we correctly say of the entire Person: God is crucified for us, God shed His blood for us; God died for us and rose from the dead, not God apart from manhood but the God who has united Himself into one Person with human nature" (Luther, *Serm. on Col. 1:18–20*, WLS I, p. 193; WA 45, 299, Roerer's notes; Ursinus, *CHC*, pp. 214–16).

Cross as Curse, Altar as Reversal

The Wood of Cross and Altar

The wood or tree became a rich metaphor encompassing both cross and altar: "He himself bore our sins in his body on the tree, so that we might die to sins and live for righteousness; by his wounds you have been healed" (1 Pet. 2:24).

The reversal of images is startling: the wood of the cross became the wood of the altar. Note the terrible irony: the cross was to this incomparable high priest his very altar. On this wood he was slain, and from it he was raised again (Heb. 11:19; Pope, *Compend.* II, p. 162), hence "we have an altar" distinguishable from that of the Levitical priesthood (Heb. 13:10). "The cross was the altar on which He, consumed by the fire of the boundless love which burned in His heart, presented the living and holy sacrifice of His body and blood to the Father" (Luther, *Eight Serm. on Psalm 110*, WLS I, p. 190; WA 41, 190f.).

Outside the Gate

Another stunning extension and reversal of the altar image is seen in

Hebrews 13: "The high priest carries the blood of animals into the Most Holy Place as a sin offering, but the bodies are burned outside the camp. And so Jesus also *suffered outside the city gate* to make the people holy through his own blood. Let us, then, go to him outside the camp, bearing the disgrace he bore. For here we do not have an enduring city, but we are looking for the city that is to come" (vv. 11–14, italics added). This act of sacrifice took place by identification with sinners in a lowly place—not where animals were sacrificed (in the Temple) but where the refuse of sacrifice was burned (outside the gate).

The Fellowship of Suffering

In this way the wood of the cross became not only the altar of sacrificial offering but also the throne of the emerging spiritual kingdom. The cross does not stand at a distance from the Christian life, but rather we are called to enter into "the fellowship of sharing in his sufferings, becoming like him in his death, and so, somehow, to attain to the resurrection from the dead" (Phil. 3:10–11; cf. Koyama, *WT,* pp. 115–29).

This interpretation of his death is riddled with irony: he who knew no sin was made sin "that in him we might become the righteousness of God" (2 Cor. 5:21). "Hence faith apprehends an acquittal in the condemnation of Christ, a blessing in his curse" whose "blood served, not only as a satisfaction, but also as a laver to wash away our corruption" (Calvin, *Inst.*, 2.16.6).

The poignant harmonies of Bach have set this tune in the heads of worshipers since the seventeenth century:

> O sacred Head, now wounded,
> With grief and shame weighed down,
> Now scornfully surrounded
> With thorns, Thine only crown;
> How pale Thou art with anguish,
> With sore abuse and scorn!
> How does that visage languish,
> Which once was bright as morn!
>
> What Thou, my Lord, hast suffered
> Was all for sinners' gain:
> Mine, mine was the transgression,
> But Thine the deadly pain.
> Lo, here I fall, my Saviour!
> 'Tis I deserve Thy place;
> Look on me with Thy favor,
> Vouchsafe me to Thy grace.

What language shall I borrow
To thank Thee, dearest Friend,
For this Thy dying sorrow,
Thy pity without end?
O make me Thine for ever;
And should I fainting be,
Lord, let me never, never
Outlive my love to Thee"

(patterned after Bernard of Clairvaux,
translated by Paul Gerhardt
into German and by
James W. Alexander into English,
MH 1939, #141; cf. *HPEC*, pp. 139–40).

The Scorn Reversed

The cross is at the same time a curse suffered by Jesus and a redemption from the curse we feel when we try to save ourselves under the ever-extending demands of the law. "Christ redeemed us from the curse of the law by becoming a curse for us, for it is written: 'Cursed is everyone who is hung on a tree'" (Gal. 3:13, quoting Deut. 21:23; cf. Rom. 8:3–4).

Hence we may "fix our eyes on Jesus" who "for the joy set before him endured the cross, scorning its shame, and sat down at the right hand of the throne of God" (Heb. 12:2). He took away the curse of the law, "nailing it to the cross. And having disarmed the powers and authorities, he made a public spectacle of them, triumphing over them by the cross" (Col. 2:14–15).

CHAPTER 11

In Our Place

The cross had to be carried and endured before it could be preached. Jesus came to become the sacrifice, not clarify the concept of sacrifice.

He did not come to teach about the cross, but to be nailed to it. He came that there might be a gospel to preach.

HOLINESS AND LOVE INCOMPARABLY JOINED

Sin dug a gulf in a relationship. The cross bridged it. Sin resulted in estrangement. The cross reconciled it. Sin made war. The cross made peace. Sin broke fellowship. The cross repaired and restored it.

A Death, Not a Concept

Death Is Not a Mode of Consciousness

The cross encounters us as an awful, actual, historical event, not an inward mode of consciousness. Death means total unresponsiveness.

Atonement is best viewed not as a conceptual problem of human speculation, but an actual event in the history of divine-human covenant. The Christian teaching of atonement is not just about the idea of dying, but about a real sacrificial death. Though his death addresses our consciousness, it cannot be reduced to the contents of consciousness. It was an event. It happened to a man from Nazareth on a particular hill on a particular day (Augustine, *Harmony of the Gospels* III.14–23, *NPNF* 1 VI, pp. 203–209).

Its Meaning

The significance of that death is not merely an expression of human hatred, avarice, pride, or of Jesus' moral courage. It accomplished an incomparable work of divine mercy for humanity and does so today even when humanity fails to respond to it.

Christianity proclaims not merely that Christ died, but that his death had significance for the otherwise apparently absurd course of human history. The Christian teaching of the cross asks what his death meant, what effect it had, how it worked for us and our salvation (Hugh of St. Victor, *OSCF,* pp. 146–47). This is the subject of atonement.

The Cross as a Unique Subject of Study

The word the cross speaks is not a word we say to ourselves. It is a word that God speaks to us through an inescapably concrete, irreversible, disturbing event.

The heart of its meaning is confessed in the creed: he died *for us* (*pro nobis, huper hemon*; Creed of 150 Fathers, *COC* II, p. 58). "He died" is a fact. "For us" is the meaning of that fact.

Reviewing Our Trajectory

The teaching of salvation began by inquiring into the unique identity of the Savior. That identity could not be adequately clarified without setting forth certain major events of his earthly ministry, all of which foreshadowed his last days and finally came to focus intensely upon the events surrounding his death.

While the inquiry into the *person* of Christ focused primarily upon the personal union of deity and humanity, the study of the *work* of Christ focuses upon what this incomparable person *did*: he served as a ransom for the sins of humanity to fulfill the compassionate will of the Father.

Soteria *Requires a* Soter

The pivotal principle that joins and correlates the study of Christ is this: *what the work of salvation required, the person of the Mediator supplied.* This unique work can only be done by this unique person. This salvation can only be accomplished by this Savior—not just anyone dying on any cross.

This principle, which holds together the varied parts of this diverse study, becomes especially important in pointing to the meaning of the cross, for in speaking of salvation as the work of Christ, we do not now leave behind or turn aside from the person. Rather we ask what the Savior (*soter*) did to merit salvation (*soteria*). The salvation question cannot be answered without asking what actually happened on the cross and why.

The Mystery of the Cross

Ancient Christian writers repeatedly warned that the work of Christ on the cross, like the incarnation, is an ever-unfolding mystery. Many questions lie outside the range not only of objective historical knowledge and speculative philosophy, but also of revealed truth. Finally it is more crucial to know *that* we are saved by the cross than precisely *how.* Yet we must ask how and why, to whatever degree it is possible to understand (Ambrose, *Of Christian Faith* II.11, *NPNF* 1 X, pp. 235–37)—questions pressed in this chapter.

The Right Ordering of Atonement Teaching

We should not expect the New Testament to supply us with a single preferred theory or view of atonement. Yet one cannot read the crucifixion narratives or apostolic Letters without pondering what this death means for humanity (F. W. Dillistone, *Christian Understanding of Atonement*). Systematic reflection must take care not to impose on the sacred texts structures foreign to them. We search for self-clarifying interpretations implicitly embedded in or explicitly stated by the texts (Stevens, *TNT,* pp. 122–32; Clarke, *OCT,* pp. 321–62; Hodge, *OOT,* pp. 401–25; Hodge, *Syst. Theol.* II, pp. 480–560).

Some sequence of argument is necessary if Christian teaching is to be cohesive, yet no particular way of organizing Christian teaching of the cross is explicated in the New Testament itself. The following sequence seeks to set forth a centrist classic Christian consensus on the meaning of Jesus' death.

The Crossroad of Christian Reflection

No Cross, No Christianity

To preach is to announce the cross. To worship is to come to the cross. To believe is to trust in the One crucified.

It is impossible to imagine Christianity without a cross. Christian worship is spatially ordered around it. The history of Western art and architecture holds the cross before us constantly. In death the graves of Christians are marked by a cross.

The Metaphorical Generativity of the Cross

Diverse metaphors strain to reflect the actual reality of the cross, as set forth by John of Damascus:

death has been brought low,
the sin of our first parent destroyed,
hell plundered,
resurrection bestowed,
the power given us to despise the things of this world and even death itself,
the road back to the former blessedness made smooth,
the gates of paradise opened,
our nature seated at the right hand of God,
and we made children and heirs of God.
By the cross all things have been set aright. . . .
It is a raising up for those who lie fallen,
a support for those who stand,
a staff for the infirm,
a crook for the shepherded,
a guide for the wandering,
a perfecting of the advanced,
salvation for soul and body,
an averter of all evils,
a cause of all good things,
a destruction of sin,
a plant of resurrection,
and a tree of eternal life

                    (John of Damascus, *OF* IV.11, *FC* 37, p. 350, spacing added).

How do such diverse metaphorical functions cohere? The point of cohesion is reconciliation. Only at this nexus are all things reconciled.

The Crimson Thread of Scripture

Although "atonement" is a word that occurs only once in the New Testament (Rom. 5:11, KJV; "reconciliation," NIV), the reconciliation of God and humanity is among the most basic themes of Scripture. Clement of Rome viewed sacrificial redemption culminating in the blood of Christ as the scarlet thread of the house of Rahab running throughout the Scripture (*First Letter* 12, *LCC* I, p. 49; cf. secs. 7, 21, 49). So central is this theme that it is no exaggeration to say that the events surrounding the cross constitute the central interest of New Testament proclamation (F. Turretin, *On the Atonement of Christ*; Berkouwer, *The Work of Christ*; Moltmann, *The Crucified God*).

The Atoning Death: Preliminary Considerations

The Procuring Cause of Salvation

The pivotal proposition of atonement teaching is that the death of

Christ is the procuring, enabling cause of salvation. Christ's death makes our salvation possible.

At the heart of the divine-human reconciliation is Christ's death (Rom. 5:10; Phil. 2:8; Heb. 2:9–14), which means the cross (Eph. 2:16; Col. 1:20), which means the giving of the lifeblood of Christ (Matt. 26:28; Mark 14:24; Eph. 1:7; 2:13; Col. 1:14; Heb. 9:12, 15; 1 John 1:7). Christ's atoning work is grounded in the Father's love (John 3:16). It manifests God's righteousness (Rom. 3:25; 2 Cor. 5:21). It forms the basis of our reconciliation with God and neighbor (Rom. 5:11; 2 Cor. 5:18–19; Lactantius, *Div. Inst.*, FC 49, pp. 309–15).

The Cross Overcame Sin

"For God was pleased to have all his fullness dwell in him, and through him to reconcile to himself all things, whether things on earth or things in heaven, by making peace through his blood, shed on the cross" (Col. 1:19–20). On this basis it is possible to speak summarily of the whole work of Christ simply as a "ministry of reconciliation" (2 Cor. 5:18) or peacemaking (Rom. 10:15; Eph. 2:14–17; Clare of Assisi, *Letter to Ermentrude*, CWS, pp. 107–108; Deotis Roberts, *Liberation and Reconciliation: A Black Theology*).

The Divine Plan Leads to the Cross

The cross occurred by divine ordering and foreknowing. According to the eternal wisdom of God's *oikonomia* (arrangement or plan), which the Father had ordained, God the Son would come to save humanity from sin by means of his sacrificial death, without ceasing to remain at one with the Father (Pearson, *EC* I, pp. 612–13).

Anglican Francis Hall tautly summarized the far-reaching plan of salvation: "The eternal Son of God took what is ours into personal union with what was His, and completed His human equipment as our Redeemer by a life of painful and exemplary obedience to the Father's will. Thus equipped, He redeemed mankind by His death and resurrection, and was thereby consecrated for a heavenly priesthood, in which He has become the Author of salvation. This salvation is accomplished through His mystical body, to which His Holy Spirit has imparted life, and in which He operates so as to enable men to work out their salvation" (*DT* VII, pp. 112–13).

The triune God arranged this great plan or *oikonomia* for our restoration through which the Father would be rightly propitiated or brought near to the sinner; the Son would be himself the means of this propitiation or bringing near; and the Holy Spirit would enkindle the heart to receive this good news (Leo, *Serm.* 77.2, *NPNF* 2 XII, p. 184). Lacking the cross, the pivotal episode of the entire economy would be missing.

The Cross Uniquely Joins Holiness and Love

The gist of atonement teaching is this: *Christ suffered in our place to satisfy the radical requirement of the holiness of God, so as to remove the obstacle to the pardon and reconciliation of the guilty. What the holiness of God required, the love of God provided in the cross.*

Atonement teaching lives out of rigorous assumptions about the relation of the holiness and love of God. Its basic premises follow.

The Holiness and Love of God Are Intrinsically Related by Being Personally Embodied

God is holy. God's holiness constrains, orders, and conditions God's love. God's love infuses, empowers, constrains, and complements God's holiness.

God would not be as holy as God is without being incomparably loving. God would not be as loving as God is without being incomparably holy. God's holiness without God's love would be unbearable. God's love without God's holiness would be unjust. God's wisdom found a way to bring them congruently together. It involved a cross (Watson, *TI* II, chaps. 19, 20, 25; Miley, *Syst. Theol.* II, pp. 65–239; Summers, *Syst. Theol.* I, pp. 215–98; N. Burwash, *Manual of Christian Theology* II, pp. 147–90; Raymond, *Syst. Theol.* II, pp. 219–307; Ralston, *ED*, pp. 193–312; S. Wakefield, *Christian Theology*, pp. 343–86).

The Resistance of Holiness to Evil

The holy God rigorously opposes moral evil. Conscience is given universally to humanity to attest to the "ought" in all that is. Conscience witnesses within us, however imperfectly, of God's own revulsion at moral evil (1 Cor. 10:25–29; 2 Cor. 1:12).

God has created a universe governed by moral law in which (socially and interpersonally conceived) the consequences of sin are guilt, loss, pain, and death, and the consequences of righteousness are freedom, happiness, well-being, and life. Sin tends inexorably to result in suffering (though often indirectly, intergenerationally, and lacking full awareness of its causes). Righteousness tends in the long run toward happiness. Human happiness consists in refracting God's holy love within the limits of human finitude (Tho. Aq., *ST* I Q26, I, pp. 142ff.; Wesley, *WJW* VI, pp. 431ff., 443ff.). This refraction has become radically distorted by the history of sin (Gustavo Gutiérrez, *A Theology of Liberation*, pp. 265–76).

The Radical Seriousness of Sin

The just God does not casually say at one moment to humanity: "when you eat of it you will surely die" (Gen. 2:17), only at the next moment to set aside the penalty after the transgression. *The holiness of God required a penalty for sin*, just as promised, otherwise there would be no way to count on the moral reliability of God's word. Lacking penalty for sin, the moral order is jeopardized. There is no approach to the mystery of the cross without this premise (Pope, *Compend.* II, pp. 253–316).

The Gospel Breaks Through the Impasse

The good news is that God through Christ has done what the law could not do: sent his Son as an offering for sin. Christ expiated sin by his own sacrificial death. The Lord laid upon him the iniquity of us all (Isa. 53:6). This is the life-giving way that the incomparably wise, holy and loving God chose to deal with the death-laden estrangement caused by sin (Tho. Aq., *ST* III Q46–51, II, pp. 2264–99).

How God's Incomparable Love Answered the Requirement of God's Incomparable Holiness in a Sinful World

God's holiness made a penalty for sin necessary. God's love endured that penalty for the transgressor and made payment of the penalty possible. It is God's holiness that manifests God's love on the cross. It is God's love that sustains and embodies God's holiness on the cross. There the holiness of the love of God is once for all clarified, and the love of the holy God is fully embodied.

By this holy love of God, sin has been atoned. It is only in the cross that Christianity finds the complete and sufficient manifestation of God's holiness that opposes sin and God's love that provides a ransom for the history of sin (Baxter, *PW* XV, pp. 218–19; Aulen, *The Faith of the Christian Church* [1960], pp. 102–30).

Love Faces Sin

Eternal love has not sought to evade the claims of righteousness but has creatively expressed them. Divine love did not plead to waive the requirements of justice but took them on directly and transmuted them. "God cannot pardon sin until provision has been made for its cure, and accomplished sin cannot be cured by mere penitence and future avoidance of sin," hence the need for expiation, "imperfect as every human explanation of it is" (Hall, *DT* VII, p. 4; cf. L. Boff, *The Way of the Cross, Way of Justice*).

It is sin that creates the controversy between God and humanity. God loved humanity in such depth that God was unwilling to see human life captive to the power of sin. Love was the divine motive; holiness the divine requirement. "God demonstrates his own love for us in this: While we were still sinners, Christ died for us" (Rom. 5:8). This love was so great that God "did not spare his own Son, but gave him up for us all" (Rom. 8:32).

The Imbalance Caused by Neglect of God's Holiness or Love

Suppose a plan of salvation in which God's holiness would be stressed but God's love neglected. If God's holiness should remain unmitigated by God's love, the supposed "salvation" could easily turn into a distorted picture of God as angry tyrant who unmercifully permits the slaying of his own Son to avenge the divine honor. Anselm's view is sometimes perceived (unfairly I think) as tending in the direction of this excess. Such exaggerations are sometimes offered as a corrective to the opposite exaggeration that accentuates God's love to the neglect of God's holiness in resisting sin (Jowett, *Essays and Dissertations*, pp. 317-69).

The Costly Congruence of Holiness and Love

The diverse divine attributes are all brought into proper equilibrium in the cross. "In the love of the Triune God is found its source, in the justice of the Triune God its necessity, and in the wisdom of the Triune God its method" (Tillett, *PS*, p. 100). It is finally on the cross that "Love and faithfulness meet together; righteousness and peace kiss each other. Faithfulness springs forth from the earth, and righteousness looks down from heaven" (Ps. 85:10-11; cf. Francis of Assisi, *Letters*, *CWS*, pp. 53-57, 68-71). By the cross the seeming conflict or (to human view) potential tension between the justice and mercy of God (or between the righteousness and compassion of God) is bridged and the two are reunited. They were never divided, but the cross expressed their congruence.

Reconciling the Theories of Reconciliation

The purpose of theories of atonement is to set forth rightly the connection between the death of Christ and the salvation of humanity. All major theories attempt this. There is considerable room within the sphere of ancient ecumenical teaching for varied interpretations of key atonement texts. Our purpose is to allow the biblical references to form the key substantive points, rather than to seek to eliminate certain views. Our concern is not with opposing but with upbuilding, not polemics but peacemaking, not dissensus but consensus emerging from Scripture and the earliest traditions.

THE REVERSAL: GOD'S OWN SACRIFICE

Christianly understood, atonement is the satisfaction made for sin by the death of Christ that makes possible the salvation of humanity (Baxter, *PW* VI, pp. 511–18).

God as Actively Reconciling and Reconciled

Kaphar

The Hebrew root words associated with atonement (*kaphar, kippurim*) had nuances of "to purge, cleanse, expiate, purify, cross out, cover, spread over, or forgive." These words ordinarily denote the expiation or satisfaction made for sin by sacrificial offerings. One makes an atonement by providing a fitting expiation or satisfaction for an injury or offense.

Human Propitiatory Initiatives Saturate the History of Religions

It is often asked how Christianity relates to other world religions. It is a distinctively modern assumption that Christianity is embarrassed by the claims of other religions. The question of atonement brings us to the heart of this issue.

Much of the history of religions is intensely concerned with expiation. Ancient and modern religions alike amply demonstrate that human beings in cultures from time immemorial have been aware of their guilt. Conscience sees to that, with as much variability as persistence.

Expiatory acts sought to remove this guilt through conciliatory actions offered to God. The expiations so commonly found in the history of religions focus upon the restoration of the damaged divine-human relationship by means of propitiatory actions initiated by penitents (Cyprian, *Epist.* 51, *ANF* V, pp. 330–32).

The Reversal of Expiatory Initiative in the Cross

The New Testament runs directly contrary to this common notion of expiation, for in Christianity it is *not humans who come to God with a compensatory gift, but rather God who comes to humanity in self-giving* in order to overcome the divine-human alienation—a very different idea of expiation indeed.

It is not that human beings conciliate God, but that "God was reconciling the world to himself in Christ" (2 Cor. 5:19). God does not passively wait to be reconciled but actively goes out, inconspicuously reaches out, and humbly suffers for others to reconcile them. God does not wait for humanity to approach but approaches humanity. God does not receive our conciliatory gifts but gives unsparingly in the way of lowliness in order to offer the gift of salvation to humanity (Augustine, *CG* XXII.22, *NPNF* 1 II, pp. 499–501; Catherine of Genoa, *Purgation and Purgatory*, *CWS*, pp. 71–80).

God Sacrifices, Not Humanity

In this way the particular sacrifice of which Christianity speaks involved a remarkable once-for-all reversal. Sacrifice thereafter does not focus primarily upon our giving God what God would not have without us, but upon our becoming totally receptive to the radical divine gift, which implies a radical human task: being for others as God is for us (Maximos, *Various Texts*, *Philokal.* II, pp. 245–49). Viewed schematically:

THE REVERSAL

Preparation for the gospel	The gospel
History of religions	The reversal of religions
Humanity approaches God	God approaches humanity
Humans suffer for God	God suffers for humanity
God receives human gifts	God gives God's own self
Sinners conciliate God	God reconciles sinners
God awaits conciliation	God actively reaches out

Atoned Life as Eucharist

This is why Christian worship and ethics focus so intently upon gratitude. The beginning point is thankful acceptance of the divine gift. Worship essentially becomes *eucharistia*. Odd as it may seem and counter to ordinary human expectations, the Christian life consists in taking the risk of allowing ourselves to be endowed with gifts from God.

Ecstatic awareness of the meaning of this reversal floods the Christian life:

> In the cross of Christ I glory,
>   Towering o'er the wrecks of time;
> All the light of sacred story
>   Gathers round its head sublime.
> When the woes of life o'ertake me,
>   Hopes deceive, and fears annoy,
> Never shall the cross forsake me;
>   Lo! It glows with peace and joy. . . .

> Bane and blessing, pain and pleasure,
>   By the cross are sanctified;
> Peace is there that knows no measure,
>   Joys that through all time abide

(John Bowring, 1825, *HPEC*, p. 135).

Distinguishable Vantage Points: Righteousness, Reconciliation, and Redemption

The atoning work may be viewed from three different vantage points as a doctrine of: God's righteousness, reconciliation between God and humanity, or the redemption of humanity. That is to say, it may be approached from the viewpoint of the divine requirement, the divine-human mediation, or the resulting condition of humanity. Each constitutes a different angle of vision upon a single event: the cross.

From the first viewpoint, *righteousness*, atonement is the revelation of the uprighting justice of God—God's own surprising and radical way of making things right—through the cross. From the second perspective, *reconciliation*, the cross is a peacemaking event in the divine-human relationship. In the cross, the sin of penitent humanity no longer remains an obstacle in the divine-human relationship. From the third, *redemption*, atonement is the liberation of the imprisoned, a redemption intended for all, yet requiring faith for its reception.

The Finished Work: Reconciliation

A Finished Work

To say that the atonement is a finished work means that in the cross the saving act has decisively occurred (John 19:30). It is a work that is objectively done and complete, a once-for-all accomplished redemption. It does not require some further sacrificial work on the part of the crucified Lord. This work consists in his obedience unto death, regarded as sacrifice for the sins of others (Gregory Nazianzen, *Fourth Theol. Orat.*, *Orat.* XXX, *NPNF* 2 VII, p. 311).

Reconciliation as an Objective Event

Reconciliation is not merely an attitudinal change on the part of individuals so as to welcome God back into congenial human company. Rather the cross is the central event of salvation history that has once for all changed the divine-human relationship. In it an unmerited divine gift is actually offered, with the intent of being received. "While we were still sinners, Christ died for us"; for "when we were God's enemies, we were reconciled to him through the death of his Son" (Rom. 5:8–10).

The Reconciliation of a Broken Relationship

Individuals do not become reconciled to God on their own initiative—rather they are being reconciled by God's own initiative to which they are being called to respond.

A reconciliation is not needed if the relationship has remained undisrupted. A massive disruption has occurred with the history of sin. In this disruption it is not merely that unholy humanity can no longer find its way back to God, but more profoundly that the Holy One is offended and estranged by the disruptions and ourtrageous injustices of willed human sin.

At-one-ment as Process and Result

Atonement includes both the reconciling means and actual reconciliation as an end. It is both the means by which the sin/guilt/punishment syndrome is broken and the end result of its being broken. The means by which the sin/death syndrome is broken is Christ's atoning death and resurrection. The end result and purpose of its having been broken is reconciliation with God.

Both of these meanings inhere in the old English term "at-one-ment"—a process and a resulting action by which two conflicting parties are reconciled, or made "at-one." The resulting reconciliation occurs by the distinctive and surprising means chosen by God's holy love—the cross.

Reconciler and Reconciled

God is both offerer and actor in the reconciling event. The world is object and recipient of this reconciliation. "God was reconciling the world to himself in Christ, not counting men's sins against them" (2 Cor. 5:19).

Reconciliation (*katallagē*) is the new relation in which the world stands to God in consequence of Christ's work. Those who had been alienated (*apallotrioō*) are now reconciled (*apokatallattō*, Col. 1:21–22).

God reconciles and is reconciled. God the Son actively reaches out in an activity of reconciliation. God the Father is reconciled to the sinful world by the one Mediator, Christ (Hilary, *Trin.* VIII.15, XI.3, *NPNF* 2 IX, pp. 141, 156). On this basis "we also rejoice in God through our Lord Jesus Christ, through whom we have now received reconciliation" (Rom. 5:11).

Reconciliation is closely related to justification. Justification pronounces a word of acquittal from guilt to the offender. Reconciliation is the restoration of the justified to communion with God.

The Call for Human Responsiveness

Reconciliation to Be Subjectively Appropriated

Communion with God is not fulfilled until those beloved of God receive the reconciling event already accomplished and become reconciled to God. "We implore you on Christ's behalf: Be reconciled to God" (2 Cor. 5:21).

The reception requires a behavioral reversal. "As God's fellow workers we urge you not to receive God's grace in vain" (2 Cor. 6:1). This is not an offer for us to reconcile ourselves to God, but to receive God's reconciling act. Until that occurs through repentance and faith, the sinner remains behaviorally unreconciled to God, even though God offers it already as a gift (Augustine, *Enchiridion* 18–20, *LCC* VII, pp. 378–86; J. Denney, *The Death of Christ*, p. 85).

Indicative Requires Imperative

The divine-human reconciliation is an objective, finished act, yet at the same time an indicative that implies an imperative. It is an actual reconciliation of humanity with God and hence a call to humanity to be reconciled with God, to lay aside enmity with God, to receive the blessing of peace with God. "All this is from God" (2 Cor. 5:18).

Christ's sacrifice is misunderstood if taken in the sense that his cross requires no cross of our own. His action does not exclude, but awakens, human responsiveness. His dying places a requirement upon our living.

The Gift Calls for Reception

This gift implies a task (Leo, *Serm.* 77, *NPNF* 2 XII, pp. 184–86). Precisely how the Holy Spirit works to apply this finished gift to believers is the subject of sanctification (to be treated in the next volume of this series). At this point we are simply trying to understand what gift is to be appropriated, the fullness of its design and the right ordering of its varied aspects.

The one atonement calls for constant appropriation in faith and obedience: "As an obedience unto death it becomes ours in justification; as a sacrifice of self-surrender, it becomes ours in sanctification" (Pope, *Compend.* II, p. 267).

Three decisive points must be held in creative tension in reflecting upon Jesus' atoning death: "(1) its *necessity*, there is no salvation except through the meritorious death of Christ; (2) it is *unlimited in extent*, it avails for all sinners and for all sin; and (3) it is *conditional* in its application, it is efficacious only for the penitent and believing sinner. The universality of the atonement is of God; its limitation is of man" (Tillett, *PS*, p. 110).

Diplomatic, Legal, Familial, and Sacrificial Metaphors of Atonement

The four spheres from which metaphors for understanding salvation were largely taken are the negotiated liberation of slaves, the fair procedures of a just courtroom, the loss of a family member, and the sacrifice offered at the Temple.

The diplomatic metaphor speaks of a ransom being paid, a price of exchange made for those imprisoned and completely unable to help themselves. The legal metaphor speaks of a court of law that has imposed a penalty due to disobedience of law, yet a substitute penalty has been offered by a friend of the court. The family metaphor speaks of a generous father who is willing to give his only son for the deliverance of many. The most important sphere from which atonement metaphors were derived is the context of Temple sacrifice, referring to a priestly mediation through which God and humanity are reconciled through a sin offering for transgressors as a propitiation of violated divine holiness.

These four metaphorical spheres intensely mesh, combine, and interface in the major texts of atonement teaching. In the court of righteousness, his perfect obedience to law discharges the duty owed to the court and fully pays the debt. The imprisoned one is liberated through the suffering and death of another. In the family of God the Son is offered for the saving of the whole human family. In the holy temple the sacrificial death of the Savior readies the sinner for meeting with God.

In the court, righteousness or justice is required. In the temple, holiness is required. In the family, love is the central motif. If one is imprisoned, what one needs most is freedom (Pearson, *EC* I, pp. 274, 611–15; Pope, *Compend.* II, pp. 253–316).

Key biblical texts develop these motifs. (1) Prisoners are liberated. "You were bought at a price" (1 Cor. 6:20) through the death of one who came to "give his life as a ransom for many" (Mark 10:45). (2) The law is obeyed and fulfilled. If one asks how Christ overcame the divine-human alienation, the general answer must be: by his obedience. "For just as through the disobedience of the one man the many were made sinners, so also through the obedience of one man the many will be made righteous" (Rom. 5:19). (3) The Son was sent on a hazardous mission for others. The whole of his life is an act of filial obedience. "This is how God showed his love among us: He sent his one and only Son into the world that we might live through him" (1 John 4:10) in a mission that required his death. (4) The divine-human conflict is ameliorated by temple sacrifice. "He did not enter by means of the blood of goats and calves; but he entered the Most Holy Place once for all by his own blood, having obtained eternal redemption" (Heb. 9:12; A. Cave, *Scriptural Doctrine of Sacrifice*).

Christ is our advocate in court, by doing what the law demands and paying the penalty for us. Christ is our priest in the temple, himself serving as the sacrifice that God accepts. Christ is the son whom the father gives for all. Christ is liberator of those in bondage (*LG*, pp. 125-27).

CHRIST'S OBEDIENCE

The unitive principle of his life work is: through his voluntary work his unique personal identity is revealed. His identity is freely made known not by fiat but precisely through his acting and suffering. *What Christ did and suffered gradually becomes the revelation of who Christ is as eternal Son.*

Atonement as Active and Passive Obedience

What He Did and Suffered

The means by which Christ rendered satisfaction was twofold: his active obedience to the law and his obedient suffering unto death (*BOC*, p. 541). The theme of Christ's obedience is extensively treated in the New Testament. This massive theme is often analyzed in terms of his *active* obedience by which he fulfilled and obeyed the law through his life, and his *passive* obedience by which he passively endured suffering unto death (Calvin, *Inst.* 2.16; Ursinus, *CHC*, pp. 212-19).

Christ's obedience countermands and amends Adam and Eve's disobedience. "For just as through the disobedience of the one man the many were made sinners, so also through the obedience of the one man the many will be made righteous" (Rom. 5:19). It is a single obedience, with active and passive aspects, by which "we have been both set free from punishment because he bore punishment for us, and given the privilege [*ius*] of eternal life, because he fulfilled the law for us" (Wollebius, *CTC* 18, *RDB*, p. 99).

Under Law and Under Its Penalty

Luther summarized: "In a twofold manner Christ put Himself under the Law. First, He put Himself under the works of the Law. He had Himself circumcised, presented, and purified in the temple. He became subject to father and mother, and the like; yet He was not obliged to do this, for He was Lord of all laws. But He did so willingly, not fearing or seeking anything for Himself in it. . . . In the second place, He also put himself under the penalty and punishment of the Law willingly" (Luther, *Serm. on Gal. 4:1-7*, WLS I, p. 189; *WA* 10 I, 1, 365f.).

In Life and in Death

The meritorious action of Christ on our behalf began with his incarnation and ended with his death, after which he makes intercession for us based upon the meritorious action complete at his death. His death finally and sufficiently merited for us our forgiveness.

"His obedience, not only in suffering and dying, but also that he in our stead was voluntarily subject to the Law, and fulfilled it by His obedience, is imputed [i.e., reckoned vicariously] to us for righteousness, so that, on account of this complete obedience, which, by deed and by suffering, in life and in death, He rendered His heavenly Father for us, God forgives our sins, regards us godly and righteous, and eternally saves us" (Formula of Concord, *Sol. Dec.* III, 14; Schmid, *DT,* p. 354; Jacobs, *SCF,* p. 173).

His obedience included not only his death, but also the fact that he endured obediently and voluntarily all the limiting conditions imposed upon him from the beginning of his incarnate life: he was born in poverty, faced hunger and thirst, was subject to parents, and so on (Calvin, *Inst.* 2.16.5). Hence his obedience is said to have begun from the moment of his birth and continued to his crucifixion, yet it is focused especially in his death and the yielding up of his spirit to God.

Viewed schematically, Christ's substitutionary act involved a twofold obedience:

ACTIVE	PASSIVE
a vicarious obedience for righteousness fulfilling the righteousness required of humanity	a vicarious punishment for sin enduring the punishment deserved by humanity

Active Obedience (His Life)

He Fulfilled the Law

By his active obedience, Christ enacted and embodied the untainted righteousness required for eternal life. Active obedience is Christ's complete compliance with and fulfillment of the law (moral, ceremonial, and forensic).

He was "born under law, to redeem those under law" (Gal. 4:4; 1 Cor. 1:30). He came not "to abolish the Law or the Prophets," "but to fulfill them" (Matt. 5:17). When John the Baptist tried to deter Jesus from being baptized, Jesus said: "Let it be so now; it is proper for us to do this to fulfill all righteousness" (Matt. 3:15).

He Fulfilled the Law for Us

According to God's reckoning, the faithful are viewed as if Christ's righteousness had become theirs (Gal. 4:4–5; Rom. 5:8; 8:3; 10:4; Phil. 3:9; Matt. 5:17). He fulfilled the law for us, so that the righteousness demanded by the law and rendered by Christ might become ours through faith. On this basis, "Christ is the end of the law so that there may be righteousness for everyone who believes" (Rom. 10:4).

The holy God could not have been reconciled to sinners had not some way been found by which it could rightly be said that sinners had satisfied the requirement of the law. Christ provided this way by fulfilling the law in our place, in order that sinners who repent and appropriate to themselves by faith this vicarious fulfillment of the law might be accounted righteous before God (Hollaz, ETA, p. 737; Schmid, DT, p. 352; Menno Simons, True Christian Faith, CWMS, p. 341).

This does not imply that the law becomes irrelevant to the Christian life, for the law, being "holy, righteous, and good" (Rom. 7:12), still judges our sin, guides the steps of faith, and prevents the civil order from self-destruction (Calvin, Inst. 2.7; Wesley, WJW V, pp. 436–64).

Jesus did not become subject to the law to win reward for himself, for that he already possessed, but to provide merit vicarously for those for whom he suffered. Hence his whole life, and not merely his death, was a chain of voluntary lowly, sacrificing, expiatory actions.

Passive Obedience (His Death)

Christ's passive obedience is his bearing on the cross the full punishment for the transgressions of sinners.

He Paid the Penalty of Others

By passive obedience is meant Christ's willingness to suffer and die. He bore the guilt of others and paid their penalties. By his suffering and death, Christ removed the discord between God and humanity (Augustine, *Enchiridion* 41, *NPNF* 1 III, p. 251; Barth, *CD* II/1, pp. 33ff.). By this means he rendered a satisfaction fully sufficient for and available to all. Merit sufficient to salvation flowed from the satisfaction rendered (Anselm, *Cur Deus Homo* I.19–II.6, *LCC* X, pp. 134–51; Quenstedt, *TDP*, III, p. 225).

His passive obedience consisted primarily in his dying act of paying the penalty due to others. He took their punishment, atoning for their sins. By his obedience, Christ freed us from the curse of the law (Gal. 3:13; John 1:29; Rom. 8:32).

Obedience Learned Through Suffering

He learned obedience through what he suffered (Heb. 5:8). The thought here is more ironic than simply saying that the Christ had to suffer. Rather it was that God "should make the author of their salvation perfect through suffering" (Heb. 2:10). It was in this surprising way that the divine requirement became fulfilled. The risen Christ chided the travelers on the road to Emmaus: "How foolish you are, and how slow of heart to believe all that the prophets have spoken! Did not the Christ have to suffer these things and then enter his glory?" (Luke 24:26).

Obedience as Sacrifice

The quintessential act of atonement was Jesus' obedience unto death, the sacrifice of his life in utter, unreserved obedience. One passage in particular unites the themes of obedience and sacrifice. Commenting upon Psalm 40:6–8, the Letter to Hebrews states: "We have been made holy through the sacrifice of the body of Jesus Christ once for all" (Heb. 10:10). Henceforth the "sacrifices and offerings," though they had been required by law, are set aside because of the one who through obedience has "come to do your will" (Heb. 10:5–10). His complete obedience is the sacrifice that makes us acceptable. It does not need to be repeated, since it is "once for all."

Complementarity of Active and Passive Obedience

Through his active life he fulfilled the divine requirement; and by his suffering death he paid the penalty for others' sins. By his active obedience he provided a completely adequate fulfillment of the law, sufficient to acquire the righteousness necessary for eternal life (Calvin, *Inst.* 2.16.5). By his passive obedience he transferred penalties to himself and endured them. As his passive obedience was necessary for the expiation of sin, his active obedience was necessary for the guidance of faith toward life eternal (Baxter, *PW* XXI, pp. 337–41; VI, pp. 511–13; Wollebius, *CTC*, p. 81; Heppe, *RD*, p. 462; cf. Brandenburg-Nürnberg Articles of 1533). One without the other would be lacking, either in pardon or righteousness. "Thus he honors obedience by his action, and proves it experimentally by his Passion" (Gregory Nazianzen, *Fourth Theol. Orat.*, *Orat.* XXX.6, *LCC* III, p. 180).

The merit of his obedience imparted to the believer is, negatively, an absolution from guilt and, positively, an imparting of the Holy Spirit who gives life. Hence these two modes of obedience must be held closely together—"What He did for us, what He suffered on account of us" (Augustine, *The Creed* 3.6, *FC* 27, p. 294).

THE CROSS AS SACRIFICE

The death of Christ was a true sacrifice. The sacrifices of the Old Testament formed an anticipatory type of the self-offering Christ was to make. John the Baptist said of Jesus: "Look, the Lamb of God, who takes away the sin of the world!" (John 1:29), attesting a sacrificial victim whose self-offering would be in the place of another.

Biblical Motifs of Sacrifice

The Principle of Sacrifice by Which the Old Testament Forms the Basis of the New

No Old Testament theme is more important to the New Testament than sacrifice. The Old Testament is most profoundly understood from the vantage point of its having been fulfilled in the New. Classic Christian exegetes did not treat Old Testament messianic promises as if they had remained unfulfilled. They could not ignore the kerygmatic premise that Old Testament messianic prophecy was fulfilled in the New. Rather they built unapologetically upon that premise.

This does not mean that we are permitted to read backward into ancient Hebraic culture conceptions derived from the New Testament, so as to prevent the Old Testament from speaking for itself. The clarification of Old Testament teaching rests primarily upon an analysis and comparison of its own contents. But this cannot rule out the procedures of classic

Christian exegesis that viewed the Old Testament as decisively illumined by its fulfillment in Jesus Christ. A major case in point is the teaching and practice of sacrifice.

Sacrifice Defined

A sacrifice is "the external offering up of a visible gift, which is destroyed, or at least submitted to an appropriate transformation, by a lawful minister in recognition of the sovereignty of God" in order to conciliate God's holy rejection of sin (Pohle-Preuss, *DT* V, p. 111; Tho. Aq., *ST* II–III, Q85.2, II, pp. 1555f.).

Sacrifice formed the core of Levitical worship and ritual. In ancient Jewish tradition, the sacrificial destruction or transformation ordinarily occurred by the death of a living animal or sometimes by the burning of foods or pouring out of fluids. The purposes of sacrifice were adoration and expiation. Sacrifices ritually acknowledged the holiness and sovereignty of God and sought to draw their offerers near to God, however keenly aware of sin they were.

The Sacrifices of Abel, Abraham, and Job

The sacrifices of Abel, Abraham, and Job were key Old Testament types that were reinterpreted in the New Testament.

Abel's Offering and Christ's

In the Hebrew mind, the practice of sacrifice dated back to very earliest humanity—Abel, who "kept flocks," "brought fat portions from some of the firstborn of his flock. The Lord looked with favor on Abel and his offering" (Gen. 4:2–4; Eusebius, *MPG* I, p. 55; Ambrose, *The Prayer of Job and David*, FC 65, pp. 416–17). The apostles preached that it was "by faith" that Abel offered this blood sacrifice, distinguished from the disapproved nonsacrificial plant offerings of Cain. The sacrifice of Abel had powerful significance for early Christian belief, for "by faith he still speaks, even though he is dead" (Heb. 11:4).

Why was Abel's offering "better" than Cain's (Heb. 11:4)? Because it occurred "by faith" in God's promise, however dimly its fulfillment was perceived. It contained an implicit acknowledgment of sin and an anticipatory faith in a coming sacrifice more fitting. And it was a costly act, as was Christ's, for the offering of this sacrifice was the indirect cause of Abel's own death at the hands of his brother. The New Testament did not miss this striking prefigurative reversal: through Abel's offering he himself was made a sacrifice.

The Offering of Isaac (Gen. 22)

The ram offered by Abraham was the prototypical vicarious offering through which another was spared—that of the *only beloved son* (Isaac) through whom the divine promise was to be fulfilled (Ambrose, *Isaac*, FC 65, pp. 10–12). The life of the ram in the thicket would be offered for the life of another. Again the Epistle to the Hebrews comments on the weighty figurative significance of this: "By faith Abraham, when God tested him, offered Isaac as a sacrifice. He who had received the promises was about to sacrifice his one and only son, even though God had said to him, 'It is through Isaac that your offspring will be reckoned.' Abraham reasoned that God could raise the dead, and figuratively speaking he did receive Isaac back from death" (Heb. 11:17–19).

The dilemma was that the very one through whom humanity was promised to be blessed (Isaac as the one and only bearer of Abraham's seed and promise) was according to God's command to be sacrificed. It took unreserved faith in God for Abraham to proceed to Mount Moriah (Augustine, *CG* XVI.24, *NPNF* I 2, pp. 323–24; Kierkegaard, *Fear and Trembling* [1954], pp. 27–37)—a faith that prefigured the resurrection faith in the sacrifice of the one and only Son. The word rendered "figuratively" (Heb. 11:19) is *parabole*, a parable or comparison or figure or type. Abraham's willingness to offer his only son and the salvation of his son were viewed parabolically as anticipatory of the Father-Son relation in the cross and resurrection of Jesus ("Hence he did get him back, by what was a parable of the resurrection," v. 19, Moffatt).

Job's Offering Exemplary

It was said to be Job's "regular custom" to "sacrifice a burnt offering" for each of his children after periods of feasting, "thinking, 'Perhaps my children have sinned and cursed God in their hearts'" (Job 1:5). This just man yearned so deeply for reconciliation with God that even on the basis of the possibility that his children might have inattentively cursed God inwardly, he offered an atoning sacrifice. Under the old law, the offering of a whole, ritually cleansed animal was understood to be a fitting atonement for potential, hidden, and inward sins of loved ones (Cyprian, *Treatises* VIII.17–18, *ANF* V, pp. 480–81). Christ's offering, too, was a plenary offering for his children in faith who cursed God in their hearts (Aphrahat, *Select Demonstrations* VI.3, *NPNF* 2 XIII, pp. 365–66).

The Levitical System of Sacrifice:
Sacrifices Prescribed Under Mosaic Law

The blood of sacrifice symbolized both the life and the death of the victim. It usually involved the violent death of a victim sacrificed in order to make the approach of amelioration. It sought a covering over of sin and the removing of defilement.

A Divinely Provided Means of Reconciliation

In the Old Testament, sacrifice was regarded as mercifully instituted by God as an expression of covenant, enabling the wayward people to draw near to God (Lev. 17:11). It was not merely a rational invention of human ingenuity or social identification. Rather, the sacrificial system was a divinely provided means of enabling the approach of sinners to God. God offered this way of reconciliation when the people had sinned, when the sanctuary, land, or a family or individual had been defiled. The sacrificial system did not, however, assume that acts of atonement could be easily applied to heinous offenses—sins committed with high-handedness (Job 21:22; Prov. 21:4; Isa. 10:12).

The Passover Lamb

The blood of the Passover lamb was given for others and put on the doorframes of the houses of the Israelites. "The blood will be a sign for you on the houses where you are; and when I see the blood, I will pass over you" (Exod. 12:13). Hence the life of the people was preserved by the death of the victim. "And when your children ask you, 'What does this ceremony mean to you?' then tell them, 'It is the Passover sacrifice to the Lord, who passed over the houses of the Israelites in Egypt and spared our homes when he struck down the Egyptians" (Exod. 12:26–27). The blood of the lamb was the life of Israel (John Chrysostom, *Hom. on John* XVII, *NPNF* 1 XIV, pp. 58–59; Augustine, *Comm. on John* LV, *NPNF* 1 VII, p. 299; Newman, *Discussions and Arguments* [1836], pp. 219–20).

Luther's language concerning Christ as lamb is particularly vivid: "He permits Himself, as the Pascal Lamb, to be killed and roasted on the tree of the cross that He may sprinkle us with His blood and that the angel of death, who had received power over us because of sin, should pass us by and do us no harm. Thus Paul well says: 'Christ, our Passover, is sacrificed for us'" (Luther, *Serm. on John 19:25–37, WLS* I, p. 191; *WA* 52, 812f., quoting 1 Cor. 5:7; cf. Menno Simons, *Foundation of Christian Doc-*

trine, CWMS, pp. 144–45). "Worthy is the Lamb, who was slain, to receive power," sang the angelic hosts of the book of Revelation, "ten thousand times ten thousand," encircling the heavenly throne (Rev. 5:11–12).

Types of Offerings

Elaborate rites of atonement developed in the postexilic period, carried out primarily by the high priest through prescribed sacrifices in the Temple. The Levitical system had five types of offerings, with which every Jew of New Testament times was doubtless familiar: the burnt offering, the cereal offering, the guilt offering, the sin offering, and the peace offering.

Each sought to reconcile the holiness of God with the conditions of alienated humanity (John Chrysostom, *Hom. on Heb.* XVIII, *NPNF* 1 XIV, pp. 451–54). The purpose of these rites was to remove the barrier of sin that inhibited the covenant relationship (*Apostolic Constitutions* IX.5–8, *ANF* VII, pp. 434–35). The Day of Atonement particularly brought the possibility of covenant renewal (Lev. 16). All of these types of sacrifice poured into New Testament assumptions concerning the Christ.

No Remission Without Shedding of Blood

The metaphor of lifeblood requires special notice. It comes from Temple sacrifice: the atoning lifeblood of the victim covers the guilt of the penitent.

Blood as Life Symbol

The metaphor of blood in the New Testament implies life being taken away violently, life offered in sacrifice. Wherever there is blood, there is life. Life is in blood. Yet blood means more than simply physical life. It means life poured out sacrificially for others (Clement of Alexandria, *Instructor* I.6, *ANF* II, p. 221; Catherine of Siena, *Pray.*, pp. 71–73, 101–103). A crucial reason why nonhuman creatures are given life, according to the Levitical system, is to replenish human life and on special ritual occasions to substitute and atone for the sins of the people (Tho. Aq., *ST* III, Q83, II, pp. 2283–93).

The Life Is in the Blood

It is not the blood itself that makes atonement, but the life or animate creation or soul in the blood that is offered as a prayer for atonement. The sacrificed victim implies not merely a death, but a death that enables life. Hence the sacrifice is not meaningless. The offering of blood is better viewed as the offering and enabling of life, not death.

The victim was slain not merely for death, but that its life – symbolized by blood – could be released for another (V. Taylor, *Jesus and His Sacrifice*, pp. 54ff.; L. Morris, *The Cross in the NT*, p. 219; Ladd, *TNT*, p. 426). This connection was clearly set forth in Levitical law: "For the life of the creature is in the blood, and I have given it to you to make atonement for yourselves on the altar; it is the blood that makes atonement for one's life" (Lev. 17:11; 16:9, 20–22; Isa. 53:4–10).

No Gift More Valuable Than Life

Blood was viewed as bearer of life. It was the most valued gift that could be offered: life. It was symbolic of the offerer's own soul or life. Blood symbolized the dedication of a life wherein one offered life substituted for the indebted life of another (Augustine, *EDQ* 49, *FC* 70, p. 84).

The Holocaust

The offerer could not actually surrender his own human life – Yahweh abhorred both suicide and human sacrifice. Hence the supplicant offered up his own life symbolically by presenting in place of his life some valued creature. The supplicant was implicitly confessing that he was unable to stand in the presence of the Holy One as sinner – so radically that he deserved to die.

This is the original meaning of holocaust (*holos*, "whole," and *kaustos*, "burnt") – a sacrifice wholly consumed by fire, a complete offering, unreservedly dedicated. It signified the destruction of sins deserving of death. Bloody sacrifice required not only a living creature and the pouring out of lifeblood, but contrition and total self-offering of the supplicant (*Jewish Encyclopedia*, III, pp. 439–42). Accordingly, Christ's death was understood as a vicarious atonement or sacrifice for the sins of humanity (Council of Ephesus Canon 10, *SCD* 122, p. 51; Trent, *Sess. Twenty-two*, 1–2, *SCD* 938–40, pp. 288–92).

Without the Shedding of Blood, No Forgiveness

No Jew, however negligent, could have failed to grasp the central point that "without the shedding of blood there is no forgiveness" (Heb. 9:22). The offerer of sacrifice, by the laying on of hands, designated the animal to be for him (or for the covenant people) a means of atonement, thanksgiving, or petition. The imposition of hands on the head of the victim symbolized that the sins of the people were being heaped upon it (Lev. 4:13–20). The atoning virtue, or power to cover sins, was assumed to reside in the shed blood.

A Covering of Sin

Essentially the sacrifice was a human gift to God, presented by those aware of their sins and hoping that the severity of divine holiness might be turned to clemency. In this sense sacrifice was something like a protective covering enshrouding the sinner in the presence of God. The idea of covering is the root idea of the Hebrew *kaphar*, "to make atonement."

Vicarious Sacrifice

The interfacing ideas of sacrifice and vicarious substitution were intimately connected. Through the death of guiltless animals, guilty sinners were saved from death. The death of the victim was vicarious, in the place of the people, and expiatory, ceremonially removing their sins as an obstacle to the divine-human relationship so as to bring God nearer (hence it was propitiatory).

The Prophets' Critique of Animal Sacrifice

The prophets protested the abuses of this sacrificial system without rejecting the system altogether. They were keenly aware of how at times it tended to neglect justice and mercy, especially to the poor (Amos 5:21ff.; Isa. 1:11; Mic. 6:7; Jer. 7:22). They repeatedly rejected the presumption that the clemency of God could be bought or traded. The virtue of the sacrifice was not determined by cost or economic value, but by the inward sincerity of the contrition that accompanied it. The Temple sacrifice system would continue in later Judaism until the destruction of the Temple in A.D. 70, when it came to an abrupt end and became transmuted in the Diaspora.

Sacrificial Law as Preparation for the Gospel

The Hebraic tradition of priestly sacrifice had gone through a lengthy period of development before New Testament times and had been influenced by diverse ideas and symbols in the history of religions. However complex that history might be, the classic Christian exegetes drew this overarching conclusion: through this sacrificial system, the people of Israel were being prepared for the incomparable act of sacrifice that was to come in Jesus Christ (Arnobius, *Ag. the Heathen* VII, *ANF* VI, pp. 518–39).

The minds of the New Testament writers were saturated with sacrificial metaphors derived from the Levitical tradition. They realized that the sacrificial system had been superseded in Christ. They also knew that they would have to use symbols from this tradition to explain how this had occurred. They sensed that "The law is only a shadow of the good things that are coming" (Heb. 10:1).

The Letters and narratives of the New Testament, however, were not finely hewn treatises of precise logic but were often written urgently under the requirement of special challenges. Hence their priestly and sacrificial images and arguments must be viewed as useful vehicles for the expression of the gospel to various audiences with various relationships to the Levitical tradition, including ignorance of it.

The writers of the New Testament returned constantly to the Psalms and prophets, searching Scripture for clarification of why Christ suffered. They found in Zechariah's smitten shepherd a metaphor for Christ (Zech. 13:7; Mark 14:27) and in Daniel's prophecy an "anointed one" who would be "cut off" and "have nothing" (Dan. 9:26). Above all they found in Isaiah 53 the suffering Servant of the Lord, who would be "pierced for our transgressions" and "crushed for our iniquities," by whose "wounds we are healed" (Isa. 53:5; cf. Luke 24:46). In John's account of Jesus' preparation of his disciples for his death, its sacrificial character became clear: "This bread is my flesh, which I will give for the life of the world" (John 6:51).

The Sacrificial Offering of Christ

How is humanity delivered from sin in a way that preserves the justice of God? God the Son offers himself "as a sacrifice of atonement" in order "to demonstrate his justice," "so as to be just and the one who justifies those who have faith in Jesus" (Rom. 3:25, 26; cf. L. Boff, *The Way of the Cross, The Way of Justice*).

Only the One Mediator Could Suffice

No blood less than that of the Son of God would have been sufficient to enable a declaration that the sins of all humanity have been forgiven (Gregory Nazianzen, *Second Orat. on Easter*, NPNF 2 VII, p. 431). No one except the God-man could be at once just and Justifier (Rom. 3:26; 1 Tim. 2:5–6).

The Law Could Not Bridge the Gulf

The law in itself did not accomplish the deliverance of humanity from sin (Rom. 8:3). Only by identifying with the sinner, by becoming an offering for sin, did the Son deliver from sin. "And so he condemned sin in sinful man, in order that the righteous requirements of the law might be fully met in us" (Rom. 8:4).

Voluntarily, the Son "gave himself up for us as a fragrant offering and sacrifice to God" (Eph. 5:2; Barth, *CD* I/1, pp. 673ff.; IV/4, pp. 158ff.; Baxter, *PW* XII, pp. 204–206). The exchange metaphor appeared frequently in the early tradition: "O the sweet exchange, O the inscrutable creation, O the unexpected benefits that the wickedness of many should be concealed in the one righteous, and the righteousness of the one should make righteous many wicked" (*Letter to Diognetus* 9, in *DWC*, p. 93).

It is from this matrix that the hymns of evangelical revival could be fashioned:

> Just as I am, without one plea,
> But that thy blood was shed for me,
> And that thou bidd'st me come to thee,
> O Lamb of God, I come.
>
> Just as I am, though tossed about
> With many a conflict, many a doubt,
> Fightings and fears within, without,
> O Lamb of God, I come
>   (Charlotte Eliott, 1840, *HPEC*, p. 121).

Jesus' Death a True Sacrifice

The essence of sacrifice lies in the self-surrendering death of the victim. Jesus voluntarily surrendered himself for the sins of the world. His blood was "poured out for many" (Mark 14:24). The blood of Christ signified his life offered to God on behalf of others (Calvin, *On Reform, SW,* p. 98).

Who Received the Sacrifice?

To whom did Christ offer this sacrifice? "God was reconciling the world to himself in Christ, not counting men's sins against them" (2 Cor. 5:19). It was God who was both offering reconciliation and receiving the reconciled. "The man Christ Jesus, though *in the form of God* He received sacrifice together with the Father, with whom He is one God, yet *in the form of a servant*, He chose rather to be than to receive a sacrifice, that not even by this instance any one might have occasion to suppose that sacrifice should be rendered to any creature. Thus He is both the Priest who offers and the Sacrifice offered" (Augustine, *CG* X.20, *NPNF* 1 II, p. 193, italics added).

Both Priest and Sacrifice

It became a key point of atonement teaching that Christ is both priest and sacrifice: "Priest and victim, then, are one" (Ambrose, *On the Christian Faith* 3.11, *NPNF* 2 X, p. 255). "For us he became to thee both Victor and Victim; and Victor because he was the Victim. For us, he was to thee both Priest and Sacrifice, and Priest because he was the Sacrifice" (Augustine, *Confessions* 10, chap. 43, *LCC* VII, p. 242). He is "both the offerer and the offering" (Augustine, *Trin.* IV.14, *NPNF* 1 III, p. 79; Chemnitz, *TNC*, pp. 337–39; Schmid, *DT*, p. 343).

Not Counting Sin Against Humanity

Paul assumed that Christ's sacrifice was a once-for-all event in history. The detailed accounting of the particulars of that event he did not have to report—that was already available in the oral traditions—though it over-reads the text to say that he found those historical details of no interest. It is clear, however, that his vital interest was focused upon the saving significance of Jesus' death—what it meant. Primarily it meant that through the cross, "God was reconciling the world to himself in Christ, not counting men's sins against them" (2 Cor. 5:19). A generation after Paul, Clement of Rome wrote: "Because of the love He bore us, our Lord Jesus Christ, at the will of God, gave His blood for us—His flesh for our flesh, His life for our lives" (Clement of Rome, *Corinthians* 49, *ECW*, p. 49).

A Once-for-All Sacrifice

Hebrews on Sacrifice

The Letter to the Hebrews provides the most complete interpretation of the sacrifice of Christ in the New Testament. Christ is viewed as high priest who transcends Levitical priesthood. Through his death sin is removed, and the approach of humanity to God made possible.

Levitical rituals must have been somewhat confusing to Gentile converts. Some Jewish Christians may have been prone to revert to Judaism. At length it must have become clear that the law of sacrifice had been transmuted and reinterpreted in the light of Jesus' death. The Letter to Hebrews provided a clear explanation of how that was being understood.

Once-for-All Offering

"Unlike the other high priests, he does not need to offer sacrifices day after day, first for his own sins, and then for the sins of the people. He sacrificed for their sins once for all when he offered himself" (Heb. 7:27). This conclusive act of self-offering is contrasted with the repetition of the Aaronic priestly rituals (Heb. 8:3; 9:26; 10:12; Gregory Nazianzen, *On the Theophany*, *NPNF* 2 VII, p. 351).

The role of high priest was understood anew in the light of Jesus Christ (Heb. 2:17; 4:14–5:10; Ps. 110:1–4). Christ "has appeared once for all at the end of the ages to do away with sin by the sacrifice of himself" (Heb. 9:26). Human beings die only once and afterward face judgment. Christ as representative Mediator "sacrificed once to take away the sins of many people; and he will appear a second time, not to bear sin, but to bring salvation to those who are waiting for him" (Heb. 9:27–28).

Christ stands not merely in the Aaronic line, but in the line of Melchizedek, a superior priesthood. Christ's offering is made in the presence of God (Heb. 9:12). It is a new and living way, a different kind of altar (Heb. 13:10). He had to go "outside the camp" to show how far God would go to reconcile lost humanity (Barth, *CD* IV/2, pp. 3ff.).

The End of Animal Sacrifice

The limitations of the Levitical animal sacrificial system were soundly criticized in Hebrews as lacking sufficient moral depth and requiring constant repetition by a professional priesthood. The Levitical sacrifices that had been instituted by God under the old covenant were efficacious in the ceremonial removal of pollution prior to Christ, but they were transcended in Jesus' ministry (Heb. 9:12–14; *Epistle of Barnabas*, 2, *ANF* I, pp. 137–38).

Christ Our Eucharist

Jesus' Death an End-time Event

When he took the cup at the first Lord's Supper, he said to his disciples: "This is my blood of the covenant. . . . I will not drink again of the fruit of the vine until that day when I drink it anew in the kingdom of God" (Mark 14:24–25). This signaled that his death was decisively associated with the coming of the kingdom of God.

Our Passover Lamb

Jesus died at virtually the same time that the pascal lambs were being slain. Paul had received the Jerusalem kerygma that had already made the decisive connection between Jesus' death and the lambs sacrificed for the Passover feast. He delivered to his hearers "as of first importance" the gospel he had received: "that Christ died for our sins" (1 Cor. 15:3–4; Gregory Nazianzen, *Second Orat. on Easter*, *NPNF* 2 VII, pp. 428–30). He understood Christ as "our Passover lamb" who "has been sacrificed" (1 Cor. 5:7). In the words of institution for the Lord's Supper as reported by

Paul—"This cup is the new covenant in my blood" (1 Cor. 11:25)—Christ's lifeblood sealed the new covenant, as sacrifice had sealed the old covenant.

Eucharist and Sacrifice

The symbolizing of internal self-oblation by an outward sacrifice has been an elementary function of religion from time immemorial. The Supper remains a perpetual reminder of the Son's own self-offering on our behalf (Jeremias, *Eucharistic Words of Jesus*, pp. 150–53). It celebrates both Christ's death and coming again: "For whenever you eat this bread and drink this cup, you proclaim the Lord's death until he comes" (1 Cor. 11:26).

The Eucharist celebrates Christ's effectual and acceptable sacrifice to God. The assumption is that the once-for-all sacrifice of the cross is the energizing grace of every Eucharist, there being in reality only one sacrifice, the cross (*Apostolic Constitutions* II.7-8, *ANF* VII, pp. 421–25; Hall, *DT* VII, pp. 123–25). Indicatively, the finished sacrifice of Jesus is complete and sufficient for all, yet imperatively in the lives of believers it is still in the process of being made complete: "By one sacrifice he has made perfect forever those who are being made holy" (Heb. 10:14).

VICARIOUS ATONEMENT

Was the sacrifice of Christ necessary? Was it sufficient?

The Unique Conditions Required for the Salvation of Humanity: Why Atonement Was Necessary

That which is *necessary* for salvation must exist as its indispensable condition. Christ's atoning death is considered an essential requisite to the salvation of humanity.

That the cross is *sufficient* for salvation means that Christ's death has provided all that is needful for redemption from sin. The cross is considered both necessary and sufficient for salvation.

A Moral Necessity, Not Externally Necessitated

In speaking of the necessity of the cross, there is no intended implication that God is under an external necessity to resolve the dilemma caused by the history of sin. The moral necessity of atonement is a requirement of God's moral will. It is necessitated only by the freedom of the holy God to love rightly.

The Cross Presupposes a History of Sin

If humanity had not sinned, the whole prospect of God providing a
dying Savior for redemption would have been futile and nonsensical,
even cruel. Salvation is God's own personal answer to the problem
created by sin. The cross is the remedy for the disease of sin. Only if one
assumes that no such disease exists is the need for the cross obviated.

Atonement is intrinsically connected with the premise that all humanity is trapped in otherwise irreversible syndromes of sin that manifest
and engender anxiety toward the future, guilt toward the past, and boredom in the present. These are intensified by idolatry that makes that
anxiety, guilt, and boredom harder to bear and easier to transmit (*SA*,
parts I–III). It is this universal condition that makes atonement necessary.

Difficulties in the Way of the Salvation of Humanity

Could Not a Better Way of Salvation Have Been Found?

It is a zealous exaggeration to say that God could not have redeemed
humanity in any other way than Christ's crucifixion (Luke 1:37; Tho. Aq.,
ST III, Q46.2, II, p. 2265). But it is difficult to imagine any alternative way
of salvation that more fully satisfies the rigorous requirements set by the
confluence of God's holiness, justice, and love amid the wretched conditions requiring reparation for the history of sin (Anselm, *Cur Deus Homo*
12–14, *LCC* III, pp. 120–23). There was no easy or cost-free way for one
man to become a substitute for the history of sin. It was necessary that
Christ be "born under law, to redeem those under law" (Gal. 4:4–5).

God does not characteristically waste precious resources. Had there
been a less costly way to reconcile sinners that could have avoided the
death of his beloved Son, that way would have been chosen (Athanasius,
Incarn. of the Word 1–5, *NPNF* 2 IV; Hall, *DT* VII, p. 142). But why this particularly harsh, narrow, difficult way of salvation, and not another milder,
broader way?

The Cross Was Consistent with God's Goodness and Human Freedom

If God were merely saving rocks or plants, the plan would have been
different—for they do not have freedom to respond and resist. The plan
of salvation had to be worthy of the character of the holy and loving God
and fitting to the conditions of human freedom so radically fallen into
distortion and self-alienation.

The plan had to be consistent with the extraordinary gifts the Creator had already bestowed upon humanity: reason, imagination, language, capacity for justice and love, and self-determining intelligence. Any design short of all these conditions would have displayed less than the incomparable wisdom of God and would have been inconsistent with all that is known of the divine character (Baxter, *PW* IX, pp. 35ff.; XX, pref.).

Redemption Congruent with Creation

The way of salvation had to be consistent with the purpose of God in creation. God could have created or not created human beings, but he in fact decided to create. God could have created companionate rational creatures with vastly different native capacities and powers but did not. Given the assumption that human beings had already vastly skewed the original purpose of their creation, God's plan of redemption had to be consistent with the original purpose of human creation (Origen, *De Principiis* II.9, *ANF* IV, pp. 291–92; Tho. Aq., *ST* I, Q47, I, p. 246).

One option was thereby negated: it would have been less fitting if God had simply started over by obliterating or demolishing botched human freedom. It was more fitting, more consistent with the character of God, that God should carry on through with the original divine plan, overcoming the fallenness of free accountable beings (Gregory Nazianzen, *Orat.* XXXVIII, *NPNF* 2 VII, pp. 346–47).

Fallen Human Freedom to Be Redeemed, Not Merely Inorganic Matter, Plants, or Beasts

The plan of salvation had to pertain to the specific conditions of self-alienated human freedom, not simply the less complicated situation of inorganic objects or plant or animal life. The natural law suited to *lifeless matter* (orderly causation) assumes that there is no capacity for response in mere air, or earth or fire or water. The conditions of renewal of inorganic life would be different from the botanic laws pertinent for *plant life*, which assume capacities (for life, growth, and reproduction) in plants that rocks do not have (although plants must live in the same orderly world with rocks, air, and water). The zoological laws pertinent for *animal life* assume capacities (mobility) that are not present in plants (although the laws pertinent to plant life also largely pertain to animal life, for animals must live in the same world with plants on whom their lives depend).

The moral laws that pertain to *human life* assume capacities (language, reason, imagination, conscience) that are not present in animals (although the laws governing animal life also shape human life, since humans have bodies, for human life is lived in the presence of and in dependence upon inorganic, plant, and animal life). Whatever would be done for the redemption of alienated human freedom would have to be consistent with the conditions of human freedom.

This means that the problem cannot be prematurely simplified by having God flatly or absolutely decree salvation apart from any intricate interaction between grace and freedom. A theology of absolute divine decrees might be a simpler theology and might appear to be more consistent, but it is lacking in the interactive complexity of the grace-freedom interface that is constantly acknowledged in Scripture in the divine-human covenant. Salvation could not simply ignore or circumvent the orderly and intelligible course of nature, so as to make the natural order less intelligible or reliable, yet it had to address human freedom uncoercively.

Rejected Options

Coercion Rejected. The God who created freedom would not act simply by fiat. If human freedom is to be honored and transformed, it cannot merely be coerced by decree but rather must be reshaped by persuasion and drawn by a convincing demonstration of unconditional love.

Pardon Without Reparation Rejected. The idea that God could have pardoned without exacting any reparation is morally insufficient and inconsistent with divine holiness.

Nonredemption Rejected. The notion that God might simply have left humanity mired in its own fallen history may be arguable on the grounds of divine righteousness, but it fails to recognize the depths of divine love. If humanity had remained forever lost in sin, then the very purpose for which humanity had been created would have been absurdly brought to nothing.

To these constraints are joined the next pivotal moral complication.

Penalty as a Consequence of Law

The Moral Necessity of Penalty

Only the fair and rightful execution of penalty guarantees the continuity and intelligibility of moral order. God does not forgive without atonement or expiation for past guilt. If God did so, God would treat his own moral order unseriously. This is why atonement was necessary.

It was necessary that the penalty be executed if violated, for to establish a just penalty for a violation of law and then to permit the violation to pass with impunity is to mock justice. Pardon without atonement would nullify justice (Ursinus, *CHC*, pp. 220–21).

The moral law given to humanity through conscience and Torah had to be with penalty. A law without penalty is merely advice. Withhold from your child or a friend all negative feedback and all resistance to evil and see what happens. It takes uncommonly optimistic assumptions about humanity to assume that all negative reinforcement can be taken away without human harm.

Impunity Mocks Justice

Suppose a legislature passed a law against theft with a specific reasonable penalty, yet the executive refused ever to enforce the law and no penalty was ever administered. Would that not have the effect of making void the law, making it a mere matter of words, thereby risking the increase of theft? Suppose God had ordered the moral universe in this way — issuing commands or requirements with penalties that were never administered — would not that result in a morally ruinous situation repugnant to moral order and law? If so, we must rule out a cheap solution to the problem of disobedience to God (Anselm, *CDH*; Grotius, *DCF*).

The Command: The Soul That Sins Shall Die

At this point it is crucial to recall the original command of God to the original human partners: "When you eat of it [the tree of the knowledge of good and evil] you will surely die" (Gen. 2:17; John Chrysostom, *Hom. on Gen.* 14, FC 74, pp. 180–93). In Ezekiel the same formula appears slightly reworded: "The soul who sins is the one who will die" (Ezek. 18:4, 20; Origen, *De Principiis* II.9, ANF IV, pp. 288–89). In Paul's Letters it reappears: "For the wages of sin is death" (Rom. 6:23; William of St. Thierry, *Romans*, CF 27, pp. 125–26). "Cursed is everyone who does not continue to do everything written in the Book of the Law" (Gal. 3:10; Deut. 26:27; John Chrysostom, *Hom. on Gal.* III, NPNF 1 XIII, pp. 26–27).

The Deepening Indebtedness

"God wills that his righteousness be satisfied; therefore, payment in full must be made to his righteousness, either by ourselves or by another. Can we make this payment ourselves? By no means. On the contrary, we increase our debt each day" (*Heidelberg Catech.* II, Q 12–13, BOConf. 4.012).

Repentance Without Grace Insufficient

Throughout the history of covenant, God has promised mercy to those who are sincerely penitent. Yet divine mercy is not premised merely upon human repentance as such, but rather upon atoning sacrifice accompanied by repentance, and this in both Testaments (Augustine, *CG, FC* 24, pp. 321–25).

"Repentance does not of itself heal this breach; nor is true repentance naturally possible for sinners, because of the blinding, hardening and weakening effect of sin upon our minds, hearts and wills" (Hall, *DT* VII, p. 132). Sinful men and women, unable to save themselves or pay this moral indebtedness, are left in their natural condition in effect "without hope and without God in the world" (Eph. 2:12). This is why atonement was required, and why it was necessary that the Son of Man come "to seek and to save what was lost" (Luke 19:10; cf. Exod. 29:21; Lev. 8:15; 17:11; Luther, *Eight Serm. on Ps. 110, WLS* I, p. 190; *WA* 41, 190f.).

Christ's Sacrifice Was Voluntary

Amid this predicament, the Son voluntarily laid down his life (Augustine, *Trin.*, *FC* 45, pp. 150–52), thereby manifesting the extent and depth of God's love for humanity, which could thereby be held in closest connection with the holiness and freedom of God. "I lay down my life — only to take it up again. No one takes it from me, but I lay it down of my own accord" (John 10:17–18).

Unlike Involuntary Animal Sacrifice

Christ's voluntary self-offering was in one respect quite different from the sacrifice of animals. The animal victim had no choice, being under the power of the one making the sacrifice. The Epistle to the Hebrews contrasts the moral efficacy of Christ's sacrifice with the morally problematic nature of animal sacrifice. "He did not enter by means of the blood of goats and calves; but he entered the Most Holy Place once for all by his own blood, having obtained eternal redemption [*lutrosis*]" (Heb. 9:12). "How much more, then will the blood of Christ, who through the eternal Spirit offered himself unblemished to God, cleanse our consciences from acts that lead to death, so that we may serve the living God" (Heb. 9:14).

Moral Repugnance of Involuntary Suffering of the Innocent

One might object to atonement teaching that it would be unjust if a government punished an innocent person and let the guilty escape — likewise by analogy God would be unjust, according to this argument, if God's innocent Son suffered for others' sin. The classical exegetes answered that it indeed would have been unjust if God had imposed the punishment of others upon his Son on the mistaken assumption that he were himself in fact guilty. That would be an *involuntary* punishment of an innocent person, hence itself an offense to the divine justice.

But that is not what happened on the cross. It would indeed be unjust if the innocent one were compelled involuntarily to suffer for what the guilty had done voluntarily. This reasoning does not apply if the innocent one has *voluntarily* consented and benevolently willed to suffer out of the compassionate motive of love toward sinners (John 10:17–18; Gal. 2:20; Eph. 5:2; Heb. 9:14; 10:7–9). To inhibit such a person from showing such compassion would be itself an act of coercion, not of freedom.

Jesus' Death Not Suicidal

The voluntary submission is a crucial factor in distinguishing Christ's death from suicide and martyrdom. Christ did not kill himself as do those who commit suicide (as if death were preferred to life). He willingly exposed himself to death only when that became the necessary implication of the way he lived his life in mission. The martyrs are like Christ in their willingness to die in witness to the truth. They are unlike Christ in that they did not have a messianic vocation and their sacrifice was not a ransom for the sins of others (John 10:17–18; Tho. Aq., *ST* III, Q22.2, II, p. 2143; Isa. 53:7).

Jesus' Death Was Vicariously Offered in Place of Sinners

Crushed for Our Iniquities

Isaiah's vision of the suffering Servant of the Lord formed the prophetic prototype of vicarious suffering. The exchange theme is portrayed with no less than eleven different metaphors of substitution in one chapter (53):

"Surely he took up our infirmities" (v. 4)
He "carried our sorrows" (v. 4)
"But he was pierced for our transgressions" (v. 5)
"He was crushed for our iniquities" (v. 5)
"The punishment that brought us peace was upon him" (v. 5)
"By his wounds we are healed" (v. 5)
"The Lord has laid on him the iniquity of us all" (v. 6)
"He was led like a lamb to the slaughter" (v. 7)
"For the transgression of my people he was stricken" (v. 8)
"The Lord makes his life a guilt offering" (v. 10)
"He will bear their iniquities" (v. 12).

New Testament Appropriation

Stricken, smitten, wounded, bruised, chastised, led to slaughter—this is the powerless one through whose stripes humanity is healed (1 Pet. 2:24). These transactional metaphors reverberate throughout major New Testament documents: He was "delivered over to death for our sins and was raised to life for our justification" (Rom. 4:25); the good shepherd "lays down his life for the sheep" (John 10:11); the innocent Messiah dies for the guilty sinners, their just punishment is remitted, his sacrificial death making satisfaction for them (BOC, p. 204; Gerhard, LT VII, I.27, chap. 2, secs. 37ff.; Schmid, DT, p. 357). We are justified "through the redemption that came by Christ Jesus" (Rom. 3:24). "In him we have redemption through his blood" (Eph. 1:7).

The Righteous for the Unrighteous

The First Epistle of Peter illustrates how the metaphors of substitution and sacrifice became interfused in early Christian preaching. The Letter was addressed to God's scattered elect who were chosen "for obedience to Jesus Christ and sprinkling by his blood" (1 Pet. 1:3). They had been "redeemed from the empty way of life" by means of "the precious blood of Christ, a lamb without blemish or defect," "through whom you believe in God" (1 Pet. 1:18–21). Recollecting Isaiah 53:9, the writer says: "'He committed no sin, and no deceit was found in his mouth.' When they hurled their insults at him, he did not retaliate; when he suffered, he made no threats. Instead, he entrusted himself to him who judges justly. He himself bore our sins in his body on the tree, so that we might die to sins and live for righteousness; by his wounds you have been healed" (1 Pet. 2:22–24). The just One died for the unjust: "For Christ died for sins once for all, the righteous for [huper] the unrighteous, to bring you to God" (1 Pet. 3:18).

Christ was punished for what sinners should have suffered. Though sinless, he died the sinner's death. Penal theories of the atonement are based upon these passages featuring the word huper: Romans 3:21–26; Galatians 3:13; and 2 Corinthians 5:21.

Substitution: Christ Died for Our Sins

Substitution occurs when one takes the place of another. Christ took the place of sinners, suffering the penalty of sin that was due them (Matt. 20:28; 2 Cor. 5:21; Gal. 2:20; 1 Pet. 3:18). Substitution is closely linked with sacrifice. It was an idea with which all observing Jews of that time would have been closely familiar.

The Substitutionary Principle Antedates the New Testament

In the Old Testament it was not uncommon for substitutes to be offered and accepted in the place of those who were guilty of offenses in God's presence. In making a burnt offering, one was instructed to "lay his hand on the head of the burnt offering, and it will be accepted *on his behalf* to make atonement for him" (Lev. 1:4, italics added). Clearly a victim was being substituted in animal sacrifice.

By sacrificing some valued creature for oneself and offering it up unreservedly to God, the supplicant acknowledged God's rightful lordship over his own life, which was symbolically being offered up and destroyed (Pohle-Preuss, *DT* V, p. 113).

The Exchange Metaphor

The language is extraordinarily specific: Christ died not only *for me* (vicariously) but *in my stead*, in place of me (as a substitute for me, or as a substitutionary sacrifice). Only because he took my place, I shall not die. Because he died in my place, I now live and may live eternally through him.

The crucial substitutionary terms are *huper*, which means "for" or "on behalf of" another, "on account of," "for the advantage of" another, or "for the benefit of," and *anti*, which means "in place of" or "instead of" another, a preposition of price, transaction, or exchange.

Love Known by Willingness to Die for Others

"This is how we know what love is: Jesus Christ laid down his life for us [*huper*]" (1 John 3:16). The indicative implies an imperative: therefore "we ought to lay down our lives for our brothers," being willing to give up what we have for those in need (1 John 3:16–17). Those who live in Christ are called to live for others.

Christ Died for Us

"The Lord Jesus, on the night he was betrayed, took bread, and when he had given thanks, he broke it and said, 'This is my body which is for you'" (*huper*, 1 Cor. 11:23–24). "Very rarely will anyone die for [*huper*] a righteous man, though for a good man someone might possibly dare to die. But God demonstrates his own love for [*huper*] us in this: While we were still sinners, Christ died for us [*Christos huper hemon apethanen*]" (Rom. 5:7–8). The vicarious act did not depend upon any merit in the offending party.

The full weight of human sin is therefore transferred to and deposited on the crucified One, according to Luther: "For we are called Christians because we may look at the Christ and say: Dear Lord, You took all my sins upon Yourself. You became Martin, Peter, and Paul, and thus You crushed and destroyed my sin. There (on the cross) I must and will seek my sin. You have directed me to find it there. On Good Friday I still clearly see my sin, but on the Day of Easter no sin is any longer to be seen" (*Easter Serm.*, Coburg, 17 April 1530, WLS I, p. 182; WA 32, 47).

The believer participates in Jesus' death, that being dead to sin, he or she may have newness of life (Rom. 6:1–11; Gal. 2:20). "He died for us" that "we may live together with him" (1 Thess. 5:10). He did what we could not do for ourselves. Since he has freely given his life for us, we can freely receive our lives from God (Calvin, *Inst.* 2.17.4).

Universal Indicative Implies Universal Imperative

The indicative that Christ died for sin, was cursed for us, and bore our iniquities, implies an imperative, that we die to sin.

The Indicative: One Died for All

As Adam represented all the human family in its previous history, Christ represented the whole of humanity in its future history under the new covenant. "We are convinced that one died for all, and therefore all died" (2 Cor. 5:14; Ursinus, *CHC*, pp. 221–25).

Christ's death was substituted for the death of all, or on behalf of all (*huper panton*), as if the others had died. There is a sense in which the death of Christ implied the death of all humanity before God—namely, the end of their judgment for sin. The death of Christ belongs to them all, just as if each person had died for his or her own sins (1 Tim. 2:6). All are heirs, as if offered title claim, by virtue of the death for them (Gregory Nazianzen, *Flight to Pontus*, NPNF 2 VII, p. 223).

In His Dying for Us, Death Has Died

Athanasius reasoned that just as a city is secured from banditry by the presence of a just, powerful ruler, so the presence of the Word in human history checks "the whole conspiracy of the enemy" against humanity, and puts away death (*Incarn. of the Word* 8–9). If one asks for evidence of the efficacy of his death, wrote Athanasius, just look at the course of history since his death. There one will find empirical evidence in the courage of the martyrs, including women martyrs, who "scoff at death, jesting at him and saying what has been written of old: 'O death, where is thy victory? O grave, where is thy sting?'" (Athanasius, *Incarn. of the Word* 27, NPNF 2 IV, p. 50).

The Imperative—Life in Christ Means Life for Others

His death for others was not an event without consequences or an indicative without imperative. He died for all "that those who live should no longer live for themselves, but for him who died for them and was raised again" (2 Cor. 5:15).

All humanity has been affected. "As there never was, is or will be any man whose nature was not assumed by our Lord Jesus Christ, so there never was, is or will be any man for whom He has not suffered; though not all are redeemed by the mystery of His passion" (Council of Quiersy, 853).

The Ransom

The atoning significance of Jesus' death was best summarized by Jesus himself: The Son of Man came "to give his life as a ransom for many [*lutron antipollōn*]" (Mark 10:45).

Lutron

A ransom (*lutron*) was a price paid to redeem prisoners from servitude. Luther thought that "redemption was not possible without a ransom of such precious worth as to atone for sin, to assume the guilt, pay the price of wrath and thus abolish sin. This no creature was able to do. There was no remedy except for God's only Son to step into our distress and himself become man" (*Epist. Serm.*, 24th Sunday After Trinity, 43, 44, SML VIII, p. 376). *Redemption* usually refers to one particular aspect of satisfaction, namely, the payment of a price by which one becomes freed, although redemption at times is used as a more general synonym for deliverance or liberation (Luke 12:28; Rom. 8:23; Eph. 4:30).

Antilutron

"There is one God and one mediator between God and men, the man Christ Jesus, who gave himself as a ransom for all men" (*antilutron huper pantōn*, 1 Tim. 2:6). The *anti* underscores substitution of one in the place of another. *Antilutron* is a substitutionary ransom—something happened to Christ, which, as a result of his action, need not happen to sinners.

Taking the Curse on Himself for Us

"Christ ransomed us from the curse pronounced in the Law, by taking the curse on himself for us" (Gal. 3:13, TCNT). "For it is written: 'Cursed is everyone who is hung on a tree'" (Gal. 3:13; cf. Deut. 21:23). "The tree of life which was planted by God in paradise prefigured this honorable Cross, for, since death came by a tree, it was necessary for life and the resurrection to be bestowed by a tree" (John of Damascus, *OF* IV.11, *FC* 37, p. 352).

The substitution did not make Christ a sinner but caused him to be viewed and dealt with as such. Christ was willing to be regarded as a sinner for our sakes. God cursed sin. If the Son was to reconcile with the Father those who had been cursed by sin, he had to become a "curse for us." It is not that he was a curse, but that "He is called so. For how can He be sin, Who setteth us free from sin?" (Gregory Nazianzen, *Orat.* XXXVI.1, *NPNF* 2 VII, p. 338). Rather, "for my sake He was called a curse, Who destroyed my curse," wrote Gregory Nazianzen. "As long then as I am disobedient and rebellious, both by denial of God and by my passions, so long Christ also is called disobedient on my account" (*Orat.* XXX.5, *NPNF* 2 VII, p. 311).

He Was Made to Be Sin for Us

How did Christ take the place of others? He died. His death constituted the penalty for the sins of humanity (Council of Ephesus, *SCD* 122ff., p. 50; see also *SCD* 160, 286, 319).

This is why Christ was treated as if a sinner, was numbered with the transgressors: "God made him who had no sin to be sin for us [*huper*]" (2 Cor. 5:21; *huper hemon hamartian epoiesen auton* implies that God made him who was sinless a sacrifice for sin; cf. Eleventh Council of Toledo, *SCD* 286, p. 111; Barth, *CD* IV/1, pp. 237ff.). Something happened on the cross that rendered God inclined to pardon sinners. "So, was the Lord turned into sin? Not so, but, since He assumed our sins, He is called sin. For the Lord is also called an accursed thing, not because the Lord was turned into an accursed thing, but because He himself took on our curse" (Ambrose, *Incarn. of Our Lord* 6.60, *FC* 44, p. 242, commenting upon 2 Cor. 5:21).

It is difficult to make the point that our sins were literally transferred to him without seeming to make him a sinner. He was not a sinner in our stead in the sense that he sinned. Nor was he righteous in such a way as to replace all need on our part for righteous response. The language of substitution must be used but cautiously and wisely.

By This Means Sin Was Condemned

God came personally to condemn sin in the flesh. "For what the law was powerless to do in that it was weakened by the sinful nature, God did by sending his own Son in the likeness of sinful man to be a sin offering. And so he condemned sin in sinful man, in order that the righteous requirements of the law might be fully met in us, who do not live according to the sinful nature but according to the Spirit" (Rom. 8:3, 4). God "did not spare his own Son, but gave him up for us all" (Rom. 8:32; Matt. 26:28; Rom. 5:6).

Consensus Sustained

Few points of ecumenical teaching have received such wide consensus as the premise that Christ's death was a sacrifice for the sin of others. Ignatius (*Letter to Smyrna, ECW,* pp. 119–23) wrote that his flesh suffered for our sins (cf. Polycarp, *Letter to Philippians, ANF* I, pp. 33–36). The *Epistle of Barnabas* argued that the blows inflicted upon the Son of God give us life and that in fulfilling the type of the sacrifice of Isaac, Jesus offered the vessel of his Spirit as a sacrifice for our sins (*Barnabas* 5–8, *ANF* I, pp. 139–42). Jesus was for us a ransom whose righteousness was capable of covering our sins (*Letter to Digonetus* 9, *ECW,* p. 180). Justin Martyr compared the blood of Christ to the pascal lamb and the scarlet thread of the house of Rahab (*Dialogue with Trypho* 95, 111, *ANF* I, pp. 247, 254; cf. Irenaeus, *Ag. Her.* III.16.9, *ANF* I, p. 444). Tertullian taught that Christ by his blood on the cross restored what Adam had lost beside the tree (*Answer to the Jews* 10–14, *ANF* III, pp. 164–73; *On Flight in Persecution* 12, *ANF* IV, pp. 123–24; for later discussions of Christ as sacrifice, see Athanasius, *On the Incarn. of the Word* 20; Gregory Nazianzen, *Orat.* XXX; Gregory of Nyssa, *ARI* 23; Basil, *Hom. on Ps. 48:3–4*; Cyril of Jerusalem, *Catech. Lect.* XIII.33; Cyril of Alexandria, *Ag. Nestorius* III.2; Ambrose, *On Flight from the World* 44; Leo, *Serm.* LXIV.3; LXVIII.3; Augustine, *Trin.* XIII.15; *Confessions* X.69; *Serm.* CCXV.4–5; Gregory the Great, *Moralia* XVII.46; John of Damascus, *OF* III.27; Bernard, *On the Errors of Abelard* 22; Anselm, *CDH*).

Answering Objections to Classical Atonement Theory

Standard objections are that God is unjust to punish his beloved Son for the sins of another; or that it is an immoral arrangement by which one receives benefit from another's suffering without moral effort or discipline; or that God is cruel to punish sin if sin is inevitable. These objections have sometimes tended either to miss or misplace the problem (the depths of the predicament of sin), the gracious character of God (his willingness to forgive), or the imperative that is embedded in the indicative of God's merciful action.

The cross itself undercuts the objection that God is cruel in punishing sin, for God the Son has voluntarily endured the penalty himself in order that sinners need not endure it. The Father gladly accepts the atoning sacrifice of the Son. In both Father and Son the opposition to sin is maintained, and the love of the sinner is demonstrated. Any theory of atonement that neglects either the opposition of God to sin or the love of God for the sinner has been traditionally judged inadequate.

SUFFICIENT SATISFACTION

God-incarnate renders infinite satisfaction for the entire enormity of the history of human sin. Christ's satisfaction, being infinite (Council of Quiersy [853], *SCD* 319, p. 127), was abundantly sufficient (Fifth Lateran Council, *SCD* 740, pp. 238–39).

Satisfaction

While expiation is a metaphor that belongs to the Temple, satisfaction is a metaphor that belongs primarily to the court of law. Satisfaction is a reparation made for the justice of the Lawgiver (Edwards, "Of Satisfaction for Sin," *Works* II, pp. 565–78). "The satisfaction of Christ is that act by which he freed us from the curse and restored eternal life to us, by being subject to the law in our place, undergoing the curse due to our sins, and perfectly performing what was required of us by the law" (Wollebius, *CTC* 18, *RDB*, p. 99).

A vicarious satisfaction requires a surrogate or substituted bondsman, by which someone else is substituted in the place of the debtor, and a payment of penalties, whereby the debtor may be declared free (*BOC*, pp. 205, 292).

There is a wide difference between an attorney and one willing to suffer for the offender. Suppose your attorney in a murder trial were willing to become a substitute for you, taking your sentence upon himself, ready to die for you. That would be much more like being your deliverer or savior than your attorney. Substitution is a much more radical form of identification than legal counsel or representation. The mediatorial work could not proceed unless the Son actually bore the penalty for those he was sent to redeem (Pearson, *EC* I, p. 255).

Christ's death is more like taking our place than giving us counsel. "His death, then, does not merely signify, but actually makes the forgiveness of sin, as a completely sufficient satisfaction" (Luther, *Lectures on Romans*, *WLS* I, p. 181; *WA* 56, 296).

Sufficiency

The sufficiency of the sacrifice is attested in eucharistic prayer: "Thou, of thy tender mercy, didst give thine only Son Jesus Christ to suffer death upon the cross for our redemption; who made there (by his one oblation of himself once offered) a full, perfect, and sufficient sacrifice, oblation, and satisfaction, for the sins of the whole world" (*BCP,* p. 80).

What Qualifies as a Substitution for Humanity's Sin?

Four conditions qualified Christ as the uniquely acceptable sacrificial victim:

his sinlessness, that the sacrifice might be spotless and undefiled;
his humanity, that he shared fully our human condition;
his deity as only beloved Son, that he might merit ransom for all;
his federal headship of humanity and identification with sinners, that
    he might be a fitting substitute for all.

Only one who fulfilled all these conditions could be offered up for the sins of all human history. There is "no other sacrifice for sin" required or sufficient (Scots Confession X, *BOC* 3.09).

The Kind and Degree of Christ's Suffering—Equivalent?

Is it being implied that Jesus suffered in the same way that every human being should have suffered for each and every sin of human history? Would not that imply the necessity of the Son of God dying over and over again or suffering eternally instead of in time?

Christ's penal satisfaction is functionally equivalent to all human sin—being *neither identical* (for Christ's taking upon himself our sin does not mean that our sin literally becomes identical with his) *nor equal* (for the death of all humanity would not be strictly speaking an equal payment for the death of the God-man, Jesus Christ). Hence the satisfaction is said to be sufficient, as functionally equivalent, and superabundantly so.

The Unique Dignity of This Person Suffices

The classical exegetes argued that it was not the intensity or precisely equivalent extent of his suffering and dying, but the dignity of his person that made his suffering sufficient for all (Gregory of Nyssa, *ARI* 17–28, *LCC* III, pp. 294–307). His sufferings were finite, but his sacrifice had infinite value due to his sonship. His suffering body and soul (the human nature) was united to the Son of God (the divine nature) so as to enable the humanity to suffer and die only once yet for all, finitely with infinite merit, in time for all time (Athanasius, *Four Discourses Ag. Arians* II.14–18, *NPNF* 2 IV, pp. 348–72; Baxter, *PW* XXI, pp. 204–206; IX, p. 35).

Only an Infinite Mediator Could Suffice

The seriousness of sin depends in part upon the one against whom it is committed. The higher the worldly authority against which an offense is committed, the greater is the guilt and punishability. Since God is infinite in majesty, an offense against God is infinitely serious and requires commensurable satisfaction. No finite creature can render adequate satisfaction for grievous sin against infinite majesty. Infinite satisfaction is rendered only by one infinite in majesty, hence none but God-incarnate (Calvin, *Inst.* 2.17; Pohle-Preuss, *DT* V, pp. 35–37). "Christ is mediator both by merit and by efficacy," wrote Wollebius. "By merit, because he made complete satisfaction for us. By efficacy, because he applies this merit to us effectively" (*CTC* 17, *RDB*, p. 97).

For Whom? The Extent of the Atoning Deed

The atonement is addressed to all humanity, intended for all, sufficient for all, yet it is effectively received by those who respond to it in faith (Wollebius, *CTC* 18, *RDB*, p. 105; Olevianus, *SFG*, pp. 67–68; Heppe, *RD*, pp. 475–79).

God Wills the Salvation of All

God primordially willed the salvation of all; the reason that some do not share in his grace must be found in their own self-determining will. Paul included both aspects in his encouragement to Timothy to trust and hope "in the living God, who is the Savior of all men, and especially of those who believe" (1 Tim. 4:10). It is not the atonement that is limited, but our receptivity to it. Our willingness to allow the Spirit to apply it to us is limited.

Universal Sufficiency Distinguished from Conditional Efficacy

As to sufficiency, the cross is *for all, for the world*. As to efficacy, the cross becomes effective *for some, for the faithful*. From this derives the distinction of universal sufficiency and conditional efficacy: *as to sufficiency it is universal; as to efficacy it is limited to those who accept God's offer of salvation through Christ*.

The *Russian Catechism* wisely holds these points in tension: "For his part, he offered himself as a sacrifice strictly for all, and obtained for all grace and salvation; but this benefits only those of us who, for their parts, of their own free will, have *fellowship in his sufferings, being made conformable unto his death* . . . through a lively and hearty faith, through the Sacraments . . . and, lastly, through the crucifixion of our flesh with its affections and lusts" (*COC* II, p. 476). It is by faith that one becomes a partaker in the atoning deed.

As to Sufficiency—"For All," "For the World"

He is a ransom "for all" (1 Tim. 2:6; Barth, *CD* I/2, pp. 360ff.; IV/3, p. 11), "For the grace of God that brings salvation has appeared to all men" (Titus 2:11). Even though only some are consciously aware of this salvation, it nonetheless is given for all and sufficient for all, and in some hidden or unknown or eschatological or presently unaware way all are already anticipatively participating in it (2 Cor. 5:14–15; Heb. 2:9; 6:4–6; 1 Cor. 8:11; 2 Pet. 2:1; 3:9). Among Johannine passages that suggest universal sufficiency are John 1:29; 3:16; 6:51; 12:47; and 1 John 2:2.

For the Lost

There is a special sense in which the atonement is given for sinners. "For I have come not to call the righteous, but sinners" (Matt. 9:12; cf. Luke 5:32). "For the Son of Man came to seek and to save what was lost" (Luke 19:10).

For All Sins

In the *Thirty-nine Articles* the sacrificial death of Christ is defined as the "perfect redemption, propitiation, and satisfaction for all the sins of the whole world, both original and actual" (*Article* XXXI, *CC*, p. 277). The atonement encompasses all sins whatever, original as well as actual, past and future, great or small, in time or eternity (Titus 2:14; 1 John 1:7; 2:2; Heb. 1:3; Wesley, *WJW* VIII, pp. 50–58). It further embraces all the penalties of sins (Gal. 3:13; Rom. 5:8–9; Heb. 2:14–15). The satisfaction is rendered, quite simply, for the sin of the world (John 1:20). All punishments are included under the general idea of *curse* (Gal. 3:13).

Not for Angels but Humanity

The speculation that Christ might have died also for fallen angels in addition to humanity (or that Christ might have assumed the form of an angel to redeem lost angels) was rejected at the Second Council of Constantinople, A.D. 553.

The Extent of Beneficial Effects of His Death

The *Russian Catechism* summarizes the three beneficial effects of Christ's death: "He, by his death on the cross, delivered us from *sin, the curse, and death.* . . . Therefore as in Adam we had fallen under sin, the curse, and death, so we are delivered from sin, the curse, and death in Jesus Christ" (*COC* II, pp. 475–76; Eph. 1:7; Gal. 3:13; Heb. 2:14, 15).

As to Efficacy—"For Many"

As to efficacy, his work addressed to all is in effect received only by some. Hence it is also rightly said that he died "for many" or "for his own."

The atonement that is sufficient for all is not effectually received by all. Hence it is said that he gave his life "as a ransom for many" (Matt. 20:28). "Christ was sacrificed once to take away the sins of many" (Heb. 9:28).

For the Faithful

"For all" means juridically and antecedently willed for all; but respecting and not coercing human freedom it means that Christ represents all who freely come to God by him. The propitiation given for all becomes effectively accepted only when the penitent responds in faith (Gal. 3:26).

Paul does not speak of a reconciliation without faith, but that "God presented him as a sacrifice of atonement, through faith in his blood" (Rom. 3:25). The atonement is addressed to all, but becomes fulfilled and appropriated among those who are united with Christ in his death and resurrection (Gal. 2:20).

It is not as though we add something to Christ's expiation by having faith in it, but that it is received for what it is when we have faith in it. The atoning work is done and completed quite independently of our acceptance of it but calls for our acceptance of it (Barth, *CD* IV/3, pp. 517ff.; IV/4, passim).

For His Own

Scripture speaks of the special efficacy of the atonement for the elect, those "called with a holy calling" (2 Tim. 1:9–10, KJV), whom "you have given me," who "see my glory, the glory you have given me because you loved me before the creation of the world" (John 17:9, 24; cf. Matt. 1:21; John 10:11; 15:13; Eph. 5:25; Heb. 2:13–14; 1 John 3:16; Turretin, *ITE* 4, Q10, 17; Fuller, *Works* II, pp. 373–74, 689ff.).

Universal Sufficiency Not Negated by Conditional Acceptance

"Christ's substitution was conditional, dependent upon the repentance and faith of sinners, with reference to the sins of men (personal sins), and unconditional with reference to the sin of the world (the guilt of the Adamic sin, collective sin)" (Bancroft, CT, p. 126; among passages that show that the universally sufficient atonement is contingent upon faithful response are John 17:9, 20, 24; Eph. 1:4; 2:1–10).

The basic distinction was well stated in a simile by the Lutheran theologian Johann Gerhard: "A hundred Christian captives are in bondage to the Turkish Emperor. A Christian prince pays a certain sum for the ransom of all. If any afterwards prefer to remain longer in captivity rather than enjoy the liberty acquired and offered them, they should ascribe this to themselves. For the universality of the ransom is not thereby invalidated" (LT IV, 178ff.; Schmid, DT, p. 365).

Sharing in His Death

Those have saving faith who answer responsively to the conditions necessary for participating in the fruits of redemption: baptism, faith, contrition, cooperation with grace, and perseverance (Council of Trent, Session VI.3).

Though Christ made sufficient satisfaction for all, each one must respond in repentance and faith in the working out of one's salvation (Tho. Aq., SCG IV.55, pp. 233–46). Though God wills antecedently that all be saved (even those who by their own choice are lost), humans will consequently to the antecedent will of God so as to elect in fact to be included in or excluded from the fruits of redemption. Since God creates and honors human freedom, God will not coerce freedom into the kingdom of light and grace.

A Time of Forbearance

To Allow for Repentance

If God's governance of history had been without mercy but with rigid adherence to the strict plumb-line of justice, the entire history of sin could have been condemned and lost and none spared. Christ's atoning death provided for a delay in the execution of the sentence against sin, a time in which God's kindness is intended to lead to repentance (Rom. 2:4; 2 Pet. 3:9), a time characterized by the continuing grace of God in the common life and God's continued guidance of history (Clement of Rome,

First Letter 7, *LCC* I, p. 47). It is this period that Paul described as a time of "passing over" or pretermission of sin: "In his forbearance, he had left the sins committed beforehand unpunished" (Rom. 3:25).

The Temporal Opportunity for Repentance Intrinsically Limited

Since repentance occurs in history, this forbearance is limited in duration. "In the past God overlooked such ignorance, but now he commands all people everywhere to repent. For he has set a day when he will judge the world with justice by the man he has appointed" (Acts 17:30–31; Barth, *CD* III/2, pp. 504–97). The urgency of preaching hinges on the limited time of repentance. No hearer has unlimited time to decide, nor does history itself continue without end.

The Salvation of Those Who Have Awaited Justice in Darkness

The patriarchs were saved by faith in the promise of God's coming. They trusted in God's mercy even when they could not see the further working out of salvation history. Of them Jesus said that "many will come from the east and the west, and will take their places at the feast with Abraham, Isaac and Jacob in the kingdom of heaven" (Matt. 8:11).

The Status of Innocents

Some have held that neonates and retarded innocents will be saved by this atonement insofar as they are judged to be incapable of refusing it and that those who do not know right from wrong cannot be said to have consented to the Adamic history of distortion (Hugh of St. Victor, *OSCF*, II.17, pp. 290–94, 461–66). Although valid baptism is generally assumed to be necessary for salvation (Tho. Aq., *ST* I, p. 1146; II, pp. 2393–2408), the intent of godly parents to have their children baptized may be accepted in lieu of actual baptism where circumstances have made actual baptism impossible (*BOC*, pp. 442–57). Reformed theology has generally held that elect children will be saved "by Christ through the Spirit, who worketh when, and where, and how he pleaseth" (Westminster Confession ch. X, *CC*, p. 206). "The promise is for you and your children and for all who are far off—for all whom the Lord our God will call" (Acts 2:39).

Vicarious Expiation and Propitiation

Propitiation Distinguished from Expiation

Propitiation is the means by which another is rendered propitious or favorable to one's cause or willing to listen to one's plea. Propitiation (*hilasmos, hilasterion*) refers to an appeasing or placating of divine anger against unrighteousness. That is propitious which renders one favorably disposed toward another who has been previously alienated. Propitiation means that which brings God near or makes God propitious or approachable.

To expiate is to make satisfaction. Christ is said to be the living expiation or "the atoning sacrifice for our sins" (1 John 2:2), enabling God and humanity to draw nearer or be made propitious or favorable.

Expiation required the removal, cleansing, or forgiveness of sin. Expiation required sacrifice in Temple ritual, where the blood of the victim was sprinkled so as to be interposed between God and our sin.

Propitiation has a different root, deriving from *prope*, "near." A propitious God is one who is near. That is propitious which brings God nearer. Propitiation is an act that enables God to come nearer to sinners (*BOC*, pp. 118, 191).

The focus of expiation is upon the removal of obstacles to the relationship. The focus of propitiation is upon the welcoming attitude of the Holy One for whom these obstacles are removed — God the Father.

Classical Christianity teaches that in the Son sin was expiated by his sacrificial offering, and the Father was propitiated in that a favorable response was elicited so that the divine-human relationship could be reconciled (Eleventh Council of Toledo, *SCD* 286, p. 111; cf. *BOC*, pp. 253, 259; Trent, *SCD* 993, p. 301).

The Appeal for Clemency

Note the context in which the idea of propitiation characteristically occurs: it is only after having been found guilty, having been sentenced by the judge, and bound over to the court for execution of sentence, that there is any need or opportunity to ask for clemency. In such cases the prisoner is better off if the aggrieved judge is rendered propitious or is disposed to show favor by some act that appeals to clemency.

Christ as Mercy-Seat

As high priest it is Christ's work both to expiate sin and to enable God to draw nearer to sinners. He had to be made like us in every way "in order that he might become a merciful and faithful high priest in service to God, and that he might make atonement for the sins of the people" (*hilaskesthai tas hamartias*, Heb. 2:17). Christ is the *hilastērion*, our Mercy-seat (*BOC*, p. 446).

The word itself (*hilastērion*) appears in the Greek Bible as a reference to the lid of the ark, the mercy-seat where the blood of atonement was sprinkled (*kapporeth*). It conveys the idea of covering, as in the covering of sin (Dodd, *Romans*, pp. 21ff.; L. Morris, *The Apostolic Preaching*, p. 172). Through the cross, God is brought near and conciliated, made propitious, or favorable to our hearing and plea. Those who have been without hope in the world have been "brought near through the blood of Christ" (Eph. 2:13).

Objections

C. H. Dodd has argued that it is not God who is appeased, nor the divine wrath conciliated, but rather characteristically in the New Testament the defilement is removed and sin atoned for. The stress accordingly is not upon propitiation as such (God being brought near by conciliation) but rather upon expiation (sin being removed; Dodd, *The Bible and the Greeks*, 1935, pp. 82–95).

The context of Paul's most important reference to *hilastērion* (Rom. 3:25), however, is the discussion of the wrath of God over sin. Hence it may be said that a propitiation is needed and offered to deliver humanity from divine wrath against ungodliness (Rom. 1:18; cf. Zech. 7:2; 8:22; Mal. 1:9). Hence it may be said that Christ is a propitiatory covering, sacrifice, or atonement for our sin effective through faith (Rom. 3:25; 1 John 2:2; 4:10; Heb. 2:17). This means that the death of Christ is the sacrificial means by which God is brought nearer or rendered propitious to one having faith, by which God becomes favorably disposed to sinners. The death of Christ secures forgiveness by its propitiatory power. It renders the aggrieved party propitious.

Meanwhile, questions about God's anger remain a stumbling block for many.

The Wrath of God Conciliated

Wrath (*orge*) differs from passionate anger, which is immediate and strong; wrath is more settled in the long term. The wrath of God suggests the continuing revulsion of the holiness of God against sin. The holy God cannot abide injustice, pride, deception, and willful diminution of the good. God's righteous wrath is directed against sin (John 3:36; Rom. 1:18; 5:9; Col. 3:6; R. V. G. Tasker, *The Biblical Doctrine of the Wrath of God*).

His anger, to speak metaphorically, is vented against all "godlessness and wickedness" (Rom. 1:18). Anger is the divine response to persistent, self-chosen human alienation, a response motivated by love. Forgiveness is made a nonevent if this deep sense of alienation is overlooked.

One cannot think of a serious parental love that makes no effort to protect the child against evil. The parent who is not revulsed by the evil that might overtake the child is not a good parent.

A remarkable reversal, however, happens in the story of the resistance of the holy God to sin. What happened in Christ was an act of substitution by which God demonstrated that his wrath had been turned aside so as to enable an entirely new relationship with humanity, not yielding to sin, but binding it up so as to make a new start.

This is quite different from the prevailing forms of conciliatory rituals in the history of religions, wherein men and women offer sacrifices to try to change a god's attitude from wrath to friendship (Arnobius, *Ag. the Heathen* VII, *ANF* VI, pp. 518–39). Rather here it is God who is taking the initiative to change the broken relationship with humanity. The picture of a human being placating an angry deity is not characteristic of New Testament teaching. More characteristic is the picture of God's quiet, costly approach to alienated humanity to overcome sin through sacrificial suffering (*Liturgy of James*, *ANF* VII, pp. 550–51).

Union and Substitution

The Bridegroom's Bestowal

Luther brought into play a marital metaphor to speak of substitution: "For it behooves Him, if He is a bridegroom, to take upon Himself the things which are His bride's, and to bestow upon her the things that are His. For if He gives her His body and His very self, how shall He not give her all that is His? And if He takes the body of the bride, how shall He not take all that is hers? . . . He by the wedding-ring of faith shares in the sins, death and pains of hell which are His bride's, nay, makes them His own, and acts as if they were His own, and as if He Himself had sinned" (Luther, *Christian Liberty*, WML II, p. 320).

Eternal Life in Union with Him

John's Gospel holds together the juxtaposed themes of the death of Christ and the eternal life of those in union with him. He came to bring eternal life (John 3:16; 6:40; 10:10; 1 John 4:9). This life is Christ, who is the life (John 1:4; 5:26; 6:25–59). Those who by faith live in union with him so as to keep his commandments (John 3:36; 5:24) share eternal life (John 10:28; 1 John 5:12). To bring humanity life, Christ died for us (John 3:14), his blood "purifies us from all sin" (1 John 1:7), as "the atoning sacrifice for our sins, and not only for ours but also for the sins of the whole world" (1 John 2:1).

Charles Wesley expressed this union warmly:

> Arise, my soul, arise;
> Shake off thy guilty fears;

The bleeding Sacrifice
  In my behalf appears.
Before the throne my Surety stands;
My name is written on his hands.

The Father hears him pray,
  His dear anointed One.
He cannot turn away
  The presence of his Son;
His Spirit answers to the blood,
And tells me I am born of God.

My God is reconciled;
  His pard'ning voice I hear;
He owns me for his child,
  I can no longer fear.
With confidence I now draw nigh,
And Father, Abba, Father, cry

("Arise My Soul," *MH*, 1966, p. 122).

CHRISTUS VICTOR

The way of salvation had to be consistent with the wisdom, majesty, and holiness of God. The cross constituted this "victory." But this forces the question as to how the cross could under any circumstances be considered a victory.

Victory by Justice, Not Power

Gregory Nazianzen knew that "the method of our new creation" must be one that would honor freedom without reinforcing pride: "all violent remedies were disapproved as not likely to persuade us, and as quite possibly tending to add to the plague through our chronic pride; but God disposed things to our restoration by a gentle and kindly method of cure," as a sapling must be slowly bent (*Orat.* XLV.12, *NPNF* 2 VII, p. 427).

The Cross Shows God's Nonviolent Way of Absorbing Violence

In no other way could we have learned, wrote Irenaeus, of God's way of redeeming humanity from sin and evil than by the death of the mediator on the cross. In a single sentence (among the most influential in early Christian teaching of salvation) Irenaeus distinguished between the violence of the Deceiver and the nonviolence of the Redeemer:

Since the apostasy tyrannized over us unjustly, and though we were by nature the property of the omnipotent God, alienated us contrary to nature, rendering us its own disciples, the Word of God, powerful in all things, and not defective with regard to His own justice, did righteously turn against the apostasy, and redeem from it His own property, *not by violent means*, (as the [apostasy] had obtained dominion over us at the beginning, when it insatiably snatched away what was not its own), *but by means of persuasion*, as became a God of counsel, who does not use violent means to obtain what He desires; so that neither should justice be infringed upon, nor the ancient handiwork of God go to destruction (*Ag. Her.* V.1.1, *ANF* I, p. 527, italics and parentheses added; cf. Rashdall, *The Idea of Atonement*, pp. 243ff.; D. Browning, *Atonement and Psychotherapy*).

In countering the Deceiver's unjust rule over humanity due to his apostasy and rebellion, God chose a just way, recovering what was his own not through coercion or by arbitrary fiat, but by way of persuasion, as was fitting to the character of God. God would redeem humanity not by force, but by taking responsibility for us, allowing the Enemy to stumble over his own follies (Martin Luther King, Jr. would later take this principle into the arena of conflict over racial injustice, *Why We Can't Wait*, pp. 36–46, 61–63).

A Just Means Required

In his treatise on the Trinity, Augustine established that there was no other more suitable way of freeing humanity from sin than incarnation and atonement. Other means were not lacking to God, but no other means were more fitting to God (*Trin.* XIII.10, *FC* 45, pp. 388–90). "By the justice of God the whole human race was delivered into the power of the devil," due to free human choice (*Trin.* XIII.12, *FC* 45, p. 391). Yet "it ought not to be understood as though God had done this [the cross] or ordered this to be done, but that He only permitted it, yet justly" (XIII.12, *FC* 45, p. 392). Even in the permission to let freedom play itself out in judgment, God continued to bestow providential blessings upon sinners.

Demonic Power Trapped by Its Lust for Power

The key to the divine economy was that "the devil was to be overcome, not by the power of God, but by His justice," for the devil had become "a lover of power"; so "it pleased God that for the sake of rescuing men from the power of the devil, the devil should be overcome not by power but by justice" (Augustine, *Trin.* XIII.13, *FC* 45, p. 393). This does not imply that power is intrinsically evil, but that it is always prone to abuse:

Would then the devil be conquered by this most just right, if Christ had willed to deal with him by power, not by righteousness? But He held back what was possible to Him [conquering by power], in order that He might first do what was fitting [conquering by powerlessness]. And hence it was necessary that He should be both man and God. For unless He had been man, He could not have been slain; unless He had been God, men would not have believed that He would not do what He could, but that He could not do what He would; nor should we have thought that righteousness was preferred by Him to power but that He lacked power (Augustine, *Trin.* XXX.14, *NPNF* 1 III, p. 177).

Viewed schematically the operative distinction between combatants in the atonement is between:

The Deceiver's way	The Son's way
Snatching	Persuading
The fall	The cross
Unjust means of bondage	Just means of redemption
Violence	Nonviolence

To Whom Was the Ransom Paid?— The Deceiver Caught by His Own Deceit

The question early arose as to whom, if a ransom metaphor is employed, would the ransom be paid? Some argued that the devil had temporarily acquired a right over the souls of free beings who had fallen into demonic syndromes not unwillingly but of their own choice. Hence it was asked whether, when God freed the captives, would it not be just and reasonable that such a temporary right be paid off?

Had the Devil Acquired a Legitimate Right to Bind Fallen Human Freedom?

Origen speculated on to whom the ransom was paid, commenting on Matthew 18:8. "Could it be then to the evil one? For he had us in his power, until the ransom for us should be given to him, even the life of Jesus, since he (the evil one) had been deceived, and led to suppose that he was capable of mastering that soul, and he did not see that to hold Him involved a trial of strength greater than he was equal to" (Origen, *Comm. on Matt. ANF* X, p. 489; cf. *Comm. on John ANF* X, pp. 349ff; Rashdall, *Idea of Atonement*, p. 261).

This theory (which never gained ecumenical acceptance) assumed that Satan had acquired a temporary quasi-legitimate right to bind human freedom since humanity had freely yielded to temptation. Hence God, according to this reasoning, justly purchased that right back by ransom of the death of the Son, wherein the Enemy did not recognize the power hidden in this ransomed Son, and the Deceiver, being deceived, was conquered.

The notion of payment to the devil of a ransom, however, never gained broad, general consent, for in Scripture, "The only payment made is described in terms of sacrifice, offered to God" (Hall, *DT* VII, p. 123; Tho. Aq., *ST* III, Q48.3, II, pp. 2284f.; cf. Alfred Cave, *The Scriptural Doctrine of Sacrifice and Atonement* [1877], II.2). The oversimplified theory that the death of Christ paid a ransom to the devil is contrary to scriptural testimony that the death of Christ was a triumph over the powers of evil (Col. 2:13-15; Heb. 2:14-15).

The Precise Equilibrium of Attributes

Gregory of Nyssa noted that "the sick do not dictate to their physicians the measures for recovery" (*Great Catech.* XVII, *NPNF* 2 V, p. 489). He provided an influential explanation of the ransom, grounded in the Irenaean premise that all the divine attributes must be seen in their intrinsic interconnectedness. The divine goodness pitied human fallenness. The divine omniscience knew the best means of rectifying it. Those means had to be completely just.

God's justice required that God not exercise "arbitrary sway over him who has us in his power, by tearing us away by a violent exercise of force from his hold, thus leaving some colour for a just complaint to him who enslaved man." He who "in His goodness had undertaken our rescue had to find no arbitrary method of recovery, but the one consonant with justice" (Gregory of Nyssa, *Great Catech.* XXII, *NPNF* 2 V, pp. 492–93). "Once we had voluntarily sold ourselves, he who undertook out of goodness to restore our freedom had to contrive a just and not a dictatorial method to do so" (Gregory of Nyssa, *ARI* 22, *LCC* III, p. 299).

Redemption could only occur through an actual history that exhibited God's wisdom (Gregory of Nyssa, *ARI* 20, *LCC* III, p. 297). "His *goodness* is evident in his choosing to save one who was lost. His *wisdom and justice* are to be seen in the way he saved us. His *power* is clear in this: that he came in the likeness of man" (Gregory of Nyssa, *ARI* 24, *LCC* III, p. 301, italics added).

The Double Irony of Demonic Deception

What method could be rightly chosen, given the severe obstacles? The Enemy, who held humanity, suffered from an intense desire to rule. It was by Satan's own inordinate pride and desire rather than God's sheer coercive power that the means of redemption were determined.

The famous metaphor Gregory of Nyssa chose may seem grotesque, but it carried the point through dramatically: "The Deity was hidden under the veil of our nature that so, as with ravenous fish, the hook of the Deity might be gulped down along with the bait of flesh; and thus, life being introduced into the house of death, and light shining in darkness, that which is diametrically opposed to life and light might vanish" (*Great Catech.* XXIV, *NPNF* 2 V, p. 494).

Satan would not have been transfixed upon the hook of deity had it not been for the inordinate desire to corrupt all flesh.

Victim as Victor

The Deceiver Justly Treated on the Basis of His Own Inordinate Desire and Deception

Some might wonder whether God might have thereby become involved in an inadvertent fraud. Gregory showed how God's atoning action was not deceptive, but just, by bringing wisdom, righteousness, and love together in a surprising and unprecedented way.

Justice means rendering to each his or her due, and "due recompense" was rendered to the Deceiver. "For it is the mark of justice to render to everyone the results of what he originally planted." In this case "the deceiver reaps the harvest of the seeds he sowed with his own free will. For he who first deceived man by the bait of pleasure is himself deceived by the camouflage of human nature. But the purpose of the action changes it into something good." An ironic medical analogy rounded off the argument: "Patients whose cure involves surgery and cautery grow incensed at their physicians when they smart under the pain of the incision. But if by these means they are restored to health and the pain of the cautery passes off, they will be grateful to those who effected their cure" (Gregory of Nyssa, *ARI* 26, *LCC* III, pp. 303–304). In this way Christ "shared in their humanity so that by his death he might destroy him who holds the power of death – that is, the devil – and free those who all their lives were held in slavery by their fear of death" (Heb. 2:14–15). Gregory's atonement centers upon the theme of the victory of Christ over the demonic (Christus Victor).

Long before Gregory, Cyprian had suggested the same basic metaphor: "The divine power of God's Son was a kind of fishhook hidden by the covering of human flesh" (Cyprian, *Expositio Symboli, MPL* 21, 354–55; translation in Chemnitz, *TNC*, p. 495). The hook metaphor derived from Job 41:1: "Can you pull in the leviathan with a fishhook?" the Lord asked Job, implying that it was beyond human power to fathom the ways of God. Leviathan later became symbolically identified with Satan.

Divine Justice Vindicated

John of Damascus corrected and extended the metaphor. He rejected both the notion that the devil had received ransom and the notion that God had unjustly given it: "God forbid that the blood of the Lord should have been offered to the tyrant. Wherefore death approaches, and swallowing up the body as a bait is transfixed on the hook of divinity, and after tasting of a sinless and life-giving body, perishes, and brings up again all whom of old he swallowed up. For just as darkness disappears on the introduction of light, so is death repulsed before the assault of life, and brings life to all, but death to the destroyer" (*OF* III.27, *NPNF* 2 IX, p. 72).

In this way the demonic grip that death held over human history was broken by the eternal Son in a way that was consistent with the justice and power of God: "Since the enemy had caught man with the bait of the hope of divinity, he himself was taken with the bait of the barrier of the flesh; and at the same time the goodness and wisdom and justice and power of God were made manifest" (*OF* III.1, *FC* 37, p. 268). In this way "destruction comes to the destroyer" (*OF* III.27, *FC* 37, p. 332; cf. Augustine, *Trin.*, *FC* 45, pp. 147–52), not as a divine deceit, for "he had done no violence, nor was any deceit in his mouth" (Isa. 53:9; *OF* III.27, *FC* 37, p. 332).

The Revulsion of the Revulsive One

The metaphorical sequence is intricate: death through sin had entered into the world. The eternal Son submitted to death to end the power of death. Humanity having offended, "it was necessary for Him to take upon Himself our redemption" (John of Damascus, *OF* III.27, *FC* 37, p. 332). The demonic Leviathan – death – was attracted to Christ's humanity, assuming the power to overcome this life as other human lives had been overcome and bound. Just at the right moment death was "pierced by the hook of the divinity," and having "tasted of the sinless and life-giving body," death was not only destroyed but was required to vomit up "all those whom it had swallowed down of old" (*OF* III.27, *FC* 37, p. 332).

Later Luther did not hesitate to adapt and develop the same metaphor: "I often delight myself with that similitude in Job, of an angle-hook that fishermen cast into the water, putting on the hook a little worm; then comes the fish and snatches at the worm, and gets therewith the hook in his jaws, and the fisher pulls him out of the water. Even so has our Lord

God dealt with the devil; God has cast into the world his only Son, as the angle, and upon the hook has put Christ's humanity, as the worm; then comes the devil and snaps at the (man) Christ, and devours him, and therewith he bites the iron hook, that is, the godhead of Christ, which chokes him, and all his power thereby is thrown to the ground. This is called *sapientia divine*, divine wisdom" (*Table Talk*, #CXCVII, *CLT*, p. 53).

Similarly Cyril of Jerusalem: "Jonah was cast into the belly of a great fish, but Christ of His own will descended to the abode of the invisible fish of death. He went down of His own will to make death disgorge those it had swallowed up, according to the Scripture: 'I shall deliver them from the power of the nether world, and I shall redeem them from death'" (*Catech. Lect.* XIV, FC 64, p. 43; Hos. 13:14). "His body, therefore, was made a bait to death, that the dragon [the Enemy], when hoping to devour it, might disgorge those also whom he had already devoured" (*Catech. Lect.* XII, FC 61, p. 236).

Silence the Only Answer to the Question "To Whom?"

Gregory Nazianzen also rejected the view that it was to the Deceiver that God had paid ransom. "To whom was that blood offered that was shed for us, and why was it shed?" To those who answer that it was offered to the devil, he replied: *pheu tes hubreos* ("fie upon the outrage"). That would imply that the thief not only received a ransom from God the Father for God the Son but was paid well for it. "If [paid] to the devil it is outrageous! The robber receives the ransom, not only from God, but a ransom consisting of God Himself. He demands so exorbitant a payment for his tyranny that it would have been right for him to have freed us altogether. But if the price is offered to the Father, I ask first of all, how? For it was not the Father who held us captive. . . . What remains to be said shall be covered with a reverent silence" (*Second Orat. on Easter Orat.* XLV.22, *NPNF* 2 VII, p. 431; see Lossky, *MTEC*, pp. 152–53).

In A.D. 569, Venantius Fortunatus envisioned the cross as the moment wherein the tempter was decisively outdone:

> Where he in flesh, our flesh who made,
> Our sentence bore, our ransom paid . . .
> The price which none but he could pay,
> And spoiled the spoiler of his prey
>
> ("The Royal Banners Forward Go,"
> trans. J. M. Neale, *HPEC*, pp. 128–29).

THE VALUE OF CHRIST'S DEATH FOR US

While the doctrines of incarnation and personal union became firmly developed consensually in the patristic period, those on redemption and atonement remained somewhat undeveloped in specific details. The essential points of the atonement were all securely embedded in Scripture texts, which were often studied, quoted, and interpreted by patristic writers. But the systematic elaboration and defense of the teaching of Christ's death as sacrifice continued to be developed through extended medieval, Reformation, and post-Reformation controversies.

Amid this lengthy history, four essential types of atonement exegesis have persistently waxed and waned through the traditions of interpretation. These four traditions are viewed in this section not as pure or exclusive types but amalgamations of overlapping themes that tend to cohere and repeat in a series of interpreters. They are the exemplar, governor, exchange, and victor motifs.

All have legitimacy, and none of itself is complete. They are best viewed as complementary tendencies rather than as cohesive schools of thought represented by a single theorist. Though Aulen has described one as classical (CV, pp. 20–33, 160–63), all four are to be found in classical Christian writings. Each approach stresses a constellation of related texts.

The Exemplar or Moral Influence Motif

Moral Aspects of Atonement in Classical Christianity

Several aspects of the example theory are well integrated into classical Christian teaching. The death of Christ is viewed in the New Testament as a demonstration of the love of God, which seeks to elicit responses of love from humanity. "For Christ's love compels us, because we are convinced that one died for all, and therefore all died. And he died for all, that those who live should no longer live for themselves but for him who died for them and was raised again" (2 Cor. 5:14-15). In addition to and in relation to vicarious, substitutionary, and sacrificial motifs, Christ's death exercises a moral influence upon believing humanity. "Be imitators of God, therefore, as dearly loved children and live a life of love, just as Christ loved us and gave himself up for us as a fragrant offering and sacrifice to God" (Eph. 5:1-2; John Chrysostom, Hom. on Eph. XVII, NPNF 2 XIII, pp. 128-32).

As Christ became obedient unto death for others, so the faithful are called to "Have this mind among yourselves, which you have in Christ

Jesus, who though he was in the form of God, did not count equality with God a thing to be grasped, but emptied himself, taking the form of a servant" and "became obedient to death—even death on a cross!" (Phil. 2:5–8). The cross is commended as a pattern of mind to have "among yourselves."

Nowhere is the deep nature and malignity of sin more truly revealed than in the cross. Also revealed there is the pattern of righteousness—the sinless life given for others—which the Christian is enabled to follow by grace. The cross reveals the love of God for sinners and makes a challenging appeal for a loving response, eliciting repentance for sin (Ignatius, *Eph.* 1, *ANF* I, p. 49; Hall, *DT* VII, p. 141). These aspects of the exemplary theory of atonement are thoroughly integrated into the classical view (Augustine, *Trin.* I.6–13, *NPNF* 1 III, pp. 22–36; Thomas à Kempis, *Imitation of Christ*; Isaac Watts, "When I Survey the Wondrous Cross," *HPEC*, p. 136). "To those who are rescued from the prisoners' yoke Redemption further procures the power of following the way of the cross by imitation" (Leo, *Serm.* LXXII.1, *NPNF* 2 XII, p. 184). Here the cross is not reduced to moral example, but has exemplary power.

The Cross in the Pelagian-Abelardian-Socinian Tradition

The tradition of Abelard and Socinus, anticipated by Pelagius, is not a consensual tradition, but a distortion that reappears in heavier or lighter tones periodically. Without denying objective aspects of the atonement altogether, this tradition has overstressed the subjective appropriation of the cross, holding that the central intent of the death of Christ was to serve as supreme example of divine love eliciting and enabling a loving human response, so as to draw humanity toward the love of the Father (J. S. Lidgett, *The Spiritual Principles of the Atonement* [1901], pp. 460–61). The moral responsibility of man is encouraged by the example of Jesus' death as a martyr. By his death he confirmed the sincerity of his teaching.

Abelard taught that the principal value of Christ's death was its exemplary effect through the responses of love that the cross elicits. Christ's death was significant because it was thought to move the beholder to repentance and faith (Abelard, *Epitome of Christian Theology*; *Comm. on Rom.*). A key moment in the history of atonement theory came in the condemnation by the Council of Sens (1141) of Abelard's tendency to speak of the efficacy of Christ's death with inordinate attention to its subjective appropriation to the neglect of objective change in the divine-human relationship (*SCD*, pp. 150–51; cf. Bernard of Clairvaux, *On the Errors of Abelard*, 22).

Similar but more radically nonconsensual was Socinus, who viewed

Christ as a prophet and teacher who saved his pupils by instruction from evil defined as ignorance and blessed them with the benefits of knowledge. His death was viewed as a final act of moral heroism, a unique example of suffering patience, eliciting repentance and faith (F. Socinus, *Praelectiones Theologicae*, xv-xxix; cf. Mozley, *Atonement*, pp. 147-51; Lidgett, *Spiritual Principle of Atonement*, pp. 474-76; Stevens, *CDS*, pp. 157-61; McDonald, *ADC*, pp. 196-99).

The Power of His God-Consciousness Demonstrated on the Cross

According to Friedrich Schleiermacher, the father of liberal theology, Christ's perfect God-consciousness is the basis for the divine-human reconciliation. Deeply compassionate for humanity, Christ identified with the lowly and exposed himself to the suffering that comes from sin, most powerfully upon the cross. As faith was elicited from others who beheld this self-giving, they were drawn into the circle of influence of his God-consciousness, sharing in his sense of sonship, relieved of the sense of God's anger, aware of God's good will (*ChrF*, secs. 100-104; Sheldon, *EC*, p. 389). "The Redeemer assumes believers into the power of his God-consciousness, and this is His redemptive activity" (*ChrF*, p. 425). Avoiding expiatory language and resisting the idea of divine wrath resting upon the Son and vicarious satisfaction, the pivotal event of Schleiermacher's atonement was "His sympathy with sin, which was strong enough to stimulate a redemptive activity sufficient for the assumption of all men into His vital fellowship" (*ChrF*, p. 462). Seeking to free atonement theory from objectivism, he overstressed the subjective side, tending "to make our poor experience the measure of what God is" (Cave, *DWC*, p. 227).

The Moral Influence of Christ's Death

Similar in tone is the Congregationalist theologian Horace Bushnell, who argued that Christ's death was offered not for the purpose of satisfying some shadowy divine justice, but to reveal God's love. He placed little stress objectively upon Christ's substitutionary suffering in our place. The cross did not change the divine-human relationship, but basically revealed to humanity God's love. His moral influence elicits repentance on the part of human recipients. Only repentance is needed for one's acceptance with God. The value of Christ's death for us lies in the influence that death exerts on human persons and through them upon the fabric of human society and history. Christ's life, teaching, works, and death serve the purpose of influencing the moral quality of life of persons and societies (Bushnell, *The Vicarious Sacrifice*; cf. Schleiermacher, *ChrF*;

Ritschl, *CDJR*; B. Jowett, *Comm. on Epist. of St. Paul*, 2d ed., 1859; Hastings Rashdall, *The Idea of Atonement*).

Objections

This emphasis upon example has led to distortions. Though the ethical emphasis has at times been somewhat neglected and has repeatedly required some form of recovery, it is always prone to being overstated. Several serious objections have been raised:

(1) This approach to atonement tends to view the death of Christ as little more than the death of a noble martyr. What redeems is finally little more than his human example of faithfulness to duty, eliciting moral responses (Wollebius, *CTC* 18, *RDB*, pp. 103–105). "To be sure, the example is precious but far too high for us; we cannot follow," Luther countered. "It is as if I were to come to some river bank where roads and highways end. I see nothing but water before me and am unable to get across. . . . There it would not help me if someone were to point out to me the goal which I must attain" (*Expos. of St. John*, John 14:6, *WLS* I, p. 186; *WA* 45, 497).

Humanity does not need merely to be instructed but to have sins forgiven, not merely enlightened but redeemed from sin, for we are not only ignorant but corrupt, not merely finite but sinners, not merely those who feel guilty but who are guilty.

Imagine a prisoner under sentence of death. Suppose one came to instruct him on the nature of justice and the values of the laws regulating capital crimes. Such instruction would not constitute a release. Christ's death means more than mere instruction. It involves the good news that the prisoner is released and can go home free since another has paid his penalty, dying in his place. "Those err who hold that Christ is a Legislator who forms moral habits and, as a sort of Socrates, proposes perfect examples of moral conduct. For although Christ does indeed give direction to actions, He first prepares and renews a man within and thereupon controls also the body, the hands and feet. For works follow faith just as the shadow follows the body" (Luther, *Lectures on Isaiah*, Isa. 52:7 [1527–1529], *WLS* I, p. 185; *WA* 25, 324). Insofar as there is no element of sacrifice or substitution in this exemplary theory, it fails to meet biblical criteria.

(2) Often the exemplary view does not say enough about who the teacher was. In the New Testament the efficacy of his work depends upon the theandric identity of his person. Classical Christianity affirms that Jesus engaged in prophetic teaching, but the crucial premise of this teaching is that he was a teacher sent from God (John 3:2). He taught them not as the scribes, but as one having authority in his own person (Mark 1:22).

There is insufficient awareness in the exemplary theory of how the triune doctrine and the teaching of the only true Mediator are crucial to the meaning and value of Christ's death (Strong, *Syst. Theol.*, pp. 728–40; Hodge, *Syst. Theol.* II, pp. 566–73; Hall, *DT* VII, pp. 33–34).

(3) Exemplary theory has too optimistically assumed that the will is not radically bound by sin and that no punishment for sin is required. The theory is based upon a weakened, diluted conception of the nature of sin. "Pelagianism credited the sinner with sufficient strength to arise after falling, nay to attain to a state of perfect sinlessness without super-natural aid, and hence denied the necessity of grace and unduly exagger-ated the moral capacity of human nature" (Pohle-Preuss, *DT* V, p. 42). The exemplary view of atonement is likely to go hand in glove with Pelagian anthropology. It may also be adapted to a humanistic pantheism that views each individual soul as a spark of divinity, so that deity is potentially incarnate in every soul, redemption thereby becoming a pro-cess of enlightenment by which one is reabsorbed into the infinite ocean of being.

Among additional problems with this tendency are: (4) It makes the life, not the death of Christ the essential focus of his work. (5) In Scrip-ture Christ does not merely suffer with humanity, but *for* humanity, a vicarious premise ignored by this theory. (6) This view fails to show how anyone born before Jesus could receive redemption, since they would have had no access to his moral teaching or influence. (7) This view locates the effective power of atonement in personal experience, yet lacks any objectivity beyond that experience. (8) The moral influence theory tends sentimentally to stress the love of God at the expense of the justice of God.

(9) More seriously, the exemplary view misses the point that finally it is not humanity only that needs to be reconciled, but primarily the holi-ness of God. The only necessity for reconciliation it discovers is found in the moral nature of humanity. It fails to grasp why the righteousness of God necessarily requires punishment of sin.

The Rector or Moral Governance Motif

The Grotian View of Atonement

Arminian Dutch jurist Hugo Grotius sought to show that Christ's death paid the penalties due for our sins without demeaning divine righ-teousness. The death of Christ demonstrates the lengths to which God will go to uphold the moral order of the universe.

The emphasis was upon the righteous governance of God, a context in which the preservation and example of order is a primary gubernatorial value and the legitimate reason for punishing sinners. "For all punishment presupposes some common good—the conservation and example of order" (Grotius, *DCF,* quoted in Cave, *DWC,* p. 206). If this aim can be achieved by the cross, it is not necessary that punishment be distributed precisely according to individual guilt. By the cross God is morally able to transmute the stern law that "those who sin must die," yet not so as to subvert the fundamental moral order. Since God is viewed as ruler (*Rector*) of this moral order, this is often called the rectoral theory.

This theory focused not upon the satisfaction offered to God, but on the moral necessities of God's government of the universe, for God's government cannot be maintained if sin is not punished. Pardoned offenders must be reminded of the high value God places upon the law and the high price of violating it, as is manifested on the cross. The necessity for atonement lies in a governmental necessity of God to punish sin or provide a substitute for such punishment compatible with God's righteous governance.

Christ's death removes the barrier to executive clemency. If God had simply forgiven humanity by fiat without the cross, that would not have had moral efficacy for humanity. Rather God chose a way to reconciliation by which both his holiness and love were manifested, sparing humanity, but in such a way that it is unthinkable that God held the punishment of sin as a small matter. God is moved to make humanity happy and blessed and chooses this as his best means. While Grotius is its chief representative (*On the Truth of the Christian Religion; DCF; LWHG*), this view is also found to some degree in Jonathan Edwards, Joseph Bellamy, Samuel Hopkins, R. W. Dale, and many Wesleyan-Arminians, such as Thomas Ralston and John Miley.

Resistance to Imputation and Propitiation

Later advocates of this approach often resisted a flattened notion of imputation—that sin was directly imputed to Christ or that the righteousness of God was imputed without further requirement or consequence to believers. They objected to an uncritical view of absolute substitution of merit and demerit that might neglect human moral responsiveness. They resisted the implication that persons are passive receptacles of salvation. They worried about the potential of moral license that might emerge out of the unconstrained idea that Christ's righteousness was unilaterally imputed to believers (Denny, *Studies in Theology,* pp. 74–99; Miley, *Syst. Theol.* I, pp. 441–530; Ralston, *ED,* pp. 123–60).

The emphasis here is upon God's compassion, not penal substitution. Since God is love, it is sometimes held that there is no need for his "wrath" to be propitiated. Sin is viewed as a challenge to the human moral order rather than primarily as an outrage against God's holiness. The strength of this view is its sturdy resistance to antinomianism. It is vigilant to show that divine mercy and forgiveness do not prompt moral irresponsibility. Christ's death manifested justice rather than expiating it, offering a penal example that served not to reinforce but to deter sin. This theory is important historically because it provides a middle ground between Socinus and satisfaction theory, combining both moral influence and transactional metaphors.

Some Objections

Some expressions of this view do not adequately account for those scriptural passages that view the cross as propitiating God himself, as the revelation of God's righteousness, and as an execution of the penalty of law. The main objection is that forgiveness rests on repentance as its ground, not objective atonement. Critics argue that this view makes the purging of sin only possible, not actual—it does not adequately account for the fact that God has already actually and objectively purged sin in the cross, failing to see the cross as the finished work of salvation, and wishing to add human repentance as necessary to the work of salvation (Hodge, *Syst. Theol.* II, pp. 578–81; Strong, *Syst. Theol.*, pp. 740–41).

Critics further argue that the work of Christ in this view has no direct effect upon God except that it renders God morally safe in forgiving sin, by awakening in sinners such a powerful sense of the evil of sin that they will turn from it in repentance. By being the source of repentance, the death of Christ removes the subjective obstacle in the way of forgiveness. Thus there is a tendency to represent repentance itself as the atoning act.

The Exchange or Satisfaction Motif

The Offense Is Against God's Holiness

Anselm emphasized the need for making reparation to God for sin, especially by use of analogies from the medieval penitential system to the idea of satisfaction in describing the Godward effect of Christ's death. The satisfaction of God's justice required that God be rendered exactly his due.

Sin is no minor offense, for God had firmly declared that the sinner must die. The penalty must be executed. Its nonexecution would be inadmissible. God would be less than holy if sin were permitted to go unpunished. It is in keeping with God's justice that sin not be cheaply remitted, but must be punished, or some satisfaction offered. Since sin is an infinite offense against divine holiness, the satisfaction for sin must be infinite. Either satisfaction or punishment was required by God's very nature. There is a real necessity for the punishment of sin in the nature of God's justice, not simply in the moral nature of humanity.

No finite being could make a sufficient satisfaction. Only one both truly God and truly human could, by taking the place of sinners, make a complete satisfaction to divine justice. In this way the death of Christ becomes understood as a debt sufficiently paid to the Father, not a ransom ambiguously paid to the devil. The death of Christ is the equivalent of all the demands of retributive justice against all for whom Christ died (Anselm, *CDH*).

The Reformed tradition has shared much of the Anselmian language and assumptions, focusing upon the themes of penal substitution and the sacrificial efficacy of the cross. Christ takes our place. Calvin argued that Christ "took upon himself and suffered the punishment that, from God's righteous judgment threatened all sinners; that he purged with his blood those evils which had rendered sinners hateful to God; that by this expiation he made satisfaction and sacrifice duly to God the Father; that as intercessor he has appeased God's wrath; that on this foundation rests the peace of God with men" (Calvin, *Inst.* 22.16.2).

Objections

In some of its expressions, this view fails to emphasize adequately the active obedience of Christ in his entire life under the law and focuses primarily upon the passive obedience of Christ in his suffering and death. Some expressions tend to exalt God's majesty or honor above God's holiness or love. Some disproportionally focus upon medieval commercial analogies (ransom, payment, debt) to the neglect of other moral, social, and familial analogies. The stress upon satisfaction of the Father's honor by the Son at times seems exaggerated. It tends toward a disjunction between an overly harsh Father and a compassionate Son. Too much is made of the divine majesty being offended, neglecting the fact that God can show mercy and forgiveness without harming his honor or majesty. Critics argue that the New Testament rather views the death of Christ not as a substituted penalty, but a substitute for a penalty (Raymond, *Syst. Theol.* II, p. 257).

The Victor or Dramatic Motif

Sometimes called the classic or dramatic theory, this view stresses those biblical texts that speak of reconciliation under metaphors of victory over demonic powers. The predicament is that sinners have chosen (through a collective history) to belong to the demonic order because of their sin. The Son pays the price of their redemption from bondage. The forces of death hungrily, avariciously, proudly took Jesus' life in the place of sinners' but could not hold him in the grave. In his resurrection he broke the power of demonic sin, guilt, and death, leaving Satan broken, though continuing to rage in history. Hostile forces are brought down. Where sin and death had reigned, righteousness and life now reign. The atonement is constituted by the fact that Christ has broken the power of evil.

The keynote of the cross is victory, Christ's victory over the powers of sin, guilt, pride, inordinate sensuality (the flesh), the devil, wrath, and death. He took away the curse of the law, "nailing it to the cross. And having disarmed the powers and authorities, he made a public spectacle of them, triumphing over them by the cross" (Col. 2:14-15). The victory has cosmic significance (Col. 1:15-23; Aulen, CV, pp. 120-31; cf. Rom. 8:18-21).

The Johannine tradition provides prime textual ground for this view, wherein "the whole world" is assumed to be "under the control of the evil one" (1 John 5:19); "The reason the Son of God appeared was to destroy the devil's work" (1 John 3:8); "Now the prince of this world will be driven out" (John 12:31). Already "the prince of this world now stands condemned" (John 16:11). "When the prince of the world is bound, all that he held in captivity is released" (Leo, Serm. XXII.4, NPNF 2 XII, p. 131).

This view, prominent among early Christian writers, was to some degree displaced by Anselm, then returned to centrality with Luther and Protestantism (notably reinterpreted by Gustaf Aulen). It is well expressed in Luther's "Ein feste Burg":

> And though this world, with devils filled,
> Should threaten to undo us,
> We will not fear, for God hath willed
> His truth to triumph through us;
> The Prince of Darkness grim,
> We tremble not for him;
> His rage we can endure,
> For lo, his doom is sure;
> One little word shall fell him
>
> (MH 1964, #20).

Aulen's influential account of this view downplays the substitution and satisfaction motifs in Scripture (Gal. 1:4; 1 Cor. 15:3; 2 Cor. 5:21); is selective in his use of sources; "establishes his point only by ignoring other facets of their accounts"; focuses inordinately upon the conflict within God; and "gives little notice to what it [salvation] cost God" (McDonald, *ADC*, pp. 263–65).

Comparison of the Complementary Tendencies

The differences between these four motifs correspond generally to what is perceived to be the deepest predicament of humanity—ignorance, misery, sin, or the bound will.

If the human predicament is conceived primarily as:

IGNORANCE	MISERY	SIN	BOUND WILL
Then the atonement is likely to be viewed as:			
Moral illumination and influence	Inauguration of a reign of happiness	Salvation by Christ in our place	Redemption from curse of sin
The corresponding social predicament is viewed as:			
Lack of education	Poverty or neurosis	Willful rebellion	Demonic captivity
The predicament of the psychosomatic interface centers more particularly, in each case, upon the:			
Ignorant mind	Sensate experience	Lost soul	Bound will
These theories of atonement have been principally formed in four related, complementary traditions:			
Pelagian-Abelardian	Grotian-Arminian	Augustinian-Anselmian	Irenaean-Cappadocian
Metaphorical focus becomes variously trained upon:			
Moral example	Executive clemency	Sacrifice	Victory

IGNORANCE	MISERY	SIN	BOUND WILL
Each is ordinarily called by its key phrase:			
Moral influence	Rectoral governance	Substitution	Christus Victor
Sometimes expressed by the summary term:			
Marturial	Rectoral	Commercial	Dramatic
The prevailing tendency is:			
Experiential, subjectivist	Legal, administrative	Penal, substitutional	Ransom-doxological
Each has a special locus of influence within Protestantism:			
Liberal	Arminian	Calvinist	Lutheran
Key advocates of this tradition in the modern period are:			
Schleiermacher	Miley	Hodge	Aulen
Each motif gives resistance to some theme regarded as potentially excessive:			
Resists original sin	Resists imputation	Resists works-righteousness	Resists commercial expressions
The potential problematic issue latent in the theory:			
Pelagian optimism	Legalistic synergism	Predestinarian decrees	Antinomianism
Thematic focus:			
Subject self	Moral reliability	Exchange	Conflict
Primary setting:			
Intrapsychic awareness	Public order	Transactional exchange	Cosmic conflict overcome
Recent inheritors include:			
Unitarianism	Liberation theology	Neoevangelical theology	Neoclassical orthodoxy

The satisfaction and Christus Victor themes come closer to being consensual approaches (in the tradition of the Irenaeus, the Cappadocians, Augustine, Anselm, and Calvin) than the others. All four need some corrective voices from the others to form an adequate teaching. They are best viewed as complementary. The scriptural and ecumenical teaching of atonement requires a good balance of the moral nature of man, moral government of God, the substitution of Christ for us in our place, and the consequent victory of Christ over demonic powers (J. K. Mozley, *The Doctrine of Atonement*; R. S. Franks, *The History of the Doctrine of the Work of Christ*, 2 vols.; L. W. Grensted, *A Short History of the Doctrine of the Atonement*; L. Morris, *The Atonement of the Death of Christ*).

THE MEANING OF DAILY SUFFERING

Anyone who understands that God suffers for humanity has come close to the heart of Christianity. The story of Jesus is essentially that of God suffering for us.

We speak of *daily* suffering to underscore that suffering is endemic to the human situation. Suffering invariably accompanies freedom, for freedom is perennially prone to anxiety, guilt, and boredom (Kierkegaard, *The Concept of Anxiety*; Niebuhr, *NDM* I; Oden, *SA*, I–III).

There is no reason to perpetuate the false impression that suffering occurs only under special conditions of stress, sickness, or tragedy. Suffering dogs the tracks of freedom. The suffering of Christ for us is primarily directed to that suffering that results from sin, from which humanity suffers daily.

Gospel as Theodicy

The recollection of Christ's suffering is itself an act by which faith participates in God's own humbling (Peter of Damascus, *Treasury, Philokal.* I, pp. 234–39). A high Christology is the key to a deep-going theodicy.

What Is Theodicy?

Theodicy is the attempt to speak rightly of God's justice (*theos-dikē*) under conditions of suffering and evil in which it is assailed. Theodicy is an intellectual discipline that seeks to clarify the hidden aspect of God's goodness despite apparent contradictions of that goodness in history. Its task is to vindicate the divine attributes of omnipotence, love, justice, and holiness in relation to the continuing existence of evil in history (Augustine, *EDQ* 21, *FC* 70, p. 48).

Just being a human being is enough to qualify one to ask the question: "Why do I suffer?" Human existence seems to require it. If this profound problem falls anywhere in the university curriculum, it falls in the lap of systematic theology. Though treated sporadically in literature and philosophy, it is not widely treated in psychology or sociology or even biblical exegesis. Universities do not appoint professors of theodicy, yet everyone suffers. The meaning of suffering was a central concern of ancient Christian writers. Without seeking it, they had their share of it.

The Difficulty of the Question

No theological question is more difficult or recurrent than why the just suffer, except for the question of why the absolutely just One has suffered absolutely.

Whatever one may theorize in response to suffering does not end suffering. The best theorists continue to suffer and even to inflict suffering upon others by means of their theories. Yet caring persons cannot simply reply with silence to the discomforting fact of suffering. In order not to say nothing, we must say something. The best Christian theodicy flows directly out of the cross.

Evil and Salvation

Framing the Question

There can be little persuasive talk of the existence of God if the evil of the world is never in any way decisively overcome, sooner or later. The alleged almightiness of God would be thrown into question if evil were in no sense overcomeable, for how could one think of God either as incomparably good or mighty if evil were more or equally powerful?

Those who cannot provide inquirers with some plausible understanding of suffering and evil in relation to God's saving activity are ill-prepared to minister to them. It is just at this point that clarity about the cross becomes a pastoral necessity (see Oden, "A Theodicy for Pastoral Practice," *Pastoral Theology* [1983]: 223–48).

Salvation as Theodicy

The gospel of salvation is intricately connected with the interfacing problems of evil and suffering. If there were no problem of evil, there would be no felt or experienced need for the gospel of salvation. The gospel is good news precisely about evil's defeat (1 John 3:8; Moltmann, *ICT*, pp. 8–13).

If evil is no problem, then there is no need of salvation. If there is no prospect of salvation from evil, then there can be no meaningful talk of a Christ of any sort. "The problem of evil only exists in relation to the conceivability of some sort of salvation" (Quick, *DC*, p. 193). Awareness of evil and suffering arouses a holy discontent that points the discontented, hungering for a saving answer in God, beyond the present sphere of human alienation (cf. Berdyaev, *Freedom and the Spirit*, pp. 158ff.).

We are clever at avoiding evidences of the subtle and recalcitrant power of evil. The awareness of evil and suffering often seems to be an obstacle to faith. They pose profound questions to which only the cross stands finally as an answer.

Doctrines of Evil Correlated with Teachings of Salvation

Various views of salvation have assumed or offered various explanations of *that pivotal form of evil that defines and shapes other evils*. Summarily, these may be schematized in this way:

THE PRIME EVIL	ITS SPHERE	PROTOTYPE	SALVATION FOUND IN
Tyranny of passions	The cosmos	Stoicism	Reason
Inability to enjoy	The passions	Epicureanism	Hedonic enjoyment
Death	Vulnerability of life	Hellenism	Immortality
Pain	The feelings	Buddhism	Nirvana
Ignorance	The intellect	Platonism	Philosophy
Property	Class alienation	Marxism	Revolution
Repression	Neurosis	Freudianism	Psychoanalysis
Sin	The will	Judeo-Christian tradition	Forgiveness

It cannot be our purpose here to set forth comparative views of evil in various developing historic traditions, however important that subject may be. It is our purpose to show that Christian theodicy exists in the context of the all-too-familiar human problem of suffering—a problem dealt with in many different traditions—and that the cross of Christ stands as the decisive event illuminating Christian theodicy.

Christianity: The Evil of the Bound Will Makes Other Evils Evil

Christianity views the pivotal evil that shapes and penetrates all other evils to be the evil of the will, especially as manifested in transgenerational sin (Quick, *DC*, pp. 193-95). Christ offers forgiveness of sin as a binding up of the evil that creates and elicts other evils.

If salvation is to attack the deepest root of evil, it must attack and deal with the problem of sin. This is not to say that all evils are unambiguously the direct result of sin, for sin does not directly cause earthquakes and floods (though it may shape our insensitivities and responses to them), but rather that willed sin is the most profound root of the wrong that human beings universally experience in history. Christians believe that if the problem of sin could be rightly dealt with (it is best not to say "solved"), then the most devastating aspects of evil would be constrained.

The good news of God's atoning work on the cross assumes that the radical evil in the world is not finally death, pain, ignorance, class conflict, or libido repression, but sin. The deepest root of evil lies in the distortions of moral self-determination.

Suffering: A Way of Summarizing the Central Human Problem

Suffering and Punishment

It may seem absurd that so much of human history and acculturation have so often been formed around the seemingly odd premise that ·suffering is a punishment. But the connection seems to appear everywhere in the history of morality and religion. The logic is unsparing: if we receive the due reward of our deeds, and if we suffer, the thought suggests itself that we suffer because of our evil deeds.

The Common Experience of Suffering for Others

The deeper level of the perplexity of suffering, however, is not when people suffer for their own sins (that has a ring of justice), but when they suffer for the sins of others (that seems unjust). Your neighbor may have to suffer innocently for something you have done (even inadvertently). Who does not know how it feels to suffer from something someone else has done? If so, there appears to be universally experienced a profoundly vicarious aspect to human suffering. It is as if all humanity had become mixed in a transgenerational stew where one person's willed evil causes others to suffer. No one comes out unhurt.

Sociality of Suffering

The premise of individualism does not help toward a solution of an enigma that is intrinsically social—the complex relational interfacing of human beings in covenant histories, the histories of families, of associations, of nations. The most profound forms of human solidarity are glimpsed in suffering. We are cursed by others, yet no one hears or discerns exactly from whose voice the curse came.

Consequences of Sin Historically Transmitted

Why has it appeared so convincingly to so many cultures that we are cursed and punished by sin? The consequences of sin, like all self-determined historical acts, become locked into causal chains. These consequences cannot be simply stopped. It does no good to pray: "Stop the world, I want to get off." To pretend that the consequences of sin could be suddenly halted would be to suspend the present natural order of cause and effect, wherein one person's bad choice causes another to suffer. To change that would be to redesign the world totally, and no one is up to that.

Athanasius argued that evil is not substantially or originally existent, but that it has emerged out of an unnecessitated history, a result of human freedom abused. Its history is basically self-determined by will, not necessitated. If so, both the views that evil is natural and that evil is coexistent with God are inadequate (Athanasius, *Contra Gentis* 2-7, NPNF 2 IV, pp. 4-7; cf. Augustine, *EDQ*, FC 70, p. 39).

Consequent Innocent Suffering

Sufferings for the most part appear to be the inevitable consequences of the corporate sins of humanity working intergenerationally to affect persons mostly but not wholly innocent of the original acts of wrongdoing. Each individual then places his or her own distinctive stamp upon the history of sin. When we make wrong uses of good creaturely gifts (like sex and power and wealth and influence), when we choose the lesser good above the greater, it is often the case that others who did not make our choices have to suffer the consequences of our bad choices.

These causal chains proceed like all natural ordering proceeds, from person to person, mother to daughter, family to family, neighbor to neighbor, seller to buyer, nation to nation. What we sow will somehow be reaped, if not by us, by others who may suffer from our choices.

Prosperity of the Wicked

In Psalm 73 the prosperity of the wicked is viewed as a temptation to faith. "Surely God is good to Israel, to those who are pure in heart. *But*"—(Ps. 73:1, italics added)—how well off are the scoffers: "They have no struggles; their bodies are healthy and strong." "Pride is their necklace." "They say, 'How can God know?'" Then comes the distinctive interpretation that faith enables: "When I tried to understand all this, it was oppressive to me till I entered the sanctuary of God; then I understood their final destiny. Surely you place them on slippery ground" (Ps. 73:4-18). That all sin stands under the penalty of death is proven by an empirical fact: There has never yet been a sinner who has not in time died.

In the apocalyptic tradition, grossly unfair distributions of rewards and punishments were viewed as proof of the anticipated end of history, the final resurrection of the just and unjust. Jesus' resurrection meant the beginning of that end time. It provided a way by which one may participate already in the end time, when all wrongs shall be righted.

Of Things Too Wonderful

Much of the Old Testament views prosperity as a sign of God's favor, and adversity as an indication of divine displeasure over sin. But such a view was inadequate to explain innocent suffering, such as that of Job. Finally lacking a formal solution to his urgent queries, Job submitted himself to the infinite majesty of God, confessing that "no plan of yours can be thwarted"; "Surely I spoke of things I did not understand, things too wonderful for me to know" (Job 42:1-4). In this way the evil of suffering led to the good of repentance.

Does Christ's Death Affect Our Daily Suffering?

Christ's Death Did Not Negate Either Our Freedom or Natural Causality

Christ's death did not change the way the world is put together as a natural order of cause and effect; causality was not banished and the chance that I might harm you was not taken away. That would have paid too high a price for freedom from sin, namely freedom from freedom, which means bondage, a parade of automatons, causal chains without self-determination in a nonhistory lacking freedom.

Christ's death does not reduce the freedom that risks causing evil and suffering. Rather Christ's death is preached as engendering freedom amid the complexities of causal chains.

This can be celebrated without attempting to pronounce in detail upon the eternal destiny of each individual. We do well to trust God to care rightly for those who have not heard adequately of divine mercy. The promise is that "He is the atoning sacrifice for our sins, and not only for ours but also for the sins of the whole world" (1 John 2:2).

God Personally Knows the Suffering from Which We Are Saved

But what is meant by punishment for sin? Above all, God knows, for God has felt the full brunt of human violence (Leo, *Serm.* LVIII, *NPNF* 2 XII, pp. 168–71; Catherine of Genoa, *Purgation and Purgatory, CSW,* pp. 72–85). God knows fully what we know partially—that sin cannot finally endure in God's world, that it must be atoned for, paid for, and has been transcended and bound up by God's love (H. W. Robinson, *Suffering Human and Divine*).

The Cross as Payment

The cross is the event in which that payment was made once for all. From the moment of Christ's last earthly breath, the world is redeemed from sin and reconciled to God, and the divine-human account is paid up—a reality in which faith may share.

This does not imply that everyone necessarily wills to share in the freedom Christ offers: "If any soul were finally and forever to put aside Him Who has vicariously borne the punishment of sin, it must bear its own punishment, for it places itself under those conditions which brought from Christ's lips the cry 'Forsaken.' . . . The alternative is this: to meet the future alone, because *forsaken,* or to be saved in Him Who was 'forsaken'" (C. C. Hall, *Does God Send Trouble?* p. 540).

The Absurdity of Continued Bondage

How is it possible that one might now continue to remain in bondage to sin, Paul asked (Rom. 6)? If actually free from sin, how could one absurdly continue to believe that God is now punishing us for sins already atoned for? To believe that is to disbelieve that God has effectively taken punishment for our sins. The cross has become for Christians a mirror through which humanity may behold both its own sin and God's willingness to share the suffering that sin creates. Through the cross, suffering is, first of all, faced and borne and, secondly, transcended by the awareness that God confronted, bore, and transcended it (*Doc. Vat. II,* pp. 24–28, 221). This is Christian theodicy.

We Were There

"Were you there when they crucified my Lord?" asks the spiritual. The faithful stand in the awareness that not only each of us was there (at the cross), but all humanity past and present was there, all sins representatively being atoned and reconciled.

Of the boy who is the main character in the novel *Bevis*, Richard Jefferies writes: "The crucifixion hurt his feelings very much: the cruel nails, the unfeeling spear: he looked at the picture a long time, and then turned over the page saying, 'If God had been there He would not have let them do it.'" But the whole point of the cross, as J. S. Whale points out, is that God was there! For it was God who was *on* the cross (*PT*, p. 45)!

The Mystery of Human Suffering Viewed in the Light of the Cross

Evil Does Not Disappear

There is never an adequate theoretical answer to the riddle of suffering because actual suffering wishes most to be solved in practice not in theory. But Christianity points to an event in relation to which suffering is transformed from absurdity to proximate meaning.

Even then, suffering remains a continuing mystery even to the faithful, as it did to Job. Paul's thorn does not go away; the daughters of Eve labor with pain; Rachel weeps. Mary the God-bearer wept. Christianity does not promise an end of pain, but a word that God shares it with us.

The Mystery Unfolds

Christianity has never at its best pretended to offer a neatly packaged answer to daily sufferers that would remove perplexities and ease all burdens. Its way is narrow. It says "take up your cross."

Gnosticism was an early competitor of Christianity that appeared to offer simpler nostrums—an instant means of escape from evil, a quick key to the secrets of the cosmos. "Mystery" for such religions meant something to be understood by a knowledge elite, which, once it is understood, would no longer be a mystery.

The mystery of the cross for Christian believers is quite the opposite: the more one knows of it the more it remains and extends as a mystery. The mystery of holy, sacrificial love is to be beheld, savored, and embraced—not resolved. "How great is the love the Father has lavished on us, that we should be called children of God!" (1 John 3:1).

Christianity Deepens the Perplexity of Evil

Christianity ironically intensifies the problems of evil and suffering (viewed as philosophical problems) by asserting that God is all-powerful and all-good. "I should be suspicious of the man who claimed to be following Christ and did not find his perplexities increased" (Robinson, *RNT*, p. 80). Suffering is not for Christians merely a conceptual problem to be theoretically solved on paper, but rather a personal challenge to be met in and through the choices of daily life.

There is never a neat or satisfactory conceptual answer for the father whose only son is brutally, senselessly killed. But Christianity points to an actual event in which the eternal Father lost his only Son in a brutal, violent death.

God's Suffering with and for Us

Rather than solving the riddle of suffering conceptually, Christianity speaks of God's actual suffering with and for us. This removes from our daily suffering our proneness to despair over its potential meaningless-ness. "But we have this treasure in jars of clay to show that this all-surpassing power is from God and not from us. We are hard pressed on every side, but not crushed; perplexed, but not in despair; persecuted, but not abandoned; struck down, but not destroyed. We always carry around in our body the death of Jesus, so that the life of Jesus may also be revealed in our body. For we who are alive are always being given over to death for Jesus' sake, so that his life may be revealed in our mortal body" (2 Cor. 4:7–11).

Luther understood how desperately the natural man wishes to avoid suffering: "He who does not know Christ does not know God hidden in suffering. Therefore he prefers works to suffering, glory to the cross, strength to weakness, wisdom to folly, and in general, good to evil. These are the people whom the apostle calls 'enemies of the cross of Christ' (Phil 3:18), for they hate the cross and suffering and love works and the glory of works" (Luther, *Heidelberg Disputation*, Thesis 21, *TGS*, p. 157).

Christ's Way of Transforming the Dilemma of Theodicy

The most profound Christian theodicy does not reason deductively but tells the story of God's suffering for us. No argument can convince the sufferer. Only the actual history of God's own coming to suffering humanity could make a difference. That is what has occurred.

God's way of coming to humanity is almost entirely unexpected, except for prophetic utterances. It is a foolish method—the cross. Christianity alone among world religions speaks of God on a cross.

Christianity is the religion of the cross. The cross is Christianity's most accurate visual summary. Yet the cross is repulsive. We turn our eyes away from a public execution. How could it have happened that Christianity could be such an aesthetic and beautiful religion and have such an ugly central symbol?

The answer is that only there do we most fully discover how far God is reaching out for us. Before beholding the cross, we were unaware that God was looking for us, seeking us, desiring to atone for our sins, ready for reconciliation. The cross is evidence that God the Son comes far out to look for us and is willing to suffer for us so as to reconcile us to the Father.

The cross hardly looks like a place where evil is being overcome. Rather it appears to be history's worst example of injustice and brutality. At least this is one aspect of the cross that is unavoidable: the brutality of sin. This world is just such a place where such things can and do happen. The innocent do suffer. This we learn from the cross, where the most undeserved suffering and the most deserving goodness meet with devastating irony (Edwards, "Christ Exalted," *Works* II, pp. 213–16).

Christ's Suffering and Ours

The Christian message does not pretend to offer an avenue of escape from temptations to will badly. To take away all possibility of temptation of sexual abuse or pride, for example, would require the taking away of the very freedom that makes us human beings.

Nor does Christianity offer an easy escape from supposed natural evil that remains a part of the risk of being human (the earth's shrinking crust in earthquakes, tidal floods for coastal inhabitants). Rather Christianity offers redemption from bondage to sin by speaking of God's own determination to overcome the barrier between humanity and God that sin has created.

The meaning of the cross is that God is there suffering for us. There he lays down his life for the life of the world. Even for those quite unaware of what God is doing, God is doing this. Christianity speaks of the surprising empathy of God who was wounded for our transgressions, who bears the sins of the world like a lamb, who offers himself as a propitiation for our sins, and not for ours only, but for the whole world. It is precisely in the middle of this historical hubris stew that God reconciles all humanity through the death of his Son.

That is not merely a theory or idea of the religious imagination, but an actual datable event in history. It occurred on a cross under Pontius Pilate and was vindicated by a resurrection witnessed by many. The cross does not provide us with an intellectually polished theory of evil or suffering. It does help us put our own suffering in focus. It enables faith to share God's own triumph over evil and suffering.

The cross is more than human agony; it is God's own agony. The cross is revelatory. It reveals the meaning of history, especially at those points in history where it does not appear as though God is truly righteous or where it appears that God may be indifferent to human suffering. In the cross we behold the decisive action of God to set things aright in a wrongly turned world.

This does not mean that the Christian acquiesces to evil or becomes passively resigned to suffering or self-pity. One of the most amazing facts about the New Testament is that it was written under conditions of radical social dislocation, oppression, injustice, war, written by people who were suffering from torture and persecution, and written to people whose lives were constantly endangered because of their faith and made more complicated because of their baptism. Yet no book is so filled with hope and joy and mutual support and encouragement. It is virtually free from the bitterness that so prevails in human life. Whatever they had to suffer, they suffered in the awareness of their sharing in the dying and rising Word of life.

What sort of victory occurred on the cross? It has been compared to a war in which the decisive battle has been won, yet skirmishes continue in history. Gregory of Nyssa used the analogy of a snake who had received "a deadly blow on the head, its coil is not at once killed," and remains "pulsing with its own life." "Similarly it is possible for evil to have been struck a mortal blow, and yet for life still to be harassed by its vestiges" (*ARI* 30, *LCC* III, p. 308).

The Christian life is a continuing war whose victory is already known and experienced, but whose ancillary battles continue in human history awaiting the last day. The warfare is deep in the human spirit, appearing in the subtle forms of pride, seduction, greed, and envy. This is not something that can be done away with by means of another march on the capitol, a more searching docudrama, stalwart investigative reporting, a revolution, or a committee for neighborhood improvement, however important those might be. "For our struggle is not against flesh and blood, but against the rulers, against the authorities, against the powers of this dark world and against the spiritual forces of evil in the heavenly realms. Therefore put on the full armor of God" so that "you may be able to stand your ground," with the belt of truth, the breastplate of righteousness, the shield of faith, the helmet of salvation, with prayer, with feet prepared for running, and with "the sword of the Spirit, which is the word of God" (Eph. 6:12–18).

Punishment and Discipline

Punishment is a legal concept; chastisement and discipline are family concepts. Chastisement and discipline are offices of the Holy Spirit (gifts of God), seeking to cleanse and make chaste our spirits and educate our moral sense. The profoundest understanding of discipline is not limited to the notion of punishment.

It is because parents love children that they discipline them. Lacking discipline they would be unprepared for the world ahead. Caring parents at times must punish children out of love and not as an end in itself, as an occasional and incomplete, but necessary corrective means.

In the Christian tradition suffering is indeed sometimes viewed as educative, sometimes as a trial of faith, sometimes as a purifying agent or means by which God's righteousness is vindicated. But all such explanations tend to fall short when we are extremely hungry or have a severe backache.

Christianity's main point concerning punishment of sin is truly a remarkable one: God knows what punishment feels like, for *God has experienced punishment for the sins of humanity.* God the Son was wounded for our transgressions (Isa. 53). The context for learning about punishment for sins is not in a legal textbook or courtroom, but at the cross, where God was willing to bear our punishment. From this vantage point, each aspect of one's own personal suffering is illumined:

> How strange that all
> The terrors, pains, and early miseries,
> Regrets, vexations, lassitudes interfused
> Within my mind, should e'er have borne a part,
> And that a needful part, in making up
> The calm existence that is mine when I
> Am worthy of myself
> > (Wordsworth, "The Prelude," Book 1).

Part IV

EXALTED LORD

The Emmaus disciples headed home after the crucifixion. "We had hoped that he was the one who was going to redeem Israel" (Luke 24:21). They had even heard of the empty tomb but had not believed (Luke 24:22–24).

When the risen Christ met them on the road home, he reprimanded them as "foolish" and "slow of heart to believe" (v. 25), a phrase that referred not to the resurrection, but of the necessity of the crucifixion, that the Christ would suffer. It was only after the resurrection that he could fully proceed to teach: "And beginning with Moses and all the Prophets, he explained to them what was said in all the Scriptures concerning himself" (Luke 24:27).

CHAPTER 12

Christus Victor

THE LIVING GOD EMBODIES THE WORD OF LIFE

With the death of Jesus an old era ends. With the resurrection of Jesus a new era begins. He who died rose. He who rose ascended. He who ascended promised to return.

The Exaltation of Christ

The Resumption of Power

Christ's exaltation (*hupsosis*, Acts 2:32; 5:31; *huperupsosis*, Phil. 2:9; *doxasis*, John 17:5; *stephanosis*, Heb. 2:9) consisted in the full resumption of the exercise of the divine powers that had been voluntarily constrained during the period from incarnation to crucifixion.

The servant form was laid aside. All limitations were withdrawn from full communication of divine attributes to the human nature of Christ. The interrupted exercise of the divine glory resumed. The full power of administering the kingdom, which he had already received through the union itself, was assumed. The exalted Christ was now free to exercise legitimate spiritual authority that rightly belonged to theandric union (Athanasius, *Four Discourses Ag. Arians* I.37–64, NPNF 2 IV, pp. 327–43).

Four Steps of Ascent

Traditionally understood, the exaltation of Christ encompasses four teachings confessed in the creed: descent to the nether world, resurrection, ascension, and session at the right hand of God. All four clauses appear in the Creed of Rufinus (ca. 404, *CC*, p. 24), and the received text of the Apostles' Creed (*CC*, p. 24). The last three clauses appear in numerous early creeds: the rule of faith of Tertullian (ca. A.D. 200, *Ag. Praxeas* 2, *CC*, p. 22), the Interrogatory Creed of Hippolytus (ca. 215), and an African Variant (ca. 400, *CC*, pp. 22–24). The return of the Lord will be discussed in the sequel to this volume.

The exaltation began hiddenly at the nadir of descent and became manifested in history in the resurrection, its context moved from earth to heaven in the ascension, and it was consummated in the session. Schematically expressed:

EXALTATION (in ascending order)

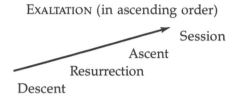

Session
Ascent
Resurrection
Descent

The Unity of the Sequence

The fourfold core of this sequence is integrally expressed in the First Letter of Peter: "For Christ died for our sins once for all, the righteous for the unrighteous, to bring you to God. He was put to death in the body but made alive by the Spirit, through whom also he went and *preached to the spirits in prison*," whose death enabled a baptism to new life that "saves you by the *resurrection* of Jesus Christ, who has *gone into heaven* and *is at God's right hand*" (1 Pet. 18–22, italics added).

This sequence was condensed into that part of the creed that states: "He descended into hell, on the third day rose again from the dead, ascended to heaven, sits at the right hand of God the Father almighty" (*CC*, p. 24).

Resurrection without descent, ascension, or intercession would be incomplete, lacking full cosmic manifestation. Rightly viewed, all four belong together as a single unity called exaltation—a cohesive classical Christian teaching, an article of faith (Acts 5:31; Wollebius, *CTC* 18, *RDB*, pp. 110–15; *Leiden Synopsis* XXVIII; Heppe, *RD*, pp. 496–501; Pope, *Compend.* II, pp. 167ff.; Strong, *Syst. Theol.*, pp. 706ff.; Barth, *CD* IV/2, pp. 132ff.). The unified purpose of Christ's resurrection, ascension, and intercession, according to the ancient account of Irenaeus (A.D. 180), is "to comprehend all things under one head [*anakephalaiosasthai*], and to raise up all flesh of all mankind" (*Ag. Her.* I, 10.1, *COC* II, pp. 13–14).

The Word of Life: Thematic Focus of Systematic Theology

At this point, the argument returns to the title theme: the Word of Life, for scripture and tradition join with reason, prophecy, history, proclamation, sacrament, prayer, and experience to attest that Christ is now alive.

The Unifying Theme: Life

The central theme of the first volume of this series was God's own life—*The Living God*. Now we speak of that same life—the source and ground of life itself—that has appeared and become known in history in an incomparable way through the Word spoken and embodied in Jesus, *The Word of Life*. This volume will be followed by another, *Life in the Spirit*, which will inquire into the community of faith brought into being by this living Word of God. Christian theology in summary concerns God's own life, God's life offered for humanity, and our life in God.

The Title Text

This volume follows the First Epistle of John in taking as its title theme "the Word of life": "That which was from the beginning, which we have heard, which we have seen with our eyes, which we have looked at and our hands have touched—this we proclaim concerning *the Word of life* [*tou logou tes zoes*]. The life appeared; we have seen it and testify to it, and we proclaim to you the eternal life, which was with the Father and has appeared to us" (1 John 1:1–2, italics added).

The Word of life, as set forth in this thematic text, is a Word that

preexisted from the beginning
was with the Father
appeared within human history
addressed alienated humanity in a hearable way
palpably became visible to human eyes
was looked upon by ordinary folk
was palpably touched
lived among us
was attested by many
proclaims eternal life
(1 John 1:1–2; cf. Clement of Alexandria, from Cassiodorus, *Fragments* 3, *ANF* II, p. 574; Pearson, *EC* I, p. 360).

According to Calvin, the ascription to Jesus of the distinctive title "the Word of life" was offered "on two accounts, [1] because he has infused life into all creatures, and [2] because he now restores life to us, which had perished" (Calvin, *Comm.* II, p. 159, numbers added). In announcing: "The life appeared" (*he zoe ephanerothe*; 1 John 1:2), the Epistle is announcing the coming of One "who is life and the fountain of life," whose "life has been openly offered to us" (Calvin, *Comm.* II, p. 160).

The Parallel with the Johannine Prologue

Dionysius, bishop of Alexandria (A.D. 190–264), pupil of Origen and head of the catechetical school of Alexandria, noted the similarity of the first verses of the Gospel of John and the First Epistle of John. He sought to establish that they were written by the same person with "the same character of writing": "Both commence the same way. For the one opens thus, 'In the beginning was the Word'; while the other opens thus, 'That which was from the beginning.' The one says: 'And the Word was made flesh, and dwelt among us,'" while the other "says the same things, with a slight alteration," that "*the Word of life*" has appeared, "which we have seen with our eyes, which we have looked at and our hands have touched," in contrast to "those who deny that the Lord is come in the flesh" (Dionysius, *Fragments, ANF* VI, p. 84, italics added).

Pauline Parallels

Our theme, "the Word of life," is alluded to also by Paul, who immediately after the epic hymn of the incarnation in Phillipians 2, instructs his readers to hold fast to the *logon zoes* ("Word of life," Phil. 2:16). He was convinced that Christ's continuing "life is at work in you" (2 Cor. 4:12), for "your life is now hidden with Christ in God" (Col. 3:3), and finally when "Christ, who is your life, appears, then you will appear with him in glory" (Col. 3:4).

To share in Christ's life is to share in his death—for we were "buried with him through baptism into death" in order that "we too may live a new life" (Rom. 6:4; Origen, *Ag. Celsus* II.69, *ANF* IV, p. 459). Having been reconciled through his death, we are now "saved through his life" (Rom. 5:10; Augustine, *Confessions* X.43, *NPNF* 1 I, p. 162). It is "not only for this life we have hope" but for a life that participates eternally in the Word of life (1 Cor. 15:19).

Christ Is Alive

In What Sense Does He "Live"?

He lives personally, not merely as a concept or symbol. He lives actually, not merely in the tenuous memories of his disciples. He lives not only in earthly history but in that eternal life that transcends history to which he ascends. He lives not in latent power or mere potentiality, but rather in full possession of blessedness and power (Wendt, *System der christliche Lehre*, p. 399). All this is meant by exaltation.

Christ Is Presently Engaged in Mission

For the support, sustenance, and completion of its mission, the church depends upon the continuing real presence of the living Lord. Without testimony to the ascension and session, the incarnate mission would be incomplete and present humanity in despair. The core of this experienced exaltation is indicated by Paul: "And God raised us up with Christ and seated us with him in the heavenly realms in Christ Jesus, in order that in the coming ages he might show the incomparable riches of his grace" (Eph. 2:6-7). If Christ were a dead body, now inorganic matter resolved into its constituents, how could he be continuing his mission?

The Participation of the Faithful in the Exaltation

Each phase of the exaltation has personal, behavioral, redemptive relevance for the life of the believer. Christ's death, descent, resurrection, ascension, and session prepare the way for the Spirit's enabling of the believer's dying to sin, conversion, faith, walking the way of holiness, and final glorification:

1. By his descent he is known to be fully empathic with our human condition in death. His descent enables us to share in his victory over the demonic powers and to face our own sin.
2. His resurrection enables the faithful to rise from the death of sin to new life in Christ.
3. With his ascension the believer is brought into the presence of the heavenly Father.
4. His session allows us access to the heavenly Father, and his intercession is for our sanctification (Cyril of Jerusalem, *Catech. Lect.* XIV, FC 64, pp. 32-52; Tho. Aq., ST III, Q52-59, II, pp. 2302-42; Anger, *MB*, p. 57).

The Meriting, Effecting, Exemplary, and Final Cause of Salvation

The scholastic exegetes followed scriptural patterns, searching for their intrinsic structures of reasoning. They drew together this overarching pattern of complementary levels of causality in salvation:

the passion is the meriting cause of our redemption,
the resurrection is the effecting cause of our regeneration,
the ascension is the exemplary cause of our sanctification,
the session is the final cause of our glorification
(Tho. Aq., *ST* III, Q56–59, II, pp. 2326–38; Garrigou-Lagrange, *CS*, pp.
    657–89; Anger, *MB*, pp. 58–59).

Faith in the Living Christ

Union with Christ

Redemption occurs not through assent to doctrine but through union
with the living Christ. It could not occur with a dead Christ. The engendering power of Christianity could not be proclaimed if Christianity
spoke only of a person who was but no longer is. If he ceased to be alive,
he could not form our present life with God.

Faith in Jesus has from its earliest inception been faith in the living
Lord. Believers are understood to be joined to the Lord in a spiritual
union and fellowship with each other that is sustained by a living Person.
The continuing life of Christ includes our life in Christ. In this union
Christ shares empathetically in our pain even now, and we share in the
fullness of his life with God the Father (Cyril of Jerusalem, *Catech. Lect.*
XXI, *NPNF* 2 VII, pp. 149–50).

Prayer to Christ

Christians from the outset have prayed to Christ, because God and
Christ are understood to be one, for Christ is nothing other than God
who has come to us for our salvation. To speak to him in prayer is to trust
that this one is God and that God is known through him.

Modern Reductionism Insufficient to Account for His Aliveness

There is hardly a point in Christian teaching at which we seem to be
further distanced from modern consciousness than the exaltation of
Jesus. When we look toward him with jaded modern eyes, we wish to
reduce him to something manageable. So modernity struggles to identify
empirically how his consciousness may have affected others' consciousness (Schleiermacher, *ChrF*, pp. 417–21). The only conception of a living
Christ that is allowable under these terms is that his influence lives in the
memory and actions of others, analogous to the way famous heroes exert
continuing influence. But it is not thereby affirmed that he acts upon us
as one who himself is personally alive. The missing element in such an
analysis is his own continuing personal life.

Christianity Not Empowered by a Dead Christ

Only a living Christ can sustain the Christian life of faith, hope, and love. The willingness to take up our cross and follow him, to suffer and die if necessary to proclaim his truth, is not plausible on the basis of a dead Christ.

The ancient ecumenical testimony is that Jesus now lives so as to engender life in us. His living presence is the real energy and force and dynamic and power of historic Christianity and present Christian life. Detached from the living Christ, the branch withers, the flower fades. Our title theme—the Word of life—echoes the celebration that he is still living.

The hinge point of human history is the dying and rising of Jesus. The study of salvation is essentially a study of what that dying and rising means. Failing to grasp the pivotal significance of this salvation event is to fail to grasp the Word of God. This is why Christian teaching has focused so intently upon these last events of Jesus' earthly ministry.

The Son Himself Is Life

To Jesus the predicate "life" has been unreservedly, almost recklessly, ascribed in Scripture (John 5:26; 11:25; 14:6; 1 John 5:20; Barth, *CD* III/2, p. 335). "In him was life, and that life was the light of men" (John 1:4; John Chrysostom, *Hom. on John* V, *NPNF* 1 XIV, pp. 21–25).

The Author of Life

Jesus is called "the Life," "our life," "the Prince of life," "Word of life" (1 John 1:1, 2; Acts 3:15; John 11:25; 2 Cor. 4:12). "For as the Father has life in himself, so he has granted the Son to have life in himself" (John 5:26). "It was his task to swallow up death. Who but the Life could do this?" (Calvin, *Inst.* 2.12.2). "God has given us eternal life, and this life is in his Son. He who has the Son has life; he who does not have the Son of God does not have life" (1 John 5:11–12).

This is why Jesus' words bring life (John 5:24; 6:68; 8:51), because they are God's own words (John 3:34; 14:10). "The words that I have spoken to you are spirit and they are life" (John 6:63).

The early preaching of Acts spoke of Jesus as "author of life" (Acts 3:15), who "gives all men life" (Acts 17:25). It was the "full message of this new life" that the apostles were called to proclaim (Acts 5:20; Henry, *CWB* 6, p. 61).

The Son Has Power to Offer Life to the World

Among prerogatives that belong only to God is the ability to give life, to be the source of all that lives. As God, the Son is called the "way of life" (John 14:6; *Didache* 1, *ECW*, p. 223; *Teaching of the Twelve Apostles* 1–2, *ANF* VII, pp. 377–78). "For as the Father raises the dead and gives them life, even so the Son gives life to whom he is pleased to give it" (John 5:20). Only God gives life. The implication is that the Son is life-giver.

The Son Has Life in Himself

The Son who dies has power to offer life (John 5:21). In the same way that God the Father has life in himself, so does the Son have life in himself (John 5:26; Novatian, *Trin.* 14, *ANF* V, p. 623). Those who have faith in the Son of God are enabled to receive eternally the life that comes from God (John 3:35; 6:47; 10:10). Everyone who "looks to the Son and believes in him shall have eternal life, and I will raise him up at the last day" (John 6:40).

The Living Word

To posit speech without a speaker is absurd. The speaker's word comes only out of the compassionate will of the speaker to communicate. The address of the Father is heard through the body language of the Son. Christ is "living Word" (*logon zonta*; Lucian of Antioch, *Rule of Faith*, *COC* II, p. 26).

The Word is meant to be heard. It is not like a candle hidden under a bushel. It is spoken, offered to humanity for the purpose of being heard, received, and answered responsively (Council of Ephesus, *SCD* 118f., p. 50; Council of Constantinople II, *SCD* 224, p. 88).

The mission to bring life to all required the death of the Son. "I tell you the truth, unless a kernel of wheat falls to the ground and dies, it remains only a single seed. But if it dies, it produces many seeds. The man who loves his life will lose it, while the man who hates his life in this world will keep it for eternal life" (John 12:23–25; see also Catherine of Siena, *Pray.*, pp. 35, 150, 160).

The Life of the World

He gives life to the world by the power of his life (Heb. 7:16; John 6:33). He came "that they may have life" (John 10:10). "For God so loved the world that he gave his one and only Son, that whoever believes in him shall not perish but have eternal life" (John 3:16).

He offers to all who would receive the "right to eat from the tree of life" (Rev. 2:7), drink "from the spring of the water of life" (Rev. 21:6), and to have their names "written in the book of life" (Rev. 20:15; Augustine, *CG*, *FC* 24, pp. 287–91). He offers the "crown of life" (Rev. 2:10). Life is offered to the world by means of repentance, faith, and baptism (Acts 11:18; John 11:25ff.; Rom. 6).

The metaphors of Life-giver, Life-enabler, and Word of life are repeatedly ascribed to Christ in the Gospels. As a vine sustains branches, Christ provides life to those who have union with him (John 15:1–8). He is like a shepherd who not only preserves the life of the flock but announces, "I give them life" (John 10:28), and who lays down his life for them (1 John 3:16). He offers "to give his life as a ransom for many" (Matt. 20:28).

To the Samaritan woman who came to the well to drink, he was ready to give "living water" (John 4:10). He spoke of himself as bread of life (John 6:35). To eat of him is to have life. The manna from heaven has come in living flesh: "Just as the living Father sent me and I live because of the Father, so the one who feeds on me will live because of me. This is the bread that came down from heaven" (John 6:57).

"God has given us eternal life, and this life is in his Son. He who has the Son has life; he who does not have the Son of God does not have life" (1 John 5:11–12). To hear him is to hear the Word of life. It is by faith active in love that "we have passed from death to life" (1 John 3:14; Baxter, *PW* XI, pp. 236–64).

DESCENT INTO THE NETHER WORLD

Between the articles on our Lord's death and his resurrection stands the confession that he descended into the abode of the dead, hades, the unseen world. "The gospel was preached even to those who are now dead" (*nekrois euēngelisthē*, 1 Pet. 4:6).

Both the Hebrew *sheol* and Greek *hades* refer to the nether world, the shadowy realm of the dead, "the place or the state of souls departed" (Isaac Barrow, *On the Creed, Serm. 28, WIB* VII, p. 275), yet without necessary reference to punishment. The descent is not into *gehenna* (the place of punishment), but into *hades* (the abode of the departed). Into this place of the dead the soul of the Lord entered while his body remained entombed.

The biblical references in addition to Psalm 16:10 may be largely grouped into Pauline texts (Eph. 4:8–10; Rom. 10:7; Col. 2:14–15), Petrine texts (1 Pet. 3:18–20; 4:4–6), and Lucan texts (Luke 23:43; 2:30–31; Acts 13:37), but ancillary references are diffused in both Testaments.

The *Russian Catechism* defines hades simply as "a place *void of light*," "the state of those spirits which are separated by sin from the sight of God's countenance, and from the light and blessedness which it confers" (*COC* II, p. 477; cf. Jude 6).

Status of the Article in the Creedal Tradition

No article of the creed is more encumbered with ambiguities than the descent into the nether world.

Dating Its Inclusion in the Creed

Although the descent into hades appears in numerous ancient creeds after A.D. 390, it does not appear directly in earlier kerygmatic or baptismal summaries. It was not mentioned in Marcellus's text of the Old Roman Symbol, but by the time of Rufinus (the Aquileian form of the creed, about A.D. 390–400) it was found in the creed that Rufinus regarded as the one traditionally committed to memory in Italy.

The descent into the abode of the dead appeared in the Athanasian Creed (Quicunque, ca. 381–428; SCD 40, p. 15) accepted by East and West, and in the received Western text of the Apostles' Creed of Caesarius of Arles (Received Text T, Western Form of the Apostolic Creed, SCD 6, p. 7; also in Pirminius, d. 753; Sacramentarium Gallicanum, seventh–eighth century, Missale Gallicanum Vetus, eighth century, and the Ordo Romanus, 950; see SCD 5n, 429, 462). It was generally affirmed by major ante-Nicene writers (Polycarp, Justin Martyr, Origen, Hermas, Irenaeus, Cyprian, Tertullian, Hippolytus, Clement of Alexandria), by major ecumenical teachers of both East and West (Athanasius, Four Discourses Ag. Arians, NPNF 2 IV, p. 424; Augustine, Letters, 164, To Evodius, FC 20, pp. 382–97), and by leading Protestants (Luther, Brief Explanation, WML II, p. 371; Calvin, Inst. 2.16.8–11; Baxter, PW XIX, pp. 77–78).

Yet it was not specifically mentioned in the creeds of the councils of Nicaea, Constantinople, or Toledo. Many scriptural passages relating to this article are obscure and difficult to interpret. One might be tempted to ignore the article altogether, were it not for its persistence in the creedal tradition.

Problems with the Article

Major reasons cited for resisting or rejecting this as an essential article of faith are that it is made up of a composite of ambiguous biblical texts, it assumes and reinforces an outmoded cosmology, and it did not regularly appear in the creeds until the fourth century.

Although these reservations should cause us to be cautiously undogmatic in statements on the descent, the consensual view generally has remained that the doctrine has sufficient biblical grounding. It has survived as a liturgical and creedal statement in many traditions for over fifteen centuries. Roman Catholics, Lutherans, Anglicans, Greek Orthodox, and many Protestants declare regularly in worship as an article of the creed: "he descended into hell."

Why the Article Is Needed

Although this phrase, Calvin thought, "did not become customary in the churches at once, but gradually," most major ancient Christian teachers discussed it. Though interpretations vary, "if it is left out, much of the benefit of Christ's death will be lost," hence "in setting forth a summary of doctrine a place must be given to it" (Calvin, *Inst.* 2.16.8). Augustine stated more firmly that none but an unbeliever would deny Christ's descent into the nether world (*Letters*, 164, *To Evodius*, FC 20, pp. 382–86).

Why the Article Touches Modern Consciousness

Modernity thinks it invented the theme of the death of God. But classical Christianity investigated the depths of this theme long before Nietzsche. Why does this phrase come closer than other articles of the creed to touching secularizing consciousness at a deep and vulnerable spot?

The disciples on the road to Emmaus were aware of the utter death of their hopes. So are those who have shared the élan of modernity often painfully aware of the death of the best human idealisms and aspirations. Good Friday is the time of the cross of God the Son. Holy Saturday is the traditional time of recollection of the death of God (viewed as God-man), that unusual moment in the Christian year when God is simply silent, absent, and hidden from view—dead—in another abode (that of the dead). The liturgy of Holy Saturday recollects this shocking entombment of the divine Son. God's Son is dead. But this does not exhaust the meaning of the descent into hell.

Theories of Descent

A Healthy Variety of Traditional Interpretations

The ambiguities and complexities of these texts have invited a broad variety of interpretations. Irenaeus argued that "the Lord observed the law of the dead, that He might become the first begotten from the dead, and tarried until the third day 'in the lower parts of the earth'" (*Ag. Her.* V.31.1, *ANF* I, p. 560; cf. IV.27.2). Clement of Alexandria proposed that Christ preached the gospel in hell to bring salvation to awaiting believers (*Stromata* VI.6, ANF II, pp. 490–92).

Tertullian wrote that Christ remained "in Hades in the form and condition of a dead man; nor did He ascend into the heights of heaven before descending into the lower parts of the earth, that He might there make the patriarchs and prophets partakers of Himself" (*On the Soul* 55, *ANF* III, p. 231). John Chrysostom argued that the descent referred to Christ's power to work miracles and to hold sway over the demonic powers (*Hom. on Matt.* LVII, *NPNF* 1 X, pp. 352–57; *Hom. on Second Cor.* XXV, *NPNF* 1 XII, pp. 394–97).

The descent article has been variously interpreted by Reformed scholastics as the *last phase of Christ's humiliation* or by Lutheran scholastics as the *first phase of Christ's exaltation* (cf. 1 Pet. 3:18, 19; Acts 2:27).

Luther argued that the descent referred primarily to the victory of Christ over the demonic powers: "I believe that He descended into hell to overthrow and take captive the devil and all his power, guile and wickedness, for me and for all who believe in Him, so that henceforth the devil cannot harm me; and that He has redeemed me from the pains of hell, and made them harmless and meritorious" (Luther, *Brief Explanation*, *WML* II, p. 371). Calvin argued that its chief reference was to the radical extent of Christ's suffering (*Inst.* 2.16.9–12). Bucer and Beza argued that it simply meant that Christ was buried (Bucer, *Enarrationes in Evangelia*, pp. 511f., 792ff.; cf. Pearson, *EC* I, p. 382). Sohnius argued that the descent referred to the entire state of humiliation of the eternal Son from incarnation to burial (*De Verbo Dei*).

Five Types

These varied views of the descent may be broadly categorized into five major types of emphasis. The first is that the confession simply meant that Jesus *died* and descended into the grave (the burial motif). The second view alleges that the descent points to Christ's *empathic suffering* and participation in the depths of human alienation (the humiliation motif). The third says it points to Christ's *victory* over the demonic powers (the exaltation motif). The fourth option is that Christ descended to *preach* in the abode of the dead (the kerygmatic motif). And the fifth is the premise of *reversal*, that the article constituted the final phase of the humiliation and the beginning phase of the exaltation (the reversal motif; cf. Pearson, *EC* I, pp. 383–89; already discussed on pp. 429ff.). Some combination of these types may emerge in future generations of orthodox exegesis as a refined, received consensus.

The Final Phase of the Humbling of God

Sheol as Simply Death

The first, most straightforward of these views holds that Jesus' entry into *sheol* simply meant nothing more or less than he died like any other human being. This anti-Docetic emphasis (held by some Reformed scholastics) stressed the truth that Jesus entered as fully into human experience in death as he did in life. Hence it was to be expected that his soul would go where all human souls go after death: to the resting place of the dead (Bucer, *Enarrationes in Evangelia*, pp. 511f., 792ff.; cf. Pearson, *EC* I, p. 382).

"The due meaning of these words may be laid down as either literal or metaphorical; the literal denotes Christ's descent into the grave or his three days continuance in that state under the lordship of death. Analogically also and metaphorically by these words may be denoted the tortures and pains of Christ borne both in the garden and on the cross" (Franciscus Burmannus, *Synopsis Theologie* V, xxi, pp. 13–14, in Heppe, *RD*, p. 492).

Yet Calvin astutely pointed to the limitation of this interpretation: it implied a "useless repetition" in the creed whose very purpose is to note "the chief points of our faith" in "the fewest possible words." It is unlikely (if descent simply means burial) that the same idea would be repeated in such a compact summary (*Inst.* 2.16.8).

The Empathic Suffering Motif

The Reformed tradition's empathic theory held that the descent into hell more specifically meant that Christ identified in an unparalleled way with the depths of human pain, suffering, and alienation. Accordingly, the descent was not a part of Christ's triumph, but constituted the last phase of Christ's humiliation, the humbling of God in suffering, absolute limitation, and in entire obedience, the final stage of the humble condescension of the Son (Ursinus, *CHC*, pp. 228–32; cf. Schmid, *DT*, pp. 397–98). There was no depth of human alienation with which our Lord was unacquainted (Calvin, *Inst.* 2.16.8–11; Baxter, *PW* XIX, pp. 77–78; G. Hedley, *The Symbol of the Faith*, pp. 70–73).

Assurance of Accompaniment Through Alienation

In this way the descent became an experiential component of the doctrine of assurance. "Why 'descended into hell'?" The *Heidelberg Catechism* teaches the confirmand to answer in a highly personal way: "That in my severest tribulations I may be assured that Christ my Lord has redeemed me from hellish anxieties and torment" (Q 44, *BOConf.* 4.044). Where the Lord has been, I may go without terror.

A variant of this view holds that what is finally signified by hell can be experientially grasped by thinking of that depth of loneliness which no word or touch of love can penetrate. Suppose one were to find oneself in such a state of abandonment that no other voice or touch could reach one anymore. That would be the sort of total unresponsiveness, abandonment, and aloneness that is symbolized by *sheol*. It was into such a state of total physical unresponsiveness that Jesus entered when he died and descended to *sheol*. Hence Christ shared the abyss of whatever abandonment humanity is capable (Ratzinger, *IC*, pp. 226–29).

Calvin taught that on behalf of the elect, Christ suffered in his soul the dreadful torments of a person condemned and irretrievably lost, thereby teaching faith to trust amid torment (*Inst.* 2.16.10; *Psychopannychia, Tracts* III, pp. 418–90). Calvin's interpretation had been anticipated by Nicolas of Cusa (*Serm. on Ps. 30:11*) and Pico della Mirandola.

The Reformed theologians viewed the descent with intense realism as "but the reverse side of this most profound humiliation, in which Christ was abandoned by the Father to the power and dominion of death. Like all human souls which separate from their bodies, even Christ's soul had to descend into Hades, because his whole divine human person was punished with real death in order that sin might be atoned for and the covenant of grace consummated" (Heppe, *RD*, p. 491). Yet he could not have been suffering physically thereby because his body was in that state of total unresponsiveness that defines and characterizes death (Hall, *DT* VII, p. 149).

Descent as Victory Over Sin and Death

The patristic and Lutheran writers put greater stress than Reformed writers on descent as victory. In his descent, Christ conquered the demonic powers, destroyed the power of hell, and seized from the Enemy all authority. This exaltation motif is found especially among those who stressed victory over demonic powers in their teaching of atonement (notably Irenaeus, Gregory of Nyssa, and Luther).

Not Humbling, but Triumphing

Accordingly, Christ did not descend into hades to suffer for us either with or under the demonic powers, for his sacrificial work had already been finished on the cross (John 19:20). His purpose rather was to triumph over the demons, as celebrated in the Apocalypse: "I am the Living One; I was dead, and behold I am alive for ever and ever! And I hold the keys of death and Hades" (Rev. 1:18; cf. Col. 2:15).

Destroying the Power of the Devil

The Letter to Hebrews strongly suggests this view. In arguing for Jesus' full humanity, it states that Christ "shared in their humanity so that by his death he might destroy him who holds the power of death – that is, the devil—and free those who all their lives were held in slavery by their fear of death. For surely it was not angels he helps, but Abraham's descendants" (Heb. 2:14-16). Christ's descent into the abode of the dead was purposefully to declare the binding up of the demonic powers and free the faithful of Abraham from their slavery and likewise all whose lives are possessed by fear of death.

Some countered that this had already occurred as a finished work on the cross; for it is "by the cross" that Christ "disarmed the powers and authorities" (Col. 2:14-15; cf. Heppe, *RD*, pp. 490-94). Exponents of the victory motif answer that the purpose of the descent was not to redo the work done on the cross, but to *announce to the depths of cosmic creation the binding up of the demonic powers.*

Thomas Aquinas stressed this distinction between his death and descent: "By the power of His Passion He delivered the saints from the penalty whereby they were excluded from the life of glory. . . . His descent into hell brought the fruits of deliverance to them only who were united to His Passion through faith quickened by charity" (Tho. Aq., *ST* III, Q52.5-6, II, pp. 2306-2307). Zechariah prophesied: "As for you, because the blood of my covenant is with you, I will free your prisoners from the waterless pit" (Zech. 9:11), a text that was taken to prefigure the sequence of Christ's Passion and descent (Tho. Aq., *ST* III, Q52.1, II, p. 2302), suggesting that the descent is an act of liberation.

Breaking Down the Gate of Hell

The visual expression of this victory motif in the history of art has been Christ breaking down the gates of hell: "He broke down the gate and 'iron bars' of hell, setting at liberty all the righteous who were held fast through original sin" (Augustine, *Serm. on the Passion* CLX, quoted in Tho. Aq., *ST* III, Q52.5, II, p. 2305).

The victory motif was celebrated by Bonaventure with poetic intensity: Christ "tore the prey away from him, broke down the gates of hell and bound the serpent. *Disarming the Principalities and Powers, he led them away boldly, displaying them openly in triumph in himself* (Col. 2:15). Then the *Leviathan was led about with a hook* (Job 40:25), his jaw pierced by Christ so that he who had no right over the Head which he had attacked, also lost what he had seemed to have over the body" (*Tree of Life, CWS*, p. 159; Job 41:1).

Remarkable Gospel references to the saints in the tombs who were raised with Jesus (Matt. 27:51-53; John 5:25-29) lend supportive evidence for this view. These souls were viewed as living evidence of Christ's liberating visitation of the abode of the dead.

The Preaching of Christ in the Nether World

Not only did he visit; he preached. A fourth motif sought to show that this article made provision for salvation for those already dead by preaching to them judgment and gospel. It was thought that the worthy dead would thereby have an opportunity to hear the preaching of Christ (Irenaeus, *Ag. Her.* V.31, *ANF* I, p. 560; cf. Hedley, *The Symbol of the Faith*, p. 68). "He showed forth His power on earth by living and dying, so also He might manifest it in hell, by visiting it and enlightening it" (Tho. Aq., *ST* III, Q52.1, II, p. 2302).

Preaching to the Dead

The First Letter of Peter is the main text for this view: "For this is the reason the gospel was preached even to those who are now dead, so that they might be judged according to men in regard to the body, but live according to God in regard to the spirit" (1 Pet. 4:6). If death is unresponsiveness, how can one preach to the dead? The assumption must be that "those who are now dead" were not totally incapable of response or, if unresponsive, were enabled by God's own awakening presence to hear the preached word.

"The true light of wisdom shone even there; it illumined hell, but was not shut up in hell," wrote Ambrose. "Even though His soul was in the depth, it is no longer there, for it is written: 'Because thou wilt not leave my soul in hell, nor wilt thou give thy holy one to see corruption" (*Incarn. of Our Lord* 5.41, *FC* 44, p. 234, quoting Ps. 15:10).

The Petrine Sequence

It is on the basis of the sequence of 1 Peter 3:18–20 that some argue that the descent occurred not before but *after* the resurrection and that it attests Christ's victory over the powers of evil. Note the sequence: "For Christ died for sins once for all, the righteous for the unrighteous, to bring you to God. He was put to death in the body but made alive by the Spirit through whom also he went and preached to the spirits in prison" (1 Pet. 3:18–19; cf. Augustine, *Letters*, 164, *To Evodius*, *FC* 20, pp. 382–97). This was a sticking point between Lutheran and Calvinist scholastics, the latter holding the reverse sequence (that the descent was before the resurrection).

Descent to Preach the Good News

Two reasons are assigned by the *Russian Catechism* for the descent into the abode of the dead: (1) to "preach his victory over death," and (2) "deliver the souls which with faith awaited his coming" (*COC* II, p. 478). The Greek Catechism was even more explicit: "While His body lay dead in the tomb, His deified soul descended into Hell, and carried to the souls which, since time began, had lain bound there, the good news of reconciliation" (*Gk. Orthodox Catech.* 37, p. 29).

There is a prevailing conviction in much classic exegesis that those who die in a state of grace remain in an intermediate place of purification until made perfect, but that when perfected they enter into the full bliss of beatific vision (Tho. Aq., *ST* III, Suppl. Q69.2; 93.1). Accordingly, then Jesus' preaching "must have brought hope to all who were not beyond the reach of saving grace" (Hall, *DT* VII, p. 153).

To Whom Was Christ Preaching?

The key passage concludes: "He went and preached to *the spirits in prison who disobeyed long ago* when God waited patiently in the days of Noah while the ark was being built. In it only a few people, eight in all, were saved through water, and this water symbolizes baptism that now saves you also" (1 Pet. 3:19–21, italics added; Luther, *Serm. on First Peter*, *LW* 30, pp. 112–15; *Torgau Serm.*, 1533, *WA* 37, pp. 35–72). The context of the passage is a plea for patience under persecution, noting that Christ himself was not exempt from suffering in making atonement for our sins as "the righteous for the unrighteous" (v. 18).

Either Christ in his preincarnate state was preaching through Noah to his disbelieving generation, or Christ between his death and resurrection was preaching to the (believing and/or disbelieving) spirits of Noah's generation. In either case, the passage shows that God's patience would allow some time for disobedience, but not forever.

Several competing interpretations may be found of the phrase "the spirits in prison." Some have argued that Christ was preaching *to the antediluvians* who had ridiculed Noah as a preacher of righteousness. "The spirits shut up in prison are the unbelievers who lived in the time of Noah, whose spirits or souls were shut up in the darkness of ignorance as in a prison; Christ preached to them, not in the flesh, for he was not yet incarnate, but in the spirit, that is, in his divine nature" (Augustine, *Letters*, 164, *To Evodius*, FC 20, pp. 382ff.).

Others say Christ was preaching *to the captives*. The Damascene summarized mature patristic teaching on the descent: "The deified soul went down into hell so that, just as the Sun of Justice rose upon those on earth, so also might the light shine upon them under the earth who were sitting in darkness and the shadow of death; so that, just as He had brought the good news of peace to those on earth, so also might He bring that of deliverance to captives and that of sight to the blind. And to them that believed He became a cause of eternal salvation. . . . And thus, having loosed them that had been bound for ages, He came back again from the dead and made the resurrection possible for us" (John of Damascus, *OF* III.29, *FC* 37, p. 334).

Other classical exegetes say Christ preached *to the patriarchs and prophets*. They view 1 Peter 3:19–21 as implying that Christ declared accomplished redemption to the souls of the patriarchs, enabling them to share in the salvation event. Tertullian wrote that Christ "descended into the inner parts of the earth, so that there he might make the patriarchs and prophets sharers of himself" (Tertullian, *Apology* 47, *ANF* III, p. 52; *On the Soul* 55, *ANF* III, p. 231; Justin Martyr, *Dialogue with Trypho* 138, 139, *ANF* I, pp. 268–69). Some say that saints of the old covenant who had believed in the coming of the Messiah were thereby vindicated by Christ. Others argue that the preaching of Christ in hades was not evangelical, but legal, not grace, but admonition. Eastern Orthodox teaching argues that Christ's preaching in *hades* was addressed to the Old Testament saints who believed in the Messiah (cf. Irenaeus, *Ag. Her* V.31, *ANF* I, p. 560; Eusebius, *CH* I.13, *NPNF* 2 I, p. 102).

Others argue that he preached *to the detained souls of the just*. Roman Catholic teaching holds that the soul of Christ descended to *limbus patrum* where the souls of the just were detained until he came to open to them the kingdom of heaven at his ascension (Eph. 4:9; 1 Pet. 3:18–20; Bellarmine, *De Christo* IV, 6–12).

Some say Christ preached *to those who had not yet heard the gospel*. Some writers have argued that the preaching of Christ according to 1 Peter 3:19 allowed for the possibility of salvation after death for those who were not given opportunity to hear the gospel in this life. This view is accompanied by the caveat that we should not "trouble ourselves with sublime and acute thoughts as to how this occurred" (Formula of Concord sec. 643, quoted in Jacobs, *SCF*, p. 150; *BOC*, p. 492).

Some say Christ simply preached *to the dead*. They were presumably captive in the absolute limitation of death. Others say that Christ preached to those who were *symbolically dead* amid the disbelief by which they were drowned in the flood, which could have been avoided by faith. Either Christ had already given them fair warning through the preaching of Noah, or Christ was returning to them to proclaim the victory of the resurrection and to declare judgment. Finally there are some who have thought that Christ was preaching *to the fallen angels* of Genesis 6:1–4.

To whomever he preached, Cyril noted that his preaching had effect, that though his descent was lonely, his ascent was in company: "He descended alone into the nether world, but ascended therefrom with a numerous company" (Cyril of Jerusalem, *Catech. Lect.* XIV, *FC* 64, p. 44). "He goes down into Hell, but He brings up the souls" (Gregory Nazianzen, *On the Son, Orat.* XXIX, *NPNF* 2 VII, p. 309).

Issues of the Descent

Several questions remain:

Are There Distinguishable Spheres Among the Dead?

Is hades to be distinguished from the places of purgation and punishment? In medieval scholasticism *hades* (*infernum*) was a broader term that could designate either (a) hell as the abode of reprobates (*gehenna*), (b) a place of purgation or cleansing after death (*purgatorium*), (c) the abode of neonates and innocents who had died unbaptized (*limbus infantium*), or (d) the abode of the just who lived in hope before the coming of Christ (*limbus patrum;* Bellarmine, *De Christo* V.8; Pohle-Preuss, *DT* V, p. 94). Much of the controversy surrounding this article has focused on which of these interpretations is preferable.

The answer of the Roman tradition has been that the only level of hades to which Christ descended was the *limbus patrum,* where the saints of the Old Testament and the just among all human history who had died in a state of grace were dwelling in expectation of beatific vision (Tho. Aq., *ST* III, Q52.7, II, p. 2307; Pohle-Preuss, *DT* V, p. 97).

The Entombed Body, Soul Descending

Which nature made the descent? Here Protestant thought reflected the patristic consensus: the divine-human person according to his human nature (Quenstedt, *TDP* III, p. 373). It is said of the God-man that he suffered, was crucified, and died as one indivisible person with two natures. Hence it must also be affirmed of his descent that one person, the God-man, descended into the nether world, yet the descent itself is predicated only of his human nature. "He was entirely in hell, because the whole Person of Christ was there by reason of the soul united with Him, and the whole Christ was then everywhere by reason of the Divine Nature," Thomas observed, adding this distinction: "Christ's Person is whole in each single place, but not wholly" (Tho. Aq., *ST* III, Q52, 3, II, p. 2304).

Did the body descend? During the three days of entombment, it has been usually argued that Jesus' soul alone descended into the unseen world where the souls of the just awaited his coming (Acts 2:27; cf. Eusebius, *Proof of the Gospel* X.8 [1920], pp. 216–37). Into the Father's hands the

Son had committed his spirit (Origen, *Dialogue with Heraclides*, LCC II, pp. 442–43). His body remained in the tomb while he continued his work in the unseen world. Yet neither his body nor his soul was separated from his deity due to the indissoluble union of his humanity and deity in one person (Tho. Aq., *ST* III, Q52, II, pp. 2302–2309). The formula of the Fourth Lateran Council stated: "He descended in soul and arose in flesh, and ascended equally in both" (*SCD*, 429, p. 169; cf. Hugh of St. Victor, *OSCF* II.1.10–11, pp. 238–49).

Was the Son Absent from Paradise in the Descent?

Hilary used the premise of theandric union to answer: "When He descended to Hades, He was never absent from Paradise (just as He was always in Heaven when He was preaching on earth). . . . Separate, if you can, from His indivisible nature a part which could fear punishment: send the one part of Christ to Hades to suffer pain, the other, you must leave in Paradise to reign" (Hilary, *Trin.* X.34, *NPNF* 2 IX, p. 190; cf. Macrina as reported to Gregory of Nyssa, *On the Soul and the Resurrection* 1, *NPNF* 2 V, pp. 430–35; Barrow, *WIB* II, pp. 479–80).

Lucan and Pauline Texts of the Descent

Luke-Acts provided much of the textuary for various interpretations concerning the article on *descensus ad infernos*.

Today in Paradise

Jesus promised the penitent thief that he would be *with him that very day* in Paradise (Luke 23:43). This suggested to some classical exegetes that the soul of Jesus immediately after his crucifixion descended to that condition in which all the dead reside (Gregory Nazianzen, *Orat.* XXIX, *On the Son* 20, *NPNF* 2 VII, p. 309; cf. Wesley, *NUNT,* p. 294).

It should be noted that in earlier Old Testament teaching, both the just and unjust went to *sheol (hades)* after death, but in some later Judaic exegesis, the righteous were assigned to a higher part of *hades,* paradise. There is evidence of controversy as to whether paradise was or was not included in *hades.* Paul thought that we are closer to God in paradise ("the eternal house in heaven") than in our earthly, bodily existence (2 Cor. 5:6–9). Tertullian believed that paradise would be not yet heaven but distinguishable from *hades,* affording rest to the souls of the righteous (*Ag. Marcion* IV.34, *ANF* III, pp. 404–406). Hence one interpretation is that Jesus went to hades to a specific part, paradise, and taught the righteous the truth of Scripture (E. C. S. Gibson, *The Thirty-Nine Articles of the Church of England,* p. 159).

His Body Did Not See Decay

One textual reference used in Acts by both Paul and Peter was the allusion to Psalm 16:10 as applied to Christ, "you will not abandon me to the grave, nor will you let your Holy One see decay" (Ps. 16:10).

Preaching at Pisidian Antioch, Paul is reported to have made a special point of preaching that "the one whom God raised from the dead did not see decay" (Acts 13:37), fulfilling the promise of Psalm 16:10. In reference to Christ's resurrection, Peter declared that David had been promised that God "would place one of his descendants on his throne. Seeing what was ahead, he spoke of the resurrection of the Christ, that he was not abandoned to the grave, nor did his body see decay" (Acts 2:30–31).

Two other Pauline texts of descent deserve mention.

He Led Captives in His Train

In making the point that each believer has grace as Christ has apportioned, the Letter to Ephesians quotes Psalm 68:18 that "When he ascended on high, he led captives in his train and gave gifts to men" (Eph. 4:7–8). This is followed by a comment: "What does 'he ascended' mean except that he also descended to the lower, earthly regions?" (Eph. 4:9). This has suggested to some exegetes that the descent into hades was available in the pre-Pauline oral tradition, and that it had as its purpose the giving of gifts, endowing those in the unseen world with gracious abilities (J. B. Lightfoot, *St. Ignatius* II, pp. 131–33). Others argue that "the lower, earthly regions" does not refer to the nether world, but simply to the earth.

Paul's Caveat on Descent

Paul joined the descent and the ascent themes together in Romans 10:6–7 (RSV), where he admonished his hearers that it not be asked who will go into the abyss to bring up Christ from the dead: "But the righteousness based on faith says, Do not say in your heart, 'Who will ascend into heaven?' (that is, to bring Christ down) or 'Who will descend into the abyss?' (that is, to bring Christ up from the dead)."

Some think that Paul thereby affirmed Christ's descent into "the abyss" as the counterpart of the ascension, taking "the abyss" as a reference to the nether world. If so, this sequence agrees with correlated texts that place the descent prior to the resurrection. Others considered "the abyss" to be simply death.

Conclusion

Noting all the difficulties of these passages, it may be concluded that there is scriptural grounding for the belief that Christ descended into the abode of the dead, but hardly for speculation in detail upon precisely how or why this descent occurred – otherwise such knowledge would have been revealed in the scriptures. "How Christ descended and when, this the Scriptures have not specially revealed to us" (John Parsimonius, quoted in Schmid, *DT*, p. 399). Hence these questions may be left open for further inquiry.

The Formula of Concord rightly warned against excessive speculation, that since this article "can be comprehended neither by our senses nor reason, but is to be received by faith alone, we unanimously advise that there be no controversy concerning this matter, but that we teach this article with the greatest simplicity . . . satisfied to know that Christ has descended to those in hell, that He has destroyed hell for all believers" (Schmid, *DT*, p. 400; Formula of Concord IX, *BOC*, p. 610).

CHAPTER 13

The Risen Lord

The creed confesses that Jesus was resurrected (*anastanta*; Lat. *resurrex-ist*, Creed of 150 Fathers, *COC* II, p. 58) on the third day (Ancient Western Form of the Apostolic Creed, *SCD* 2, p. 5; see also *SCD* 13, 16, 20, 40, 54).

The truth about Jesus was not finally revealed until his resurrection. The resurrection was the seal and confirmation of Christ's saving activity on the cross.

The Gospels do not explain the resurrection. The resurrection alone is what can explain the Gospels.

The redemptive value of his death for others was made effective by his resurrection. The resurrection is that mystery by which the value of his death for others is realized. Resurrection is the necessary complement and sequel to the incarnation.

"After his suffering, he showed himself to these men and gave many convincing proofs that he was alive. He appeared to them over a period of forty days and spoke about the kingdom of God" (Acts 1:3).

THE LORD IS RISEN INDEED

What had looked like the collapse and defeat of God's mission turned out to be its most signal victory. God's saving event stood contrary to every normal human expectation. The best human intelligence could not have predicted this reversal. The signs that pointed toward it were dis-believed.

Every aspect of his teaching that had earlier seemed to be a "hard say-ing" (John 6:60) was now in the light of his resurrection viewed as a source of joy. The resurrection threw instant light upon all that had preceded it.

Modern chauvinism assumes the inferiority of premodern insight.

When modern chauvinism looks at the resurrection, it sees nothing but absurdities and obstacles. When classical Christianity looks at the resurrection, it beholds clarity, revelation, plausibility, and evidence of the highest order.

Resurrection Defined

Jesus' resurrection is that event in which the Messiah was raised from the dead, his body brought to life to demonstrate to the disciples the completed work of redemption (Augustine, *CG, FC* 24, pp. 68-71, 423-32).

His Death for Others Made Effective

The redemptive value of his death for others was made plain by his resurrection.

The root meaning of resurrection (*anastasis; exanastasis;* verbs: *anístēmi, egeirō*) is simply to raise or arise from the dead. The resurrection of Christ is the arising (vivification, reanimation) of his body on the third day after his death. Resurrection is God's own way of demonstrating the defeat of death. God brought forth his body reunited with his soul and so appeared before the disciples risen from the tomb (Hilary, *Trin.* IX.9-18, *NPNF* 2 IX, pp. 158-60; Innocent III, *Eius Exemplo, SCD* 422, p. 167; see also *SCD* 462).

Thereafter Christians have sought to "know Christ and the power of his resurrection and the fellowship of sharing in his sufferings, becoming like him in his death, and so, somehow, to attain to the resurrection from the dead" (Phil. 3:10; Gregory Nazianzen, *Orat.* I, *NPNF* 2 VII, pp. 203, 235ff.).

A Temporal Event Revealing the Hidden Meaning of Universal History

Christians understand the resurrection together with the cross to be history's most important event. The despair of all past history is reversed by it. The hope of all future history is enabled by it. It is of all events the most illuminating disclosure of God's plan of salvation (C. F. D. Moule, *The Significance of the Message of the Resurrection for Faith in Jesus Christ*). To understand the resurrection is to understand the meaning of history from its end.

"The Lord has risen indeed" (Luke 24:34, RSV) has thereafter been the hallmark of Christian testimony. The appearances occurred at particular places and times, beginning from a stone sepulchre near Golgotha (John 19:41) and continuing for forty days. Yet they had universal historical significance (Lactantius, *Div. Inst.*, FC 49, pp. 297-99).

The Raising of Humanity

By rising from the grave the Lord raised human nature and honored humanity in an unparalleled way (Rom. 5:15–19; Acts 2:24; 1 Cor. 15:20–23; John 15:1–6). By the resurrection, the drama of God's coming was brought to an astounding climax and resolution.

Ancient exegetes taught that God became human that humanity might become God and that through union with Christ our humanity is deified. That did not imply that we cease being creatures or lose our humanity in God, but that we in faith become partakers of, participants in, or members of Christ's own resurrected body. His resurrection points to what we are to become and makes possible the intended and fitting consummation of our humanity (Irenaeus, *Ag. Her.* III.19.1; V.16.2; V.21.1, *ANF* I, pp. 448, 544, 548; Athanasius, *On the Incarn.*, 54; John of Damascus, *OF* III.17).

Sufficiently Attested

The witnesses were numerous, competent, and willing to suffer for their testimony. The testimony of the apostles was accompanied by God's own testimony: "This salvation, which was first announced by the Lord, was confirmed to us by those who heard him. God also testified to it by signs, wonders and various miracles, and gifts of the Holy Spirit" (Acts 2:3–4). The Spirit continues to bear witness to the truth of this saving event in our hearts (Rom. 8:11–17).

Each Sunday Service Attests Resurrection

Sabbath observance for Christians is on Sunday, resurrection day, as a continuing testimony of the church every week to the centrality of the resurrection. The resurrection is not celebrated on Easter alone but every Lord's Day. The phrase "the first day of the week" was not found in Jewish tradition until the Gospel writers (Matt. 28:1; Mark 16:2, 9; Luke 24:1; John 20:1, 9; see Acts 20:7; 1 Cor. 16:2).

Death and Resurrection Inseparable, Viewed as Integral Salvation Event

It is best to think of Christ's death and resurrection as a single event or complex of events, rather than two separable events. For "He was delivered over to death for our sins and was raised to life for our justification" (Rom. 4:25). The cross "contains in itself the mystery of Easter" (Leo, *Serm.* LXXI.1, *NPNF* 2 XII, p. 182). Cyril of Jerusalem understood that one sees Jesus' death most clearly through the lens of the resurrection: "I confess the Cross, because I know of the Resurrection" (*Catech. Lect.* XIII, FC 64, p. 6).

As cross is inseparable from resurrection, so is resurrection inseparable from the cross: "So then, let us remember that whenever mention is made of his death alone, we are to understand at the same time what belongs to his resurrection. Also, the same synecdoche applies to the word 'resurrection': whenever it is mentioned separatedly from death, we are to understand it as including what has to do especially with his death" (Calvin, *Inst.* 2.16.13).

"'Sin was taken away by his death; righteousness was revived and restored by his resurrection.' For how could he by dying have freed us from death if he had himself succumbed to death?" But "thanks to his resurrection – his death manifested its power and efficacy to us" (Calvin, *Inst.* 2.16.13).

THE HOPE OF RESURRECTION

Beliefs prior to Jesus about the general resurrection shaped the New Testament interpretation of Jesus' resurrection.

The Context: Resurrection and Universal History

The Event in Apocalyptic Context

To understand why the resurrection is so decisive for Christianity, it is necessary to think about the meaning of universal history. The resurrection is best understandable as a historical event in the context of apocalyptic hopes.

History as Revelation

Universal history is the most comprehensive horizon of the human imagination. The revelation of God cannot be grasped apart from the end of universal history. If God is revealed in history, history as God's address cannot be finally revealed until it is over. Universal history, if its intent could be grasped, would constitute the decisive revelation of God.

The Meaning of Universal History as Theology's Subject Matter

The task of theology is to search for the meaning of history. The creeds of the churches have sought to interpret the whole of history from beginning to end, not merely a part of history. The meaning of universal history is the proper subject matter of theology. What the resurrection is all about is the meaning of universal history.

Final Revelation Is Knowable Only at History's End

If the whole of history is revelation, then revelation is complete only at the end of history, for it is only then that one may hear "what history says" or behold to what conclusion history has come.

History could come to an end at any moment. At no point in history is there an empirical guarantee that it will continue. Whatever its duration, *it is only from the end of history that its final meaning can be discerned*. Julian of Norwich grasped the decisive analogy: "We can never fully know ourself until the last moment" (*Aphorisms, IAIA,* p. 191). As a person's life is only interpretable when one's last responsible decision is made, so is the life of history only interpretable on its last day.

We may theorize about what all of history means, yet all such talk remains within the parentheses of continuing history, hence is tentative and incomplete, for the course of future history could always reverse our theories about it. It is precisely of this point that the concept of resurrection speaks.

Resurrection in the Light of Apocalyptic

The Apocalyptic Focus upon the End

The apocalyptic movements of late Judaism were keenly aware of the incompleteness of history. They understood how limited and distorted were the prevailing visions of humanity under the power of sin. The meaning of history was not to be derived from past or present history, but only from the last day of history.

Apocalyptic understandings of history in the late intertestamental period sought to reflect anticipatively and imaginatively upon the end, for only then would the meaning of history be apparent or even possible to grasp. Hence the whole of history is not interpretable from any of its parts, which could be reversed on the last day. History is interpretable only from its final day. For that day apocalyptic prayed.

All subsequent philosophies of history have been decisively shaped by these writers. Apocalyptic discovered the idea of universal history by focusing in an unprecedented way upon the end of history. Until apocalyptic, there was, strictly speaking, no idea of universal history.

End-time Expectation Saturated the Environment in Which the New Testament Was Written

For apocalyptic writings and for late Judaic consciousness generally, the resurrection is the key for grasping the meaning of the whole of his-

tory (Pannenberg, *TKG*, pp. 51ff.). Jesus' resurrection does not make sufficient sense if artificially abstracted from this actual history of expectation.

Many first-century documents attest intense expectation that the
general resurrection (hence the end of history) was imminent. This is
seen in the Qumran scrolls and late Judaic apocalypticism. A quarter century after Jesus' death, Paul was still expecting that the general resurrection (the end of history) would occur soon (1 Thess. 4:15–17; 1 Cor. 15:51).

Why an Existentialist Interpretation of History Is Constricted

For those who become fixated primarily upon here-and-now decisions instead of objective history, the meaning of universal history tends
to become collapsed into our present experience. In psychological and
existentialist interpretations, the revealing whole of history is misplaced
and we remain in our introversions.

The contemporary study of Christ needs urgently to transcend a subjectivist existentialist exegesis that collapses history into introverted
inwardness or subjective decision (Bultmann). On the other hand, it cannot take flight into a suprahistorical view that sees salvation history as
existing over and above universal history. Both tendencies resist revelation as universal history and have been rightly resisted in our time by Pannenberg (*Revelation as History*), as they were previously resisted by
Irenaeus (*Ag. Her.*), Lactantius (*Div. Inst.*), and Augustine (*CG*). "All theological questions and answers are meaningful only within the framework
of the history which God has with humanity and through humanity with
his whole creation – the history moving toward a future still hidden from
the world but already revealed in Jesus Christ" (Pannenberg, *BQT* I, p. 15).

How Jesus Transformed the End-time Expectation

Jesus' Ministry Constantly Pointed to Its End

During his entire earthly ministry, Jesus' identity (according to his
own testimony) awaited future confirmation. He did not play into the
hands of those who sought to force him into an instant identification. He
often taught that the confirmation of his ministry would be revealed in
future events.

When the Pharisees demanded a sign from heaven, Jesus resisted
their demand, not because there was no way to legitimize his claims, but
because the time for their confirmation was not yet (Mark 8:11–12; Matt.
12:38–42; 16:1–4; Luke 11:16, 29–32; 12:54–56). At that stage Jesus merely
pointed to his deeds as preliminary verification of his claim to authority
(in his response to John's disciples, Matt. 11:5ff., and in Luke 11:20). But

the final confirmation, he said, would have to await the resurrection and the coming judgment of the Son of Man.

The apocalyptic understanding of history was radically reformulated by the history of Jesus. He did not invent apocalyptic but modified it decisively both through his proclamation and especially through his own bodily resurrection. He spoke of the future of God as at hand and of himself as the sign of its imminent coming.

What the Resurrection Meant to Jesus' Contemporaries

First-century Jews commonly knew that resurrection means the end of history. Resurrection is the event that occurs at the end of history. Resurrection *is* the end of history.

Thus *if the resurrection takes place in our midst, then we are already at the end*. In an individual's resurrection, the beholders are being given a glimpse of the end and therefore the meaning of history; therefore they have received final revelation and the word history is speaking from its end. Resurrection is the word God speaks from the end of history.

Jesus' Resurrection Was Understood as an Event in the Context of Apocalyptic Expectations

Jesus' resurrection was understood out of a history of expectation prior to him. Jesus' resurrection finds its deepest meaning in relation to a specific history of expectation about the final events of history.

The resurrection of Jesus was not viewed simply as a fact without interpretation. Rather it was a fact laden with end-time significance. Its meaning was understood in the light of a history of expectation concerning *the* distinctive final event—resurrection. Those untrained in the tradition concerning the resurrection could hardly be expected to grasp all the nuances of Jesus' resurrection or even to understand what it meant in its context. But the disciples of Jesus were not thus untrained, as we moderns are.

What Would a Resurrection Have Meant to Them?

The testimony to the resurrection cannot be discounted as unreliable history, for it is clear that witnesses to it were radically transformed by what they saw. It requires some empathic effort for modern persons to understand what an actual resurrection would have instantly and self-evidently meant to Jesus' contemporaries. *The resurrection would have meant that the end time had begun.*

The general resurrection event was a way of speaking about the universal awakening at the end of time of those who sleep (Dan. 12:2–3;

1 Thess. 4:13ff.; cf. Baruch 30:1; 4 Ezra). Resurrection was the event of the consummation of history. It was God's own doing. The end of the world would not be something human beings create or consummate, but God's own fitting consummation of what God has created, however distorted by human willing.

Jesus' Resurrection in the Light of Apocalyptic Hopes

Jesus shared with apocalyptic the intense focus upon the end. Jesus came proclaiming a particular understanding of the end—namely, that it was immediately at hand and already being anticipated in his own ministry of healing and proclamation. When he rose from the dead, he confirmed what had been anticipated in his proclamation.

In Jesus the End Is Now

Jesus' ministry is a *prolepsis*, or "pre-receiving" anticipation of the end time. In him the end event is already anticipatively experienced in the present. The end occurs in a sense "ahead of time" as a "foretaste of the age to come," as if the end were already being taken into the present or received already. The end was not only conceptualized in advance but it was in effect "happening in advance" (proleptically). Whether hearers would participate in God's saving event therefore depended upon what they decided about Jesus and whether they participated in his life, death, and resurrection.

The Risen Lord Meant the End, the Final Revelation

In Jesus' resurrection the disciples understood themselves to be hearing the final word that history was to speak. To anyone who earnestly shared the apocalyptic hope in the general resurrection, the resurrection of Jesus would have revealed the meaning of universal history. It glimpsed the end of history. The meaning of the whole was made known through the lens of this one end-time event (Pannenberg, *JGM*, pp. 53–88; Moltmann, *ICT*, pp. 194–214; *HP*, pp. 31–55).

The moment the disciples were met by the risen Jesus, they understood that they were already standing at the beginning of the end time, the last days, the general resurrection. The event communicated to them its own message. It stood as confirmation of Jesus' living and dying ministry.

In an instant it became clear to them that the end had indeed appeared and begun and that Jesus was "the firstfruits of those who have fallen asleep" (1 Cor. 15:20). This recognition was not a matter of gradual or lengthy development. *The kernel of Christology was fully formed in the single instant of meeting the risen Lord.*

Resurrection as Event

Either the resurrection was an event in history or the whole of Christianity is pitiable. Pannenberg backs into this conclusion cautiously: if the emergence of Christian proclamation can be understood "only if one examines it in the light of the eschatological hope for a resurrection from the dead, then that which is so designated is a historical event, even if we do not know anything more particular about it" (Pannenberg, *JGM*, p. 98). Those who attested the resurrection did not have to use such guarded language.

Firstfruits of the General Resurrection

Jesus' resurrection was instantly recognized as the firstfruits of general resurrection (1 Cor. 15:20; Col. 1:18). Jesus was regarded as the first born from the dead, the one through whom the believing community learned to look for the final coming of the kingdom of God, and the fulfillment of the apocalyptic hope.

Resurrection Distinguished from Resuscitation

Due to this matrix of historical expectation, resurrection did not mean simply a resuscitation of an individual corpse. A resuscitation such as that of Lazarus could (like Jesus' resurrection) point toward the end, but it was not the end, for Lazarus had no signs of being called to messianic sonship. He lacked theandric identity.

Resurrection is a more intricately layered event (framed by prophetic expectation) than simple resuscitation. When a dead body is resuscitated, there is a temporary revitalization of a single individual from the dead, yet that one would be destined to die again. In resurrection, there is a major difference—the resurrected one lives on. The same body is transformed into a glorified body for which there is no future death—imperishable (1 Cor. 15:35–56). The general resurrection was expected as a universal historical event, not something that happens only to one or a few resuscitated individuals who were themselves again bound to die.

Resurrection as Confirmation of Jesus' Identity as Anointed One

The Identification Confirmed

Any Jew who beheld the resurrected Jesus would have made the connection easily: in the risen Jesus, God was confirming that Jesus really was who he was suspected of being—Son of Man, sent of God, Anointed One. The claims that before the resurrection seemed blasphemous to

Jewish ears now seemed to be confirmed in God's own distinctive, eventful way.

The Son of Man Identified

If before the resurrection there had been some debate as to whether Jesus was regarded as Son of Man or regarded himself as such, there can be no doubt that soon after the resurrection he was viewed as Son of Man, an identity confirmed by an event—resurrection. After the resurrection the conclusion was unavoidable: we have met on earth the Son of Man who will come again to consummate history in a fitting way.

Final Revelation Made Known

If true, the resurrection would have meant to pious Jewish beholders that God is finally revealed. It is a reliable tenet of Hebraic logic that if the Messiah is risen, then God is unsurpassably revealed, for only at the end of history is the meaning of history knowable. But the end of history is already in a sense present in Jesus' resurrection. The general resurrection is foretasted in Jesus' resurrection. In this way, *Jesus' divinity is implied from his resurrection*. If risen, then Son of Man, Son of God.

Confidence Amid History's Continuing Ambiguities

All who shared the expectation of a general resurrection felt themselves grasped by the end time in the presence of the risen Jesus. They acquired an incredibly confident and otherwise implausibly courageous attitude toward history, suffering, and life's ambiguities. Why was the New Testament community so confident about the historical process? Because in Jesus' resurrection, the end was already beheld. The resurrection is thus the clue to the whole of history, through which God is finally made known (Pannenberg, *JGM*; cf. Oden, *ATW*, pp. 66–69; Moltmann, *ICT*, pp. 194–214).

"Jesus' unity with God was not yet established by the claim implied in his pre-Easter appearance, but only by his resurrection from the dead" (Pannenberg, *JGM*, p. 53). Pannenberg criticizes all who accept any indications of divinity prior to the resurrection. He thinks the Christological titles were due exclusively to faith in the risen Lord (*JGM*, p. 54). John Henry Cardinal Newman had similarly argued that there is no reason for supposing that prior to his resurrection the disciples adequately grasped that He was God in our human nature (*SD*, pp. 138–41).

New Testament Teaching of the General Resurrection

The New Testament taught that a general resurrection of the just and the unjust was to be expected. The vital connection between the general resurrection and Christ's resurrection was strongly indicated by Paul: "If there is no resurrection of the dead, then not even Christ has been raised" (1 Cor. 15:13).

Paul specifically rejected the view that the resurrection is past. He said of Hymenaeus and Philetus, whose teaching might "spread like gangrene," that they "have wandered away from the truth. They say that the resurrection has already taken place, and they destroy the faith of some" (2 Tim. 2:17–18; cf. Calvin, *TAAAL*, pp. 112–13, 146–48, 292–98).

Jesus himself taught and expected a general resurrection of the just and the unjust. John reported that Jesus taught that "a time is coming when all who are in their graves will hear his [the Son's] voice and come out—those who have done good will rise to live, and those who have done evil will rise to be condemned" (John 5:28; see also John 6:39–44; 11:24–25; 1 Thess. 4:13–16; 2 Cor. 5:1–10).

When questioned by Sadducees who denied the resurrection on the grounds that it was not in the Pentateuch, Jesus regarded them as lacking in their understanding of Scriptures and the power of God: "Now about the dead rising—have you not read in the book of Moses, in the account of the bush, how God said to him, 'I am the God of Abraham, the God of Isaac, and the God of Jacob'? He is not the God of the dead, but of the living. You are badly mistaken" (Mark 12:26–27; see also Gen. 50:24; Exod. 2:24; 6:3–8; Lev. 26:42). What does resurrection have to do with Abraham, Isaac, Jacob, and Joseph? These accounts contain proleptic resurrection narratives at their decisive moments—Isaac rose from the knife, Joseph from the pit.

THE MEANING OF HIS RESURRECTION

The Atoning Value of His Death Confirmed

His Prophetic Teaching Ratified

The resurrection ratified Jesus' messianic teaching, for he had explained "plainly" to his disciples in advance that "the Son of Man must suffer many things and be rejected by the elders, chief priests and teachers of the law, and that he must be killed and after three days rise again" (Mark 8:31).

His Sacrificial Self-Offering Accepted

Through the resurrection it was made clear that his sacrificial offering of himself for others had been accepted. His atonement for humanity was

462 EXALTED LORD

received of God, and humanity brought near to God. The resurrection confirmed the atoning value of his death. It attested that he suffered for the sins of the world, the just for the unjust (Cyril of Jerusalem, *Catech. Lect.* XIV, *NPNF* 2 VII, pp. 94–103).

His Suffering Vindicated

His resurrection thereby vindicated the Father's sending of the Son, the Son's suffering death. The resurrection stands as the key to the Christian understanding of suffering, for it is God the Son who comes to share our human suffering and the triune God who vindicates that mission.

His Victory over Sin Demonstrated

Thereby human history has become the setting in which God's final pledge of victory over sin and death has once for all been demonstrated (Hilary, *Trin.* I.13–14, *NPNF* 2 IX, pp. 43–44; Tho. Aq., *ST* III, Q53, II, pp. 2309–13). The humbling of the Son in the incarnation was vindicated in the exaltation of the Son in the resurrection (Barth, *CD* III/2, pp. 442ff.). "God raised him from the dead, vindicating him as Messiah and Lord. The victim of sin became victor, and won the victory over sin and death for all men" (Confession of 1967, I.A.1, *BOConf.* 9.08). The suffering of the cross was not absurd.

His Messianic Sonship Ratified

Above all, in the light of the tradition of resurrection expectation, Jesus' resurrection was understood as the unmistakable confirmation of his messianic kingship, his rightful authority to receive the kingdom of God and to govern (by guidance and protection) the kingdom of God (Calvin, *Inst.* 2.16.13–16). The resurrection reversed the sentence of death and vindicated the ministry of the suffering Servant.

The Davidic Promise Fulfilled

The hope of resurrection that had long remained quietly buried in the Psalms was now brought to life. Peter understood Jesus' resurrection in the light of the Davidic promise of Psalm 16: "David died and was buried, and his tomb is here to this day. But he was a prophet and knew that God had promised him on oath that he would place one of his descendants on his throne. Seeing what was ahead, he spoke of the resurrection of the Christ, that he was not abandoned to the grave, nor did his body see decay" (Acts 2:29–31).

His Authority Made Clear

Christ became exalted as messianic king through the resurrection. From the tomb he arose to give his disciples the Great Commission wherein the legitimate authority of the resurrected Lord became clear: "All authority in heaven and on earth has been given to me. Therefore go . . ." (Matt. 28:18).

Peter proclaimed that the risen Christ had "commanded us to preach to the people and to testify that he is the one whom God appointed as judge of the living and the dead. All the prophets testify about him that everyone who believes in him receives forgiveness of sins through his name" (Acts 10:40–43).

His Divinity Demonstrated

The resurrection serves as proof and eventful demonstration of his divinity (Hilary, *Trin.* VI.12, *NPNF* 2 IX, p. 122). The *Russian Catechism* asks: "What is the first proof and earnest [pledge] given by Jesus Christ that his sufferings and death have wrought salvation for us men?" Answer: "This: that he rose again, and so laid the foundation for our like blessed resurrection" (*COC* II, p. 477).

The Death of Death

The relevance of the resurrection of Jesus was absolutely extensive, saturating every aspect of early Christian preaching.

Power to Live Now

The resurrection became for Christians the power not only to face the future, but to live this life. The believer has died to the old way of life and risen to the new with Christ. Eternal life in Christ begins in the here and now and hopes to be fully shaped by the love of God in eternity.

His Exaltation Made Recognizable

The resurrection was the first evidence of the ascent of the humbled Son, the descent being complete in the *descensus ad infernos*. But no one could see his descent into the abode of the dead; the resurrection was beheld. Descent and resurrection are correlated as victory hidden and victory revealed.

His death having culminated his descent (from preexistent glory through incarnation to birth, ministry, death and burial, and descent), his resurrection began his ascent (from the empty tomb, resurrected, ascended to heaven, to intercede and sit at the right hand of God). His life and death embodied the full measure of obedience to the Father (actively through his life, passively through his death). His resurrection vindicated his suffering and death. Thereafter history would be divided into promise and fulfillment of the Christ, the old and new law, the prophetic anticipation and the messianic fulfillment of divine promise.

Material Creation Redeemed

It was a resurrection of the body. Resurrection (consistent with incarnation) thereby demonstrates that the living God is being vindicated in and through material creation. It is not merely as if God were acting apart from the body or above it or circumventing it (Origen, *Dialogue with Heraclides*, LCC II, pp. 440–41).

More generally stated, resurrection declares that God remains sovereign in material creation. The divine purpose is being fulfilled in the resurrection in a way that is consistent with the purpose of God in creation and with the incarnation. Resurrection is not counter to the purpose and order of creation, but God's way of redeeming humanity by utilizing fleshly creation (Isa. 26:19; Rom. 1:4). Furthermore, cosmic history is being brought toward a redemption that involves the whole of creation and not merely human history (Rom. 8:19–23).

A Bodily Event Unique to Christian Testimony

The creed contains two distinct references to the resurrection: "I believe in Jesus Christ . . . who . . . the third day rose from the dead" and "in the resurrection of the body" (no other salvific term is mentioned twice).

Jesus' resurrection was a bodily event. So is the resurrection of believers, whose lives are hid in Christ, a resurrection of the body (*sarkos anastasin*; COC II, p. 55).

There is no direct parallel in the history of religions of a founder whose bodily resurrection from the dead confirms and ratifies his life and teaching and enables followers to enter eternal life.

On the Third Day

He rose on the third day (*tertia dei*; Creed of 150 Fathers, COC II, p. 58). Like "suffered under Pontius Pilate," this phrase of the creed reminds us that the redemption of the world was a datable event, an occurrence in history, not an abstract idea.

In Jewish calculation, each day in which he was dead, whether part or whole, is counted as a day, hence he died and was buried on Good Friday (the fourteenth of Nisan), remained in the tomb on Holy Saturday (paschal sabbath), and arose on Easter morning (the sixteenth of Nisan). It was customary to count each new day as beginning at sunset. Thus Christ was in the sepulchre during part of two days, and the full day between (Augustine, *Trin.* IV, *FC* 45, p. 157).

Neither More Nor Less

Three days of burial, no less, no more, were required to establish the truth of his death. Athanasius set forth reasons why the resurrection could not reasonably have been sooner or later than the third day. It could not be sooner or his death would have been denied. If only two days, "the glory of his incorruption would have been obscure." It had best not be later because the witnesses to his death would disperse and the identity of his body placed in question (*Incarn. of the Word*, 26, *NPNF* 2 IV, p. 50).

"For if He had risen directly after death, it might seem that His death was not genuine and consequently neither would His Resurrection be true. But to establish the truth of Christ's death, it was enough for His rising to be deferred until the third day, for within that time some signs of life always appear in one who appears to be dead whereas he is alive" (Tho. Aq., *ST* III, Q53.2, II, p. 2310).

Anticipations of the Third Day Motif

The eighth-century B.C. prophet Hosea had used this figure of the healing of Israel: "on the third day he will restore us, that we may live in his presence" (Hos. 6:2; cf. 1 Sam. 30:12; 2 Kings 20:5, 8; Lev. 7:17–18). The risen Christ himself "opened their minds so they could understand the Scriptures. He told them, 'This is what is written: The Christ will suffer and rise from the dead on the third day'" (Luke 24:45–46).

The third day was connected with the wave offering, when "on the day after the Sabbath" the Levitical priest was instructed to "wave the sheaf before the Lord" (each person having brought the priest "a sheaf of the first grain you harvest"); for "On the day you wave the sheaf, you must sacrifice as a burnt offering to the Lord a lamb" (Lev. 23:9–12). The sheaves were waved as a sign to the people that the sacrifice had been accepted. Similarly it occurred in the case of the resurrection, that God's own sign of acceptance (analogous to sheaf-waving) occurred on the day after the Sabbath, namely Easter Sunday (Pope, *Compend.* II, pp. 169ff.).

The Sign of Jonah

Another prefigurative type that entered into the memory of the proclaiming church was Jonah. Jesus had said that no sign would be given to his "wicked and adulterous generation" "except the sign of the prophet Jonah. For as Jonah was three days and three nights in the belly of a huge fish, so the Son of Man will be three days and three nights in the heart of the earth" (Matt. 12:39–40). Jesus' death and resurrection was like Jonah's entombment in and disgorgement from the great fish (Ambrose, *Flight from the World*, FC 65, pp. 296–97).

> Love's redeeming work is done,
> Fought the fight, the victory won,
> Jesus' agony is o'er,
> Darkness veils the earth no more. . . .
> Made like him, like him we rise;
> Ours the cross, the grave, the skies
> (C. Wesley, "Christ the Lord Is Risen Today," *HPEC*, p. 161).

The Latin poet Venantius Fortunatus wrote:

> 'Tis thine own third morning! rise, O buried Lord! . . .
> Loose the souls long prisoned, bound with Satan's chain;
> All that now is fallen raise to life again. . . .
> Bloom in every meadow, leaves on every bough,
> Speak his sorrow ended, hail his triumph now
> (trans. John Ellerton, *HPEC*, pp. 155–57).

THE POWER OF HIS RESURRECTION

In Christian teaching two structures of interpretation constantly intermesh: resurrection and triunity.

The Triune Premise

The resurrection was the act of the triune God—not only of the Father, but also of Son and Spirit. Since God is three in one, it is not inappropriate to say that "God raised him from the dead" (Col. 2:12; cf. 1 Cor. 15:4; cf. Acts 2:24; 13:30); therefore it is fitting to say at the same time he is raised by the glory of the Father, by the Son's own power, through the Spirit.

Through the Glory of the Father

Christ was "raised from the dead through the glory of the Father" (Rom. 6:4). God the Father, who gives "the Spirit of wisdom," "raised him from the dead" (Eph. 1:20; cf. Pearson, *EC* 1, p. 430).

By the Son's Own Power

It is not inconsistent, according to the triune premise, also to affirm that Jesus rose by his own power. For the Son, being God, had power to raise himself. Christ explicitly stated of himself that he had authority to lay down his life and "authority to take it up again" (John 10:18). This implied a voluntary act of surrendering his life in death, and an equally voluntary act of resuming his life (Eleventh Council of Toledo, *SCD* 286, p. 111). When his detractors demanded that he prove his authority to them, Jesus answered in a way that assumed that he himself was the agent of raising in the resurrection: "Destroy this temple, and I will raise it again in three days" (John 3:19).

This distinction is useful: *when the resurrection is viewed as the vindication of Jesus' own divine power, it is viewed as the act of the Son. When the resurrection is viewed as the confirmation by the Father of the Son's life and death, it is viewed as the work of the Father. The triune premise remains: "Whatever the Father does the Son also does"* (John 5:19; John Chrysostom, *Hom. on John* XXXVIII, *NPNF* 1 XIV, pp. 134–36).

Through the Spirit

Finally, it was "through the Spirit," said Paul, that Christ Jesus was "declared with power to be the Son of God by his resurrection from the dead" (Rom. 1:4). "And if the Spirit of him who raised Jesus from the dead is living in you, he who raised Christ from the dead will also give life to your mortal bodies through his Spirit, who lives in you" (Rom. 8:11). Peter preached that the same God who "anointed Jesus of Nazareth with the Holy Spirit and power" was the very one God who "raised him from the dead" (Acts 10:38, 40). Only the triune premise makes these statements possible and intelligible.

The Status of Christ's Humanity Following the Resurrection

Several technical questions have emerged out of this triune premise in relation to resurrection.

Was the Trinity Changed or Enriched by the Resurrection?

Can it be rightly said that the Son brought back to the triune God an enriched Trinity, enhanced by his human experience? Has he who was sent out of pretemporal communion with the Father into the hazard of history brought out of history a new experience to the deity?

It has not been thought fitting to say that God learned something from incarnation or crucifixion, due to the premise of foreknowledge—the all-wise God foreknew all that was to be known about the unfolding historical events that the disciples witnessed. Being eternal, God lives in eternal simultaneity with all events past and future. So what is to learn? Yet since God and humanity are one in Jesus Christ, the costly, hard won experiences of being human are brought back and received again into the eternal memory of the Godhead.

Is Jesus' Humanity Received into the Trinity?

Assuming the permeant logic of the theandric union, in the history of the Son, there is now a person in the Trinity in whom human experience has become indissolubly united with the eternal God, "so that the heart of man and the heart of God beat in the risen Lord" (Mackintosh, *PJC*, p. 371).

Was the Same Incarnate Body Raised?

The same body Jesus received from Mary was raised, glorified, and transformed. "He showed us the conditions of our resurrection in His own flesh, by restoring in His Resurrection the same body which He had from us" (Novatian, *Trin.* 10, FC 67, p. 46; cf. Ursinus, *CHC*, pp. 234–39). The Council of Constantinople (A.D. 543) rejected the Origenist teaching of the ethereal nature and sphericity of the risen body. The glorified state was a real reunion of Christ's soul with his body (Pohle-Preuss, *DT* V, p. 104).

Did His Deity or Humanity Rise Again?

Only the hypothesis of theandric union could have enabled the kind of reasoning we find embedded in the language of Ambrose: "For the same one suffered and did not suffer; died and did not die; was buried and was not buried; rose again and did not rise again; for the body proper took on life again; for what fell, this rose again; what did not fall, did not rise again. He rose again, therefore, according to the flesh, which, having died, rose again. He did not rise again according to the Word, which had not been destroyed on earth, but remained always with God" (Ambrose, *Incarn. of Our Lord* 5.36, FC 44, p. 232).

Was the Risen Body Able to Suffer?

At a very early date Ignatius had grasped a pivotal dialectic: "Son of Mary and Son of God" was "first able to suffer" as crucified, "and then unable to suffer" as exalted (Ignatius of Antioch, *Eph.* 3, FC 1, p. 90). "The body was made impassible, which it had been possible to crucify" (Leo, *Serm.* LXXI, *NPNF* 2 XII, p. 183).

Were the Wounds Assumed with the Risen Body?

Thomas Aquinas sorted out the reasons why it was fitting that the soul of Christ reassume the wounded body so as to retain the wounds: to confirm the disciples in their faith in the resurrection; in order rightly to intercede for humanity, to be able to show the Father what had been suffered for humanity; to demonstrate that it was the same body that had been crucified that was glorified; and to be able to exhibit on the last day the justice of judgment upon the disbelieving and mercy for the redeemed, "as an everlasting trophy of His victory" (Tho. Aq., *ST* III, Q54.4, II, pp. 2316–17; Augustine, *CG* XXII, *NPNF* 1 II, pp. 479ff.; Bede, *Comm.* on Luke 24:40, *MPL* 92, sec. 27).

An Event Without Analogy

Distinguishing Jesus' Resurrection from Analogous Events

Of everyone else it is understandable that healthy skepticism might assume the high improbability of resurrection from the dead. But in Jesus' case, we are not talking of the usual human situation, for he is the unique theandric surprise unexpectedly embodied in time who breaks through our native skepticism.

The Presumption in Favor of Resurrection Derives from His Distinctive Theandric Identity

The more one learns about Jesus, the more the presumption reasonably shifts in favor of his resurrection—precisely due to who he is. It's as if to say: how could it be otherwise than that such a person rise if dead? How could this one be conquered by death (cf. McDonald, *ADC*, p. 33)?

The church was attesting not the resurrection of just anyone, but of Jesus Christ. It is only because of who he was—his identity as Son of God—that he had the power to raise himself up. (This is a deductive argument based upon the premise of theandric union.)

The Cases of Enoch and Elijah Distinguished from Jesus' Resurrection

Different distinctions applied to Enoch and Elijah: "Recall that Henoch [Enoch] was translated; but Jesus ascended," and "Elia [Elijah] ascended *as* into heaven, but Jesus, into heaven" (Cyril of Jerusalem, *Catech. Lect.* XIV, *FC* 64, p. 49; Gen. 5:24; 2 Kings 2:11). In neither Enoch nor Elijah do we have the crucial premises of theandric union and messianic vocation.

What of the Resurrection of Lazarus and Others?

In three miracles in the Gospels Jesus is reported as raising others from the dead: the son of the widow of Nain (Luke 7:11–18), the daughter of Jairus (Matt. 9:18–26; Mark 5:22–24, 35–43; Luke 8:40–56), and Lazarus (John 11:43). All point anticipatively toward the coming unparalleled resurrection of the Son of God.

Yet all three are quite unlike the resurrection of Jesus in that those raised *all died again*! The primary occurrence attested in these narratives is that Christ speaks and the dead hear as if they could hear his voice from the abode of the dead. This suggests that somehow the dead in the tombs were able or made able to hear and obey him.

Thomas Aquinas pointed out that one may be restored to life in one of two ways: first, as in the case of Lazarus, where one lives anew having been dead, but is still subject to future death—he "had to die again"; and second, as in the case of Christ, where one "is not only rescued from death, but from the necessity, nay more, from the possibility of dying again" (Tho. Aq., *ST* III, Q.53.3, II, p. 2311). "For we know that since Christ was raised from the dead, he cannot die again; death no longer has mastery over him" (Rom. 6:9).

Only by Jesus may it be claimed: "I have authority to lay [my life] down and to take it up again" (John 10:18). This is what most sharply distinguishes Jesus' resurrection from all others. They have been raised by a power not their own. Jesus was raised by his own power, God's own power. This is why his resurrection is without analogy.

The Untombed at Jesus' Death

It is in this light that Matthew's startling account of the moment of Jesus' death must be understood: "The tombs broke open and the bodies of many holy people who had died were raised to life. They came out of the tombs, and after Jesus' resurrection they went into the holy city and appeared to many people" (Matt. 27:52–53). This does not imply that they rose before Jesus' resurrection, assuming that he was "the firstfruits of those who have fallen asleep" (1 Cor. 15:20). Nor does the passage imply that these believers either continued thereafter to live immortally on earth or ascended into heaven, but rather that "they rose to die again" (Tho. Aq., *ST* III, Q53.3, II, p. 2312; following Augustine, *Letters*, 164, *To Evodius*, FC 20, pp. 382–98).

Such events were regarded as anticipatory of the resurrection of the dead or evidences of the power of the resurrection. While all of these who rose again from the dead anticipated and prefigured (or, in the case of

Tabitha, attested the power of) Jesus' resurrection, none was of the same genre as the bodily resurrection of Jesus on earth and in heaven.

Birth, cross, and resurrection all join in pointing to the uniqueness of this event, as sung in H. W. Farrington's simple hymn:

> I know not how that Bethlehem's Babe
> Could in the Godhead be;
> I only know the manger Child
> Has brought God's life to me.
>
> I know not how that Calvary's cross,
> A world from sin could free;
> I only know its matchless love
> Has brought God's love to me.
>
> I know not how that Joseph's tomb
> Could solve death's mystery;
> I only know a living Christ,
> Our immortality
>
> (*MH* 112).

The Necessity of the Resurrection

Resurrection is not merely an optional addendum or incidental epilogue to the gospel. It is intrinsic to the gospel, affirming, attesting, and validating the otherwise enigmatic earthly ministry of Jesus (Pearson, *EC* I, pp. 433–45).

Why Was the Resurrection Necessary?

Thomas Aquinas formulated five reasons why resurrection is a necessary Christian teaching:

1. because justice required that the humbled be exalted (Luke 1:52);
2. because faith in his divinity is thereby kindled (2 Cor. 13:4);
3. because it gives believers hope that they too will rise again (1 Cor. 15:12);
4. because by it we too may die to sin and walk in newness of life (Rom. 6:4); and
5. because only by the resurrection is God's saving work on the cross confirmed (Tho. Aq., *ST* III, Q53.1, II, p. 2309).

Lacking Resurrection, Faith in Vain

So central was the resurrection in defining the meaning of history that Paul wrote: "If Christ has not been raised, our preaching is useless and so is your faith" (1 Cor. 15:14). The gospel depended upon an event—resurrection—to validate the ministry of the person—Jesus as the Christ. Paul pressed further: "More than that, we are then found to be false witnesses about God, for we have testified about God that he raised Christ from the dead" (v. 16). Testimony to Christ and faith in Christ could not proceed without the resurrection as event.

Christianity without resurrection is a pitiable thing: "If Christ has not been raised, your faith is futile; you are still in your sins" (v. 17). The reduction of Christianity to humanistic hope is rejected in the strongest terms: "If only for this life we have hope in Christ, we are to be pitied more than all men" (v. 19).

BELIEVERS' PARTICIPATION IN CHRIST'S RESURRECTION

The resurrection forms the basis for the believer's hope amid death. By sharing in Christ's resurrection by faith, the believer is delivered from the power of death.

Benefits of the Resurrection

Righteousness Given, Immortality Pledged, Life Renewed

Calvin summarized major benefits that accrue from the resurrection: "For by it righteousness is obtained for us (Rom. 4:24); it is a sure pledge of our future immortality (1 Cor. 15); and even now by its virtue we are raised to newness of life, that we may obey God's will by pure and holy living (Rom. 6:4)" (Calvin, Catech. of the Church of Geneva, LCC XXII, p. 100; cf. Augustine, Trin., FC 45, pp. 382–87; Ursinus, CHC, pp. 238–41).

Luther wrote of the believer's new life quickened with him: "I believe that He rose on the third day from the dead, to give me and to all who believe in Him a new life; and that He has thereby quickened us with Him, in grace and in the Spirit, that we may sin no more, but serve Him alone in every grace and virtue" (Brief Explanation, WML II, p. 370; cf. J. Macquarrie, Principles of Christian Theology).

Moral Implications of the Resurrected Life

Faith in the resurrection implies the self-constraint of the flesh and calls for "the sanctification of the whole life" (Leo, Serm. LXXI.6, NPNF 2 XII, p. 184). Living the resurrected life was compared to awakening to a new day—the wayfarer is counseled to "wake up from your slumber" and "put aside the deeds of darkness," to "behave decently," so as to "not think about how to gratify the desires of the sinful nature" (Rom. 13:11-14).

After-death Expectation in Judaism

Although ancient Hebraic religion characteristically accepted death as the limit of human bodily finitude, there were nonetheless important Old Testament expressions about life beyond death. Since doubt has been cast upon whether there was any hope of life after death in the Old Testament, it is necessary to establish this point.

Textuary of the Resurrection Hope

Sheol in the Old Testament in its most elementary sense ordinarily meant simply the abode of the dead and did not include later images of punishment or purgation. There were significant Old Testament witnesses to the expectation that God would deliver the soul from death. Hannah sang: "The Lord brings death and makes alive; he brings down to the grave and raises up" (2 Sam. 2:6). This raising from nothing is characteristically what the Lord does (as in raising up Israel from nothing), stated in parallelism with raising up the poor from the dust, lifting the needy from the ash heap, and bringing children to barren women — bringing life from death (1 Sam. 2:4–8).

Isaiah prophesied: "But your dead will live; their bodies will rise. You who dwell in the dust, wake up and shout for joy. Your dew is like the dew of the morning; the earth will give birth to her dead" (Isa. 26:19; cf. Barth, CD III/2, p. 619; see also Jer. 18:3–6; Ps. 88:10). The Psalms anticipated personal resurrection (Pss. 17:10–11; 73:24): "God will redeem my life from the grave; he will surely take me to himself" (Ps. 49:15; cf. Ps. 16:10). The final human destiny was not simply resting in the abode of the dead (Pss. 17:15; 73:24–25; Prov. 23:14). Job assumed that "After my skin has been destroyed, yet in my flesh I will see God" (Job 19:25–27).

In the "dry bones" prophecy, Ezekiel declared: "This is what the Sovereign Lord says: O my people, I am going to open your graves and bring you up from them; I will bring you back to the land of Israel. Then you, my people, will know that I am the Lord, when I open your graves and bring you up from them. I will put my Spirit in you and you will live" (Ezek. 37:12–14). The hope of individual resurrection was clearly expressed in Daniel: "Multitudes who sleep in the dust of the earth will awake: some to everlasting life, others to shame and everlasting contempt" (Dan. 12:2, cf. Rev. 20:4–6; Apocalypse of Enoch 22:10–12).

Classic exegesis worked constantly upon the cross-illumination of promise and fulfillment in the two Testaments. Luther summarized: "The light of faith in the resurrection of the dead shone also in the Old Testament, although not so plentifully and clearly as in the New Testament.

Christ says: 'God is not the God of the dead, but of the living' [Matt. 22:32]. Therefore all the fathers, who hoped in God, without a doubt also believed the resurrection of the dead" (*Lectures on Gen.*, Gen. 40:12–15, *WLS* III, p. 1216; *WA* 44, 385).

Late Judaic Views of Afterlife

Though immortality of the soul was much more characteristically a Hellenistic idea, it had gradually penetrated into Jewish religion long before the coming of Jesus. Among Jews of intertestamental times, some rejected the resurrection and immortality, accepting death as an untranscendable limit (as the Samaritans, and the Sadducees who accepted only the Pentateuch; cf. Ecclus. 30:4–6; 1 Macc. 2:49–70). Some accepted the belief in the immortality of the soul (*Jub.* 23:31; *Wisd. of Sol.* 3:1–4). Others looked forward to the resurrection (2 Macc. 7:9).

The expectation of a universal resurrection of the just and unjust was assumed in *Enoch* 51 (cf. 4 Ezra 7:29ff.; *Syriac Baruch* 50:2ff.). The Pharisees expected only a resurrection of the just (Josephus, *Jewish War* II.viii.14; *Antiquities of the Jews* XVIII.i.3; *Contra Apionem* 2, 30). It was in a context in which general resurrection was piously expected that primitive Christianity emerged.

Immortality and Resurrection

The hope of immortality is not denied in Christian literature but viewed in the light of the hope of resurrection.

Immortality Defined

Immortality means deathlessness, immunity to death, not being subject to death or to any corrupting influence that might lead to death. The resurrection of Jesus provided for Christian faith the hope of imperishable life, the death of death, the hope of eternal life (Origen, *OFP*, pp. 181–85, 325–27).

Immortality Brought to Light Through the Gospel

While being diffusely prophesied in the Old Testament, the meaning of the future life was not fully developed. The full knowledge of immortality was brought to light through the gospel. "This grace was given us in Christ Jesus before the beginning of time, but it has now been revealed through the appearing of our Savior, Christ Jesus, who has destroyed death and has brought life and immortality [*aphtharsian*] to light through the gospel" (2 Tim. 1:9–10). In destroying death, Christ brought the hope of imperishable life to light and transmuted the hypothesis of the immortality of the soul, not ending or eliminating or negating the theme of immortality, but viewing it in the light of the gospel of the resurrection (Augustine, *Trin.*, FC 45, pp. 382–87). Those who set immortality and resurrection in direct opposition, as if contraries, have misplaced this correlation.

The Imperishable Inheritance

By this gospel, Christians have been born "into a living hope through the resurrection of Jesus Christ from the dead, and into an inheritance that can never perish [*kleronomian apartharton*], spoil or fade – kept in heaven for you, who through faith are shielded by God's power" (1 Pet. 1:3–4). "For you have been born again, not of perishable seed, but of imperishable, through the living and enduring word of God" (1 Pet. 1:23).

Hope of Immortality Transformed

The resurrection thereby confirmed the perennial human hope for immortality by transforming it into the assurance that through Christ the future life transcends death and corruption (Augustine, CG, FC 14, pp. 457–549). "In Christ's death, death died. Life dead slew death; the fullness of life swallowed up death; death was absorbed in the body of Christ" (Augustine, *Comm. on John* XII.11, NPNF 1 VII, p. 85).

Death Overcome

What is the death that is overcome? "It is twofold: bodily, when the body loses the soul which quickened it; and spiritual, when the soul loses the grace of God, which quickened it with the higher and spiritual life. Can the soul, then, die as well as the body? It can die, but not so as the body. The body, when it dies, loses sense, and is dissolved; the soul, when it dies by sin, loses spiritual light, joy, and happiness, but is not dissolved nor annihilated" (*Longer Catech. of the Eastern Church*, COC II, pp. 469–70).

Since human beings are "not only flesh, but flesh and soul, the flesh alone suffers the inroads of dissolution and death; whereas the soul, which is not liable to the laws of dissolution and death, remains obviously uncorrupted," for "the immortal soul cannot be killed" (Novatian, *Trin.* 25, FC 67, p. 89).

This is congruent with the explicit saying of Jesus in Matthew: "Do not be afraid of those who kill the body but cannot kill the soul. Rather, be afraid of the One who can destroy both the soul and body in hell" (Matt. 10:28). The text does not say that the soul *is* destroyed in hell, but that

God (not Satan) *is capable of* doing so, being all-powerful, for whom nothing is impossible. The saying does not imply that the soul is annihilated, but that its spiritual vitality is subject to divine judgment. Of this the living do well to stand in awe.

The Laughter of Women at Death

Attitudes toward death were changed by the resurrection. Before the resurrection, death was thought to be terrible, "and all wept for the dead as though they perished. But now that the Saviour has raised His body, death is no longer terrible," for believers truly "know that when they die they are not destroyed, but actually begin to live, and become incorruptible through the Resurrection" (Athanasius, *Incarn. of the Word* 27, NPNF 2 IV, p. 51).

Athanasius offered as sufficient evidence of this radical change the incontestable historical fact that *courageous women were empowered to martyrdom without fear.* Every Christian who had lived through the Diocletian persecution (A.D. 303–305, as had Athanasius himself) knew this to be a fact. Two analogies were offered to show the courage of these women. The first is their laughter at a bound tyrant: the women of the persecution laughed at death "as when a tyrant has been defeated by a real king, and bound hand and foot, then all that pass by laugh him to scorn," "no longer fearing his fury." As women laugh at a bound tyrant, so do Christians laugh at death. The second analogy is the fearless touching of fire: the martyred women who shared in Christ's resurrection learned to "despise even what is naturally fearful," as those persons from India who handle fire, touching it but unafraid, as stubble enclosed in asbestos no longer needs to dread the fire (Athanasius, *Incarn. of the Word* 27, 44, NPNF 2 IV, pp. 51, 61).

The Pauline Tradition Concerning the Afterlife

God Alone Is Immortal

The premise of Paul's teaching of afterlife is: God "alone is immortal," "who lives in unapproachable light, whom no one has seen or can see" (1 Tim. 6:16). Whatever immortality human beings share is shared with God, who alone is intrinsically deathless. God is not subject to corruption, diminution, or decay (Rom. 1:23; 1 Tim. 1:17).

The General Resurrection

All human beings will experience a personal afterlife, according to Paul. All must "appear before the judgment seat of Christ, that each one may receive what is due him for the things done while in the body, whether good or bad" (2 Cor. 5:10). Paul was here transmitting the received early Christian kerygma that Christ, who was judged in our place, would be the end-time judge of all.

Being Clothed with Heavenly Dwelling

Paul wrote of the future life in which the mortal body would be clothed in a heavenly dwelling: "Now we know that if the earthly tent we live in is destroyed, we have a building from God, an eternal house in heaven, not built by human hands. Meanwhile we groan, longing to be clothed with our heavenly dwelling, because when we are clothed, we will not be found naked. For while we are in this tent, we groan and are burdened, because we do not wish to be unclothed but to be clothed with our heavenly dwelling, so that what is mortal [*thnēton*] may be swallowed up by life [*zōes*]" (2 Cor. 5:1–4). The crown of life awarded to the faithful is imperishable (1 Cor. 9:25).

Sharing Christ's Resurrection

All thoughts of afterlife are transmuted by the hope of resurrection. In Paul's writings, the afterlife is portrayed as a participation in Christ's resurrection, wherein the faithful are clothed in spiritual bodies and share in Christ's resurrected life (1 Cor. 15:42–54). *Athanasia* ("immortality," "deathlessness") is attested in the Corinthian Letters as the incorruptible life of the resurrection, the resurrection body not subject to death (1 Cor. 15:53–54; Bonaventure, *CQLS* III.19, Art. 1, Q1).

Participation in the mystery of Christ's resurrected body remains an anticipated mystery to be revealed in the future life of the believer: "Listen, I tell you a mystery: We will not all sleep, but we will all be changed – in a flash, in the twinkling of an eye, at the last trumpet. For the trumpet will sound, the dead will be raised imperishable, and we will be changed. For the perishable must clothe itself with the imperishable, and the mortal with immortality. When the perishable has been clothed with the imperishable, and the mortal with immortality, then the saying that is written will come true: 'Death has been swallowed up in victory'" (1 Cor. 15:51–54, quoting Isa. 25:8; Tho. Aq., *SCG* IV, pp. 163–67, 297–99, 318–21).

Faith Looks Toward Resurrection Without Anxiety

Paul himself eagerly awaited the future life. "For to me, to live is Christ and to die is gain. If I am to go on living in the body, this will mean fruitful labor for me. Yet what shall I choose? I do not know! I am torn between the two: I desire to depart and be with Christ, which is better by far; but it is more necessary for you that I remain in the body. Convinced of this, I know that I will remain" (Phil. 1:21–25).

Characteristics of the Risen Body: The Same Body Glorified

After the forty days of resurrection appearances and the ascension, the Lord's body passed into its glorified state. "What that state is we know only so far as may be learned from what the Apostle teaches from the nature of the bodies with which believers are to be invested after the resurrection" (Hodge, *Syst. Theol.* II, p. 628). The resurrected life of the believer is like Christ's glorified body (Phil. 3:21).

In his humbled incarnate life, John says that Jesus "had not yet been glorified" (John 7:39), since his hour had not yet come. During his earthly ministry he did not fully exercise the divine attributes fitting to his divine sonship; in his post-resurrection ministry he did more freely exercise them.

The showing of marks or signs (*tekuria*) on his hands and feet, eating, and drinking with his disciples pointed to the mystery of his risen body. He was the same, yet glorified, "of the same nature but of different glory" (Tho. Aq., *ST* III, Q55.6, II, p. 2323).

The Same Jesus

The same Jesus who died was raised. Jesus' risen body was a real (not a phantom or ethereal) body, capable of eating, and demonstrating its corporeality to the disciples: "Look at my hands and my feet. It is I myself! Touch me and see; a ghost does not have flesh and bones, as you see I have" (Luke 24:39). He was seen "by us who ate and drank with him after he rose from the dead" (Acts 10:41). The risen Lord was not a different person from the one who had been crucified. The body was not a substitute (John 20:27). Jesus' risen body bore the marks of his crucifixion to assure believers that the one crucified was the same who was risen.

Changed

Nonetheless, his risen body was also described as a changed body, a "glorious body" (Phil. 3:21), a body for eternity, a body that could move through doors and walls at any time and appear and disappear; and even those who knew him well did not always recognize him quickly (Luke 24:15–16, 31). The resurrection body had direct continuity with the body that had died, but it now appeared in a changed state of glory. It was not merely flesh and blood physically resuscitated, but a glorified body (Origen, *OFP*, pp. 252–54).

The body was the same, yet changed, retaining the print of the nails, yet glorified. He was mistaken for the gardener until he called Mary by name (John 20:15). He was not recognized by travelers until he was made known in the breaking of bread (for "they were kept from recognizing him," Luke 24:16). He was capable of appearing and disappearing, of moving through graveclothes undisturbed, of moving from one state to the other while sustaining the identity with the earthly body, and vanishing instantly (Luke 24:31, 36). He truly ate, yet without need (Leo IX, *Symbol of Faith*, SCD 344, p. 140; see also SCD 422; Bede on Luke 24:41: "Christ ate because He could, not because He needed," in Tho. Aq., *ST* III, Q55.6, II, p. 2323). It was to the mystery of this spiritual body that the resurrection narratives pointed when they spoke of Christ entering a room through closed doors (John 20:19) or vanishing (Luke 24:31) or suddenly appearing (Mark 16:12; cf. 1 Cor. 15:51–52).

> Secrets of thy kingdom learn,
>   Read the vision open spread,
> Feel thy word within us burn,
>   Know thee in the broken bread
>   (J. Mason, *HPEC*, p. 165).

The Resurrected Body of Believers

The Resurrected Body in Apocalyptic Literature

Some apocalyptic expectation had held that the resurrected righteous would be changed into a radiance that would "shine like the brightness of the heavens" (Dan. 22:3; 12:3; cf. 1 Enoch 48:10; 52:4; 4 Ezra 7:97; *Syriac Baruch* 51:5, 10). This apocalyptic expectation offered Paul an available language for designating his meeting with the Lord as resurrection (Acts 9:3–19; 17:18, 32; cf. Pannenberg, *JGM*, p. 81).

Christ's Resurrection and Ours

His life enables life in the faithful. "And if the Spirit of him who raised Jesus from the dead is living in you, he who raised Christ from the dead will also give life to your mortal bodies through his Spirit, who lives in you" (Rom. 8:11). Paul wrote to Corinth that we know "that the one who raised the Lord Jesus from the dead will also raise us with Jesus and present us with you in his presence" (2 Cor. 4:14).

Shall flesh and blood inherit the kingdom? In answering no (1 Cor. 15:50), Paul was not repudiating the resurrection of the body, but rather saying that those guilty of sinful acts of flesh and blood are not rightly prepared to receive the kingdom. "Neither doth this corruptible body inherit that incorruptible kingdom" (Wesley, *NUNT*, p. 639).

The Resurrected Body

Paul wrote that at the Lord's future coming he will "transform our lowly bodies so that they will be like his glorious body" (Phil. 3:21). In that day those who share in Christ's resurrection will share in his "spiritual body," which is to be "raised imperishable": "So will it be with the resurrection of the dead. The body that is sown is perishable; it is raised imperishable; it is sown in dishonor, it is raised in glory; it is sown in weakness, it is raised in power; it is sown a natural body, it is raised a spiritual body" (1 Cor. 15:42–44; Calvin, *Inst.* 2.16.13).

Continuity Yet Transformation

The resurrected body is characterized both by *continuity with* the old earthly body, yet at the same time a *transformation of* it so that a changed (not wholly different!) body is given life. The old body is to the resurrected body as seed is to plant (1 Cor. 15:37). It exists in an unbroken connection, yet changed, glorified (Tho. Aq., *ST* III, Q54–55, II, pp. 2313–24; cf. Pearson, *EC* I, pp. 642–44). The glorified body will display a recognizable continuity with the earthly body, yet it will be given an incorruptibility not possible within the conditions of earthly existence (Leo, *Serm.* LXXI.4, *NPNF* 2 XII, p.183).

Christ's resurrection makes possible the conversion of our corruptible bodies into spiritual bodies in which body becomes completely consecrated to the spirit. The resurrected body participating in Christ is freed to be devoted to those holy employments for which the body from the outset was created and purposed (Tho. Aq., *SCG* IV, p. 180; Pearson, *EC*, pp. 381–85; Simpson, *RMT*, chap. 22; Hall, *DT* VII, p. 256).

The Glorified Body

From **Soma Psuchikon** to **Soma Pneumatikon**

In the resurrection, Jesus' body was changed from a natural body (*soma psuchikon*) to a spiritual body (*soma pneumatikon*), a body entirely subject to *pneuma*. In 1 Corinthians 15, Paul contrasts a preresurrection *soma psuchikon* (human soul-body interface, or natural body) with the postresurrection *soma pneumatikon* (pneumatic, spiritual body). The former is characterized by the simple enlivening or animation of the body. The latter is characterized by the subjection of body to spirit, hence the spiritualization of the body, or glorified body (1 Cor. 15:43–54; Tho. Aq., *SCG* IV, pp. 178–79).

Neither *psuche* (soul) nor *pneuma* (spirit) is itself physical-material substance, but *soma* (body) is capable of becoming enlivened by *psuche* and inspirited by *pneuma*. *Psuche* gives life to the otherwise unresponsive body; *pneuma* inspires the body and allows it to enter into a relation with God's own Spirit. If in this life the body is fundamentally controlled by the lower animal soul, in the end it will be inspirited. The change to a glorified body will "endow the *soma* with immortality and incorruptibility, imparting to it the power which flesh and blood does not naturally possess, the power to inherit the kingdom of God" (Hall, *DT* VII, pp. 181–82, cf. pp. 239–40). The glorified body of those whose lives are hid in Christ is to become *soma pneumatikon* (spiritual body), like the body of the risen Lord.

The Spiritual Body

The familiar soul/body (psychosomatic, *soma psuchikon*) interface of our present human existence is thereby transmuted in the resurrection into the spirit/body (pneumasomatic, *soma pneumatikon*) interface of the resurrected body—the spiritual body that is formed by the Spirit that raised Christ from the dead (Tho. Aq., *ST* III, Q56, II, p. 2324). The psychosomatic body that we now experience is adapted to the body-soul interface operative in all animal existence yet intensified by the self-determination distinctive of human freedom. The *soma pneumatikon* is a body existing in continuity with our present body but one that does not inherit incorruption (1 Cor. 15:50–53). The spiritual body does not lack body, but is embodied in a glorified manner.

The Plasticity, Agility, Impassibility, and Luminosity of the Glorified Body

The change from natural body to spiritual body is from dishonor, weakness, corruptibility, and mortality to glory, power, incorruption, and immortality (1 Cor. 15:42–44; 2 Cor. 5:4). Scholastic exegetes held that there are four qualities of the glorified body:

plasticity or subtlety: the glorified body is entirely subject to employment by Spirit ("raised a spiritual body," 1 Cor. 15:44);

agility: the glorified body has abundant energy and ability to move ("raised in power," 1 Cor. 15:43);

impassibility: the glorified body does not suffer ("raised imperishable," 1 Cor. 15:42, 52); and glory: the glorified body is luminous ("the righteous will shine like the sun in the kingdom," Matt. 13:43; cf. Tho. Aq., *ST* III, Q64, 65; cf. III, Suppl. Q83–88; *SCG* IV, pp. 179–80); it is in this glorified state that the human body finally fulfills its intended higher dignity and spiritual purpose (Milligan, *The Resurrection of Our Lord*, pp. 7–14; H. P. Liddon, *Easter in St. Paul's*, pp. 80–83; Hall, *DT* VII, pp. 238–40).

The Transcending of the Passions

The resurrected body neither marries nor is given in marriage, in Jesus' teaching (Matt. 22:30). It does not struggle with the passions that belong to the present psychosomatic interface (Augustine, *CG*, *FC* 24, pp. 458–72; Tho. Aq., *SCG* IV, pp. 311–29).

Luther explained: "It will be the body of a human being, just as it was created; but the body will have a different appearance and use. It will not eat, drink, digest, procreate children, keep house, etc. It will need none of the things that pertain to this transient life and bodily sustenance. . . . The difference between man and woman, which God established in creation, will continue just as grain keeps its nature and its characteristics. Nothing but a blade of wheat grows from a kernel of wheat; nothing but a blade of barley grows from a kernel of barley, and so on. Each kernel retains its nature and kind" (Luther, *Serm. on 1 Cor. 15:39–44* [1544], *WLS* III, p. 1218; *WA* 49, 4529f.).

The Present Christian Life in Christ

The Christian presently lives a life hid in Christ—born from above by the power of the Spirit, embodying and declaring the good news, going about doing good, willing to die for the truth, living in newness of life and in hope of the resurrection at the last day.

"We were buried with him through baptism into death in order that, just as Christ was raised from the dead through the glory of the Father, we too may live a new life. If we have been united with him like this in his death, we will certainly also be united with him in his resurrection. For we know that our old self was crucified with him so that the body of sin might be done away with, that we should no longer be slaves to sin—because anyone who has died has been freed from sin. Now if we died with Christ, we believe that we will also live with him" (Rom. 6:5–8). "In the same way count yourselves dead to sin but alive to God in Christ Jesus" (Rom. 6:11; see also Eph. 1:18–20; Phil. 3:10, 11; Col. 2:13; Tho. Aq., *ST* III, Q56.2, II, p. 2326).

IS RESURRECTION EVIDENCE SUFFICIENT?

Is the empty tomb a psychological "rationalization" of the early Christian community that is not "open to empirical verification" (Tillich, *Syst. Theol.* II, pp. 127, 155–58)? To answer this question, the evidence needs to be fairly presented, as it might be in a fair trial under unprejudiced conditions.

He Appeared to Many

The texts do not support the case that one must have had faith before one could have seen the risen Lord. Thomas had to be convinced visibly prior to his confession. The resurrected body of Jesus was seen by those who had not yet come to faith. The despairing Emmaus travelers saw him and spoke with him before they recognized him and believed (Luke 24:13–32). Mary Magdalene mistook him for a gardener (John 20:15).

No one can read the New Testament without becoming aware of how frequently it refers to the risen Lord. All four Gospels report numerous accounts. He was seen by Mary Magdalene (Matt. 28:1; Mark 16:9; John 20:11–18); the women returning from the tomb (Matt. 28:8–10); Peter (1 Cor. 15:5; Luke 24:34); the Emmaus travelers (Mark 16:12, 13; Luke 24:33–35); the disciples, excepting Thomas, assembled in Jerusalem (Luke 24:36–43), and including Thomas on the next Sunday night (Mark 16:14; John 20:26–29); seven disciples (including Peter, Thomas, Nathanael, James, and John) beside the Sea of Galilee (John 21:1–24); "more than five hundred of the brothers at the same time, most of whom are still living" (1 Cor. 15:6); James (1 Cor. 15:7); and all those who witnessed the ascension (Matt. 28:18–20; Mark 16:19; Acts 1:3–12). Paul added to his list: "and last of all he appeared to me also" as to one "untimely born" (1 Cor. 15:8, KJV; for Cyril of Jerusalem's account of this sequence, see *Catech. Lect.* XIV, FC 64, p. 46). Acts reported that these appearances spanned forty days (1:3). There may have been other appearances unrecorded.

Luther summarized the types of testimony: "The resurrection of the Lord Christ is made certain (1) by the testimony of His adversaries, (2) by the testimony of His friends, (3) by the testimony of the Lord Himself, and (4) by the testimony of dear prophets and of Holy Scripture" (Luther, *WLS* I, p. 181, *WA* 28, 434; Chemnitz, *TNC*, pp. 343–44; 431ff.).

The Tomb Was Empty

On Easter morning, women visited the sepulchre where he had been laid. They were astonished to find his body not there. The first layer of evidence is simply an empty tomb.

Shortly thereafter the apostles were actively proclaiming that Jesus had risen. It is hardly convincing that they could have gotten by with inventing this story if it could have been easily squelched by producing the body. But no one could produce the body. Several contrary objections must be taken seriously.

Maybe He Never Died

Could it be that Jesus did not die on the cross? Perhaps he only fainted? (Thomas Huxley, *Christianity and Agnosticism*, pp. 76–80; cf. W. Milligan, *The Resurrection of Our Lord*, pp. 43–44). This hypothesis is deficient on several grounds: (1) The evidence of his death seemed sufficient to his enemies and to civil officials. The centurion reportedly assured Pilate that Jesus was dead, in effect officially verifying the death (Mark 15:44–45). The reason the soldiers did not break Jesus' legs is that they "found that he was already dead" (John 19:33). It was after this that "the soldiers pierced Jesus' side with a spear" (v. 34). (2) Joseph of Arimathea "asked Pilate for the body" (John 19:38). "With Pilate's permission, he came and took the body away" (John 19:38). He was accompanied by Nicodemus. If he were still alive, no one would have described him as "the body." (3) His body had gone through a complex burial process: "Taking Jesus' body, the two of them wrapped it, with the spices, in strips of linen" in accordance with "Jewish burial custom," and there was "in the garden a new tomb" in which Jesus was laid (John 19:40–42).

Hence it is implausible to imagine that all during this time Jesus was not dead. Surely his heartbeat or breath would have been noticed. It is implausible that he could have survived being wrapped in linen and then had strength to remove the boulder that had been set to seal the tomb precisely to prevent any loose talk about a possible resurrection or that he could have done all this and still not disturbed the Roman guard.

Suppose They Looked in the Wrong Place

This seems implausible since two of the women (Mary Magdalene and Mary the mother of Jesus) had seen where Jesus was laid (Mark 15:47; Luke 23:55) and witnessed the burial, "sitting there opposite the tomb" (Matt. 27:61; Simpson, *RMT*, pp. 45–46; cf. K. Lake, *Historical Evidence for the Resurrection*, pp. 246–53).

Perhaps the Body Was Stolen

Could someone have removed the body? (1) It is unlikely that the disciples would or could have covertly removed the body, because a specific plan had been initiated by Pilate to prevent just that (Simpson, *RMT*, pp. 40–43). The chief priests and Pharisees told Pilate: "We remember that while he was still alive that deceiver said, 'After three days I will rise again.' So give the order for the tomb to be made secure until the third day. Otherwise, his disciples may come and steal the body and tell the people that he has been raised from the dead." Pilate ordered his guards to "'make the tomb as secure as you know how.' So they went and made the tomb secure by putting a seal on the stone and posting the guard" (Matt. 27:62–66). In fact Matthew reported that a conspiracy had taken place to bribe the guards. Further, the chief priests and elders devised a plan to give "the soldiers a large sum of money, telling them, 'You are to say, "His disciples came during the night and stole him away while we were asleep,"'" a story which has been "widely circulated among the Jews to this very day" (Matt. 28:12–15). Augustine mused: "You bring forward as witnesses men who were sleeping. Truly, it is you who have fallen asleep, you who have failed in examining such things. If they were sleeping, what could they have seen? If they saw nothing, how are they witnesses?" (*Expos. on Ps. 64* 13, *NPNF* 1 VIII, p. 266).

(2) It is implausible that thieves could have deceived the guards, moved the huge boulder, and *taken the body but left the graveclothes*—what possible motive could be conceived for that? Alternative explanations strain credulity (Daniel Whitby, *Logos tes pisteos*, p. 394, in *Angl.*, p. 270).

(3) If the authorities themselves had removed the body, then they would have had at their disposal the means of silencing the earliest proclaimers of resurrection—and they would have had sufficient motive to do so—if they only had a body. But they did not. The tomb was empty.

If the authorities had it in their power to disprove the resurrection, the vitality of the church would have been quickly dissipated. But it was not within their power to disprove the resurrection because they did not have a body. Their very silence gives weight and plausibility to the kerygma. "We know that his resurrection was confirmed by the testimony of his enemies" (Scots Confession X, *BOConf.* 3.10).

All these theories are inadequate. Classical exegetes thought that none is more plausible than the straightforward narrative we have, told by persons who hardly can be charged with either psychosis or insincerity. Their testimony was simple: God raised Jesus up to authenticate his messianic mission, to prove his divine sonship.

Finally historical judgment must fall on one side or the other: either the remembering community brought to life the deceptive story of a risen Christ or a living risen Christ brought to life the remembering community. There is no middle way.

Were the Graveclothes Left Collapsed and Undisturbed?

Careful unpacking of the evidence presented by John 20:1-9 yields a remarkable conclusion: Jesus' body was not there, but the graveclothes were there precisely in the place and in the exact form in which he had been lain. The account bears peculiar marks of a direct eyewitness account in its precision and detail. John reached the tomb first and looked in, but Peter entered it first. John entered the tomb and saw something that immediately convinced him that Jesus had risen.

The account is precise: he "went inside. He saw and believed" (John 20:8). But exactly what evidence did he see that elicited instant belief? Not just the absence of the body, but the *particular way the graveclothes were lying*, precisely as they would have been as if on the body but now collapsed without the body and left in an undisturbed condition. Joseph and Nicodemus had wound the linen around the body, inserting spices in the folds, and used a separate linen for the head (John 20:40).

The evidence in John's Gospel indicates that the body simply disappeared, leaving the linens as they were. The resurrected Lord passed through the graveclothes leaving them limp. There was a space between the head napkin and the body clothes. "He saw the strips of linen lying there, as well as the burial cloth that had been around Jesus' head. The cloth was folded up by itself, separate from the linen" (John 20:6-7; cf. Cyril of Jerusalem, *Catech. Lect* XIV, FC 64, p. 46)! This is what they saw that elicited belief instantly. The linens had not been disturbed by anyone and lay limply like a discarded cocoon (Leo, *Serm.* LXXI.3, *NPNF* 2 XII, p. 182; Stott, *BC*, p. 53). His body apparently exhaled through them (H. Latham, *The Risen Master*, chaps. 1-3). It is astonishing that we have such a precise description of such a crucial moment by an eyewitness that has survived twenty centuries.

"The linen clothes also, which enveloped Him and which He left behind when He rose" were early regarded as silent "witnesses." Three centuries later, Cyril of Jerusalem was confident that the specific location of this sepulchre had been correctly remembered and identified, "the spot itself, still to be seen" (namely, the site of the Church of the Holy Sepulchre, the very place where Cyril was offering his catechetical lectures, *Catech. Lect.* XIV, FC 64, p. 46).

Invention and Hallucination Hypotheses

If the testimony had been sporadic or dubious, these reports might be easier to dismiss. But one must search for some explanation of the extensive testimonies to Jesus' resurrection. Three hypotheses seem to exhaust the possibilities: they were either inventions, hallucinatory projections, or true. The first is sometimes called the impostor theory, and the second the enthusiast or projection or vision theory. That these are not late nineteenth-century challenges is seen in the long history of exegesis, where these challenges have repeatedly reappeared and have had to be fended off.

If one believes from the outset that there cannot under any circumstances be a third alternative (that he truly rose), then one must scramble hard for some way to support one of the other two hypotheses. If one rules out from the beginning the possibility that any resurrection can ever occur in any sense, then one is no longer looking at historical evidence concerning the resurrection—there is no need of that—but rather imposing a predisposing philosophical bias upon historical investigation.

The Hypothesis of Invention

The problem with *the hypothesis of invention* is that the narratives are exceedingly graphic and enriched by specific touches of an eyewitness. They show every evidence of being the testimony of people who were there and were candidly reporting what they saw. The narratives of the discovery of the empty tomb seem to be too particularized to be fabricated, too molded by specific detail to have been invented.

If the Easter narratives were invented, we would say that they were not very good inventions. If someone had wanted to contrive a resurrection story, would it sound like the meeting on the Emmaus road? If one were inventing the story, one might at least have played down the resistance and anxieties of the disciples. The noncanonical narratives of the resurrection indeed do display many such embellishments, but they do not have the palpability and concreteness of the New Testament narratives, which do not float expansively toward symbolic interpretation.

The Hypothesis of Hallucination or Projection

A hallucination is the supposed perception of an object that does not exist. Did all these above-named people see a risen Christ that was not there? The problem with *the hypothesis of hallucination or projection* is that it requires two elements missing in the Gospel narratives: intensified wish projection and memory-eliciting occasions.

The core of the projection theory is found in Hegel, anticipating Freudian views of wish projection: "The need for religion finds its satisfaction in the risen Jesus" (Hegel, *The Spirit of Christianity*, OCETW, p. 292). The projection theory requires that there be a strong disposition on the part of the rememberers in a particular, predisposing direction.

EXALTED LORD

The texts indicate the opposite tendency, "because their hearts were not disposed so as to accept readily the faith in the Resurrection. Then He says Himself [Luke 24:25]: O foolish and slow of heart to believe; and [Mark 16:14]: He upbraided them with their incredulity" (Tho. Aq., *ST* III, Q55.6, II, p. 2322).

(1) No sequel to death was expected. The body was received by friends and bound in linen. There seems to be no doubt that Jesus was dead and buried. The tomb was sealed. Burial rites began Friday and were still continuing on Sunday ("the day after the Sabbath") when the women came to the sepulchre. If large numbers of disciples had been expecting some sequel, there surely would have been some indication that they were eagerly awaiting it.

Rather, they came to the tomb to proceed with the burial. They did not come expecting to find the tomb empty. If they had been expecting the resurrection, they surely would not have done as the text of Mark indicates: "Trembling and bewildered, the women went out and fled from the tomb. They said nothing to anyone, because they were afraid" (Mark 16:8).

(2) The disciples were hard to convince. When the appearances were first reported, the disciples had an exceptionally hard time convincing anyone that they were true: "They did not believe it" (Mark 16:11). Luke's account stated the point more strongly: "But they did not believe the women, because their words seemed to them like nonsense" (Luke 24:11). Subsequently when "Jesus himself stood among them and said to them, 'Peace be with you,'" "they were startled and frightened" (Luke 24:36). Jesus "rebuked them for their lack of faith and their *stubborn refusal to believe* those who had seen him after he had arisen" (Mark 16:14, italics added). That hardly sounds like the disciples were predisposed to expect a resurrection so intensely that they fabricated it from whole cloth.

Thomas even more stubbornly refused to credit the reports—"Unless I see the nail marks in his hands and put my finger where the nails were, and put my hand into his side, I will not believe it" (John 20:25)! Far from being portrayed as intensely expecting the resurrection, the disciples were portrayed as stubbornly resistant, cautious, and skeptical. Jesus indicated their resistance when he described them as "slow of heart to believe" (Luke 24:25).

John's Gospel specifically notes that at the time Peter and "the other disciple" (himself) reached the empty tomb to inspect it, "They still did not understand from Scripture that Jesus had to rise from the dead" (John 20:9). Only if the opposite were true could the hallucination premise gain plausibility.

(3) The hallucinatory hypothesis also requires another element distinctly missing in the narratives: a memory-eliciting occasion. The hallucinatory argument might have been strengthened if any of these appearances had happened in a sacred location where it might have been plausible that the hallucination would have been elicited or the subconscious hope cathected. But the random and miscellaneous circumstances under which Jesus appeared to the numerous people were the most ordinary of circumstances—not special places with hallowed memories to be reawakened: some were walking on a road away from Jerusalem; some were out fishing on the Sea of Tiberias; others were on a mountain in Galilee; others were at some nondescript point between the Garden and the city of Jerusalem.

The range of moods in which the disciples were found by the risen Lord were extremely varied: grief (Mary Magdalene), skepticism (Thomas), fear (the women), remorse (Peter). Some appearances were to persons alone, others to small groups, others to large groups. There is no pattern in the situations of the appearances and no plausible psychosocial evidence on which to base a theory of hallucinatory projection. So the hallucinatory hypothesis must itself press and stretch the evidence in order to pretend plausibility.

The Account Is True

The only remaining option is that the account is true. According to Thomas Aquinas's analysis, Jesus sufficiently manifested the truth of his resurrection by showing that he had (1) a physical body after death (by eating); (2) an emotive life capable of interpersonal relationships (by greeting and talking with others); (3) an intellectual life (by dialogue and discoursing on Scripture); and (4) the divine nature (by working the miracle of the draft of fishes, and by ascending). Each of these testimonies or proofs "was sufficient to its own class," so as to maintain a correspondence between the testimony of human observers and testimony of Scriptures (Tho. Aq., ST III, Q55.6, II, p. 2323). Daniel Whitby reasoned: "'Tis equally incredible that they [the disciples] should deceive or be deceived" (Logos tes pisteos, p. 400, in Angl., p. 271).

Something Must Have Changed Their Lives

The radically changed behavior of the disciples after the resurrection is the best evidence of the resurrection. They do not intend or propose that we look at their behavior—all they want us to do is look at the evidence on which they base their testimony. But their behavior itself becomes an overriding argument for the authenticity of their testimony.

Before and After

Their lives were completely reversed by the resurrection. They were different persons after the resurrection. They had left the burial with a deep sense of loss, facing the collapse of what they had hoped would be the decisive event in Israel's history. Suddenly the persons we see portrayed in Acts are those willing to "risk their lives for the name of our Lord Jesus Christ" (Acts 15:26), who were proceeding to turn the world upside down to attest the living Lord (Acts 17:6; Moltmann, *ICT*, pp. 202–206). Their behavioral change was instantaneous, radical, and enduring.

What caused this radical change? They understood it to be the coming of the Holy Spirit that coincided with the ascension of the resurrected Lord.

Two Cases in Point—Peter and James

What caused Peter's change? During the trial Peter had denied that he had ever known Jesus—three times! Peter and the other disciples had anxiously met "together, with the doors locked for fear of the Jews" (John 20:19). Within days he was preaching with such extraordinary power that "three thousand people were added to their number that day" and baptized (Acts 2:41). "He spoke of the resurrection of the Christ, that he was not abandoned to the grave, nor did his body see decay. God has raised this Jesus to life, and we are all witnesses of the fact" (Acts 2:31–32). Soon he was calling all hearers to repentance, healing the lame, challenging the Sanhedrin, and suffering persecution on behalf of this testimony. What had happened? It is not just that something had happened, but that everything had changed. It is unconvincing to hypothesize that a non-event, a cipher elicited this change.

What caused James's change? He was one of the relatives of the Lord who had resisted him, who "did not believe in him" (John 7:5). But after the resurrection, James became a major figure among those attesting the resurrection. Paul specifically noted that "he appeared to James" at some point after he had appeared to the five hundred (1 Cor. 15:7).

The primary evidence for the resurrection today remains: changed lives, walking testimonies, people willing to proclaim the good news the world over. "It is prodigious to think that a poor ignorant young man, of meanest birth and breeding of a most hateful nation, and hated by that nation to the death, because pretending that He was a prophet sent from God, and after this His death, only avouched to be so by twelve fishermen, pretending with loud boasts of miracles, false as God is true, to testify His Resurrection through a greater falsehood, and promising to all that would believe it nothing besides this power of working miracles but death and miseries at present, which their experience proved to be true; I say, it is prodigious to think that He and His disciples should with no other charms work such a lasting faith in all the wisest part of men, that neither time nor vice, though most concerned to do so, should ever be able to deface it" (Daniel Whitby, *Logos tes pisteos*, p. 400, *Angl.*, p. 272).

The Test of Gamaliel

After Jesus' resurrection, many religious leaders desired to stamp out any sign of the preaching of his resurrection. But the wise rabbi Gamaliel urged caution in applying this test: "Let them go! For if their purpose or activity is of human origin, it will fail. But if it is from God, you will not be able to stop these men; you will only find yourselves fighting against God" (Acts 5:38–39). The truth of the resurrection passes this test.

THE NATURE OF RESURRECTION EVIDENCE

The most indisputable evidence for the resurrection is the Christian community itself. Some hypothesis is necessary to make plausible the transformation of the disciples from grieving followers of a crucified messiah to those whose resurrection preaching turned the world upside down. That change could not have happened, according to the church's testimony, without the risen Lord. There would have been no community to remember the cross, had there not been those whose lives were transformed by their meeting with the risen Lord.

It is only a living Christ, thought Athanasius, who could be empowering the witness of martyrs who do not flinch from torture. The demonstration of his resurrection lies in factually embodied evidence—that of persons whose lives have been decisively changed by the One who is alive. One dead ceases to influence. Christ's death increased his influence. The works of costly witness and service are not "of one dead, but of one that lives" (Athanasius, *Incarn. of the Word* 30, *NPNF* 2 IV, p. 52).

Attested as a Fact

Jesus' resurrection is not considered myth or symbol in the New Testament documents but simply a fact attested by credible witnesses: "God has raised this Jesus to life, and we are all witnesses of the fact" (Acts 2:32).

Occurrence, Not Imagination

The church did not receive its life from a moral teacher whose body was decomposing in the grave, but from one whose incomparable power made him known as risen Lord. The assumption that the resurrection actually occurred as event, not merely as a figment of imagination, is integral to the gospel.

It was not the case that the resurrection narratives were contrived and foisted upon the remembering community some months or years after Jesus' death. The resurrection testimony could not have exercised the power that it did in the lives of the disciples if it were not rooted in an actual occurrence immediately attested. Its truth value for its attestors depended entirely upon its authenticity as historical occurrence.

Differences in Detail of Resurrection Reports Enrich Their Authenticity

An event without analogy would strain language, since ordinary language would depend heavily upon analogy. Those who were reporting the resurrection were reporting an event for which they had no adequate language.

Of such an event it is not to be expected that the reports will display logical coherence in every detail. Whether there were one or two angels (Mark 16:5; Luke 24:4) or whether the resurrection appearances were all in Jerusalem (Mark) or Galilee (Luke) or in both places (Matthew and John) remains a matter of textual analysis that takes into account the sources and purposes of the writers.

There was no fixation upon neatly harmonizing the chronologies. This reveals the confidence of the attestors in the authenticity of the accounts. Differences of detail were due to the fact that each Evangelist was selecting from numerous testimonies, traditions, and recollections available to him that would correspond to his purpose with his own audience. Many witnesses were still alive at the time Paul wrote to Corinth. They were available to correct statements made about these appearances.

Witness to the Resurrection a Criterion of Apostolicity

When it became necessary to choose someone to replace Judas among the Twelve after his apostasy, the stated criterion was that he must have "been with us the whole time," "beginning from John's baptism to the time when Jesus was taken up from us. For one of these must become a witness with us of his resurrection" (Acts 1:21–22). Matthias was chosen. On a special basis Paul was regarded as an apostle, for "Last of all, as to one untimely born, he appeared also to me" (1 Cor. 15:8, RSV).

The Willingness to Die a Premise of Testimony to the Resurrection

Witness to this event necessarily called for the witnesses' readiness to die for this truth. Those willing to attest the resurrection in fact did so at the risk of their lives. This makes it more than casual testimony. Cyril wrote: "Twelve disciples were witnesses of his resurrection, and the measure of their witness is not their winning speech, but their striving for the truth of the resurrection unto torture and to death" (Cyril of Jerusalem, *Catech. Lect.* IV.12, *LCC* IV, p. 106). Their witness to his death sealed their own death. Their witness to his resurrection sealed their own resurrection.

Difficulties of Belief

Ordinary Experience Resists Resurrection Testimony

Analogy-bound naturalistic reasoning puts up stiff resistance to the very idea of resurrection. Understandably so, for "no article so contradicts experience as this one does. For our eyes see that all the world is swept away by death. . . . Therefore it is necessary for every Christian to have before him the testimony of the Holy Scripture concerning the resurrection" (Luther, *Serm. on John 20:1* [1529], *WLS* III, pp. 1216-17; *WA* 28, 429ff.).

Resurrection No Less Possible Than Creation

God is portrayed in Scripture as creating the cosmos—bringing the world to life—simply by speaking a word, "Let it be," and it was done. Is it more difficult to believe that God can create renewed life out of death than out of nothing? When compared to the miracle of creation, resurrection does not look so implausible.

Both creation and resurrection are finally a matter of God speaking a word: "If you ask reason to explain this, you will never believe it. But then God will prove His divine power and majesty. Thus He did when He created heaven and earth out of nothing. He spoke only one word, and immediately they stood there. So it will be at the time of the resurrection" (Luther, *Serm. on the Death of Elector Frederick, WLS* III, p. 1217).

Modesty in Evidentiary Presentation

No Validation by Analogy to Physical Evidence

Belief that Jesus rose from the dead is further complicated by the fact that attestors can never expect to reach absolute knowledge in detail of this event or find a language adequate to express it. It is too much to ask of this event that it be historically validated according to the analogy of laboratory experiment. Historical argument generally proceeds without the types of verification required in natural science and would be hampered by them.

The resurrection was a unique event without analogy in human experience. There was no other instance with which the witnesses could compare it. "Therefore the generalizations and rules of historical inquiry cannot, when *exclusively* employed, enable us either to demonstrate its reality or to overthrow its credibility" (Hall, *DT* VII, p. 170).

This is why a general principle of modesty and toleration is fitting to this subject. There remains an element of mystery in all historical events, and not only those attesting divine revelation. Historical inquiry is rightly and necessarily to be used where useful, but at best it does not claim to have absolute or omnicompetent usefulness.

Even if we should possess complete statements written down by every original eyewitness, the differences of opinion about what happened would not and need not be entirely eliminated. No presentation of evidence is totally devoid of subjective interpretation, however well-intended and truthful (as seen in any courtroom).

Caveat on Objective Investigation of the Resurrection

It is demeaning to the resurrection narratives to treat them as if they are merely objective reporting. Hegel's admonition, though overstated, should be carefully weighed: "To consider the resurrection of Jesus as an event is to adopt the outlook of the historian, and this has nothing to do with religion. Belief or disbelief in the resurrection as a mere fact deprived of its religious interest is a matter for the intellect whose occupation (the fixation of objectivity) is just the death of religion, and to have recourse to the intellect means to abstract from religion. But, of course, the intellect seems to have a right to discuss the matter" (*OCETW*, p. 292).

The Resurrection Cannot Be Protected by Objectivizing Evidence

Gregory Nazianzen plunged deeper. He thought that the limits of historical argument would be inevitably met in the mystery of the empty tomb, so that God's strength would be made perfect through our weakness: "For when we leave off believing and protect ourselves by mere strength of argument, and destroy the claim which the Spirit has upon our faith by questionings, and then our argument is not strong enough for the importance of the subject (and this must necessarily be the case, since it is put in motion by an organ of so little power as is our mind), what is the result? The weakness of the argument appears to belong to the mystery" (*Orat.* XXIX.21, *NPNF* 2 VII, p. 309). If one appeared to present an airtight case of evidence for resurrection, so that the argument appears stronger than the event it attests (so that the human ability to present evidence towers over the event itself), that would detract from the

mystery to which the intrinsically limited evidence seeks to point (Kierkegaard, *TC*, II).

The Resurrection as Evidence That Jesus Is the Christ

Yet the need to present evidence accurately is not obviated by the presence of mystery. That makes the need for careful, modest evidentiary presentation even greater.

The Gospels Set Forth Resurrection Evidences

The resurrection provided evidence to the disciples that Jesus is the
Christ (Tertullian, *Ag. Marcion* V.9–10, *ANF* III, pp. 447–52; Barth, *CD* III/2,
pp. 360, 379, 384). A major reason for writing the Gospels was to sum-
mon up this evidence (John 20:31). The gospel Paul proclaimed far and
wide was summarized simply as "the good news about Jesus and the
resurrection" (Acts 17:19). The apostles thought that those who rejected
the resurrection were thereby rejecting the whole revelation of the Son of
God (Tertullian, *On the Resurrection of the Flesh*, *ANF* III, pp. 545–94). "He
enlightened our faith with proofs," wrote Bonaventure (*Tree of Life*, *CWS*,
p. 16).

To refuse to consider the evidence is not only biased historical inquiry,
it amounts to a fundamental decision about the meaning of history. "The
decision to accept Jesus as Lord cannot be made without historical
evidence—yes, historical—about Jesus. If it were a decision without any
historical evidence it would not be about Jesus (a historical person) but
only about an ideology or an ideal" (C. F. D. Moule, *The Phenomenon of the
NT*, p. 78).

No Event of Jesus' Life Musters More Evidence Than His Resurrection

No aspect of Jesus' ministry was more minutely recorded than his
resurrection. Due to the pivotal importance of his resurrection, the evidence for it appears to have been assiduously collected, transmitted, and
embedded in the essential proclamation of salvation attested by the earliest Christian communities. The Gospel narratives seem to be saying to us
that if we cannot credit the last validating episode of his life, we are not
likely to grasp anything else said about him (Augustine, *CG* XXII.12–22,
NPNF 1 II, pp. 493–501).

Resurrection as Demonstrative Proof

The resurrection was generally thought to be an evidentiary demonstration of Jesus' messianic identity. This notion of proof comes directly

from Jesus himself. Jesus clearly indicated that he would rise from the dead within three days.

Luke, who said that he had "carefully investigated everything from the beginning," and who reported things "just as they were handed down to us by those who from the first were eyewitnesses" (Luke 1:2–3), insisted that "After his suffering, he showed himself [*parestēsen heauton*] to these men and *gave many convincing proofs* [*en pollois tekmēriois*] that he was alive. He appeared to them over a period of forty days" (Acts 1:3, italics added).

The proof of Christ's deity was to come not by rational argument but by events which would stand as *tekmērion* ("infallible proofs," KJV), "an evident sign affording positive proof." This eventful proof was embedded anticipatively in prophetic Scripture, for "it was from the authority of the Sacred Scriptures that He proved to them the truth of His Resurrection" (Tho. Aq., *ST* III, Q55.6, II, p. 2322). The resurrection was the event that proved the truth already attested in Scripture.

Resurrection the Proof of Lordship

The first Christian confession was the simple, straightforward proclamation "Jesus is Lord." Such a statement could never have been plausibly made lacking the proof of resurrection, without the risen Jesus finally clarifying his identity as eternal Son. That Jesus is Lord meant that he now lives, despite his death, as living God. The Gospels were written to proclaim the kingdom of God known through the resurrection, not to satisfy voyeuristic, judgmental, picayune, or ideological interests of social, historical, or literary criticism centuries later.

Paul had received and passed on the tradition of preaching that Christ Jesus was "a descendant of David" who "through the Spirit of holiness was declared with power to be the Son of God by his resurrection from the dead" (Rom. 1:4). The declaration of his sonship occurred through an event: resurrection. This event constitutes our justification: "He was delivered over to death for our sins and was raised to life for our justification" (Rom. 4:25).

The Manner of His Coming and Leaving

His birth and death were natural. He really was born and really died in a way familiar to human existence. His conception and resurrection were preternatural: he was conceived and raised in a way without analogy.

There is strong congruity and mutual reinforcement between the nativity and resurrection accounts. What occurs at the end could have been virtually anticipated from the beginning. If he were indeed the unique eternal Son of the annunciation, would not one expect that he would leave the world in a surprising way, just as he entered it unexpectedly and miraculously? Would not one expect his entry and leaving of the world to be consistent with everything else we know of him?

The Earliest Testimony: 1 Corinthians 15:3-7

Suppose it could be demonstrated that we have in hand a source exceptionally close to the event itself. That would mute the argument that the resurrection has its source in a much later remembering church rather than an event on the first Easter. We do have such an account. The most primitive written source attesting the resurrection is Paul's Letter to Corinth. There are several reasons why this source is of very early date.

"What I Received"

Paul was by his own attestation using language that had been passed on to him. "For what I received I passed on to you" (1 Cor. 15:3). By usual calculations, Paul was converted about A.D. 33 or shortly thereafter. Hence we have an account of what the church already considered to be an established tradition less than forty months after the event itself.

Paul an Untimely Witness to Resurrection

The fact that the early church accepted Paul's description of himself as a recipient of a resurrection appearance—probably about three or four years after the other disciples—also attests to the exceptionally early date of this tradition: "and last of all he appeared to me also, as to one abnormally born" (v. 8).

God's Own Initiative

Paul's repeated use of the phrase "he appeared" suggests that the risen Lord took the initiative of self-presentation to the disciples. The alternative hypothesis would assume that the initiative was being taken by the disciples first to hope for a risen Lord and then to attribute risenness to a desperate hope.

Why the Testimony of Women Omitted

Ironically, the probable reason why the attestations of women were not in Paul's account of 1 Corinthians 15 is that Paul was here attempting to provide an account that would be acceptable under the specific conditions of a court of law of his time. Since women were not admitted as official witnesses in a court of law, the appearances to women were not mentioned. Paul's omission thereby indicates that he had deliberately shortened his list to provide the most officially acceptable evidence available. This does not mean that the women's testimony was questionable or that Paul had discounted it, but that it did not have sufficient standing in formal court testimony.

But it did not escape the notice of the classic exegetes that it was to women that Christ appeared first. Women were "first to see and proclaim the adorable mystery of the Resurrection; thus womankind has procured absolution from ignominy, and removal of the curse" (Tho. Aq., *ST* III, Q55.1, II, p. 2318, in reference to Cyril on John 20:17).

Why were women, not men, the first beholders? "Because the women whose love for our Lord was more persistent," thought Thomas, "did not depart" after the others had withdrawn from the sepulchre—hence "were the first to see Him rising in glory" (Tho. Aq., *ST* III, Q55.1, II, p. 2318; cf. Phoebe Palmer, *The Promise of the Father*; Elisabeth Schüssler-Fiorenza, *In Memory of Her*).

The Modern Mythographers: Redoing the Texts According to Naturalistic Reductionism

Is the Resurrection Merely the Rise of Faith?

If one begins by entirely eliminating the possibility of resurrection, then the project of Christology is effectively immobilized. This has in fact happened in the tradition from David Friedrich Strauss to Bultmann. Bultmann concluded that "The resurrection itself is not an event of past history." "The real Easter faith is faith in the word of preaching. If the event of Easter Day is in any sense an historical event additional to the event of the cross, it is nothing else than the rise of faith in the risen Lord, since it was this faith which led to the apostolic preaching" (*New Testament and Mythology, KM*, p. 42).

Tillich specifically denied that the resurrection of Jesus had "the character of a revived (and transmuted) body"—rather it was thought to have had the character of only a diffuse "spiritual presence," not a body (*Syst. Theol.* II, p. 157). The only "event" he can identify is that which occurs in the minds of the disciples when they connected Jesus with the reality of the New Being, and it is that "event" that became "interpreted through the symbol 'Resurrection.'" This "restitution" had its locus in the impact Jesus' unity with God had "on the minds of the apostles" (*Syst. Theol.* II, p. 157).

The Interdiction of Evidence

A prevailing assumption of much modern historical interpretation is that nothing preternatural can happen or ever has. Almost anything can be alleged as a historical event except an event that alleges a divine cause. Yet the Bible constantly alleges God as causal factor in events. Hence the conflict between modern historicism and the Bible.

The habits of modern historicism can result in a systematic neglect of certain types of evidence. Such a procedure is as absurd as if in a court of law the judge would say: "We are ruling out all words that begin with the letter *B* or all statements that are made by brown-eyed women." Such an interdiction of evidence is arbitrary.

In the parable of the beggar Lazarus, Jesus pictured Lazarus as saying to Abraham: "If someone from the dead goes to them"–those who find their righteousness in the law–"they will repent." Abraham answered: "If they do not listen to Moses and the Prophets, they will not be convinced even if someone rises from the dead" (Luke 16:30–31). Here is an anticipation in the Lucan account that some would not be prepared to listen to evidence—*even the evidence of one risen from the dead*! Such is the case with modern historicism.

The Reductionist Bias

The kind of evidentiary presentation that is so painstakingly displayed in the New Testament is peremptorily ruled out in advance on the basis of a rigid philosophical commitment to naturalistic reductionism. This preempting takes place largely in the modern university only–seldom in the worshiping congregation or even in the general modern populace.

If one begins by first deciding that resurrection cannot occur and that no evidence could ever convince one that a resurrection had happened or ever could, then there is little sense in trying to convince such a person of this resurrection. One had best seek to show such a person that such a premise amounts to a predecided prejudice, a prejudgment, a bias based on philosophical grounds prior to the presentation of evidence.

Much of the effort of New Testament studies of the last century has proceeded under just this bias and with this handicap. No amount of evidence for an event will persuade one who remains doggedly committed to a philosophical predisposition that has already in advance precluded the possibility of that event's occurrence.

The trick then becomes to explain the New Testament without the resurrection or to assert reasons for a plausible belief in resurrection yet without a resurrection. For over a hundred years, this line of reasoning has been applied to the debunking of the bodily resurrection by means of criticism and psychological analysis.

If one depends exclusively upon a historical method that starts with a postulate that begs the question by assuming that an alleged event cannot happen if not seen and tested empirically, then that method has ceased to study history and has begun to assert untested axiomatic philosophical predispositions.

Modern skepticism approaches the resurrection narratives with a predisposition to disbelief, sometimes with absolutely fixed unconvincability, not unlike the Athenians who first heard of the resurrection from Paul: "When they heard about the resurrection of the dead, some of them sneered" (Acts 17:32). Luther found the same response in his time: "Moreover, to this day there are many who laugh all the more at this article, consider it a fable, and do so publicly, the greater their mind and learning are" (Luther, *Bondage of the Will* [1525], WLS III, p. 1216; WA 18, 663).

History Not Duplicable

The natural sciences cannot, without overleaping their method, put the resurrection (or any historical event) under duplicable conditions, for history is not reduplicable. That is where history differs from science. Good natural science is aware of its own limits and does not transgress them. When the natural sciences claim that nothing can be observed or be said to exist except that which comes within empirical observation, "they venture into an extra-scientific field and indulge in an *a priori* dogmatism for which their specialized methods of inquiry afford no basis" (Hall, *DT* VII, p. 166).

Why Was He Not Seen by All?

No Historical Event Is Seen by All

Jesus appeared to numerous witnesses (Acts 10:40). But why not to everyone, instead of some? The resurrection in this sense is more rather than less like other historical events—seen only by some (Tho. Aq., *ST* III, Q55.1, II, p. 2318). What other historical event was seen by all?

Peter preached that "God raised him from the dead on the third day and caused him to be seen. He was not seen by all the people, but by witnesses whom God had already chosen—by us who ate and drank with him after he rose from the dead" (Acts 10:40-41). That this event was attested only by some, not all, humanity qualifies rather than disqualifies it as a historical event, for an event alleged to be seen by all could hardly have been an event in history.

Identification with the Lowly

Jesus showed himself not to power brokers, movers and shakers, but rather to the broken-hearted, the meek and lowly, those who loved and had traveled and faced hazard with him.

The appearance narratives suggest that he was avoiding the impression among the populace that he was a worker of prodigious miracles (John 6:26–27). He deliberately sought to avoid being trapped by the nationalistic vision of the messiah (John 6:14–15). He taught that those who always desire a special divine sign as a condition of faith thereby show their lack of faith (Matt. 12:38–39). When the decisive event comes, it comes quietly, personally, in low key, and like ordinary events it happens in the presence of some and not others.

Attested by Those Who Doubted

Those who beheld were those who had traveled far in faith, yet whose belief had been crushed by the cross (Luke 24:18–32). Among these was Thomas who doubted, but in his doubt did not doubt so as to preclude all possibility of belief (John 20:24–28).

The evidences for the resurrection ask of the examiner a certain degree of spiritual discernment, without which, however splendid one's intellectual gifts, one cannot finally or correctly weigh the evidence (Clement of Alexandria, *Stromata* I.12, *ANF* II, pp. 312–13). "The man without the Spirit does not accept the things that come from the Spirit of God, for they are foolishness to him, and he cannot understand them, because they are spiritually discerned" (1 Cor. 2:14).

CHAPTER 14

Ascension and Session

THE ASCENDED LORD

Judging by the New Testament, the ascension cannot be an incidental or minor episode in Christian memory (Bultmann, *TNT* I, p. 45). It is recalled in all four Gospels, again in the Acts, in Paul, First Peter, and Revelation. None of the creeds neglected the confession: he ascended into heaven (*ascendit in coelum*; Creed of 150 Fathers, *COC* II, p. 58; *SCD* 2ff., 13, 20, 54, 86, 255).

From the finite world of space, time, and matter into the transcendent heavenly sphere the Son moved in the ascension (1 Pet. 3:18–22; Heb. 1:3; 4:14; 9:24; Rev. 12:5; 19:11). His glorified body rose above both the visible sphere and the invisible sphere, to enter into the presence of the Father (Lactantius, *Div. Inst.*, FC 49, pp. 300–301). Jesus' ascension signified his triumph as victor over sin and death.

Preparation for the Ascension

The Promise of the Father

Jesus had asked his disciples not to leave Jerusalem but to "wait for the gift my Father promised, which you have heard me speak about. For John baptized with water, but in a few days you will be baptized with the Holy Spirit" (Acts 1:4–5). At their last meeting the disciples asked him, "'Lord, are you at this time going to restore the kingdom to Israel?' He said to them: 'It is not for you to know the times or dates the Father has set by his own authority. But you will receive power when the Holy Spirit comes on you'" (Acts 1:6–8).

The Forty-Day Interval of Teaching

"Why did Jesus Christ after his resurrection show himself to the Apostles during the space of forty days? During this time he continued to teach them the mysteries of the kingdom of God" (*Russian Catech.*, *COC* II, p. 479; Ursinus, *CHC*, p. 244).

What was he teaching? Jesus "opened to them all things which were about to happen," especially the destruction of Jerusalem, to ready them for yet unfolding history, according to the tradition that Lactantius had received (*Div. Inst.* IV.21, *ANF* VII, p. 123). During the forty-day interval between the first Easter and ascension (Acts 1:3) the disciples were gradually weaned away from dependence upon his visible presence and prepared for the climactic event of salvation history: his exaltation to the Father by ascension.

That he would ascend was already foreshadowed in his first resurrection appearance, according to John's Gospel: "Do not hold on to me, for I have not yet returned to the Father. Go instead to my brothers and tell them, 'I am returning to my Father and your Father, to my God and your God'" (John 20:17).

He Ascended

Witness to the Ascension Embedded in the Earliest Kerygma

The earliest written testimony to the ascension is found in Paul, for whom the ascension implied the filling of the whole universe with the reconciling love of God: "He who descended is the very one who ascended higher than all the heavens, in order to fill the whole universe" (Eph. 4:10; cf. Eph. 1:20; Rom. 10:6-7). It was almost certainly a part of the earliest Christian kerygma received by Paul (Phil. 2:6-11).

Similar echoes of the earliest preaching are also found in John: "No one has ever gone into heaven except the one who came from heaven— the Son of Man. Just as Moses lifted up the snake in the desert, so *the Son of Man must be lifted up*, that everyone who believes in him may have eternal life" (John 3:13, italics added; cf. 6:62). In Mark's account the ascension is not explicitly narrated but implied in the saying that the Son of Man will sit "at the right hand of the Mighty One" (Mark 14:62).

The Lucan Narrative

Luke's account of the ascension is succinct: "When he had led them out to the vicinity of Bethany, he lifted up his hands and blessed them. While he was blessing them, he left them and was taken up into heaven. Then they worshiped him and returned to Jerusalem with great joy. And they stayed continually at the temple, praising God" (Luke 24:50-53). Cyril noted that the ascension bore evidences that the earliest proclaiming community was also at the same time a worshiping community: "Christ is no sooner crucified than he begins to be worshiped" (Cyril of Jerusalem, *Catech. Lect.* IV.12, *LCC* IV, p. 107).

Luke summarized Jesus' earthly ministry as "the whole time the Lord Jesus went in and out among us, beginning from John's baptism to the time when Jesus was taken up from us" (Acts 1:21–22). It was this whole time, which was completed by the ascension, in which one must have participated in order to be counted among the original apostolic witnesses (Acts 1:23).

Prefigured by the Transfiguration

Distinguished from the transfiguration, which had only three witnesses, the ascension was attested by a large company. The transfiguration had prepared the disciples for the coming exaltation and fulfillment of Christ's ministry. Both transfiguration and ascension narratives made use of the metaphor of departure (*exodos*) from a mountain surrounded by clouds (cf. Luke 9:1–34; Acts 1:1–12; J. G. Davies, *He Ascended into Heaven*, 1958, p. 40).

Attested as a Visible Event for Faith's Recollecting

Ascension did not imply merely a disappearance or evanescence to mere invisibility but rather was attested as a visible lifting up, a rising to transcend all earthly categories and historical realities (Augustine, *CG*, *FC* 24, pp. 423–32). He "ascended into heaven by His own power, first of all by His Divine power, and secondly by the power of His glorified soul moving His body at will" (Tho. Aq., *ST* III, Q57.3, II, p. 2330).

The meaning of the ascension, however, is not constricted to its character as an attested visible event. As was said of the resurrection so it may be said of the ascension: "Blessed are those who have not seen and yet have believed" (John 20:29). "Though you have not seen him, you love him; and even though you do not see him now, you believe in him and are filled with an inexpressible and glorious joy, for you are receiving the goal of your faith, the salvation of your souls" (1 Pet. 1:8, 9).

The Meaning of the Ascension

Ascension is the upward corollary of the downward movement of incarnate descent, as exaltation is the counterpart of humiliation. It is the exaltation that validates, clarifies, and makes understandable the lowly earthly mission (Chemnitz, *TNC*, pp. 426–28; Newman, *MD*, pp. 532–34).

Ascension marked a decisive transition: it showed that the period of Christ's resurrected bodily appearances had come to an end and that he had returned exalted to the Father to intercede, establish, and consummate his divine governance. His earthly mission is complete, his heavenly ministry had begun (Athanasius, *Incarn. of the Word* 26–30, NPNF 2 IV, pp. 50–52; cf. J. G. Davies, *He Ascended into Heaven*).

The teaching of the ascension focuses on several points:

The Same Body

The body that rose and ascended is not a different body than was crucified and rose: "On the third day he arose from the dead, with the same body in which he suffered, with which also he ascended into heaven, and there sitteth" (Westminster Confession VIII, CC, p. 204). He ascended to session, body and soul: the Son of God "on the fortieth day after the resurrection with the flesh in which He arose and with His soul ascended" (Council of Lyons, SCD 462, p. 183; see also SCD 344, 429, 709), to be seated at the right hand of the Father in the flesh (Innocent III, *Eius Exemplo*, SCD 422, p. 166; see also SCD 73, 462, 709), according to a natural manner of existing (Council of Trent, SCD 874, p. 266).

The Bodily Evidence of Atonement Presented

Luke's account of the ascension portrays the Son returning to God, taking into God's presence the evidence of atonement—his own body! He ascended "so that, seated at the right hand of Majesty, he might show to the glorious face of his Father the scars of the wounds which he suffered for us" (Bonaventure, *Tree of Life*, CWS, p. 162).

It could not be a chimerical body that Jesus took into the presence of God as evidence of atonement: "He suffered a true passion in the flesh, died His own true bodily death, rose again by a true resurrection of His flesh and the true resumption of His body by His soul. He ate and drank in His risen flesh, and then ascended to heaven and is seated at the right hand of the Father. In the same flesh He will come to judge the living and the dead" (Innocent III, *Profession of Faith Prescribed to the Waldensians* [1208], CF, p. 175; Tho. Aq., ST III, Q59, II, pp. 2336–38). He remained truly human in his ascension (Gregory Nazianzen, *On Pentecost*, NPNF 2 VII, p. 380).

The Believer's Appropriation of Christ's Ascension

The event of ascension has ethical and behavioral consequences. Those who are raised with Christ are instructed to "set your hearts on things above, where Christ is seated at the right hand of God" (Col. 3:1).

The ascension of the faithful to the celestial city is inaugurated by Christ's ascension. The way to that abode is made by his going to prepare a place for us (John 14:2). "I believe that He ascended," Luther wrote. "Therefore, He can help me and all believers in all our necessities against all our adversaries and enemies" (*Brief Explanation*, *WML* II, p. 371).

Benefits of Christ's Ascension

The *Heidelberg Catechism* in its usual way emphasizes the benefits received from Christ's ascension: "First, that he is our Advocate in the presence of his Father in heaven. Second, that we have our flesh in heaven as a sure pledge that he, as the Head, will also take us, his members, up to himself. Third, that he sends us his Spirit as a counterpledge by whose power we seek what is above, where Christ is, sitting at the right hand of God, and not things that are on earth" (Q 49, *BOC* 4.049; cf. Wollebius, *CTC* 18, *RDB*, p. 112; Pearson, *EC* I, p. 459).

Might It Have Been More Fitting for Christ to Remain?

It was "not fitting that Christ should remain upon earth after the Resurrection," for his incorruptible body belonged in an incorruptible dwelling (Tho. Aq., *ST* III, Q57.1, II, p. 2328).

By ascending, he did not abandon his disciples (Leo, *Serm.* LXXIV, *NPNF* 2 XII, pp. 187–89), but rather increased their faith in that which is unseen, gave them hope of following him, and thus the withdrawal of his bodily presence "was more profitable for us than His bodily presence would have been" (Tho. Aq., *ST* III, Q57.1, II, p. 2328). "Christ left us in such a way that his presence might be more useful to us." In ascending he did not "cease to be present with believers still on their earthly pilgrimage, but to rule heaven and earth with a more immediate power" (Calvin, *Inst.* 2.16.13).

Absent in Flesh, Present in Spirit

"Do not think that because He is absent in the flesh He is therefore absent in the spirit; He is here in the midst of us, listening to what is said of Him, seeing our thoughts, searching our hearts and souls; He is ready even now to present all of you, as you come forward for Baptism in the Holy Spirit, to the Father" (Cyril of Jerusalem, *Catech. Lect.* XIV, *FC* 64, p. 52). "For at his departure He had endowed them with power and strength" (Lactantius, *Div. Inst.* IV.21, *ANF* VII, p. 123).

With respect to the flesh of Jesus that was "nailed to the tree, let down from the cross, enveloped in a shroud, laid in the sepulchre" (Augustine, *Comm. on John*, *NPNF* 1 VII, p. 282), it is right that we accept his word: "You will not always have me" (Mark 14:7, in contrast to my poor who will remain to be served). His bodily resurrection was "for the purpose of beholding" until his ascension into heaven. He is there now, "and He is here also, having never withdrawn the presence of His glory. In other words, in respect of His divine presence we always have Christ; in respect of His presence in the flesh it was rightly said to the disciples, 'Me ye will not have always'" (Augustine, *Comm. on John*, NPNF 1 VII, p. 282).

Was the Human Nature Exalted?

One technical problem that vexed early interpreters is whether it was the divine or human nature that was exalted. The consensual answer gradually emerged on the premise of theandric union: according to his human nature he was exalted by laying aside all infirmities (hunger, thirst, fatigue, pain, social rejection, mortality) and resuming powers associated with the divine-human union. According to his divine nature, he was not exalted by acquiring any new dignity or power (for that already belonged to him), but rather by the manifestation of his majesty which had been constrained under his servant form (Ursinus, *CHC*, pp. 243–45; Wollebius, *CTC*, p. 85; Heppe, *RD*, p. 495; cf. Calvin, *Inst.* 2.16.14).

Descended as God, Ascended as Man

On the premise of his personal union, it may be said that He descended as God, ascended as man (Ambrose, *MPL* XV, p. 1225). "Christ as God, together with the Father and the Holy Ghost, reigns from eternity by means of His essential omnipotence; Christ as man, or according to His assumed human nature, reigns not from eternity, but from the time of His exaltation" (Quenstedt, *TDP* III, p. 384; Schmid, *DT*, p. 405; Hollaz, *ETA*, p. 788; cf. Newman, *SN*, p. 304).

To Heaven

The ascension begins on earth and ends in heaven. It begins in the presence of the disciples and ends in the presence of the Father. It begins in the thick of human history and ends in the abode of blessed spirits (John 14:2).

Metaphors of Heaven

The predominating metaphor is that of the throne of God (Isa. 66:1). Heaven receives Christ as a country receives a beloved Son returning from a long and hazardous journey. Associated images include the Father's house (John 14:2), the celestial city (Heb. 12:22), the transcendent Jerusalem (Gal. 4:26), the abode of angels (Matt. 6:9–10), the place not made with hands (Heb. 9:24), and paradise (Luke 23:43).

Heaven is the abode of God, that which exists on the other side of space and time. This is the abode prepared for believers (John 14:2). Augustine advised that "it is sheer curiosity and a waste of time to inquire as to the 'where' and 'how' of the Lord's body in heaven; we have only to believe" (*Faith and the Creed* 6.13, FC 27, p. 329).

Directionality and Heaven

Recent criticism, led by Bultmann, has imagined that it has done away with all "three-storey worlds" and "above" and "below" language with one fell swoop by consigning such language to outdated mythology. Yet it is doubtful that the language of descent and ascent in the New Testament ever really intended such a flat, unmetaphorical, literal three-story picture, even in the first century, for descent into the nether world does not imply a particular spatial or outward direction (Augustine, "Is There an 'Above' and a 'Below' in the Universe?" *EDQ*, 29, FC 70, p. 54). In the most important text of Christ's abasement, his cry from the cross, there is no hint of directionality. The heavens into which Christ ascended are not to be thought of as subsisting within time-space categories as a palpable temporal place, but as the ethereal sphere in which the God of glory is eternally manifested (Augustine, *Trin.*, FC 45, pp. 23–24, 438–46).

Above All Rule and Authority

Paul preached that God had "raised him from the dead and seated him at his right hand in the heavenly realms, far above all rule and authority, power and dominion, and every title that can be given, not only in the present age but also in the one to come. And God placed all things under his feet and appointed him to be head over everything for the church, which is his body, the fullness of him who fills everything in every way" (Eph. 1:20–23).

"For he 'has put everything under his feet.' Now when it says that 'everything' has been put under him, it is clear that this does not include God himself, who put everything under Christ" (1 Cor. 15:27). Paul is here recalling and interpreting the psalm wherein "man" or "the Son of Man" is "crowned with glory and honor" (Ps. 8:6; cf. Heb. 2:6–8). Jesus is representative man in whom humanity's appointed destiny is being fully manifested. "When we say that our nature rose from the dead and ascended and sat at the right hand of the Father, we do not imply that all human persons arose and sat at the right hand of the Father, but that our entire nature did so in the Person of Christ" (John of Damascus, *OF* III.6, FC 37, p. 281; Eph. 2:6).

Peter's earliest known preaching stated: "He must remain in heaven until the time comes for God to restore everything, as he promised long ago through his holy prophets" (Acts 3:21). Now it is sufficient to know that "God has highly exalted him" (Phil. 2:9).

Descent of the Spirit

He withdrew visibly in order that he might send the Holy Spirit (John 16:7). The sending of the Spirit could not be fully manifested until the Son had ascended, for in the triune *oikonomia*, Pentecost would not come until after ascension (Tho. Aq., *ST* III, Q57.6, II, p. 2332). Jesus himself had indicated that the Spirit would be given only when he was glorified (John 7:39).

In the ensuing volume of this series we will discuss the application of the work of Christ by the Holy Spirit. At this point it is fitting to place the descent of the Spirit in right order in the history of salvation. The sequence is—on earth: following the ascension, the descent of the Spirit; in heaven: the session at the right hand of God in heaven, including Christ's intercession and cosmic reign, looking toward his coming again (Baxter, *PW* XIX, pp. 81–83).

It was necessary that his sacrifice be presented to the Father before the Spirit was sent forth. Before his departure, Jesus had stated: "It is for your good that I am going away. Unless I go away, the Counselor will not come to you; but if I go, I will send him to you" (John 16:7).

The Descent Prophesied

The psalmist had anticipated the gift of the Spirit following a victorious ascension: "When you ascended on high, you led captives in your train; you received gifts from men, even from the rebellious—that you, O Lord God, might dwell there" (Ps. 68:18). It is this psalm to which Paul refers in his interpretation of the ascension: "When he ascended on high, he led captives in his train and gave gifts to men" (Eph. 4:8).

Jesus had received the gifts of the Spirit constantly throughout his life, but more particularly in his conception, baptism, temptation, Passion, death, resurrection, and ascension. The mission of the Son complete, the Father and the Son sent the Spirit, who descended upon the apostles to apply the work of Christ to ensuing human history.

The Descent at Pentecost

Luke's account of the descent of the Spirit is dramatic: "When the day of Pentecost came, they were all together in one place. Suddenly a sound like the blowing of a violent wind came from heaven and filled the whole house where they were sitting. They saw what seemed to be tongues of fire that separated and came to rest on each of them. All of them were filled with the Holy Spirit and began to speak in other tongues as the Spirit enabled them" (Acts 2:1–4). "After the Resurrection, with the sending of the Holy Spirit, the gift of tongues was granted –'that they may serve the Lord with one accord'" (Cyril of Jerusalem, *Catech. Lect.* XIII, FC 64, p. 36; Zeph. 3:10, LXX).

The Descent Interpreted

Peter interpreted Pentecost in this way: "God has raised this Jesus to life, and we are all witnesses of the fact. Exalted to the right hand of God, he has received from the Father the promised Holy Spirit and has poured out what you now see and hear" (Acts 2:32–33). The gift of the Holy Spirit at Pentecost confirmed the truth of the ascension and began the new era of the Spirit.

Pannenberg almost got it right: "A Gentile *mission* seems to have arisen for the first time as a result of the conviction that the resurrected Jesus had now already been exalted to Lordship in heaven and consequently the news of his Lordship is to be carried to all nations" (*JGM*, p. 71). The mission, however, did not arise from human conviction, but from the resurrection that called forth that conviction.

SEATED AT THE RIGHT HAND OF THE FATHER

Why the Celestial Session?

Dominion Over All

He sits at the right hand of the Father (*sedet ad desteram Patrus*; Creed of 150 Fathers, *COC* II, p. 58; *SCD* 1, 2, 3ff.). Christ's session, or sitting at the right hand of God, means that Christ governs in the kingdom of power, grace, and glory, reigns eternally, has dominion over all things (Calvin, *Catech. of the Church of Geneva*, LCC XXII, p. 101; Ursinus, *CHC*, pp. 254–57). To sit on the right hand of the Father means to participate fully in God's majesty imparted through the exaltation (Matt. 24:30; 25:31; Luke 22:69; Heb. 1:3; Augustine, *On the Creed* 11, *NPNF* 1 III, p. 373).

To Sit Is to Judge

Sitting is a judicial metaphor, for "it is the judge's place to sit" (Gregory I, *Hom. 29 on the Ascension, Homiliarum in Evangelia Libri* II, *MPL* 76, sec. 3, quoted in Tho. Aq., *ST* III, Q58, II, p. 2333). "Sitting denotes either abiding, or royal or judiciary dignity. Hence, to sit on the right hand of the Father is nothing else than to share in the glory of the God-head with the Father, and to possess beatitude and judiciary power" (Tho. Aq., *ST* III, Q58.2, II, p. 2334), "exalted in rank above every crea-ture" (Tho. Aq., *Compend.* 240, p. 295).

The Name Above Every Name

It is this glory of which Jesus prayed when he said: "And now, Father, glorify me in your presence with the glory I had with you before the world began" (John 17:5). It is of this power that Peter preached when he said: "God has made this Jesus, whom you crucified, both Lord and Christ" (Acts 2:36). This is the vision that comforted Stephen in his death—he saw the Son of Man on the right hand of God (Acts 7:56; Cal-vin, *Inst.* 2.16.15). It is this same authority that was anticipated in the commission: "All authority in heaven and on earth has been given to me" (Matt. 28:18).

Therein Jesus is given that name above every name, that at his name every knee should bow and every tongue confess that he is Lord (Phil. 2:6–11). "To which of the angels did God ever say, 'Sit at my right hand'?" (Heb. 1:13; Ps. 110:1). In session Christ gloriously performs and fulfills his destined offices of prophet, priest, and king (Calvin, *Inst.* 2.16.15).

Sacrifice and Session

The priestly sacrifice makes way for the governing session. "We do have such a high priest, who sat down at the right hand of the throne of the Majesty in heaven, and who serves in the sanctuary" (Heb. 8:1–2; see also 12:2). "But when this priest had offered for all time one sacrifice for sins, he sat down at the right hand of God. Since that time he waits for his enemies to be made his footstool, because by one sacrifice he has made perfect forever those who are being made holy" (Heb. 10:12–14).

The Creedal Sequence Viewed from the Session

Chemnitz summarized the creedal sequence: "For in *incarnation* there occurred a hypostatic union of the Godhead of the *logos* with assumed humanity, in which the whole fulness of the Godhead dwelt personally from the first moment of conception. But by reason of *self-renunciation*, its employment and manifestation were for a time postponed, and, as it were suspended, so that it did not exercise itself through the assumed humanity immediately and always. Moreover, by the *ascension*, infirmi-ties being laid aside and self-renunciation removed, He left the mode of life according to the conditions of this world, and departed from the world. Moreover, by *sitting* at the Right Hand of God, He entered upon the full and public employment and display of the power, virtue, and glory of the Godhead" (Chemnitz, *TNC*, XXXII, pp. 475–85; Schmid, *DT*, p. 387; cf. Pearson, *EC* I, pp. 463–66).

Why the "Right Hand"?

An Empowerment Metaphor

"We do not hold that the right hand of the Father is an actual place. For how could He that is uncircumscribed have a right hand limited by place?" (John of Damascus, *OF* IV.2, *NPNF* 2 IX, p. 74; see Chemnitz, *TNC*, pp. 407–408). Neither "right hand" nor "sit" is to be taken literally (John of Damascus, *OF* IV.2, *FC* 37, p. 336).

"Right hand" means the almighty power and majesty of God. "Your right hand, O Lord, was majestic in power. Your right hand, O Lord, shattered the enemy" (Exod. 15:6). "Your arm is endued with power, your hand is strong, your right hand exalted" (Ps. 89:13). The Deuteronomic preface to the Decalogue employs this empowerment metaphor in recalling that "you were slaves in Egypt and that the Lord your God brought you out of there with a mighty hand, and an outstretched arm" (Deut. 5:15).

The place of highest honor was normally on the right hand of the ruler (1 Kings 2:19; Ps. 45:10; Matt. 20:21). "The expression 'at the right hand' must therefore be understood in this sense: to exist in a state of perfect blessedness, where there is justice and peace and joy" (Augustine, *Faith and the Creed* 7.14, *FC* 27, p. 330; Tho. Aq., *ST* III, Q58, II, pp. 2333–36).

What Does the Ascended Mediator Do?

His life in session is filled with activity: "He therefore sits on high, transfusing us with his power, that he may quicken us to spiritual life, sanctify us by his Spirit, adorn his church with divers gifts of his grace, keep it safe from all harm by his protection, restrain the raging enemies of his cross and of our salvation by the strength of his hand, and finally hold all power in heaven and on earth" (Calvin, *Inst.* 2.16.16; cf. Barth, *CD* II/1, pp. 397ff.; IV/2, pp. 132ff.).

The ascended Lord "sits at the right hand of the Father and wills our salvation both as God and as man. And, while He acts as God by working the providence, preservation, and government of all things, He acts as man in remembering His labors on earth and in seeing and knowing that He is adored by all rational creation" (John of Damascus, *OF* IV.1, *FC* 37, p. 335).

Why the Heavenly Intercession?

The principal feature of the session of Christ is that he enters into an intercessory ministry for humanity in the presence of the Father, pleading humanity's case before the Father (Hilary, *Hom. on Psalms* 53:4, *NPNF* 2 IX, p. 244). In him "we have one who speaks to the Father in our defense" (1 John 2:1).

Empathic Intercession

Only one who has known empathically what it means to suffer in the world can make this intercession rightly (Heb. 2:14–16). The intercession occurs in heaven (Heb. 6:19–20), and continues forever (Heb. 9:11–28).

Mediation Assumes Access

"The work of mediation between God and man depended on the entrance into heaven of the mediator, as the intercessory nature of the Jewish high priest depended on his gaining access to the holy of holies" (Guthrie, *NTT*, p. 399).

Access for believers to the Father is a chief benefit of the ascended Lord in session. The faithful take comfort in this eternal access to the Father, that their prayers may be heard, that they will be kept from evil (John 17:15), that Christ's sacrifice is sufficient (Heb. 9:23–24), that where Christ is they may be also and that they may behold God's glory (John 17:24). Our prayers are offered in his name, and are made acceptable to the Father (John 14:6, 13). The essential pattern of Christ's intercessory ministry is already anticipated in the high-priestly prayer of John 17 (Pearson, *EC* I, p. 451).

His once for all entry into heaven is contrasted with repetitive priestly seasonal rituals: "Nor did he enter heaven to offer himself again and again, the way the high priest enters the Most Holy Place every year with blood that is not his own" (Heb. 9:25).

Adoration of the Word

Our worship is addressed not to the flesh as such, but to the theandric union, for "His flesh is not adorable, in so far as it is created. When, however, it has been united with God the Word, it is adorable" (John of Damascus, *OF* IV.3, *FC* 37, p. 336). "And He ascended, not leaving behind on the earth as a useless piece of clothing His human nature; but carrying it inseparable from Himself and incorruptible and endowed with such nobility as was to be expected from human nature united with the divine one" (*Gk. Orthodox Catech.* 39, p. 30).

Christ's teaching office continues through the contemporary body of Christ, the church, whom he promised to be with "always, to the very end of the age" (Matt. 28:20), to whom the deposit of faith is entrusted. With the apostolic teaching the church is readied for varied cultural situations or historical revolutions to respond whatever the times or changes or pretenses of change. No error is completely novel or surprising to those thoroughly instructed by the apostolic witness and ecumenical teaching. No distortion is so great that it cannot be corrected "with antidotes from her spiritual pharmacopoeia" (Pohle-Preuss, *DT* V, p. 148).

CHRIST THE KING

Although legitimate authority was pretemporally given to the Son, he did not exercise that authority directly during his humiliation but awaited its proper reception at the conclusion of his earthly ministry.

The Kingdom Brought Forth by His Death and Resurrection

The Way to the Kingdom

Christ entered into messianic kingship through an entirely unexpected route: suffering, cross, death, and burial. The rightful authority of Christ is based on his sacrificial death. This kingship is assigned to Christ by virtue of his sacrifice.

He led the covenant people from bondage, analogous to Moses. Yet the emergent rule of God is not intended for a single racial stock or nation but for all. The governance of Christ is his rightful lordship over the future fulfillment and application of the redemption made possible through his suffering (Creed of Epiphanius, *SCD* 13, p. 9; cf. *SCD* 333, 2194ff.).

His Death the Premise of His Kingship

The essential order of salvation was taught on the Emmaus road: "Did not the Christ have to suffer these things and then enter his glory?" (Luke 24:26). It was only through his Passion and death that he entered into the exercise of all power in heaven and earth (Matt. 28:18). Legitimate governance was conferred in his resurrection and ascension, whereupon he sent forth his apostles to declare the emergent reign of God and call all to enter it. "For Christ did not enter a man-made sanctuary that was only a copy of the true one; he entered heaven itself, now to appear for us in God's presence" (Heb. 9:24). In this way Christ's spiritual kingship became closely bound with his priestly task.

Guiding and Guarding

In the spiritual community he brought forth, Christ does what governors and rulers do: *gubernatio* ("governance, rulership, guidance") and *defensio* ("protecting, guarding from harm"), yet without coercion. He guides by his Word and guards by his Spirit. Through this guiding and guarding activity, Christ orders, directs, and preserves the church (Lactantius, *Div. Inst.*, FC 49, pp. 298–300; Bucer, *De Regno Christi*, LCC XIX, pp. 177ff., 262ff.). "The royal office is to rule and preserve the church" (Wollebius, *CTC* 17, *RDB*, p. 98).

Although masculine images predominate in traditional regal language, classic exegetes were able to use feminine images, especially in the protecting role of Christ as ruler. Luther spoke of the ascended Christ as a "Shelter, beneath whom we hide ourselves as young chicks do under the wings of the clucking hen" (*Serm. on John 15:23–30*, 1522, WLS I, p. 150; WA 10 III, 136f.).

Benefits of His Governance

The benefits conferred by Christ's kingdom were summarized by Calvin: "we are accorded freedom of conscience for pious and holy living, are provided with his spiritual riches, and also armed with strength sufficient to overcome the perpetual enemies of our souls" (Calvin, *Catech. of the Church of Geneva*, LCC XXII, p. 96). "Such is the nature of his rule, that he shares with us all that he has received from the Father. Now he arms and equips us with his power, adorns us with his beauty and magnificence, enriches us with his wealth" (Calvin, *Inst.* 2.15.4).

Exalted Lord as King

The Right Use of Power

His prophetic and priestly offices were an expression of his humble, self-effacing servanthood. His ruling office, however, was precisely to be exalted and glorified in resurrection, ascension, and session (Gregory Nazianzen, *Fourth Theol. Orat.*, *Orat.* XXX, NPNF 2 VII, pp. 310–11). While the priestly office required self-sacrifice and compassion, the office of governance would require infinite wisdom and care in the right use of power by ordering, judging, legislating, and perfecting the community of faith.

Kingship Defined

A king (*basileus*) is a sovereign invested with supreme authority, "that he may rule over a certain people, according to just laws, that he may have power to reward the good and punish the evil, and that he may defend his subjects, not having any one superior or above him" (Baxter, *PW* II, pp. 207–209; Proba, *Cento* 406–409).

"The King of Kings is Christ, who was immediately ordained of God, that he might govern, by his word and Spirit, the church which he purchased with his own blood, and defend her against all her enemies" (Ursinus, *CHC*, p. 176).

Christ's governance continues in heavenly session while his prophetic and priestly offices were primarily focused upon his earthly life. The Greek Orthodox Catechism defined these periods temporally: "His Prophetic Offices lasted for three years; for during three years our Lord travelled throughout Palestine teaching His unique truths like the Prophets of old. His Sacerdotal Office lasted during the three days of His Passion, when He offered Himself as a victim for the redemption of the world. But His Royal Office does not know eclipse, and will continue forever and ever" (*Gk. Orthodox Catech.* 39, p. 30; Wollebius, *CTC* 18, *RDB*, pp. 113–15).

His Manner of Ruling

Christ's way of being a ruler is as guide of souls. He is shepherd and bishop of our souls (1 Pet. 2:25). The rulership referred to is spiritual, not political. He came to establish a spiritual kingdom or governance.

His Kingdom Not of This World

The form of this governance is of a spiritual sort. His kingdom is not like kingdoms that are ruled by force (Augustine, *CG*, *FC* 24, pp. 63–66). This kingdom is governed by the Spirit, by self-giving love (Calvin, *Inst.* 2.15.3–4).

The kingdom is therefore hiddenly within us and does not come by force or external observation (Luke 17:20–21). It consists in "righteousness, peace, and joy in the Holy Spirit" (Rom. 14:17). These are the gifts conferred by his governance (Calvin, *Inst.* 2.14.4).

Rendering to Caesar

Jesus' kingdom is a purely spiritual rulership. He never sought to establish a coercive, political, earthly kingdom. After the multiplication of the loaves, when the people "intended to come and make him a king by force," he "withdrew again to a mountain by himself" (John 6:15). He acknowledged the Roman emperor as legitimate temporal ruler when he taught: "Give to Caesar what is Caesar's, and to God what is God's"

(Matt. 22:21; Tertullian, *On Idolatry* XV, *ANF* III, p. 70; *The Chaplet* XII, *ANF* III, p. 101).

He refused to be a judge of secular affairs, as for example, when a man and his brother came to him with a question about inheritance. He replied: "Man, who appointed me a judge or an arbiter between you?" (Luke 12:14). This was not the task to which he was anointed. He spoke as king but never courted power or popularity (Newman, *PPS* I, pp. 297–98).

The Exchange with Pilate

Jesus summed up the disavowal of political power in the presence of Pilate: "My kingdom is not of this world. If it were, my servants would fight to prevent my arrest by the Jews. But now my kingdom is from another place" (John 18:36). Pilate, confused, retorted: "You are a king, then!" Jesus: "You are right in saying I am a king. In fact, for this reason I was born, and for this I came into the world, to testify to the truth" (John 18:37).

This decisive exchange established four key points of Christian teaching: He is indeed a king. He is not a worldly king. His kingdom is spiritual, from above. His mission was to attest that coming, spiritual kingdom.

Eternal Kingship Maintained amid Temporal Poverty

The Mediator never staked out a claim for economic advantage. He lived in such abject poverty that he had "no place to lay his head" (Luke 9:58). He did not disavow the right to acquire possessions, and in fact he possessed such simple things as his own sandals and clothing. But his intent was never to gain worldly power or political ascendancy. "Christ is not concerned with political and domestic economy" (Luther, *Table Talk*, *WLS* I, p. 201; *WA Tischreden* 1, No. 1 932). "He is not a worldly king, and has no worldly kingdom" (Luther, *Ascension Serm.* [1534], *WLS* I, p. 201; *WA* 37, 3395, Roeher's notes).

His Essential and Humbled Kingship

As long as he was lowly, poor, and limited by assuming human flesh, the Son refrained from the full use and exercise of the authority he was rightly due. Christ remained king while he was being despised and rejected, while the world received him not (John 1:11; Barth, *CD* IV/2, pp. 155ff.). Thus a distinction is maintained between Christ's essential or eternal kingship, which is preexistent from all eternity, and his personal and humble kingship, which is a part of his office as Mediator during his earthly ministry beginning with the incarnation.

The Undivided Kingdom

Being a spiritual kingdom, this kingdom does not diminish as do earthly kingdoms. It "is not divided by the number of those who reign; nor lessened by being shared, nor disturbed by its magnitude, nor disordered by its inequality of ranks, nor circumscribed by space, nor changed by motion, nor measured by time" (Bonaventure, *Tree of Life, CWS*, p. 169).

Kingship Prefigured in the Law and Prophets

The expectation of messianic kingship emerged through a gradual history of the covenant community.

An Expectation of Messianic Kingship Developed in the History of Israel

Christ's kingly rule was alluded to in the Protevangelium in the Garden (where Yahweh promised to crush the head of the tempter, Gen. 3:15). It was promised to Abraham ("through your offspring, all nations on earth will be blessed, because of your faith," Gen. 22:17); anticipated in David's kingdom ("your throne will be established forever," 2 Sam. 7:16); and foretold by the prophets, especially in Isaiah 53. The prophets "predicted the sufferings of Christ and the glories that would follow" (1 Pet. 1:11).

Yahweh chose the seed of Abraham and Sarah as his own, electing them to covenant relation: "Now if you obey me fully and keep my covenant, then out of all nations you will be my treasured possession. Although the whole earth is mine, you will be for me a kingdom of priests and a holy nation" (Exod. 19:5–6). For the guidance and defense of this kingdom, Yahweh provided for the ordaining of kings, priests, and prophets. All of these became enduring institutions that stood as anticipatory indications of what was to happen in Jesus' messianic coming.

Prefigured in Messianic Promises

Messianic expectations focused upon a messianic king of whom it was promised: "I will establish his kingdom. He is the one who will build a house for my name, and I will establish the throne of his kingdom forever. I will be his father, and he will be my son" (2 Sam. 7:11–14; cf. Pss. 2; 30; 37; 45; 72; 109; Isa. 9:6ff.; Dan. 7:13ff.; Zech. 9). These prophecies were fulfilled in Jesus, yet spiritually transformed in their very fulfillment.

The Fulfillment Announced

The expected kingdom was immediately heralded by John the Baptist who announced: "Repent, for the kingdom of heaven is near" (Matt. 3:2). To Mary it was promised that her son Jesus would be "called the Son of the Most High. The Lord God will give him the throne of his father David, and he will reign over the house of Jacob forever; his kingdom will never end" (Luke 1:32–33).

The Spiritual Reign Begun

Jesus' Distinctive Embodiment of the Regal Office

Jesus began his public ministry by proclaiming the reign of God at hand. Yet it was not until the very end of his ministry in the events surrounding his death that he received that kingdom and undertook its governance.

His glorification was anticipated in his high-priestly prayer. He was portrayed as praying just before his arrest: "Father, the time has come. Glorify your Son, that your Son may glorify you. For you granted him authority over all people that he might give eternal life to all those you have given him." "I brought you glory on earth by completing the work you gave me to do. And now, Father, glorify me in your presence with the glory I had with you before the world began" (John 17:1–5).

Dominion Received

Through his death he redeemed humanity from bondage to sin. As he approached the cross, he prepared himself for the struggle toward the promised victory: "Now is the time for judgment on this world; now the prince of this world will be driven out" (John 12:31). It was indeed by force that the demonic powers had to be cast out (Mark 3:27), but ironically by their own force being spent on the death of the Son (Gregory of Nyssa, ARI 20–24, LCC III, pp. 297–301). The dominion given the Son by the Father, the reign of God, was a gift to the Son, having fulfilled his messianic mission. Having become obedient to death, "God exalted him to the highest place and gave him the name that is above every name, that at the name of Jesus every knee should bow, in heaven and on earth and under the earth, and every tongue confess that Jesus Christ is Lord, to the glory of God the Father" (Phil. 2:9–11; Augustine, Trin., FC 45, pp. 22–32).

His resurrection and ascension signaled to the disciples that the reign of God had begun and that Jesus had decisively received the hidden kingdom now being openly revealed. His great commission upon departing from his disciples was: "All authority in heaven and on earth has been given to me. Therefore go and make disciples of all nations" (Matt. 28:18–19). The work that began on the cross continues in the life of the world and will be consummated at the end of history.

Exaltation as Enthronement

His ascension was understood as the formal possession of his royal throne and authority. As royal judge he will reappear in the final days to judge the living and the dead. The faithful expect "the appearing of our Lord Jesus Christ, which God will bring about in his own time – God, the blessed and only Ruler, and King of kings and Lord of lords" (1 Tim. 6:14–15; Augustine, *Trin.*, FC 45, pp. 38–49).

The Kingdom to Come

The messianic kingship established through his exaltation is an eternal kingdom that will endure forever (Heb. 10:12). Yet this kingship will pass through a series of phases before its consummation. The regal office is universal-historical in scope, pretemporally foreseen and decreed, yet only finally to be concluded in the end time. Remaining issues relating to the kingdom of Christ are to be considered in the sequel to this volume under the headings of the Spirit, the church, and the end time.

The Mystery of Location and Ubiquity

Secret Things Not Revealed

Many questions remain unanswered and to some degree unanswerable. Can we speak of a locus of this exalted, ascended, reigning, judging activity, and if so how is such a locus related to the ubiquity assumed? How can the ascended body be the same as the earthly body? Amid these and other mysteries, the classic exegetes appealed to the Deuteronomic distinction: "The secret things belong to the Lord our God, but the things revealed belong to us and to our children forever" (Deut. 29:29). Preaching is not free to speak about what is not revealed.

Filling the Universe

Christ "ascended higher than all the heavens, in order to fill the whole universe" (Eph. 4:10). Classic exegetes have treated the cosmic reign or session as having a transcendent reality beyond time and space, so as not to become dissipated in a ubiquitous diffusion that would result in the disappearance of Christ in ubiquitarianism. Christ, who according to humanity is now in heaven, is everywhere according to divinity (Hugh of St. Victor, *OSCF* II.17–18, pp. 451–76; *BOC*, p. 590).

The commonsense premise that one who is everywhere can be nowhere is transcended by Christ. Christ sits at God's right hand in heaven, not everywhere, but the effect and influence of the reign is everywhere (Eusebius, *MPG* I, p. 189). That Christ is in heaven does not imply that he is not at the same time present in the church by his Spirit.

Where Is Heaven?

If asked, "Where is heaven?" or "Where is hell?" it is best to answer that heaven is where our Lord's glorified body is, and hell where the dead not yet in a state of grace remain. Heaven cannot be said to be nowhere. To be a body is to be somewhere, though that "somewhere" may transcend our time-space categories. We are not told in Scripture where heaven is, aside from the general metaphorical direction of "up" (as in the case of the rich man and Lazarus, Luke 16:22–26). But "up" in this case is not a finite spatial referent, but an infinite transcendent referent. It is that sphere from which the incarnate Son descended and to which the resurrected Son ascended.

Kingdom of Power, Grace, and Glory

His governance in this life is called the kingdom of power or grace, in reference either to the world or the church. In the future life it is called the kingdom of glory. These three designations are required to show that the governance of Christ pertains distinguishably to the present world, the present church, and the future of history (Schmid, *DT*, pp. 370–72; Quenstedt, *TDP*, III, pp. 260–64; Gerhard, *LT* III, 578; Hollaz, *ETA*, pp. 763–64).

In sum: the kingdom of power exists amid the dying world in which hiddenly Christ reigns amid and beyond the death of human cultures and artifacts. The church is the kingdom of grace in history, and glory beyond history.

The Kingdom of Power

The *kingdom of power* is that sovereignty through which Christ exercises sustaining governance over the world, disposes all things in heaven and earth, for the preservation, calling, and salvation of his people. All things are sustained by the word of his power. His dominion extends over all (Pss. 2:9; 8:6; 110:2; 1 Cor. 15:25–27; Eph. 1:20–21; Heb. 2:8).

This legitimate power is acquired by Christ's death for all. Only one who dies for all has a right to rule over all. Only God the Son could die efficaciously for all (Athanasius, *Four Discourses Ag. Arians* II.14, *NPNF* 2 IV, 350–53).

There is a sense in which the coming Christ has jurisdiction over the world's destiny. The providential governance of the world is in Christ's hands, all things being quietly ordered for the guidance and protection of the emerging new humanity which Christ is calling and gathering. God rules over the demonic powers whose exercise of evil power is permitted only for a time (Origen, *OFP*, pp. 52ff., 242–50).

The power of the triune God (the power through which "the God of our Lord Jesus Christ, the glorious Father, may give you the Spirit," Eph. 1:17), was described in plenary terms as "above all rule": "That power is like the working of his mighty strength, which he exerted in Christ when he raised him from the dead and seated him at his right hand in the heavenly realms, far above all rule and authority, power and dominion, and every title that can be given, not only in the present age but also in the one to come. And God placed all things under his feet and appointed him to be head over everything for the church, which is his body, the fullness of him who fills everything in every way" (Eph. 1:19–23)!

The Kingdom of Grace

The *kingdom of grace* is that sovereignty through which the Son bestows spiritual blessings in this life through word and sacrament. He awakens, calls, empowers, and preserves the church. The subjects of the dominion of grace are believers united to Christ through word and sacrament. The dominion of grace is the church, which Christ enables, furnishes, equips with gifts requisite to mission, and defends against ever-incipient temptation and apostasy (Matt. 25:34; 28:20; John 3:5; 17:17, 24; Titus 3:5; Manas Buthelezi, "In Christ," *African Journal of Theology* 7 [1978]:33–42).

The arena in which this kingdom is present is the inner life. It is not a physical or economic sphere subject to empirical identification or material measurement. "For the kingdom of God is not a matter of eating and drinking, but of righteousness, peace and joy in the Holy Spirit" (Rom. 14:17). It is ruled by the Spirit under the new covenant in which God has promised: "I will put my laws in their minds and write them on their hearts" (Heb. 8:1; cf. Jer. 31:33).

The kingdom of grace is governed by preaching the gospel, teaching the covenant community the truth, continuing the restraint of sin by law, providing what is necessary for salvation, pardoning the penitent, justifying by grace, converting through repentance and faith, and sanctifying through the Spirit.

The kingdom of grace is at the same time a kingdom of heaven (because Christ intercedes in heaven) and a kingdom already expectantly received here on earth (because Christ enables citizens of this kingdom to enjoy the fruits of his guidance and protection already in present history). Jesus taught his disciples to pray: "Your kingdom come, your will be done on earth as it is in heaven" (Matt. 6:10; John Chrysostom, *Hom. on Matt.* XIX, *NPNF* 1 X, pp. 134–35). And yet the kingdom is not to be simply equated with the visible church, which within history remains plagued by tares among the wheat, blemished and tainted by unholy egocentrism and sin.

The Kingdom of Glory

The *kingdom of glory* is that future fulfillment of the messianic mission through which the wrongs of history will be righted. It is portrayed as a blessed governance by the exalted Savior of the faithful in eternity. "Father, I want those you have given me to be with me where I am, and to see my glory, the glory you have given me because you loved me before the creation of the world" (John 17:24).

In eternity, the kingdom of Christ is changed from glory to glory, from grace within history to completion beyond history, in a kingdom of peace and righteousness without end (Luke 1:33). "But each in its own turn: Christ, the firstfruits; then, when he comes, those who belong to him. Then the end will come, when he hands over the kingdom to God the Father after he has destroyed all dominion, authority and power" (1 Cor. 15:23–24).

A creative form of deconstruction accompanies the completion of history, namely, the destruction of all obstacles to the reign of grace and righteousness. Then the period of history requiring prophecy and priestly intercession will cease—prophecies will be done away with, tongues shall cease, and knowledge will pass away (1 Cor. 13:8). Christ will have completed the reconciliation once for all, the kingdom of Christ being scrubbed clean of all defilement. The church will have been made holy, cleansed "by the washing of water through the word," that it might be presented "to himself as a radiant church, without stain or wrinkle, or any other blemish, but holy and blameless," in the same way that husbands and wives may love each other purely and without defilement by other loves (Eph. 5:25–29).

Hence Christ's governance extends to the church in particular and to the world in general, which are preserved through grace until the final days. Within history Christ's kingdom is in but not of the world, hidden in a world sustained by divine providence. Christ's kingly rule is manifested among those who have union with him, the church, which in history includes both wheat and tares (Matt. 13:25–40). The kingdom is already begun, yet awaiting its consummation; in time, yet eternal. Citizens of this kingdom exist paradoxically in two cities, the world and the church, earth and heaven, present conflicts of power and future righteousness (Augustine, *CG* XV.1–9, *NPNF* 1 II, pp. 284–90).

"In putting everything under him, God left nothing that is not subject to him. Yet at present we do not see everything subject to him. But we see Jesus" (Heb. 2:8–9). Even amid this present distorted world, Jesus Christ is Lord and King, and even when we cannot see his kingdom reigning, we can still behold his glory and participate in the promise of his kingdom, quietly growing like a tiny mustard seed or yeast in bread.

Quenstedt summed up the varied spheres and means of Christ's governance: "Christ reigns in the world by power, in the Church by grace, in heaven by glory, and in hell by justice" (*TDP* III, p. 264). Evil is permitted, but only for a time. Even during this limited time, it is curbed and restrained by grace. It will finally be overcome in the last days. Meanwhile, all things work together for good for those who love God.

The last scene in the drama of the kingdom is the final judgment: "When the Son of Man comes in his glory, and all the angels with him, he will sit on his throne in heavenly glory. All the nations will be gathered before him, and he will separate the people one from another as a shepherd separates the sheep from the goats" (Matt. 25:31–32). The final rejection of evil, despair, and disbelief is to be expected in the future reign of glory.

> For lo! the days are hastening on,
>   By prophets seen of old,
> When with the ever-circling years,
>   Shall come the time foretold,
> When the new heaven and earth shall own
>   The Prince of Peace their King,
> And the whole world send back the song
>   Which now the angels sing
>
> (Edmund H. Sears, 1846, HPEC, p. 70).

THE EXPECTATION OF CHRIST'S RETURN

The coming of the Son having been accomplished, his Second Coming is expected. The present age begins with the ascension and ends with the Parousia ("return, coming again"). This age is the age of the risen and ascended Lord, awaiting the returning Lord. It is an article of baptismal faith that he shall come again (*et iterum venturus est*; Creed of 150 Fathers, *COC* II, p. 58).

Luke's account deliberately connected Christ's ascension with Christ's return: "This same Jesus, who has been taken from you into heaven, will come back in the same way you have seen him go into heaven" (Acts 1:9-11). Similarly John: "If I go and prepare a place for you, I will come back and take you to be with me that you also may be where I am" (John 14:3).

In heavenly session, Christ begins his reign (1 Cor. 15:20-28). This reign extends not merely to the elect or believers, but over the cosmos itself (Rom. 8:18-25; Col. 1; A. Galloway, *The Cosmic Christ*). In him the fullness of the deity dwells (Col. 2:9). Under this emergent divine governance, a new heaven and a new earth is being created.

The reign will continue until all enemies are overcome, including sin, guilt, and death (1 Cor. 15:20-28; Rom. 8:9-11). Finally it shall be said that: "The kingdom of the world has become the kingdom of our Lord and of his Christ, and he will reign for ever and ever" (Rev. 11:15).

> He shall reign from pole to pole
> With illimitable sway;
> He shall reign when, like a scroll,
> Yonder heavens have passed away
>
> (James Montgomery, 1818, *HPEC*, p. 92).

Cyril ended his *Catechetical Lecture* on the exalted Lord with this prayer: "May [God] raise you up together with Him from your dead sins to His heavenly gift, and deem you worthy to 'be caught up in clouds to meet the Lord in the air,' in His good time; and until that time of His glorious second coming arrives, may He write all your names in the book of the living, and after writing them, never blot them out" (XIV, *FC* 64, p. 52).

The exaltation of Jesus was tantamount to his being enthroned as messianic king. The messianic reign of the promised Davidic heir had thereby begun. The blessings of the messianic age were already beginning to be experienced. They await a future consummation in the return of the messianic king. The Son rules conjointly with the Father and the Spirit in the heavenly kingdom in a governance that will not reach its completion until the last day when all creation will live ordinately in relation to God.

The New Testament ends on a note of expectancy with Christ's own benediction and promise: "'Yes, I am coming soon.' Amen. Come, Lord Jesus" (Rev. 22:20-21).

ADDENDUM
A Modest Proposal for Christological Reform:
The Theandric Person as History

Historical inquiry into Jesus has not yet rigorously begun in our time. It will not begin until the premise of theandric union—truly God, truly human—is entertained as a serious hypothesis by historians.

The incarnate Son is always greater than our methods of investigating him. The living Lord breaks through the very historical limitations to which he voluntarily submitted. This is why historical inquiry is always to some degree puzzled by Jesus, for he is intrinsically puzzling to reductionist and rationalistic inquiry.

The notion that novelty is proof of error—so prevalent in early Christianity—has been reversed in modern times by the conviction that novelty is proof of truth. This is often linked with the judgment that all premodern reflection is prone to error precisely because of its antiquity.

Modernity is over, fully corrupted by its own premises. We are now in a postmodern, postcritical situation, wherein the assumptions of modernity are no longer credible apart from tiny, introverted elites. Within this situation, Jewish and Christian scholars are challenged to reappropriate and renew a classic critique of modernity, without cynicism and with charity toward all.

The Value of Historical Method

The study of Jesus cannot rightly proceed without historical inquiry, since he lived in history. Nowhere is the case better stated than by Francis Hall: "The historical method is indispensable for adequate study of our Lord's human life, and the remedy for its misuse is its abundant proper use" (*DT* VI, p. 316; cf. Baxter, *PW* XIII, pp. 408-14).

Sincere Christian advocates have at times been tardy in grasping the decisive importance of careful, honest historical inquiry. This may be because these methods were developed out of an ethos of rationalist polemic against orthodoxy, and indeed much of the result has been cynical and destructive. Yet however distorted in practice by reductive philosophical predispositions, the historical method itself is of great value in the study of Jesus Christ (Barth, *Evangelical Theology: An Introduction*, pp. 176-78; *CD* III/3, pp. 374-76). Stuhlmacher has argued that Jesus himself was a model of "critical scriptural exposition" (*HCTIS*, p. 23). The same could be claimed of Tertullian *contra* Marcion and Athanasius *contra* Arius or Augustine *contra* the Manicheans.

Hence it is unwise to reject prematurely historical method in defense of faith, even where historical method has been grossly abused. Historical method has an enduring and continuing role in the inquiry into Jesus (Ebeling, *WF*, pp. 22-24, 56). That does not mean that Christianity must gullibly accept all fanciful or hypothesized conclusions drawn by advocacy historians or interest-laden investigations.

Historical method must be better protected from abuse and extended to include forms of inquiry able to take seriously the assumptions of pre- and postmodern Jewish and Christian orthodoxy. Postcritical Christology need not imply a disavowal of historical critical study. It commends a form of historical inquiry that transcends fatuous secularizations and naturalisms, one that listens to all, not selected bits of filtered evidence.

Spirituality and History

The deepest piety does not impatiently try to turn historical scholarship into piety. Yet there is no need for piety to be overwhelmed or intimidated by the pretenses of modern historical research, whose methods have often been unself-critically imperialistic and distorted by unexamined philosophical predispositions.

A life such as Kepler's or Einstein's would require some technical and mathematical knowledge to understand. Similarly, a life such as Jesus' requires a certain level of spiritual discernment to understand. One who is already bored with poetry is not likely to penetrate very deeply into William Blake—so one who lacks spiritual discernment cannot adequately treat Jesus' life. One who is tone deaf cannot be a music critic. An adequate account of Jesus is not likely to be given by one who begins by assuming that God cannot become flesh or save humanity from sin.

Accurate historical inquiry is presupposed in the study of holy writ. Historical inquiry seeks to state accurately what transpired and what was said in what context using what language and with what nuances of meaning (Baxter, *PW* XIII, pp. 408-14; cf. P. Ricoeur, *Essays on Biblical Interpretation*). It is not necessary to deny the careful findings of historical research in order to affirm the historic Christian faith. Yet there is need for realism about the tendency of pretentious criticism to exaggerate its own competencies (F. Hahn, "Probleme historischer Kritik," *Zeitschrift für die Neutestamentliche Wissenschaft* 63 [1972], 1–17).

The usefulness of historical research depends upon the fairness with which it is applied. In its grossly biased forms, it does not deserve to be trusted in the current era following the decline of modernity. Although historical research is limited in its aims and competencies (notably in the presence of the divine address), it deserves to play a key role in Christian reflection about Jesus, since Jesus is a person in history, not merely an idea.

Is the History of Jesus Crucial to the Teaching of Salvation?

The history of Jesus is the point of constant reference for the Christian teaching of salvation, for Christianity is not merely about the *idea* of deliverance, but of *a person* through whom this deliverance appears. "He who says, 'Jesus' says also 'history'" (Neill, *TGI*, p. 71; Cone, *BTL*, p. 212).

The history of Jesus is from first to last the history of a unique theandric person. Historical inquiry into Jesus will not resume until that premise is grasped. To attempt a history of Jesus without the theandric premise is like attempting sculpture without materials or mathematics without using numbers.

The Good News Is an Event in History

It is not in nature but in history that the revelation decisive for Christianity has occurred. Although nature may speak by the negative way of the existence of God, it remains mute on the crucial themes of forgiveness, spiritual rebirth, and reconciliation of sinners with God.

The good news occurs in history and is reported as a definite historical event. The history of Jesus must be studied in the same arena in which any past event is studied: by historical methods. Yet this is a history that challenges and tests ordinary methods of investigation.

Does Salvation Depend upon Historical Study?

However important, historical research cannot yield saving faith. One does not come closer to faith by piling up historical evidence. Historical science is not competent to save one from sin.

While history cannot establish or prove faith, the study of history is nonetheless an essential companion to the study of faith, insofar as faith attests revelation in history, and asks for historical evidences for its judgments about history (Braaten, *History and Hermeneutics*, pp. 11–53; P. Ricoeur, *The Reality of the Historical Past*).

Christ was a historical person, not merely an idea. His earthly life requires historical investigation using rigorous methods of inquiry. His life deserves investigation in relation to its historical context, political and social context, linguistic and philological traditions, geography, archeology, social customs, and special audiences. He did not live a life unrelated to a particular historical period, but within an unrepeatable setting: Judaism just before the Roman destruction of Jerusalem.

The incarnation requires that the humbling of God be viewed under the impact of historical limitations and in relation to particular historical circumstances. Today the language of classical Christology must be made as understandable as possible to those committed to historical critical methods. Postcritical Christology reaches out especially to those already well-instructed in historical methods, who nonetheless continue to experience the hunch that the living Christ is not made uncomfortable by unprejudiced historical inquiries into his earthly ministry.

Historicist Demands on Christology

By historicism I mean the view that turns historical study into an inquiry controlled by the historian rather than by the events under consideration. Historicism is made by and for interested academicians. The appropriate study of history is open to any fair-minded inquirer, just as the study of philosophy is not restricted to those who attend professional philosophical associations. The reform of Christology cannot proceed without offense to historicism.

Nineteenth-century Jesus research ended with the self-congratulatory feeling that liberal Christianity had come to know Jesus "as no other age," and that criticism had "placed constructive thought in a more advantageous position" (Fairbairn, PCMT, p. 20; pref., viii). The twentieth century, which began with Schweitzer's devastating eschatologically oriented critique of liberal assumptions about Jesus, is now ending with the slow death of radical critical exegesis. More and more layers of fact have been uncovered about a less and less well-defined kerygmatic figure who has become further and further distanced by the very methods that were supposed to bring him near.

The waning momentum of modernity still wishes to reduce the Christ event to historical determinants, explaining the theandric mystery in terms of the gradual historical development of antecedent ideas or themes in the history of religions.

Since Jesus comes to us as a concrete historical person, he must be studied historically. But he breaks through our sin-laden assumptions about what is possible amid the history of sin. The incarnation is a historical event, but a unique and unparalleled historical event that Christians

believe marks the pivotal point of history and furnishes the key to understanding all other developments in history.

Admittedly it is impossible to identify the very words of Christ (*ipsis-
sima verba*) with precise certainty, but little else can be known with precise
certainty. There is far more known of Jesus Christ on the basis of historical evidence than ever was known of Sophocles or Plato or Epictetus, yet
no one doubts that these figures existed, had powerful historical
influence, and have to some extent made themselves known. Those who
demean the Christian tradition for lacking hard evidence of the actual
words of Jesus sometimes stretch this point so as to try to use that lack as
a means of discrediting his proclamation altogether or minimizing any
revelatory dimension of his coming.

Can History Contain a Revelation?

Can anything be of enduring value that is floating in the ceaseless flux
of history? Is it foolish for Christians to fixate upon a single event? Does not
the salvation event have multiple and dubious interpretations? Is one ill-
advised to base one's whole life-truth upon a single happening amid the
great sweep of history? Can any single event become absolutely important
in a history that is far from over? Is there reliable evidence that these alleged "saving events" really happened? Is faith based on historical fact? Can
faith's historical groundedness be demonstrated sufficiently? These questions perennially have vexed Christological reasoning (Kierkegaard, *Concluding Unscientific Postscript*; Harvey, *HB*). From ancient Greeks to modern
Buddhists the idea of revelation in and through history has been thought
to be a dubious idea. The premise that God is revealed in history is placed
constantly on the defensive within the matrix of fading modernity.

Lessing despaired that "accidental truths of history can never become
the proof of necessary truths of reason" ("On the Proof of the Spirit and
of Power," *Lessing's Theological Writings* [1956], p. 53). He wondered if any
eternal truth could ever be contained in fragile, passing, fleeting, unsub-
stantial historical events. It was in response to this that Kierkegaard wrote
Philosophical Fragments, seeking to show that a historical point of
departure—namely, the incarnation—is possible for eternal happiness.
No modern interpreter has been a more steady or reliable companion to
this writer than Kierkegaard. It is doubtful that a Kierkegaardian
Christology has ever been written. If this study does not suffice, at least
it celebrates much of the core of Kierkegaard's intent (as expressed in
Phil. Frag., Concluding Unscientific Postscript, TC, Christian Discourses, and
The Point of View of My Work as an Author), yet aware that with him the pen-
dulum has swung too far in a subjectivist direction.

Classical Antecedents of Modern Critical Inquiry

It should not be imagined that critical inquiry into the history of Jesus began in the nineteenth century. In its early centuries, apostolic teaching had to stand up to the searching criticisms of Marcion, Celsus, Valentinus, Praxeus, Lucian, and other probing minds who challenged the apostolic teaching with variant interpretations, each of which had to be answered carefully by apologists such as Irenaeus, Hippolytus, Cyprian, Arnobius, and Eusebius.

Christian teaching has in several periods of its long history set itself intensively to the task of using the available resources of historical (as well as social and philosophical) investigation to inquire reasonably into its own historical foundations. This occurred in the thirteenth and sixteenth centuries notably, with Thomas and Luther, but even more fundamentally in the fourth and fifth centuries (with Eusebius, Athanasius, the Cappadocians, Rufinus, Augustine, and Jerome, Paula and company).

There is a profound moral requirement upon faith that it speak historical truth and not lie or dissemble about facts. This is a commitment that requires daily renewal. Even though this commitment has sometimes plunged faith into empiricist or rationalistic excesses, the respect for evidence remains an important means by which the Holy Spirit protects the worshiping community from petty innovations and erroneous teachings (Baxter, *PW* XIII, pp. 376–78, 408–14).

The distinctively modern mutations of criticism that have emerged since the Enlightenment are best viewed in the light of previous patristic, medieval, and Renaissance textual, contextual, and literary cirticism. In the eighteenth century the deistic and Enlightenment critiques of Reimarus, Hume, Voltaire, and others, in the nineteenth those of Hegel, Baur, and Strauss, and in the twentieth the tradition from Weiss to Braun, have all been providential challenges for the strengthening of faith.

Through these varied streams, the history of Jesus has not suffered from a lack of criticism. We are now concerned only about the adequacy and depth of recent criticism.

Amid reductionist debates the onion has never been peeled to nothing, nor could it ever be. Any salvation that can be destroyed by historical criticism is not God's own coming to humanity. After all these critical inquiries, it seems more evident than ever that faith in Jesus continues. Jesus continues to meet people of today personally on his own terms. He was never the product of a series of redactive errors, ideological distortions, or literary deceptions.

Circumventing the Offense

Biblical critics imagine that they have found legitimate ways of circumventing the theandric offense. Echoing the tradition that followed Hegel, they pretend to treat the question of Christ exclusively as a critique of the ideas of those who remembered Jesus, hence as having little to do with the person himself. But the person keeps on intruding on the historical reverie.

Liberal theology has long sought to overleap the theandric offense by writing the life of Jesus from the viewpoint of late nineteenth-century Kantian-dominated ethics—until Schweitzer. The Bultmannian school sought to avoid the offense by positing a mere *Dass*, the formal assertion *that* Jesus did appear, but little could be known of him since the memory of him is so fundamentally distorted by his followers. In effect this line of thought circumvents the historical Jesus almost altogether by speaking only of the remembered kerygma. Pannenberg's heroic attempt at recovery sought to ground Christology in the history of Jesus by developing a Christology *von unten*, "from below," i.e., through history. All of these attempts are due to be succeeded by a recovery of classic Christological exegesis on its own terms, unintimidated by modernity.

H. R. Mackintosh described the prevailing dilemma of biblical studies accurately a generation ago: "There has never been a Christianity in the world which did not worship Christ the Lord as personally identical with Jesus of Nazareth. A criticism, therefore, which after repudiating His exaltation, strives to disinter the real Jesus from the mounds of untrustworthy legend, is reduced for lack of matter to constructions of a subjective and imaginary character. These constructions proceed on lines which almost by definition make valid results impossible; for, resting as they do in partially naturalistic assumptions, they are led to argue, first, that no transcendent Person such as the Christ of faith could possibly exist, and secondly, that even if He did, it is inconceivable that a subsequent age should be credibly informed of His reality" (*PJC*, p. 318). This is the road that has finally come to an end.

The Needed Cohesion

These attempts have failed finally to come to terms with the single most elementary affirmation of the New Testament proclamation, that Jesus *is* the Christ (as distinguished markedly from the view that Jesus is merely *proclaimed* as the Christ, or that Jesus *became* the Christ through a remembering process, or that the Christ is reducible to a modern rendering of the *moral teaching* of Jesus). Christ comes to us only in the palpable form of this person—Jesus. Jesus comes to us only as the Christ, and short of that affirmation we have not yet begun to deal with the history of Jesus.

Paul thought that Jesus had been declared the Christ not by his followers but by God (Rom. 1:4). That is a startling fact far greater in significance than that there may be stages of development leading to that declaration. An event must not be confused with its historical development.

The Life of Jesus Is That of the Incarnate Lord

The account of Jesus' earthly ministry cannot be told as if it were purely a heavenly or transhistorical event, for it is the story of a human being. Nor can it be told as if it were merely the story of a human being, for it is the account of God's own coming. His life story is a thoroughly human story, but at the same time the story of God's coming.

How are we to proceed to account for this particular life? Certainly by making full use of historical inquiry. But not by preemptively weeding out all reference to the divine initiative and thereby destroying the central datum to be investigated.

Historical judgment is not abandoned when the apostolic teaching is understood as having been raised up by the risen Lord. The apostles remembered better than they understood (V. Taylor, *PC*; T. W. Manson, *Studies in the Gospels and Epistles*). We are able to know him now because they knew him and reported him with sufficient adequacy—sufficient for human salvation.

The burden of Christology is to show or disprove that Christ was who he said he was. If he was indeed God incarnate, then an inquiry that circumvented or accidentally missed that fact would be inadequate.

The truth of his life—that he was God incarnate—was not fully realized by his closest disciples during his earthly life. It was only adequately realized after his resurrection. Once grasped, it became the fulcrum of apostolic teaching.

The events of his life were events of the God-man. Apart from this fact, these narratives remain enigmatic and baffling. Any attempt to account for his life without accounting for this fact is, according to apostolic testimony, pitiable and untrue.

Logos became *sarx*, flesh, historical person. The uncreated One assumed the life of a creature. God entered history and became a single individual in it. If so, the meaning of history is to be found not in ideas, not in the history of earthly power, but in a man born of woman, a particular man as Son of God, Son of God as a particular man. Let this theandric premise be taken seriously and the study of the historical Jesus can once again be resumed.

The Systematic Study of God's Coming

It is best to disavow pretentious expectations or conclusions. This study has had a limited purpose. It emerges out of a constrained, self-limiting systematic method. It has tried not to promise what would not be delivered—political wisdom or psychotherapy or economic analysis or original historical research or detailed textual exegesis. Rather this is theology, more particularly the pivotal Christological phase of classic Christian teaching, the creed's second article.

Some account is required of that prevailing understanding of the systematic study of Christ that has emerged out of this ecumenical, consensual tradition. This is best done by stating four disclaimers that distinguish systematic theology, classically conceived, from other disciplines and then stating positively the systematic way of classic Christology.

What Christology Is Not

Four distinct disclaimers indicate what classic Christology is not.

Christology Is Not Exegesis

The systematic way of classic Christology has always presupposed rigorous examination of contexts and texts of Scripture but itself is distinguishable from strict exegesis as such, however valuable that may be. Our method of study has been not primarily an exegetical but a systematic method. Its chief purpose is not to unpack for readers the historical development or social or cultural location or interpretation of particular texts, though this is useful at points. Rather, as systematic inquiry, it wishes to organize and place the truth of the canonical texts in fitting order and systematic arrangement—fitting in relation to the pattern of baptismal formulae, creeds, conciliar decisions, confessions, catechesis, and normative homilies.

This does not imply that exegetical interest is lacking, for there is need to unpack in some detail certain crucial texts like Philippians 2:6–11, John 1, Hebrews 10, and various texts in Romans, Galatians, and Acts, since these texts remain so important for Christological definition.

One reason that critical exegesis has been so centerless in our time, prone to exaggerated radicalism, captive to historical skepticism, and tempted to inordinate speculation is that modern exegesis has not had rigorous enough partners in either ancient ecumenical or systematic theology. Meanwhile modern exegetes have been so busy disavowing the classic exegetes that they have by now almost entirely quit reading them—a premise easily tested by examining the footnotes of Bultmann, Tillich, Kümmel, Käsemann, Perrin, and Marxsen (Barth, Meyendorff, and Pannenberg being among the happy exceptions). A new era of exegesis is called for by exegetes who have carefully read Athanasius, John Chrysostom, Ambrose, Augustine, Jerome, and Calvin, and not just commentaries postdating Schweitzer.

The result of the detachment of exegesis from ecumenical consensus is that exegetical issues have become grossly contorted and imbalanced by speculative theories of oral and editorial transmission. Whatever the speculated or real historical development of a particular biblical text may be, it deserves treatment by systematic theology as a canonical text, a passage from the book of the church, as normative record of revelation.

Some resist systematic theology on the grounds that it inevitably distorts the texts, which do not lend themselves to systematization. Classical Christian teaching has respected the discrete texts, but that respect has itself called the church to consistent reflection about the whole of Scripture. Every discrete canonical text is legitimately a part of this reflection, even if at some distance from the center of our interest.

The better system may learn even from its least systematic elements. There is an aesthetic quality about systematic cohesion that wishes to include all without coercing any, that looks intently for how any text of Scripture holographically reflects the whole. Robert Herrick savored this aesthetic connection when he observed:

> A careless shoe-string, in whose tie
> I see a wild civility,
> Do more bewitch me, than when art
> Is too precise in every part
> ("Delight in Disorder").

Christology Is Not History

What is said of exegesis may also be said generally of historical method. While respecting the value of historical inquiry, we have not proceeded by making it normative for Christian teaching. This disclaimer is especially needed in an era in which historical inquiry is so undisciplined. Pannenberg's work is the most heroic (and I believe the best, although with wrenching pathos because he finally had to disavow the canonical textuary of systematics) example of an attempt at dogmatics that wished to be entirely and consistently faithful to historical method. I believe this to be finally a fatal flaw prone to the idolatry of historical science.

What must be recovered is systematic method unenslaved by historical method. Historical study asks: how did the history of the transmission of the tradition occur? Systematic theology asks an entirely distinguishable (though not separable) question: what is the truth of the Christian faith, and how is it best ordered in relation to the history of revelation? Since revelation has a history (indeed *is* a history!), it requires that systematic theology be well instructed in exegetical and historical method and issues (Irenaeus, *Ag. Her.* I.1-10, *ANF* I, pp. 315-32), but that cannot be limited to the most recent discussions of exegesis and history, which are too largely lacking in spiritual depth. The exegesis and historical study that becomes the absorbing interest of systematics as here defined is the exegesis of classical Christian teachers. We have searched for the path of consensus of those early teachers who have best articulated the mind of the believing church. This study seeks to be unremittingly and intensively grounded in exegetical and historical wisdom, yet not so as to become preoccupied with contemporary exegetical or current historical methods or procedures.

Our purpose is not to attempt to fix an exact order in the sequence of events or the precise manner of transmission of religious ideas into or out of the first, fifth, or fifteenth centuries. That is the prerogative of intellectual historians and has no right to imperialize upon systematic theology.

Conceivably each subheading of this study could have been accompanied by a longer treatise on the history of its development. That is an appropriate task, but not the subject of this modest inquiry. However intriguing, it could easily become the excuse for not engaging Christian teaching systematically at all. Writers like Dorner, Barth, Weber, Thielicke, Rahner, and Pannenberg have sought admirably to include extensive historical materials in their systematic discussions, but unfortunately the price they paid was the inordinate burdening of systematic discussions with ever-extending historical excursi, with their resulting tediousness, accompanied by a certain tendency to inconclusiveness and evasion.

Christology Is Not Sociology

Christology is not politics or cultural analysis or social work. However much one may enjoy political talk or be morally committed to social change, this is not an inquiry into political ethics or contemporary culture or class analysis. The methods of social ethics, political theology, sociology of religion, and psychology of religion seek to apply learnings from (mostly modern, seldom ancient) politics, ethics, and sociological insight to the study of Christian truth. These are all legitimate exercises, but they are only indirectly related to our specific intent. If Christ is Lord, this must impinge upon politics; yet there can be no such impingement without first understanding what "Christ is Lord" means—*that* remains our subject.

To disavow that political-cultural issues are central to our present intention does not imply that they lack interest or importance. These disciplines suffer now from a lack of dialogue with classical Christianity. It is because exegetical theology has so often abandoned its text and historical theology has forgotten the varying ways the texts have been transculturally remembered, and systematic theology has fled from both *systema* and *theos*, that the theological ethicist has been left bereft of dialogue.

In the post-Tillichian period that promised so much for a theology of culture, the disciplines that should bridge to and from theology now have no path to follow, nowhere to go to find the city of theology (which smoulders in ruins), hence no partner with which to dialogue. Tillich's method of correlation had the comically unintended effect of totally disenfranchising and immobilizing a theology of culture. The unwished outcome has suffered from Tillich's own unclear understanding of canon and lack of empathy with the church.

It is time to seek a renewal and deepening of psychology and sociology of religion, but not one that continues detached from classic Christian teaching. Someday the dialogue between theology and the social sciences will bloom, but not until theology has mended its prodigal ways. Until then, there is no companion voice with which sociology and psychology may dialogue—only a faint echo. Now theology lacks identity and remains a catatonic, inarticulate partner in the dialogue—a cipher, a somewhat pretentious nonentity.

The time will come when a Christian political theology will emerge as something more than a faint echo of twisted and destructive contemporary secular (often Marxist) political fantasies but will rather be shaped by the distinctive political wisdom of the history of revelation. Now Christian political theology is captive, confused, and made relatively impotent by the thin voice of systematic theology, which has understandably lost and has not yet reearned a hearing.

Systematic theology and apologetics seek to account for the same faith with different audiences. Systematic inquiry assumes that it does not have to repeat all the detailed work of *apologetics*, which is seeking to make the truth of the Christian faith plausible to a varied range of cultured despisers, critics, inquirers, and the pious of varied world religions, as well as agnostics and atheists. While a work of systematic theology cannot presume well-formed faith on the part of readers, it does assume at least some preliminary form of faith and cannot be diverted from its major purpose—to serve the community of faith by leading it toward greater clarity concerning its confession. Apologetics addresses a different audience—not faith, but unfaith or pseudofaith or diluted faith or disbelief or doubt that may or may not seek to become inquiring preliminary belief. Hence I am undisturbed if theology remains relatively unattended in my time, since I am confident that a decade will come when the roots of faith will deepen and the thirst for grounded theology will be intense.

Christology Is Not Praxis

We have proceeded not by a pragmatic method, which would seek practically to apply the truth of Christianity to problems of pastoral care, worship, preaching, and the ministry of the laity. That this writer believes that these are worthy and important subjects should be evident, having spent much of a lifetime of professional energies teaching and researching issues of pastoral care and ministry. But systematic theology must stand on its own methodological ground and not be inordinately dependent for its legitimation upon whether it preaches well, enhances church growth, or enlivens worship. A better ordered systematic theology would indeed assist preaching greatly, deepen worship profoundly, and form the basis of a more effective pastoral care. But these practical outcomes cannot define the essential work and task of systematic theology.

Note that in these four points we have made reference to each of four basic areas of theological curriculum. Having argued that systematic method differs from biblical studies, historical studies, studies in church and culture (or religion and society), and studies in practical theology, each with its own method—exegetical, historical, ethical (including socio-

logical, cultural, and political studies), and pragmatic methods of application—if systematic theology is none of these, what is it? If its method is
not finally borrowed from any of these, what method does it employ?

The Systematic Way Defined

The systematic pathway is indicated by its defining term—*systema*
(from *sunistanai*, "to place together"). Systematic theology wishes to
bring together in connected order and sequential arrangement the
organic whole of Christian teaching, showing the order of the whole and
the right relation of each part to the whole. Christology wishes to do this
with respect to the study of Christ. It builds upon the resources of all
these companion disciplines, seeking to bring them into a cohesive statement and plausible clarification of the truth of Christ.

Systematic theology seeks order, right organization, fitting arrangement, logical consistency. Admittedly the other disciplines have these
values in mind as well, for pastoral theology wishes to be well organized,
exegesis wishes to be properly ordered, and so on. But there is a difference. Systematic theology has as its main purpose and chief aim the right
organization of all the disparate materials of the varied types of theological inquiry. That is not the purpose of exegesis, church history, ethics, or
homiletics. If they did that single-mindedly and in a thoroughgoing way,
they would be engaging in systematic theology. Systematic theology
wishes to know something about almost everything going on in all quar-
ters of the theological curriculum in order that it may do this one task
well. A good systematician cannot merely say: I am doing systematics so
do not bother me now with exegesis, pastoral care, history, or politics. It
is because one is trying to be a good systematician that one is going to
search for the cohesion that can only emerge out of dialogue in all of
these inquiries, so as to serve the life of the Christian community with
the ordered truth of that community.

While distinguishing itself from exegesis, systematics listens attentively and critically to the exegetes, both historical and contemporary.
While not becoming captive to historical method, systematics seeks to
understand historical research and have a wide data base for reasoning
historically. While critically resisting the seductive aspects of the method
of correlation with all its fascinating points of contact with modern consciousness, systematics seeks to understand its modern hearers in the
light of revealed truth and to be attentive to the context to which the gospel is addressed. While not becoming captive to a pragmatic theology
that would always judge the value of truth exclusively by its practical out-

comes, systematic theology must serve the living church in its own distinctive way by its own particular method. It will best energize the worshiping community, deepen pastoral caring, and serve to improve preaching by its distinctive form of truth-telling—faith's cohesive reasoning.

This is the modest service that systematic theology hopes to render. There is an aesthetic quality and intent in the effort to refract the truth of Christ in a way that corresponds with the intellectual beauty of that truth. Rhetoric is no small part of the task, and the best theologians have often been the best rhetoricians—Gregory Nazianzen, Augustine, Leo, Luther, and Kierkegaard among the most gifted.

Hence what one must love, if one is to serve as systematic theologian, is the peace and unity of the church and the truth that enables that peace and unity. Systematics has an unceasing eros for the unity of the community and seeks to draw the community together in a single, cohesive hymn of faith, a single intelligible baptism, a single table of the Lord shared by all who confess that faith. Hence systematic theology is by definition an ecumenical task. Any systematic theology that intends to serve only its denominational ethos is by definition profoundly unsystematic, since it prefers not to listen to the Christian community in those other times and places.

Systematics hungers for that bread that is offered in a single loaf. The pastor who wishes to think and preach systematically needs a steady temperament for this irenic, unifying search for internal cohesion of the whole church's witness, shared in all times and places by the faithful community (Vincent of Lerins, *Comm.*). Among writers of the modern period who had this temperament, I commend especially William Burt Pope; among classic Protestant writers the best systematic minds were John Calvin, John Pearson, and Martin Chemnitz; among medieval writers none excels Anselm or Thomas Aquinas; among patristic writers the systematic mind is best exemplified by all eight great doctors of the church, none more profoundly than Gregory of Nazianzus. All of these exemplify Pascal's beautiful maxim: "God orders all things with gentleness, and His way is to plant religion in the mind by argument and in the heart by grace" (*Pensées*, Concerning True Religion, 1, H. F. Stewart transl., *TGS*, p. 213).

The vocation of the theologian is not to gain cost-free acceptance with modern hearers but to try to point intelligibly to that Word that is able to save from sin and death. If the modern reader must clash with Christianity, may the theologian at least bear sufficiently accurate witness to the truth that the clash is made possible. The theologian's vocation is not to cower, discover convenient ploys, rearrange favorable terms, or expect some better outcome provided the audience is entertained at the expense of the truth.

Some may feel that this argument, if taken seriously, would set theology back a hundred years. I would hope not—I would prefer a thousand or more.

ABBREVIATIONS AND REFERENCES

AAS   *Acta Apostolicae Sedis*. Rome, 1909ff.

ACW   *Ancient Christian Writers: The Works of the Fathers in Translation*. Edited by J. Quasten, J. C. Plumpe, and W. Burghardt. 44 vols. New York: Paulist Press, 1946–.

ADC   *The Atonement of the Death of Christ*. H. D. McDonald. Grand Rapids, MI: Baker, 1985.

AEG   *Ante-Nicene Exegesis of the Gospels*. Edited by Harold D. Smith. 6 vols. London: S. P. C. K., 1925.

AF   *The Apostolic Fathers*. Edited by J. N. Sparks. New York: Nelson, 1978.

AFT   *Agenda for Theology*. Thomas C. Oden. San Francisco: Harper & Row, 1979.

Ag.   Against

ANF   *Ante-Nicene Fathers*. Edited by A. Roberts and J. Donaldson. 10 vols. 1885–1896. Reprinted ed., Grand Rapids, MI: Eerdmans, 1979. Book (in Roman numerals) and chapter or section number (usually in Arabic numerals), followed by volume and page number.

Angl.   *Anglicanism, The Thought and Practice of the Church of England*. Edited by P. E. More and F. L. Cross. London: S. P. C. K., 1935.

APD   *The Apostolic Preaching and Its Developments*. C. H. Dodd. New York: Harper, 1954.

Ari.   *The Arians. Works of John Henry Cardinal Newman*. Edited by Joseph Rickaby. Westminster, MD: Christian Classics, 1977.

ARI   *An Address on Religious Instruction*. Gregory of Nyssa. *LCC* III, pp. 268–326.

AST   *Abstract of Systematic Theology* (1887). James Peitigru Boyce. Reprint edition. Louisville, KY: n.p., n.d.

Ath.   *St. Athanasius. Works of John Henry Cardinal Newman*. Edited by Joseph Rickaby. 2 vols. Westminster, MD: Christian Classics, 1977.

ATW   *After Therapy What? Lay Therapeutic Resources in Religious Perspective.* Finch Lectures by Thomas C. Oden, with Responses by N. Warren, K. Mulholland, C. Schoonhoven, C. Kraft, W. Walker. Edited by Neil C. Warren. Springfield, IL: Thomas, 1974.

BC   *Basic Christianity.* John Stott. Grand Rapids, MI: Eerdmans, 1964.

BCP   *Book of Common Prayer* (1662). Royal Breviar's edition. London: S. P. C. K., n.d.

BCSP   *The Beginnings of Christology: A Study of Its Problems.* Willi Marxsen. Philadelphia: Fortress, 1969.

Bever.   Henry Beveridge translation. Calvin. *Institutes of the Christian Religion.* 2 vols. London: Clarke, 1953.

BHT   *The Bible in Human Transformation.* Walter Wink. Philadelphia: Fortress, 1973.

Bk.   Book

BMW   *The Bible in the Modern World.* James Barr. London: SCM, 1973.

BOC   *The Book of Concord* (1580). Edited by T. G. Tappert. Philadelphia: Muhlenberg Press, 1959.

BOConf.   *The Book of Confessions.* New York: United Presbyterian Church, 1966. Part I of *The Constitution of the United Presbyterian Church.* No page references, only section numbers.

BQT   *Basic Questions in Theology.* Wolfhart Pannenberg. 3 vols. Philadelphia: Westminster, 1970–1973.

BSG   *The Birth of the Synoptic Gospels.* Jean Carmignac. Translated by Michael J. Wrenn. Chicago: Franciscan Herald Press, 1987.

BTL   *A Black Theology of Liberation.* James H. Cone. Philadelphia: J. D. Lippincott, 1970.

Catech.   Catechism or Catechetical

CC   *Creeds of the Churches.* Edited by John Leith. Richmond, VA: John Knox, 1979.

CD   *Church Dogmatics.* Karl Barth. Edited by G. W. Bromiley, T. F. Torrance, et al. 4 vols. Edinburgh: Clark, 1936–1969.

CDH   *Cur Deus Homo.* Anselm. Translated by S. N. Deane. Lasalle, IN: Open Court, 1966.

CDJR   *The Christian Doctrine of Justification and Reconciliation.* Albrecht Ritschl. Edited by H. R. Mackintosh. London, 1900.

CDS   *The Christian Doctrine of Salvation.* G. B. Stevens. Edinburgh: Clark, 1909.

CEJC   *The Christology of Early Jewish Christianity.* Richard N. Longenecker. London: SCM, 1970.

CF   *The Christian Faith in the Doctrinal Documents of the Catholic Church.*

Edited by J. Neuner and J. Dupuis. New York: Alba House, 1982, revised edition.

CFS   *Cistercian Fathers Series*. 44 vols. to date. Kalamazoo, MI: Cistercian Publications, 1968–.

CG   1 *City of God*. Augustine. *NPNF* 1 II. 2 *The Christ of the Gospels*. William West Holdsworth. London: Kelly, 1911.

CGTC   Cambridge Greek Testament Commentary. Cambridge: Cambridge University Press.

CH   *Church History*. Eusebius of Caesarea. *NPNF* 2, I.

CHC   *Commentary on the Heidelberg Catechism*. Zacharius Ursinus. Cincinnati: T. P. Bucher, 1851.

Chr.   Christian

ChrD   1 *Christian Dogmatics*. Edited by Carl E. Braaten and Robert W. Jensen. 2 vols. Philadelphia: Fortress Press, 1984. 2 *Christian Doctrine*. J. S. Whale. London: Collins, 1957.

ChrF   1 *The Christian Faith*. Olin A. Curtis. New York: Methodist Book Concern, 1905. 2 *The Christian Faith*. Friedrich Schleiermacher. Edinburgh: Clark, 1928.

CLT   *A Compend. of Luther's Theology*. Edited by H. T. Kerr. Philadelphia: Westminster, 1953.

CNT   *Christology of the New Testament*. Oscar Cullmann. Philadelphia: Westminster, 1959.

COC   *Creeds of Christendom*. Edited by P. Schaff. 3 vols. New York: Harper, 1919.

Comm.   1 *Commentary*. 2 *Calvin's Commentaries*. John Calvin. 22 vols. Grand Rapids, MI: 1981. Originally printed for The Calvin Translation Society, Edinburgh. 3 *Commentaries*, Bede. *Complete Works*. Edited by J. Giles. 12 vols. London, 1843–1844. See *MPL* 90–95. 4 *Commonitory*. Vincent of Lerins. *NPNF* 2 XI. *LCC* VII.

Compend.   1 *Compendium*. 2 *Compendium of Christian Theology*. William Burt Pope. 3 vols. New York: Phillips and Hunt, n.d. 3 *Compendium of Theology*. Thomas Aquinas. New York: Herder, 1947.

CQLS   *Commentaria in Quator Libros Sententiarum*. *Works of Bonaventure*. Translated by Jose de Vinck. 5 vols. Patterson, NJ: St. Anthony Guild Press, 1960–1970.

CR   *Corpus Reformatorum, Philippi Melanchthonis opera*. Edited by C. G. Bretschneider and H. E. Bindsell. 28 vols. Halis Saxonium, 1834–1860.

CS   *Christ the Savior*. Reginald Garriogou-Lagrange. London: B. Herder, 1950.

CT   *Christian Theology.* Emery H. Bancroft. Edited by Ronald B. Majors. Grand Rapids, MI: Zondervan, 1976.

CTC   *Christianae Theologiae Compendium.* Johnannes Wollebius. Edited by Ernst Bizer. Neukirchen, 1935. English translation by John Beardslee, in *RDB.*

CTP   *Contemporary Theology and Psychotherapy.* Thomas C. Oden. Philadelphia: Westminster, 1967.

CV   *Christus Victor.* Gustaf Aulen. New York: Macmillan, 1958.

CWB   *A Commentary on the Whole Bible.* Matthew Henry. 6 vols. Iowa Falls, IA: World Bible Publishers, n.d.

CWMS   *Complete Writings of Menno Simons.* Edited by John C. Wenger. Scottdale, PA: Herald Press, 1956.

CWS   *Classics of Western Spirituality.* Edited by Richard J. Payne et al. 30 vols. to date. Mahwah, NJ: Paulist Press, 1978–. Volumes unnumbered.

CWST   *Complete Works of St. Teresa.* Teresa of Avila. Edited by E. Allison Peers. 3 vols. London: Sheed and Ward, 1946.

DC   *Doctrines of the Creed.* Oliver C. Quick. London: Nisbet, 1938.

DCF   *A Defence of the Catholic Faith Concerning the Satisfaction of Christ Against Faustus Socinus* (1617). Hugo Grotius. Translated by F. H. Foster. London: Draper, 1889.

Div. Inst.   *Divine Institutes.* Lactantius. *ANF* VII. *FC* 49.

DL   *The Divinity of Our Lord.* H. P. Liddon. London: Rivingtons, 1875.

Doct.   Doctrine

Doc. Vat. II   *The Documents of Vatican II.* Edited by W. M. Abbott. New York: Guild Press, 1966.

DS   *Enchridion Symbolorum.* Edited by H. Denzinger and Clem. Bannwart. Friburg: Herder and Co., 1922.

DT   **1** *Dogmatic Theology.* Francis Hall. New York: Longmans, Green, 1907–1922. **2** *Dogmatic Theology.* Joseph Pohle. Edited by Arthur Preuss. 12 vols. St. Louis, MO: B. Herder, 1922. **3** *Doctrinal Theology of the Evangelical Lutheran Church.* Heinrich Schmid. 3d ed. Minneapolis, MN: Augsburg, 1899.

DWC   *The Doctrine of the Work of Christ.* Sidney Cave. Nashville, TN: Cokesbury, 1937.

EC   **1** *Exposition of the Creed* (1659). John Pearson. Edited by Edward Burton. London, 1833. **2** *Evangelical Christology.* Bernard Ramm. Nashville, TN: Nelson, 1985. **3** *The Essentials of Christianity.* Henry Clay Sheldon. New York: Doran, 1922.

ECW   *Early Christian Writers: The Apostolic Fathers.* Translated by Maxwell Staniforth. London: Penguin, 1968.

ED   *Elements of Divinity*. Thomas N. Ralston. New York: Abingdon, 1924.

EDQ   *Eighty-three Different Questions*. Augustine. *FC* 70.

EHCM   *The End of the Historical-Critical Method*. Gerhard Maier. St. Louis, MO: Concordia, 1977.

ENOT   *Explanatory Notes Upon the Old Testament*. John Wesley. 3 vols. Salem, OH: Schmul, 1975.

ENTT   *Essays in New Testament Themes*. Ernst Käsemann. Studies in Biblical Theology, no. 41. London: SCM, 1964.

Epist.   Epistle(s)

ETA   *Examen Theologicum Acroamaticum* (1707). David Hollaz (or Hollatz). Leipzig: Brietkopf, 1763.

Evang.   Evangelical

Expos.   Exposition

FC   *The Fathers of the Church: A New Translation*. Edited by R. J. Deferrari. 73 vols. to date. Washington, DC: Catholic University Press, 1947–.

FGG   *From Glory to Glory, Texts from Gregory of Nyssa's Mystical Writings*. Translated by H. Musurillo. New York: Scribner, 1961.

FNTC   *The Foundation of New Testament Christology*. Reginald H. Fuller. New York: Scribner, 1965.

FP   *First Principles*. Origen. Boston: Peter Smith, 1985.

GA   *Grammar of Assent. Works of John Henry Cardinal Newman*. Edited by Joseph Rickaby. Westminster, MD: Christian Classics, 1977.

Gk.   Greek

GRA   *God, Revelation, and Authority*. Carl F. H. Henry. Waco, TX: Word, 1976.

GWC   *God Was in Christ*. Donald M. Baillie. London: Faber & Faber, 1956.

Harmony   *Harmony of the Evangelists*. John Calvin, *Commentaries* XVI, XVII. See *Comm.*

HB   *The Historian and the Believer*. Van A. Harvey. New York: Macmillan, 1966.

HCTIS   *Historical Criticism and Theological Interpretation of Scripture*. Peter Stuhlmacher. Translated by Roy Harrisville. Philadelphia: Fortress, 1977.

Heb.   Hebrew

Her.   Heresies

Hom.   *Homily* or *Homilies*

HP   *Hope and Planning*. Jürgen Moltmann. New York: Harper & Row, 1971.

HPC   *A Harmony of Protestant Confessions*. Edited by Peter Hall. London: J. F. Shaw, 1842.

HPEC   *Hymnal, Protestant Episcopal Church.* New York: Church Pension Fund, 1916.

IAIA   *Juliana of Norwich: An Introductory Appreciation and an Interpretative Anthology.* Edited by P. Franklin Chambers. New York: Harper, 1955.

IBHJ   *I Believe in the Historical Jesus.* I. Howard Marshall. Grand Rapids, MI: Eerdmans, 1977.

IC   *Introduction to Christianity.* Joseph Ratzinger. New York: Herder & Herder, 1970.

ICT   *Introduction to Christian Theology.* Jürgen Moltmann. Lectures at Duke Divinity School. Edited by Douglas Meeks. Durham, NC: Duke Divinity School, 1968 (mimeographed).

Incarn.   Incarnation

Inst.   *Institutes of the Christian Religion.* John Calvin. *LCC,* 20–21. References by book, chapter, and section numbers.

Intro.   Introduction

ITE   *Institutio Theologiae elencticae.* Francis Turretin. Utrecht and Amsterdam, 1701.

ITLC   *Institutiones Theologicae seu Locorum Communium Christiane Religionis.* Guelielmus Bucanus. Geneva: le Preux, 1609. English translation: *Institutions of the Christian Religion.* London: Snowden, 1606.

JGM   *Jesus—God and Man.* Wolfhart Pannenberg. Philadelphia: Westminster, 1968.

JN   *Jesus of Nazareth.* Gunther Bornkamm. London: Hodder and Stoughton, 1960.

KC   *Kerygma and Counseling.* Thomas C. Oden. San Francisco: Harper & Row, 1978.

KM   *Kerygma and Myth: A Theological Debate with Contributions by Rudolf Bultmann, et al.* Edited by H. W. Bartsch. London: S. P. C. K., 1957.

KJKEK   *Das Kruez Jesu und die Krise der Evangelischen Kirche.* S. Findeisen, H. Frey, W. Johanning. Bad Liebenzell: Verlag der Liebenzeller Mission, 1967.

KJV   King James Version, 1611.

Lat.   Latin

LCC   *The Library of Christian Classics.* Edited by J. Baillie, J. T. McNiell, and H. P. Van Dusen. 26 vols. Philadelphia: Westminster, 1953–1961.

LCF   *The Later Christian Fathers.* Edited by H. Bettenson. Oxford: Oxford University Press, 1970.

Lect.   Lecture or lectures

LF   *A Library of the Fathers.* Edited by E. B. Pusey, J. Kebel, J. H. Newman, C. Marriott. 50 vols. Oxford: J. H. Parker, 1838–1888.

LG   *The Living God, Systematic Theology: Volume One.* Thomas C. Oden. San Francisco: Harper & Row, 1987.

LibT   *Liberation Theology.* Leonardo and Clodovis Boff. San Francisco: Harper & Row, 1986.

LMJ   *The Life and Ministry of Jesus.* Vincent Taylor. Nashville, TN: Abingdon, 1955.

LPT   *Library of Protestant Thought.* Edited by John Dillenberger. 13 vols. New York: Oxford University Press, 1964–1972.

LT   **1** *Loci Theologici* (1591). Martin Chemnitz. 3 vols. Frankfurt: N. Hoffmann, 1606. **2** *Loci Theologici* (1610–1621). John Gerhard. 22 vols. Tübingen: n.p., 1762–1787.

LTJM   *The Life and Times of Jesus the Messiah.* Alfred Edersheim. Grand Rapids, MI: Eerdmans, 1953.

LW   *Luther's Works.* Edited by J. Pelikan and H. T. Lehmann. 54 vols. to date. St. Louis, MO: Concordia, 1953–.

LWHG   *The Life and Works of Hugo Grotius.* London: Grotius Society, 1925.

LXX   Septuagint

MB   *The Doctrine of the Mystical Body of Christ According to the Principles of Theology of St. Thomas Aquinas.* Joseph Anger. Translated by John J. Burke. New York: Benziger, 1931.

MC   *On the Meaning of Christ.* John Knox. New York: Scribner, 1947.

MD   *Meditations and Devotions. Works of John Henry Cardinal Newman.* Edited by Joseph Rickaby. Westminster, MD: Christian Classics, 1977.

Med.   *The Mediator.* Emil Brunner. Philadelphia: Westminster, 1947.

MH   *The Methodist Hymnal.* Nashville, TN: Methodist Publishing House, 1939.

Mir.   *Essays on Miracles. Works of John Henry Cardinal Newman.* Edited by Joseph Rickaby. Westminster, MD: Christian Classics, 1977.

Mix.   *Discourses to Mixed Congregations. Works of John Henry Cardinal Newman.* Edited by Joseph Rickaby. Westminster, MD: Christian Classics, 1977.

MPG   *Patrologia Graeca.* Edited by J. B. Migne. 162 vols. Paris: Migne, 1857–1876.

MPL   *Patrologia Latina.* Edited by J. B. Migne. 221 vols. Paris: Migne, 1841–1865. General Index, Paris, 1912.

MPNTC   *A Modern Pilgrimage in New Testament Christology.* Norman Perrin. Philadelphia: Fortress, 1974.

MTEC *Mystical Theology of the Eastern Church*. Vladimir Lossky. London: J. Clarke, 1957.

MTM *More Than Man: A Study in Christology*. Russell F. Aldwinkle. Grand Rapids, MI: Eerdmans, 1976.

NDM *The Nature and Destiny of Man*. Reinhold Niebuhr. 2 vols. New York: Scribner, 1941, 1943.

NJ *The Names of Jesus*. Vincent Taylor. London: Macmillan, 1953.

NIV New International Version

NPNF *A Select Library of the Nicene and Post-Nicene Fathers of the Christian Church*. 1st series, 14 vols. 2nd series, 14 vols. Edited by H. Wace and P. Schaff. New York: Christian, 1887–1900. References are by title and book or chapter, subsection, and *NPNF* series no., volume, and page number.

NQHJ *A New Quest for the Historical Jesus*. James M. Robinson. Naperville, IL: Allenson, 1959.

NT New Testament

NTDC *New Testament Doctrine of Christ*. A. E. J. Rawlinson. London: Longmans, Green, 1926.

NTI *New Testament Introduction*. Donald Guthrie. Downers Grove, IL: InterVarsity, 1971.

NTT *New Testament Theology*. Donald Guthrie. Downers Grove, IL: InterVarsity, 1981.

NUNT *Explanatory Notes Upon the New Testament*. John Wesley. London: Epworth, 1950.

OC *The Origin of Christology*. C. F. D. Moule. London: Cambridge University Press, 1977.

OCD *Outlines of Christian Dogma*. Darwell Stone. New York: Longmans, Green, 1900.

OCETW *On Christianity: Early Theological Writings*. Friedrich Hegel. New York: Harper, 1948.

OCT *An Outline of Christian Theology*. William Newton Clarke. Edinburgh: Clark, 1913.

OF *On the Orthodox Faith*. John of Damascus. *NPNF* 2 IX. FC 37.

OFP *On First Principles. Origen, Selected Works*. Translated by Rowan Greer. CWS. New York: Paulist Press, 1979.

ONTC *The Origins of New Testament Christology*. I. Howard Marshall. Downers Grove, IL: InterVarsity, 1976.

OOT *Outlines of Theology*. Archibald Alexander Hodge. Grand Rapids, MI: Eerdmans, 1928.

Orat. Oration or orations

OSCF *On the Sacraments of the Christian Faith*. Hugh of St. Victor. Cambridge, MA: Mediaeval Academy of America, 1951.

OT Old Testament

OTR *Of True Religion*. Augustine. Chicago: Henry Regnery, 1959, unless otherwise noted as *LCC* VI.

PC **1** *The Person of Christ*. Vincent Taylor. London: Macmillan, 1958. **2** *The Person of Christ*. David F. Wells. Westchester, IL: Crossway, 1984.

PCMT *The Place of Christ in Modern Theology*. A. M. Fairbairn. New York: Scribner, 1900.

PG *Preparation for the Gospel*. Eusebius. 2 vols. Grand Rapids, MI: Baker, 1981.

Philokal. *The Philokalia*. Compiled by Nikodimos of the Holy Mountain and Makarios of Corinth. 3 vols. London: Faber & Faber, 1979–1984.

Phil. Frag. *Philosophical Fragments*. Søren Kierkegaard. Princeton, NJ: Princeton University Press, 1962.

PJC *The Doctrine of the Person of Jesus Christ*. H. R. Mackintosh. New York: Scribner, 1931.

PPH *The Power of the Poor in History*. Gustavo Gutiérrez. Maryknoll, NY: Orbis, 1983.

PPJC *Person and Place of Jesus Christ*. P. T. Forsyth. London: Independent Press, 1930.

PPS *Parochial and Plain Sermons. Works of John Henry Cardinal Newman*. Edited by Joseph Rickaby. 8 vols. Westminster, MD: Christian Classics, 1977.

Pray. *The Prayers of Catherine of Siena*. New York: Paulist, 1984.

PS *Personal Salvation*. Wilbur Tillett. Nashville, TN: Barbee and Smith, 1902.

PT *The Protestant Tradition*. J. S. Whale. Cambridge: Cambridge University Press, 1955.

PW *Practical Works*. Richard Baxter. 23 vols. London: James Duncan, 1830.

RD *Reformed Dogmatics*. Heinrich Heppe. Translated by G. T. Thomson. London: Allen and Unwin, 1950.

RDB *Reformed Dogmatics: Seventeenth-Century Reformed Theology Through the Writings of Wollebius, Voetius, and Turretin*. Edited by John W. Beardslee III. Grand Rapids, MI: Baker, 1965.

RDL *Revelations of Divine Love*. Julian [Juliana] of Norwich. Translated by M. L. del Mastro. New York: Doubleday, 1977.

Relig.   Religion

RMT   *The Resurrection and Modern Thought.* W. J. S. Simpson. London: Longmans, Green, 1911.

RNT   *Redating the New Testament.* J. A. T. Robinson. Phildelphia: Westminster, 1976.

RO   *Radical Obedience: The Ethics of Rudolf Bultmann.* Thomas C. Oden. Philadelphia: Westminster, 1966.

RSV   Revised Standard Version

SA   *The Structure of Awareness.* Thomas C. Oden. Nashville, TN: Abingdon, 1968.

SCD   *Sources of Christian Dogma (Enchiridion Symbolorum).* Edited by Henry Denzinger. Translated by Roy Deferrari. New York: Herder, 1954.

SCF   *A Summary of the Christian Faith.* Henry E. Jacobs. Philadelphia: General Council of Publications, 1905.

SCG   *On the Truth of the Catholic Faith, Summa contra Gentiles.* Thomas Aquinas. 4 vols. (with subvolumes). New York: Doubleday, 1955–1957. Referenced by book, chapter, and page number.

SD   **1** *The Sickness unto Death.* Søren Kierkegaard. Princeton, NJ: Princeton University Press, 1954. **2** *Sermons on Subjects of the Day. Works of John Henry Cardinal Newman.* Edited by Joseph Rickaby. Westminster, MD: Christian Classics, 1977.

Sent.   *Sentences of Peter Lombard. Commentaria in Quator Libros Sententiarum. Works of Bonaventure.* Translated by Jose de Vinck. 5 vols. Patterson, NJ: St. Anthony Guild Press, 1960–1970.

Serm.   Sermon or sermons

SFG   *De Substantia Foederis Gratuiti.* Gaspar Olevianus. Geneva, 1585.

SML   *Sermons of Martin Luther.* Edited by J. N. Lencker [1905–1909]. 8 vols. Grand Rapids, MI: Baker, 1988.

Sol. Dec.   Solid Declaration. Part II of Formula of Concord. *BOC*, pp. 501–636.

SN   *Sermon Notes. Works of John Henry Cardinal Newman.* Edited by Joseph Rickaby. Westminster, MD: Christian Classics, 1977.

ST   *Summa Theologica.* Thomas Aquinas. Edited by English Dominican Fathers. 3 vols. New York: Benziger, 1947. References include part, subpart, question number, volume and page number of Benziger edition.

SW   *John Calvin, Selections from His Writings.* Edited by John Dillenberger. Missoula, MT: Scholars' Press, 1975.

Syst.   Systematic

Syst. Theol.   **1** *Systematic Theology.* Charles Hodge. 3 vols. 1877. Grand Rapids, MI: Eerdmans, reprinted 1968. **2** *Systematic Theology.* John

Miley. 2 vols. New York: Eaton & Mains, 1892. **3** *Systematic Theology.* Miner Raymond. 2 vols. Cincinnati: Hitchcock & Walden, 1877. **4** *Systematic Theology.* A. H. Strong. 3 vols. in one [1907]. Old Tappan, NJ: Fleming H. Revell, reprinted 1979. **5** *Systematic Theology.* Thomas O. Summers. 2 vols. Nashville, TN: Publishing House of the Methodist Episcopal Church South, 1888. **6** *Systematic Theology.* Paul Tillich. 3 vols. Chicago: University of Chicago Press, 1951–1963.

TAAAL *Treatises Against the Anabaptists and Against the Libertines.* John Calvin. Edited by B. W. Farley. Grand Rapids, MI: Baker, 1982.

TATT *St. Thomas Aquinas Theological Texts.* Edited by Thomas Gilby. London: Oxford University Press, 1955.

TC *Training in Christianity.* Søren Kierkegaard. Princeton, NJ: Princeton University Press, 1941.

TCBM *The Truth of Christmas—Beyond the Myths: The Gospels of the Infancy of Christ.* Rene Laurentin. Petersham, MA: St. Bede's Publications, 1985.

TCGNT *A Textual Commentary on the Greek New Testament.* Bruce M. Metzger. New York: United Bible Societies, 1971.

TCNT The Twentieth Century New Testament

TDNT *Theological Dictionary of the New Testament.* Edited by G. Kittel. Translated by G. W. Bromiley. 9 vols. Grand Rapids, MI: Eerdmans, 1964–1974.

TDP *Theologia Didactico-Polemica.* Friedrich Quenstedt. 4 Parts in 1 vol. Wittenberg: J. L. Quensted, 1691.

TEV Today's English Version

TGI *The Truth of God Incarnate.* Edited by Michael Green. Grand Rapids, MI: Eerdmans, 1977.

TGS *Theology of God—Sources.* Edited by K. Kehoe. New York: Bruce, 1971.

Theol. Theology or Theological

Tho. Aq. Thomas Aquinas

TI *Theological Institutes.* Richard Watson. Edited by John M'Clintock. 2 vols. New York: Carlton & Porter, 1850.

TIR *Trinity, Incarnation, and Redemption.* Anselm of Canterbury. Translated by Jasper Hopkins and Herbert Richardson. New York: Harper & Row, 1969.

TJC *The Titles of Jesus in Christology.* Ferdinand Hahn. London: Lutterworth, 1969.

TKG *Theology and the Kingdom of God.* Wolfhart Pannenberg. Edited by R. J. Neuhaus. Philadelphia: Westminster, 1971.

TNC   *The Two Natures in Christ*. Martin Chemnitz. Translated by J. A. O. Preus. St. Louis, MO: Concordia, 1971.

TNT   **1** *Theology of the New Testament*. Rudolf Bultmann. 2 vols. New York: Scribner, 1952. **2** *An Outline of the Theology of the New Testament*. Hans Conzelmann. Philadelphia: Fortress, 1983. **3** *A Theology of the New Testament*. George E. Ladd. Grand Rapids, MI: Eerdmans, 1974. **4** *The Theology of the New Testament*. George B. Stevens. Edinburgh: Clark, 1908.

TPA   *Theologia Positiva Acroamatica* (1664). John Frederick Koenig. Rostock: Joachim Wild, 1687.

TPW   *Taylor's Practical Works*. Jeremy Taylor. 2 vols. London: L. G. Bohn, 1854.

Tracts   *Tracts and Treatises*. John Calvin. 3 vols. Grand Rapids, MI: Eerdmans, 1958.

Trin.   Trinity

US   *Oxford University Sermons. Works of John Henry Cardinal Newman*. Edited by Joseph Rickaby. Westminster, MD: Christian Classics, 1977.

v.   verse

VCOS   *On the Virgin Conception and Original Sin*. Anselm. *TIR*.

Vulg.   Vulgate

WA   *Weimarer Ausgabe. Dr. Martin Luthers Werke. Kritische Gesamtausgabe*. Weimar: Hermann Boehlau, 1883–.

WF   *Word and Faith*. Gerhard Ebeling. London: SCM, 1963.

WIB   *Works of Isaac Barrow*. 3 vols. New York: John C. Riker, 1845.

WJW   *Works of the Reverend John Wesley*. Edited by Thomas Jackson. 14 vols. London: Wesleyan Conference Office, 1872.

WJWB   *The Works of John Wesley*. Edited by Frank Baker. Bicentennial Edition. 8 vols. to date. Nashville, TN: Abingdon, 1975– (formerly published by Oxford University Press).

WLS   *What Luther Says*. Edited by E. Plass. 3 vols. St. Louis, MO: Concordia, 1959.

WML   *Works of Martin Luther: An Anthology*. Philadelphia edition. 6 vols. Philadelphia: Muhlenberg Press, 1943.

Works   **1** *The Works of Jonathan Edwards*. 2 vols. Carlisle, PA: Banner of Truth Trust, 1984. **2** *Works of Andrew Fuller*. 8 vols. Charlestown, MA: Collier, 1820–1825.

WT   *Waterbuffalo Theology*. Kosuko Koyama. Maryknoll, NY: Orbis, 1974.

Name Index

Aaron, 138, 282, 285, 306, 312–14
Abelard, Peter, 385, 404
Abraham, 38, 39, 71, 73, 113, 122, 143, 150, 153, 169, 211, 230, 232, 313–14, 363–64, 392, 443, 461, 499, 518
Adam, 79, 104–5, 110, 115, 118–19, 122, 128, 136–37, 147, 149, 151, 153, 241, 243, 252, 264, 313, 358, 382, 385, 390
Africanus, 145, 154–55
Agatho, 191, 192
a Kempis, Thomas, 404
Aldwinckle, R., 176, 187, 257
Alexander VIII, 254
Alexander, J. W., 343
Alexander of Alexandria, 51
Alexander the Great, 2
Alfaro, J., 139
Ambrose, xvii, 8, 74, 86–87, 95, 98, 101, 103, 115, 119, 154, 161, 205, 265, 283, 287, 289, 306, 309, 312–13, 333, 340, 346, 363–64, 371, 384–85, 444, 466, 468, 507, 536
Anderson, H., 199
Anger, J., 163, 240, 433, 434
Anna, 144, 158, 163, 233
Anselm, 87, 95, 97, 106, 159, 351, 361, 374, 377, 385, 409–11, 414, 541
Aphrahat, 364
Archelaus, 93, 229, 244
Aristotle, 103
Arius, 37, 50–51, 224

Arnobius, 99, 368, 395
Athanasius, xvi, xvii, 2, 9, 16, 18, 30, 36, 43, 50–51, 58, 68, 71, 89–90, 95–96, 103, 127–31, 156, 169, 178, 189, 197, 201, 205, 224, 226, 235, 241, 269, 328–32, 340, 374, 382–83, 385, 388, 419, 429, 438, 453, 465, 476, 491, 522, 536
Athenagoras, 201
Augustine, xvii, 1, 8, 11–12, 16–18, 21, 25, 34, 36, 38, 41, 43–49, 53, 56–58, 60, 64, 66–67, 69, 71–72, 77, 79, 82–83, 91, 93–95, 98–107, 109, 111–13, 115–18, 124, 126–29, 134, 145, 146, 152, 158, 160, 163, 168, 172–75, 182, 191, 197, 205, 224–25, 230, 235–39, 240, 243, 245, 247–50, 253, 260, 264, 269, 271, 279, 282, 287, 290, 297, 298, 301, 304, 306, 309, 316–19, 331, 344, 353, 356, 361–67, 370, 371, 378, 385, 397–98, 401, 404, 414, 419, 432, 436, 438, 439, 443–45, 452, 456, 465, 469, 470, 472, 475, 482, 485, 495, 504–8, 510, 512, 516, 519–20, 524, 536, 541
Aulen, G., 350, 403, 411–13

Baillie, D., 88, 98
Baltimore, Lord, 222
Barclay, W., 324
Barnabas, 43, 108, 372, 385
Barrett, C. K., 63

Barrow, Isaac, 437
Barth, K., 12, 51–52, 55, 71, 81, 88, 96, 98, 102, 106, 133, 157, 181, 191, 207, 235, 240, 244, 258, 267, 276, 287, 301–2, 309–10, 313, 317, 330, 361, 370, 372, 384, 389–92, 430, 435, 456, 462, 473, 495, 512, 517, 536–37
Bartsch, H. W., 224
Basil, xvii, 90, 385
Bauer, F. C., 200
Baxter, Richard, 52, 95, 102, 107, 163, 222, 243, 245, 248, 265–67, 290, 301, 307, 317, 350, 352, 362, 370, 375, 388, 437, 438, 441, 509, 516
Bede, 268, 294, 469, 479
Benedict XV, 90
Benedict XIV, 116
Berdyaev, N., 416
Berger, P., 10
Berkouwer, G. C., 99, 166, 347
Bernard of Clairvaux, 232, 343, 385, 404
Biedermann, A. E., 200
Blumhardt, C., 8
Boff, Leonardo and Clodovis, 78, 80, 139
Bonaventure, 233, 238–40, 266, 299, 326–27, 338, 443, 477, 495, 505, 518
Bonhoeffer, D., 11, 257
Bornkamm, G., 199, 202, 203, 236, 262, 296, 322, 324, 328
Borsch, F. H., 264

Subject Index

A priori argument, 212, 302, 500
Abba, 58, 68, 276, 396. *See also* Father
Abrahamic covenant, 38–39, 71, 73, 113, 122, 143, 150, 153, 169, 211, 230, 232, 313–14, 363–64, 392, 443, 461, 499, 518. *See also* Israel, Circumcision
Absolute, 45, 84, 119, 152, 203, 376, 408, 441, 446, 493
Action, divine-human activity, xiii, 2, 17–19, 22, 25, 57, 64, 73, 86–87, 99, 173, 174, 181–82, 191–92, 197, 200, 206, 264, 280, 287, 292–94, 296, 305, 307, 319, 322, 327, 355–56, 359, 362, 382–83, 385, 400, 405, 415, 425, 451, 491, 512, 515, 520. *See also* Agent, Operations, Will
Adam, 79, 104–5, 110, 115, 118–19, 122, 128, 136–37, 147, 149, 151, 153, 241, 243, 252, 264, 313, 358, 382, 385, 390. *See also* Eve, Fallenness, Original Sin
Adoption, adoptionism, 58, 107, 241–42
Adoration of Christ, 40, 46, 130, 194, 363, 513, 525
Advent, 57, 101
Agent, agency, 37, 53, 70, 73, 118, 119, 133, 138, 225, 242, 274, 303, 426, 467. *See also* Action
Albigenses, 112

Altar, 284, 304, 306–8, 341–42, 367, 372. *See also* Levitical system, Sacrifice, Tree metaphor
Analogy, 68, 87, 111, 113, 142, 156, 172, 174, 178, 182, 183, 223, 232, 245, 276, 302, 311, 313, 318, 378, 393, 400, 425, 455, 469–70, 492–94, 496. *See also* Metaphor
Angels, angelic, 52, 59, 73, 101, 107, 119–20, 125, 138–41, 149, 163, 270, 365–66, 389, 492, 507. *See also* Eternity, Heaven
Anger, 124, 163, 317, 392, 394, 405. *See also* Judgment, Wrath
Anima, 173. *See also* Psuche, Soul
Animal, 48, 125–26, 189, 285, 363–64, 367–68, 372, 375–76, 378, 481. *See also* Life, Plant, Human
Anoint, Anointed One, 22, 206, 209, 237, 268, 269, 271, 274, 279, 284, 287, 302, 369, 396, 459. *See also* Messiah, Oil, Unction
Antecedent will, 391. *See also* Consequent will of God, Will
Anthropology, 106, 116, 407
Antinomianism, 409, 413. *See also* Law, Requirement
Apocalyptic, 202, 203, 263, 271, 420, 454–59, 479. *See also* End, History, Resurrection

Apollinarianism, 125
Apostle, apostolic, xi, 49–52, 134, 160–62, 213, 273, 283, 292, 313, 338, 346, 366, 373, 394, 438, 451, 492, 498, 504. *See also* Mission, World
Apostles' Creed, 15, 16, 22, 52, 134, 198, 327, 430, 438
Apostolic Constitutions, 366, 373
Apparition, 124
Arians, Arianism, 18, 36, 50, 51, 58, 68, 82, 89–90, 96, 103, 127, 130–31, 156, 169, 173, 186, 189, 235, 241, 259, 388, 429, 438, 522. *See also* Council of Chalcedon, Nicaea, Son, Uncreated One
Arminianism, 407, 412, 413. *See also* Dort, Freedom, Grace, Synergism
Arrest of Jesus, 71, 296, 326, 329, 517, 519. *See also* Trial
Art, Christ in the history of, 49, 139, 149, 158, 191, 268, 275, 329, 342, 346, 389, 443, 477, 536
Ascension, Ascent, 21, 91, 293, 307, 309, 429–30, 433, 434, 446, 449, 478, 483, 490, 502–25. *See also* Descent, Exaltation, Resurrection, Session of Christ
Assent, 177, 434
Assumptio carnis, 95, 96
Assumptions, ix, xi, xii, 35, 70, 207, 211, 216, 221–22,

Majesty of God (*continued*)
  also Attributes of God,
  Sovereignty
Maleness, Masculine, 8,
  117–18, 134, 137, 144,
  146–47, 154, 230, 232, 249,
  250. *See also* Adam,
  Female
Man, doctrine of, human-
  ity, 6, 8–14, 18, 24, 31,
  36–42, 46–49, 52, 57,
  61–62, 65, 66, 68–69, 71,
  76, 79–119, 124, 128–40,
  144, 146, 156–59, 162,
  165–78, 181–92, 203–6, 213,
  215, 220, 225, 235,
  239–242, 251–67, 271–73,
  275, 277, 289, 296, 300–3,
  310, 318, 322–28, 331–33,
  337, 340–41, 344, 357–58,
  364, 369, 370, 374, 378,
  381, 383, 385, 387, 389,
  392, 398–402, 404, 406,
  414, 422–23, 436, 439,
  447, 457–61, 466–68, 482,
  490, 501, 503, 507–8,
  511–14, 517, 521, 524. *See
  also* Anthropology, Compositum, Human,
  Humanity
Marriage, 115, 129, 138, 154,
  175, 250–51, 482. *See also*
  Celibacy, Sexuality
Martyrdom, 2, 48, 202, 221,
  266, 379, 476
Marxism, 55, 64, 221, 226, 539
Mary, 15, 24, 31, 59, 89, 93,
  96, 109–10, 117, 125,
  133–41, 144, 145, 148–63,
  169, 186, 232–33, 301, 341,
  422, 468, 479, 483–84, 489,
  519. *See also* Birth, Eve,
  Theotokos, Virgin
Matter, material reality, xiii,
  3, 25, 32, 59, 83, 95, 112,
  122, 151, 155, 159, 175,
  180, 183, 202, 210, 246–47,
  275, 324, 330, 335, 375,
  377, 408, 433, 450, 454,
  458, 464, 481, 492–94, 502,
  522. *See also* Causality,
  Cosmos, Physical, World
Mediator, xix, 6, 17–19,
  21–22, 25–26, 79, 82, 90,
  100–108, 118–24, 127, 147,
  159, 160, 167–68, 181, 184,
  192–93, 205, 221, 235, 258,
  274, 277, 279, 280, 283,

285, 289, 294, 304, 306,
  308, 334, 341, 345, 355,
  369, 372, 382–83, 388, 396,
  407, 512–13, 517. *See also*
  Divine-Human, Atone,
  Natures of Christ, Person
  of Christ, Theandric
Medieval tradition, xiv, xv,
  12, 72, 95, 159, 221, 224,
  403, 409, 410, 447, 541. *See
  also* Scholasticism
Memory, 2, 22, 25, 61, 63,
  116, 149, 208–13, 223, 324,
  434, 438, 465, 468, 487,
  489, 498, 502. *See also*
  Time, Remembering
  community
Memory-eliciting occasion,
  489
Mercy, 72, 101, 118, 283,
  298, 308, 310, 313, 345,
  351, 368, 377, 387, 391–93,
  409–10, 420, 469. *See also*
  Grace, Love, Pardon
Merit, 129, 147, 150, 231,
  291, 310, 345, 360–62, 381,
  387–88, 408. *See also*
  Grace, Law
Messiah, xiii, xiv, 4, 6,
  10–11, 13, 15, 21, 36, 49,
  52, 55, 63, 118, 145, 147,
  154, 199, 207, 220, 237–41,
  252–53, 261–74, 277, 284,
  287, 318, 321, 328–29, 380,
  446, 452, 460, 462, 491,
  501. *See also* Anointed,
  Davidic, King, Lord
Messianic Secret, 61, 262,
  273, 274
Metaphor, xix, 55, 56, 76,
  77, 84, 150, 205, 230, 247,
  326, 328, 341, 357, 366,
  369–70, 381, 386, 395, 398,
  400–401, 504, 507, 510,
  512, 520. *See also* Parable,
  Symbol
Method, theological, xv,
  xvii, xix, xx, 95, 97, 115,
  226, 351, 396, 399, 423,
  500, 535, 537–41. *See also*
  Authority, Hermeneutic,
  System, Vincentian
Minister, ministry, xii, 3, 5,
  13, 20, 31–36, 62–63, 67,
  74–79, 91, 121, 160, 175–76,
  183, 197–98, 200, 205,
  208–13, 229, 235–38,
  242–44, 249, 252, 257–65,

272–87, 290–304, 309–13,
  318–20, 329–30, 345, 348,
  363, 372, 415, 435, 456,
  458, 462–63, 471–72, 478,
  495, 504–5, 513–19, 539.
  See also Earthly, Ordination, Servant
Miracle, 13, 35, 62, 88,
  151–52, 184–85, 191, 192,
  214, 272–73, 290, 293, 298,
  299–303, 325, 335–37, 440,
  453, 470, 489–91, 501. *See
  also* Earthly, Healing,
  Resurrection
Mission, x, xviii, 1, 5, 9,
  18–19, 24, 35–37, 41, 58,
  60, 65–66, 77, 81–82,
  85–91, 114, 117, 143–44,
  147, 183–85, 193, 212–13,
  234, 238, 240, 242–43, 249,
  250–54, 257, 261–66, 271,
  273–74, 281, 293–95, 298,
  300, 302, 305, 323, 326,
  336, 358, 379, 433, 436,
  451, 462, 485, 504–5,
  509–10, 517, 519, 522–23.
  See also Apostolate
Modernity, xi, xii, xiii, xvi,
  199, 202, 204, 221–23, 225,
  250, 434, 439. *See also*
  Criticism, Reductionism,
  Science, Secularization
Modern period, modern
  theology, ix, xi–xx, 2,
  8–9, 17, 22, 30, 35, 42, 49,
  54, 63–65, 68, 98, 112, 129,
  131, 137, 146, 161–62, 185,
  199–205, 208, 212, 216,
  221–26, 242, 250–51, 273,
  302, 321, 352, 413, 434,
  439, 451–52, 457, 498–500,
  536, 538, 540–41
Monarchianism, 82
Monogenes, xix, 23, 24, 57,
  58, 94, 108. *See also* Begetting, Only-begotten, Son
Monophysitism, 175
Monothelitism, 190
Moral theology, morality,
  xiii, 2, 3, 9, 10, 33, 37, 48,
  52, 55, 80, 83, 94, 129, 131,
  132, 135, 163, 192,
  199–201, 206, 213, 227,
  232, 235, 244–46, 248, 254,
  256, 257, 259, 290, 291,
  303, 344, 349, 350, 360,
  372, 373, 375–78, 385,
  403–10, 412–14, 418, 426,

Scripture Index